X-MEN AG… X

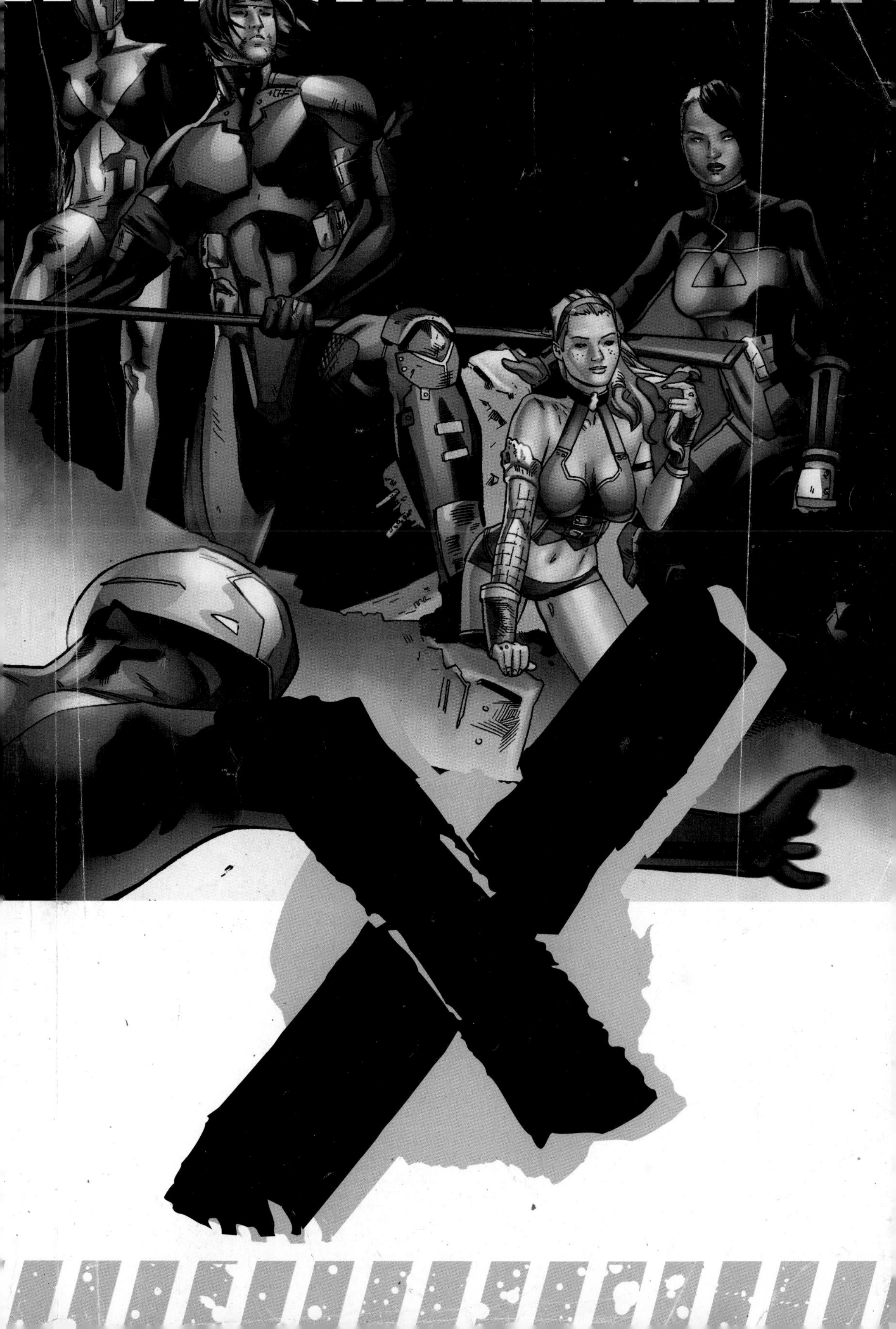

AGE OF X: ALPHA

WRITER: Mike Carey
ARTISTS: Mirco Pierfederici,
Gabriel Hernandez Walta,
Carlo Barberi & Walden Wong,
Paco Diaz and Paul Davidson
COLORISTS: Mirco Pierfederici,
Gabriel Hernandez Walta,
Antonio Fabela, Matt Milla
& Brian Reber
LETTERER: VC's Joe Caramagna
COVER ART: Chris Bachalo
& Tim Townsend

X-MEN LEGACY #245-247

WRITER: Mike Carey
PENCILER: Clay Mann
INKER: Jay Leisten
COLORIST: Brian Reber
LETTERER: VC's Cory Petit
COVER ART: Leinil Yu &
Marte Gracia and Mico Suayan
& Marte Gracia

NEW MUTANTS #22-24

WRITER: Mike Carey
PENCILER: Steve Kurth
INKER: Allen Martinez
COLORIST: Brian Reber
LETTERERS: VC's Chris
Eliopoulos & Joe Caramagna
COVER ART: Mico Suayan &
Marte Gracia and Leinil Yu
& Marte Gracia

AGE OF X: UNIVERSE #1-2

WRITERS: Simon Spurrier,
Jim McCann & Chuck Kim
ARTISTS: Khoi Pham &
Tom Palmer, Paul Davidson
and Gabriel Hernandez Walta
COLORISTS: Sonia Oback,
Antonio Fabela &
Gabriel Hernandez Walta
LETTERER: VC's Joe Sabino
COVER ART: Simone Bianchi
& Simone Peruzzi

ASSISTANT EDITORS:
Sebastian Girner & Jake Thomas
EDITOR: Daniel Ketchum
GROUP EDITOR: Nick Lowe

COLLECTION EDITOR:
Jennifer Grünwald
ASSISTANT EDITORS:
Alex Starbuck & Nelson Ribeiro
EDITOR, SPECIAL PROJECTS:
Mark D. Beazley
SENIOR EDITOR, SPECIAL PROJECTS:
Jeff Youngquist
SENIOR VICE PRESIDENT OF SALES:
David Gabriel
**SVP OF BRAND PLANNING &
COMMUNICATIONS:**
Michael Pasciullo
BOOK DESIGNER:
Rodolfo Muraguchi

EDITOR IN CHIEF: Axel Alonso
CHIEF CREATIVE OFFICER: Joe Quesada
PUBLISHER: Dan Buckley
EXECUTIVE PRODUCER: Alan Fine

X-MEN: AGE OF X. Contains material originally published in magazine form as AGE OF X: ALPHA, X-MEN LEGACY #245-247, NEW MUTANTS #22-24 and AGE OF X UNIVERSE #1-2. First printing 2011. ISBN# 978-0-785-5290-3. Published by MARVEL WORLDWIDE, INC., a subsidiary of MARVEL ENTERTAINMENT, LLC. OFFICE OF PUBLICATION: 135 West 50th Street, New York, NY 10020. Copyright © 2010 and 2011 Marvel Characters, Inc. All rights reserved. $24.99 per copy in the U.S. and $27.99 in Canada (GST #R127032852); Canadian Agreement #40668537. All characters featured in this issue and the distinctive names and likenesses thereof, and all related indicia are trademarks of Marvel Characters, Inc. No similarity between any of the names, characters, persons, and/or institutions in this magazine with those of any living or dead person or institution is intended, and any such similarity which may exist is purely coincidental. **Printed in the U.S.A.** ALAN FINE, EVP - Office of the President, Marvel Worldwide, Inc. and EVP & CMO Marvel Characters B.V.; DAN BUCKLEY, Publisher & President - Print, Animation & Digital Divisions; JOE QUESADA, Chief Creative Officer; DAVID BOGART, SVP of Business Affairs & Talent Management; TOM BREVOORT, SVP of Publishing; C.B. CEBULSKI, SVP of Creator & Content Development; DAVID GABRIEL, SVP of Publishing Sales & Circulation; MICHAEL PASCIULLO, SVP of Brand Planning & Communications; JIM O'KEEFE, VP of Operations & Logistics; DAN CARR, Executive Director of Publishing Technology; SUSAN CRESPI, Editorial Operations Manager; ALEX MORALES, Publishing Operations Manager; STAN LEE, Chairman Emeritus. For information regarding advertising in Marvel Comics or on Marvel.com, please contact John Dokes, SVP Integrated Sales and Marketing, at jdokes@marvel.com. For Marvel subscription inquiries, please call 800-217-9158. **Manufactured between 11/24/2011 and 12/13/2011 by QUAD/GRAPHICS, DUBUQUE, IA, USA.**

10 9 8 7 6 5 4 3 2 1

AGE OF X: ALPHA

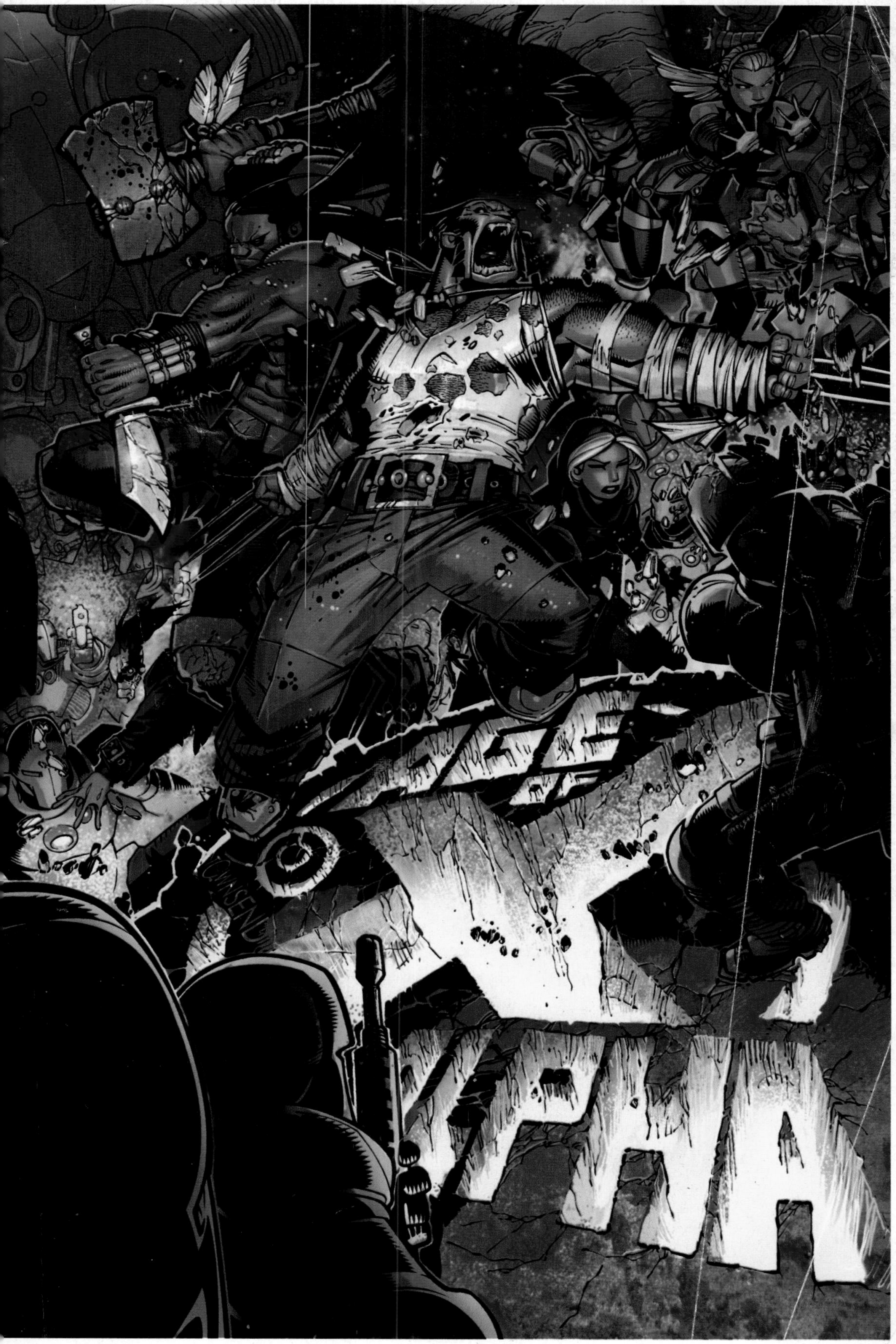

In a world where the X-Men never existed and mutantkind has been hunted to extinction, the few remaining mutants band together to make their last stand. The final war starts here...

AGE of X
ALPHA

WRITTEN by MIKE CAREY

ART by MIRCO PIERFEDERICI

BASILISK
ART by GABRIEL HERNANDEZ WALTA

CANNONBALL AND HUSK
PENCILED by CARLO BARBERI
INKED by WALDEN WONG
COLORED by ANTONIO FABELA

WOLVERINE
PENCILED and INKED by PACO DIAZ
COLORED by MATT MILLA

MAGNETO
PENCILED and INKED by PAUL DAVIDSON
COLORED by BRIAN REBER

LETTERED by VC'S JOE CARAMAGNA
COVER ART by CHRIS BACHALO and TIM TOWNSEND
VARIANT COVER ART by OLIVIER COIPEL, MARK MORALES and LAURA MARTIN
LOGO DESIGN by JARED FLETCHER

Production: IRENE Y. LEE
Assistant Editor: JAKE THOMAS
Editor: DANIEL KETCHUM
Consulting Editor: NICK LOWE
Editor in Chief: JOE QUESADA
Publisher DAN BUCKLEY
Executive Producer: ALAN FINE

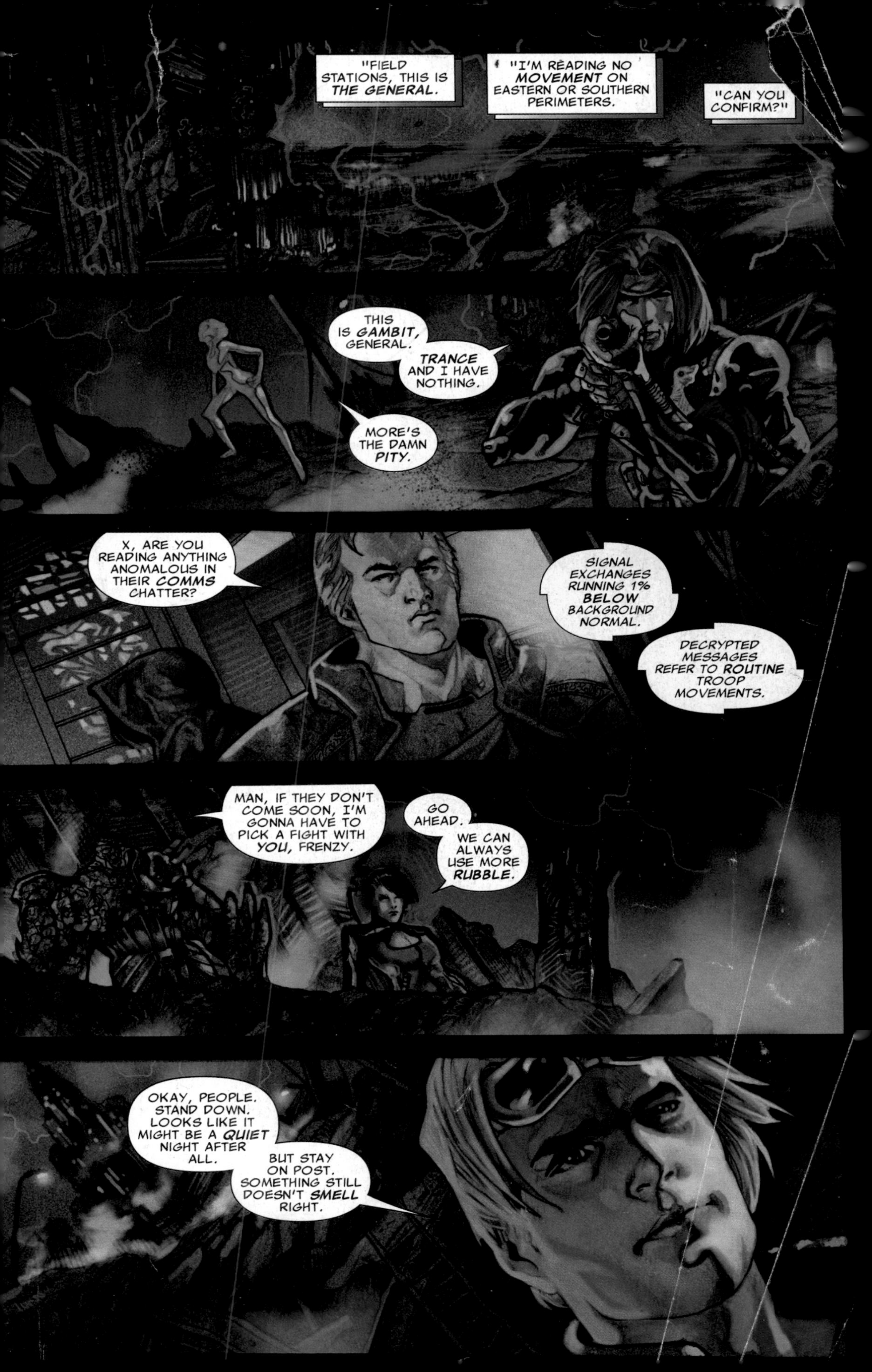
"FIELD STATIONS, THIS IS THE GENERAL.
"I'M READING NO MOVEMENT ON EASTERN OR SOUTHERN PERIMETERS.
"CAN YOU CONFIRM?"
THIS IS GAMBIT, GENERAL.
TRANCE AND I HAVE NOTHING.
MORE'S THE DAMN PITY.
X, ARE YOU READING ANYTHING ANOMALOUS IN THEIR COMMS CHATTER?
SIGNAL EXCHANGES RUNNING 1% BELOW BACKGROUND NORMAL.
DECRYPTED MESSAGES REFER TO ROUTINE TROOP MOVEMENTS.
MAN, IF THEY DON'T COME SOON, I'M GONNA HAVE TO PICK A FIGHT WITH YOU, FRENZY.
GO AHEAD.
WE CAN ALWAYS USE MORE RUBBLE.
OKAY, PEOPLE. STAND DOWN. LOOKS LIKE IT MIGHT BE A QUIET NIGHT AFTER ALL.
BUT STAY ON POST. SOMETHING STILL DOESN'T SMELL RIGHT.

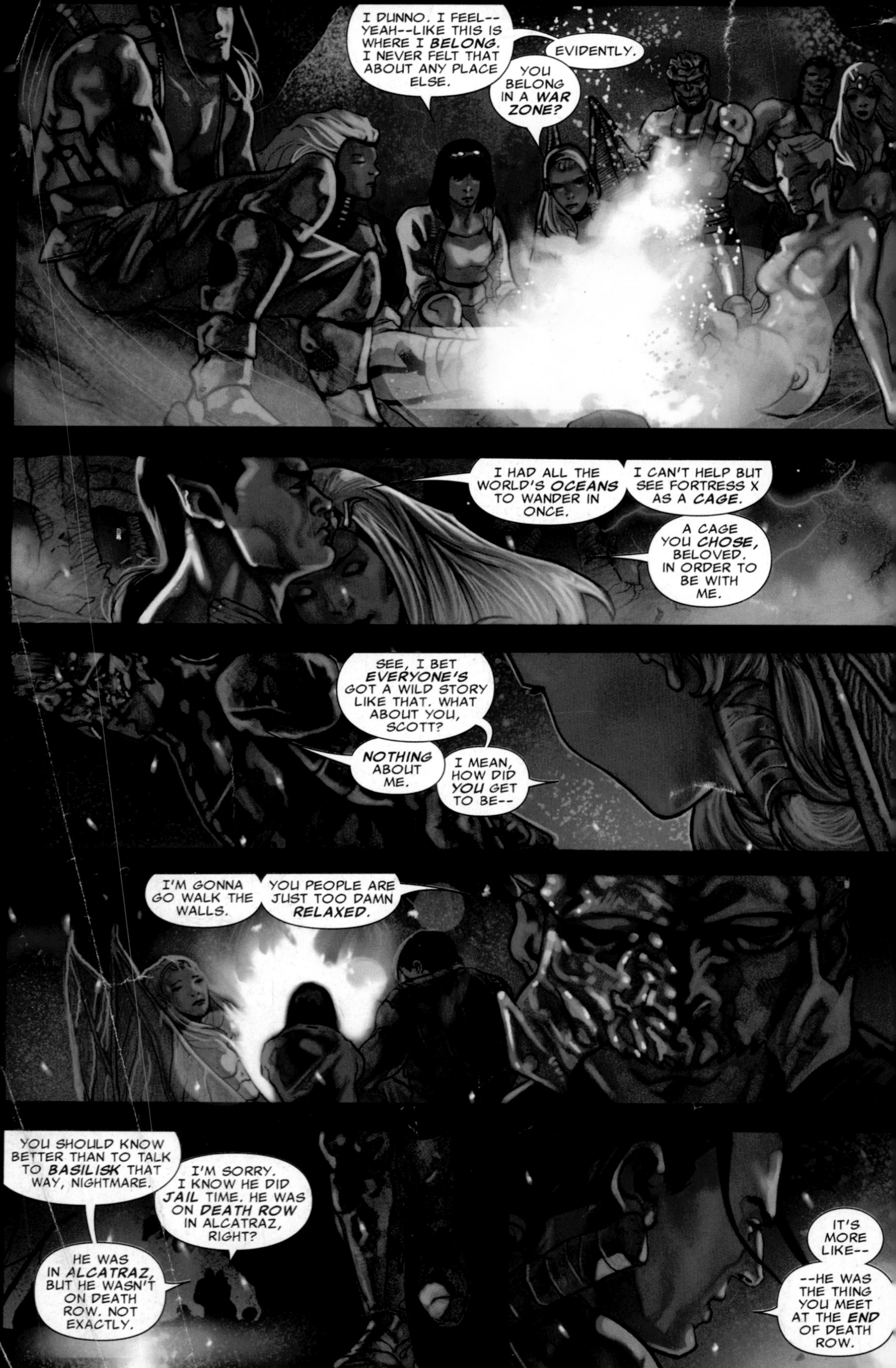
I DUNNO. I FEEL-- YEAH--LIKE THIS IS WHERE I BELONG. I NEVER FELT THAT ABOUT ANY PLACE ELSE.
EVIDENTLY.
YOU BELONG IN A WAR ZONE?
I HAD ALL THE WORLD'S OCEANS TO WANDER IN ONCE.
I CAN'T HELP BUT SEE FORTRESS X AS A CAGE.
A CAGE YOU CHOSE, BELOVED. IN ORDER TO BE WITH ME.
SEE, I BET EVERYONE'S GOT A WILD STORY LIKE THAT. WHAT ABOUT YOU, SCOTT?
NOTHING ABOUT ME.
I MEAN, HOW DID YOU GET TO BE--
I'M GONNA GO WALK THE WALLS.
YOU PEOPLE ARE JUST TOO DAMN RELAXED.
YOU SHOULD KNOW BETTER THAN TO TALK TO BASILISK THAT WAY, NIGHTMARE.
I'M SORRY. I KNOW HE DID JAIL TIME. HE WAS ON DEATH ROW IN ALCATRAZ, RIGHT?
HE WAS IN ALCATRAZ, BUT HE WASN'T ON DEATH ROW. NOT EXACTLY.
IT'S MORE LIKE--
--HE WAS THE THING YOU MEET AT THE END OF DEATH ROW.

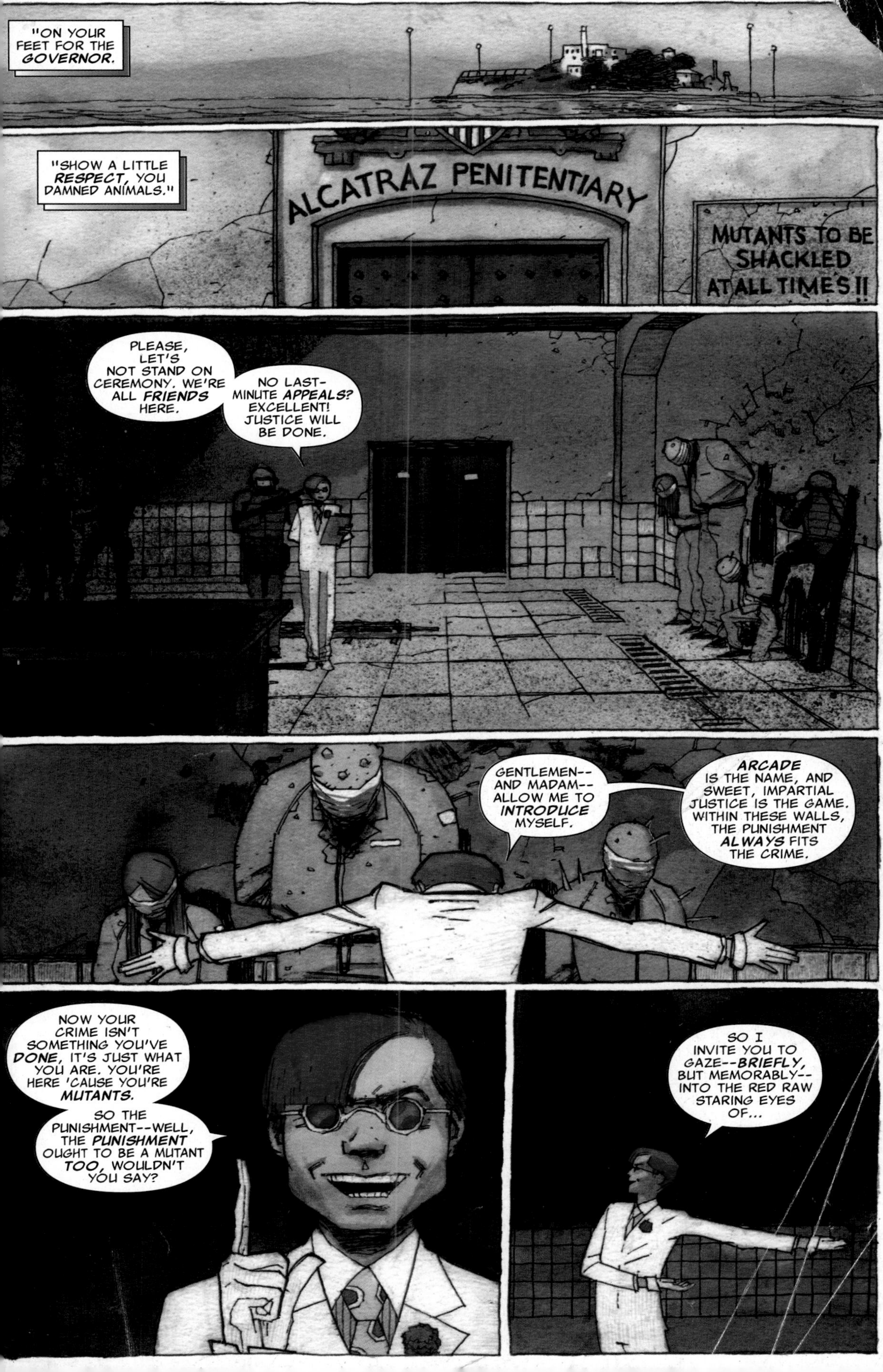

"ON YOUR FEET FOR THE GOVERNOR.
"SHOW A LITTLE RESPECT, YOU DAMNED ANIMALS."
ALCATRAZ PENITENTIARY
MUTANTS TO BE SHACKLED AT ALL TIMES!!
PLEASE, LET'S NOT STAND ON CEREMONY. WE'RE ALL FRIENDS HERE.
NO LAST-MINUTE APPEALS? EXCELLENT! JUSTICE WILL BE DONE.
GENTLEMEN-- AND MADAM-- ALLOW ME TO INTRODUCE MYSELF.
ARCADE IS THE NAME, AND SWEET, IMPARTIAL JUSTICE IS THE GAME. WITHIN THESE WALLS, THE PUNISHMENT ALWAYS FITS THE CRIME.
NOW YOUR CRIME ISN'T SOMETHING YOU'VE DONE, IT'S JUST WHAT YOU ARE. YOU'RE HERE 'CAUSE YOU'RE MUTANTS.
SO THE PUNISHMENT--WELL, THE PUNISHMENT OUGHT TO BE A MUTANT TOO, WOULDN'T YOU SAY?
SO I INVITE YOU TO GAZE--BRIEFLY, BUT MEMORABLY-- INTO THE RED RAW STARING EYES OF...

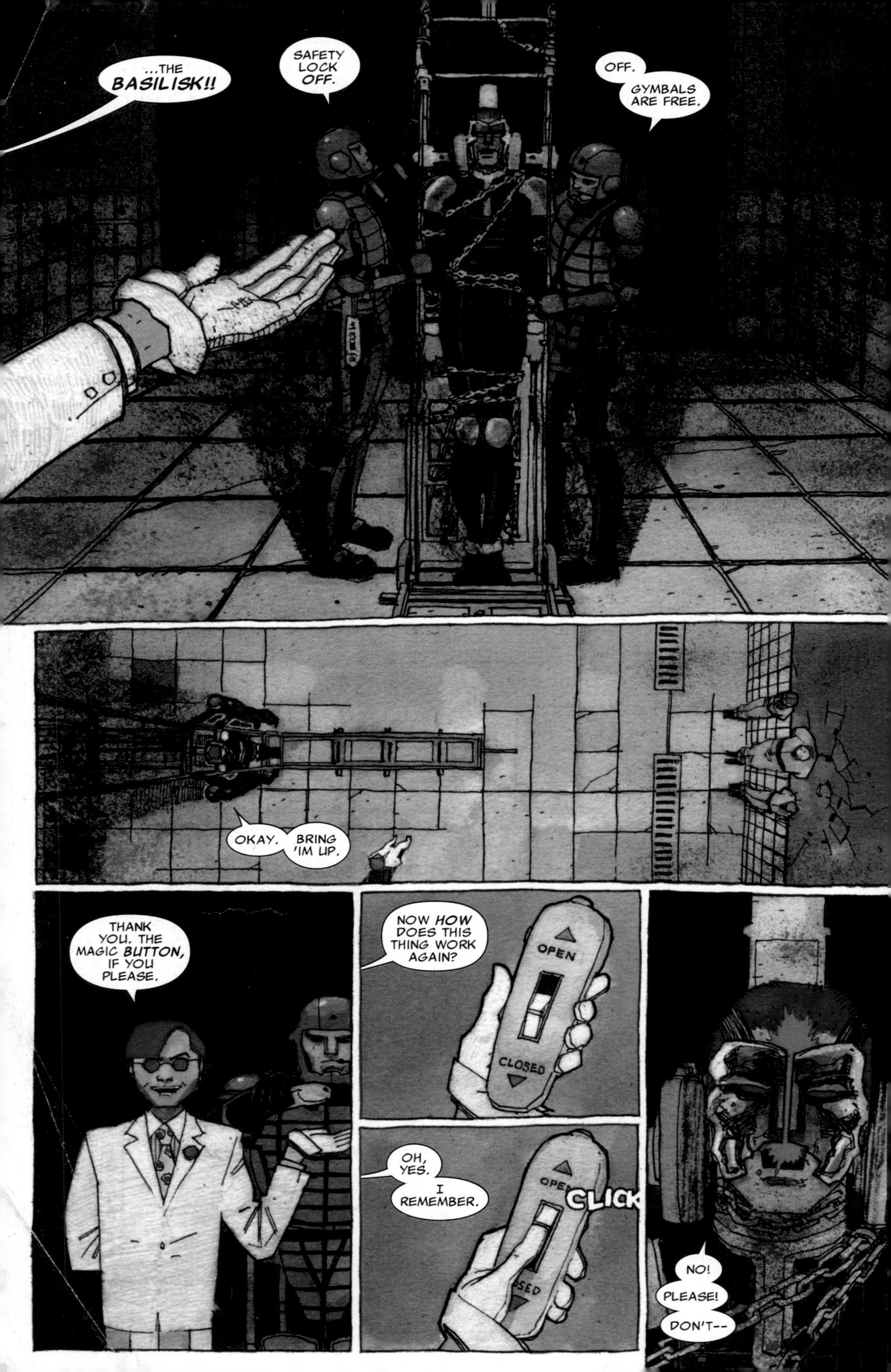
...THE BASILISK!!
SAFETY LOCK OFF.
OFF.
GYMBALS ARE FREE.
OKAY.
BRING 'IM UP.
THANK YOU. THE MAGIC BUTTON, IF YOU PLEASE.
NOW HOW DOES THIS THING WORK AGAIN?
OPEN
CLOSED
OH, YES.
I REMEMBER.
CLICK
NO!
PLEASE!
DON'T--

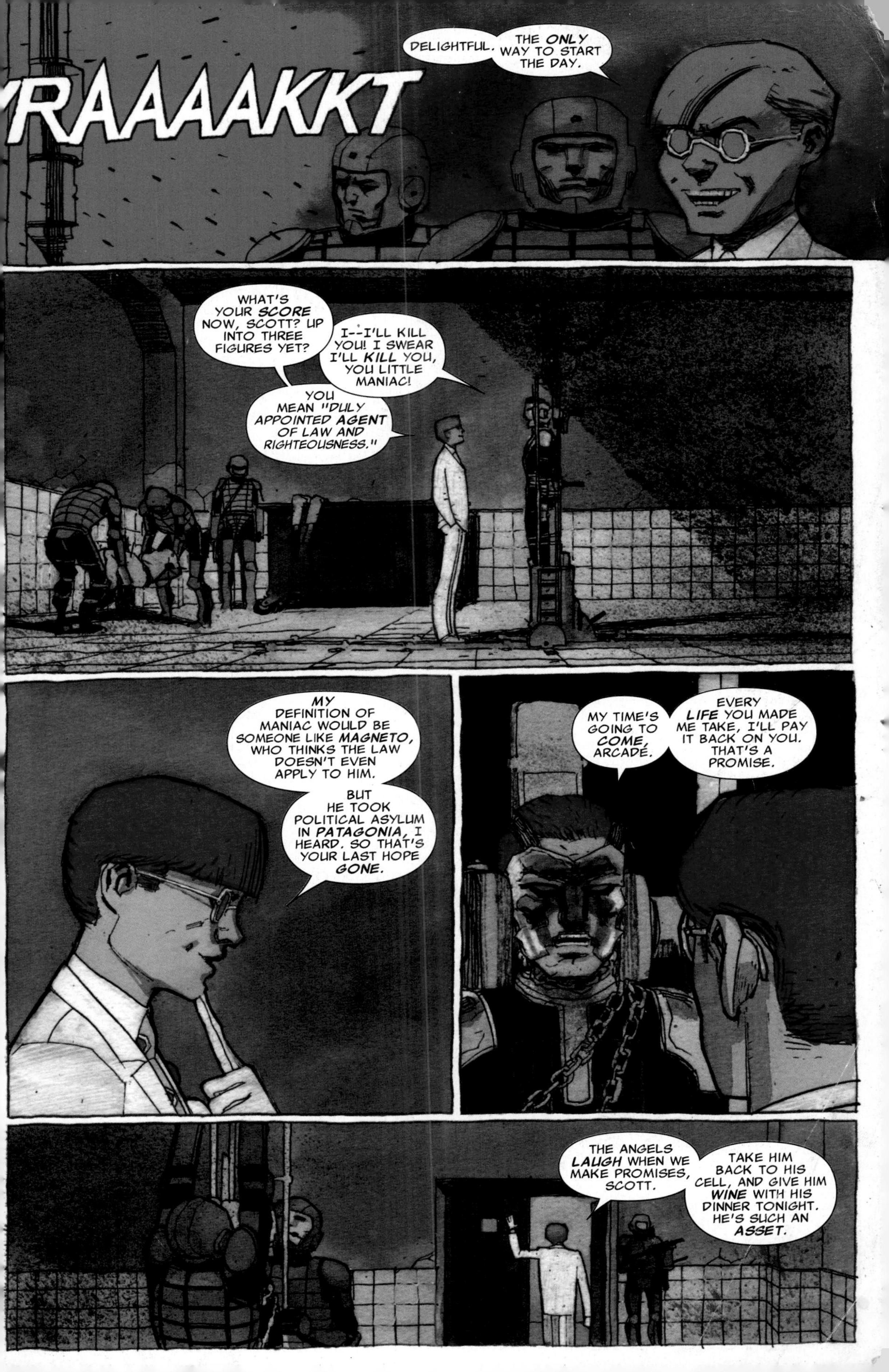
RAAAAKKT
DELIGHTFUL.
THE ONLY WAY TO START THE DAY.
WHAT'S YOUR SCORE NOW, SCOTT? UP INTO THREE FIGURES YET?
I--I'LL KILL YOU! I SWEAR I'LL KILL YOU, YOU LITTLE MANIAC!
YOU MEAN "DULY APPOINTED AGENT OF LAW AND RIGHTEOUSNESS."
MY DEFINITION OF MANIAC WOULD BE SOMEONE LIKE MAGNETO, WHO THINKS THE LAW DOESN'T EVEN APPLY TO HIM.
BUT HE TOOK POLITICAL ASYLUM IN PATAGONIA, I HEARD. SO THAT'S YOUR LAST HOPE GONE.
MY TIME'S GOING TO COME, ARCADE.
EVERY LIFE YOU MADE ME TAKE, I'LL PAY IT BACK ON YOU. THAT'S A PROMISE.
THE ANGELS LAUGH WHEN WE MAKE PROMISES, SCOTT.
TAKE HIM BACK TO HIS CELL, AND GIVE HIM WINE WITH HIS DINNER TONIGHT. HE'S SUCH AN ASSET.

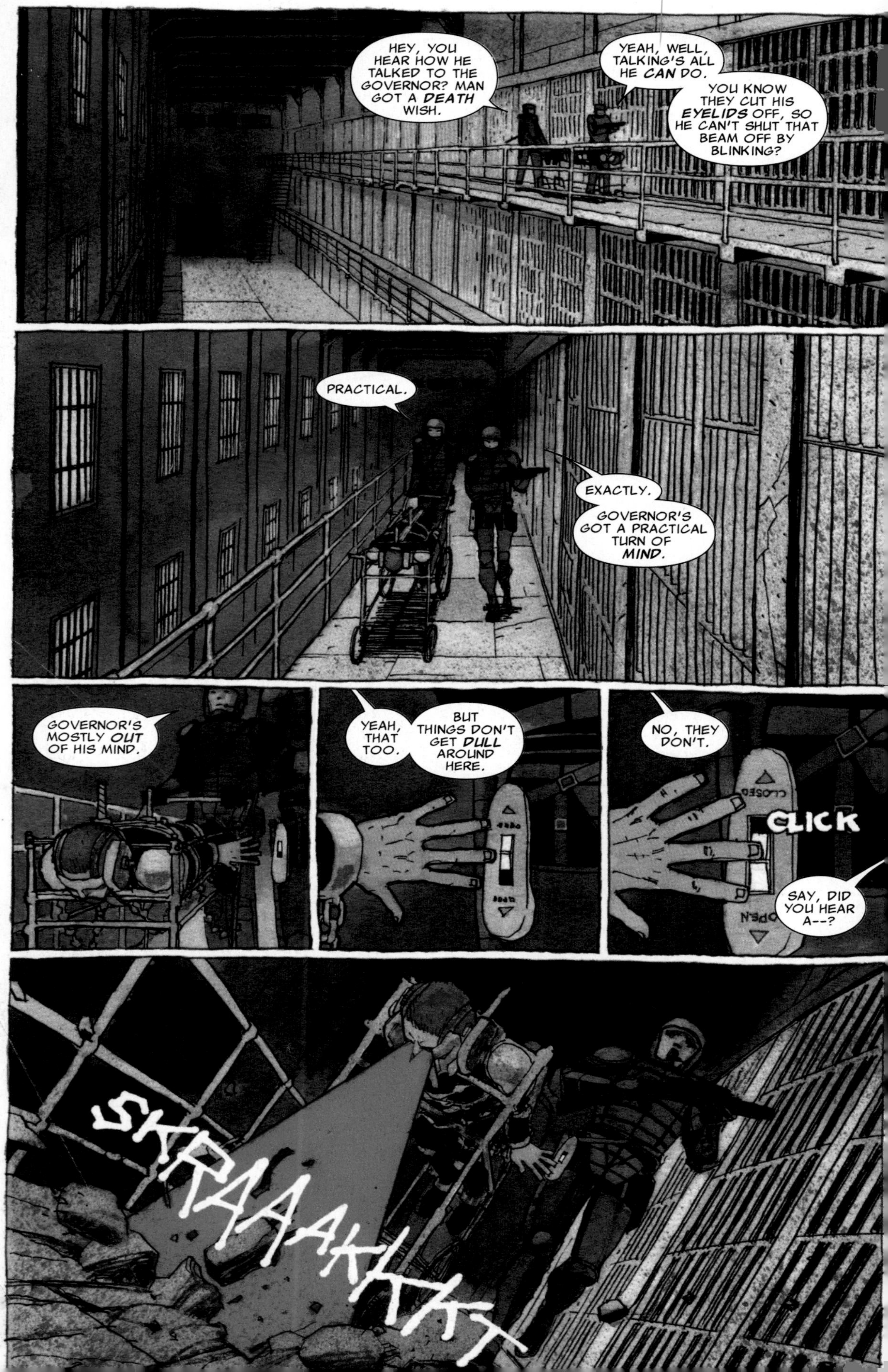
HEY, YOU HEAR HOW HE TALKED TO THE GOVERNOR? MAN GOT A DEATH WISH.
YEAH, WELL, TALKING'S ALL HE CAN DO.
YOU KNOW THEY CUT HIS EYELIDS OFF, SO HE CAN'T SHUT THAT BEAM OFF BY BLINKING?
PRACTICAL.
EXACTLY.
GOVERNOR'S GOT A PRACTICAL TURN OF MIND.
GOVERNOR'S MOSTLY OUT OF HIS MIND.
YEAH, THAT TOO.
BUT THINGS DON'T GET DULL AROUND HERE.
NO, THEY DON'T.
CLOSED
OPEN
CLICK
SAY, DID YOU HEAR A--?
SKRAAAKKKT

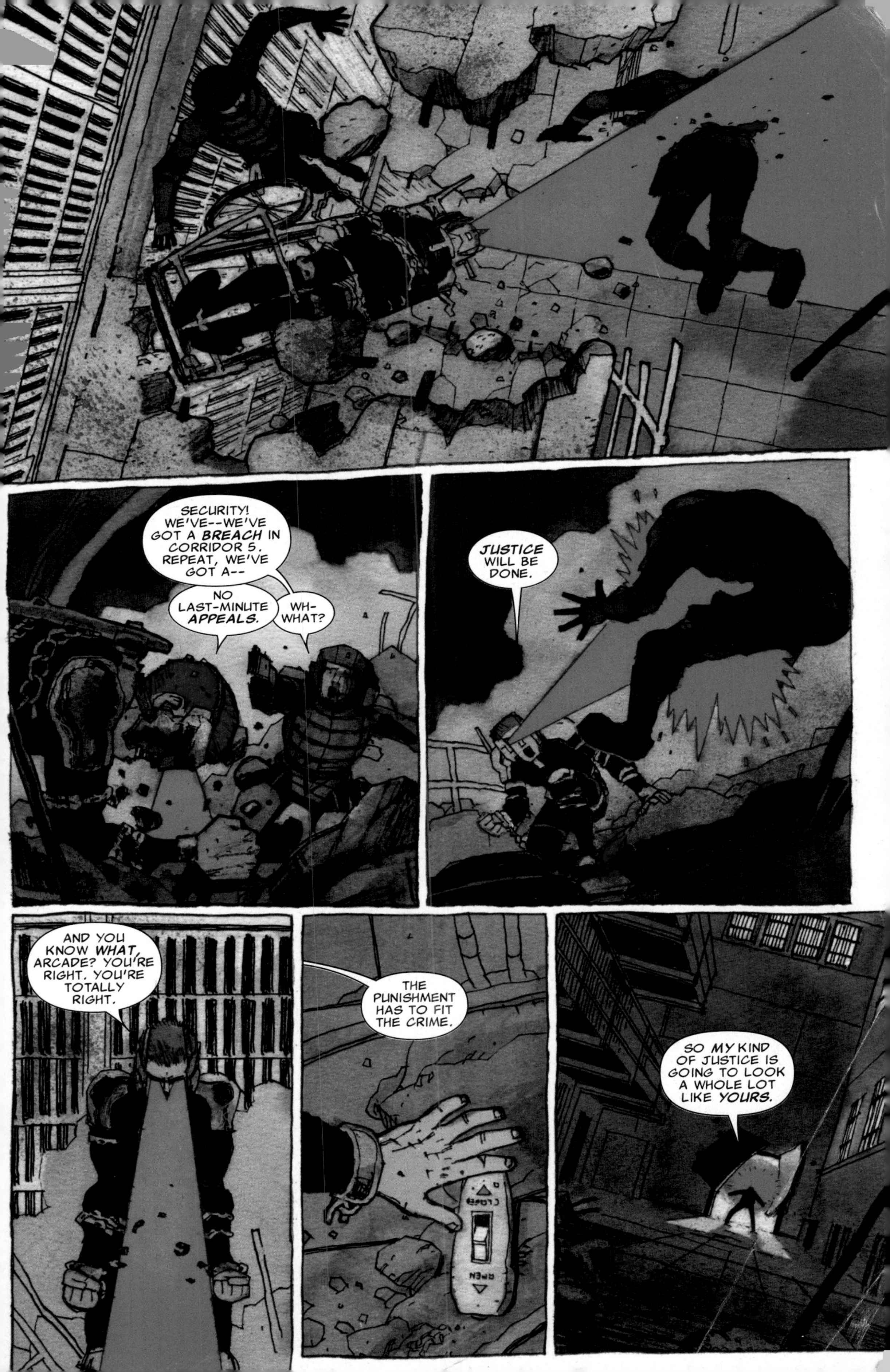
SECURITY! WE'VE--WE'VE GOT A BREACH IN CORRIDOR 5. REPEAT, WE'VE GOT A--
NO LAST-MINUTE APPEALS.
WH-WHAT?
JUSTICE WILL BE DONE.
AND YOU KNOW WHAT, ARCADE? YOU'RE RIGHT. YOU'RE TOTALLY RIGHT.
THE PUNISHMENT HAS TO FIT THE CRIME.
SO MY KIND OF JUSTICE IS GOING TO LOOK A WHOLE LOT LIKE YOURS.

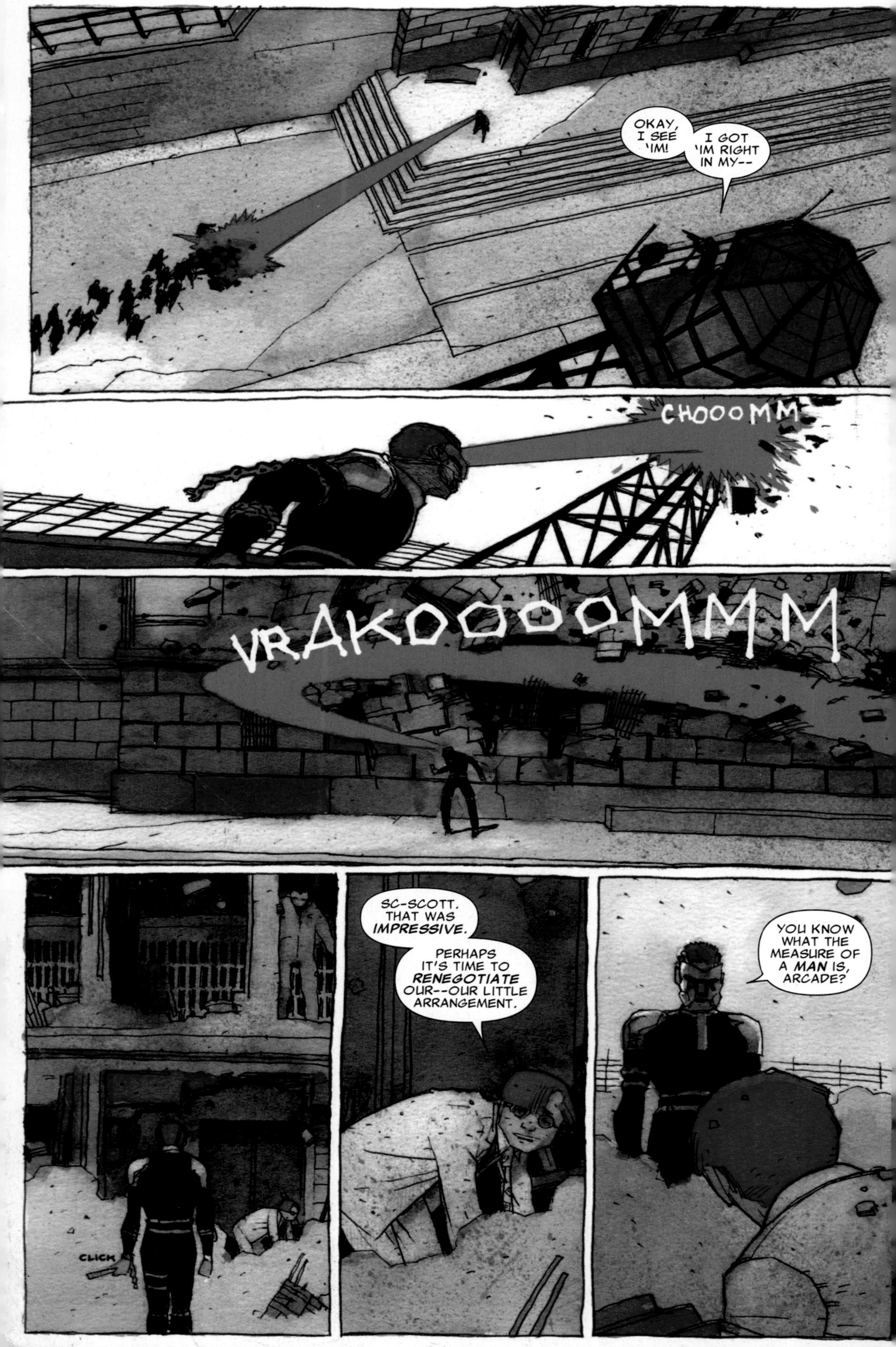
OKAY, I SEE 'IM!
I GOT 'IM RIGHT IN MY--
CHOOOMM
VRAKOOOOMMM
CLICK
SC-SCOTT. THAT WAS IMPRESSIVE.
PERHAPS IT'S TIME TO RENEGOTIATE OUR--OUR LITTLE ARRANGEMENT.
YOU KNOW WHAT THE MEASURE OF A MAN IS, ARCADE?

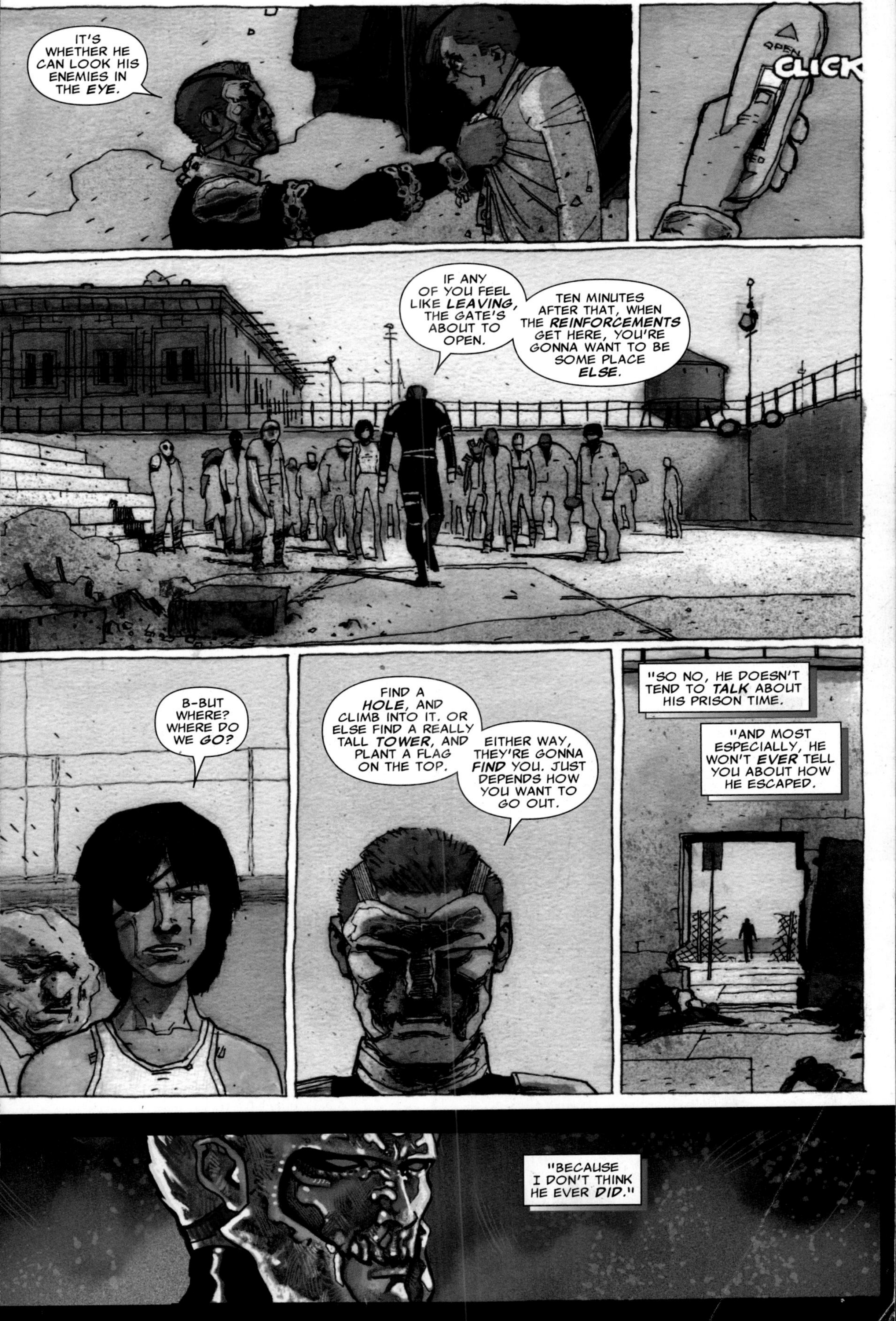
IT'S WHETHER HE CAN LOOK HIS ENEMIES IN THE EYE.
OPEN
CLICK
IF ANY OF YOU FEEL LIKE LEAVING, THE GATE'S ABOUT TO OPEN.
TEN MINUTES AFTER THAT, WHEN THE REINFORCEMENTS GET HERE, YOU'RE GONNA WANT TO BE SOME PLACE ELSE.
B-BUT WHERE? WHERE DO WE GO?
FIND A HOLE, AND CLIMB INTO IT. OR ELSE FIND A REALLY TALL TOWER, AND PLANT A FLAG ON THE TOP.
EITHER WAY, THEY'RE GONNA FIND YOU. JUST DEPENDS HOW YOU WANT TO GO OUT.
"SO NO, HE DOESN'T TEND TO TALK ABOUT HIS PRISON TIME.
"AND MOST ESPECIALLY, HE WON'T EVER TELL YOU ABOUT HOW HE ESCAPED.
"BECAUSE I DON'T THINK HE EVER DID."

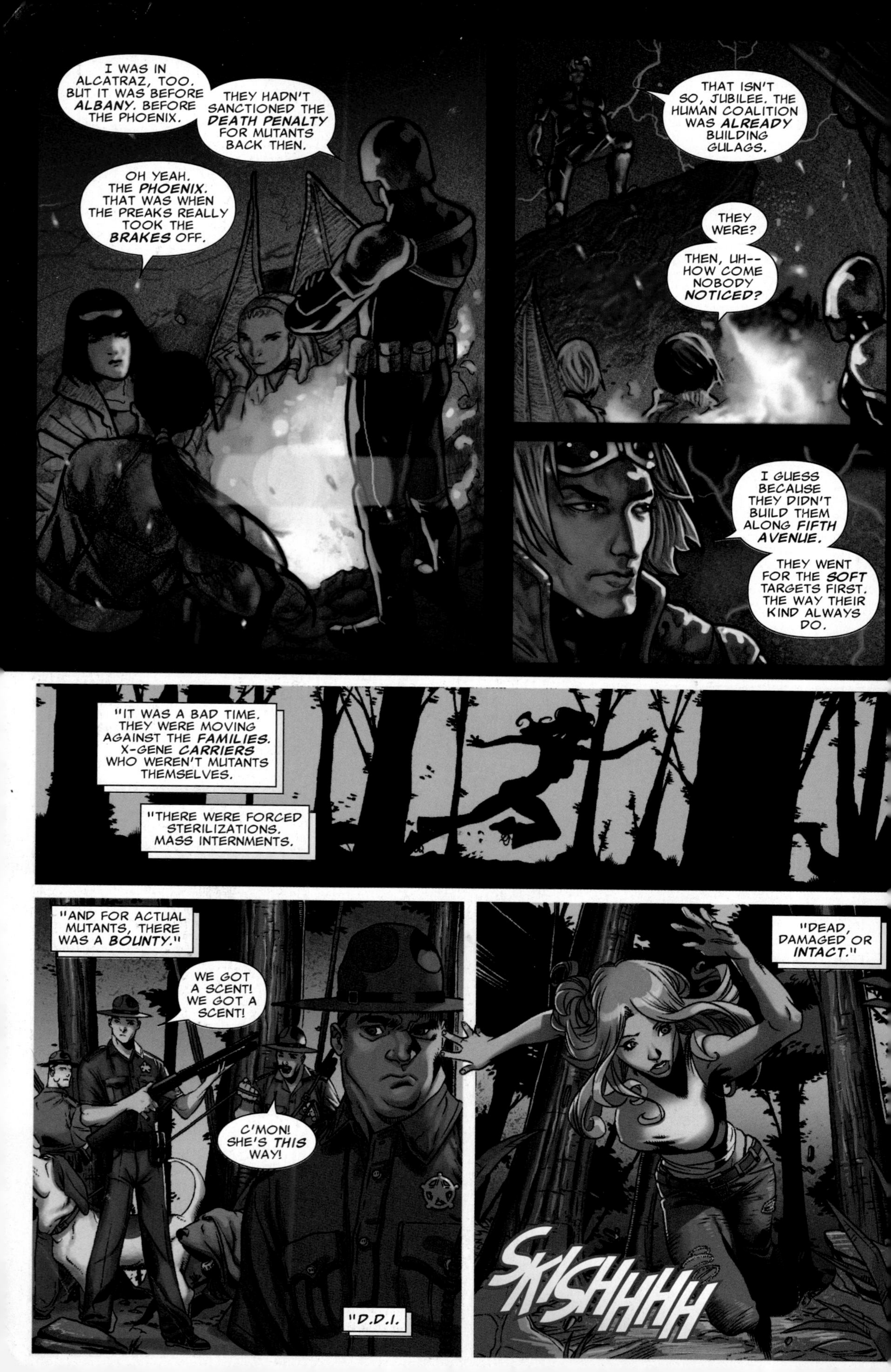

I WAS IN ALCATRAZ, TOO. BUT IT WAS BEFORE ALBANY. BEFORE THE PHOENIX.
THEY HADN'T SANCTIONED THE DEATH PENALTY FOR MUTANTS BACK THEN.
OH YEAH. THE PHOENIX. THAT WAS WHEN THE PREAKS REALLY TOOK THE BRAKES OFF.
THAT ISN'T SO, JUBILEE. THE HUMAN COALITION WAS ALREADY BUILDING GULAGS.
THEY WERE?
THEN, UH-- HOW COME NOBODY NOTICED?
I GUESS BECAUSE THEY DIDN'T BUILD THEM ALONG FIFTH AVENUE.
THEY WENT FOR THE SOFT TARGETS FIRST. THE WAY THEIR KIND ALWAYS DO.
"IT WAS A BAD TIME. THEY WERE MOVING AGAINST THE FAMILIES. X-GENE CARRIERS WHO WEREN'T MUTANTS THEMSELVES.
"THERE WERE FORCED STERILIZATIONS. MASS INTERNMENTS.
"AND FOR ACTUAL MUTANTS, THERE WAS A BOUNTY."
WE GOT A SCENT! WE GOT A SCENT!
C'MON! SHE'S THIS WAY!
"D.D.I.
"DEAD, DAMAGED OR INTACT."
SKISHHHH

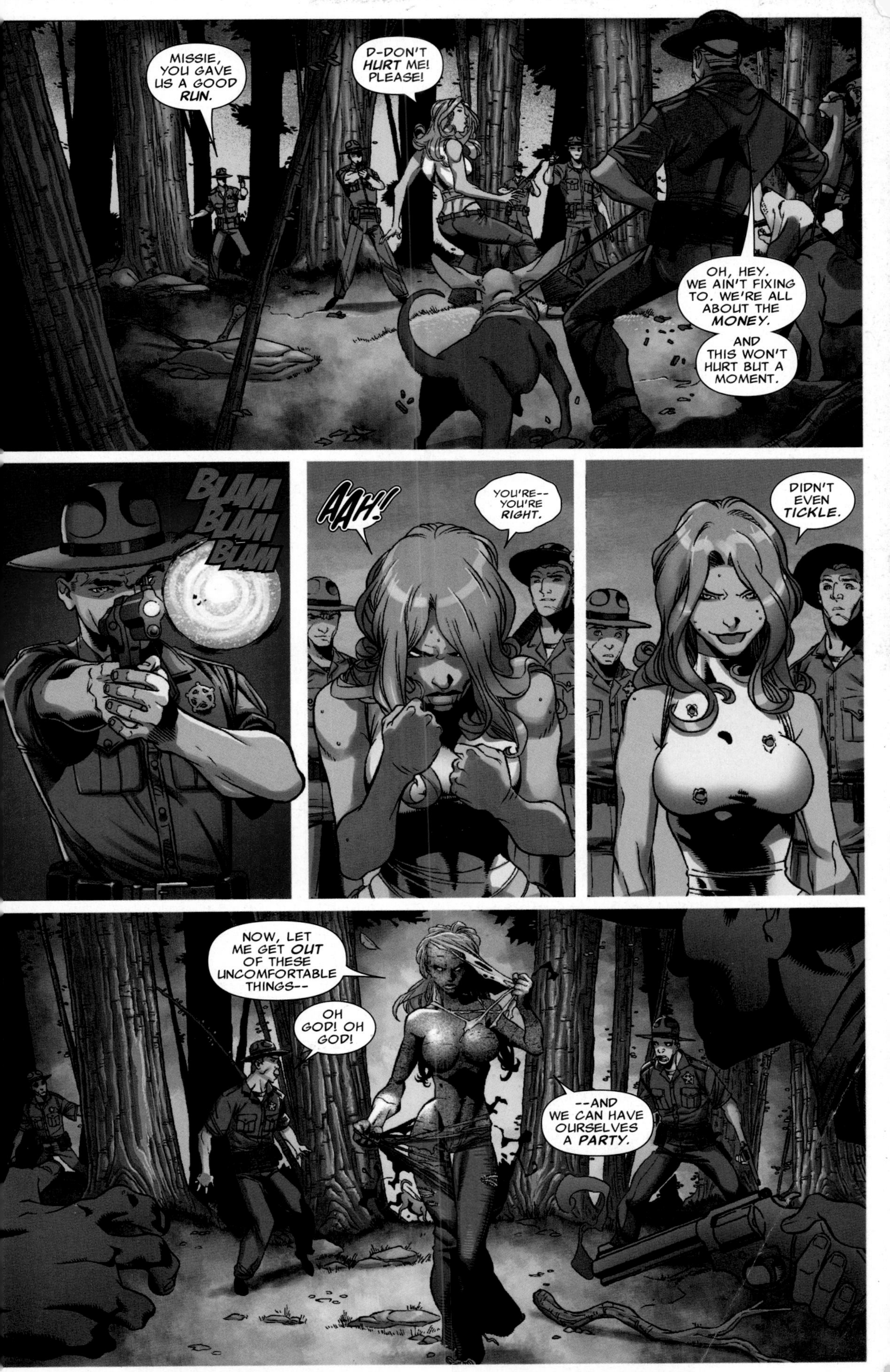
MISSIE, YOU GAVE US A GOOD RUN.
D-DON'T HURT ME! PLEASE!
OH, HEY. WE AIN'T FIXING TO. WE'RE ALL ABOUT THE MONEY.
AND THIS WON'T HURT BUT A MOMENT.
BLAM BLAM BLAM
AAH!
YOU'RE-- YOU'RE RIGHT.
DIDN'T EVEN TICKLE.
NOW, LET ME GET OUT OF THESE UNCOMFORTABLE THINGS--
OH GOD! OH GOD!
--AND WE CAN HAVE OURSELVES A PARTY.

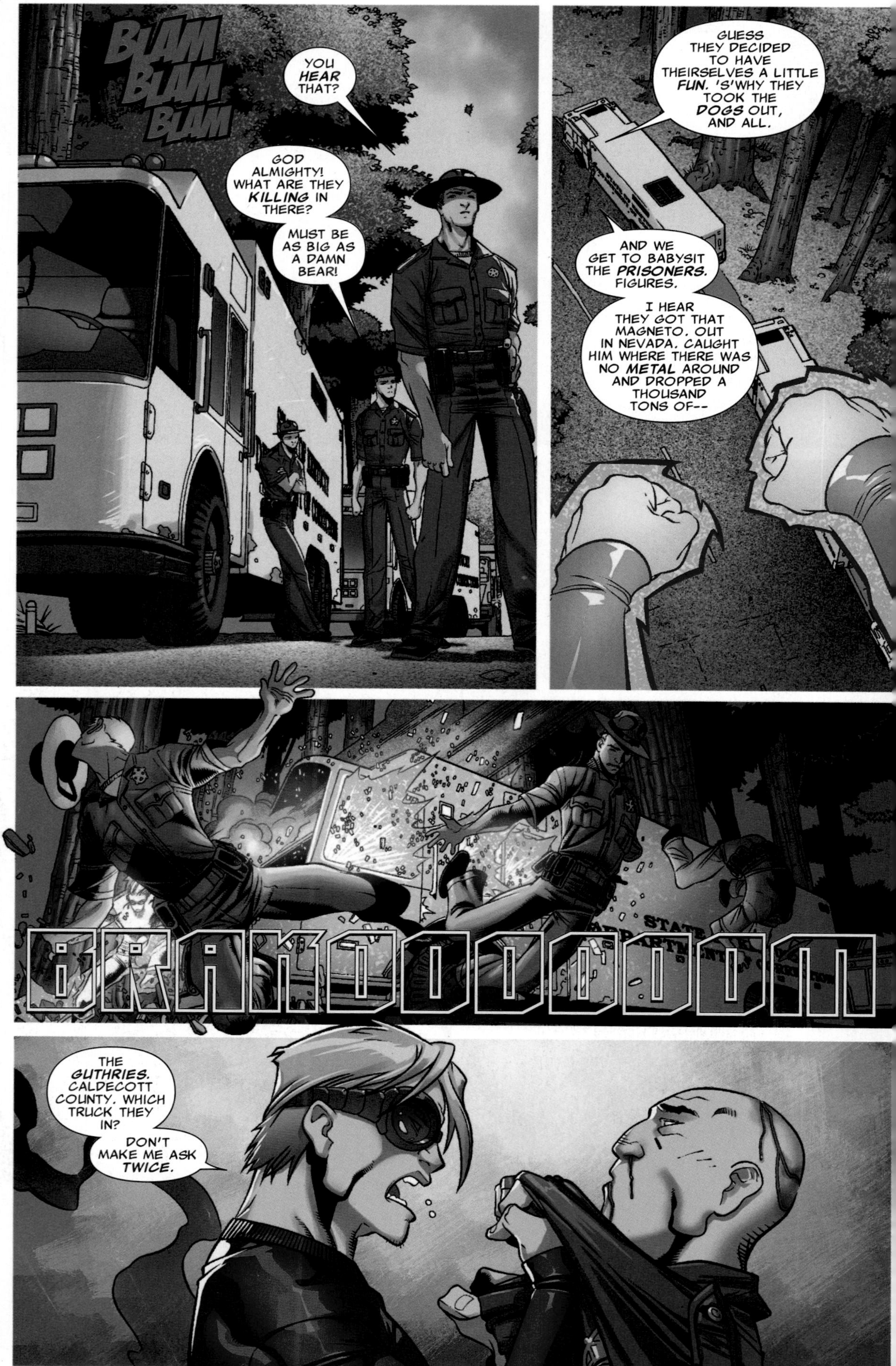
BLAM BLAM BLAM
YOU HEAR THAT?
GOD ALMIGHTY! WHAT ARE THEY KILLING IN THERE?
MUST BE AS BIG AS A DAMN BEAR!
GUESS THEY DECIDED TO HAVE THEIRSELVES A LITTLE FUN. 'S'WHY THEY TOOK THE DOGS OUT, AND ALL.
AND WE GET TO BABYSIT THE PRISONERS. FIGURES.
I HEAR THEY GOT THAT MAGNETO. OUT IN NEVADA. CAUGHT HIM WHERE THERE WAS NO METAL AROUND AND DROPPED A THOUSAND TONS OF--
BRAKOOOOOOM
THE GUTHRIES. CALDECOTT COUNTY. WHICH TRUCK THEY IN?
DON'T MAKE ME ASK TWICE.

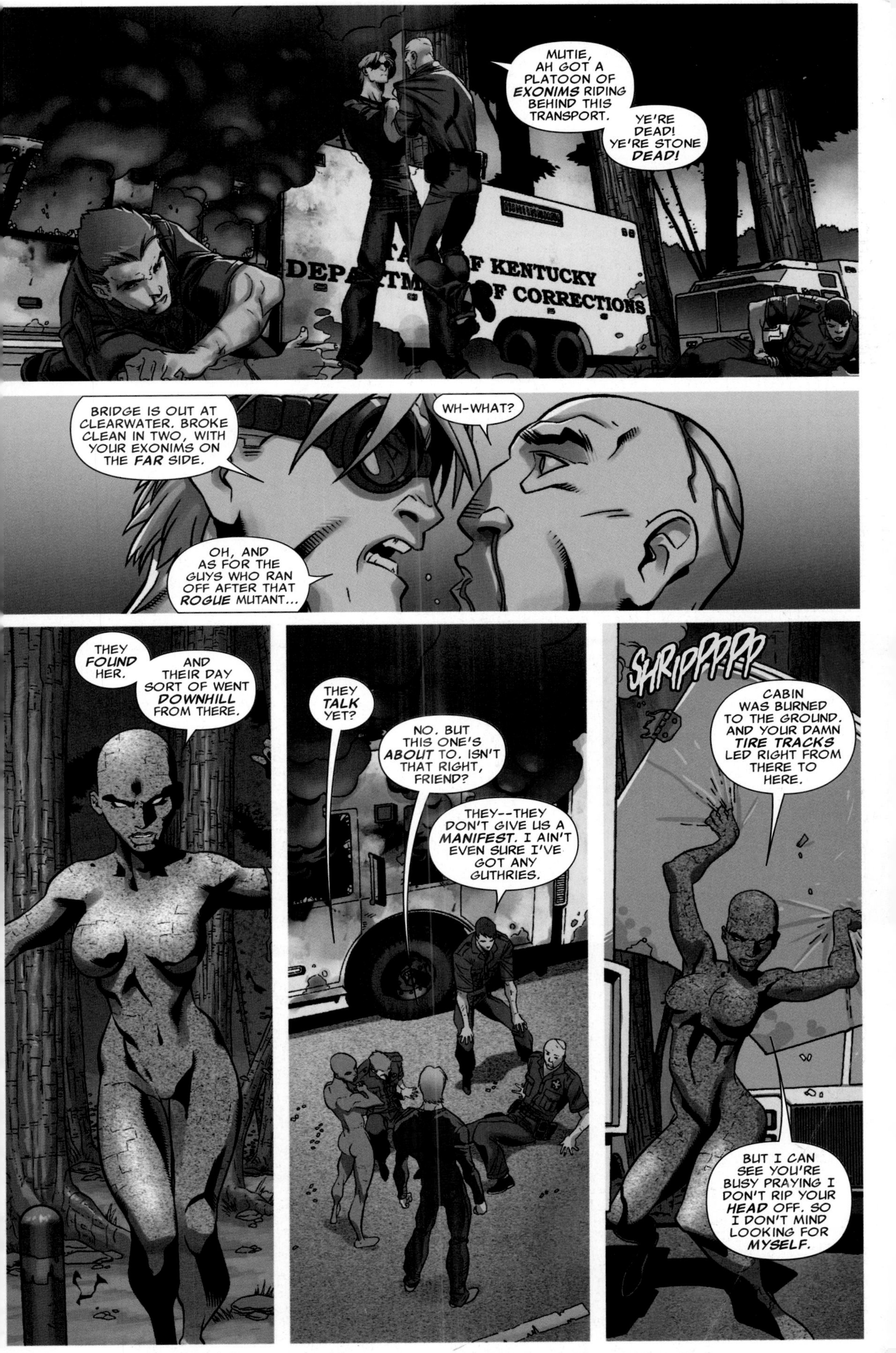
MUTIE, AH GOT A PLATOON OF EXONIMS RIDING BEHIND THIS TRANSPORT.
YE'RE DEAD! YE'RE STONE DEAD!
STATE OF KENTUCKY DEPARTMENT OF CORRECTIONS
BRIDGE IS OUT AT CLEARWATER. BROKE CLEAN IN TWO, WITH YOUR EXONIMS ON THE FAR SIDE.
WH-WHAT?
OH, AND AS FOR THE GUYS WHO RAN OFF AFTER THAT ROGUE MUTANT...
THEY FOUND HER.
AND THEIR DAY SORT OF WENT DOWNHILL FROM THERE.
THEY TALK YET?
NO. BUT THIS ONE'S ABOUT TO. ISN'T THAT RIGHT, FRIEND?
THEY--THEY DON'T GIVE US A MANIFEST. I AIN'T EVEN SURE I'VE GOT ANY GUTHRIES.
SHRIPPPP
CABIN WAS BURNED TO THE GROUND. AND YOUR DAMN TIRE TRACKS LED RIGHT FROM THERE TO HERE.
BUT I CAN SEE YOU'RE BUSY PRAYING I DON'T RIP YOUR HEAD OFF. SO I DON'T MIND LOOKING FOR MYSELF.

MA? JEB? LUCINDA? ANY OF YOU *HEAR* ME?

WH–WHO *ARE* YOU? PLEASE DON'T KILL US!

I'M NOT GONNA *TOUCH* YOU.

MA, COME ON OUT!

OKAY.

TRY THE *NEXT* ONE.

YOU *REALLY* WANT TO MAKE HER MADDER THAN SHE ALREADY IS?

I T–TOLD YOU. I DON'T *KNOW* THE NAMES.

IT'S JUST *MUTIE* TRANSPORT. THEY NEVER TELL US THE NAMES.

MA LEWIS! JOELLE!

COME *ON,* YOU GUYS. WE GOTTA GET CLEAR BEFORE THE *EXONIMS* CATCH UP WITH US!

STATE OF KENTUCKY DEPARTMENT OF CORRECTIONS

AND THEN THERE WAS *ONE.* BUT I DON'T RECKON YOU KEEP PRISONERS IN A––

...

––*DUMP* TRUCK?

N–NOBODY WANTED THIS, MISTER. SOME IDIOT SQUEEZED OFF A *SHOT,* AND––YOU KNOW HOW IT IS.

THAT SET EVERYONE *ELSE* TO SHOOTING.

WHAT?

OH GOD. OH SWEET GOD.

R-REST IN PEACE.

REST IN PEACE, MA.

ALL OF YOU.

PAIGE, ARE THEY--?

THEY'RE DEAD. THEY'RE ALL DEAD.

STAND AWAY FROM HIM.

STATE OF KENTUCKY DEPARTMENT OF CORRECTIC

JUST AN ITCHY TRIGGER FINGER, HEY, MISTER?

THAT WAS IT. EXACTLY.

I SEE THAT. IT'S AN AFFLICTION. BUT IT'S OKAY.

THERE'S A CURE.

GYARRRRHHH!

SKRUNCH

PAIGE.

GO AWAY, SAM. GO AWAY AND DON'T LOOK.

THIS PLACE IS GOING TO BE A DESOLATION. I'M GOING TO KILL THEM ALL, THEN I'M GONNA KILL THE ONES WHO SENT THEM.

NO, YOU'RE NOT. WE'RE RESPONSIBLE FOR THESE PEOPLE NOW, AND THE EXONIMS ARE ON THEIR WAY.

THERE AIN'T NO TIME FOR VENGEANCE.

OUR KIN, SAM. THEY KILLED OUR KIN! THEN THREW THEM IN A WAGON LIKE SO MUCH GARBAGE.

YOU THINK I DON'T FEEL THAT?

CHRIST'S MERCY, PAIGE! EVERY ONE OF THESE PEOPLE IS SOMEONE'S KIN, AND WE'RE THE ONLY HOPE THEY'VE GOT.

FINE, THEN. BUT YOU DON'T HAVE A HEART, SAM GUTHRIE. YOU DON'T HAVE A DAMN SOUL, EVEN, THE ONE THING THAT EVERYTHING HUMAN'S MEANT TO HAVE.

AND I WON'T BE FLESH AND BLOOD AGAIN UNTIL I SEE YOU BREAK AND WEEP FOR WHAT YOU DID THIS DAY.

YOU WON'T GET FAR, MUTIES! THE HUMAN COALITION'S CALLED THE NUMBER ON YOUR KIND!

THERE'S NO HOUSE IN THIS WORLD THAT'LL TAKE YOU IN.

STATE OF KENTUCKY
DEPARTMENT OF CORRECTIONS

DARE SAY YOU'RE RIGHT.

SO I GUESS WE'LL HAVE TO BUILD ONE.

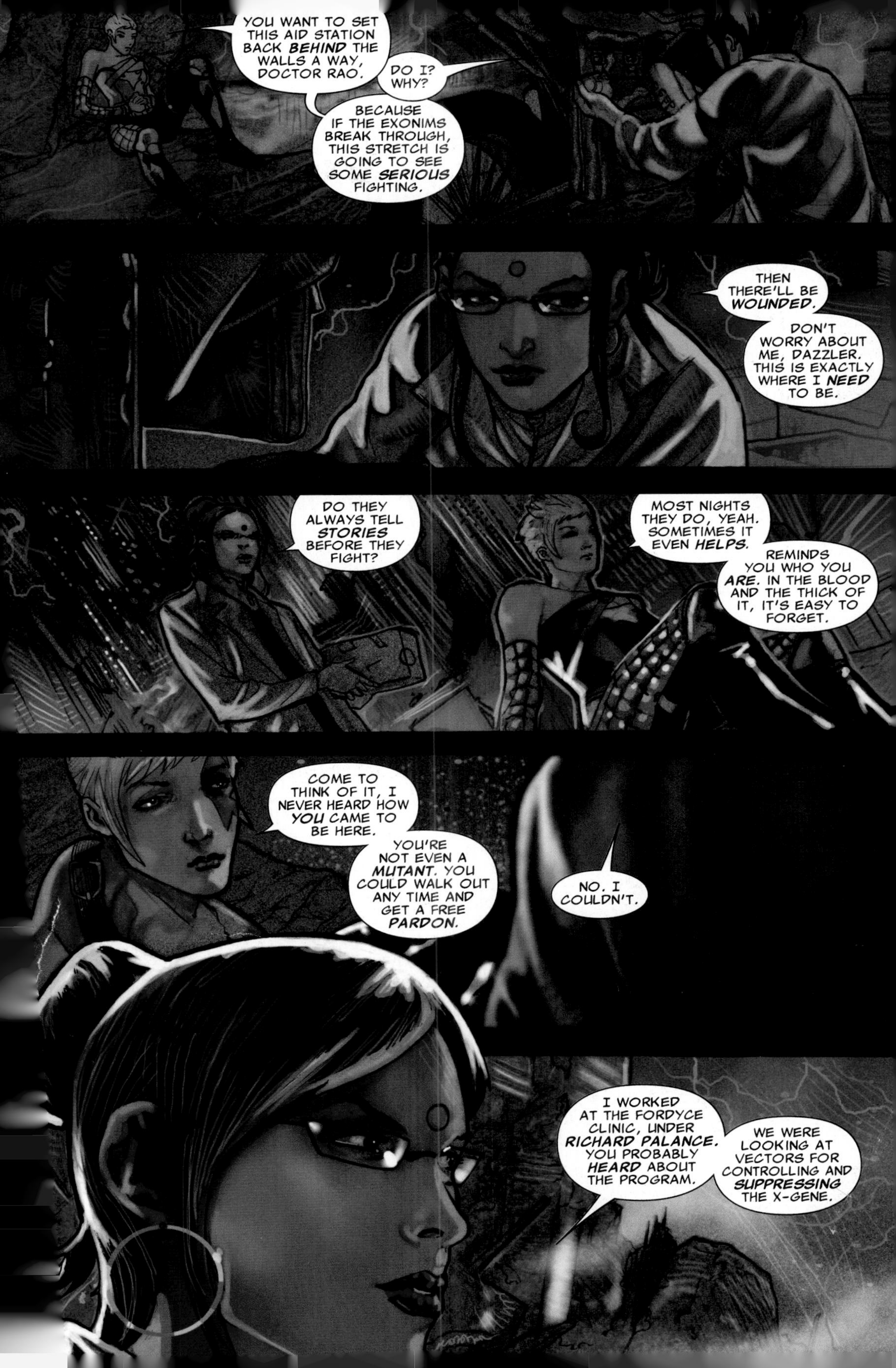

YOU WANT TO SET THIS AID STATION BACK BEHIND THE WALLS A WAY, DOCTOR RAO.
DO I? WHY?
BECAUSE IF THE EXONIMS BREAK THROUGH, THIS STRETCH IS GOING TO SEE SOME SERIOUS FIGHTING.
THEN THERE'LL BE WOUNDED.
DON'T WORRY ABOUT ME, DAZZLER. THIS IS EXACTLY WHERE I NEED TO BE.
DO THEY ALWAYS TELL STORIES BEFORE THEY FIGHT?
MOST NIGHTS THEY DO, YEAH. SOMETIMES IT EVEN HELPS.
REMINDS YOU WHO YOU ARE. IN THE BLOOD AND THE THICK OF IT, IT'S EASY TO FORGET.
COME TO THINK OF IT, I NEVER HEARD HOW YOU CAME TO BE HERE.
YOU'RE NOT EVEN A MUTANT. YOU COULD WALK OUT ANY TIME AND GET A FREE PARDON.
NO. I COULDN'T.
I WORKED AT THE FORDYCE CLINIC, UNDER RICHARD PALANCE. YOU PROBABLY HEARD ABOUT THE PROGRAM.
WE WERE LOOKING AT VECTORS FOR CONTROLLING AND SUPPRESSING THE X-GENE.

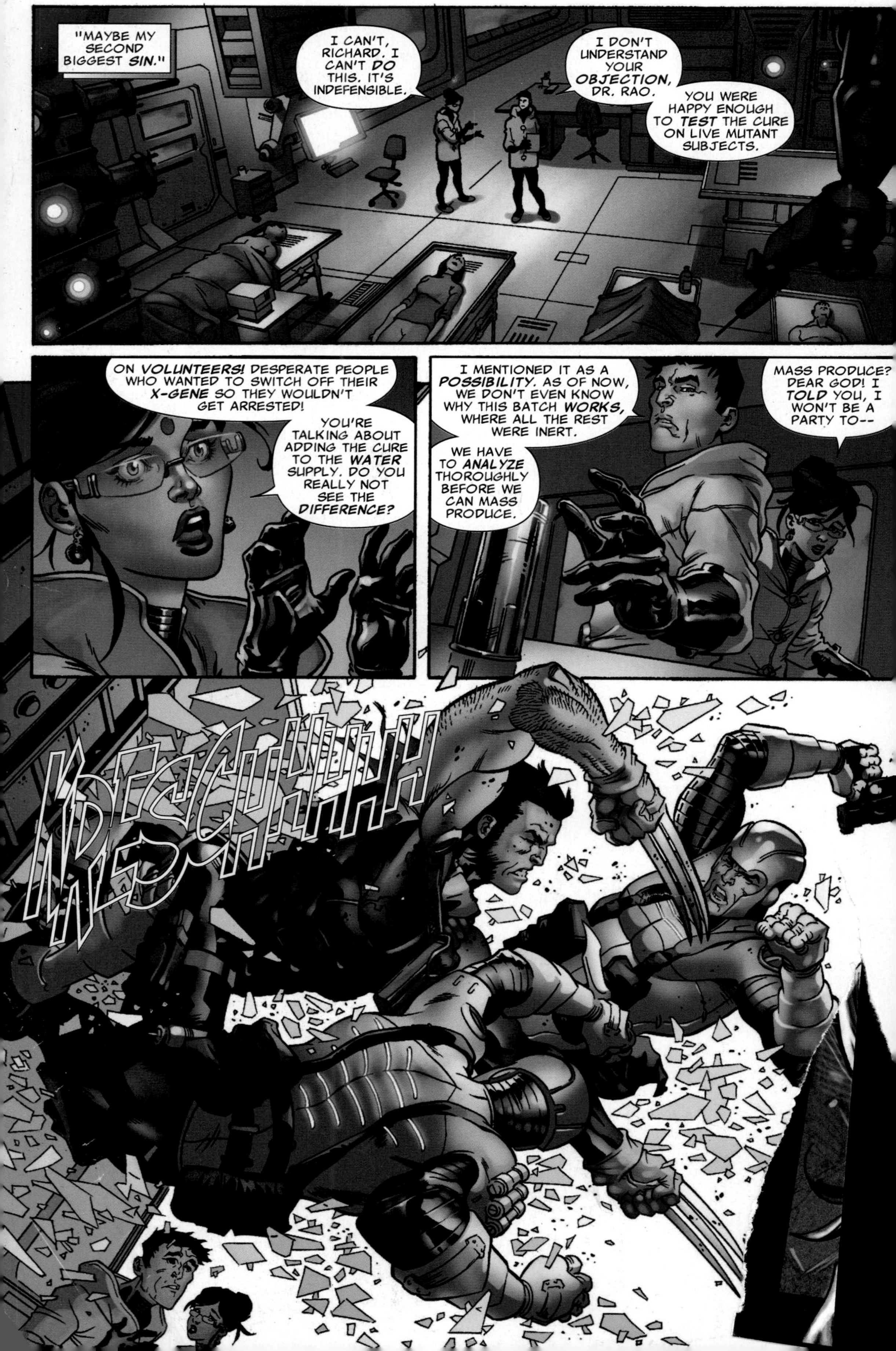

"MAYBE MY SECOND BIGGEST SIN."
I CAN'T, RICHARD. I CAN'T DO THIS. IT'S INDEFENSIBLE.
I DON'T UNDERSTAND YOUR OBJECTION, DR. RAO.
YOU WERE HAPPY ENOUGH TO TEST THE CURE ON LIVE MUTANT SUBJECTS.
ON VOLUNTEERS! DESPERATE PEOPLE WHO WANTED TO SWITCH OFF THEIR X-GENE SO THEY WOULDN'T GET ARRESTED!
YOU'RE TALKING ABOUT ADDING THE CURE TO THE WATER SUPPLY. DO YOU REALLY NOT SEE THE DIFFERENCE?
I MENTIONED IT AS A POSSIBILITY. AS OF NOW, WE DON'T EVEN KNOW WHY THIS BATCH WORKS, WHERE ALL THE REST WERE INERT.
WE HAVE TO ANALYZE THOROUGHLY BEFORE WE CAN MASS PRODUCE.
MASS PRODUCE? DEAR GOD! I TOLD YOU, I WON'T BE A PARTY TO--
KRESSHHHHH

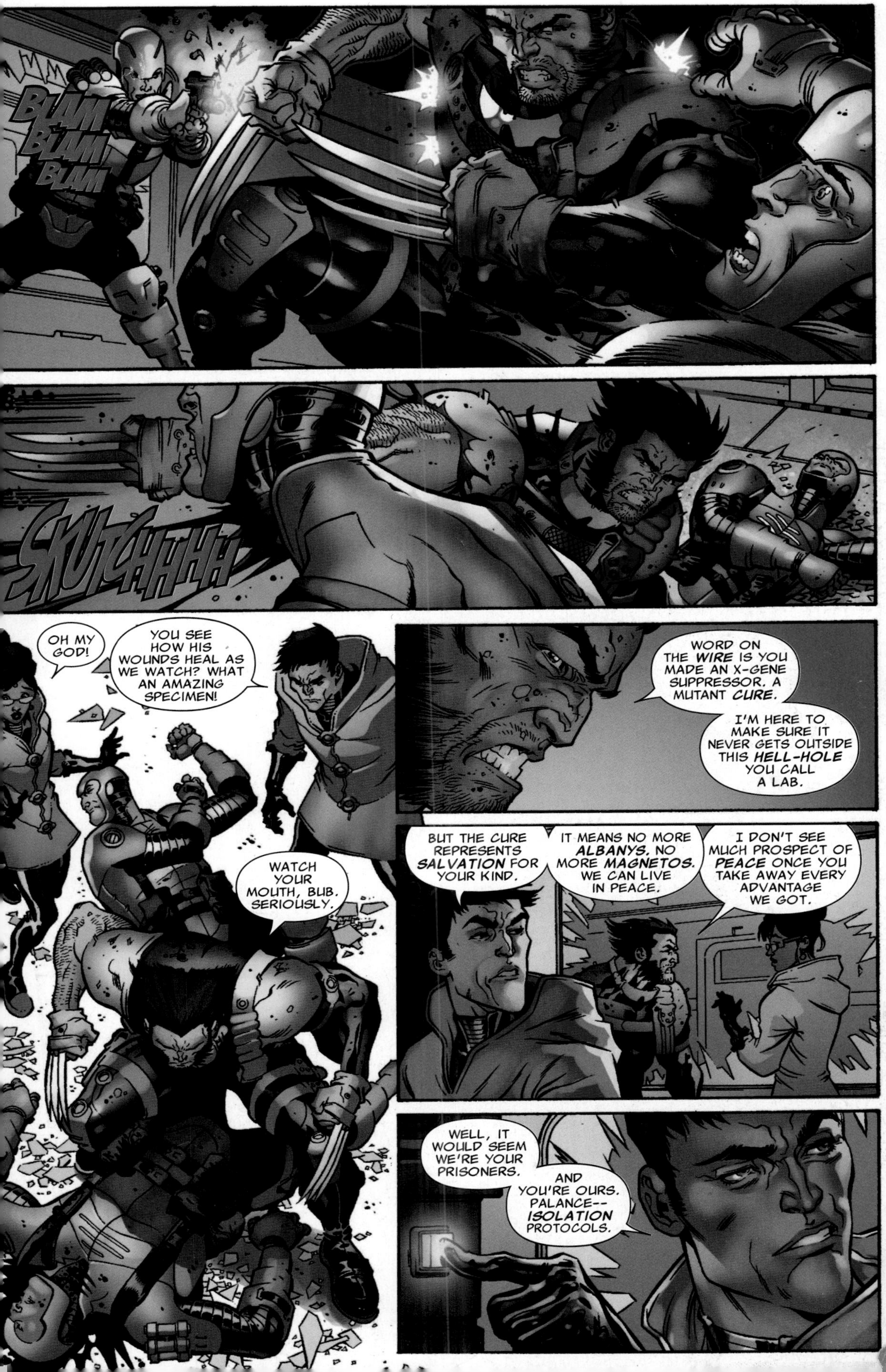

BLAM
BLAM
BLAM
SKUTCHHHH
OH MY GOD!
YOU SEE HOW HIS WOUNDS HEAL AS WE WATCH? WHAT AN AMAZING SPECIMEN!
WATCH YOUR MOUTH, BUB. SERIOUSLY.
WORD ON THE WIRE IS YOU MADE AN X-GENE SUPPRESSOR. A MUTANT CURE.
I'M HERE TO MAKE SURE IT NEVER GETS OUTSIDE THIS HELL-HOLE YOU CALL A LAB.
BUT THE CURE REPRESENTS SALVATION FOR YOUR KIND.
IT MEANS NO MORE ALBANYS. NO MORE MAGNETOS. WE CAN LIVE IN PEACE.
I DON'T SEE MUCH PROSPECT OF PEACE ONCE YOU TAKE AWAY EVERY ADVANTAGE WE GOT.
WELL, IT WOULD SEEM WE'RE YOUR PRISONERS.
AND YOU'RE OURS. PALANCE-- ISOLATION PROTOCOLS.

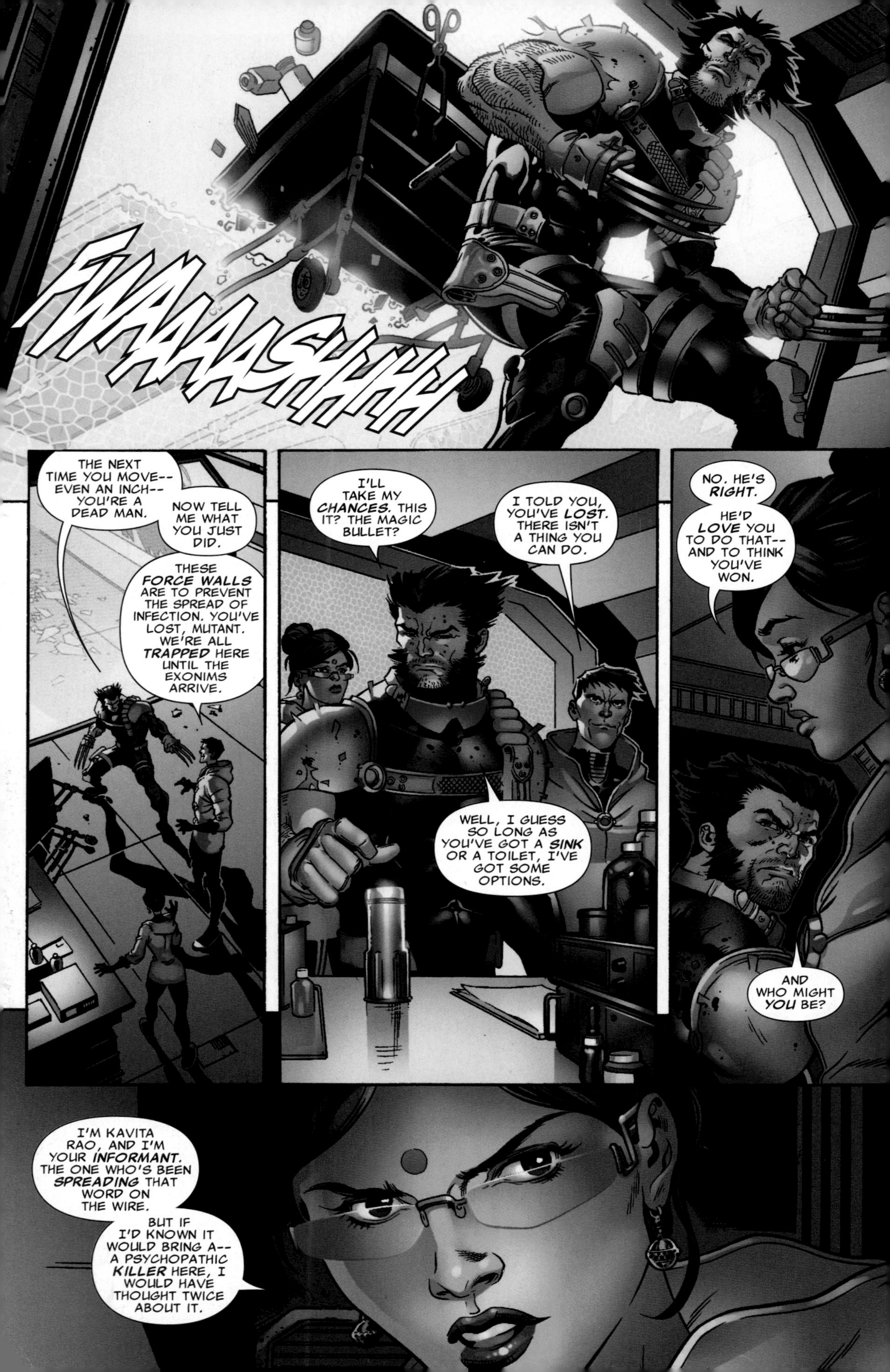
FWAAASHHH
THE NEXT TIME YOU MOVE-- EVEN AN INCH-- YOU'RE A DEAD MAN.
NOW TELL ME WHAT YOU JUST DID.
THESE FORCE WALLS ARE TO PREVENT THE SPREAD OF INFECTION. YOU'VE LOST, MUTANT. WE'RE ALL TRAPPED HERE UNTIL THE EXONIMS ARRIVE.
I'LL TAKE MY CHANCES. THIS IT? THE MAGIC BULLET?
I TOLD YOU, YOU'VE LOST. THERE ISN'T A THING YOU CAN DO.
WELL, I GUESS SO LONG AS YOU'VE GOT A SINK OR A TOILET, I'VE GOT SOME OPTIONS.
NO. HE'S RIGHT.
HE'D LOVE YOU TO DO THAT-- AND TO THINK YOU'VE WON.
AND WHO MIGHT YOU BE?
I'M KAVITA RAO, AND I'M YOUR INFORMANT. THE ONE WHO'S BEEN SPREADING THAT WORD ON THE WIRE.
BUT IF I'D KNOWN IT WOULD BRING A-- A PSYCHOPATHIC KILLER HERE, I WOULD HAVE THOUGHT TWICE ABOUT IT.

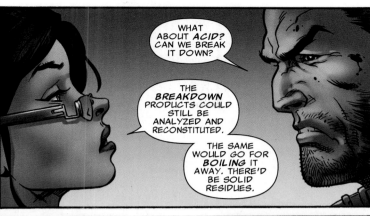

YOUR CAREER IS *OVER*, RAO. AS OF NOW, IT'S OVER.

SO WHAT AM I *MISSING*?

WHAT ABOUT *ACID*? CAN WE BREAK IT DOWN?

THE *BREAKDOWN* PRODUCTS COULD STILL BE ANALYZED AND RECONSTITUTED.

THE SAME WOULD GO FOR *BOILING* IT AWAY. THERE'D BE SOLID RESIDUES.

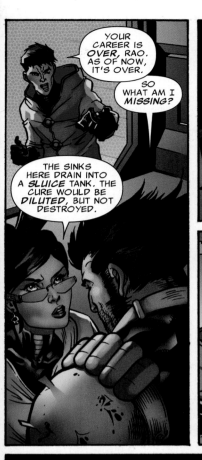

THE SINKS HERE DRAIN INTO A *SLUICE* TANK. THE CURE WOULD BE *DILUTED*, BUT NOT DESTROYED.

THIS IS ACTUALLY *AMUSING*. A LOCKED ROOM MYSTERY, WITH NO *SOLUTION*.

COME ON, DOC. YOU'RE THE *EXPERT*. THERE'S GOT TO BE A WAY TO *DITCH* THIS STUFF.

IN THE *TIME* WE'VE GOT? I CAN ONLY THINK OF ONE THING.

YOU COULD *METABOLIZE* IT.

NO!

SAY WHAT?

IT'S THE ONLY WAY. IT'S A MASSIVE *OVERDOSE*, BUT YOUR HEALING FACTOR SHOULD HELP YOU *SURVIVE*.

UNLESS THE CURE *OVERWHELMS* YOUR POWERS QUICKLY ENOUGH TO KILL YOU.

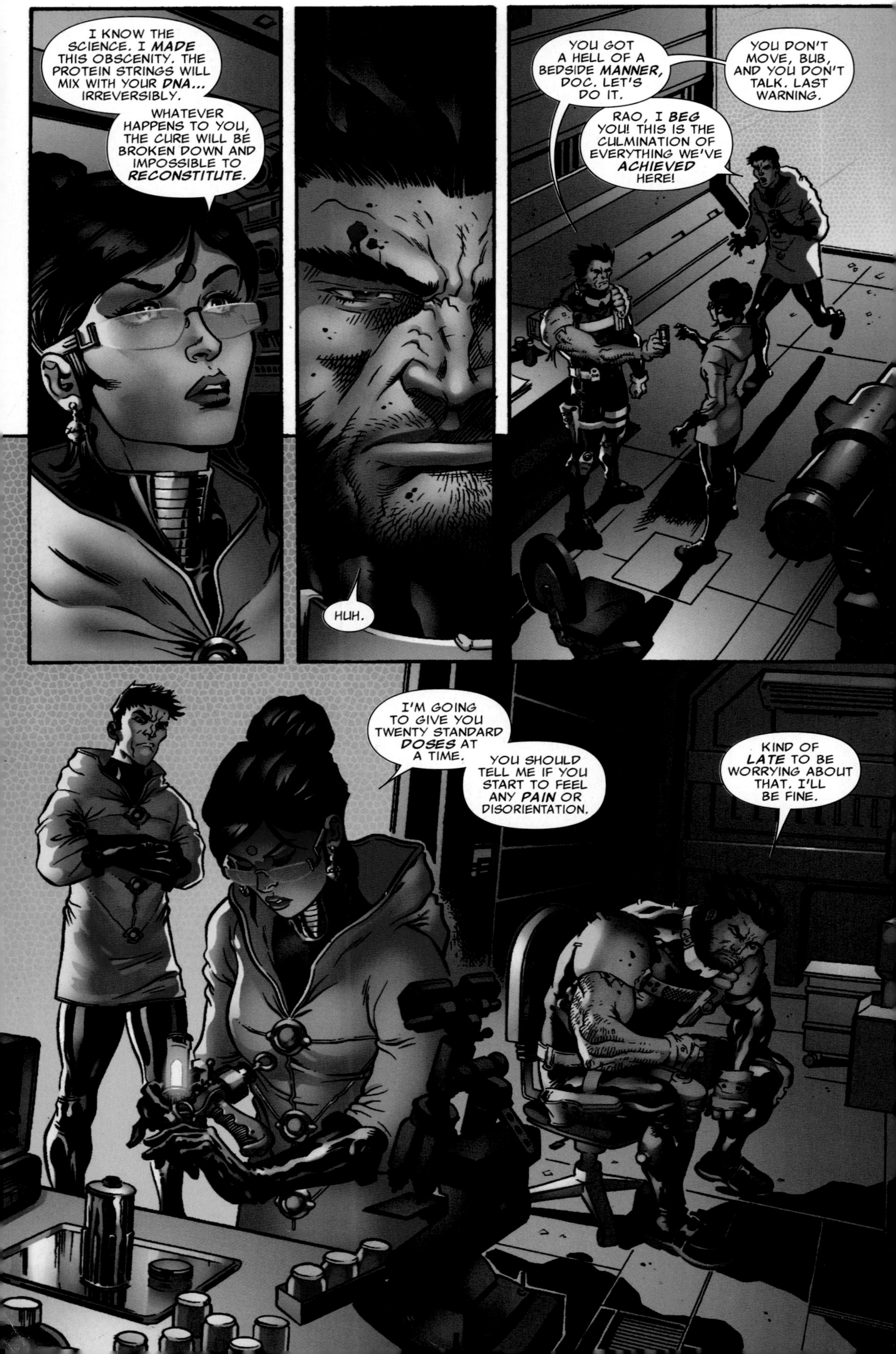
I KNOW THE SCIENCE. I MADE THIS OBSCENITY. THE PROTEIN STRINGS WILL MIX WITH YOUR DNA... IRREVERSIBLY.
WHATEVER HAPPENS TO YOU, THE CURE WILL BE BROKEN DOWN AND IMPOSSIBLE TO RECONSTITUTE.
HUH.
YOU GOT A HELL OF A BEDSIDE MANNER, DOC. LET'S DO IT.
YOU DON'T MOVE, BUB, AND YOU DON'T TALK. LAST WARNING.
RAO, I BEG YOU! THIS IS THE CULMINATION OF EVERYTHING WE'VE ACHIEVED HERE!
I'M GOING TO GIVE YOU TWENTY STANDARD DOSES AT A TIME.
YOU SHOULD TELL ME IF YOU START TO FEEL ANY PAIN OR DISORIENTATION.
KIND OF LATE TO BE WORRYING ABOUT THAT. I'LL BE FINE.

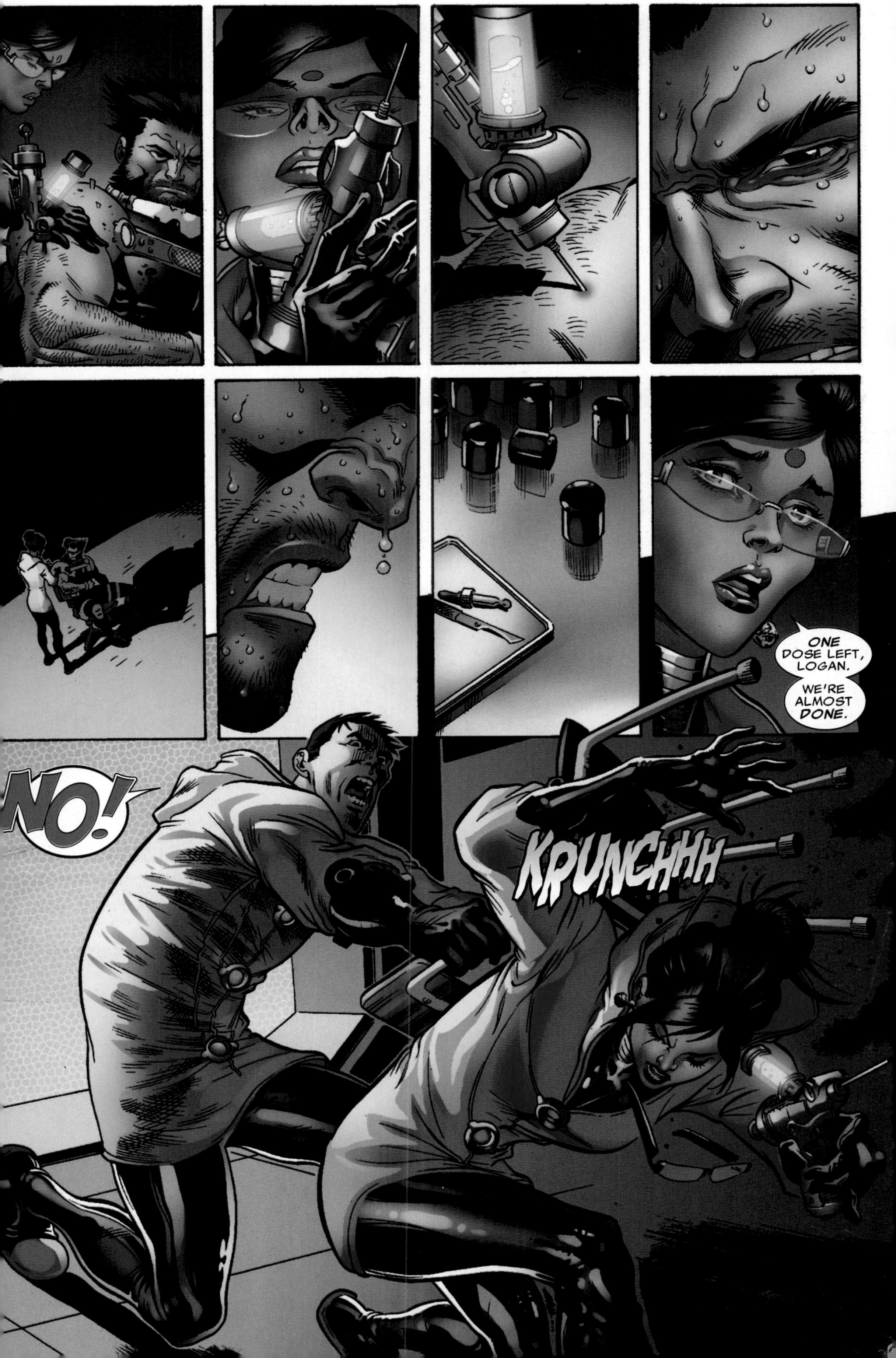
ONE DOSE LEFT, LOGAN.
WE'RE ALMOST DONE.
NO!
KRUNCHHH

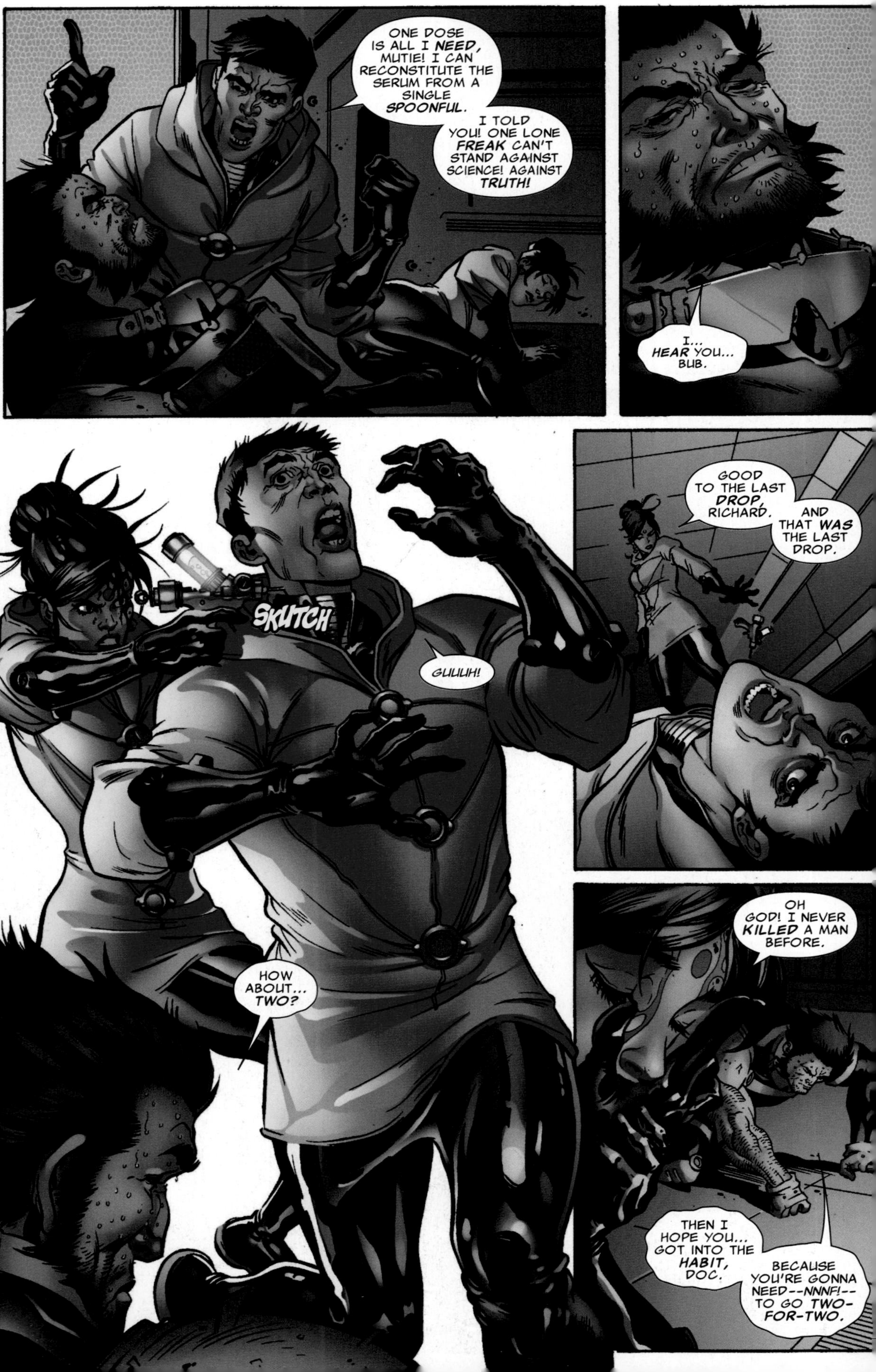

ONE DOSE IS ALL I NEED, MUTIE! I CAN RECONSTITUTE THE SERUM FROM A SINGLE SPOONFUL.
I TOLD YOU! ONE LONE FREAK CAN'T STAND AGAINST SCIENCE! AGAINST TRUTH!
I... HEAR YOU... BUB.
SKUTCH
GUUUH!
HOW ABOUT... TWO?
GOOD TO THE LAST DROP, RICHARD.
AND THAT WAS THE LAST DROP.
OH GOD! I NEVER KILLED A MAN BEFORE.
THEN I HOPE YOU... GOT INTO THE HABIT, DOC.
BECAUSE YOU'RE GONNA NEED--NNNF!--TO GO TWO-FOR-TWO.

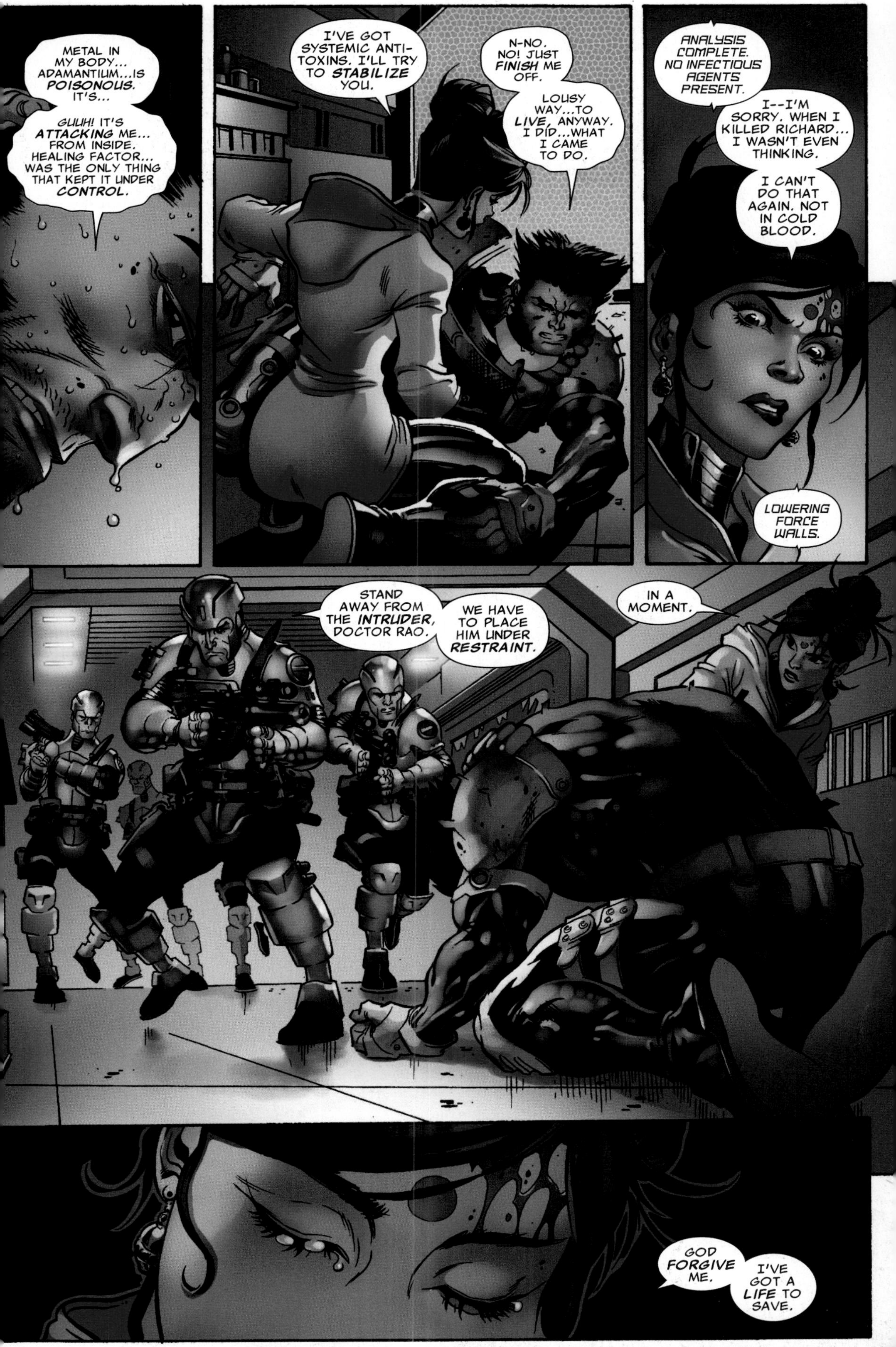
METAL IN MY BODY... ADAMANTIUM...IS POISONOUS. IT'S...
GUUH! IT'S ATTACKING ME... FROM INSIDE. HEALING FACTOR... WAS THE ONLY THING THAT KEPT IT UNDER CONTROL.
I'VE GOT SYSTEMIC ANTI-TOXINS. I'LL TRY TO STABILIZE YOU.
N-NO. NO! JUST FINISH ME OFF.
LOUSY WAY...TO LIVE, ANYWAY. I DID...WHAT I CAME TO DO.
ANALYSIS COMPLETE. NO INFECTIOUS AGENTS PRESENT.
I--I'M SORRY. WHEN I KILLED RICHARD... I WASN'T EVEN THINKING.
I CAN'T DO THAT AGAIN. NOT IN COLD BLOOD.
LOWERING FORCE WALLS.
STAND AWAY FROM THE INTRUDER, DOCTOR RAO.
WE HAVE TO PLACE HIM UNDER RESTRAINT.
IN A MOMENT.
GOD FORGIVE ME.
I'VE GOT A LIFE TO SAVE.

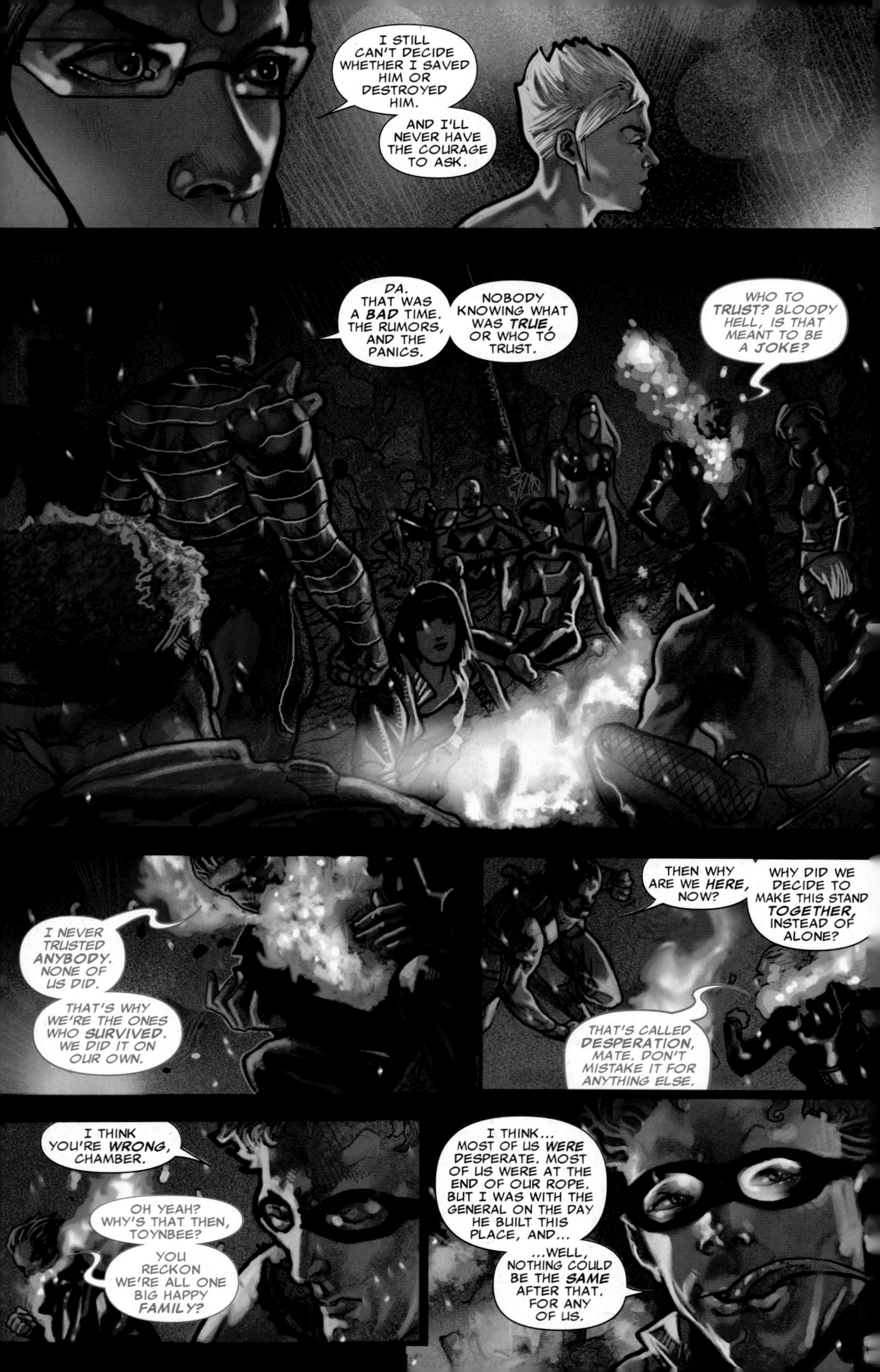
I STILL CAN'T DECIDE WHETHER I SAVED HIM OR DESTROYED HIM.
AND I'LL NEVER HAVE THE COURAGE TO ASK.
DA. THAT WAS A BAD TIME. THE RUMORS, AND THE PANICS.
NOBODY KNOWING WHAT WAS TRUE, OR WHO TO TRUST.
WHO TO TRUST? BLOODY HELL, IS THAT MEANT TO BE A JOKE?
I NEVER TRUSTED ANYBODY. NONE OF US DID.
THAT'S WHY WE'RE THE ONES WHO SURVIVED. WE DID IT ON OUR OWN.
THEN WHY ARE WE HERE, NOW?
WHY DID WE DECIDE TO MAKE THIS STAND TOGETHER, INSTEAD OF ALONE?
THAT'S CALLED DESPERATION, MATE. DON'T MISTAKE IT FOR ANYTHING ELSE.
I THINK YOU'RE WRONG, CHAMBER.
OH YEAH? WHY'S THAT THEN, TOYNBEE?
YOU RECKON WE'RE ALL ONE BIG HAPPY FAMILY?
I THINK... MOST OF US WERE DESPERATE. MOST OF US WERE AT THE END OF OUR ROPE. BUT I WAS WITH THE GENERAL ON THE DAY HE BUILT THIS PLACE, AND...
...WELL, NOTHING COULD BE THE SAME AFTER THAT. FOR ANY OF US.

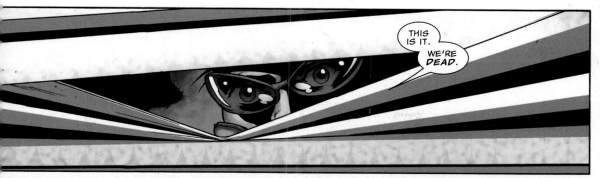

THIS IS IT. WE'RE DEAD.

THERE ARE **CHILDREN** HERE, MR. TOYNBEE.

I'M SORRY, MS...**REYES**, WAS IT? BUT TAKE A LOOK OUT THERE.

THEY'VE GOT US **SURROUNDED** SEVEN WAYS FROM SUNDAY.

NOW THAT THE COALITION HAS SLAIN **MAGNETO**, THEY'RE MOVING TO CRUSH THE LAST VESTIGES OF MUTANT **RESISTANCE**.

I THINK ONE OF YOU MAY HAVE BEEN **FOLLOWED** HERE.

IT COULD WELL HAVE BEEN **ME**. I AM OF UNUSUAL AND SUSPECT APPEARANCE. PERHAPS IF I GO DOWN AND **SURRENDER**--

NO.

"BELIEVE ME, SOORAYA--

"--AT THIS STAGE, THAT'S NOT LIKELY TO MAKE MUCH **DIFFERENCE**."

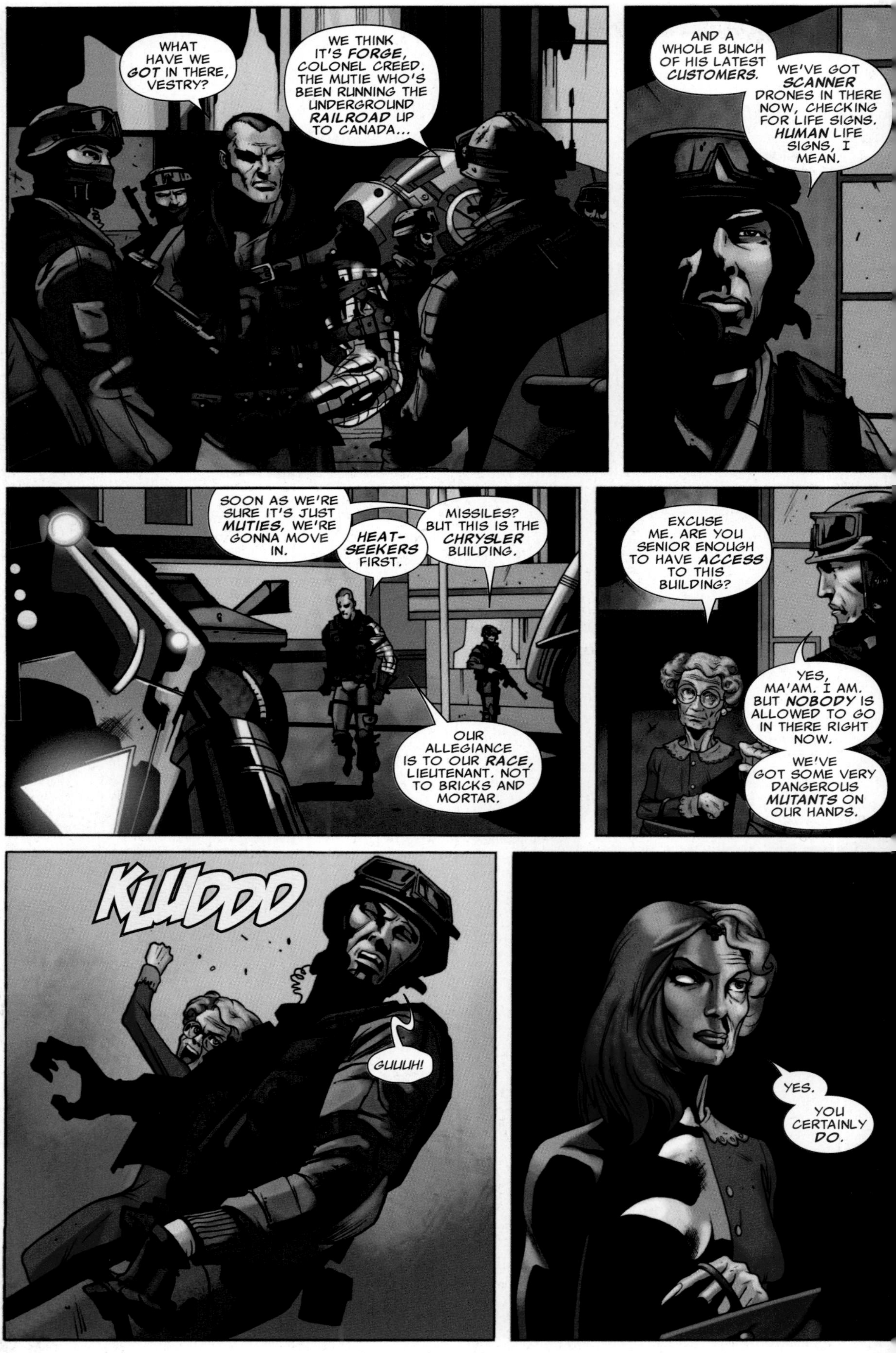
WHAT HAVE WE GOT IN THERE, VESTRY?
WE THINK IT'S FORGE, COLONEL CREED. THE MUTIE WHO'S BEEN RUNNING THE UNDERGROUND RAILROAD UP TO CANADA...
AND A WHOLE BUNCH OF HIS LATEST CUSTOMERS.
WE'VE GOT SCANNER DRONES IN THERE NOW, CHECKING FOR LIFE SIGNS. HUMAN LIFE SIGNS, I MEAN.
SOON AS WE'RE SURE IT'S JUST MUTIES, WE'RE GONNA MOVE IN.
HEAT-SEEKERS FIRST.
MISSILES? BUT THIS IS THE CHRYSLER BUILDING.
OUR ALLEGIANCE IS TO OUR RACE, LIEUTENANT. NOT TO BRICKS AND MORTAR.
EXCUSE ME. ARE YOU SENIOR ENOUGH TO HAVE ACCESS TO THIS BUILDING?
YES, MA'AM. I AM. BUT NOBODY IS ALLOWED TO GO IN THERE RIGHT NOW.
WE'VE GOT SOME VERY DANGEROUS MUTANTS ON OUR HANDS.
KLUDDD
GUUUH!
YES.
YOU CERTAINLY DO.

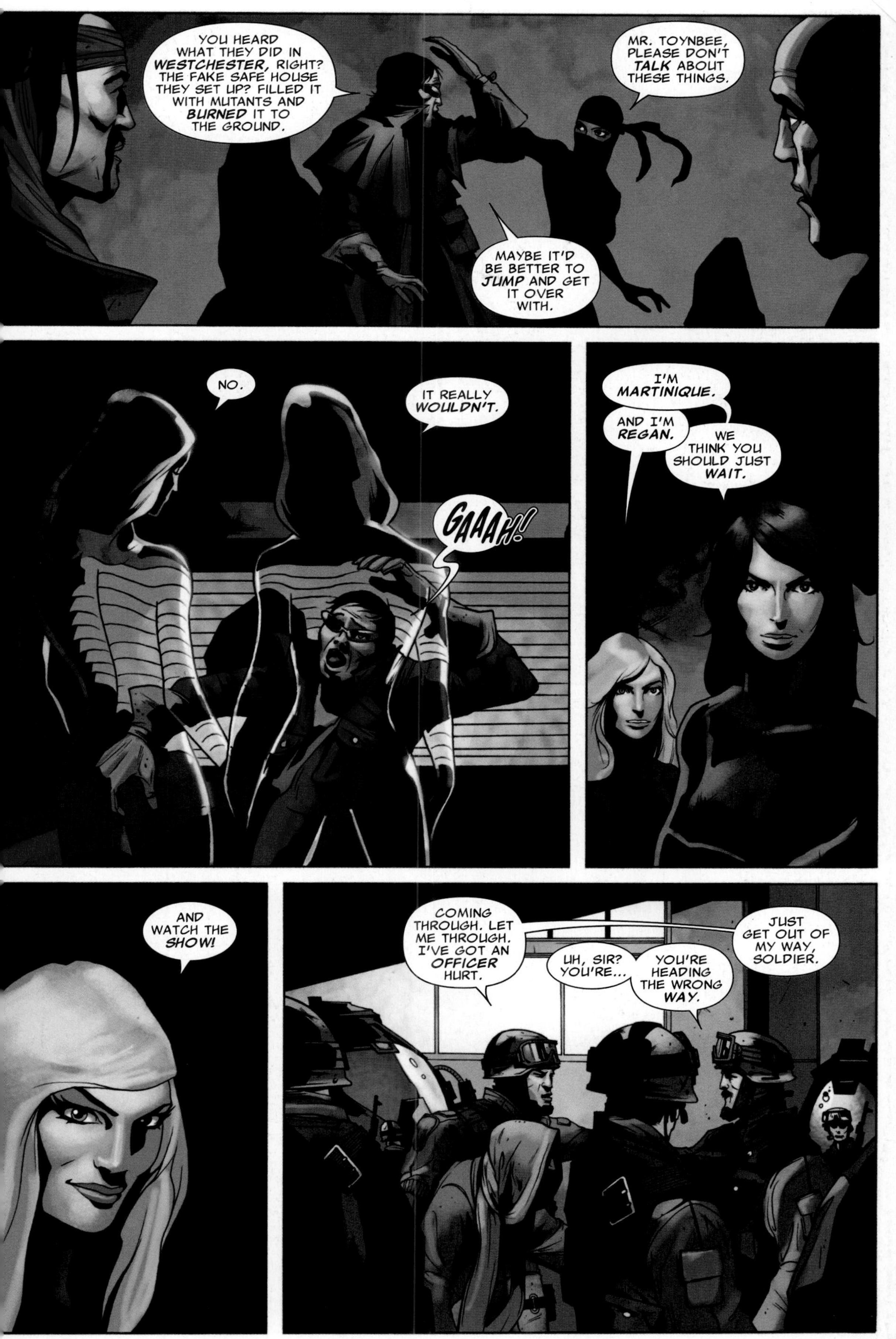
YOU HEARD WHAT THEY DID IN WESTCHESTER, RIGHT? THE FAKE SAFE HOUSE THEY SET UP? FILLED IT WITH MUTANTS AND BURNED IT TO THE GROUND.
MR. TOYNBEE, PLEASE DON'T TALK ABOUT THESE THINGS.
MAYBE IT'D BE BETTER TO JUMP AND GET IT OVER WITH.
NO.
IT REALLY WOULDN'T.
GAAAH!
I'M MARTINIQUE.
AND I'M REGAN.
WE THINK YOU SHOULD JUST WAIT.
AND WATCH THE SHOW!
COMING THROUGH. LET ME THROUGH. I'VE GOT AN OFFICER HURT.
JUST GET OUT OF MY WAY, SOLDIER.
UH, SIR? YOU'RE...
YOU'RE HEADING THE WRONG WAY.

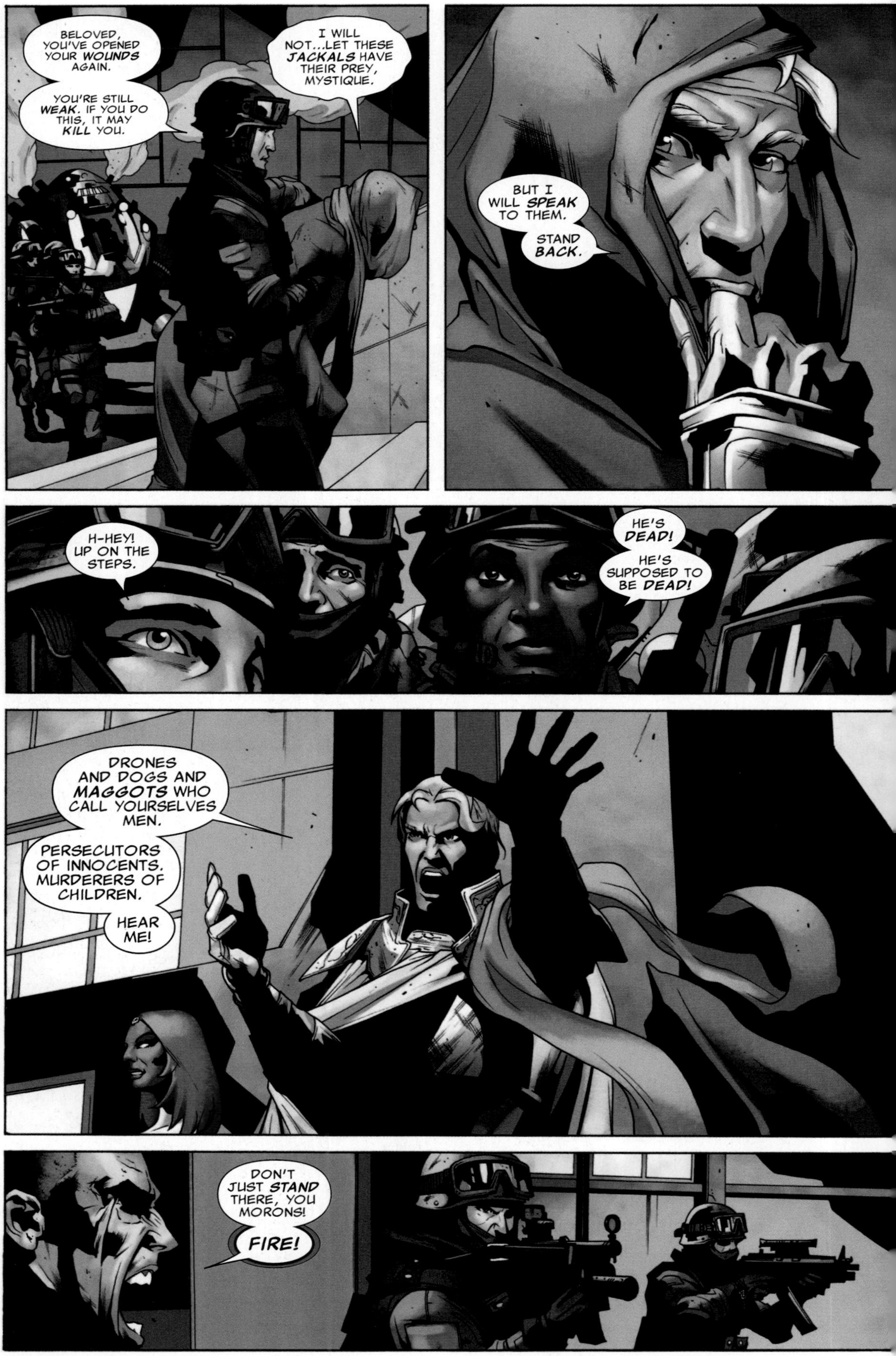
BELOVED, YOU'VE OPENED YOUR WOUNDS AGAIN.
YOU'RE STILL WEAK. IF YOU DO THIS, IT MAY KILL YOU.
I WILL NOT...LET THESE JACKALS HAVE THEIR PREY, MYSTIQUE.
BUT I WILL SPEAK TO THEM.
STAND BACK.
H-HEY! UP ON THE STEPS.
HE'S DEAD!
HE'S SUPPOSED TO BE DEAD!
DRONES AND DOGS AND MAGGOTS WHO CALL YOURSELVES MEN.
PERSECUTORS OF INNOCENTS. MURDERERS OF CHILDREN.
HEAR ME!
DON'T JUST STAND THERE, YOU MORONS!
FIRE!

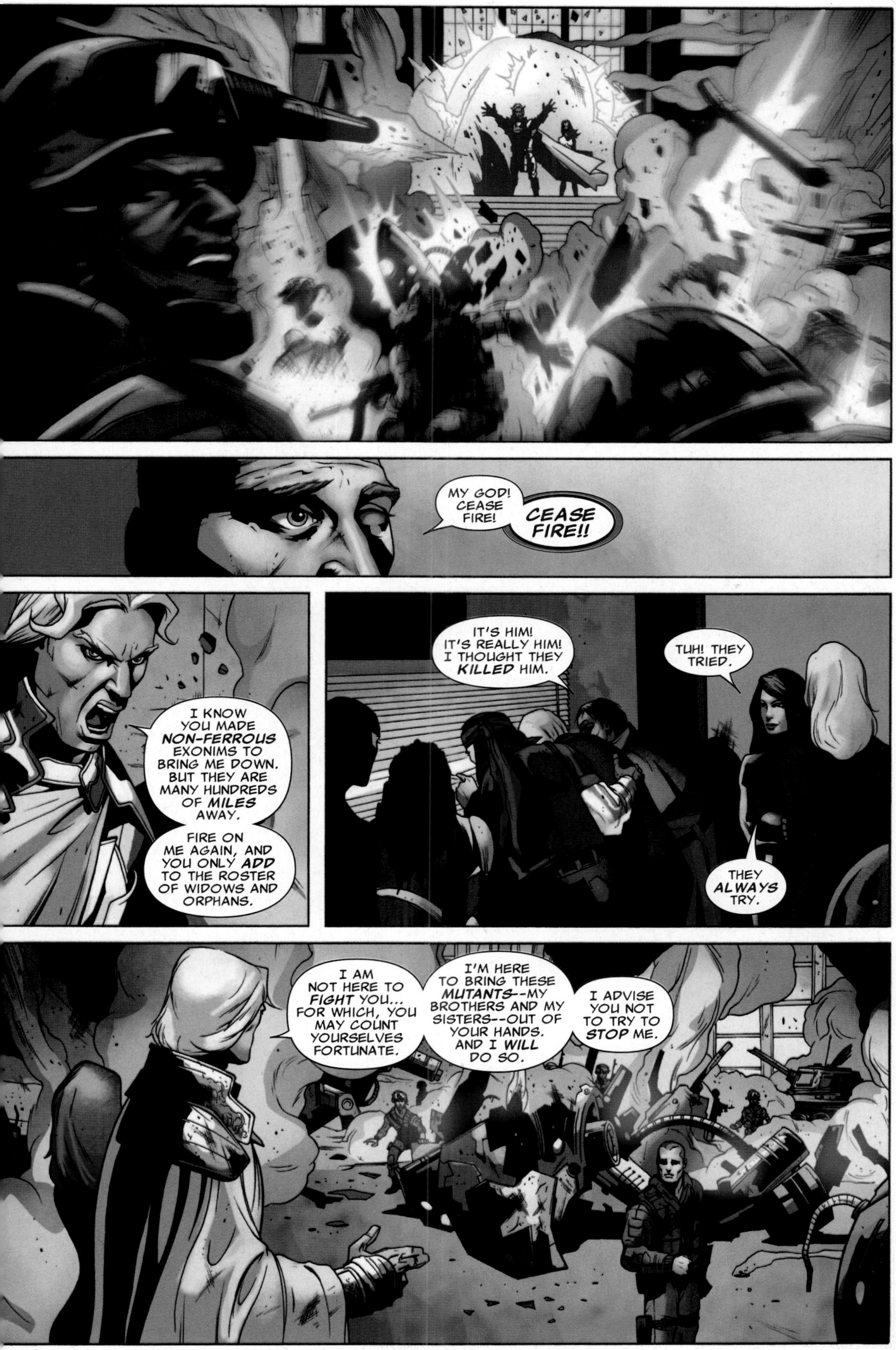
MY GOD! CEASE FIRE!
CEASE FIRE!!
I KNOW YOU MADE NON-FERROUS EXONIMS TO BRING ME DOWN. BUT THEY ARE MANY HUNDREDS OF MILES AWAY.
FIRE ON ME AGAIN, AND YOU ONLY ADD TO THE ROSTER OF WIDOWS AND ORPHANS.
IT'S HIM! IT'S REALLY HIM! I THOUGHT THEY KILLED HIM.
TUH! THEY TRIED.
THEY ALWAYS TRY.
I AM NOT HERE TO FIGHT YOU... FOR WHICH, YOU MAY COUNT YOURSELVES FORTUNATE.
I'M HERE TO BRING THESE MUTANTS--MY BROTHERS AND MY SISTERS--OUT OF YOUR HANDS. AND I WILL DO SO.
I ADVISE YOU NOT TO TRY TO STOP ME.

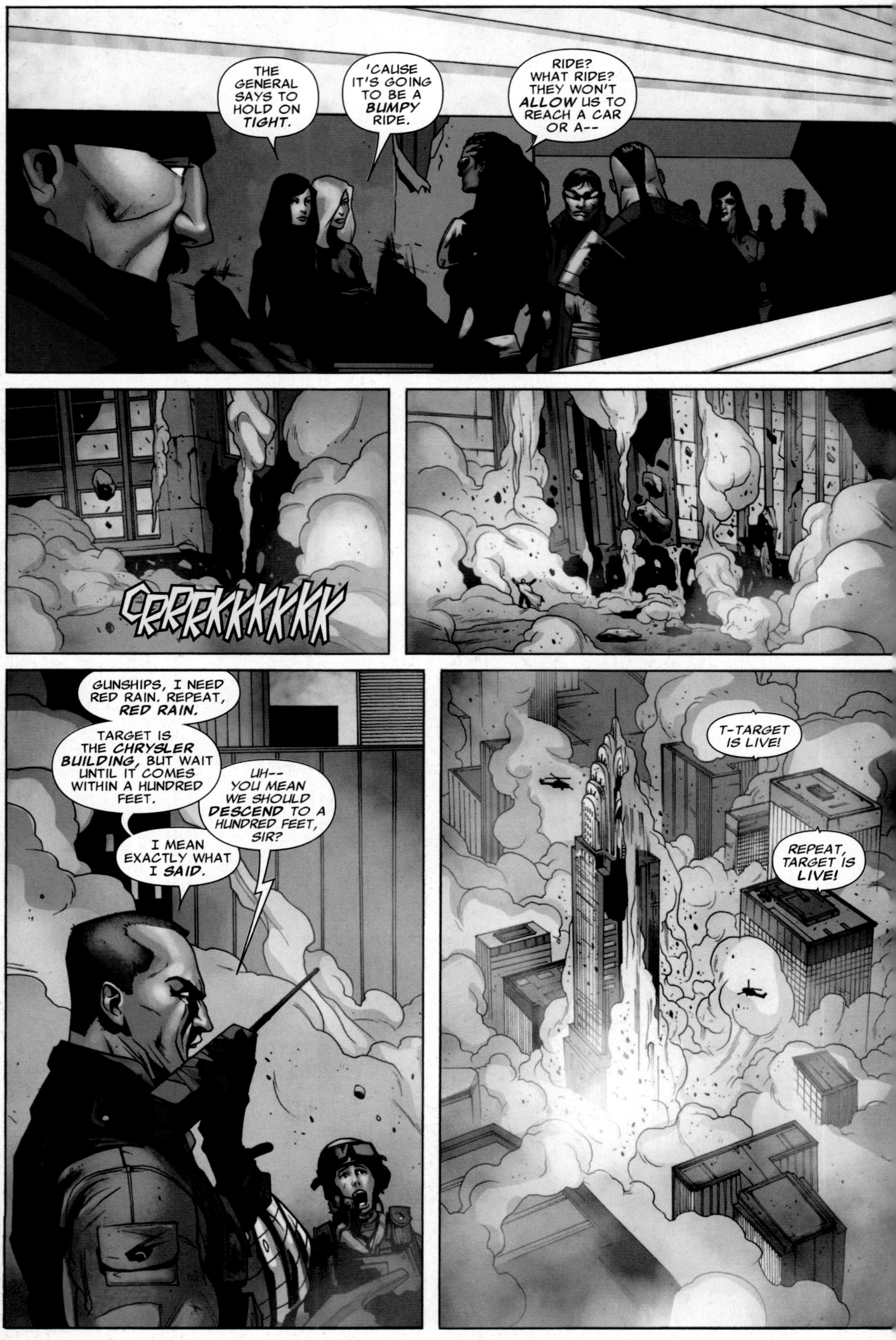
THE GENERAL SAYS TO HOLD ON TIGHT.
'CAUSE IT'S GOING TO BE A BUMPY RIDE.
RIDE? WHAT RIDE? THEY WON'T ALLOW US TO REACH A CAR OR A--
CRRRKKKKKKK
GUNSHIPS, I NEED RED RAIN. REPEAT, RED RAIN.
TARGET IS THE CHRYSLER BUILDING, BUT WAIT UNTIL IT COMES WITHIN A HUNDRED FEET.
UH-- YOU MEAN WE SHOULD DESCEND TO A HUNDRED FEET, SIR?
I MEAN EXACTLY WHAT I SAID.
T-TARGET IS LIVE!
REPEAT, TARGET IS LIVE!

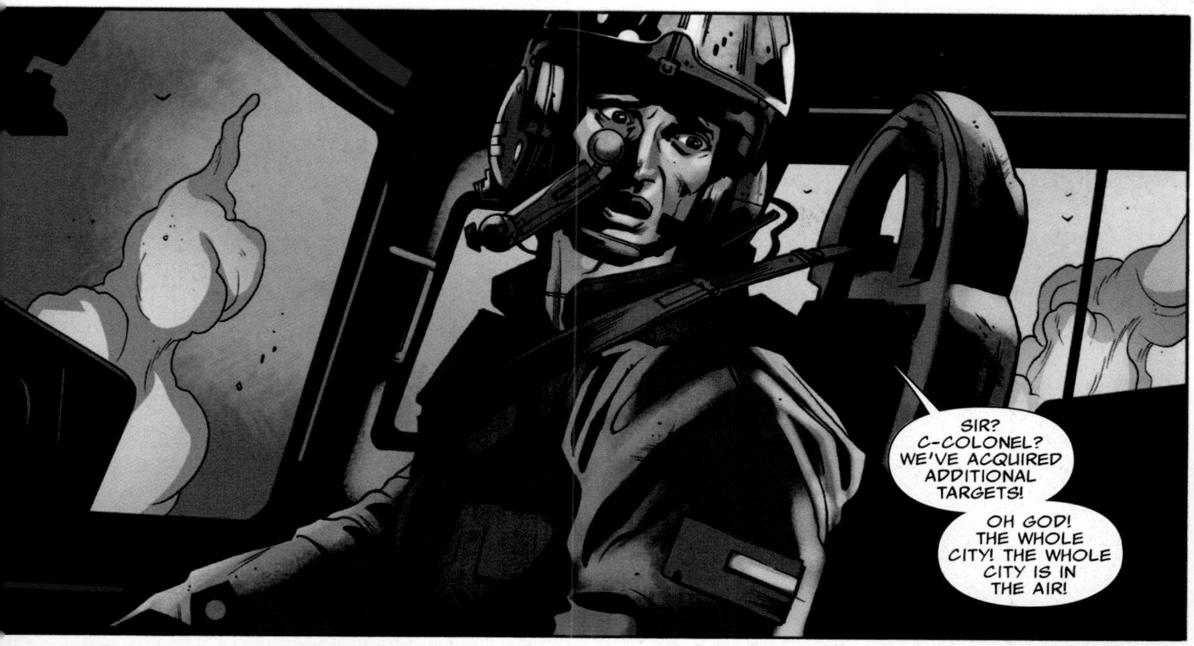
SIR? C-COLONEL? WE'VE ACQUIRED ADDITIONAL TARGETS!
OH GOD! THE WHOLE CITY! THE WHOLE CITY IS IN THE AIR!

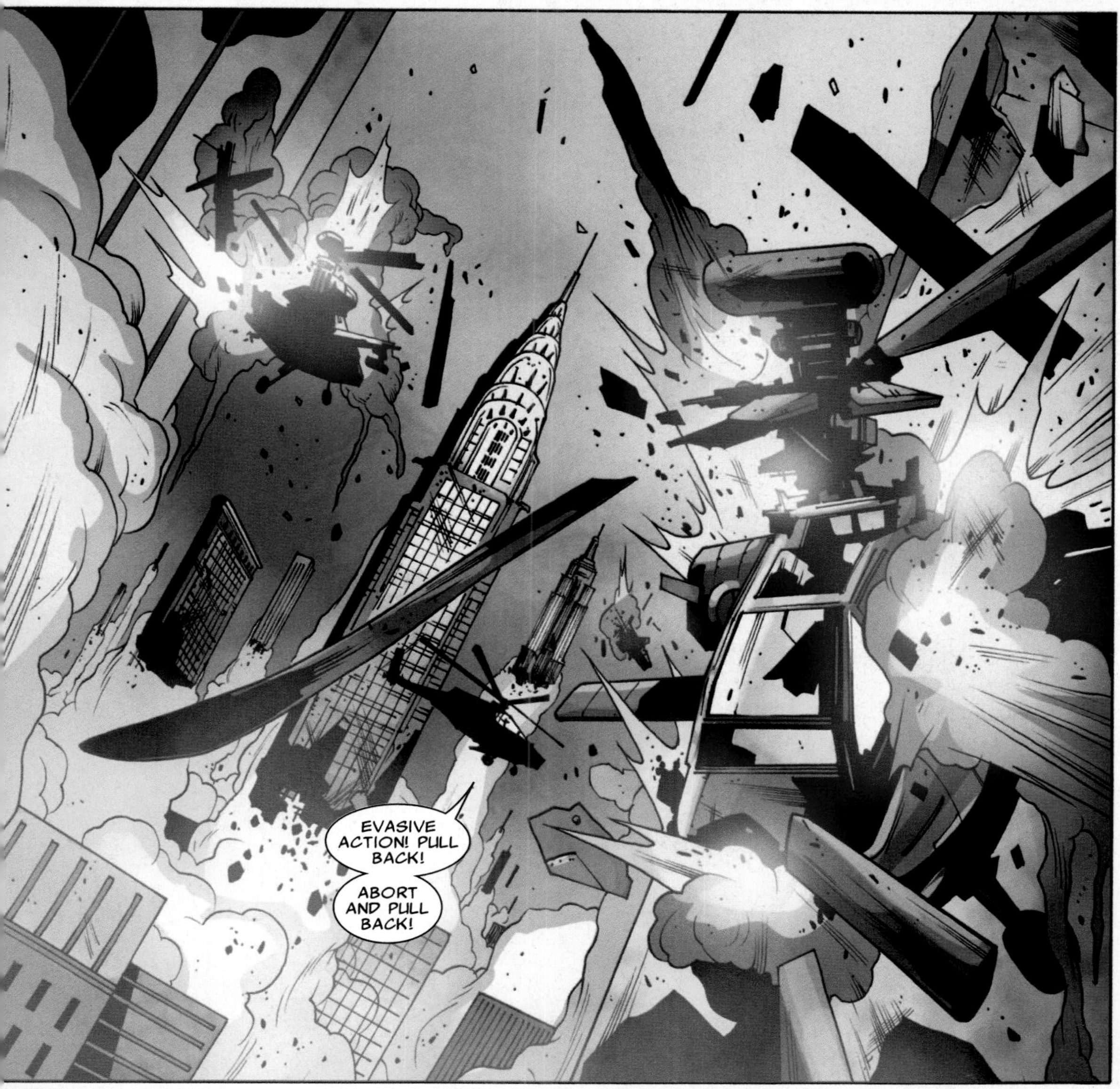
EVASIVE ACTION! PULL BACK!
ABORT AND PULL BACK!

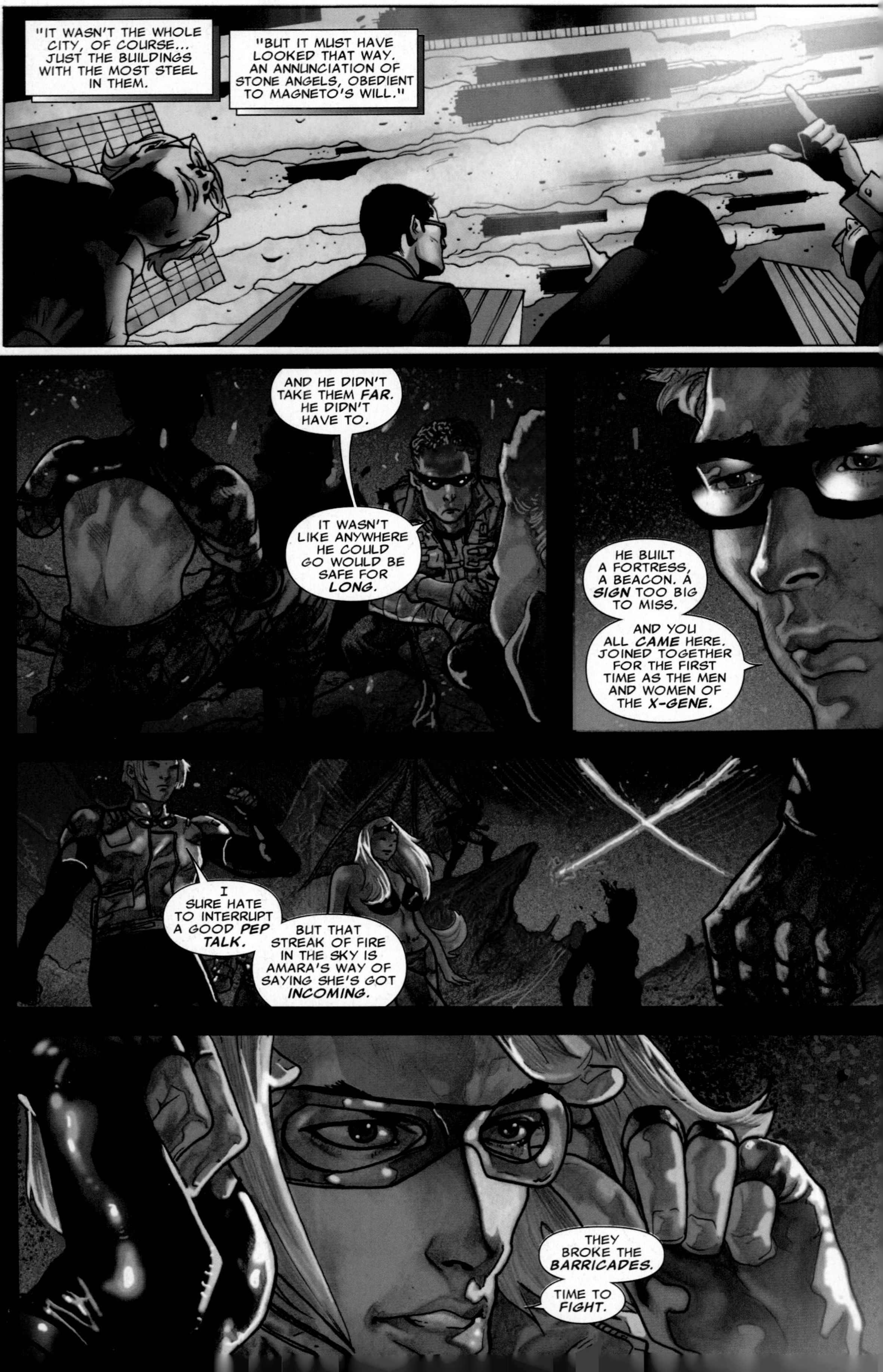
"IT WASN'T THE WHOLE CITY, OF COURSE... JUST THE BUILDINGS WITH THE MOST STEEL IN THEM.
"BUT IT MUST HAVE LOOKED THAT WAY. AN ANNUNCIATION OF STONE ANGELS, OBEDIENT TO MAGNETO'S WILL."
AND HE DIDN'T TAKE THEM FAR. HE DIDN'T HAVE TO.
IT WASN'T LIKE ANYWHERE HE COULD GO WOULD BE SAFE FOR LONG.
HE BUILT A FORTRESS, A BEACON. A SIGN TOO BIG TO MISS.
AND YOU ALL CAME HERE. JOINED TOGETHER FOR THE FIRST TIME AS THE MEN AND WOMEN OF THE X-GENE.
I SURE HATE TO INTERRUPT A GOOD PEP TALK.
BUT THAT STREAK OF FIRE IN THE SKY IS AMARA'S WAY OF SAYING SHE'S GOT INCOMING.
THEY BROKE THE BARRICADES.
TIME TO FIGHT.

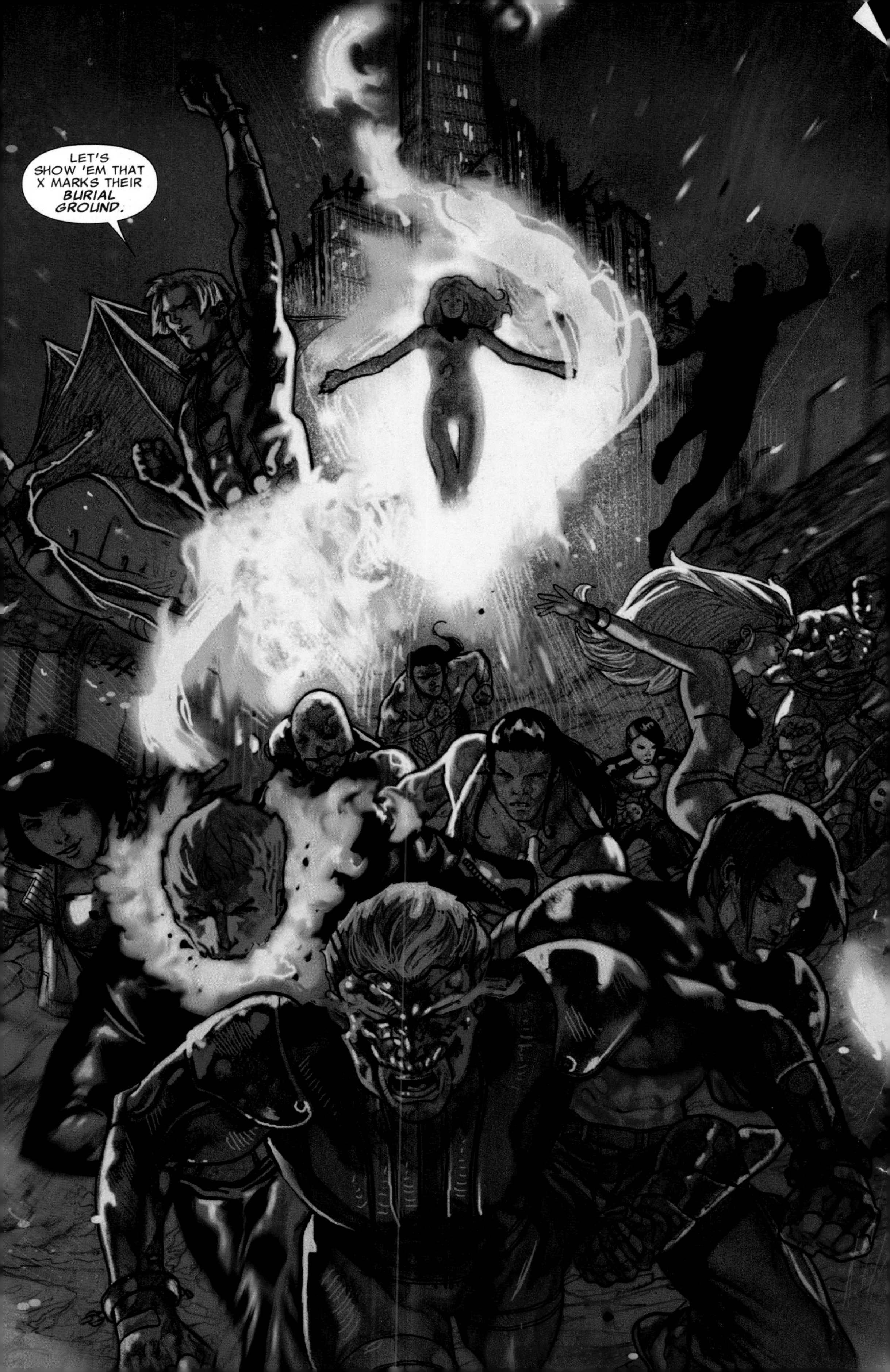
LET'S SHOW 'EM THAT X MARKS THEIR BURIAL GROUND.

X-MEN LEGACY #245

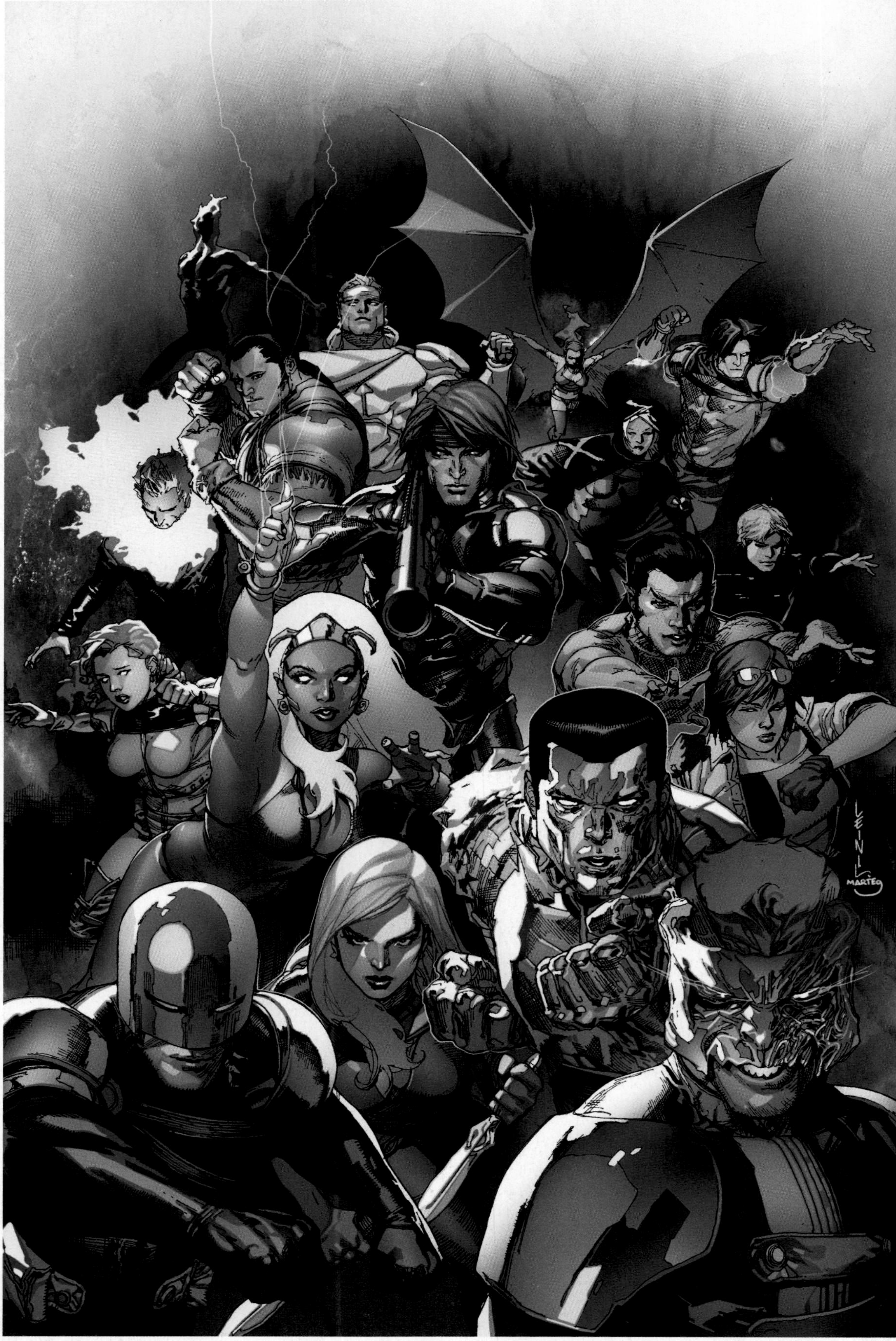
LEINIL
MARTEG

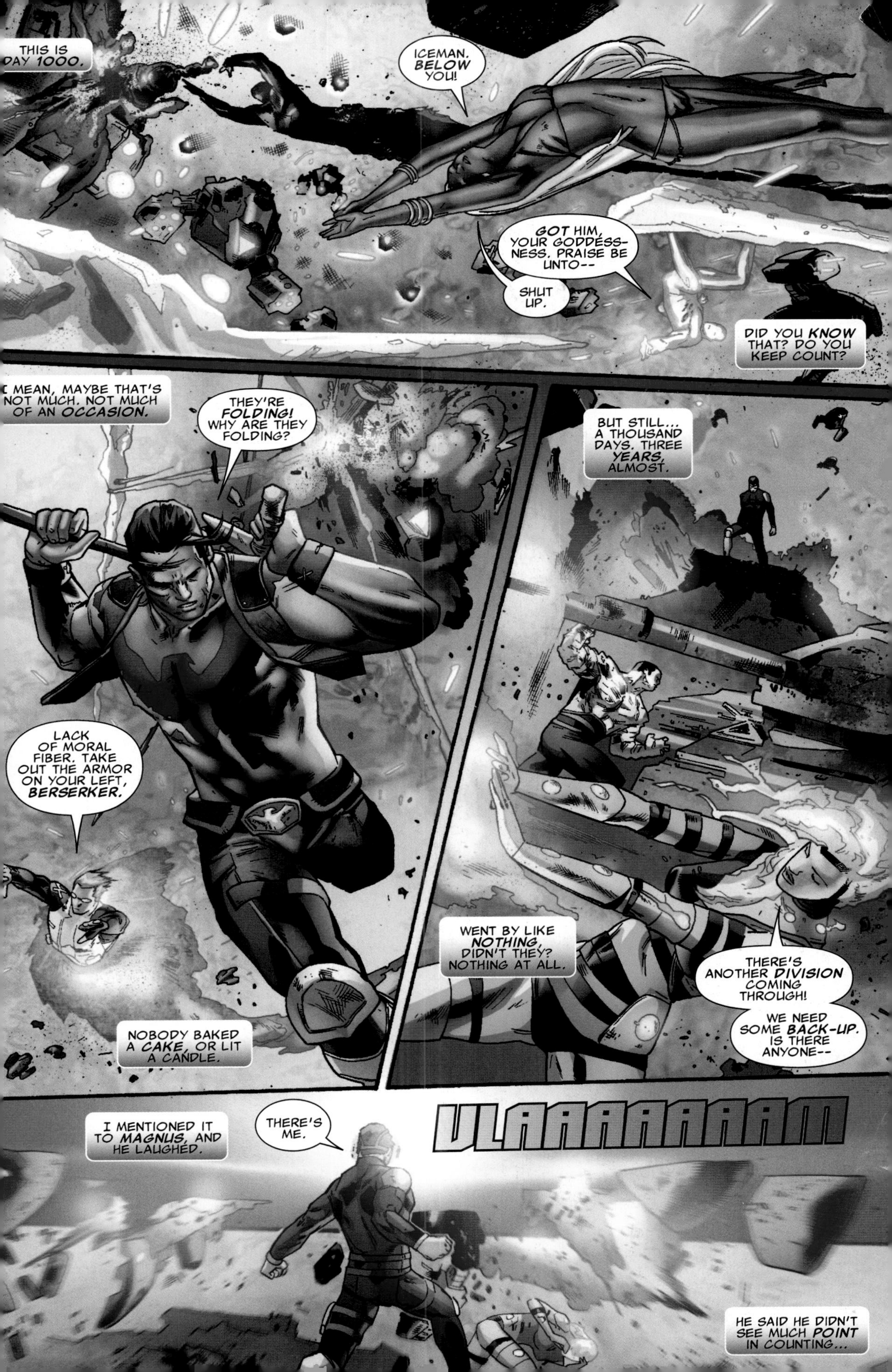

THIS IS DAY 1000.
ICEMAN. BELOW YOU!
GOT HIM, YOUR GODDESS-NESS. PRAISE BE UNTO--
SHUT UP.
DID YOU KNOW THAT? DO YOU KEEP COUNT?
I MEAN, MAYBE THAT'S NOT MUCH. NOT MUCH OF AN OCCASION.
THEY'RE FOLDING! WHY ARE THEY FOLDING?
LACK OF MORAL FIBER. TAKE OUT THE ARMOR ON YOUR LEFT, BERSERKER.
NOBODY BAKED A CAKE, OR LIT A CANDLE.
BUT STILL... A THOUSAND DAYS. THREE YEARS, ALMOST.
WENT BY LIKE NOTHING, DIDN'T THEY? NOTHING AT ALL.
THERE'S ANOTHER DIVISION COMING THROUGH!
WE NEED SOME BACK-UP. IS THERE ANYONE--
I MENTIONED IT TO MAGNUS, AND HE LAUGHED.
THERE'S ME.
VLAAAAAAAAM
HE SAID HE DIDN'T SEE MUCH POINT IN COUNTING...

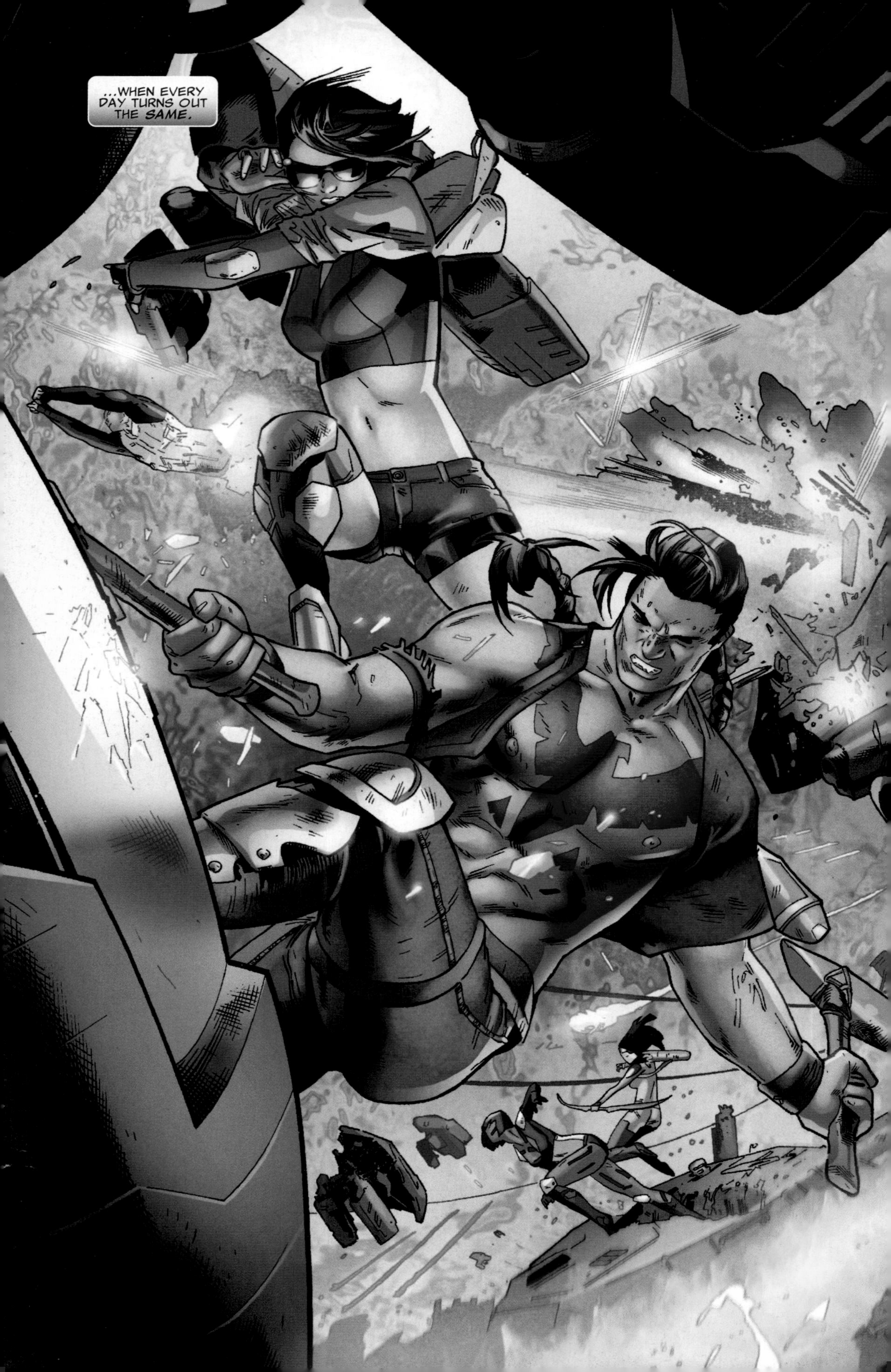
...WHEN EVERY DAY TURNS OUT THE SAME.

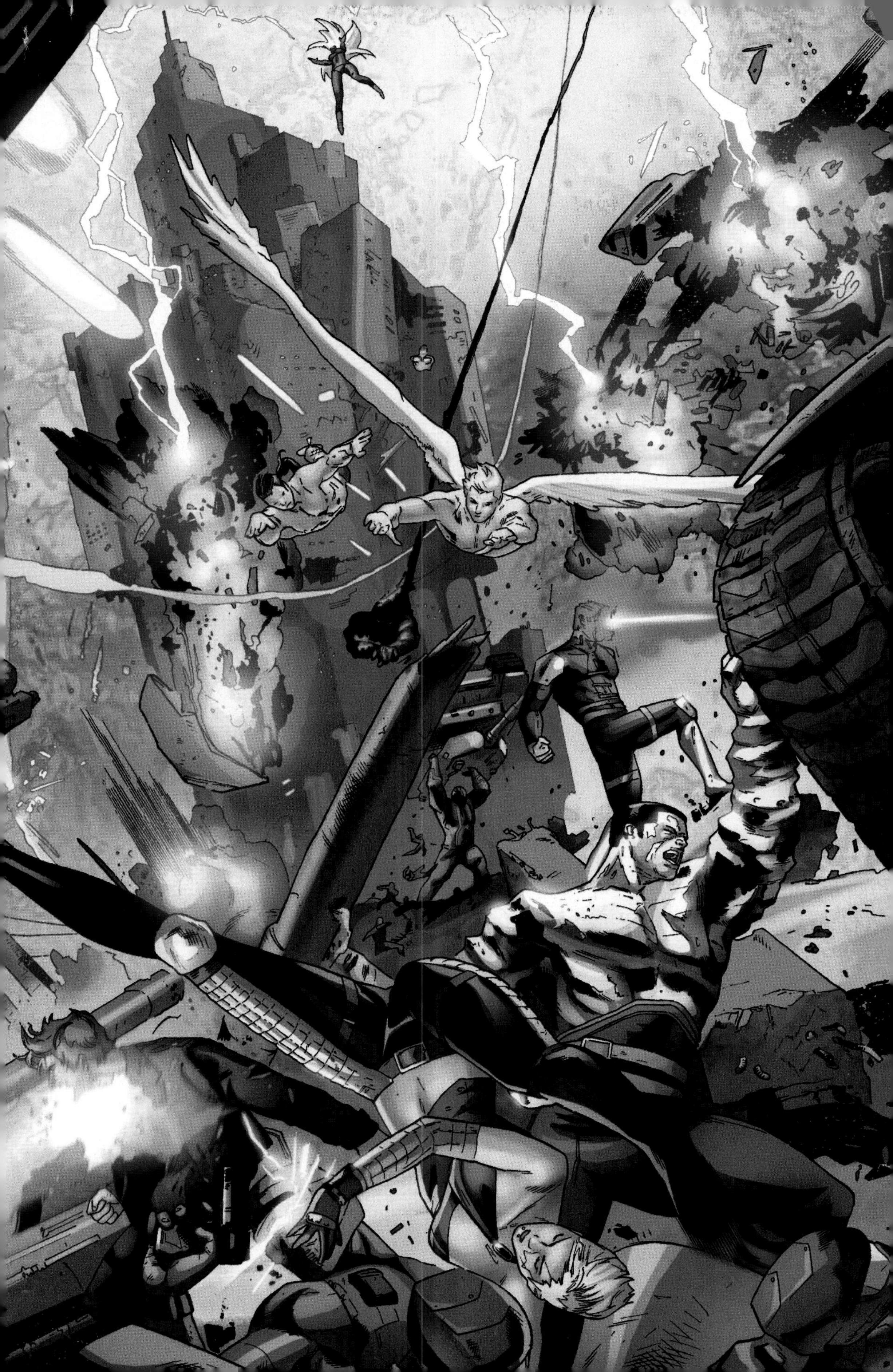

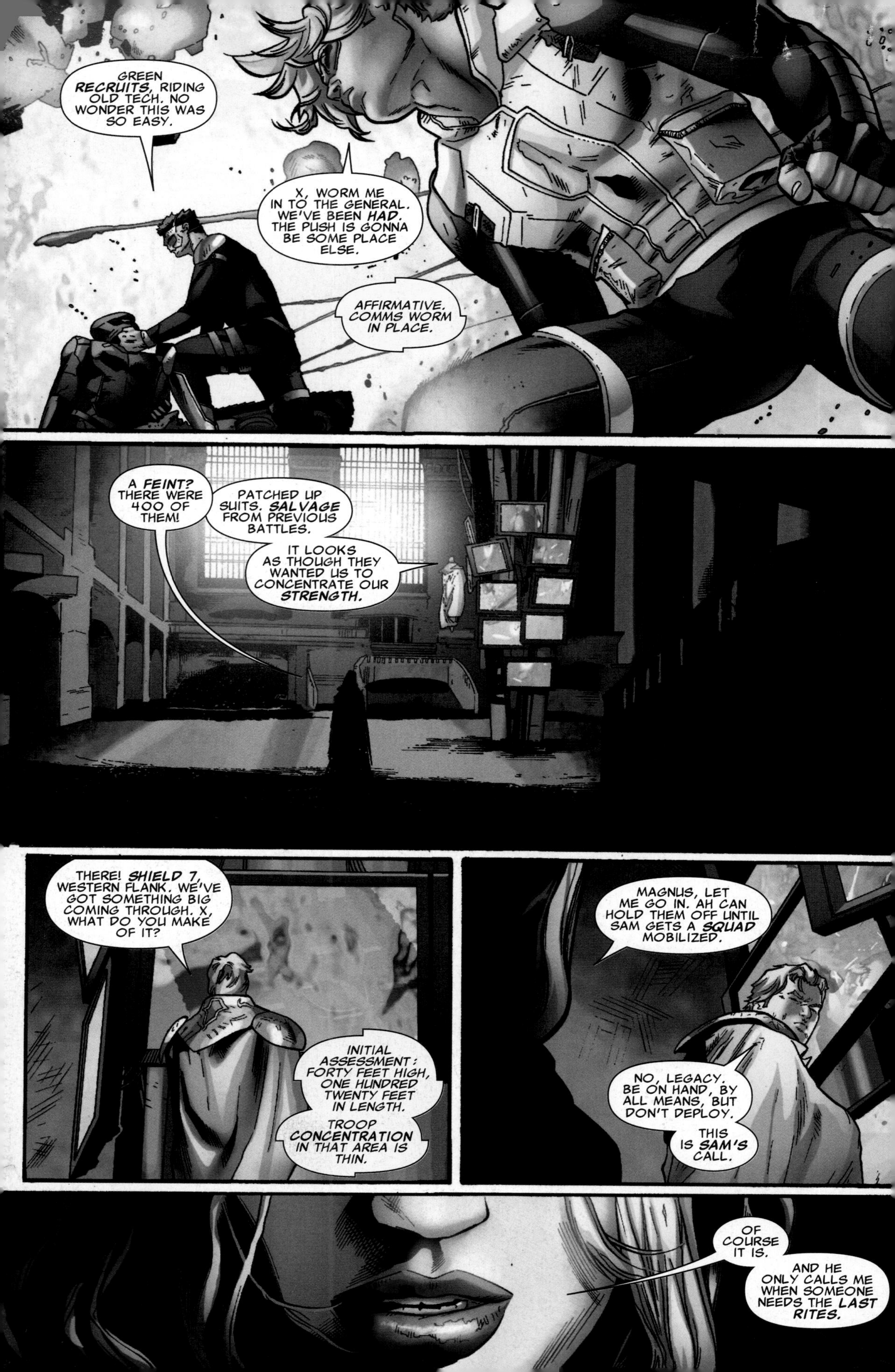
GREEN RECRUITS, RIDING OLD TECH. NO WONDER THIS WAS SO EASY.
X, WORM ME IN TO THE GENERAL. WE'VE BEEN HAD. THE PUSH IS GONNA BE SOME PLACE ELSE.
AFFIRMATIVE. COMMS WORM IN PLACE.
A FEINT? THERE WERE 400 OF THEM!
PATCHED UP SUITS. SALVAGE FROM PREVIOUS BATTLES.
IT LOOKS AS THOUGH THEY WANTED US TO CONCENTRATE OUR STRENGTH.
THERE! SHIELD 7, WESTERN FLANK. WE'VE GOT SOMETHING BIG COMING THROUGH. X, WHAT DO YOU MAKE OF IT?
INITIAL ASSESSMENT: FORTY FEET HIGH, ONE HUNDRED TWENTY FEET IN LENGTH.
TROOP CONCENTRATION IN THAT AREA IS THIN.
MAGNUS, LET ME GO IN. AH CAN HOLD THEM OFF UNTIL SAM GETS A SQUAD MOBILIZED.
NO, LEGACY. BE ON HAND, BY ALL MEANS, BUT DON'T DEPLOY.
THIS IS SAM'S CALL.
OF COURSE IT IS.
AND HE ONLY CALLS ME WHEN SOMEONE NEEDS THE LAST RITES.

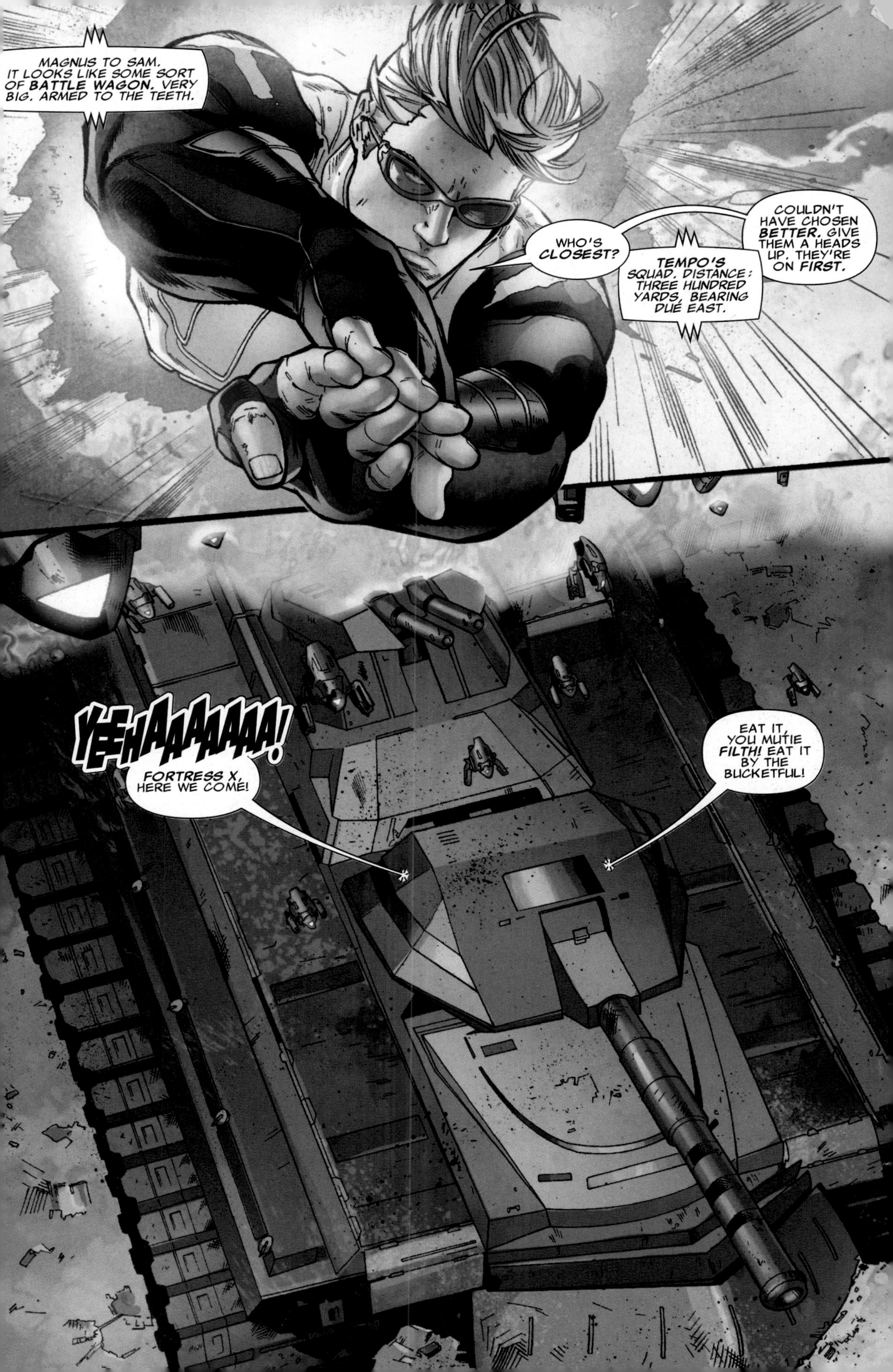
MAGNUS TO SAM. IT LOOKS LIKE SOME SORT OF **BATTLE WAGON.** VERY BIG. ARMED TO THE TEETH.
WHO'S **CLOSEST?**
TEMPO'S SQUAD. DISTANCE: THREE HUNDRED YARDS, BEARING DUE EAST.
COULDN'T HAVE CHOSEN **BETTER.** GIVE THEM A HEADS UP. THEY'RE ON **FIRST.**
YEEHAAAAAAA!
FORTRESS X, HERE WE COME!
EAT IT, YOU MUTIE **FILTH!** EAT IT BY THE BUCKETFUL!

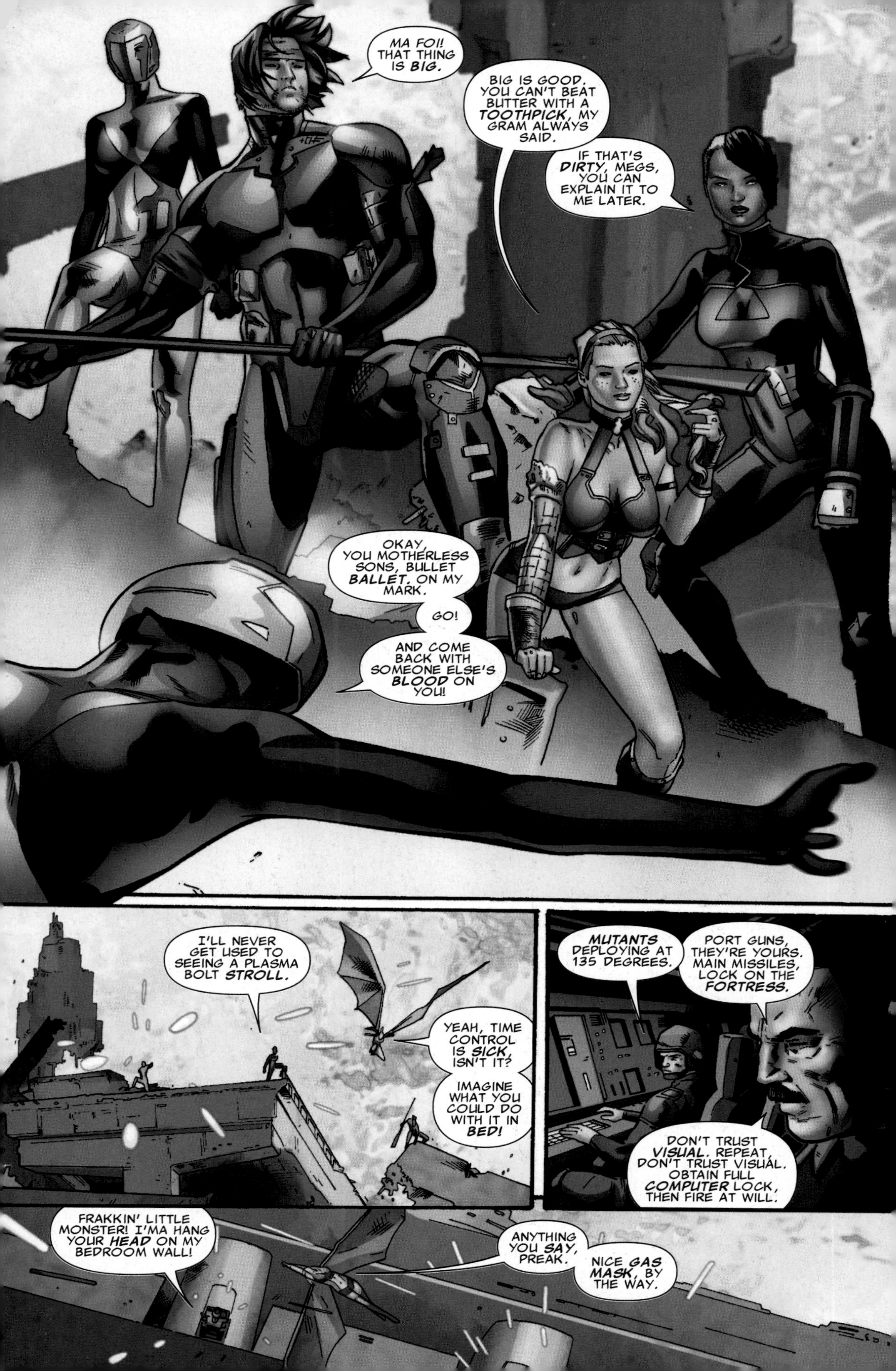
MA FOI! THAT THING IS BIG.
BIG IS GOOD. YOU CAN'T BEAT BUTTER WITH A TOOTHPICK, MY GRAM ALWAYS SAID.
IF THAT'S DIRTY, MEGS, YOU CAN EXPLAIN IT TO ME LATER.
OKAY, YOU MOTHERLESS SONS, BULLET BALLET. ON MY MARK.
GO!
AND COME BACK WITH SOMEONE ELSE'S BLOOD ON YOU!
I'LL NEVER GET USED TO SEEING A PLASMA BOLT STROLL.
YEAH, TIME CONTROL IS SICK, ISN'T IT?
IMAGINE WHAT YOU COULD DO WITH IT IN BED!
MUTANTS DEPLOYING AT 135 DEGREES.
PORT GUNS, THEY'RE YOURS. MAIN MISSILES, LOCK ON THE FORTRESS.
DON'T TRUST VISUAL. REPEAT, DON'T TRUST VISUAL. OBTAIN FULL COMPUTER LOCK, THEN FIRE AT WILL.
FRAKKIN' LITTLE MONSTER! I'MA HANG YOUR HEAD ON MY BEDROOM WALL!
ANYTHING YOU SAY, PREAK.
NICE GAS MASK, BY THE WAY.

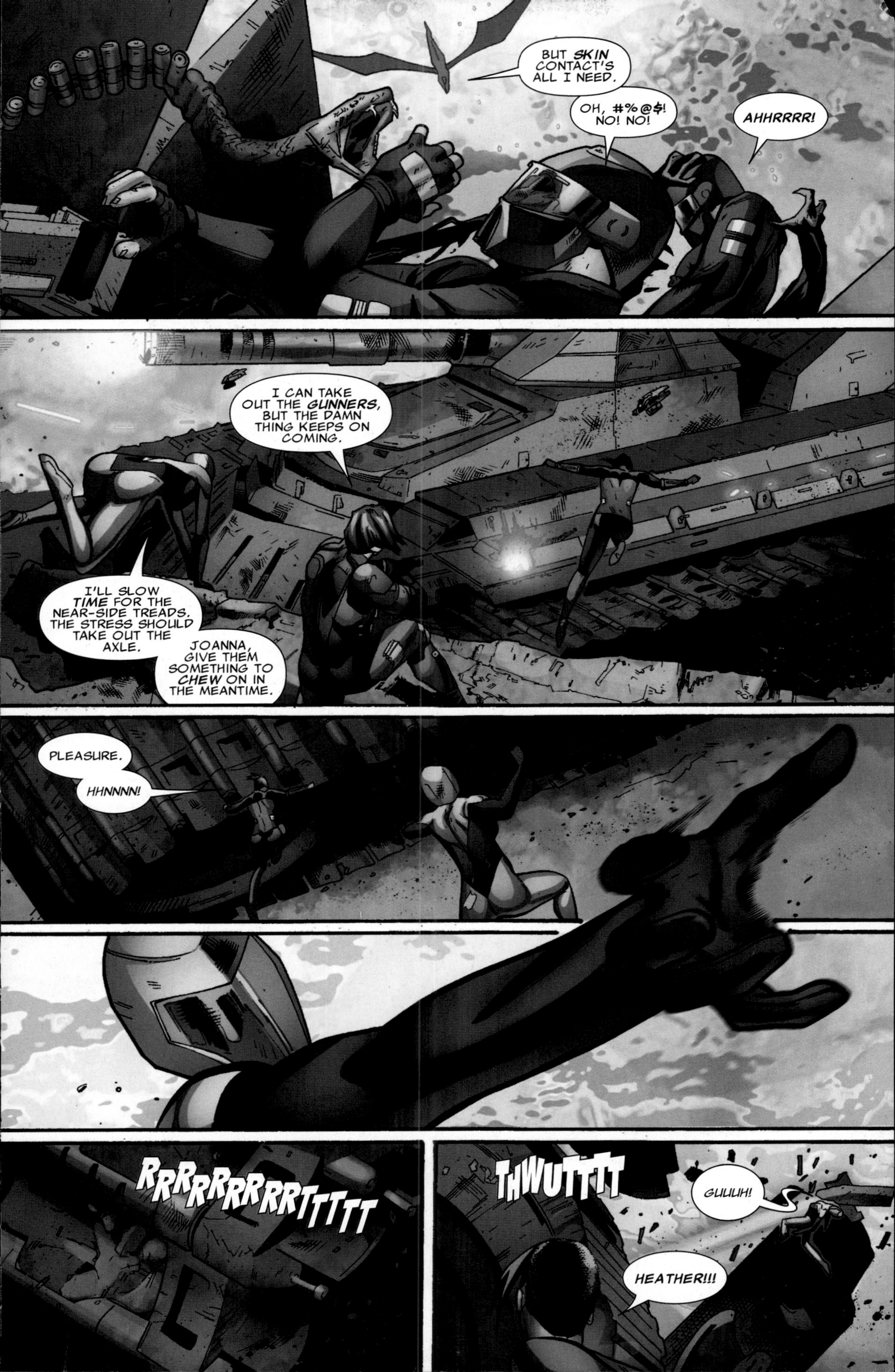
BUT SKIN CONTACT'S ALL I NEED.
OH, #%@$! NO! NO!
AHHRRRR!
I CAN TAKE OUT THE GUNNERS, BUT THE DAMN THING KEEPS ON COMING.
I'LL SLOW TIME FOR THE NEAR-SIDE TREADS. THE STRESS SHOULD TAKE OUT THE AXLE.
JOANNA, GIVE THEM SOMETHING TO CHEW ON IN THE MEANTIME.
PLEASURE.
HHNNNN!
RRRRRRRRRTTTTTT
THWUTTTT
GUUUH!
HEATHER!!!

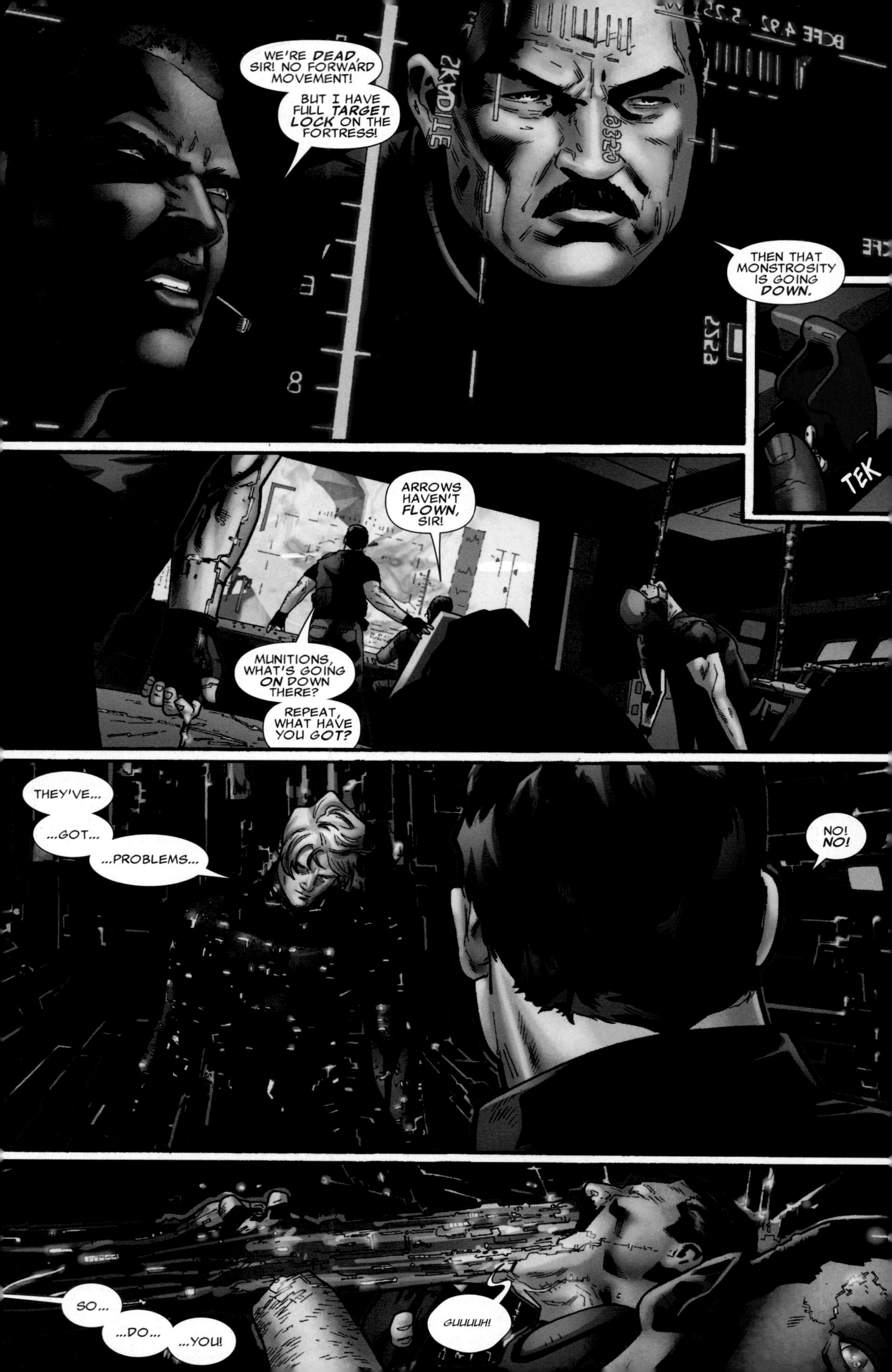

WE'RE DEAD, SIR! NO FORWARD MOVEMENT!
BUT I HAVE FULL TARGET LOCK ON THE FORTRESS!
THEN THAT MONSTROSITY IS GOING DOWN.
TEK
ARROWS HAVEN'T FLOWN, SIR!
MUNITIONS, WHAT'S GOING ON DOWN THERE?
REPEAT, WHAT HAVE YOU GOT?
THEY'VE...
...GOT...
...PROBLEMS...
NO! NO!
SO...
...DO...
...YOU!
GUUUUH!

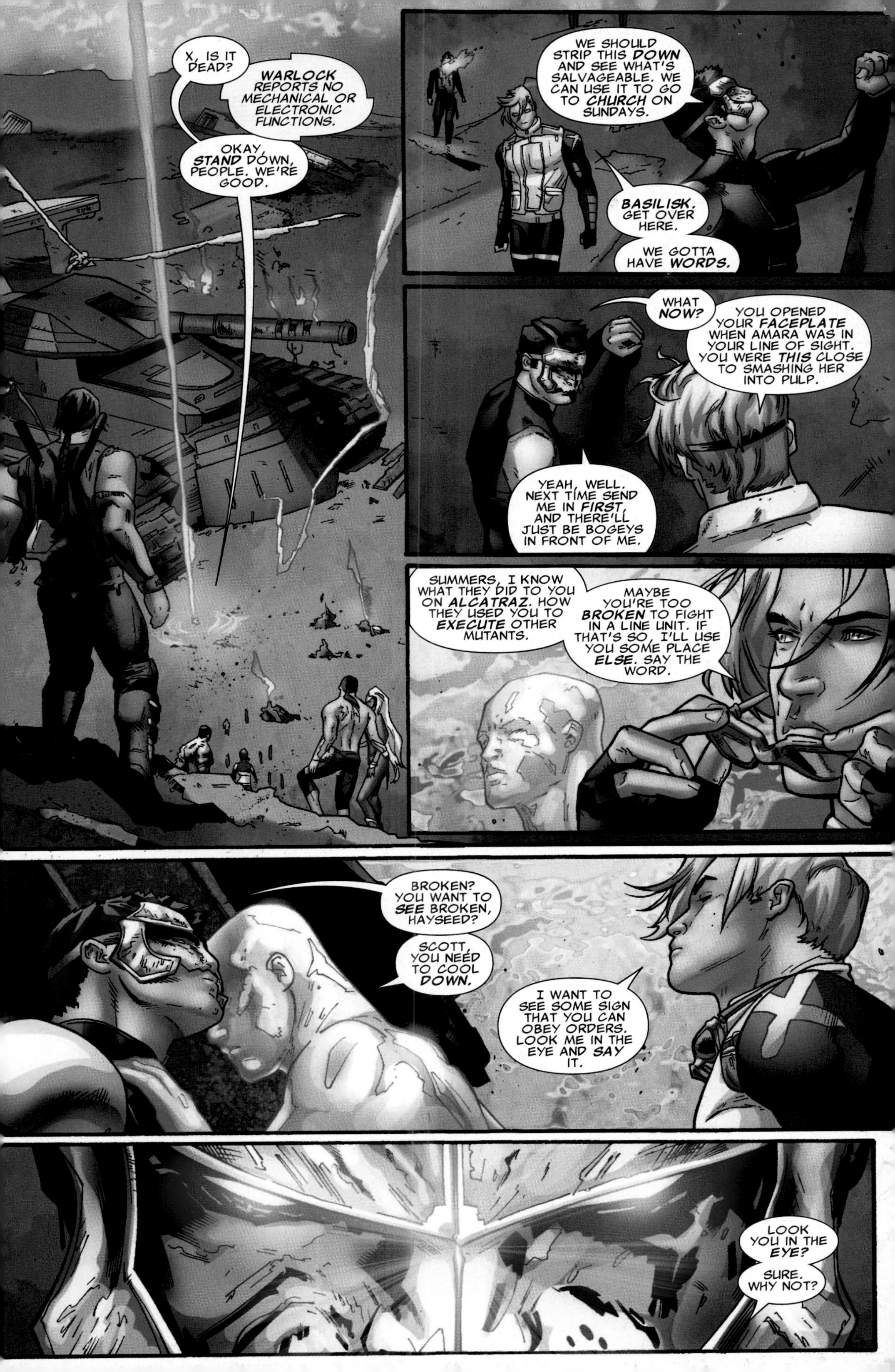
X, IS IT DEAD?
WARLOCK REPORTS NO MECHANICAL OR ELECTRONIC FUNCTIONS.
OKAY, STAND DOWN, PEOPLE. WE'RE GOOD.
WE SHOULD STRIP THIS DOWN AND SEE WHAT'S SALVAGEABLE. WE CAN USE IT TO GO TO CHURCH ON SUNDAYS.
BASILISK. GET OVER HERE.
WE GOTTA HAVE WORDS.
WHAT NOW?
YOU OPENED YOUR FACEPLATE WHEN AMARA WAS IN YOUR LINE OF SIGHT. YOU WERE THIS CLOSE TO SMASHING HER INTO PULP.
YEAH, WELL. NEXT TIME SEND ME IN FIRST, AND THERE'LL JUST BE BOGEYS IN FRONT OF ME.
SUMMERS, I KNOW WHAT THEY DID TO YOU ON ALCATRAZ. HOW THEY USED YOU TO EXECUTE OTHER MUTANTS.
MAYBE YOU'RE TOO BROKEN TO FIGHT IN A LINE UNIT. IF THAT'S SO, I'LL USE YOU SOME PLACE ELSE. SAY THE WORD.
BROKEN? YOU WANT TO SEE BROKEN, HAYSEED?
SCOTT, YOU NEED TO COOL DOWN.
I WANT TO SEE SOME SIGN THAT YOU CAN OBEY ORDERS. LOOK ME IN THE EYE AND SAY IT.
LOOK YOU IN THE EYE?
SURE. WHY NOT?

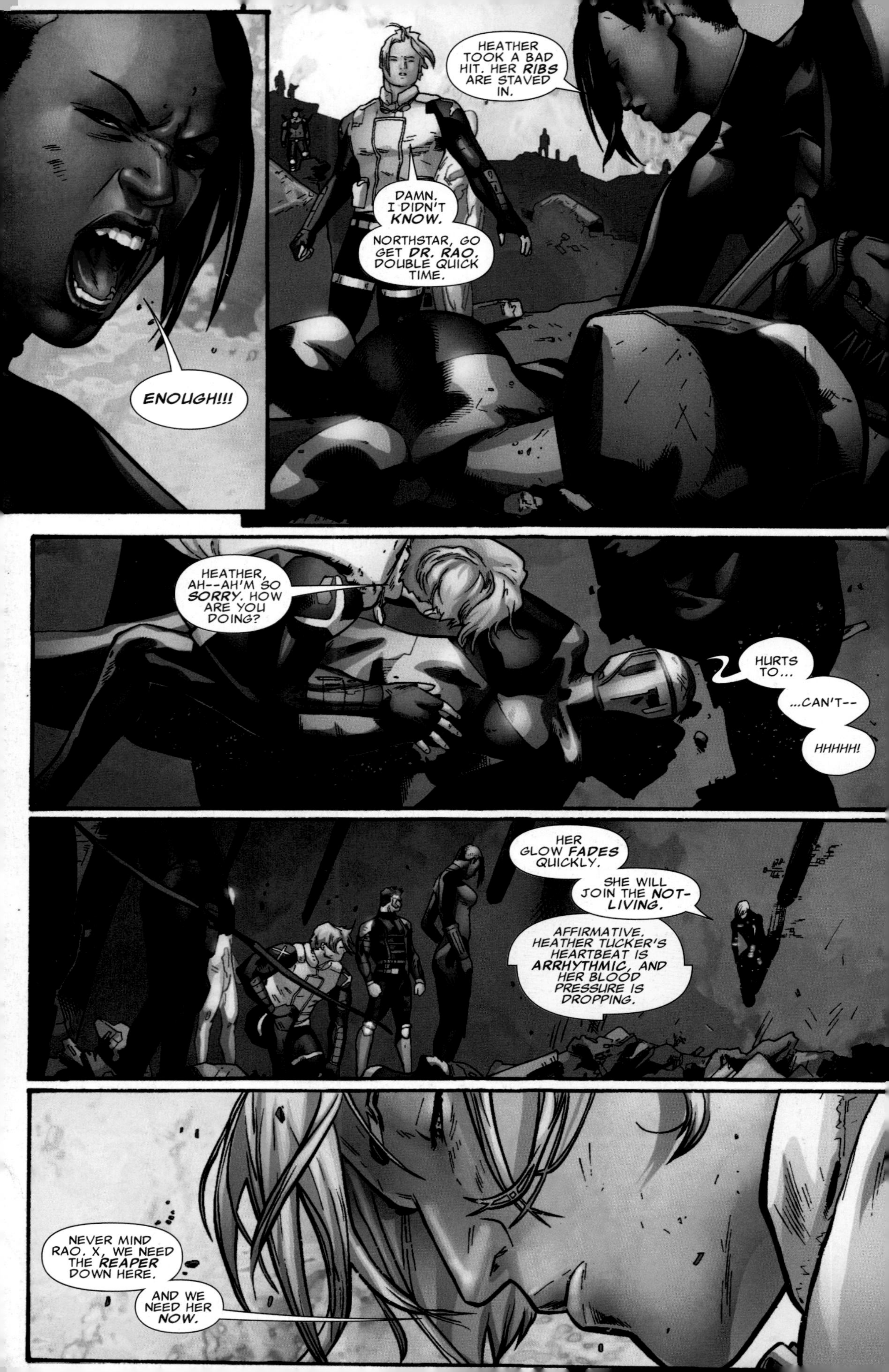
ENOUGH!!!
HEATHER TOOK A BAD HIT. HER RIBS ARE STAVED IN.
DAMN. I DIDN'T KNOW.
NORTHSTAR, GO GET DR. RAO. DOUBLE QUICK TIME.
HEATHER, AH--AH'M SO SORRY. HOW ARE YOU DOING?
HURTS TO...
...CAN'T--
HHHHH!
HER GLOW FADES QUICKLY.
SHE WILL JOIN THE NOT-LIVING.
AFFIRMATIVE. HEATHER TUCKER'S HEARTBEAT IS ARRHYTHMIC, AND HER BLOOD PRESSURE IS DROPPING.
NEVER MIND RAO. X, WE NEED THE REAPER DOWN HERE.
AND WE NEED HER NOW.

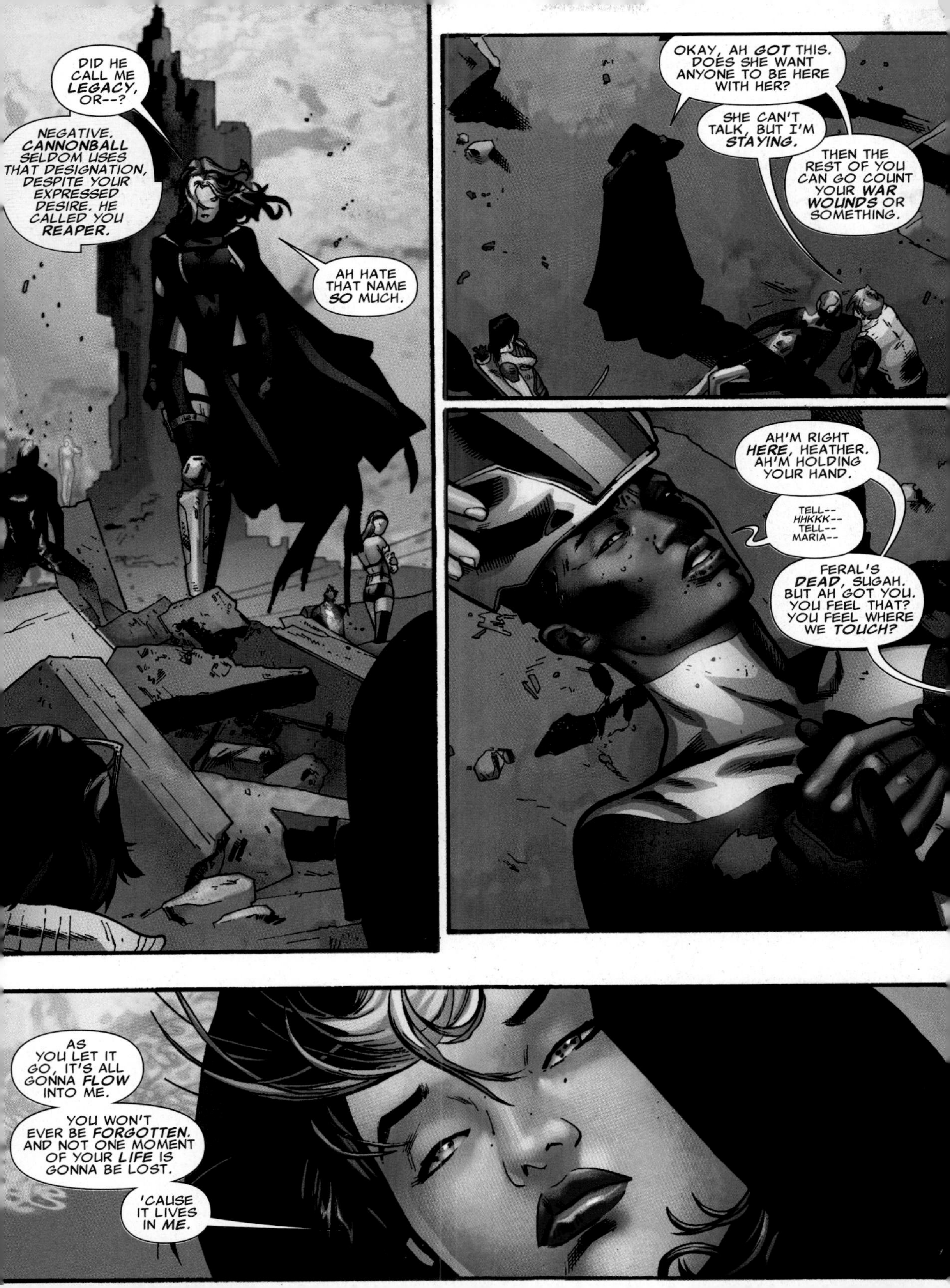
DID HE CALL ME LEGACY, OR--?
NEGATIVE. CANNONBALL SELDOM USES THAT DESIGNATION, DESPITE YOUR EXPRESSED DESIRE. HE CALLED YOU REAPER.
AH HATE THAT NAME SO MUCH.
OKAY, AH GOT THIS. DOES SHE WANT ANYONE TO BE HERE WITH HER?
SHE CAN'T TALK, BUT I'M STAYING.
THEN THE REST OF YOU CAN GO COUNT YOUR WAR WOUNDS OR SOMETHING.
AH'M RIGHT HERE, HEATHER. AH'M HOLDING YOUR HAND.
TELL-- HHKKK-- TELL-- MARIA--
FERAL'S DEAD, SUGAH. BUT AH GOT YOU. YOU FEEL THAT? YOU FEEL WHERE WE TOUCH?
AS YOU LET IT GO, IT'S ALL GONNA FLOW INTO ME.
YOU WON'T EVER BE FORGOTTEN. AND NOT ONE MOMENT OF YOUR LIFE IS GONNA BE LOST.
'CAUSE IT LIVES IN ME.

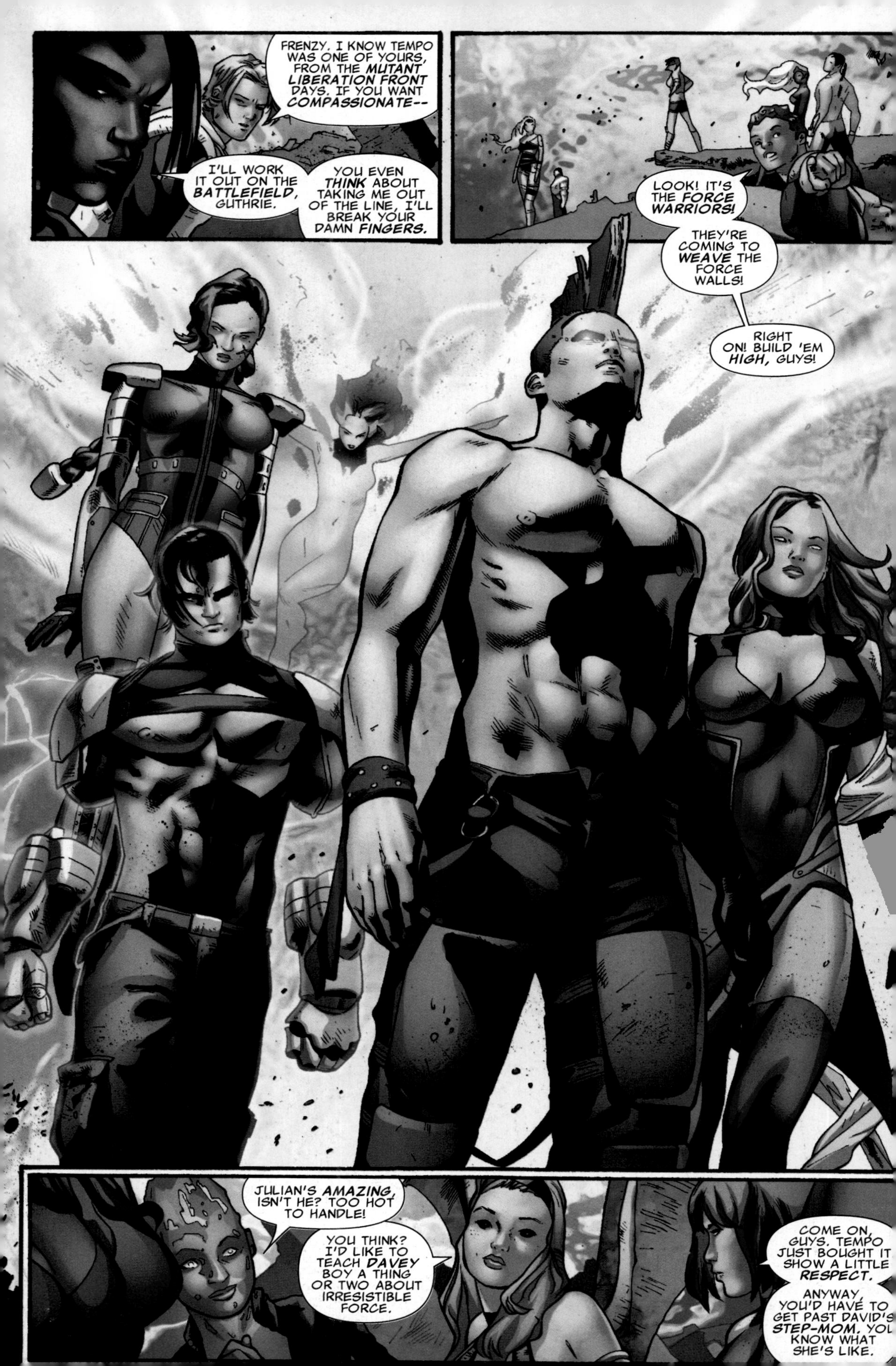
FRENZY. I KNOW TEMPO WAS ONE OF YOURS, FROM THE MUTANT LIBERATION FRONT DAYS. IF YOU WANT COMPASSIONATE--
I'LL WORK IT OUT ON THE BATTLEFIELD, GUTHRIE.
YOU EVEN THINK ABOUT TAKING ME OUT OF THE LINE, I'LL BREAK YOUR DAMN FINGERS.
LOOK! IT'S THE FORCE WARRIORS!
THEY'RE COMING TO WEAVE THE FORCE WALLS!
RIGHT ON! BUILD 'EM HIGH, GUYS!
JULIAN'S AMAZING, ISN'T HE? TOO HOT TO HANDLE!
YOU THINK? I'D LIKE TO TEACH DAVEY BOY A THING OR TWO ABOUT IRRESISTIBLE FORCE.
COME ON, GUYS. TEMPO JUST BOUGHT IT. SHOW A LITTLE RESPECT.
ANYWAY, YOU'D HAVE TO GET PAST DAVID'S STEP-MOM. YOU KNOW WHAT SHE'S LIKE.

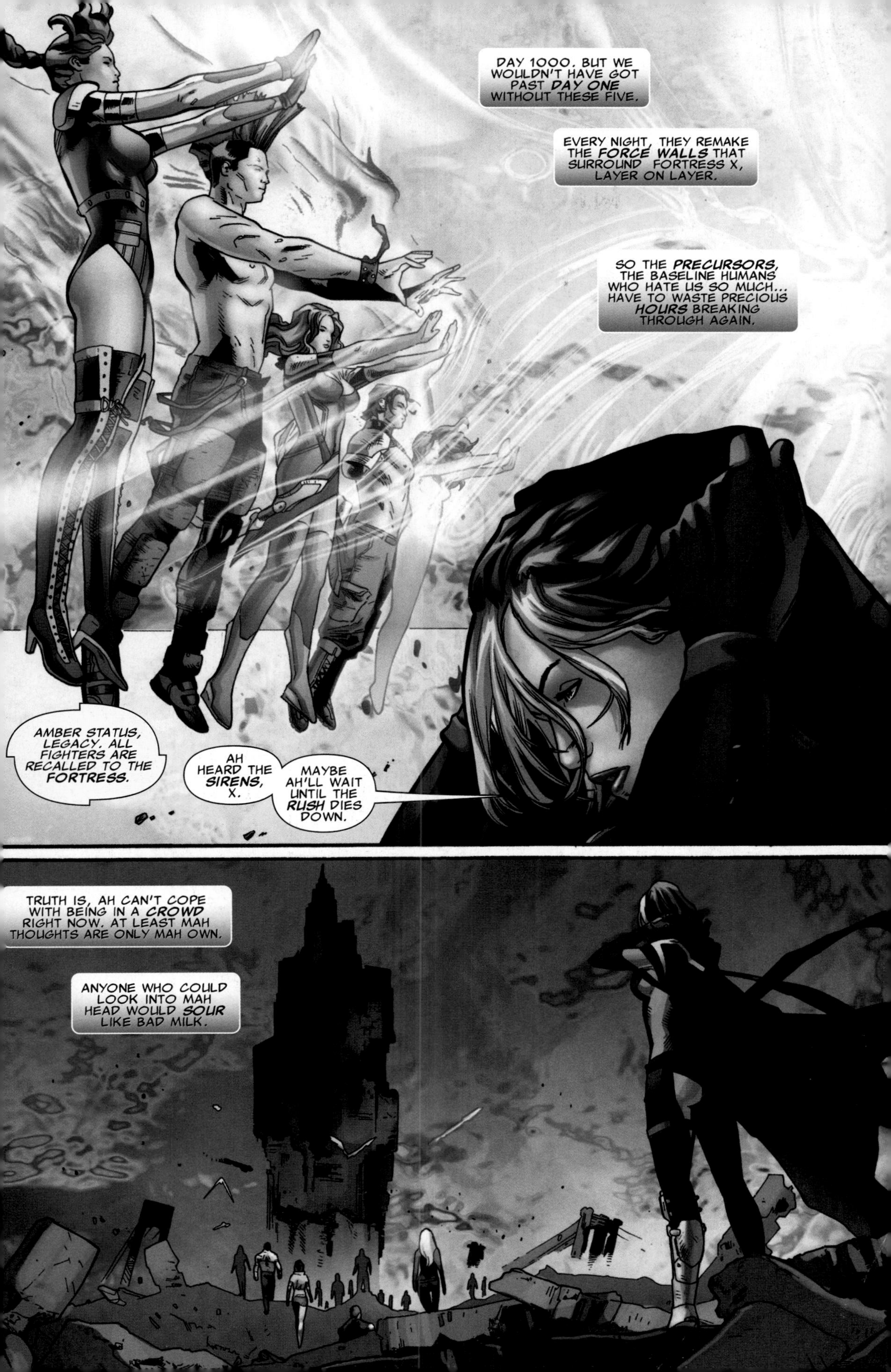
DAY 1000. BUT WE WOULDN'T HAVE GOT PAST DAY ONE WITHOUT THESE FIVE.
EVERY NIGHT, THEY REMAKE THE FORCE WALLS THAT SURROUND FORTRESS X, LAYER ON LAYER.
SO THE PRECURSORS, THE BASELINE HUMANS WHO HATE US SO MUCH... HAVE TO WASTE PRECIOUS HOURS BREAKING THROUGH AGAIN.
AMBER STATUS, LEGACY. ALL FIGHTERS ARE RECALLED TO THE FORTRESS.
AH HEARD THE SIRENS, X.
MAYBE AH'LL WAIT UNTIL THE RUSH DIES DOWN.
TRUTH IS, AH CAN'T COPE WITH BEING IN A CROWD RIGHT NOW. AT LEAST MAH THOUGHTS ARE ONLY MAH OWN.
ANYONE WHO COULD LOOK INTO MAH HEAD WOULD SOUR LIKE BAD MILK.

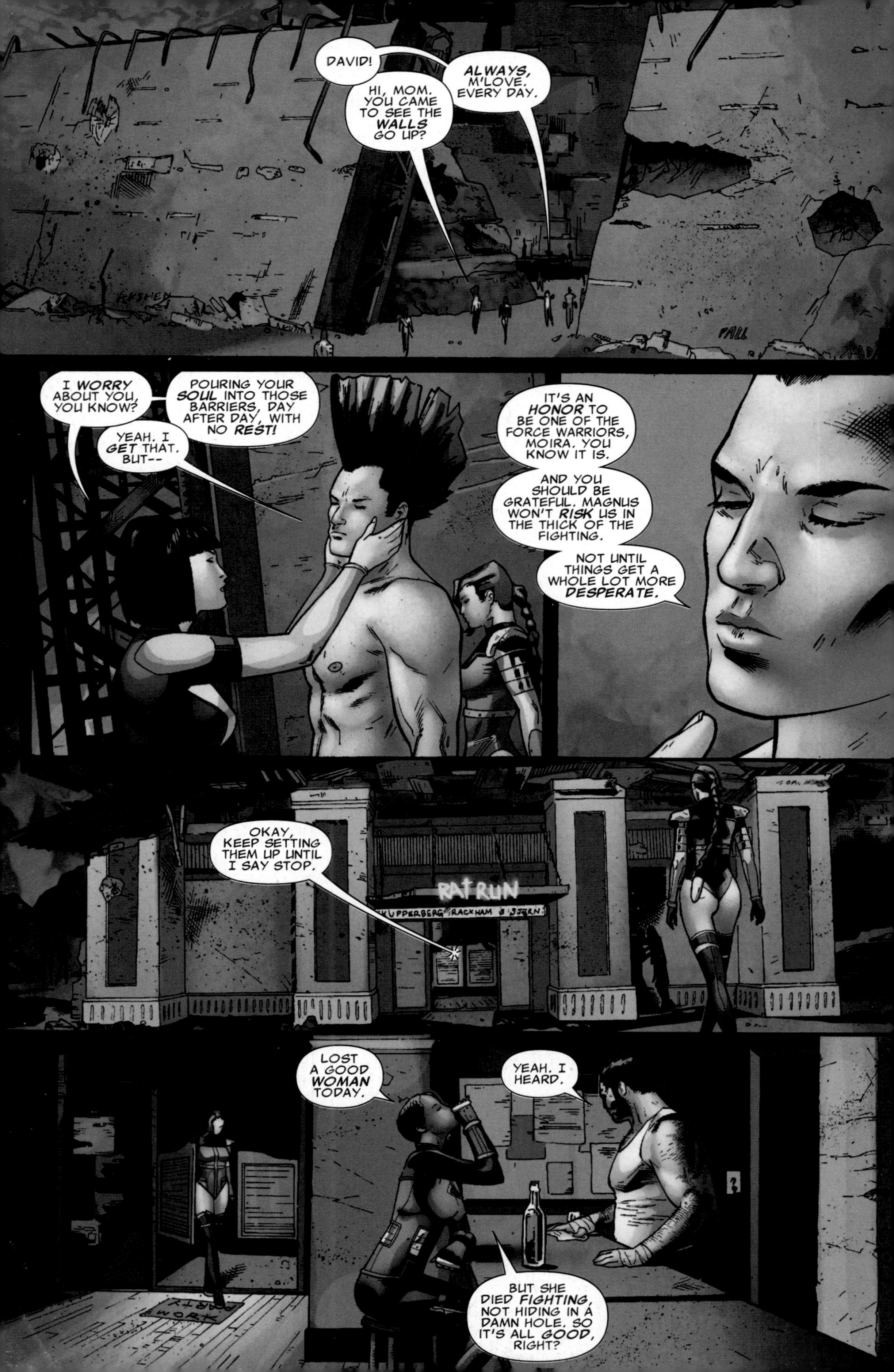

DAVID!
HI, MOM. YOU CAME TO SEE THE WALLS GO UP?
ALWAYS, M'LOVE. EVERY DAY.
I WORRY ABOUT YOU, YOU KNOW?
POURING YOUR SOUL INTO THOSE BARRIERS, DAY AFTER DAY, WITH NO REST!
YEAH. I GET THAT. BUT--
IT'S AN HONOR TO BE ONE OF THE FORCE WARRIORS, MOIRA. YOU KNOW IT IS.
AND YOU SHOULD BE GRATEFUL. MAGNUS WON'T RISK US IN THE THICK OF THE FIGHTING.
NOT UNTIL THINGS GET A WHOLE LOT MORE DESPERATE.
OKAY, KEEP SETTING THEM UP UNTIL I SAY STOP.
RAT RUN
KUPPERBERG RACKHAM & STERN
LOST A GOOD WOMAN TODAY.
YEAH. I HEARD.
BUT SHE DIED FIGHTING, NOT HIDING IN A DAMN HOLE. SO IT'S ALL GOOD, RIGHT?

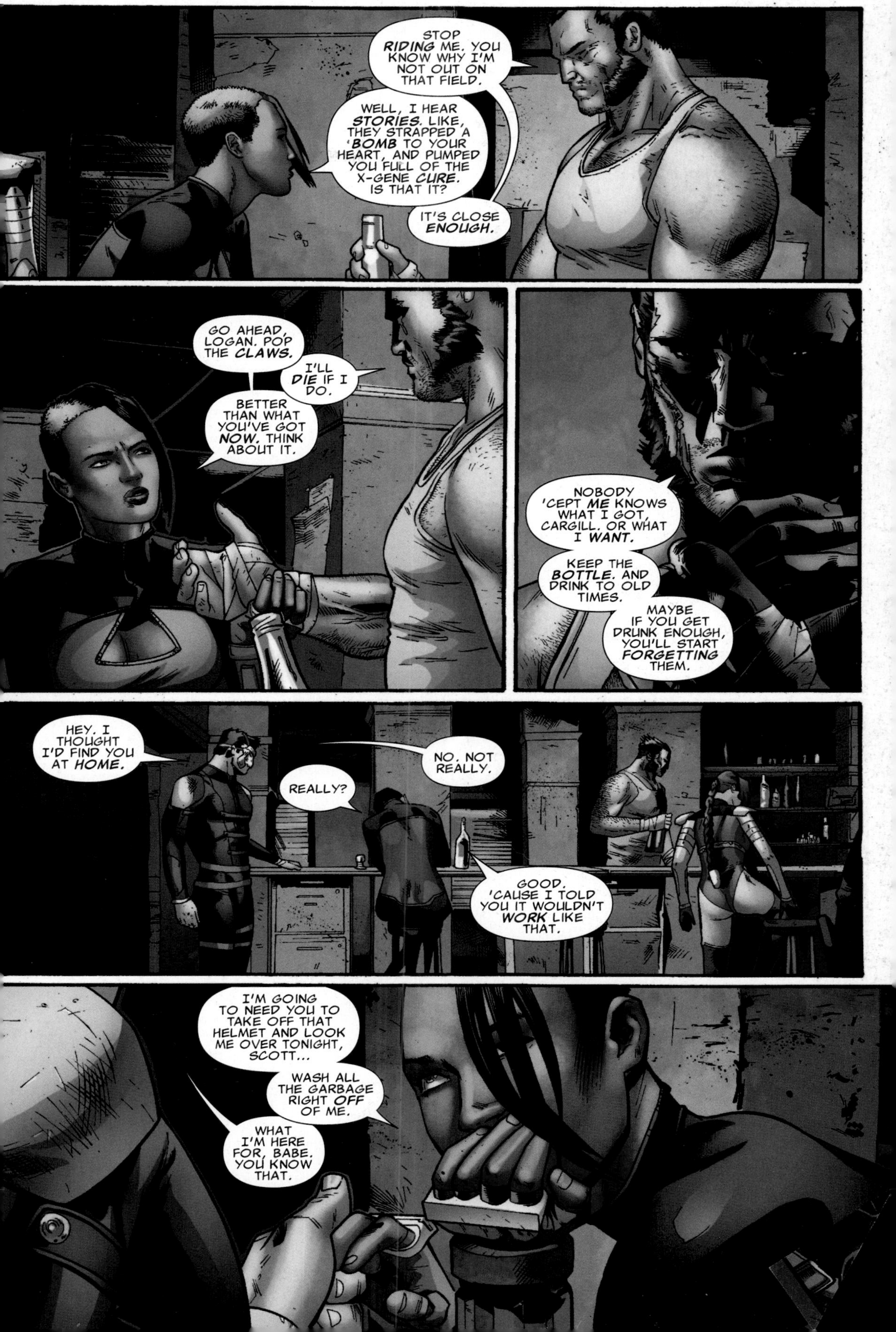
STOP RIDING ME. YOU KNOW WHY I'M NOT OUT ON THAT FIELD.
WELL, I HEAR STORIES. LIKE, THEY STRAPPED A 'BOMB TO YOUR HEART, AND PUMPED YOU FULL OF THE X-GENE CURE. IS THAT IT?
IT'S CLOSE ENOUGH.
GO AHEAD, LOGAN. POP THE CLAWS.
I'LL DIE IF I DO.
BETTER THAN WHAT YOU'VE GOT NOW. THINK ABOUT IT.
NOBODY 'CEPT ME KNOWS WHAT I GOT, CARGILL. OR WHAT I WANT.
KEEP THE BOTTLE. AND DRINK TO OLD TIMES.
MAYBE IF YOU GET DRUNK ENOUGH, YOU'LL START FORGETTING THEM.
HEY. I THOUGHT I'D FIND YOU AT HOME.
REALLY?
NO. NOT REALLY.
GOOD. 'CAUSE I TOLD YOU IT WOULDN'T WORK LIKE THAT.
I'M GOING TO NEED YOU TO TAKE OFF THAT HELMET AND LOOK ME OVER TONIGHT, SCOTT...
WASH ALL THE GARBAGE RIGHT OFF OF ME.
WHAT I'M HERE FOR, BABE. YOU KNOW THAT.

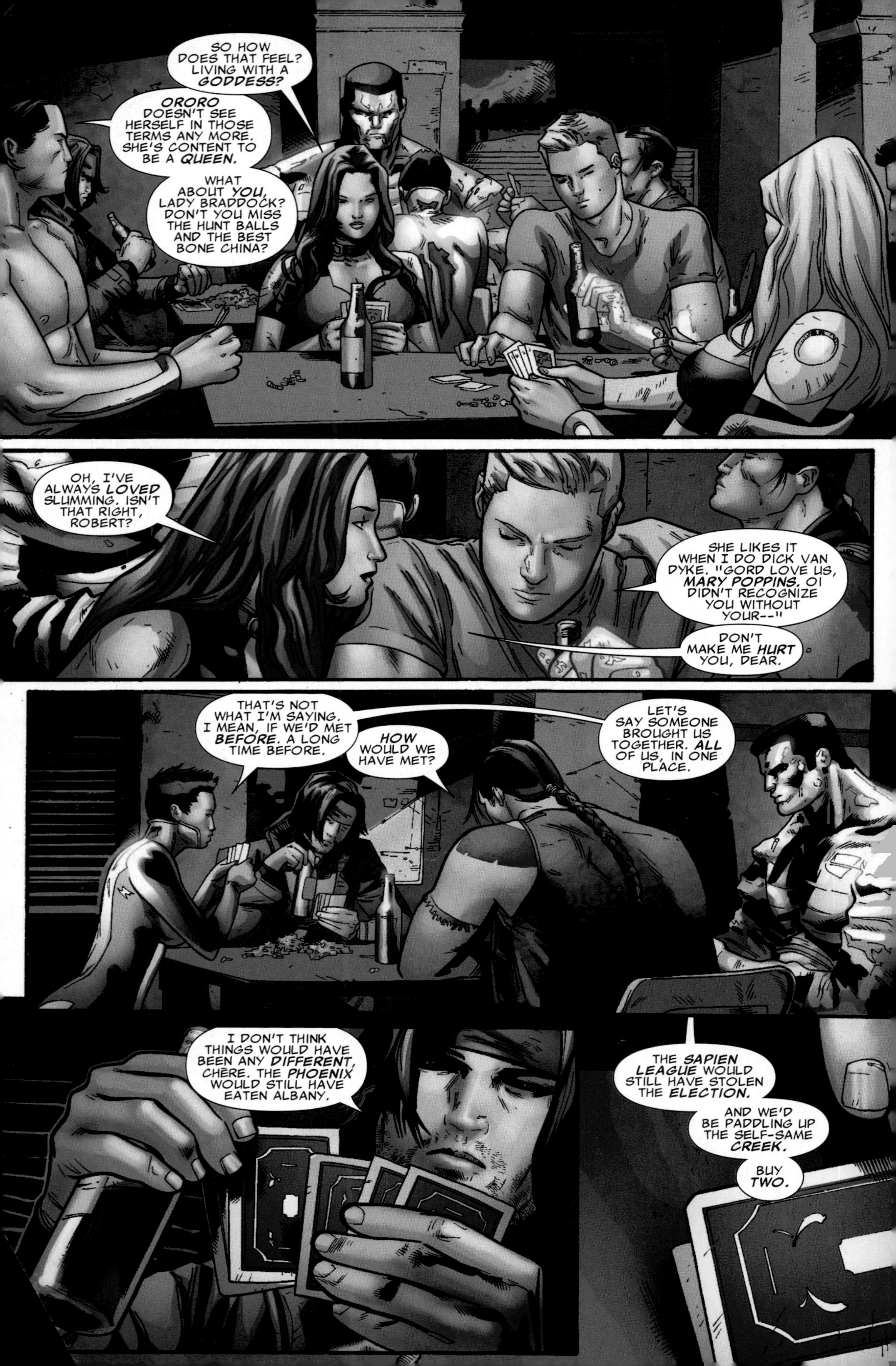
SO HOW DOES THAT FEEL? LIVING WITH A GODDESS?
ORORO DOESN'T SEE HERSELF IN THOSE TERMS ANY MORE. SHE'S CONTENT TO BE A QUEEN.
WHAT ABOUT YOU, LADY BRADDOCK? DON'T YOU MISS THE HUNT BALLS AND THE BEST BONE CHINA?
OH, I'VE ALWAYS LOVED SLUMMING. ISN'T THAT RIGHT, ROBERT?
SHE LIKES IT WHEN I DO DICK VAN DYKE. "GORD LOVE US, MARY POPPINS. OI DIDN'T RECOGNIZE YOU WITHOUT YOUR--"
DON'T MAKE ME HURT YOU, DEAR.
THAT'S NOT WHAT I'M SAYING. I MEAN, IF WE'D MET BEFORE. A LONG TIME BEFORE.
HOW WOULD WE HAVE MET?
LET'S SAY SOMEONE BROUGHT US TOGETHER. ALL OF US, IN ONE PLACE.
I DON'T THINK THINGS WOULD HAVE BEEN ANY DIFFERENT, CHÈRE. THE PHOENIX WOULD STILL HAVE EATEN ALBANY.
THE SAPIEN LEAGUE WOULD STILL HAVE STOLEN THE ELECTION.
AND WE'D BE PADDLING UP THE SELF-SAME CREEK.
BUY TWO.

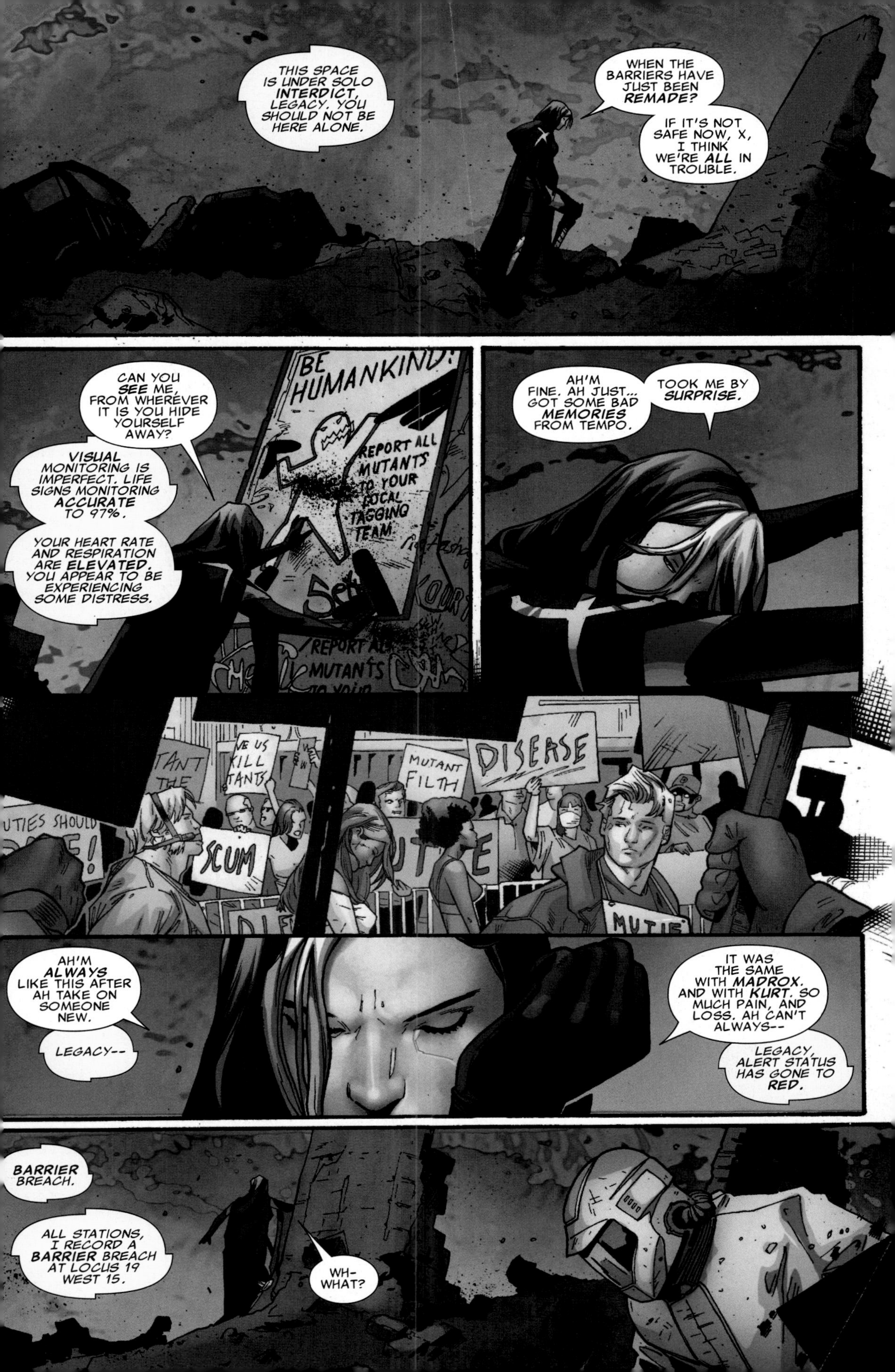
THIS SPACE IS UNDER SOLO **INTERDICT**, LEGACY. YOU SHOULD NOT BE HERE ALONE.
WHEN THE BARRIERS HAVE JUST BEEN **REMADE?**
IF IT'S NOT SAFE NOW, X, I THINK WE'RE **ALL** IN TROUBLE.
CAN YOU **SEE** ME, FROM WHEREVER IT IS YOU HIDE YOURSELF AWAY?
VISUAL MONITORING IS IMPERFECT. LIFE SIGNS MONITORING **ACCURATE** TO 97%.
YOUR HEART RATE AND RESPIRATION ARE **ELEVATED.** YOU APPEAR TO BE EXPERIENCING SOME DISTRESS.
BE HUMANKIND!
REPORT ALL MUTANTS TO YOUR LOCAL TAGGING TEAM
AH'M FINE. AH JUST... GOT SOME BAD **MEMORIES** FROM TEMPO.
TOOK ME BY **SURPRISE.**
MUTANT FILTH
DISEASE
SCUM
AH'M **ALWAYS** LIKE THIS AFTER AH TAKE ON SOMEONE NEW.
LEGACY--
IT WAS THE SAME WITH **MADROX.** AND WITH **KURT.** SO MUCH PAIN, AND LOSS. AH CAN'T ALWAYS--
LEGACY, ALERT STATUS HAS GONE TO ***RED.***
BARRIER *BREACH.*
ALL STATIONS, I RECORD A ***BARRIER*** *BREACH AT LOCUS 19 WEST 15.*
WH- WHAT?

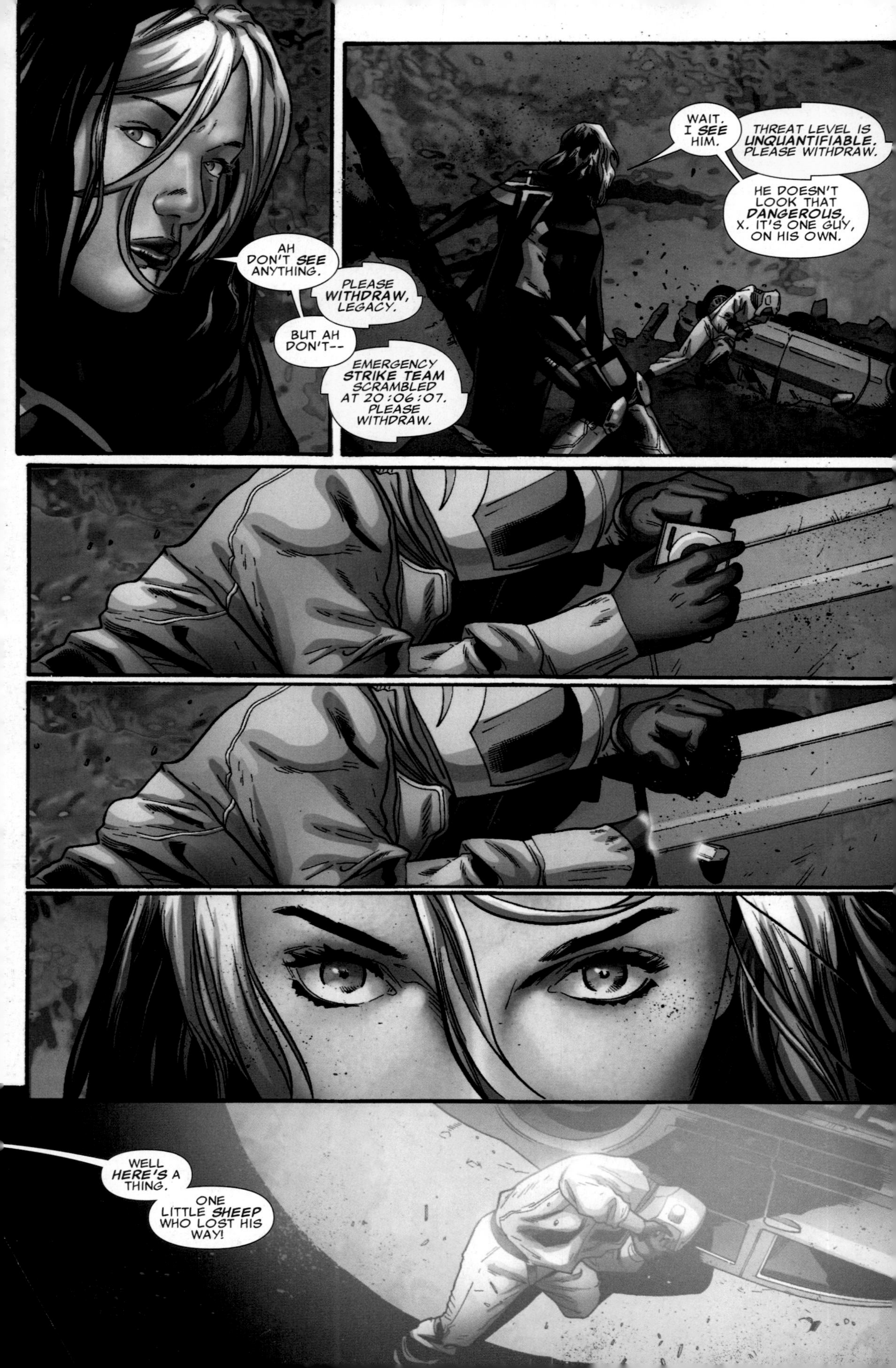
AH DON'T SEE ANYTHING.
PLEASE WITHDRAW, LEGACY.
BUT AH DON'T--
EMERGENCY STRIKE TEAM SCRAMBLED AT 20:06:07. PLEASE WITHDRAW.
WAIT. I SEE HIM.
THREAT LEVEL IS UNQUANTIFIABLE. PLEASE WITHDRAW.
HE DOESN'T LOOK THAT DANGEROUS, X. IT'S ONE GUY, ON HIS OWN.
WELL HERE'S A THING.
ONE LITTLE SHEEP WHO LOST HIS WAY!

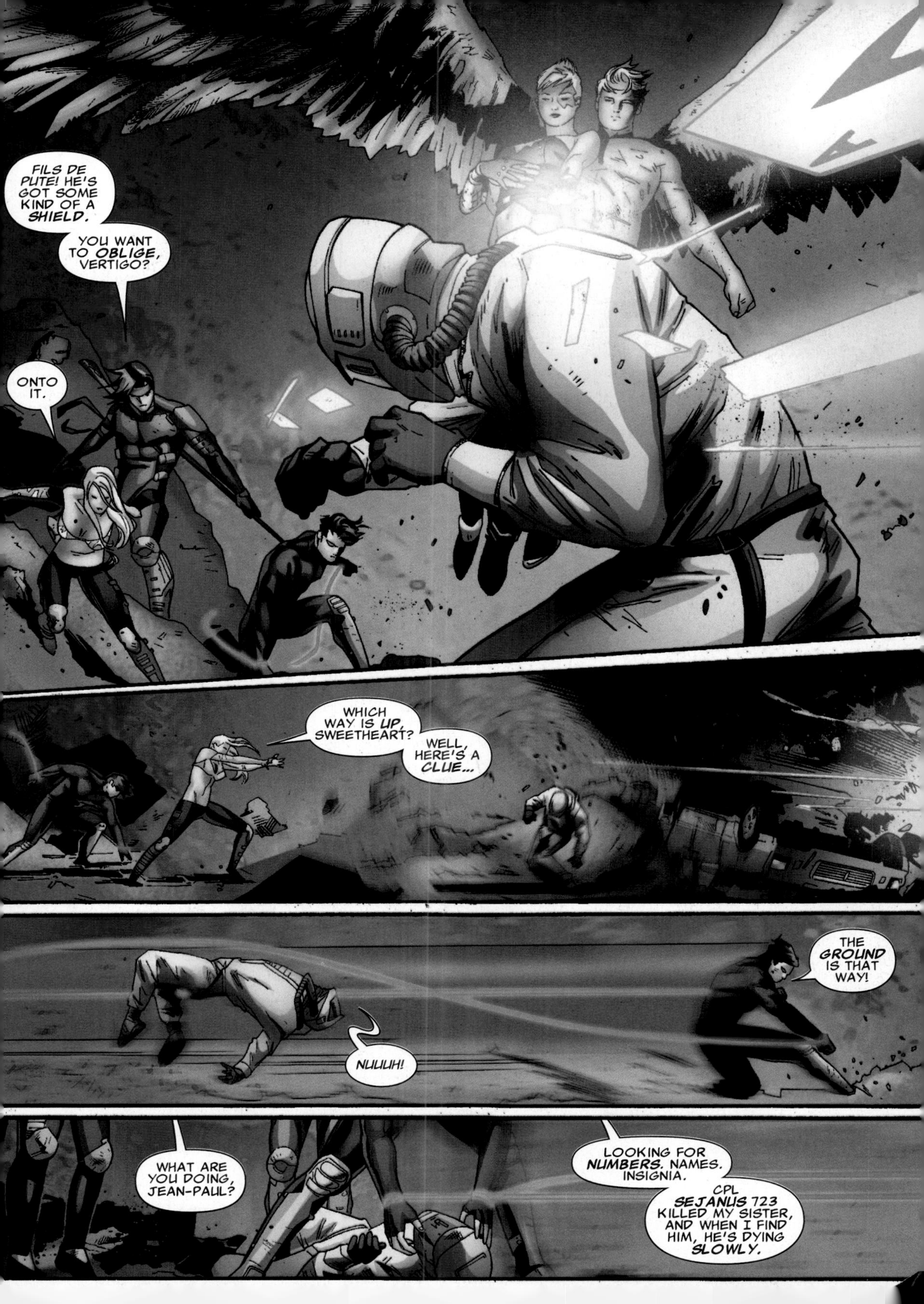
FILS DE PUTE! HE'S GOT SOME KIND OF A SHIELD.
YOU WANT TO OBLIGE, VERTIGO?
ONTO IT.
WHICH WAY IS UP, SWEETHEART?
WELL, HERE'S A CLUE...
THE GROUND IS THAT WAY!
NUUUH!
WHAT ARE YOU DOING, JEAN-PAUL?
LOOKING FOR NUMBERS. NAMES. INSIGNIA.
CPL SEJANUS 723 KILLED MY SISTER, AND WHEN I FIND HIM, HE'S DYING SLOWLY.

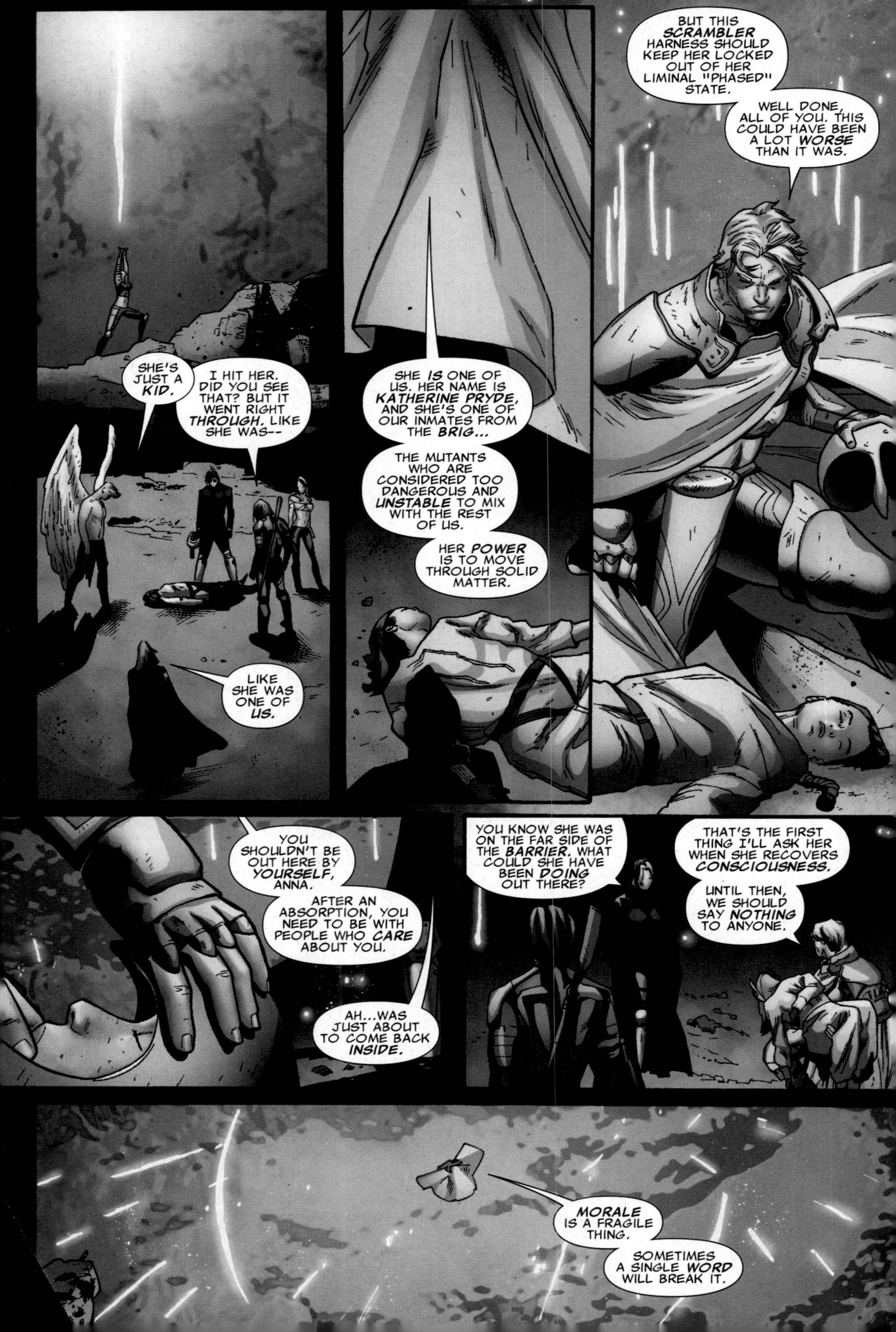
SHE'S JUST A KID.
I HIT HER. DID YOU SEE THAT? BUT IT WENT RIGHT THROUGH. LIKE SHE WAS--
LIKE SHE WAS ONE OF US.
SHE IS ONE OF US. HER NAME IS KATHERINE PRYDE, AND SHE'S ONE OF OUR INMATES FROM THE BRIG...
THE MUTANTS WHO ARE CONSIDERED TOO DANGEROUS AND UNSTABLE TO MIX WITH THE REST OF US.
HER POWER IS TO MOVE THROUGH SOLID MATTER.
BUT THIS SCRAMBLER HARNESS SHOULD KEEP HER LOCKED OUT OF HER LIMINAL "PHASED" STATE.
WELL DONE, ALL OF YOU. THIS COULD HAVE BEEN A LOT WORSE THAN IT WAS.
YOU SHOULDN'T BE OUT HERE BY YOURSELF, ANNA.
AFTER AN ABSORPTION, YOU NEED TO BE WITH PEOPLE WHO CARE ABOUT YOU.
AH...WAS JUST ABOUT TO COME BACK INSIDE.
YOU KNOW SHE WAS ON THE FAR SIDE OF THE BARRIER. WHAT COULD SHE HAVE BEEN DOING OUT THERE?
THAT'S THE FIRST THING I'LL ASK HER WHEN SHE RECOVERS CONSCIOUSNESS.
UNTIL THEN, WE SHOULD SAY NOTHING TO ANYONE.
MORALE IS A FRAGILE THING.
SOMETIMES A SINGLE WORD WILL BREAK IT.

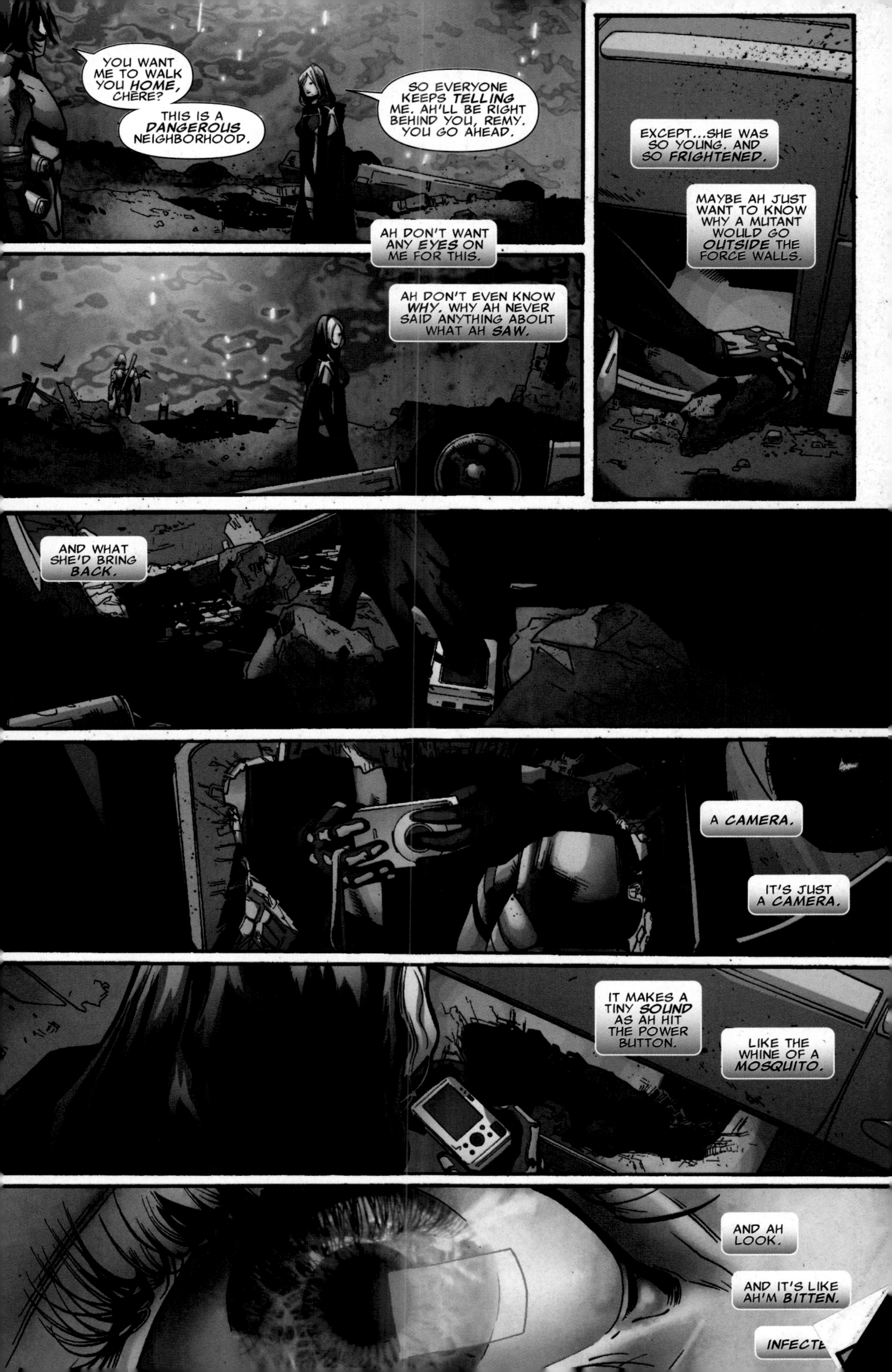

YOU WANT ME TO WALK YOU HOME, CHÈRE?
THIS IS A DANGEROUS NEIGHBORHOOD.
SO EVERYONE KEEPS TELLING ME. AH'LL BE RIGHT BEHIND YOU, REMY. YOU GO AHEAD.
AH DON'T WANT ANY EYES ON ME FOR THIS.
AH DON'T EVEN KNOW WHY. WHY AH NEVER SAID ANYTHING ABOUT WHAT AH SAW.
EXCEPT...SHE WAS SO YOUNG. AND SO FRIGHTENED.
MAYBE AH JUST WANT TO KNOW WHY A MUTANT WOULD GO OUTSIDE THE FORCE WALLS.
AND WHAT SHE'D BRING BACK.
A CAMERA.
IT'S JUST A CAMERA.
IT MAKES A TINY SOUND AS AH HIT THE POWER BUTTON.
LIKE THE WHINE OF A MOSQUITO.
AND AH LOOK.
AND IT'S LIKE AH'M BITTEN.
INFECTE

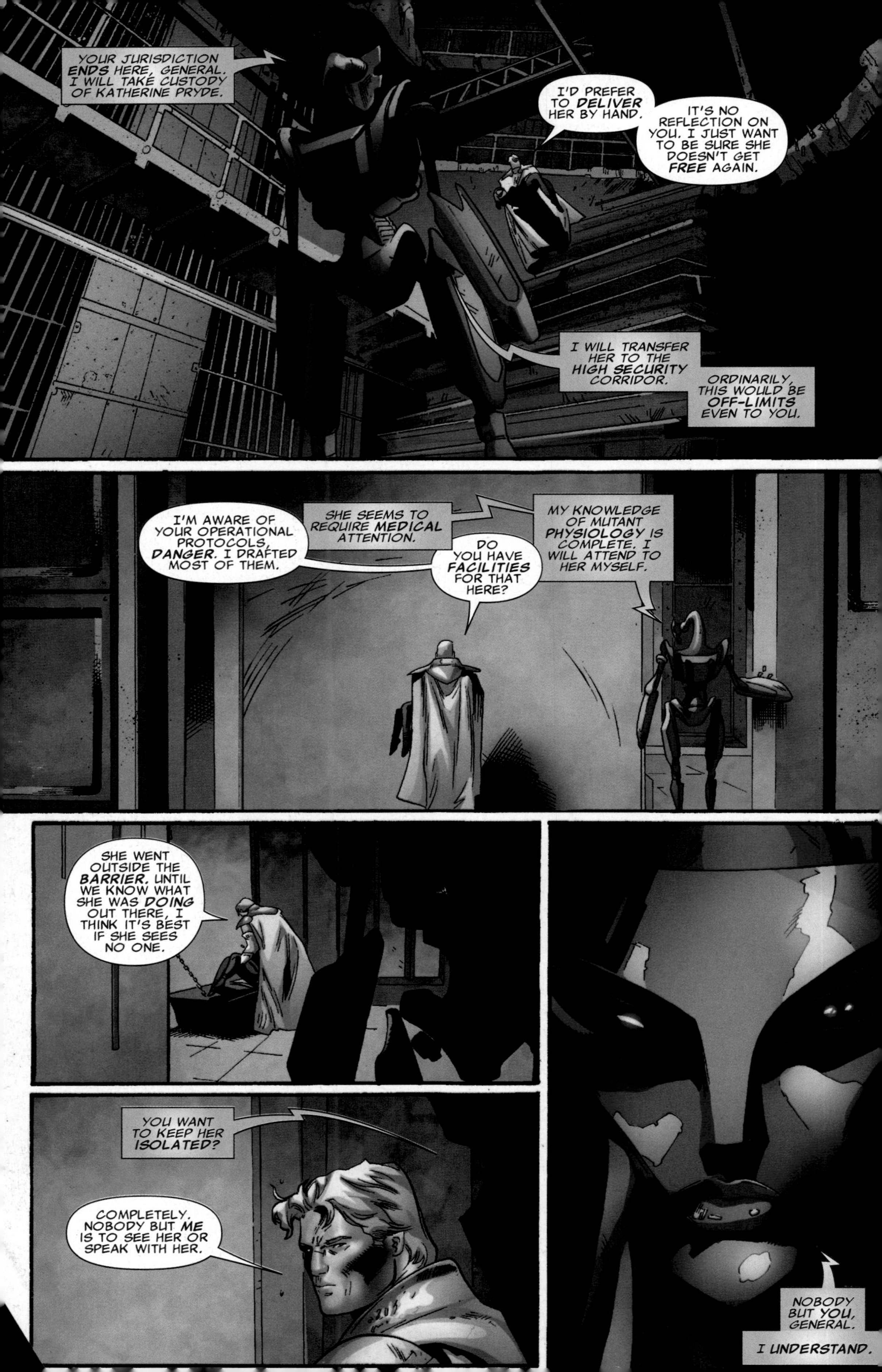
YOUR JURISDICTION ENDS HERE, GENERAL. I WILL TAKE CUSTODY OF KATHERINE PRYDE.
I'D PREFER TO DELIVER HER BY HAND.
IT'S NO REFLECTION ON YOU. I JUST WANT TO BE SURE SHE DOESN'T GET FREE AGAIN.
I WILL TRANSFER HER TO THE HIGH SECURITY CORRIDOR.
ORDINARILY, THIS WOULD BE OFF-LIMITS EVEN TO YOU.
I'M AWARE OF YOUR OPERATIONAL PROTOCOLS, DANGER. I DRAFTED MOST OF THEM.
SHE SEEMS TO REQUIRE MEDICAL ATTENTION.
DO YOU HAVE FACILITIES FOR THAT HERE?
MY KNOWLEDGE OF MUTANT PHYSIOLOGY IS COMPLETE. I WILL ATTEND TO HER MYSELF.
SHE WENT OUTSIDE THE BARRIER. UNTIL WE KNOW WHAT SHE WAS DOING OUT THERE, I THINK IT'S BEST IF SHE SEES NO ONE.
YOU WANT TO KEEP HER ISOLATED?
COMPLETELY. NOBODY BUT ME IS TO SEE HER OR SPEAK WITH HER.
NOBODY BUT YOU, GENERAL.
I UNDERSTAND.

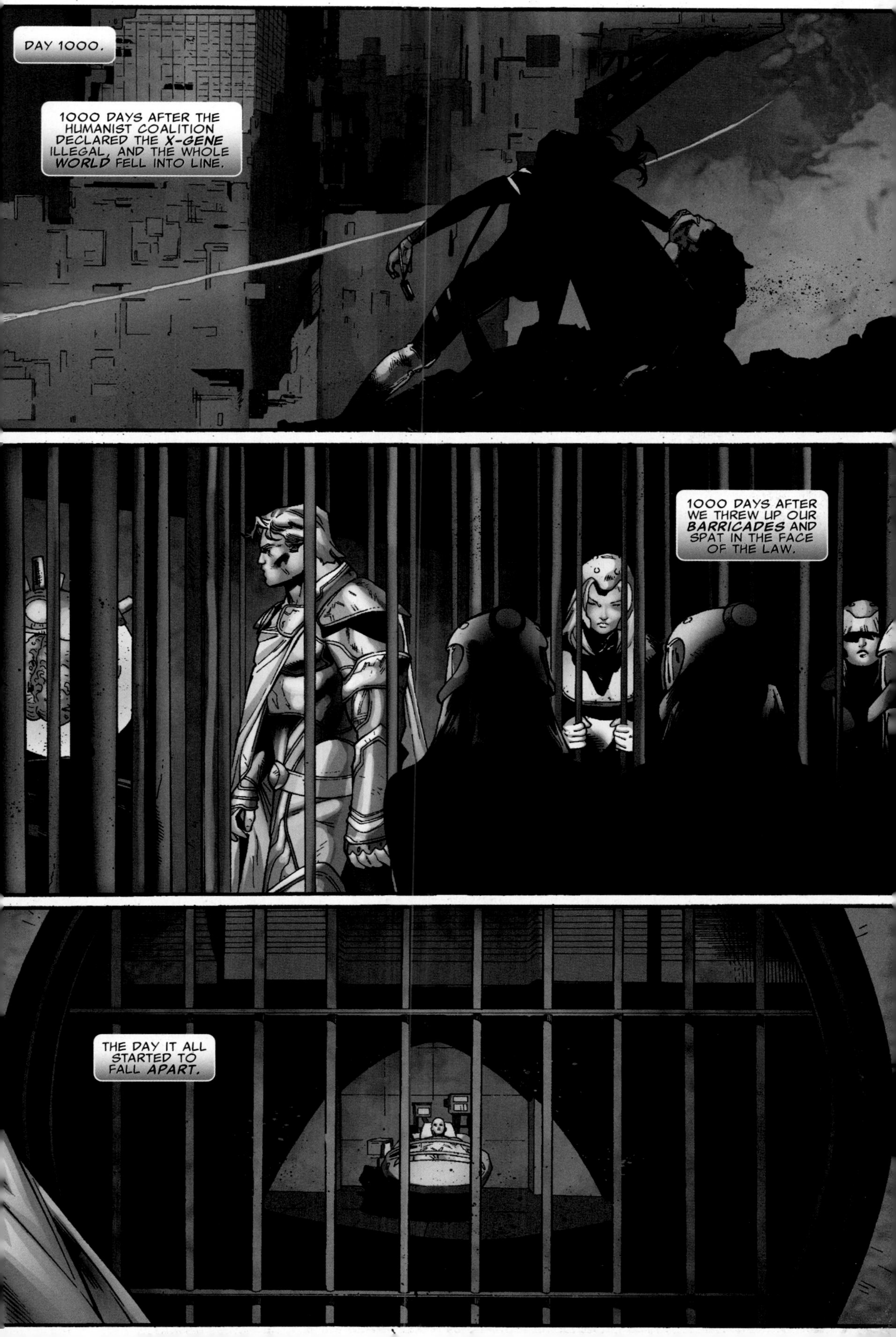
DAY 1000.
1000 DAYS AFTER THE HUMANIST COALITION DECLARED THE X-GENE ILLEGAL, AND THE WHOLE WORLD FELL INTO LINE.
1000 DAYS AFTER WE THREW UP OUR BARRICADES AND SPAT IN THE FACE OF THE LAW.
THE DAY IT ALL STARTED TO FALL APART.

NEW MUTANTS #22

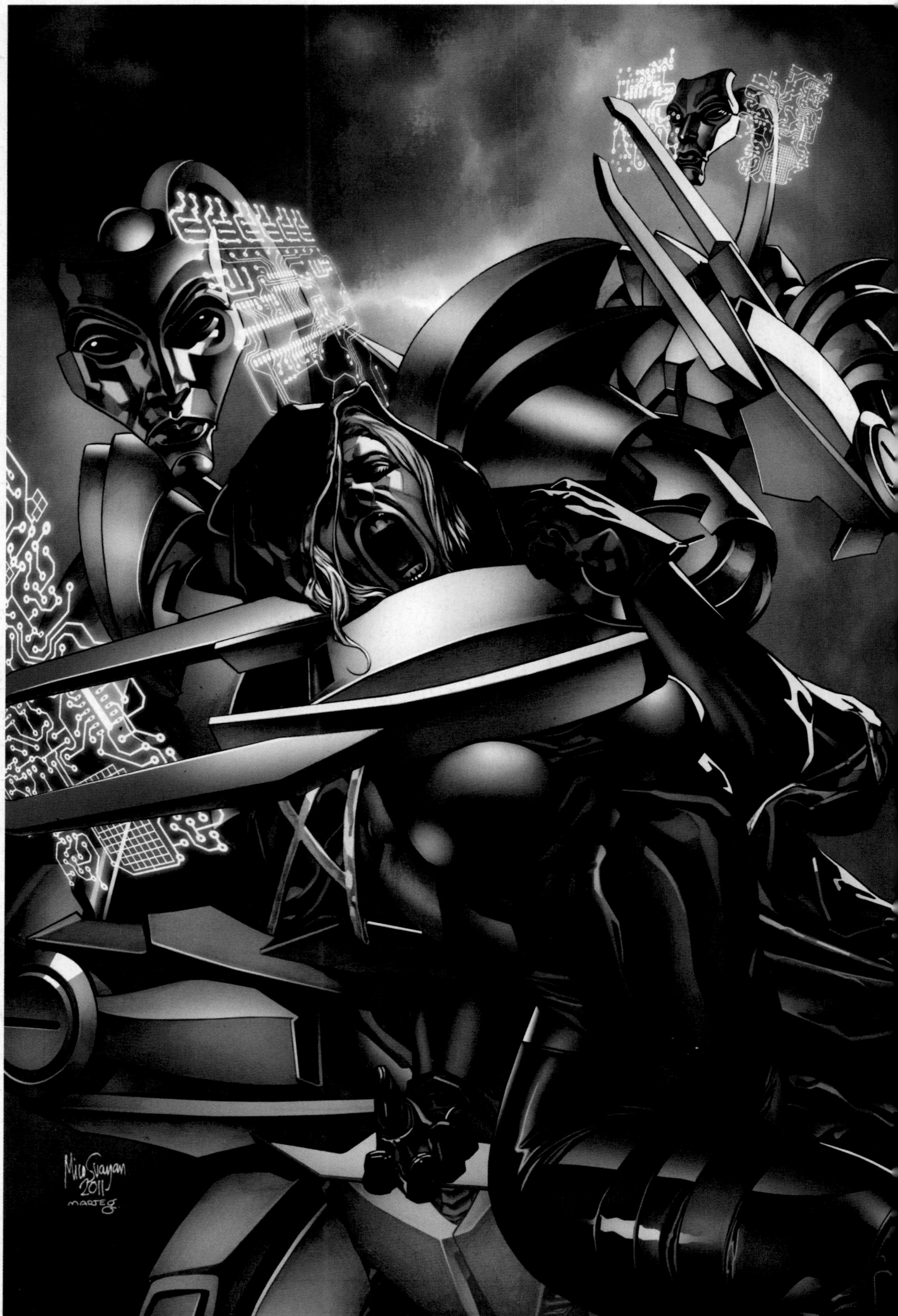

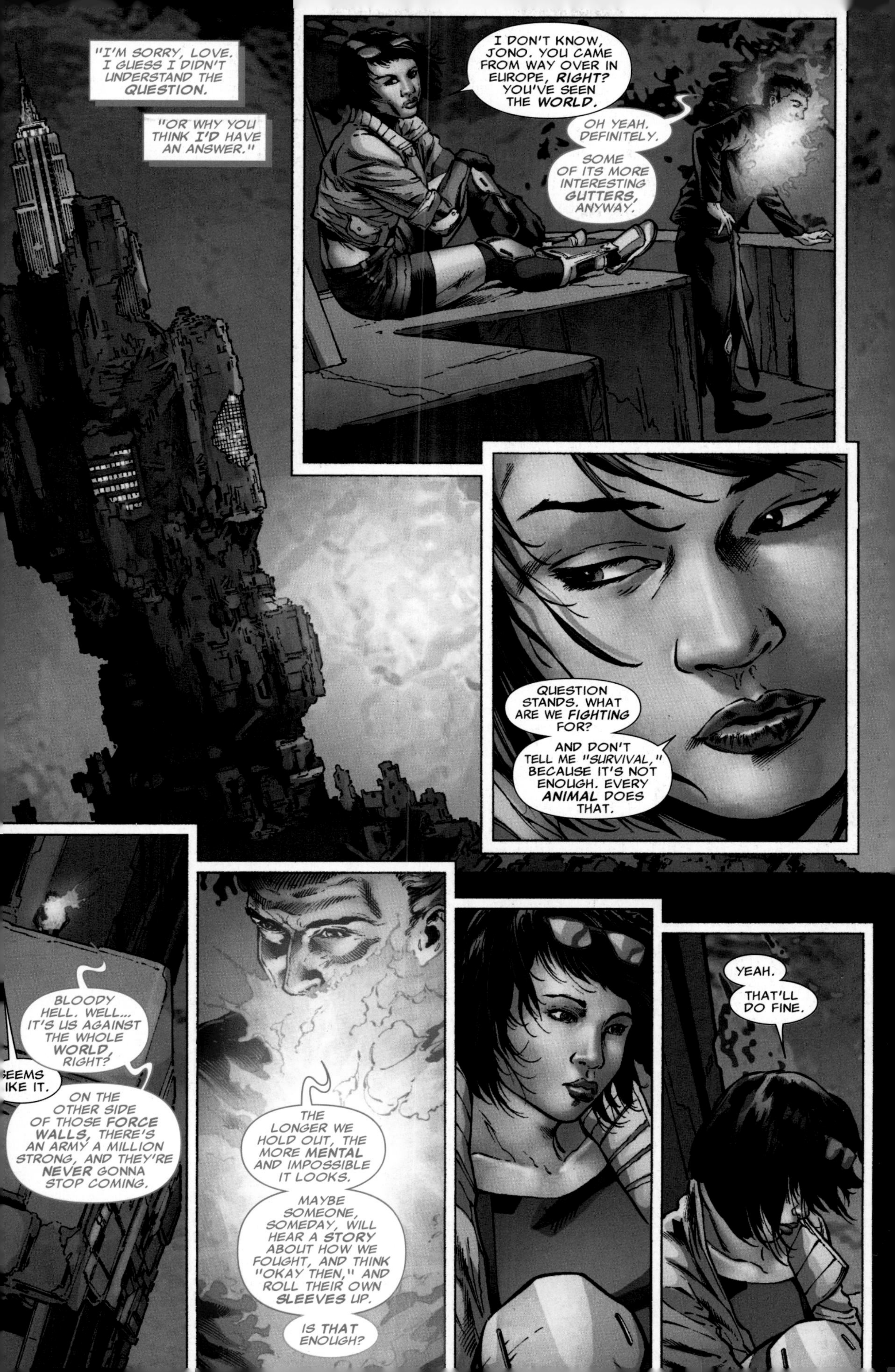
"I'M SORRY, LOVE. I GUESS I DIDN'T UNDERSTAND THE QUESTION.
"OR WHY YOU THINK I'D HAVE AN ANSWER."
I DON'T KNOW, JONO. YOU CAME FROM WAY OVER IN EUROPE, RIGHT? YOU'VE SEEN THE WORLD.
OH YEAH. DEFINITELY.
SOME OF ITS MORE INTERESTING GUTTERS, ANYWAY.
QUESTION STANDS. WHAT ARE WE FIGHTING FOR?
AND DON'T TELL ME "SURVIVAL," BECAUSE IT'S NOT ENOUGH. EVERY ANIMAL DOES THAT.
BLOODY HELL. WELL... IT'S US AGAINST THE WHOLE WORLD, RIGHT?
SEEMS LIKE IT.
ON THE OTHER SIDE OF THOSE FORCE WALLS, THERE'S AN ARMY A MILLION STRONG, AND THEY'RE NEVER GONNA STOP COMING.
THE LONGER WE HOLD OUT, THE MORE MENTAL AND IMPOSSIBLE IT LOOKS.
MAYBE SOMEONE, SOMEDAY, WILL HEAR A STORY ABOUT HOW WE FOUGHT, AND THINK "OKAY THEN," AND ROLL THEIR OWN SLEEVES UP.
IS THAT ENOUGH?
YEAH.
THAT'LL DO FINE.

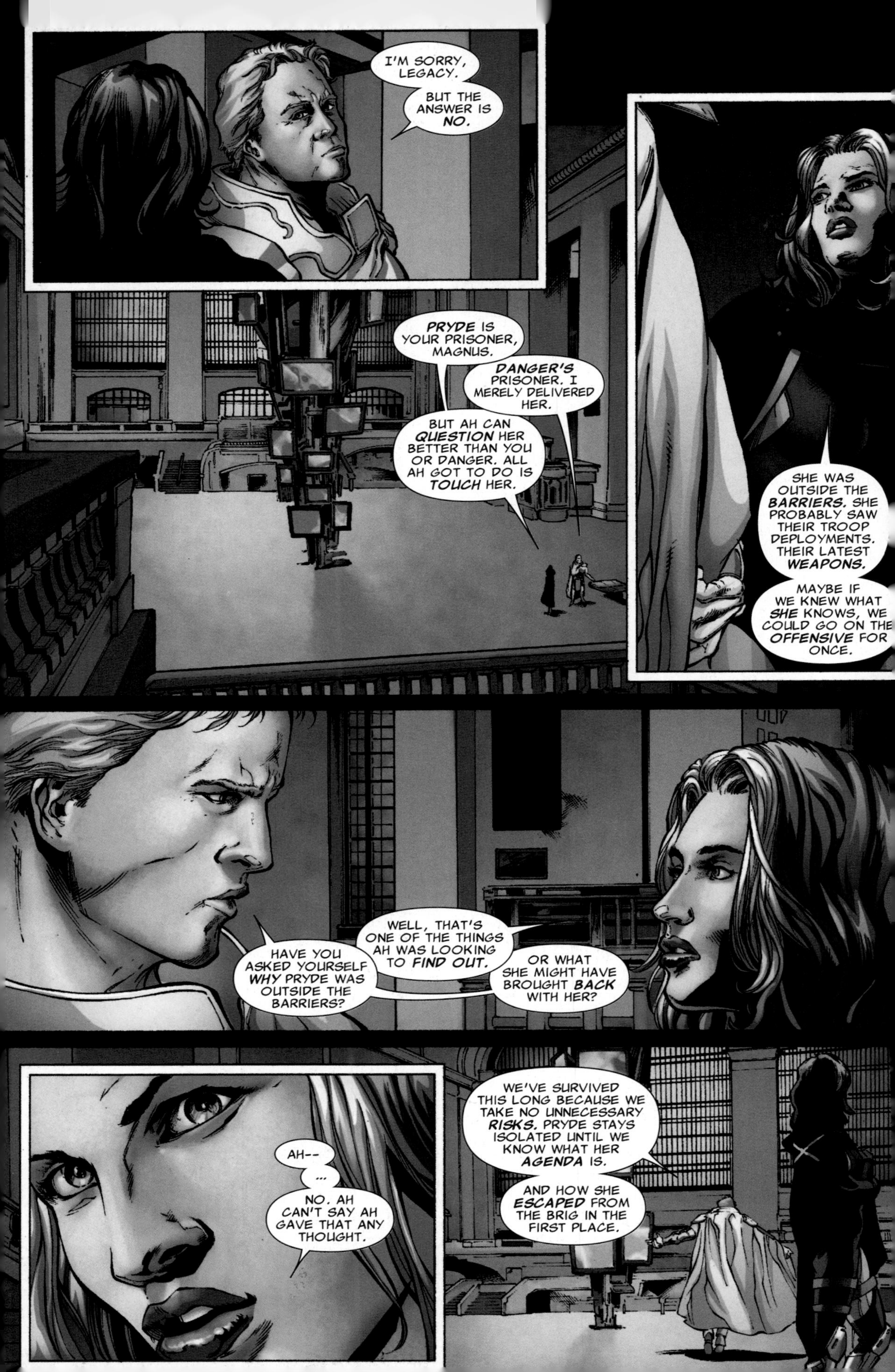
I'M SORRY, LEGACY.
BUT THE ANSWER IS NO.
PRYDE IS YOUR PRISONER, MAGNUS.
DANGER'S PRISONER. I MERELY DELIVERED HER.
BUT AH CAN QUESTION HER BETTER THAN YOU OR DANGER. ALL AH GOT TO DO IS TOUCH HER.
SHE WAS OUTSIDE THE BARRIERS. SHE PROBABLY SAW THEIR TROOP DEPLOYMENTS. THEIR LATEST WEAPONS.
MAYBE IF WE KNEW WHAT SHE KNOWS, WE COULD GO ON THE OFFENSIVE FOR ONCE.
HAVE YOU ASKED YOURSELF WHY PRYDE WAS OUTSIDE THE BARRIERS?
WELL, THAT'S ONE OF THE THINGS AH WAS LOOKING TO FIND OUT.
OR WHAT SHE MIGHT HAVE BROUGHT BACK WITH HER?
AH--
...
NO. AH CAN'T SAY AH GAVE THAT ANY THOUGHT.
WE'VE SURVIVED THIS LONG BECAUSE WE TAKE NO UNNECESSARY RISKS. PRYDE STAYS ISOLATED UNTIL WE KNOW WHAT HER AGENDA IS.
AND HOW SHE ESCAPED FROM THE BRIG IN THE FIRST PLACE.

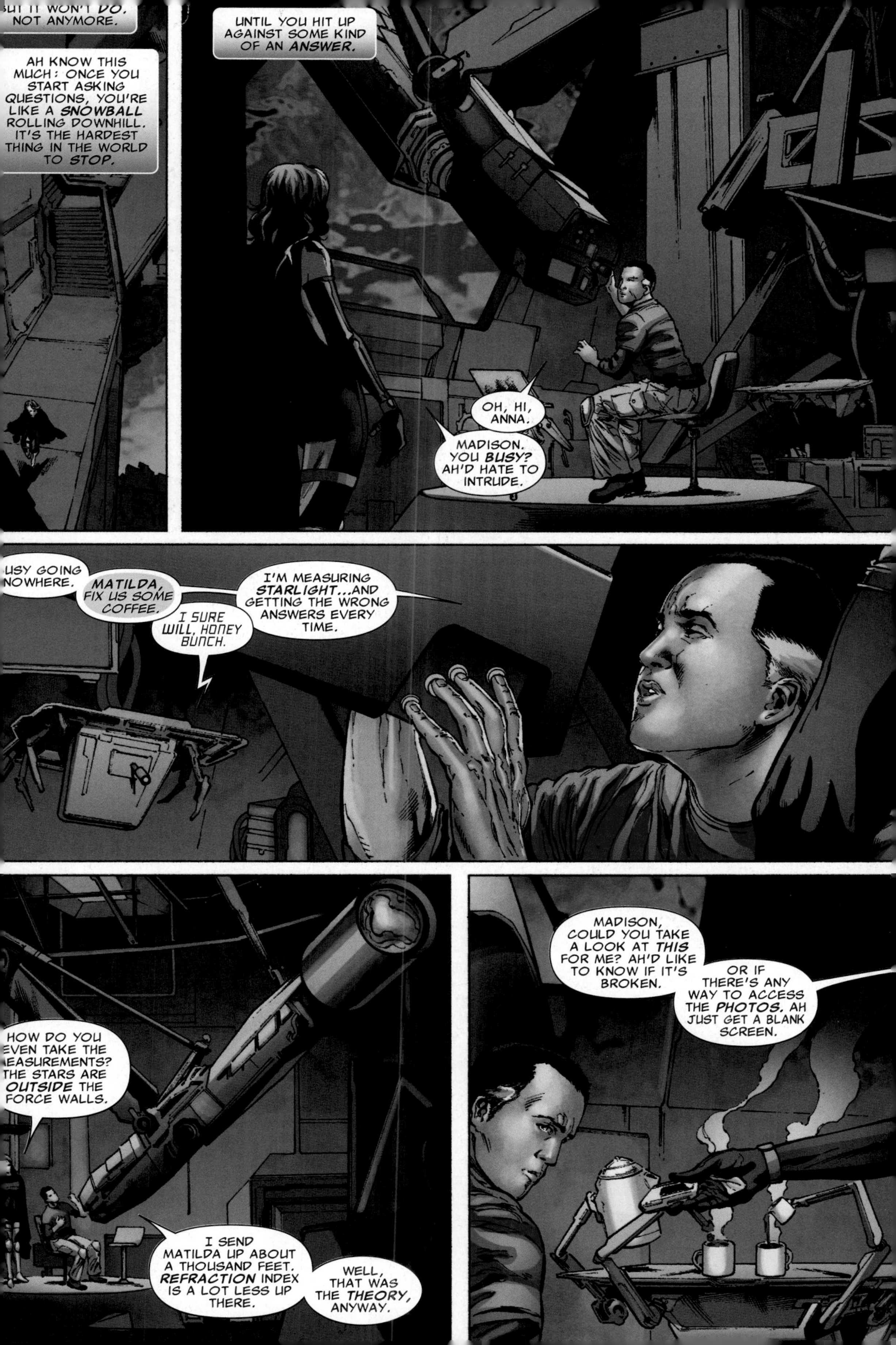

BUT IT WON'T DO. NOT ANYMORE.
AH KNOW THIS MUCH: ONCE YOU START ASKING QUESTIONS, YOU'RE LIKE A SNOWBALL ROLLING DOWNHILL. IT'S THE HARDEST THING IN THE WORLD TO STOP.
UNTIL YOU HIT UP AGAINST SOME KIND OF AN ANSWER.
OH, HI, ANNA.
MADISON. YOU BUSY? AH'D HATE TO INTRUDE.
USY GOING NOWHERE.
MATILDA, FIX US SOME COFFEE.
I SURE WILL, HONEY BUNCH.
I'M MEASURING STARLIGHT...AND GETTING THE WRONG ANSWERS EVERY TIME.
HOW DO YOU EVEN TAKE THE EASUREMENTS? THE STARS ARE OUTSIDE THE FORCE WALLS.
I SEND MATILDA UP ABOUT A THOUSAND FEET. REFRACTION INDEX IS A LOT LESS UP THERE.
WELL, THAT WAS THE THEORY, ANYWAY.
MADISON, COULD YOU TAKE A LOOK AT THIS FOR ME? AH'D LIKE TO KNOW IF IT'S BROKEN.
OR IF THERE'S ANY WAY TO ACCESS THE PHOTOS. AH JUST GET A BLANK SCREEN.

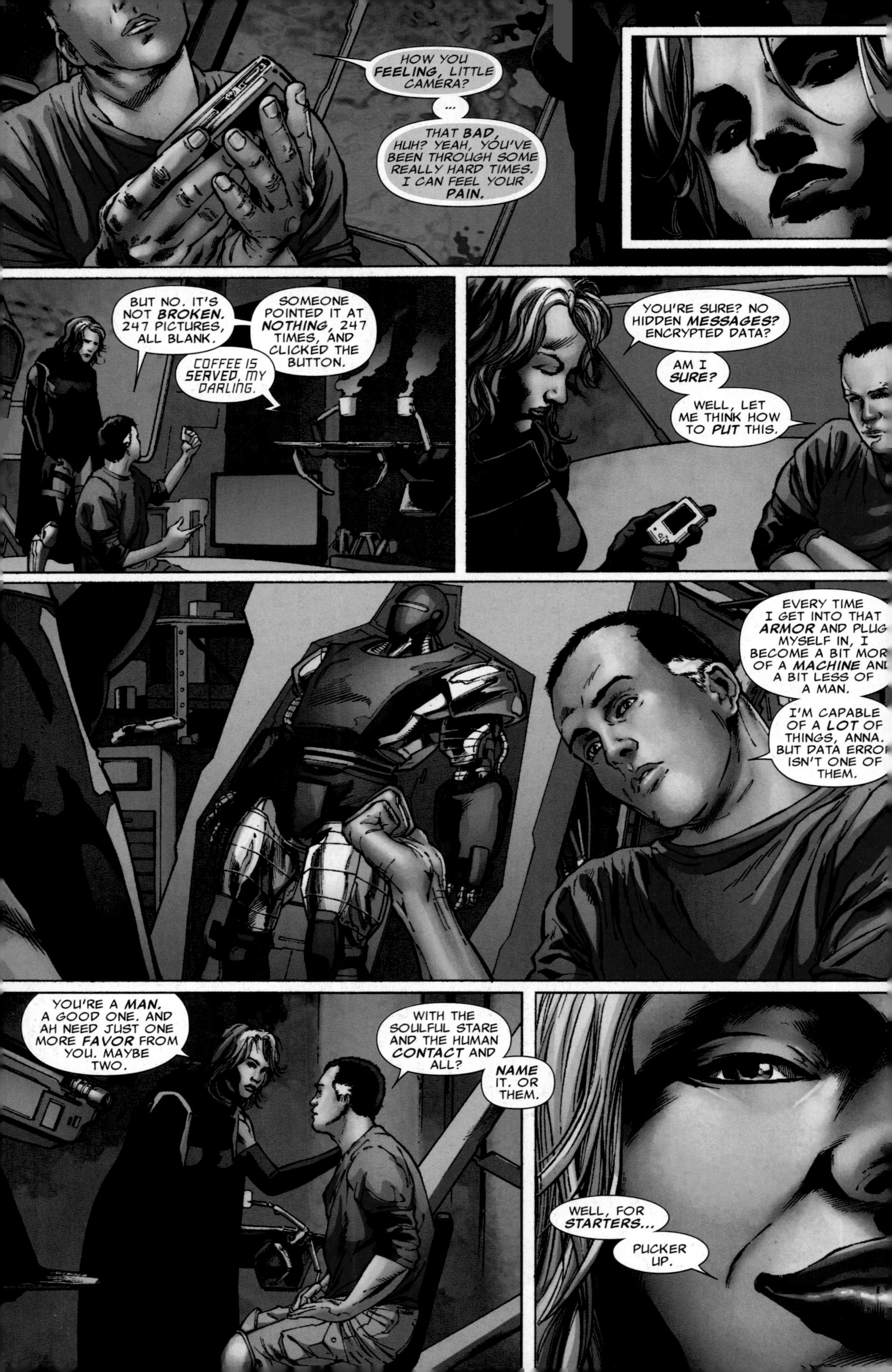
HOW YOU FEELING, LITTLE CAMERA?
...
THAT BAD, HUH? YEAH, YOU'VE BEEN THROUGH SOME REALLY HARD TIMES. I CAN FEEL YOUR PAIN.
BUT NO. IT'S NOT BROKEN. 247 PICTURES, ALL BLANK.
SOMEONE POINTED IT AT NOTHING, 247 TIMES, AND CLICKED THE BUTTON.
COFFEE IS SERVED, MY DARLING.
YOU'RE SURE? NO HIDDEN MESSAGES? ENCRYPTED DATA?
AM I SURE?
WELL, LET ME THINK HOW TO PUT THIS.
EVERY TIME I GET INTO THAT ARMOR AND PLUG MYSELF IN, I BECOME A BIT MOR OF A MACHINE AN A BIT LESS OF A MAN.
I'M CAPABLE OF A LOT OF THINGS, ANNA. BUT DATA ERRO ISN'T ONE OF THEM.
YOU'RE A MAN. A GOOD ONE. AND AH NEED JUST ONE MORE FAVOR FROM YOU. MAYBE TWO.
WITH THE SOULFUL STARE AND THE HUMAN CONTACT AND ALL?
NAME IT. OR THEM.
WELL, FOR STARTERS...
PUCKER UP.

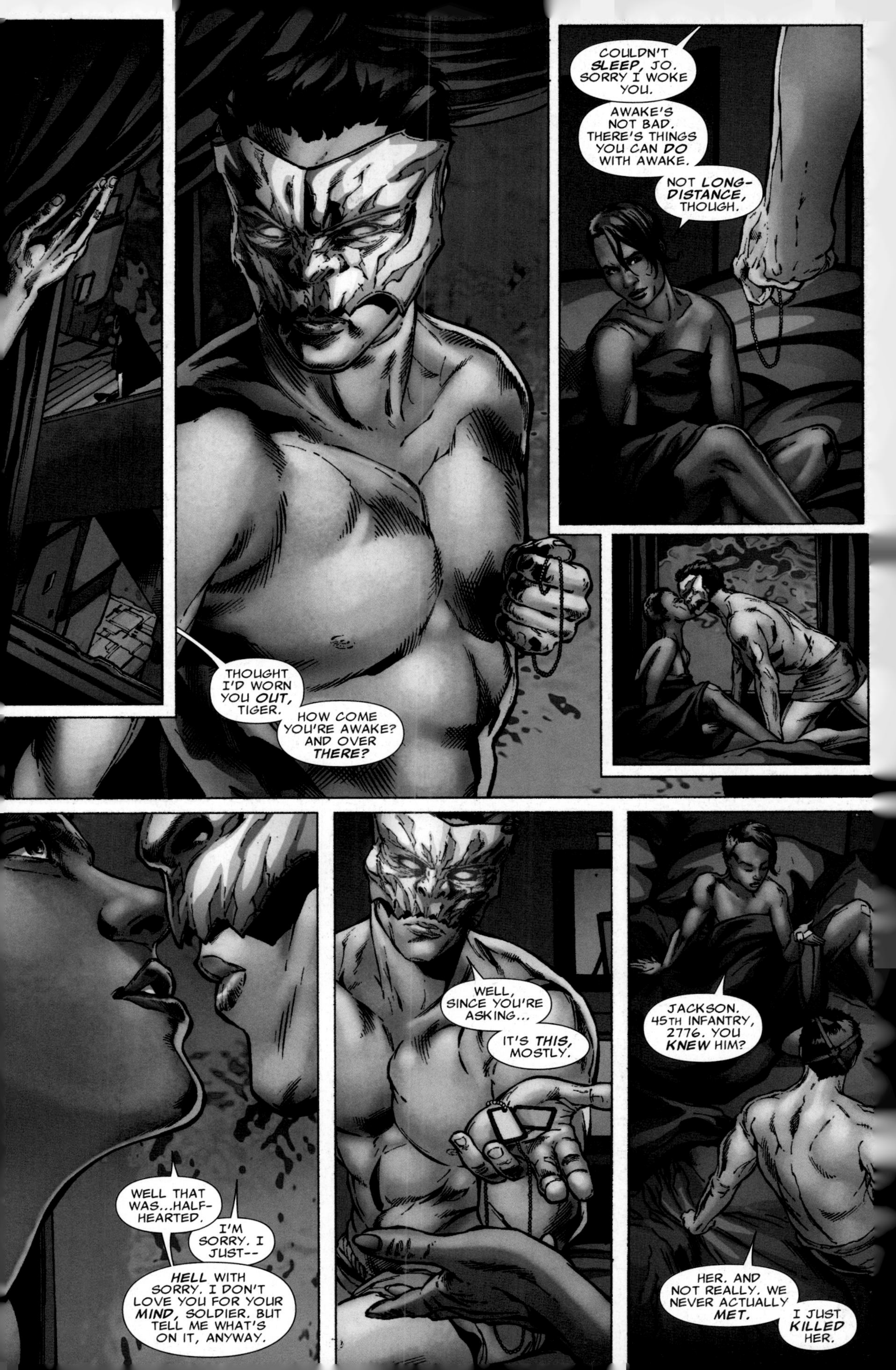

COULDN'T SLEEP, JO. SORRY I WOKE YOU.
AWAKE'S NOT BAD. THERE'S THINGS YOU CAN DO WITH AWAKE.
NOT LONG-DISTANCE, THOUGH.
THOUGHT I'D WORN YOU OUT, TIGER.
HOW COME YOU'RE AWAKE? AND OVER THERE?
WELL THAT WAS...HALF-HEARTED.
I'M SORRY. I JUST--
HELL WITH SORRY. I DON'T LOVE YOU FOR YOUR MIND, SOLDIER. BUT TELL ME WHAT'S ON IT, ANYWAY.
WELL, SINCE YOU'RE ASKING...
IT'S THIS, MOSTLY.
JACKSON. 45TH INFANTRY, 2776. YOU KNEW HIM?
HER. AND NOT REALLY. WE NEVER ACTUALLY MET.
I JUST KILLED HER.

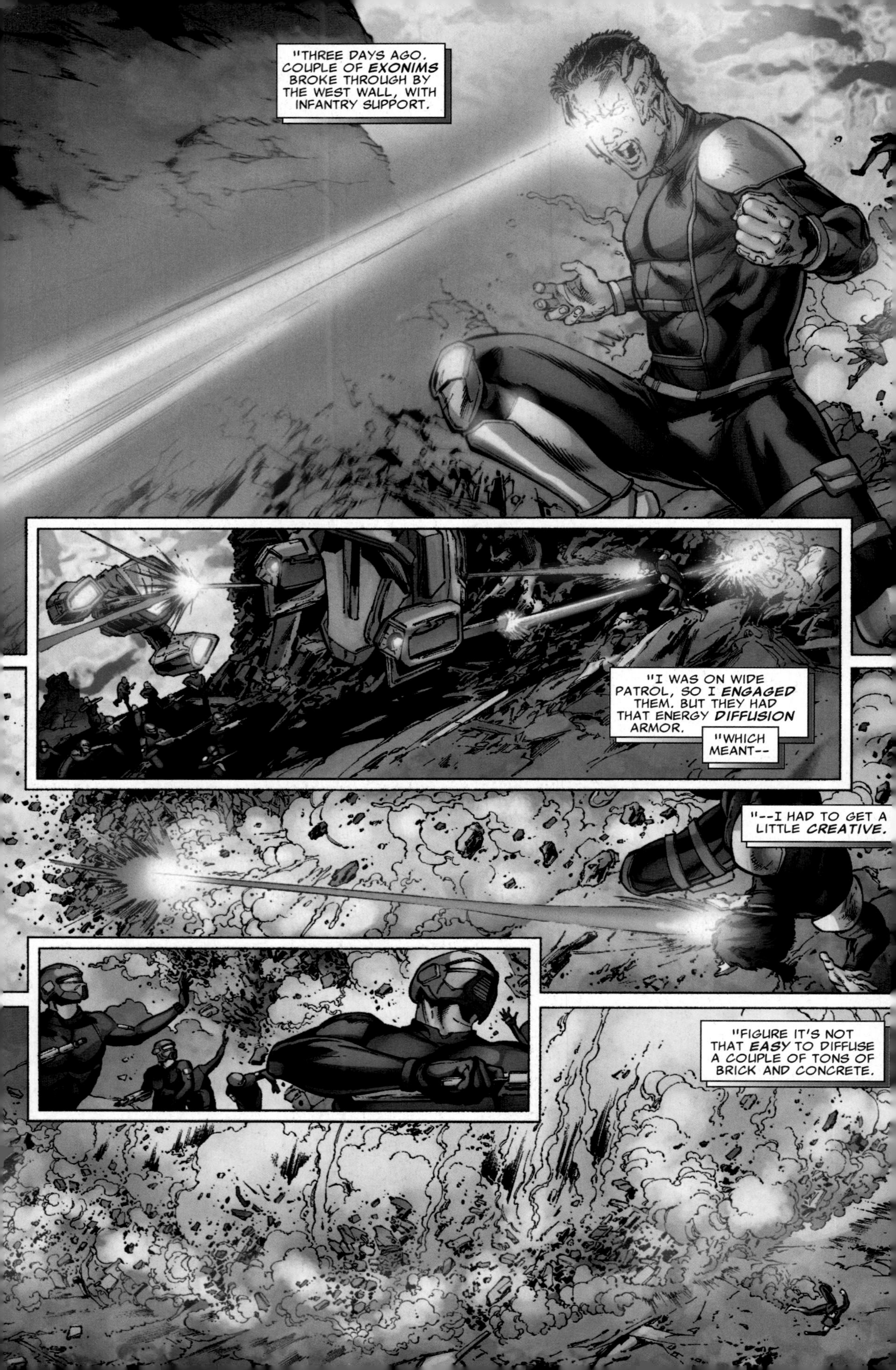
"THREE DAYS AGO. COUPLE OF EXONIMS BROKE THROUGH BY THE WEST WALL, WITH INFANTRY SUPPORT.
"I WAS ON WIDE PATROL, SO I ENGAGED THEM. BUT THEY HAD THAT ENERGY DIFFUSION ARMOR.
"WHICH MEANT--
"--I HAD TO GET A LITTLE CREATIVE.
"FIGURE IT'S NOT THAT EASY TO DIFFUSE A COUPLE OF TONS OF BRICK AND CONCRETE.

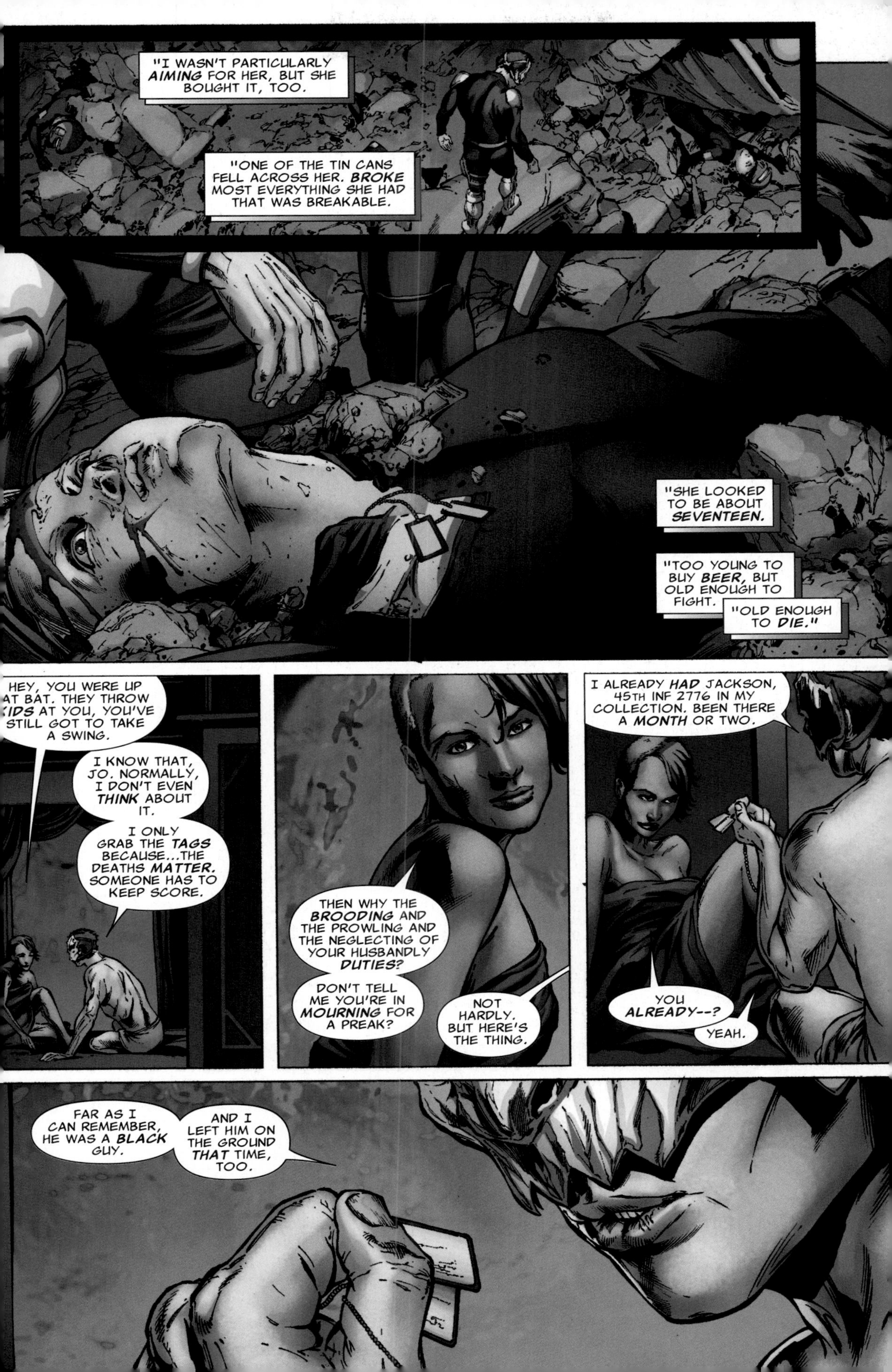
"I WASN'T PARTICULARLY AIMING FOR HER, BUT SHE BOUGHT IT, TOO.
"ONE OF THE TIN CANS FELL ACROSS HER. BROKE MOST EVERYTHING SHE HAD THAT WAS BREAKABLE.
"SHE LOOKED TO BE ABOUT SEVENTEEN.
"TOO YOUNG TO BUY BEER, BUT OLD ENOUGH TO FIGHT.
"OLD ENOUGH TO DIE."
HEY, YOU WERE UP AT BAT. THEY THROW KIDS AT YOU, YOU'VE STILL GOT TO TAKE A SWING.
I KNOW THAT, JO. NORMALLY, I DON'T EVEN THINK ABOUT IT.
I ONLY GRAB THE TAGS BECAUSE...THE DEATHS MATTER. SOMEONE HAS TO KEEP SCORE.
THEN WHY THE BROODING AND THE PROWLING AND THE NEGLECTING OF YOUR HUSBANDLY DUTIES?
DON'T TELL ME YOU'RE IN MOURNING FOR A PREAK?
NOT HARDLY. BUT HERE'S THE THING.
I ALREADY HAD JACKSON, 45TH INF 2776 IN MY COLLECTION. BEEN THERE A MONTH OR TWO.
YOU ALREADY--?
YEAH.
FAR AS I CAN REMEMBER, HE WAS A BLACK GUY.
AND I LEFT HIM ON THE GROUND THAT TIME, TOO.

SECURE HOLDING FACILITY
NO ADMITTANCE

HAVEN'T DONE THAT IN A WHILE. *KISSED* A MAN TO BORROW HIS POWERS. USED TO BE MY THING BACK WHEN I WAS YOUNG AND *STUPID.*

THESE DAYS AH'M MOSTLY THE *REAPER.* AND DEATH DOESN'T FLIRT.

ID SCAN INITIATED.

THERE'S NOBODY HERE.

ID SCAN TERMINATED.

OPEN UP. THEN *ERASE* ACTIVITY LOG.

VIFFFFFFFFF

THANK YOU KINDLY.

CAMERAS, LOOK AWAY.

NOTHING TO SEE HERE.

AH NEED A MAP.

WHERE'S KATHERINE PRYDE?

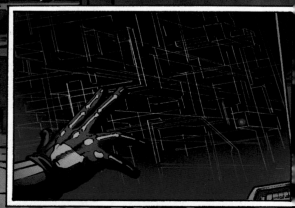

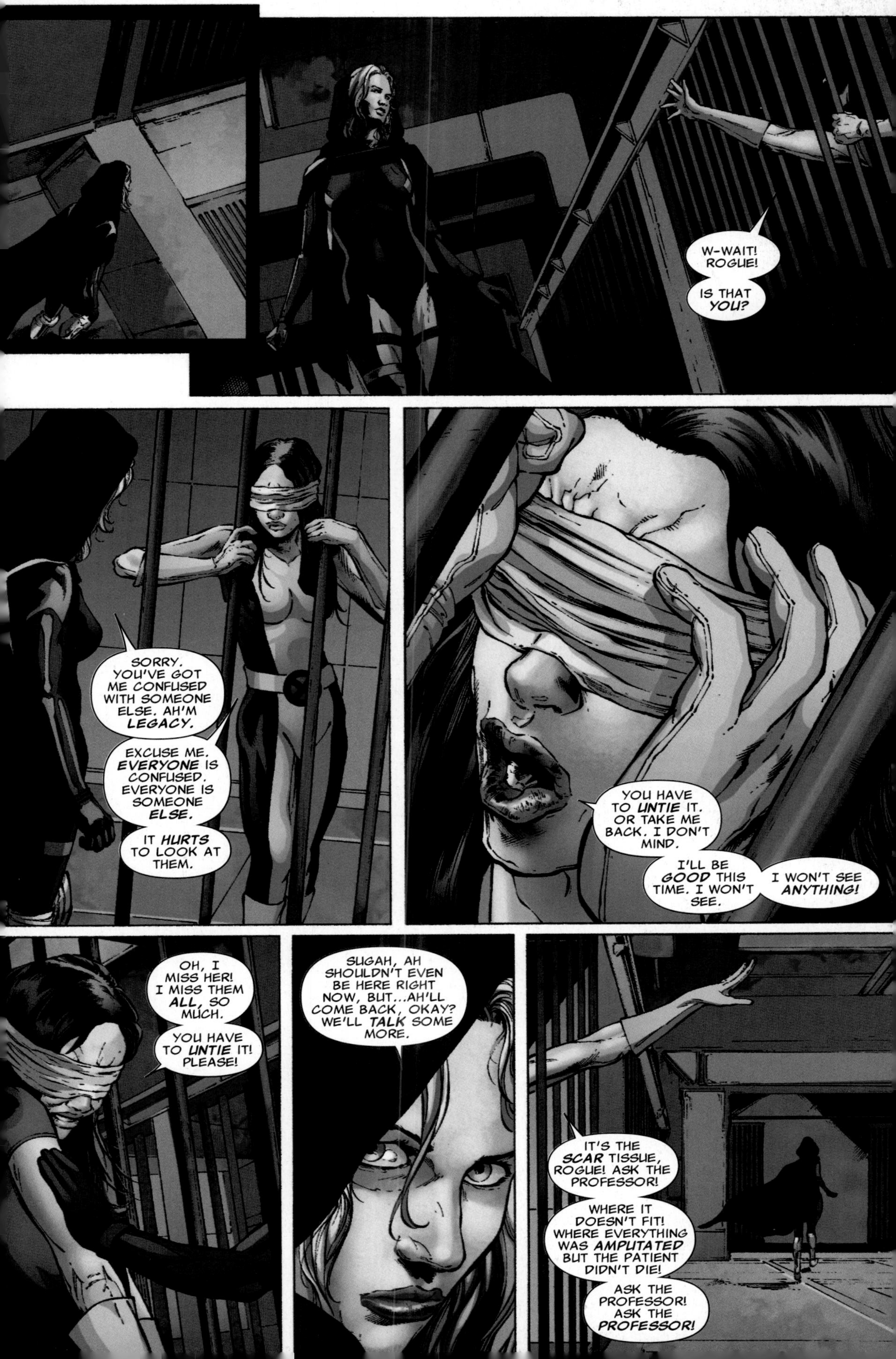

W-WAIT! ROGUE!
IS THAT YOU?
SORRY. YOU'VE GOT ME CONFUSED WITH SOMEONE ELSE. AH'M LEGACY.
EXCUSE ME. EVERYONE IS CONFUSED. EVERYONE IS SOMEONE ELSE.
IT HURTS TO LOOK AT THEM.
YOU HAVE TO UNTIE IT. OR TAKE ME BACK. I DON'T MIND.
I'LL BE GOOD THIS TIME. I WON'T SEE.
I WON'T SEE ANYTHING!
OH, I MISS HER! I MISS THEM ALL, SO MUCH.
YOU HAVE TO UNTIE IT! PLEASE!
SUGAH, AH SHOULDN'T EVEN BE HERE RIGHT NOW, BUT...AH'LL COME BACK, OKAY? WE'LL TALK SOME MORE.
IT'S THE SCAR TISSUE, ROGUE! ASK THE PROFESSOR!
WHERE IT DOESN'T FIT! WHERE EVERYTHING WAS AMPUTATED BUT THE PATIENT DIDN'T DIE!
ASK THE PROFESSOR! ASK THE PROFESSOR!

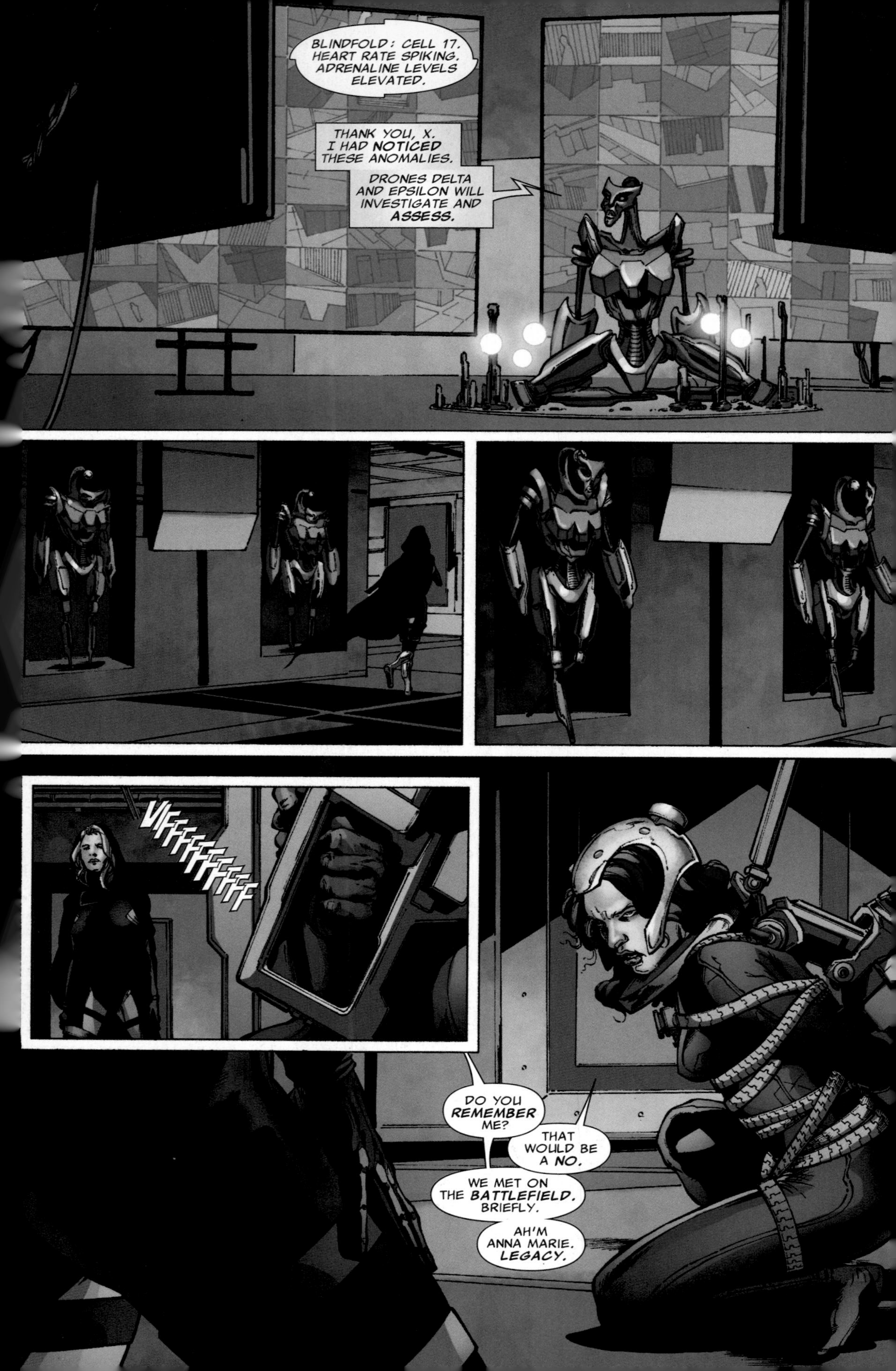
BLINDFOLD: CELL 17. HEART RATE SPIKING. ADRENALINE LEVELS ELEVATED.
THANK YOU, X. I HAD NOTICED THESE ANOMALIES.
DRONES DELTA AND EPSILON WILL INVESTIGATE AND ASSESS.
VIFFFFFFFFFFFF
DO YOU REMEMBER ME?
THAT WOULD BE A NO.
WE MET ON THE BATTLEFIELD. BRIEFLY.
AH'M ANNA MARIE. LEGACY.

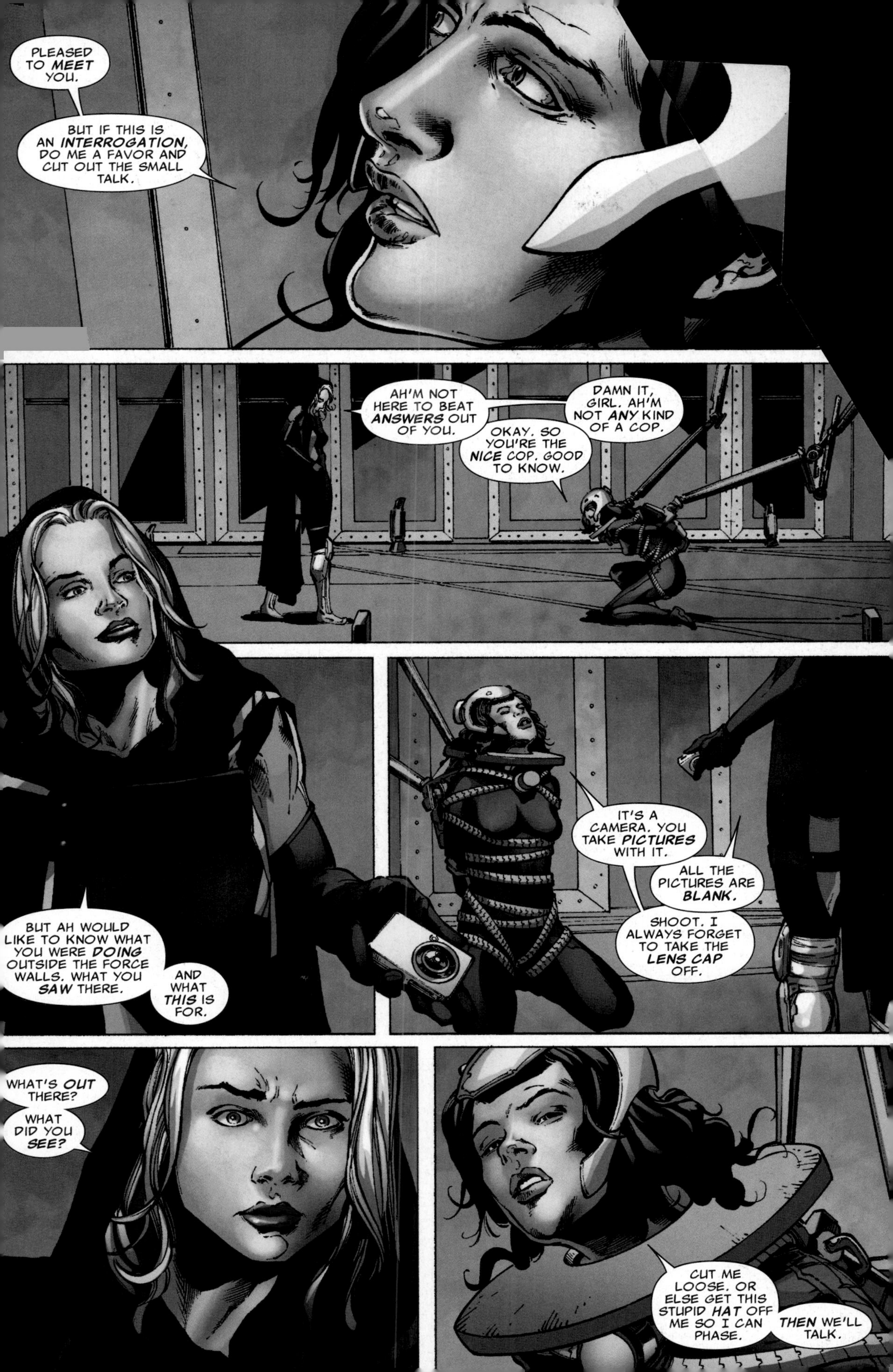
PLEASED TO MEET YOU.
BUT IF THIS IS AN INTERROGATION, DO ME A FAVOR AND CUT OUT THE SMALL TALK.
AH'M NOT HERE TO BEAT ANSWERS OUT OF YOU.
OKAY. SO YOU'RE THE NICE COP. GOOD TO KNOW.
DAMN IT, GIRL. AH'M NOT ANY KIND OF A COP.
BUT AH WOULD LIKE TO KNOW WHAT YOU WERE DOING OUTSIDE THE FORCE WALLS. WHAT YOU SAW THERE.
AND WHAT THIS IS FOR.
IT'S A CAMERA. YOU TAKE PICTURES WITH IT.
ALL THE PICTURES ARE BLANK.
SHOOT. I ALWAYS FORGET TO TAKE THE LENS CAP OFF.
WHAT'S OUT THERE?
WHAT DID YOU SEE?
CUT ME LOOSE. OR ELSE GET THIS STUPID HAT OFF ME SO I CAN PHASE.
THEN WE'LL TALK.

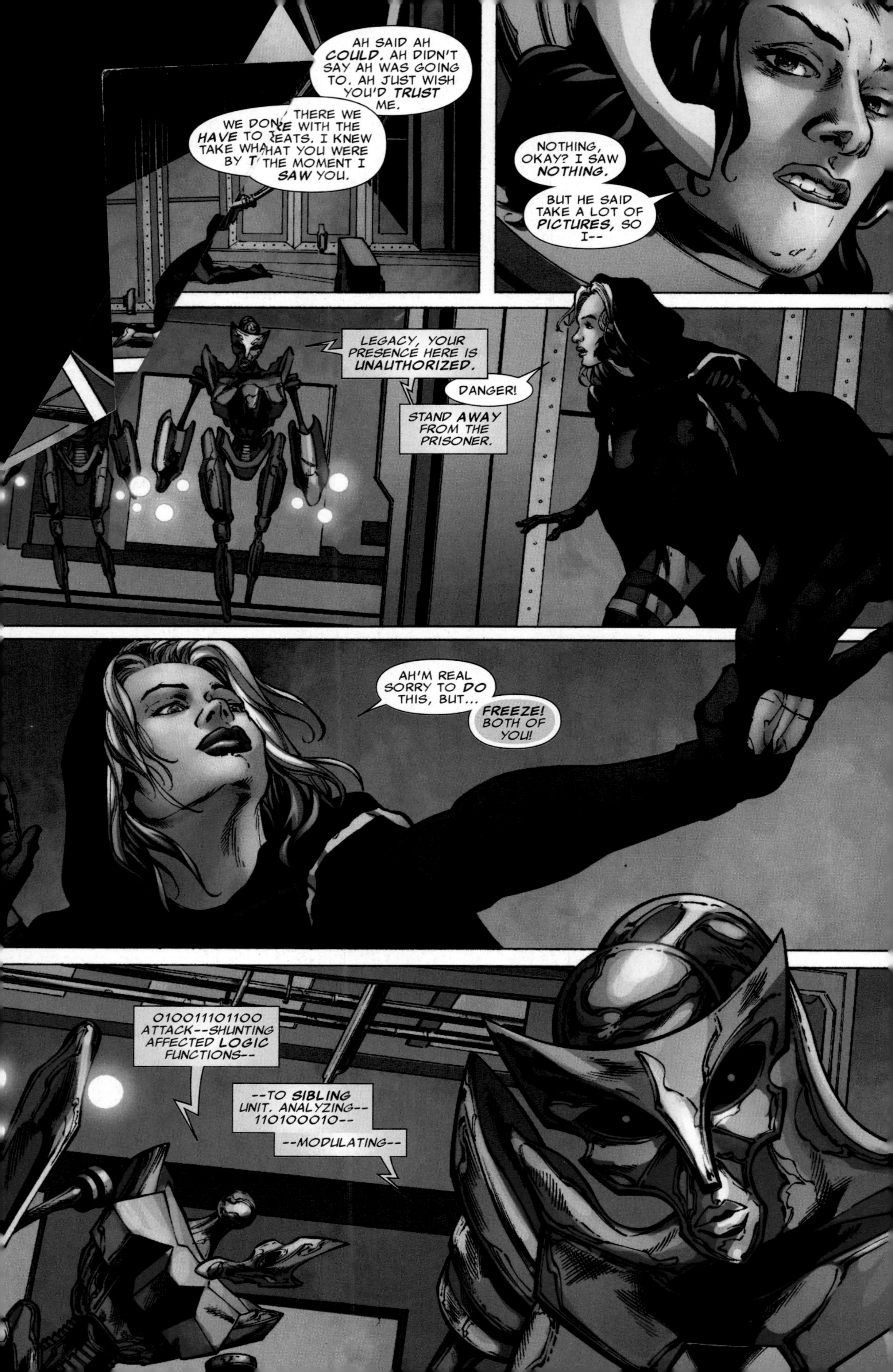

AH SAID AH COULD. AH DIDN'T SAY AH WAS GOING TO. AH JUST WISH YOU'D TRUST ME.
WE DON HAVE TO TAKE WHA BY T
THERE WE E WITH THE EATS. I KNEW HAT YOU WERE THE MOMENT I SAW YOU.
NOTHING, OKAY? I SAW NOTHING.
BUT HE SAID TAKE A LOT OF PICTURES, SO I--
LEGACY, YOUR PRESENCE HERE IS UNAUTHORIZED.
DANGER!
STAND AWAY FROM THE PRISONER.
AH'M REAL SORRY TO DO THIS, BUT...
FREEZE! BOTH OF YOU!
010011101100 ATTACK--SHUNTING AFFECTED LOGIC FUNCTIONS--
--TO SIBLING UNIT. ANALYZING-- 110100010--
--MODULATING--

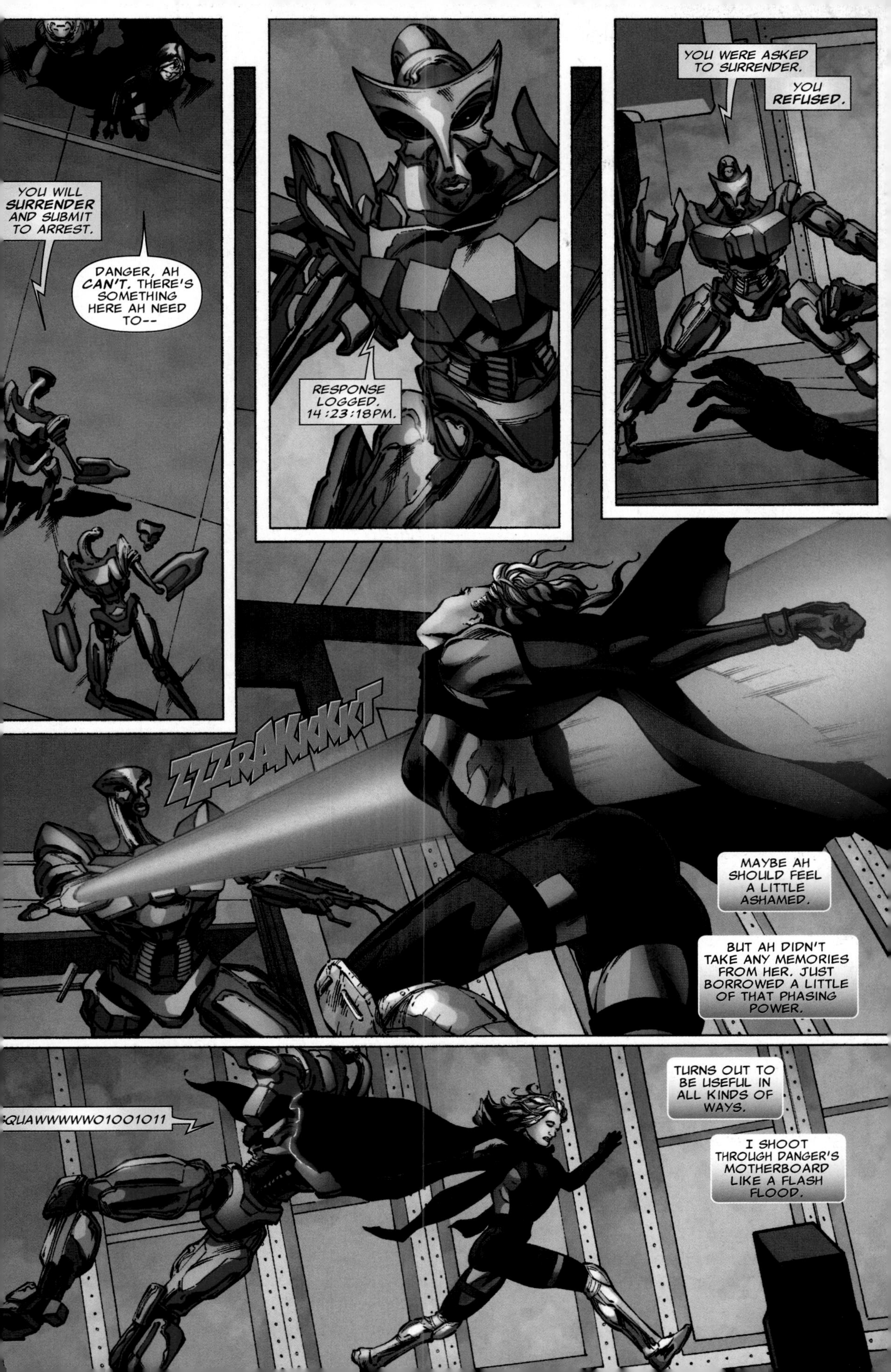

YOU WILL SURRENDER AND SUBMIT TO ARREST.
DANGER, AH CAN'T. THERE'S SOMETHING HERE AH NEED TO--
RESPONSE LOGGED. 14:23:18PM.
YOU WERE ASKED TO SURRENDER.
YOU REFUSED.
ZZZRAKKKKT
MAYBE AH SHOULD FEEL A LITTLE ASHAMED.
BUT AH DIDN'T TAKE ANY MEMORIES FROM HER. JUST BORROWED A LITTLE OF THAT PHASING POWER.
SQUAWWWWWO1001011
TURNS OUT TO BE USEFUL IN ALL KINDS OF WAYS.
I SHOOT THROUGH DANGER'S MOTHERBOARD LIKE A FLASH FLOOD.

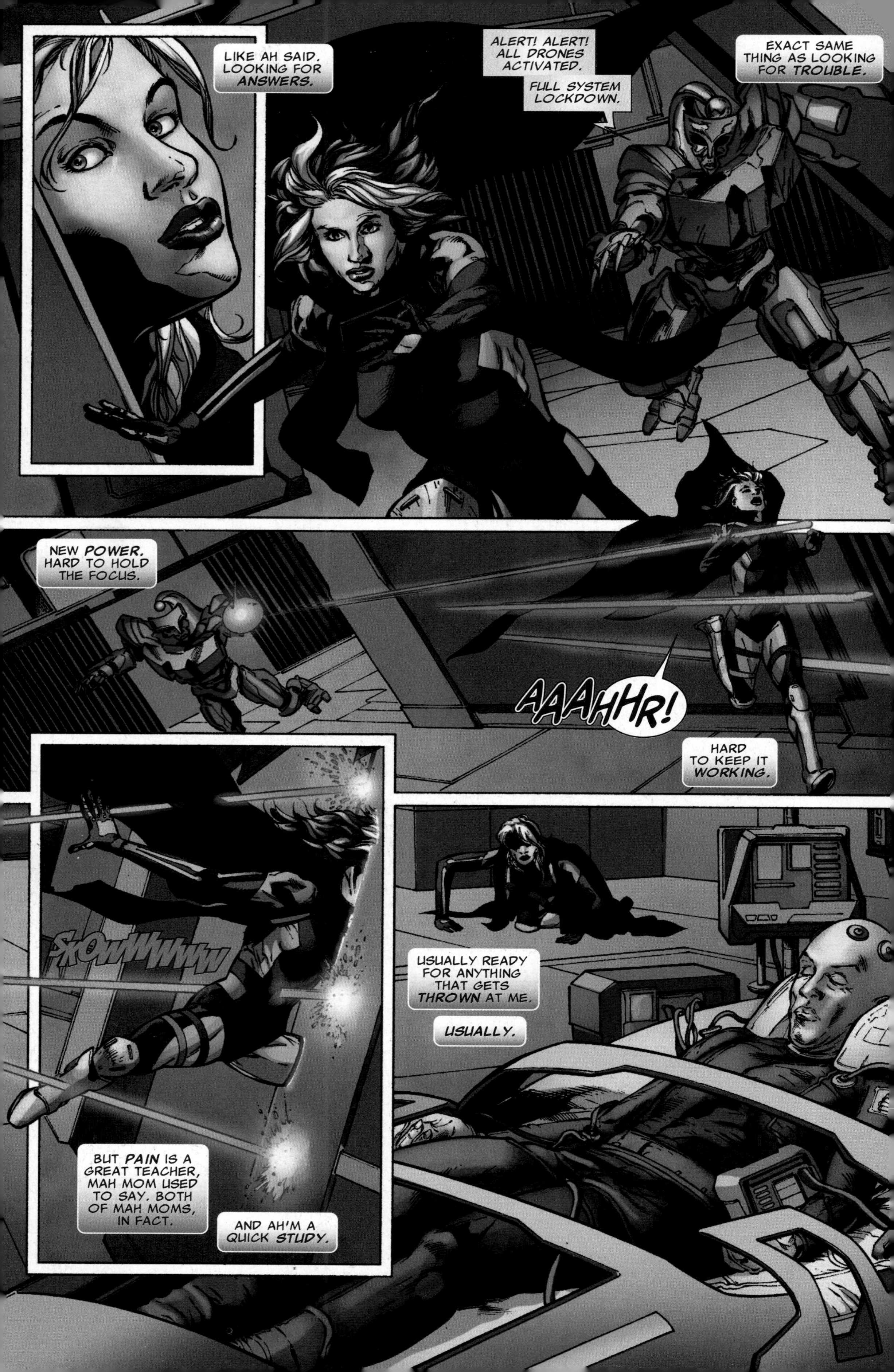
LIKE AH SAID. LOOKING FOR ANSWERS.
ALERT! ALERT! ALL DRONES ACTIVATED.
FULL SYSTEM LOCKDOWN.
EXACT SAME THING AS LOOKING FOR TROUBLE.
NEW POWER. HARD TO HOLD THE FOCUS.
AAAHHR!
HARD TO KEEP IT WORKING.
SKOWWWWWW
BUT PAIN IS A GREAT TEACHER, MAH MOM USED TO SAY. BOTH OF MAH MOMS, IN FACT.
AND AH'M A QUICK STUDY.
USUALLY READY FOR ANYTHING THAT GETS THROWN AT ME.
USUALLY.

THIS IS INSANE. AH'M PRETTY SURE AH NEVER *SAW* THIS MAN IN MAH LIFE BEFORE.

BUT A *NAME* STIRS RIGHT AT THE BASE OF MAH BRAIN, AND IT'S--

--CHARLES?

CHARLES *XAVIER?*

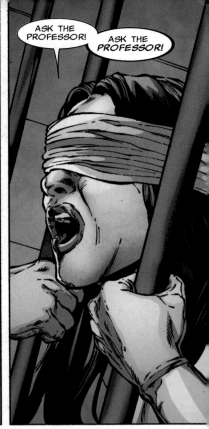

ASK THE PROFESSOR!

ASK THE PROFESSOR!

NO *PROMISES* THIS TIME. NO HOLDING BACK.

AH GOT TO *KNOW.* ALTHOUGH MAH HAND IS SHAKING LIKE AH GOT *MALARIA,* AND MAH HEART IS IN MAH MOUTH.

AH GOT TO *KNOW.*

NUUUUH!

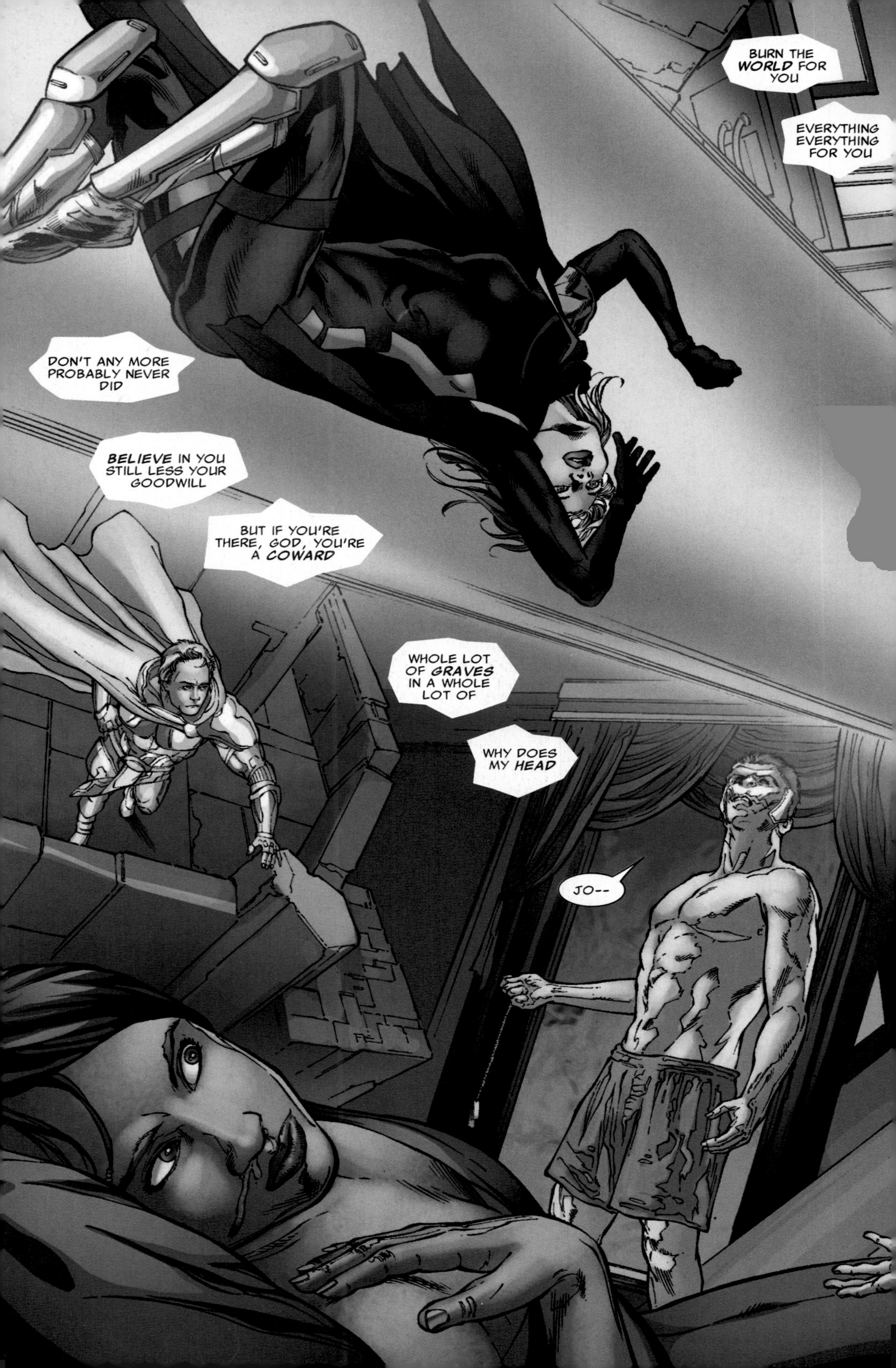

BURN THE WORLD FOR YOU
EVERYTHING EVERYTHING FOR YOU
DON'T ANY MORE PROBABLY NEVER DID
BELIEVE IN YOU STILL LESS YOUR GOODWILL
BUT IF YOU'RE THERE, GOD, YOU'RE A COWARD
WHOLE LOT OF GRAVES IN A WHOLE LOT OF
WHY DOES MY HEAD
JO--

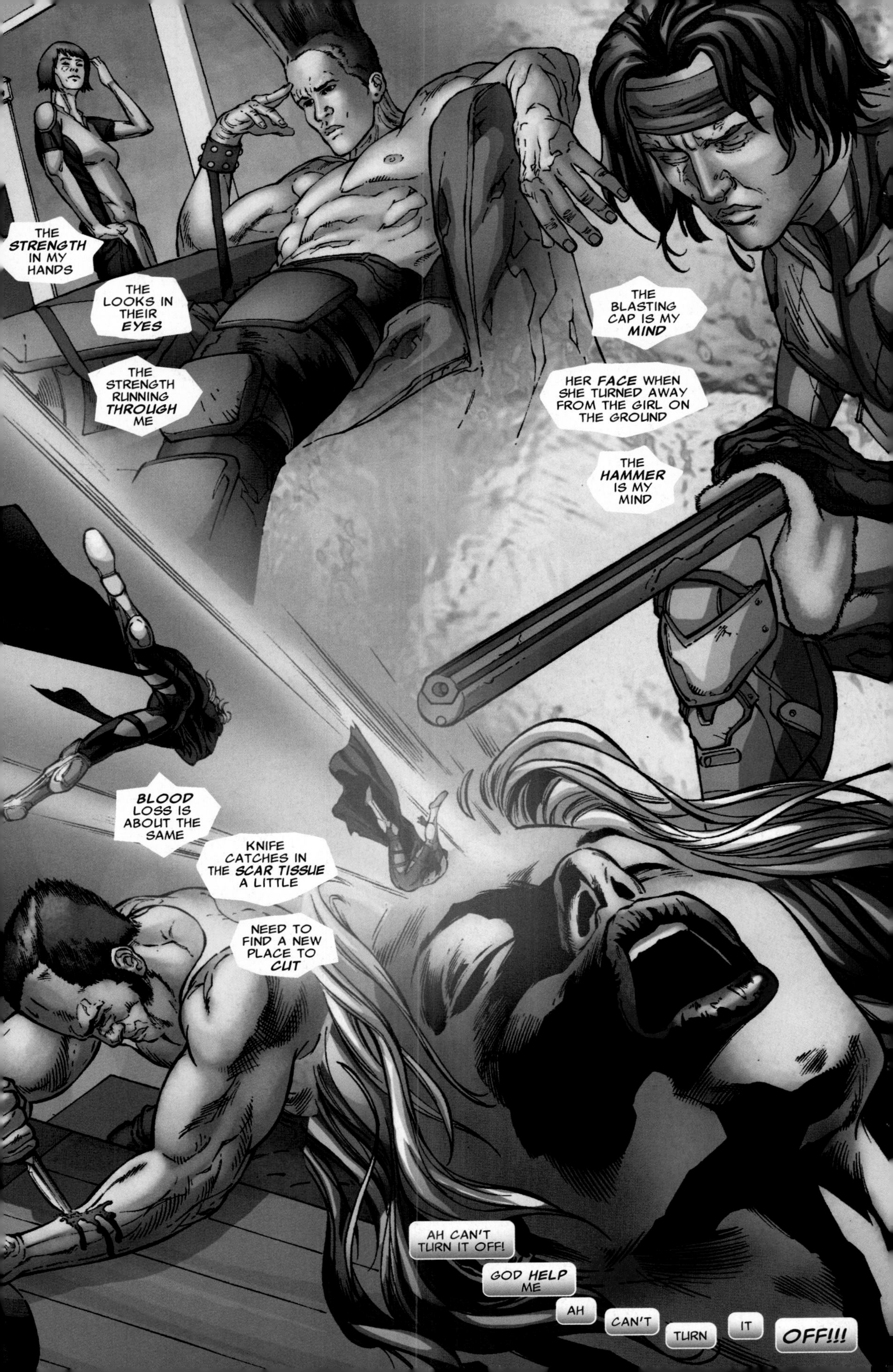

THE STRENGTH IN MY HANDS
THE LOOKS IN THEIR EYES
THE STRENGTH RUNNING THROUGH ME
THE BLASTING CAP IS MY MIND
HER FACE WHEN SHE TURNED AWAY FROM THE GIRL ON THE GROUND
THE HAMMER IS MY MIND
BLOOD LOSS IS ABOUT THE SAME
KNIFE CATCHES IN THE SCAR TISSUE A LITTLE
NEED TO FIND A NEW PLACE TO CUT
AH CAN'T TURN IT OFF!
GOD HELP ME
AH
CAN'T
TURN
IT
OFF!!!

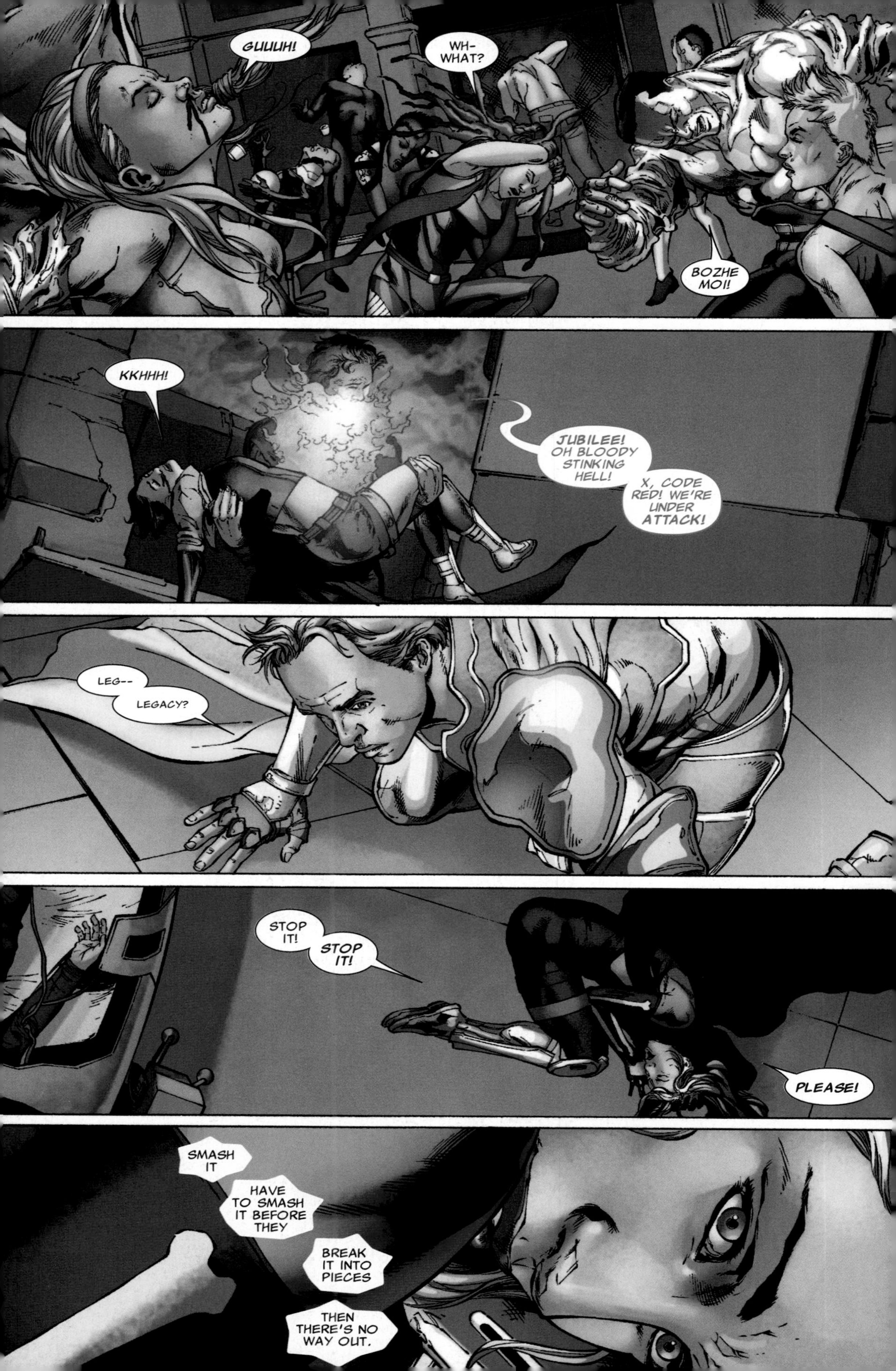
GUUUH!
WH-
WHAT?
BOZHE MOI!!
KKHHH!
JUBILEE! OH BLOODY STINKING HELL!
X, CODE RED! WE'RE UNDER ATTACK!
LEG--
LEGACY?
STOP IT!
STOP IT!
PLEASE!
SMASH IT
HAVE TO SMASH IT BEFORE THEY
BREAK IT INTO PIECES
THEN THERE'S NO WAY OUT.

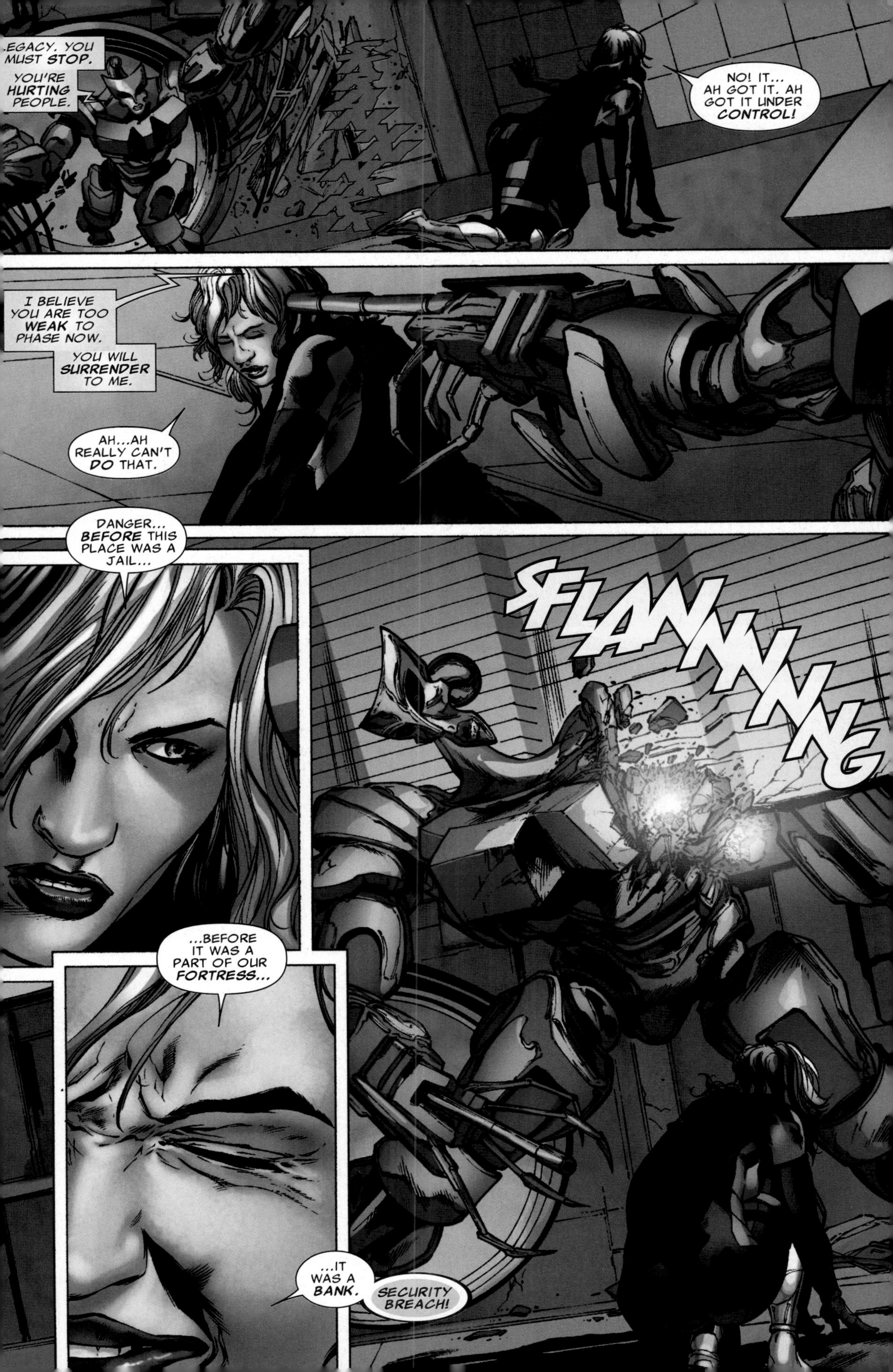
.EGACY. YOU MUST STOP.
YOU'RE HURTING PEOPLE.
NO! IT... AH GOT IT. AH GOT IT UNDER CONTROL!
I BELIEVE YOU ARE TOO WEAK TO PHASE NOW.
YOU WILL SURRENDER TO ME.
AH...AH REALLY CAN'T DO THAT.
DANGER... BEFORE THIS PLACE WAS A JAIL...
SFLANNNNNG
...BEFORE IT WAS A PART OF OUR FORTRESS...
...IT WAS A BANK.
SECURITY BREACH!

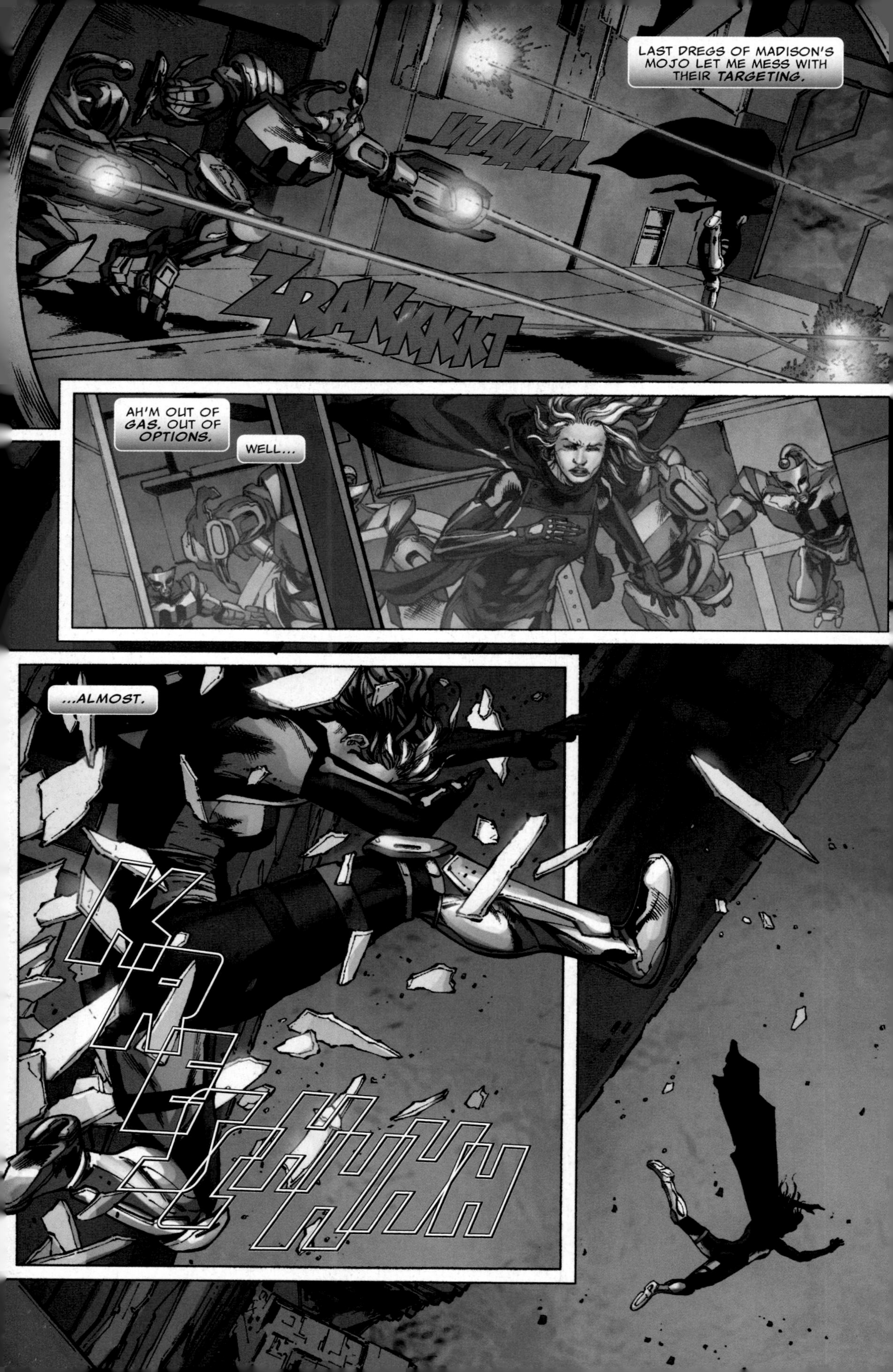
LAST DREGS OF MADISON'S MOJO LET ME MESS WITH THEIR TARGETING.
VLAAM
ZRAKKKKKT
AH'M OUT OF GAS. OUT OF OPTIONS.
WELL...
...ALMOST.
KRRSHHHH

AS FAR AS CAN BE ASCERTAINED, LEGACY DID NOT TOUCH ANY MUTANTS WITH THE POWER OF FLIGHT.

VERIFIED. SHE DID NOT. BUT SENSORS AT GROUND LEVEL HAVE NOT LOCATED HER BODY.

DANGER TO ALL STATIONS, VIA X. FUGITIVE ALERT.

"LEGACY HAS *ATTACKED* ALL INHABITANTS OF FORTRESS X WITH A MUTANT POWER WHOSE MODALITY IS UNKNOWN.

"SHE ALSO ATTEMPTED A *RESCUE* OF KATHERINE PRYDE, CURRENTLY IN ISOLATION ON MAGNETO'S ORDERS."

SET ME DOWN ON THE *LEDGE*, MATILDA, GENTLY.

WELL, THAT WOULD BE MY *PLEASURE*, LEGACY. ANY FRIEND OF MADISON'S IS A FRIEND OF MINE.

YOUR ORDERS, MAGNETO?

STANDARD PROCEDURE DICTATES--

YES.

APPREHEND LEGACY. BRING HER IN.

USING ALL NECESSARY FORCE.

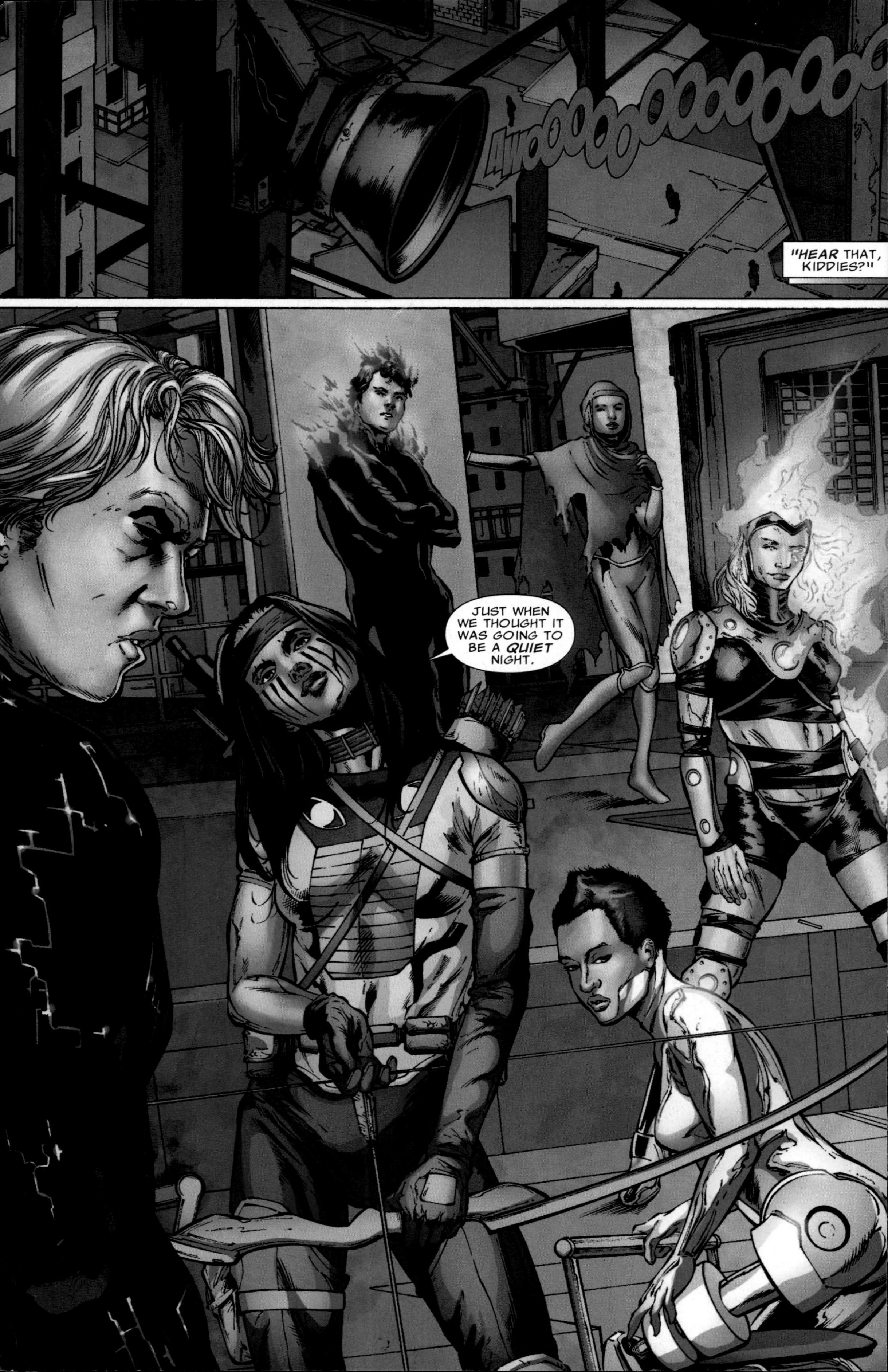
AWOOOOOOOOOOOOOO
"HEAR THAT, KIDDIES?"
JUST WHEN WE THOUGHT IT WAS GOING TO BE A QUIET NIGHT.

X-MEN LEGACY #246

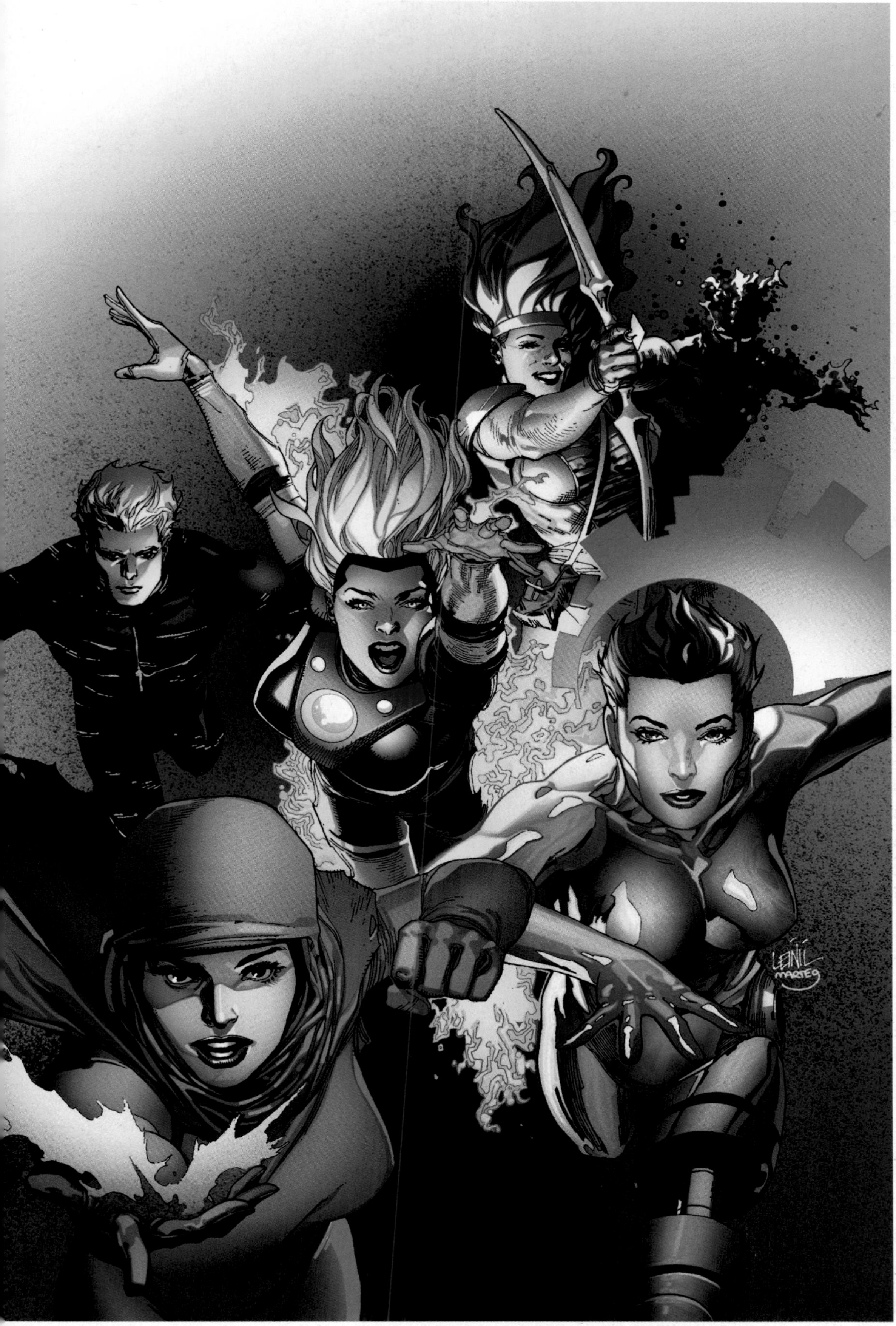

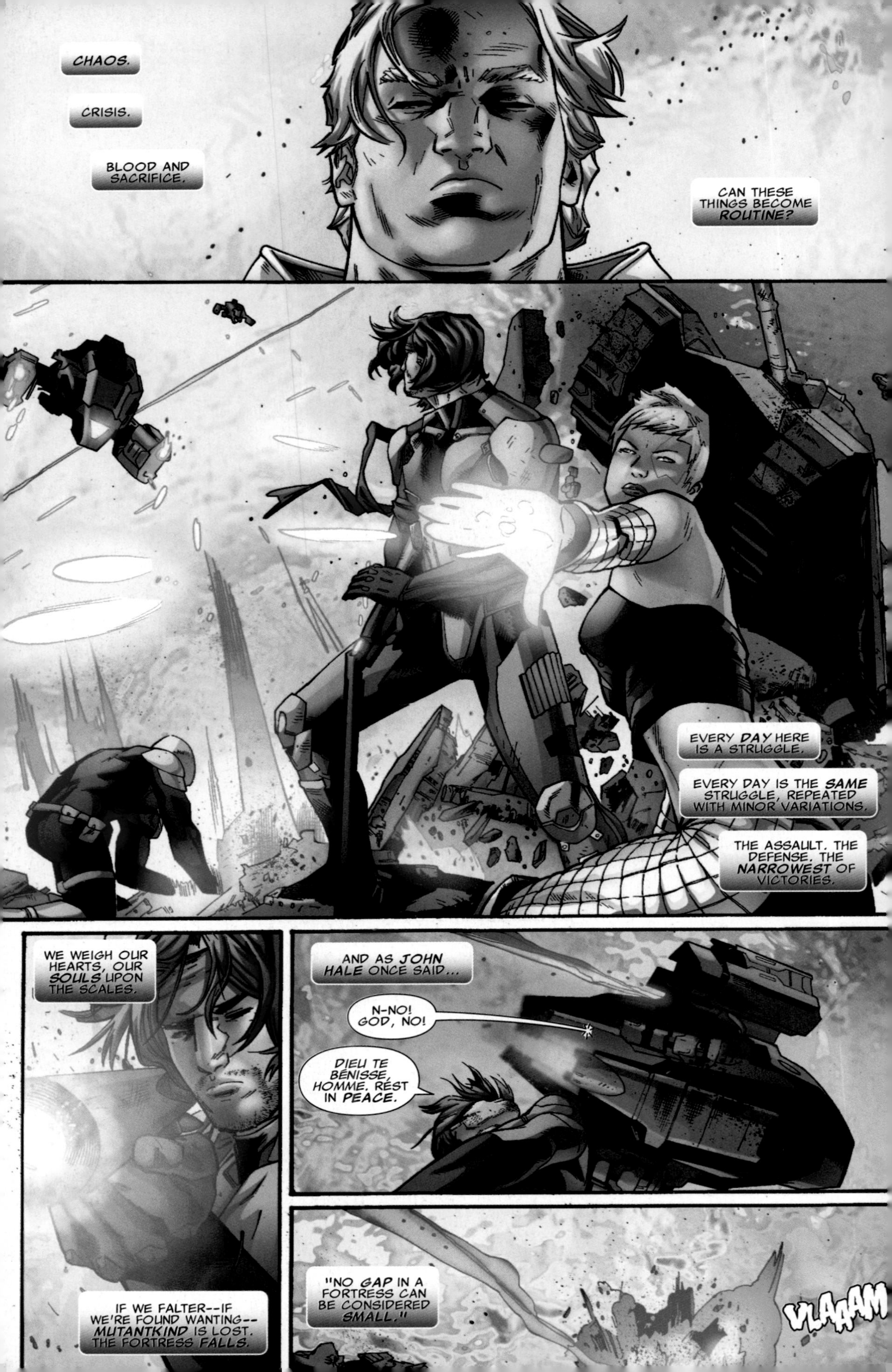
CHAOS.
CRISIS.
BLOOD AND SACRIFICE.
CAN THESE THINGS BECOME ROUTINE?
EVERY DAY HERE IS A STRUGGLE.
EVERY DAY IS THE SAME STRUGGLE, REPEATED WITH MINOR VARIATIONS.
THE ASSAULT. THE DEFENSE. THE NARROWEST OF VICTORIES.
WE WEIGH OUR HEARTS, OUR SOULS UPON THE SCALES.
IF WE FALTER--IF WE'RE FOUND WANTING--MUTANTKIND IS LOST. THE FORTRESS FALLS.
AND AS JOHN HALE ONCE SAID...
N-NO! GOD, NO!
DIEU TE BÉNISSE, HOMME. REST IN PEACE.
"NO GAP IN A FORTRESS CAN BE CONSIDERED SMALL."
VLAAAM

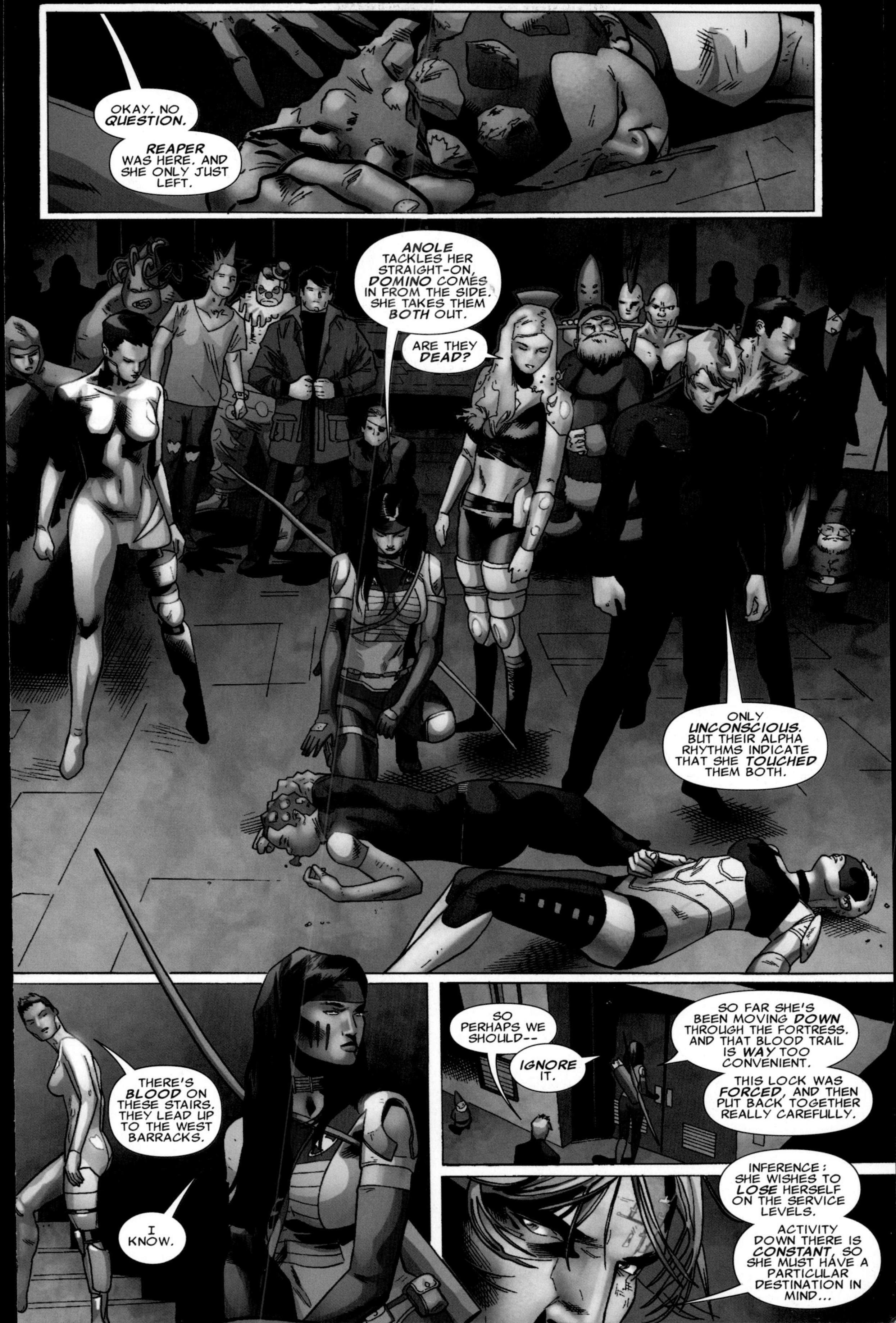

OKAY. NO QUESTION.
REAPER WAS HERE, AND SHE ONLY JUST LEFT.
ANOLE TACKLES HER STRAIGHT-ON, DOMINO COMES IN FROM THE SIDE. SHE TAKES THEM BOTH OUT.
ARE THEY DEAD?
ONLY UNCONSCIOUS. BUT THEIR ALPHA RHYTHMS INDICATE THAT SHE TOUCHED THEM BOTH.
THERE'S BLOOD ON THESE STAIRS. THEY LEAD UP TO THE WEST BARRACKS.
I KNOW.
SO PERHAPS WE SHOULD--
IGNORE IT.
SO FAR SHE'S BEEN MOVING DOWN THROUGH THE FORTRESS. AND THAT BLOOD TRAIL IS WAY TOO CONVENIENT.
THIS LOCK WAS FORCED, AND THEN PUT BACK TOGETHER REALLY CAREFULLY.
INFERENCE: SHE WISHES TO LOSE HERSELF ON THE SERVICE LEVELS.
ACTIVITY DOWN THERE IS CONSTANT, SO SHE MUST HAVE A PARTICULAR DESTINATION IN MIND...

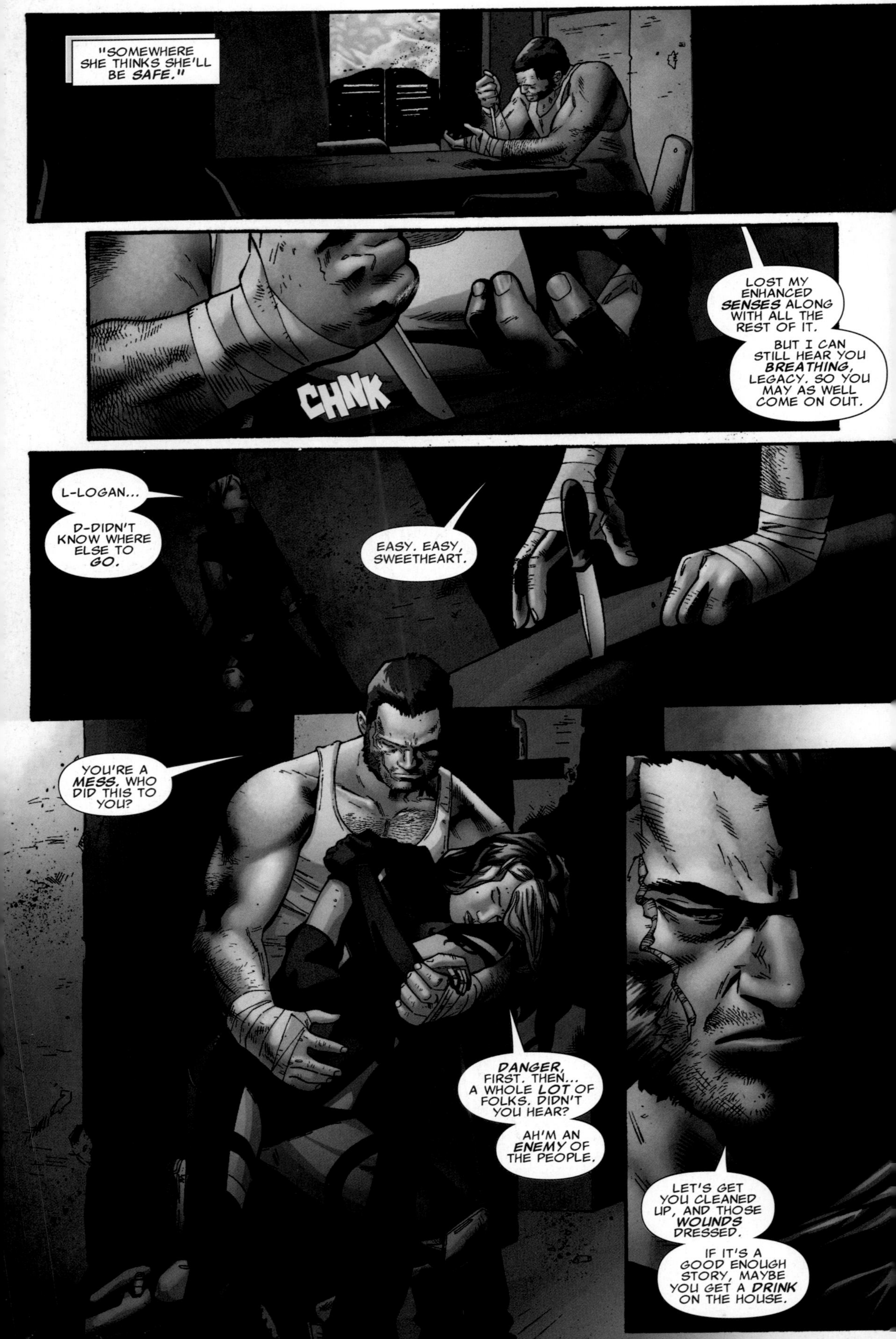
"SOMEWHERE SHE THINKS SHE'LL BE SAFE."
LOST MY ENHANCED SENSES ALONG WITH ALL THE REST OF IT.
BUT I CAN STILL HEAR YOU BREATHING, LEGACY. SO YOU MAY AS WELL COME ON OUT.
CHNK
L-LOGAN...
D-DIDN'T KNOW WHERE ELSE TO GO.
EASY. EASY, SWEETHEART.
YOU'RE A MESS. WHO DID THIS TO YOU?
DANGER, FIRST. THEN... A WHOLE LOT OF FOLKS. DIDN'T YOU HEAR?
AH'M AN ENEMY OF THE PEOPLE.
LET'S GET YOU CLEANED UP, AND THOSE WOUNDS DRESSED.
IF IT'S A GOOD ENOUGH STORY, MAYBE YOU GET A DRINK ON THE HOUSE.

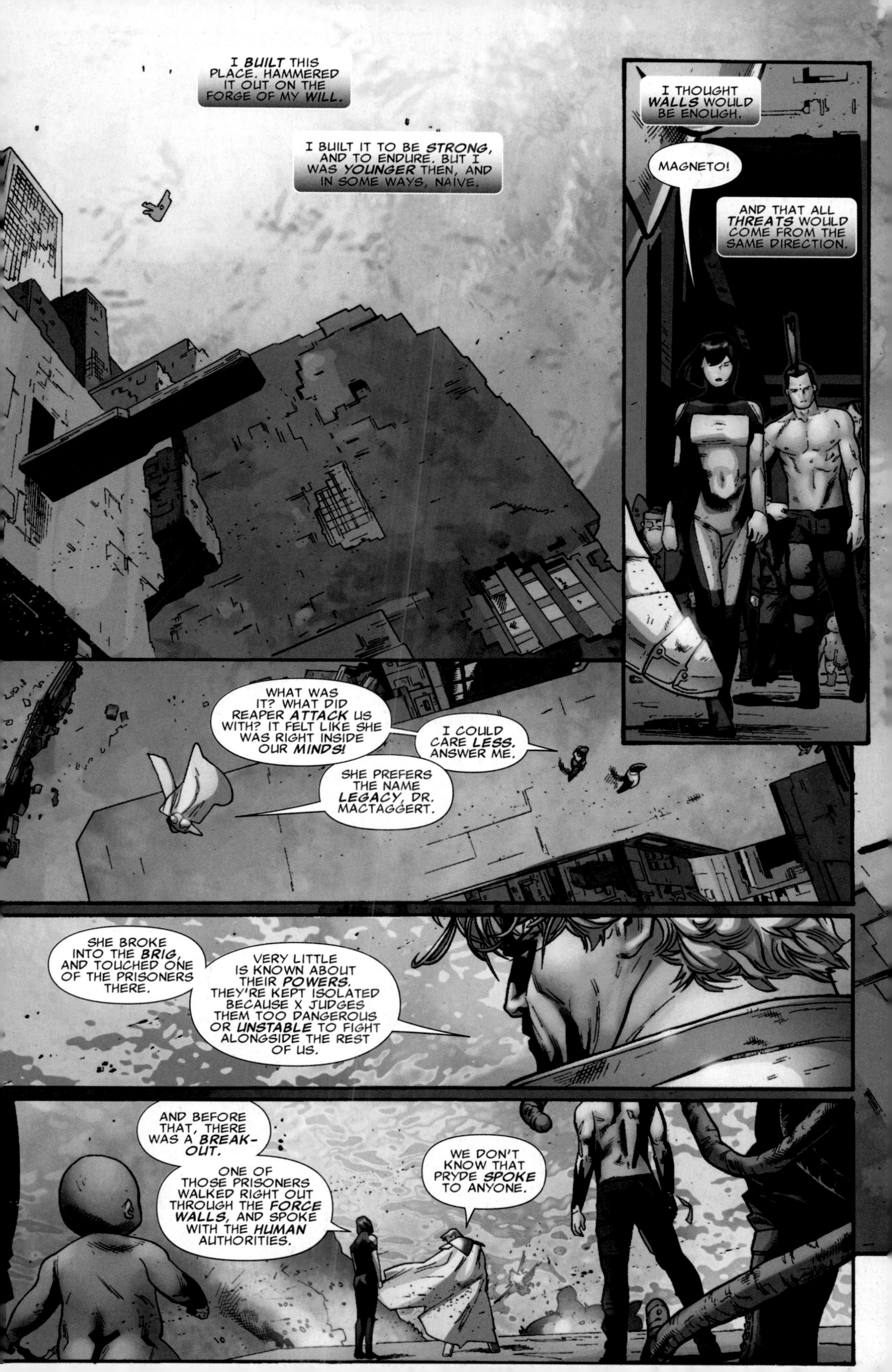
I BUILT THIS PLACE. HAMMERED IT OUT ON THE FORGE OF MY WILL.
I BUILT IT TO BE STRONG, AND TO ENDURE. BUT I WAS YOUNGER THEN, AND IN SOME WAYS, NAIVE.
I THOUGHT WALLS WOULD BE ENOUGH.
MAGNETO!
AND THAT ALL THREATS WOULD COME FROM THE SAME DIRECTION.
WHAT WAS IT? WHAT DID REAPER ATTACK US WITH? IT FELT LIKE SHE WAS RIGHT INSIDE OUR MINDS!
I COULD CARE LESS. ANSWER ME.
SHE PREFERS THE NAME LEGACY, DR. MACTAGGERT.
SHE BROKE INTO THE BRIG, AND TOUCHED ONE OF THE PRISONERS THERE.
VERY LITTLE IS KNOWN ABOUT THEIR POWERS. THEY'RE KEPT ISOLATED BECAUSE X JUDGES THEM TOO DANGEROUS OR UNSTABLE TO FIGHT ALONGSIDE THE REST OF US.
AND BEFORE THAT, THERE WAS A BREAK-OUT.
ONE OF THOSE PRISONERS WALKED RIGHT OUT THROUGH THE FORCE WALLS, AND SPOKE WITH THE HUMAN AUTHORITIES.
WE DON'T KNOW THAT PRYDE SPOKE TO ANYONE.

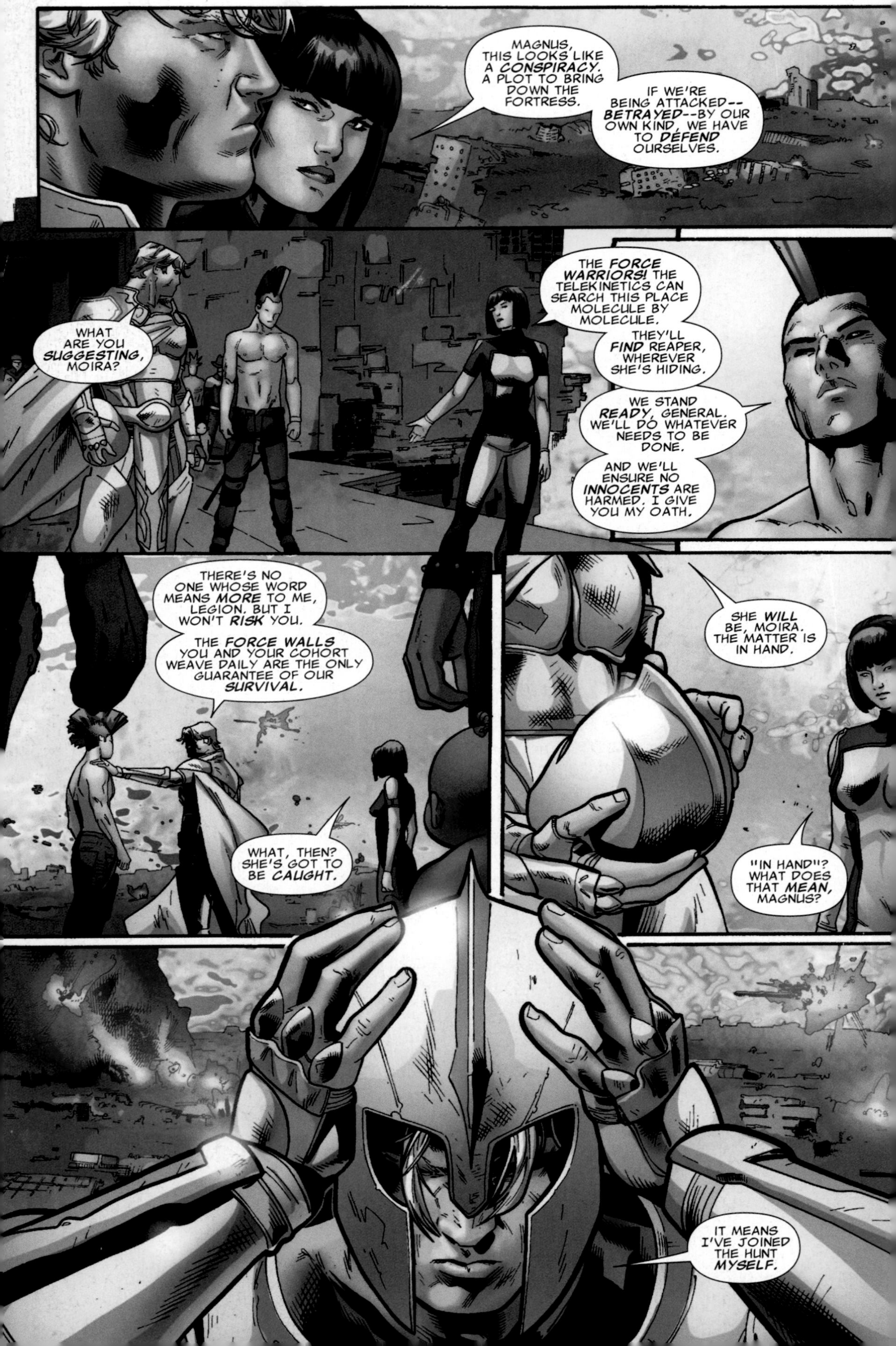
MAGNUS, THIS LOOKS LIKE A CONSPIRACY. A PLOT TO BRING DOWN THE FORTRESS.
IF WE'RE BEING ATTACKED--BETRAYED--BY OUR OWN KIND, WE HAVE TO DEFEND OURSELVES.
WHAT ARE YOU SUGGESTING, MOIRA?
THE FORCE WARRIORS! THE TELEKINETICS CAN SEARCH THIS PLACE MOLECULE BY MOLECULE.
THEY'LL FIND REAPER, WHEREVER SHE'S HIDING.
WE STAND READY, GENERAL. WE'LL DO WHATEVER NEEDS TO BE DONE.
AND WE'LL ENSURE NO INNOCENTS ARE HARMED. I GIVE YOU MY OATH.
THERE'S NO ONE WHOSE WORD MEANS MORE TO ME, LEGION. BUT I WON'T RISK YOU.
THE FORCE WALLS YOU AND YOUR COHORT WEAVE DAILY ARE THE ONLY GUARANTEE OF OUR SURVIVAL.
WHAT, THEN? SHE'S GOT TO BE CAUGHT.
SHE WILL BE, MOIRA. THE MATTER IS IN HAND.
"IN HAND"? WHAT DOES THAT MEAN, MAGNUS?
IT MEANS I'VE JOINED THE HUNT MYSELF.

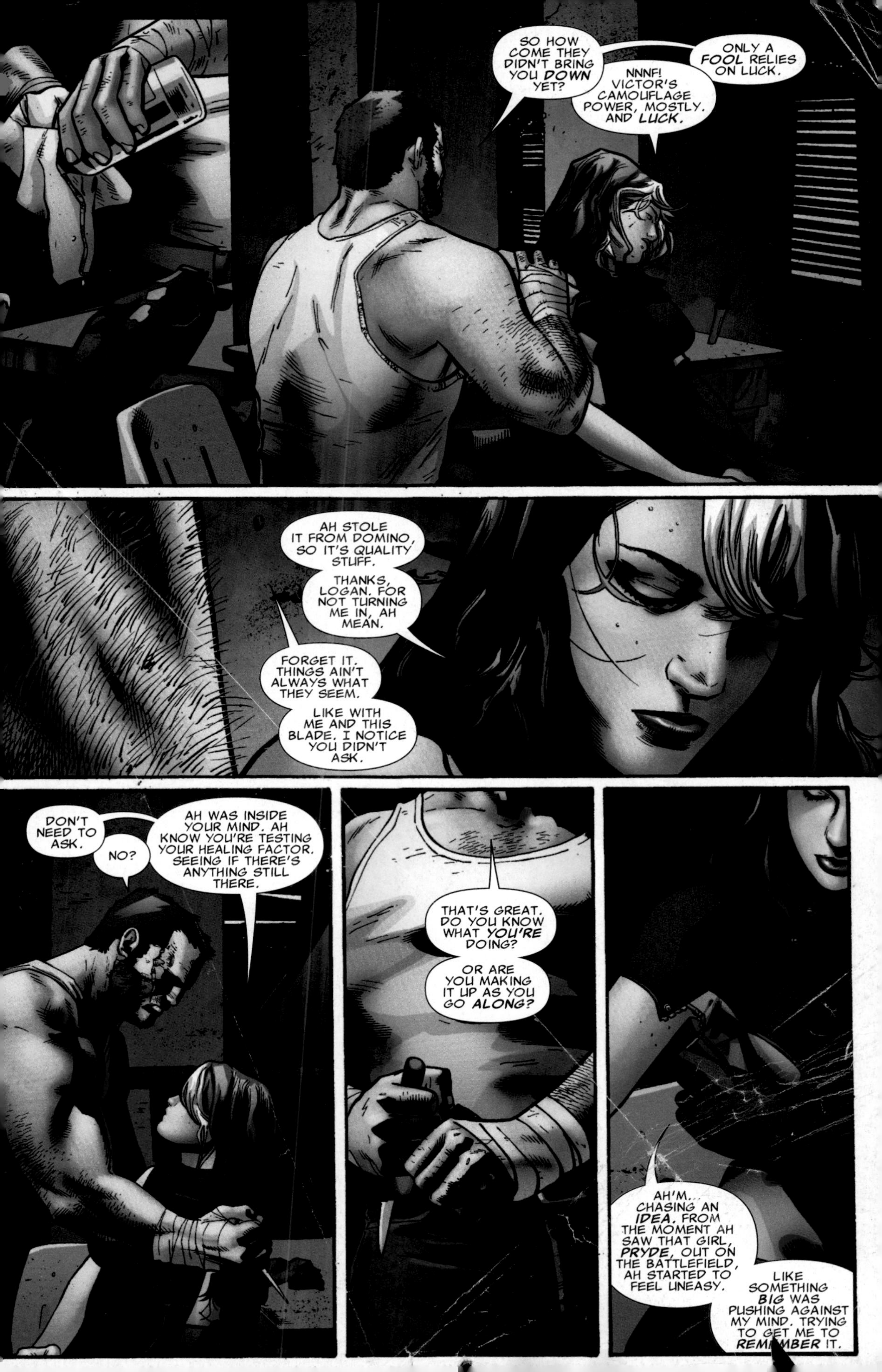
SO HOW COME THEY DIDN'T BRING YOU DOWN YET?
NNNF! VICTOR'S CAMOUFLAGE POWER, MOSTLY. AND LUCK.
ONLY A FOOL RELIES ON LUCK.
AH STOLE IT FROM DOMINO, SO IT'S QUALITY STUFF.
THANKS, LOGAN. FOR NOT TURNING ME IN, AH MEAN.
FORGET IT. THINGS AIN'T ALWAYS WHAT THEY SEEM.
LIKE WITH ME AND THIS BLADE. I NOTICE YOU DIDN'T ASK.
DON'T NEED TO ASK.
NO?
AH WAS INSIDE YOUR MIND. AH KNOW YOU'RE TESTING YOUR HEALING FACTOR. SEEING IF THERE'S ANYTHING STILL THERE.
THAT'S GREAT. DO YOU KNOW WHAT YOU'RE DOING?
OR ARE YOU MAKING IT UP AS YOU GO ALONG?
AH'M... CHASING AN IDEA. FROM THE MOMENT AH SAW THAT GIRL, PRYDE, OUT ON THE BATTLEFIELD, AH STARTED TO FEEL UNEASY.
LIKE SOMETHING BIG WAS PUSHING AGAINST MY MIND. TRYING TO GET ME TO REMEMBER IT.

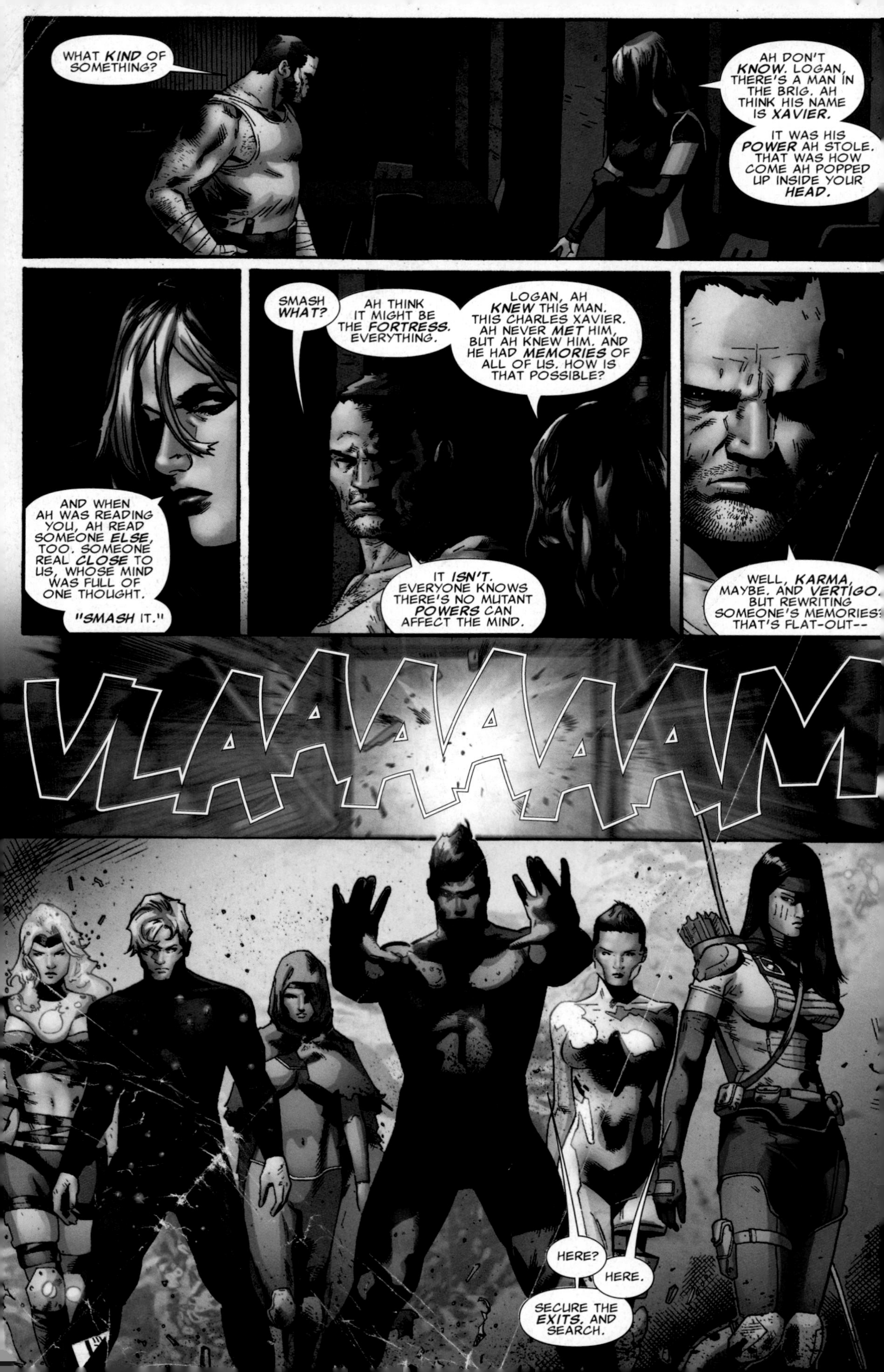
WHAT KIND OF SOMETHING?
AH DON'T KNOW. LOGAN, THERE'S A MAN IN THE BRIG. AH THINK HIS NAME IS XAVIER.
IT WAS HIS POWER AH STOLE. THAT WAS HOW COME AH POPPED UP INSIDE YOUR HEAD.
AND WHEN AH WAS READING YOU, AH READ SOMEONE ELSE, TOO. SOMEONE REAL CLOSE TO US, WHOSE MIND WAS FULL OF ONE THOUGHT.
"SMASH IT."
SMASH WHAT?
AH THINK IT MIGHT BE THE FORTRESS. EVERYTHING.
LOGAN, AH KNEW THIS MAN. THIS CHARLES XAVIER. AH NEVER MET HIM, BUT AH KNEW HIM. AND HE HAD MEMORIES OF ALL OF US. HOW IS THAT POSSIBLE?
IT ISN'T. EVERYONE KNOWS THERE'S NO MUTANT POWERS CAN AFFECT THE MIND.
WELL, KARMA, MAYBE. AND VERTIGO. BUT REWRITING SOMEONE'S MEMORIES: THAT'S FLAT-OUT--
VLAAAAAM
HERE?
HERE.
SECURE THE EXITS, AND SEARCH.

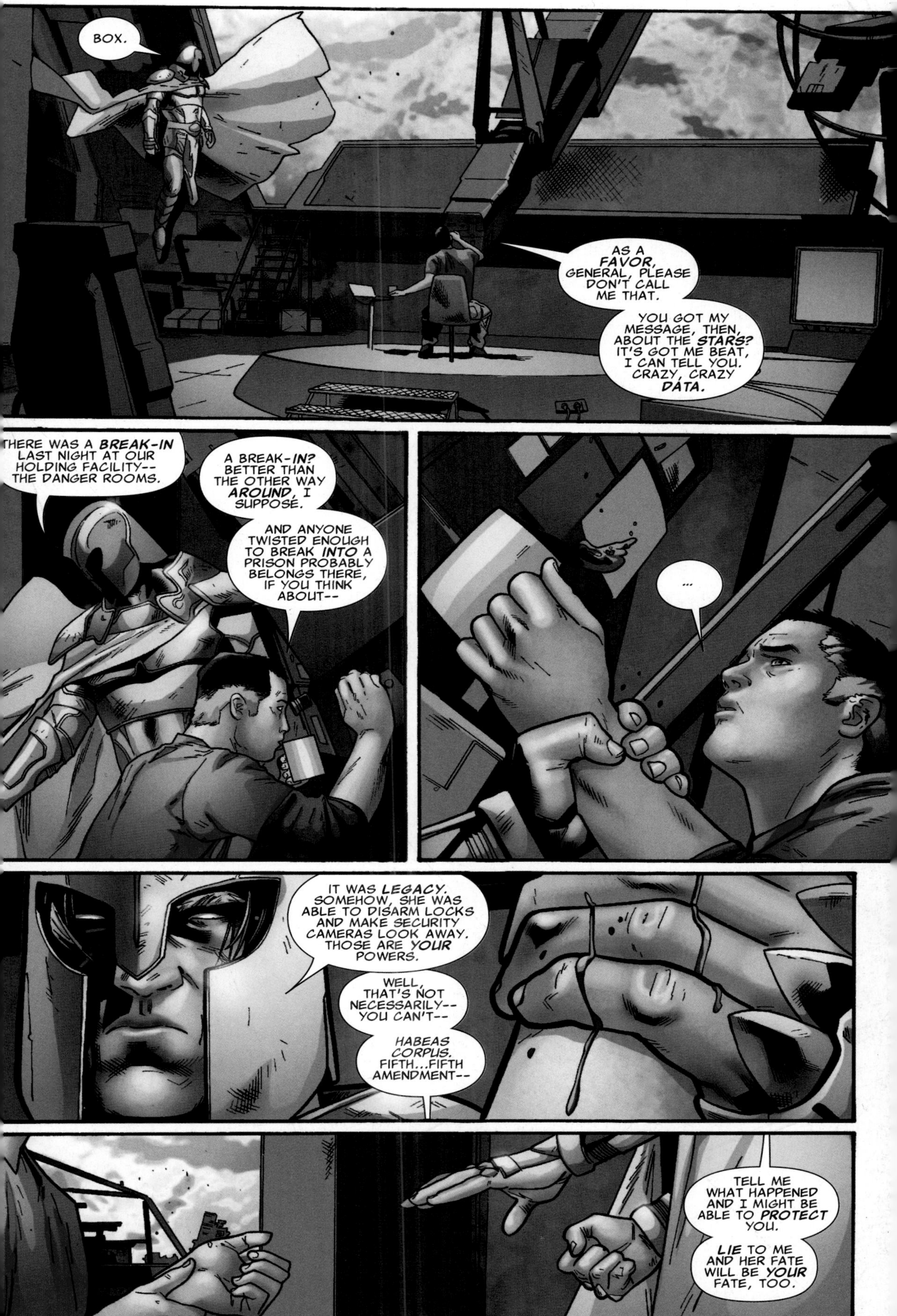
BOX.
AS A FAVOR, GENERAL, PLEASE DON'T CALL ME THAT.
YOU GOT MY MESSAGE, THEN, ABOUT THE STARS? IT'S GOT ME BEAT, I CAN TELL YOU. CRAZY, CRAZY DATA.
THERE WAS A BREAK-IN LAST NIGHT AT OUR HOLDING FACILITY-- THE DANGER ROOMS.
A BREAK-IN? BETTER THAN THE OTHER WAY AROUND, I SUPPOSE.
AND ANYONE TWISTED ENOUGH TO BREAK INTO A PRISON PROBABLY BELONGS THERE, IF YOU THINK ABOUT--
...
IT WAS LEGACY. SOMEHOW, SHE WAS ABLE TO DISARM LOCKS AND MAKE SECURITY CAMERAS LOOK AWAY. THOSE ARE YOUR POWERS.
WELL, THAT'S NOT NECESSARILY-- YOU CAN'T--
HABEAS CORPUS. FIFTH...FIFTH AMENDMENT--
TELL ME WHAT HAPPENED AND I MIGHT BE ABLE TO PROTECT YOU.
LIE TO ME AND HER FATE WILL BE YOUR FATE, TOO.

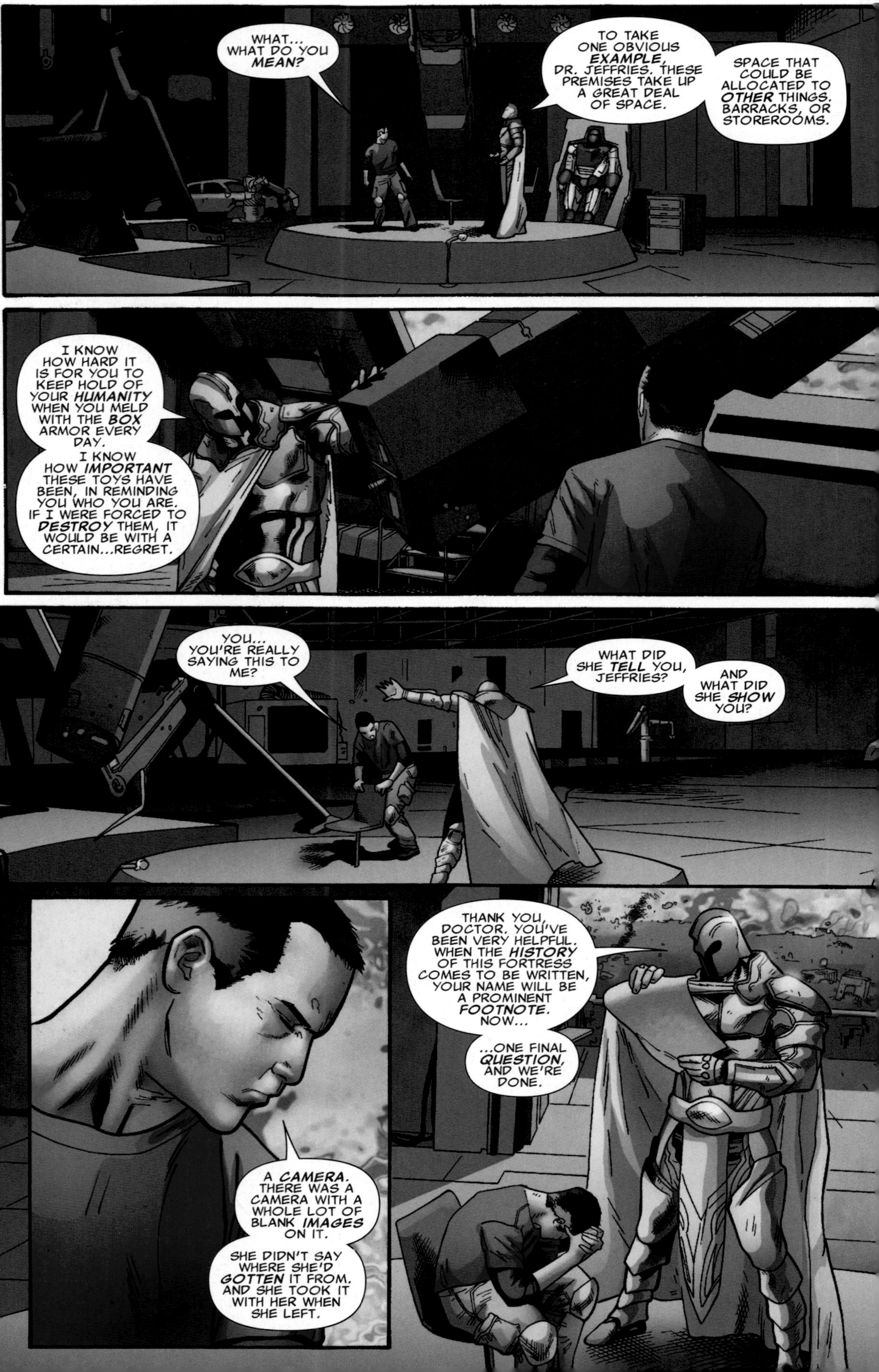
WHAT... WHAT DO YOU MEAN?
TO TAKE ONE OBVIOUS EXAMPLE, DR. JEFFRIES. THESE PREMISES TAKE UP A GREAT DEAL OF SPACE.
SPACE THAT COULD BE ALLOCATED TO OTHER THINGS. BARRACKS, OR STOREROOMS.
I KNOW HOW HARD IT IS FOR YOU TO KEEP HOLD OF YOUR HUMANITY WHEN YOU MELD WITH THE BOX ARMOR EVERY DAY.
I KNOW HOW IMPORTANT THESE TOYS HAVE BEEN, IN REMINDING YOU WHO YOU ARE. IF I WERE FORCED TO DESTROY THEM, IT WOULD BE WITH A CERTAIN...REGRET.
YOU... YOU'RE REALLY SAYING THIS TO ME?
WHAT DID SHE TELL YOU, JEFFRIES?
AND WHAT DID SHE SHOW YOU?
A CAMERA. THERE WAS A CAMERA WITH A WHOLE LOT OF BLANK IMAGES ON IT.
SHE DIDN'T SAY WHERE SHE'D GOTTEN IT FROM. AND SHE TOOK IT WITH HER WHEN SHE LEFT.
THANK YOU, DOCTOR. YOU'VE BEEN VERY HELPFUL. WHEN THE HISTORY OF THIS FORTRESS COMES TO BE WRITTEN, YOUR NAME WILL BE A PROMINENT FOOTNOTE. NOW...
...ONE FINAL QUESTION, AND WE'RE DONE.

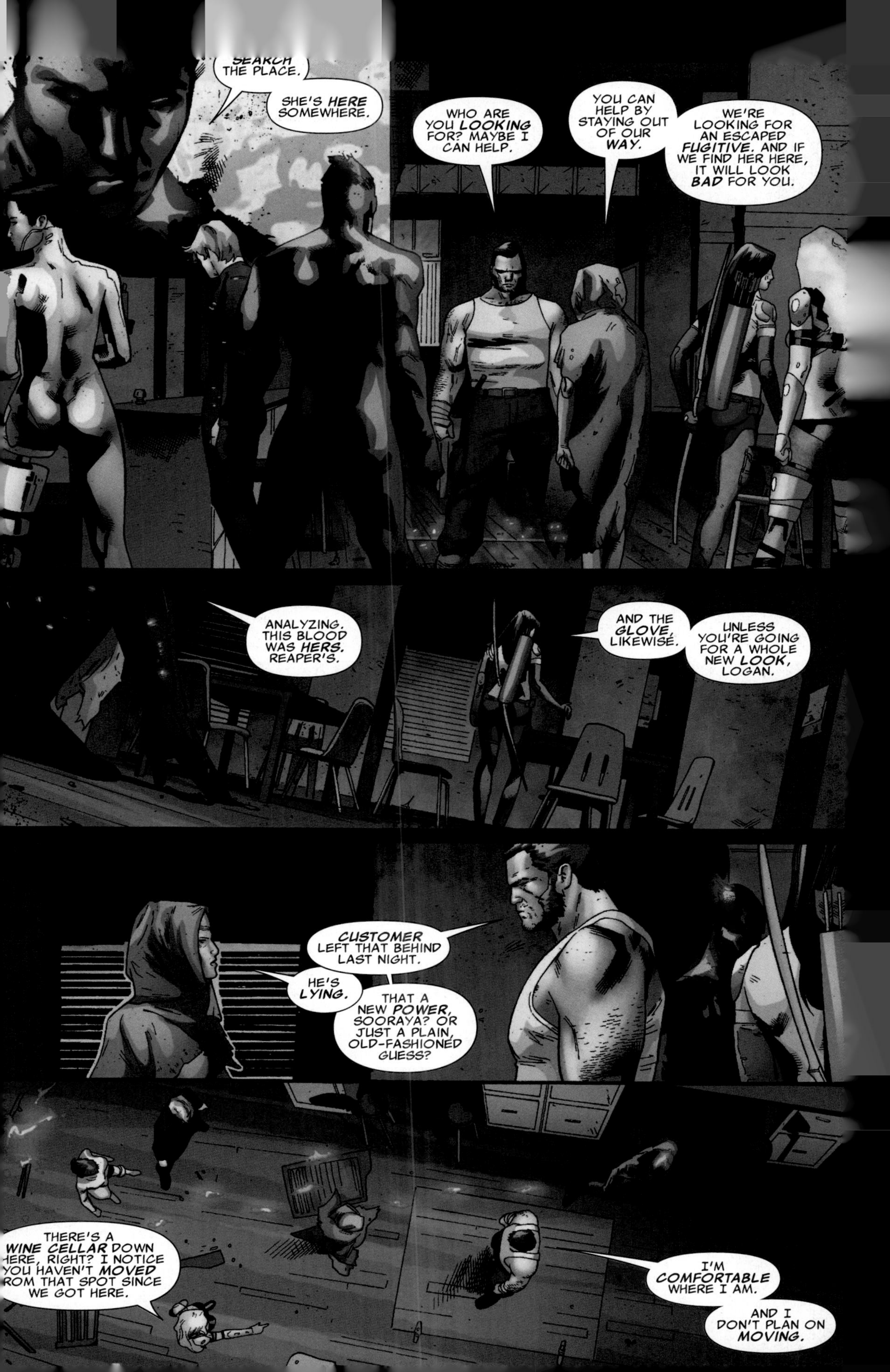

SEARCH THE PLACE.
SHE'S HERE SOMEWHERE.
WHO ARE YOU LOOKING FOR? MAYBE I CAN HELP.
YOU CAN HELP BY STAYING OUT OF OUR WAY.
WE'RE LOOKING FOR AN ESCAPED FUGITIVE. AND IF WE FIND HER HERE, IT WILL LOOK BAD FOR YOU.
ANALYZING. THIS BLOOD WAS HERS. REAPER'S.
AND THE GLOVE, LIKEWISE.
UNLESS YOU'RE GOING FOR A WHOLE NEW LOOK, LOGAN.
CUSTOMER LEFT THAT BEHIND LAST NIGHT.
HE'S LYING.
THAT A NEW POWER, SOORAYA? OR JUST A PLAIN, OLD-FASHIONED GUESS?
THERE'S A WINE CELLAR DOWN HERE, RIGHT? I NOTICE YOU HAVEN'T MOVED ROM THAT SPOT SINCE WE GOT HERE.
I'M COMFORTABLE WHERE I AM.
AND I DON'T PLAN ON MOVING.

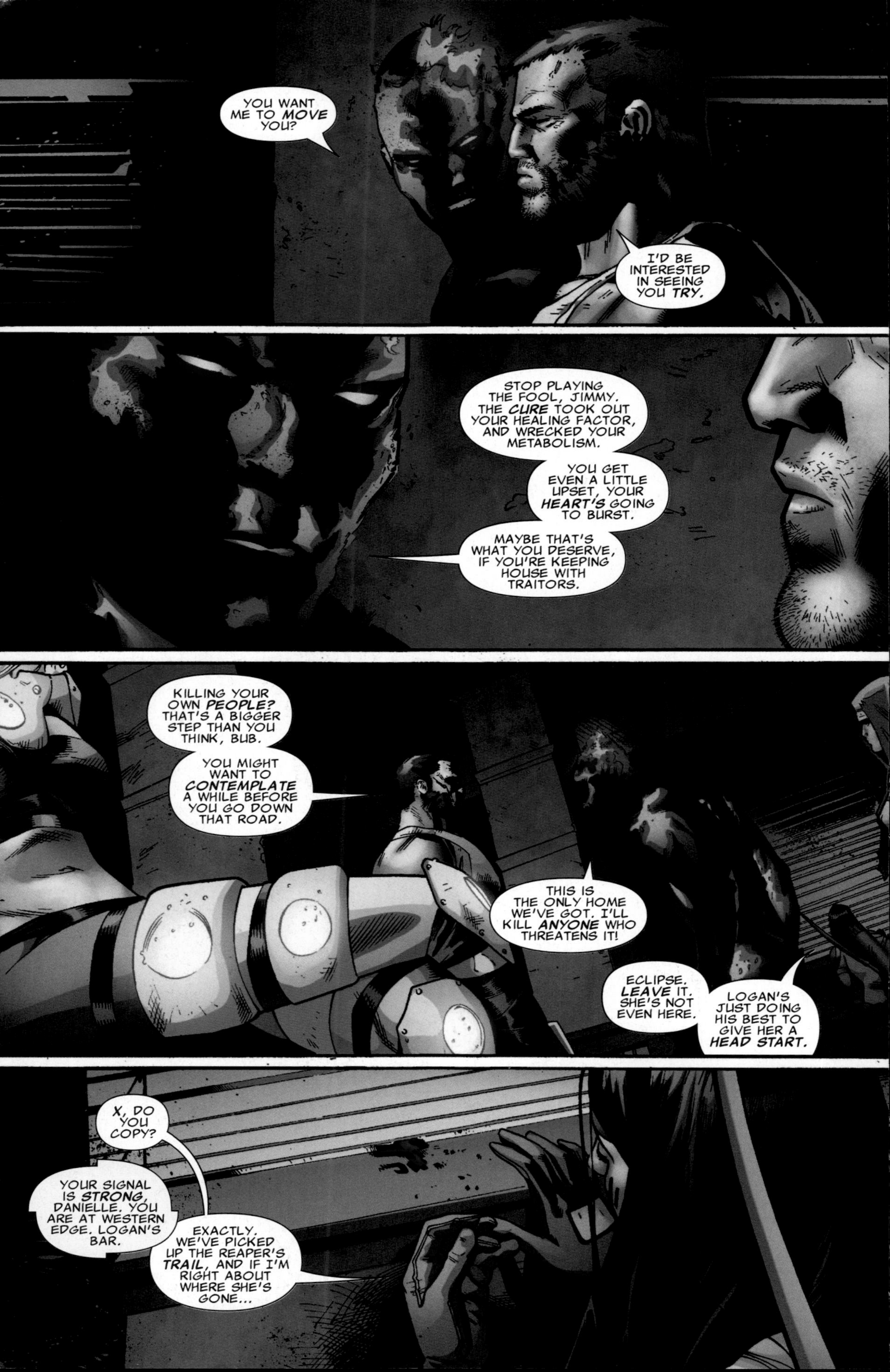
YOU WANT ME TO MOVE YOU?
I'D BE INTERESTED IN SEEING YOU TRY.
STOP PLAYING THE FOOL, JIMMY. THE CURE TOOK OUT YOUR HEALING FACTOR, AND WRECKED YOUR METABOLISM.
YOU GET EVEN A LITTLE UPSET, YOUR HEART'S GOING TO BURST.
MAYBE THAT'S WHAT YOU DESERVE, IF YOU'RE KEEPING HOUSE WITH TRAITORS.
KILLING YOUR OWN PEOPLE? THAT'S A BIGGER STEP THAN YOU THINK, BUB.
YOU MIGHT WANT TO CONTEMPLATE A WHILE BEFORE YOU GO DOWN THAT ROAD.
THIS IS THE ONLY HOME WE'VE GOT. I'LL KILL ANYONE WHO THREATENS IT!
ECLIPSE. LEAVE IT. SHE'S NOT EVEN HERE.
LOGAN'S JUST DOING HIS BEST TO GIVE HER A HEAD START.
X, DO YOU COPY?
YOUR SIGNAL IS STRONG, DANIELLE. YOU ARE AT WESTERN EDGE. LOGAN'S BAR.
EXACTLY. WE'VE PICKED UP THE REAPER'S TRAIL, AND IF I'M RIGHT ABOUT WHERE SHE'S GONE...

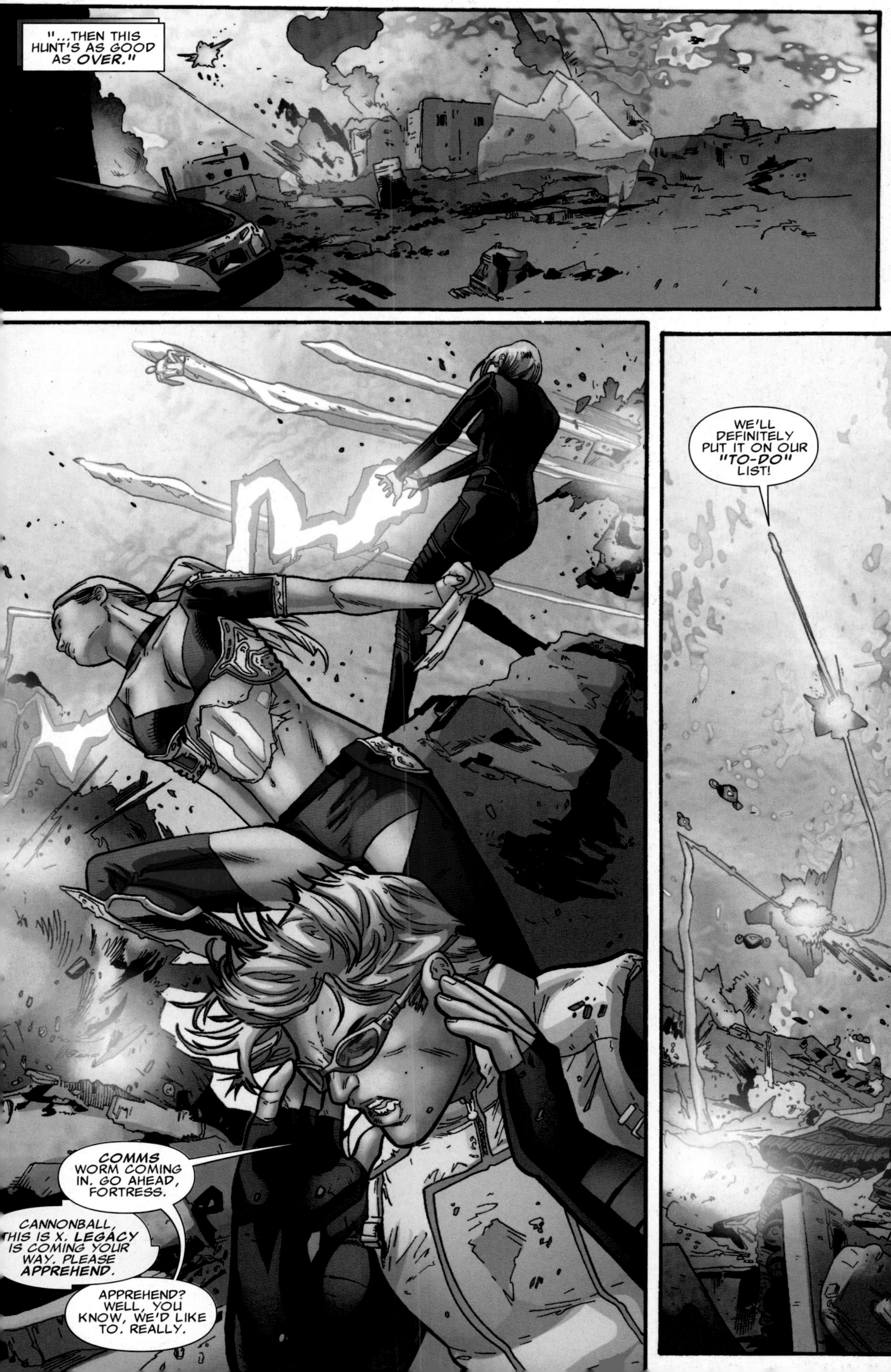
"...THEN THIS HUNT'S AS GOOD AS OVER."
COMMS WORM COMING IN. GO AHEAD, FORTRESS.
CANNONBALL, THIS IS X. LEGACY IS COMING YOUR WAY. PLEASE APPREHEND.
APPREHEND? WELL, YOU KNOW, WE'D LIKE TO. REALLY.
WE'LL DEFINITELY PUT IT ON OUR "TO-DO" LIST!

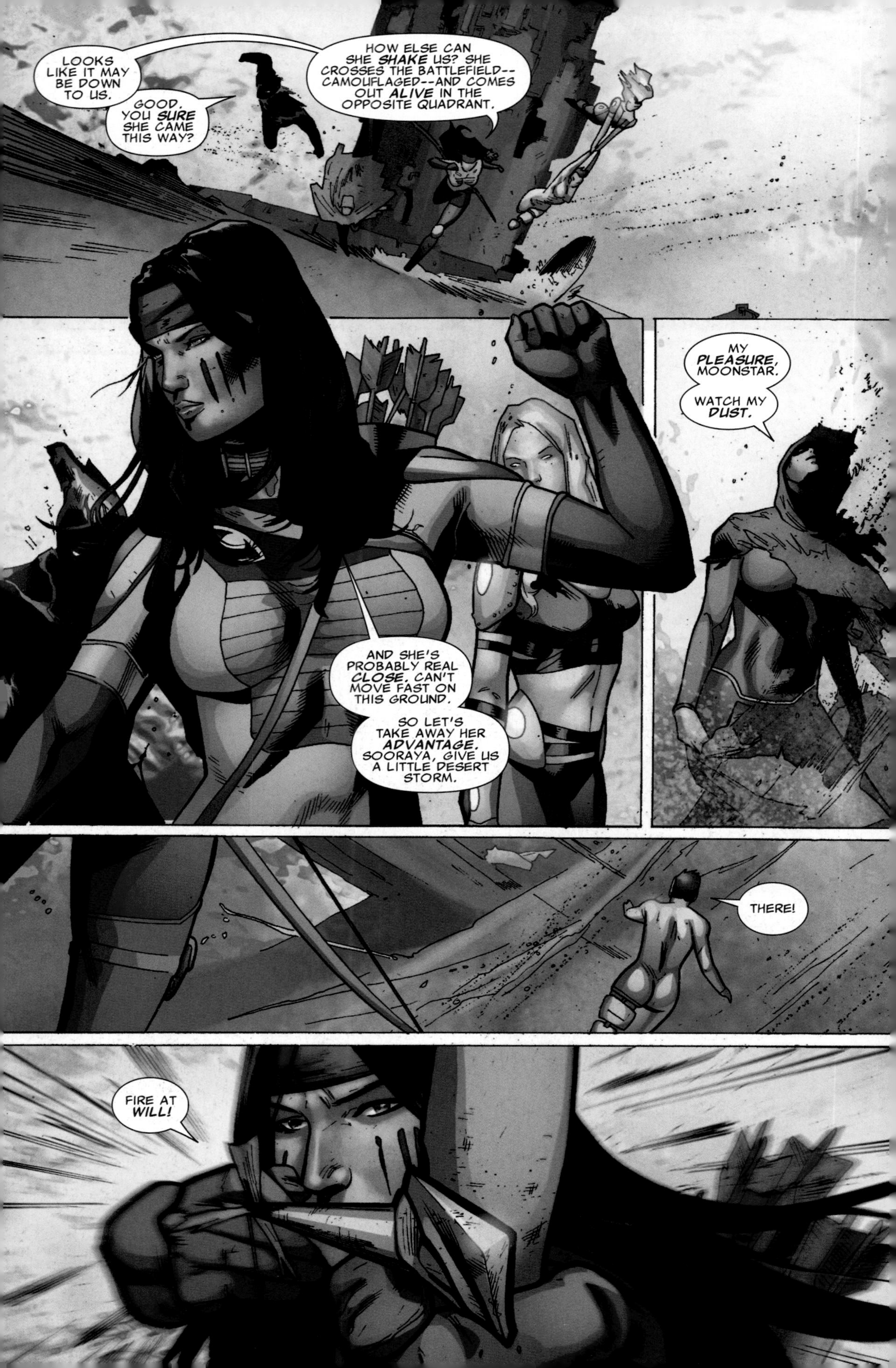
LOOKS LIKE IT MAY BE DOWN TO US.
HOW ELSE CAN SHE SHAKE US? SHE CROSSES THE BATTLEFIELD--CAMOUFLAGED--AND COMES OUT ALIVE IN THE OPPOSITE QUADRANT.
GOOD. YOU SURE SHE CAME THIS WAY?
AND SHE'S PROBABLY REAL CLOSE. CAN'T MOVE FAST ON THIS GROUND.
SO LET'S TAKE AWAY HER ADVANTAGE. SOORAYA, GIVE US A LITTLE DESERT STORM.
MY PLEASURE, MOONSTAR.
WATCH MY DUST.
THERE!
FIRE AT WILL!

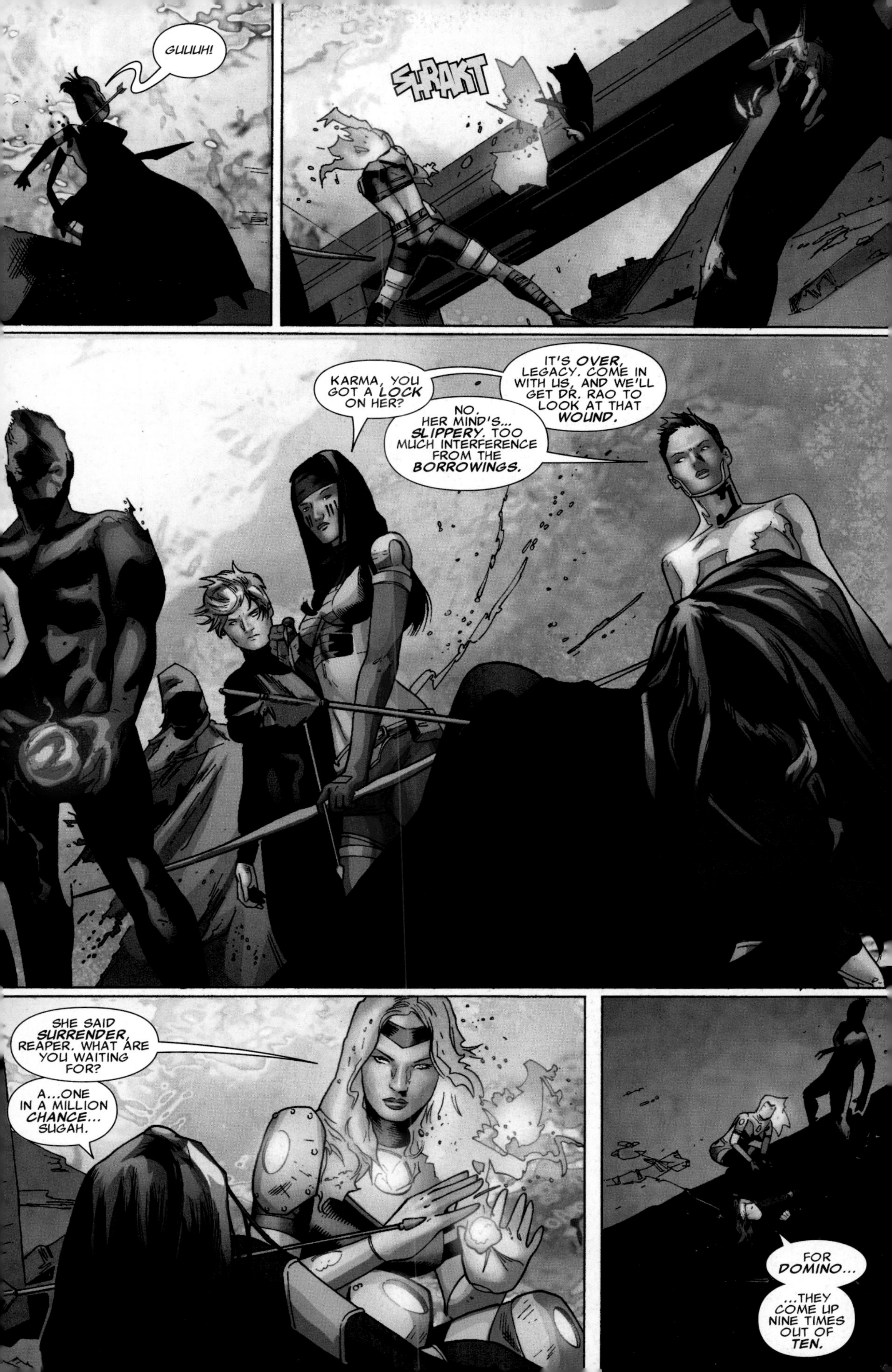
GUUUH!
SHRAKT
KARMA, YOU GOT A LOCK ON HER?
IT'S OVER, LEGACY. COME IN WITH US, AND WE'LL GET DR. RAO TO LOOK AT THAT WOUND.
NO. HER MIND'S... SLIPPERY. TOO MUCH INTERFERENCE FROM THE BORROWINGS.
SHE SAID SURRENDER, REAPER. WHAT ARE YOU WAITING FOR?
A...ONE IN A MILLION CHANCE... SUGAH.
FOR DOMINO...
...THEY COME UP NINE TIMES OUT OF TEN.

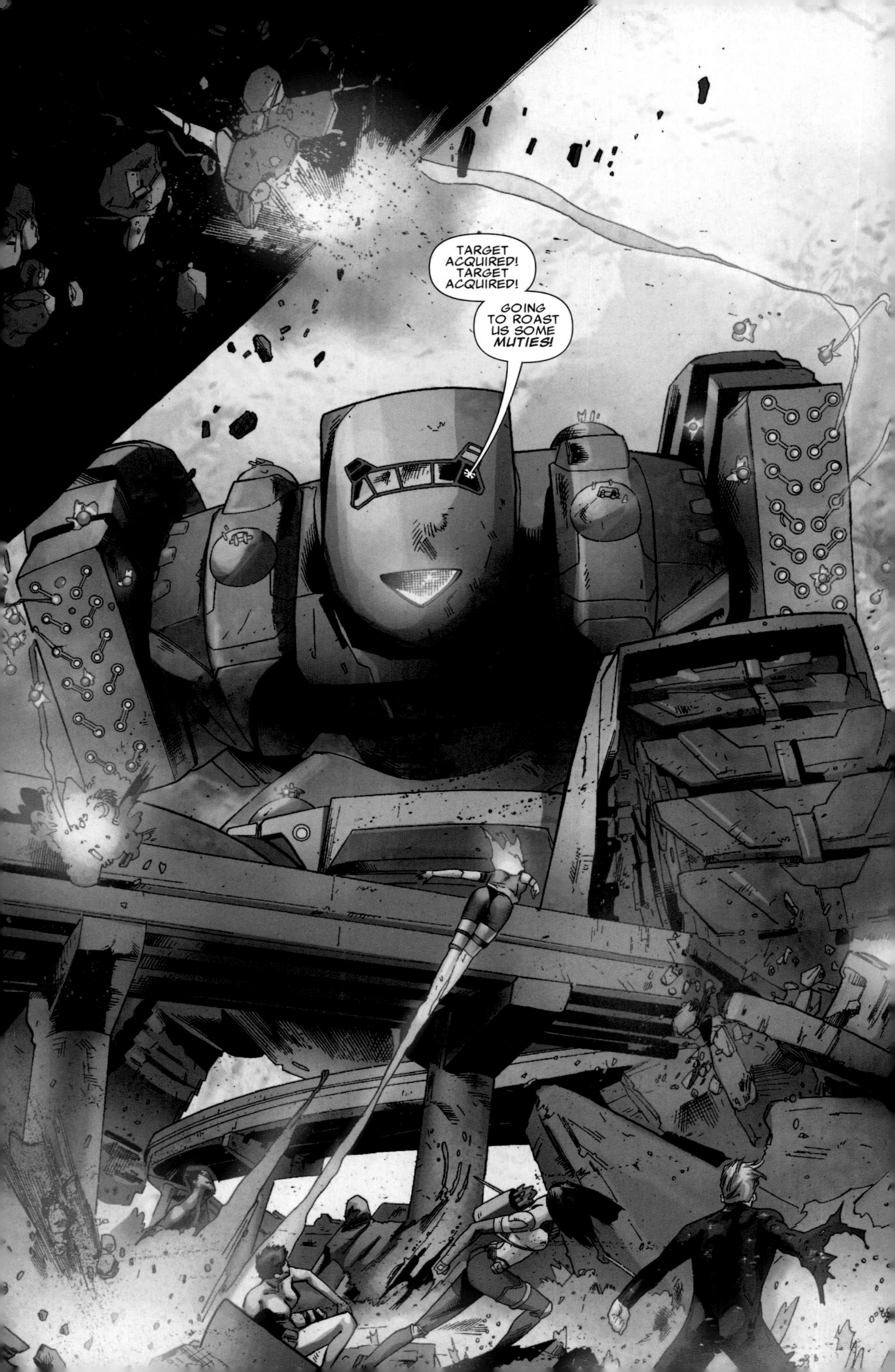
TARGET ACQUIRED! TARGET ACQUIRED!
GOING TO ROAST US SOME MUTIES!

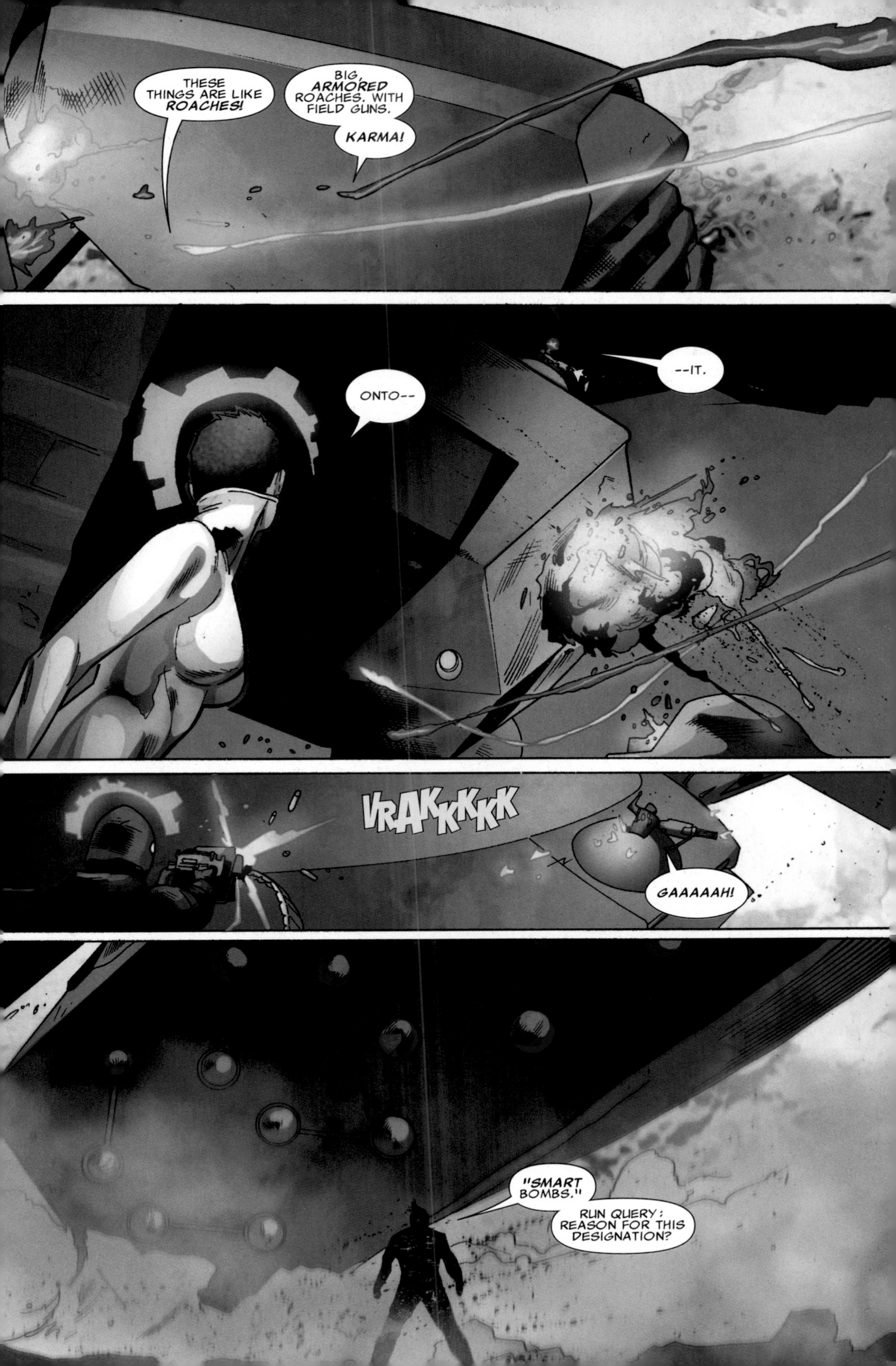
THESE THINGS ARE LIKE ROACHES!
BIG, ARMORED ROACHES. WITH FIELD GUNS.
KARMA!
ONTO--
--IT.
VRAKKKKK
GAAAAAH!
"SMART BOMBS."
RUN QUERY: REASON FOR THIS DESIGNATION?

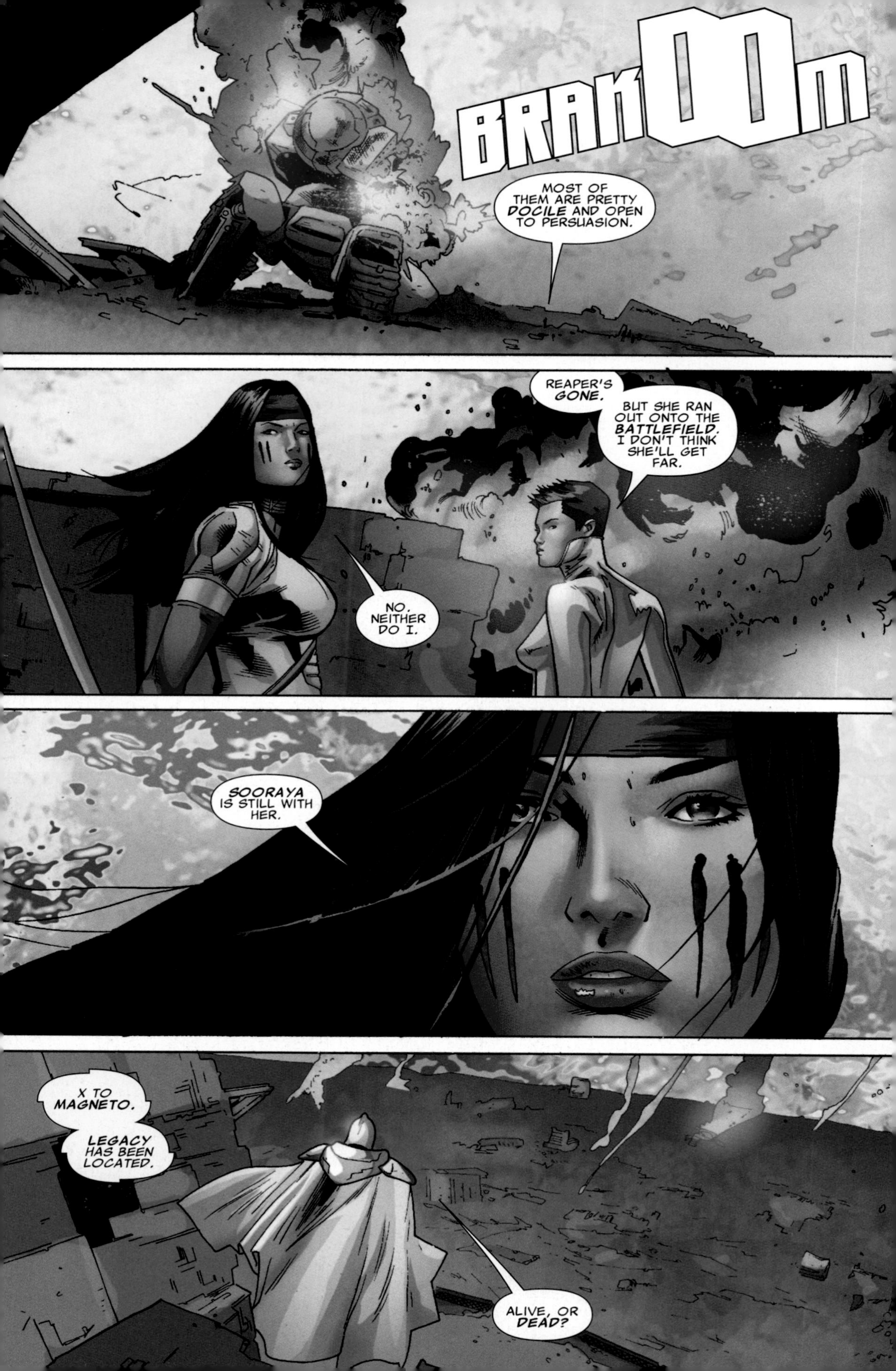
BRAKOOM
MOST OF THEM ARE PRETTY DOCILE AND OPEN TO PERSUASION.
REAPER'S GONE.
BUT SHE RAN OUT ONTO THE BATTLEFIELD. I DON'T THINK SHE'LL GET FAR.
NO. NEITHER DO I.
SOORAYA IS STILL WITH HER.
X TO MAGNETO.
LEGACY HAS BEEN LOCATED.
ALIVE, OR DEAD?

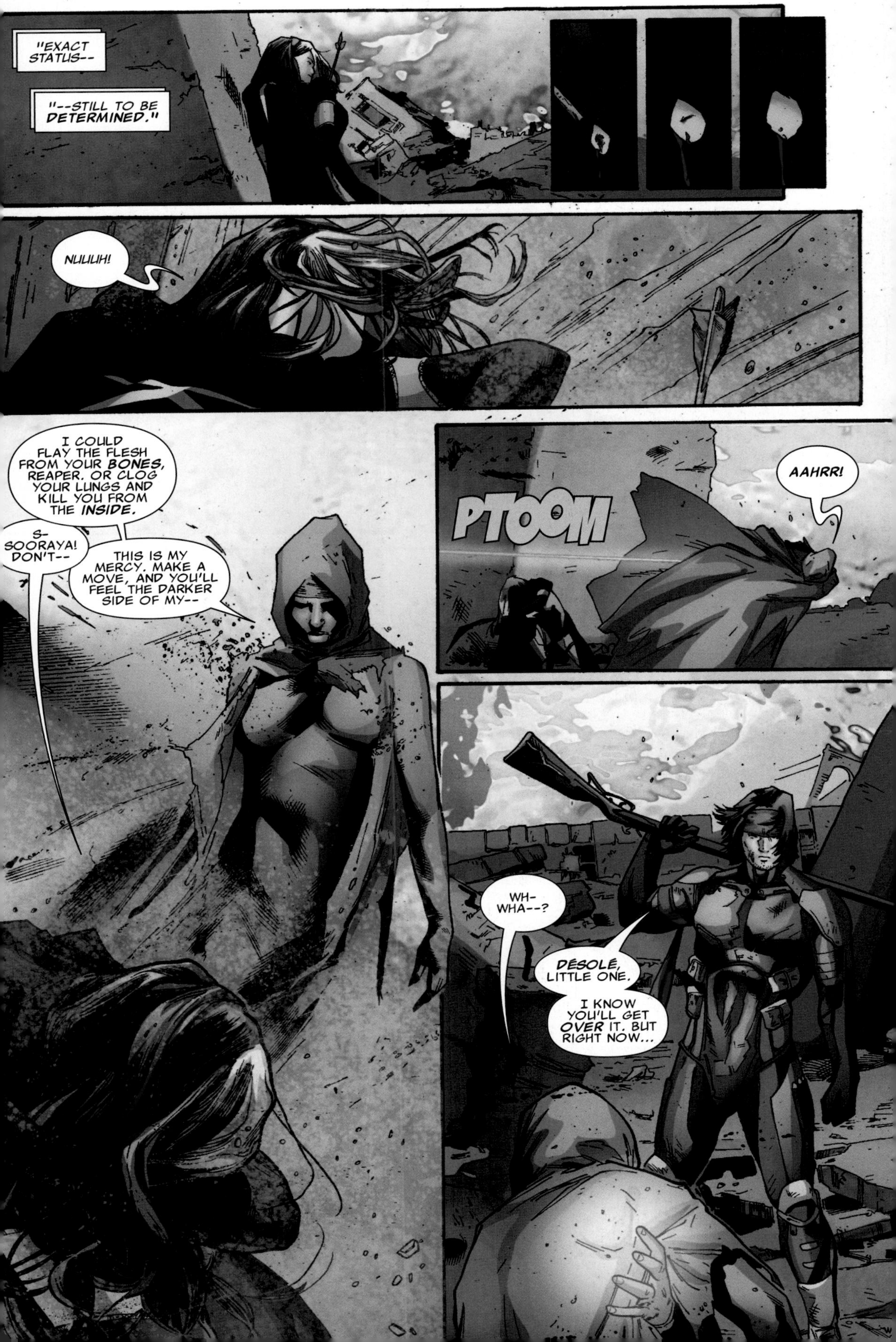
"EXACT STATUS--
"--STILL TO BE DETERMINED."
NUUUH!
I COULD FLAY THE FLESH FROM YOUR BONES, REAPER. OR CLOG YOUR LUNGS AND KILL YOU FROM THE INSIDE.
S-SOORAYA! DON'T--
THIS IS MY MERCY. MAKE A MOVE, AND YOU'LL FEEL THE DARKER SIDE OF MY--
PTOOM
AAHRR!
WH-WHA--?
DÉSOLÉ, LITTLE ONE.
I KNOW YOU'LL GET OVER IT. BUT RIGHT NOW...

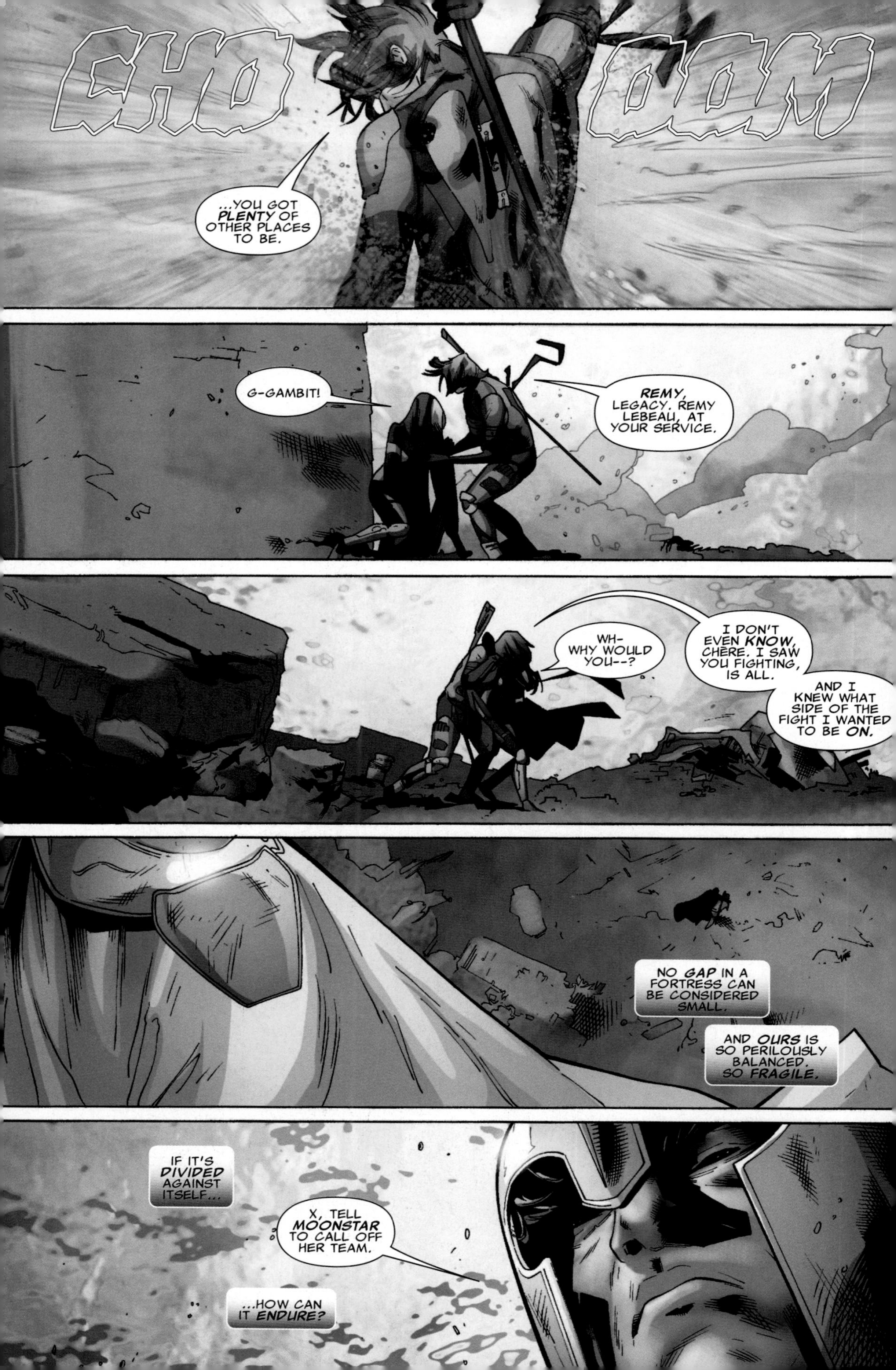
CHO
OOM
...YOU GOT PLENTY OF OTHER PLACES TO BE.
G-GAMBIT!
REMY, LEGACY. REMY LEBEAU, AT YOUR SERVICE.
WH- WHY WOULD YOU--?
I DON'T EVEN KNOW, CHÈRE. I SAW YOU FIGHTING, IS ALL.
AND I KNEW WHAT SIDE OF THE FIGHT I WANTED TO BE ON.
NO GAP IN A FORTRESS CAN BE CONSIDERED SMALL.
AND OURS IS SO PERILOUSLY BALANCED. SO FRAGILE.
IF IT'S DIVIDED AGAINST ITSELF...
X, TELL MOONSTAR TO CALL OFF HER TEAM.
...HOW CAN IT ENDURE?

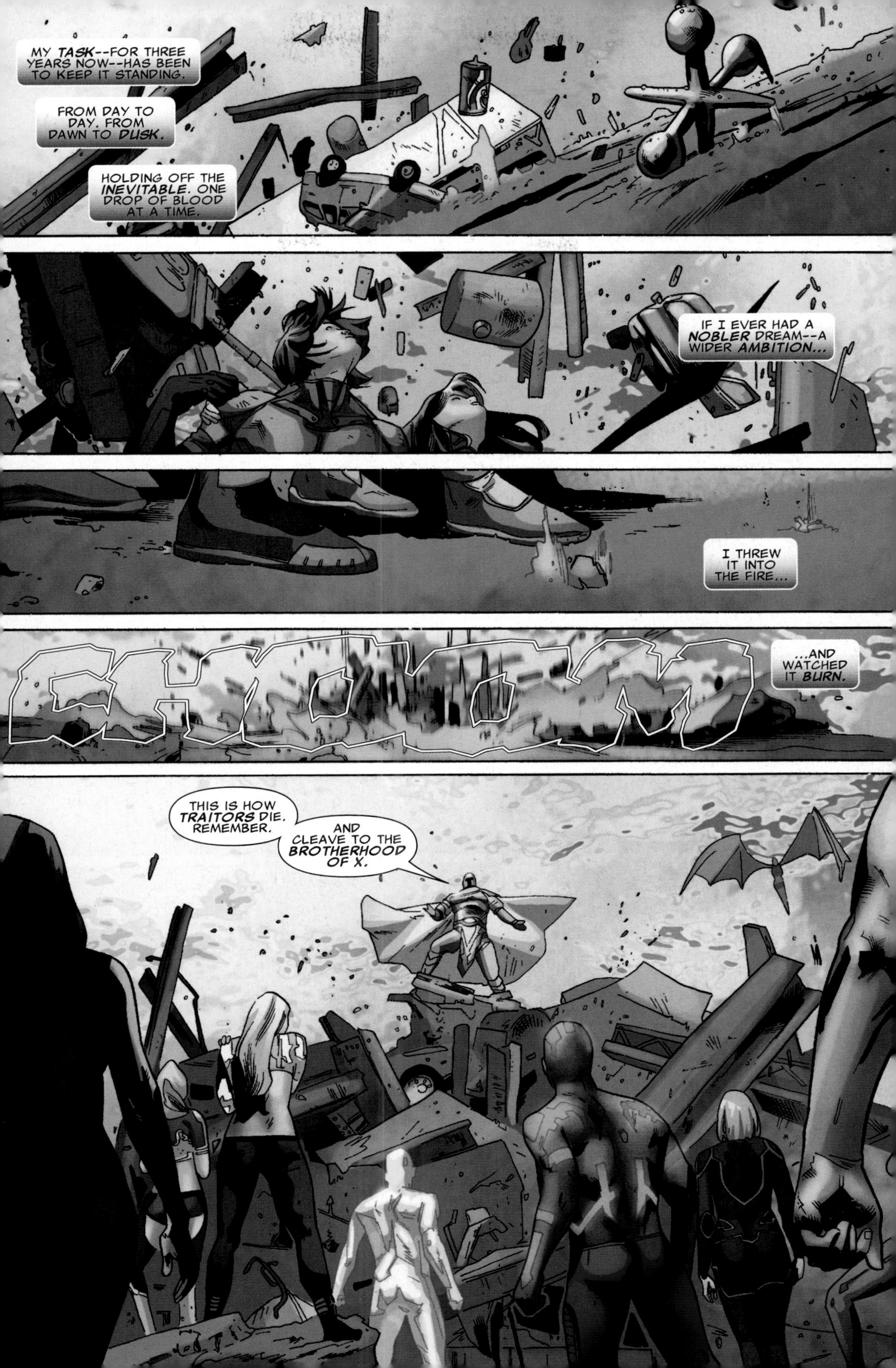
MY TASK--FOR THREE YEARS NOW--HAS BEEN TO KEEP IT STANDING.
FROM DAY TO DAY. FROM DAWN TO DUSK.
HOLDING OFF THE INEVITABLE. ONE DROP OF BLOOD AT A TIME.
IF I EVER HAD A NOBLER DREAM--A WIDER AMBITION...
I THREW IT INTO THE FIRE...
CHOOOM
...AND WATCHED IT BURN.
THIS IS HOW TRAITORS DIE. REMEMBER.
AND CLEAVE TO THE BROTHERHOOD OF X.

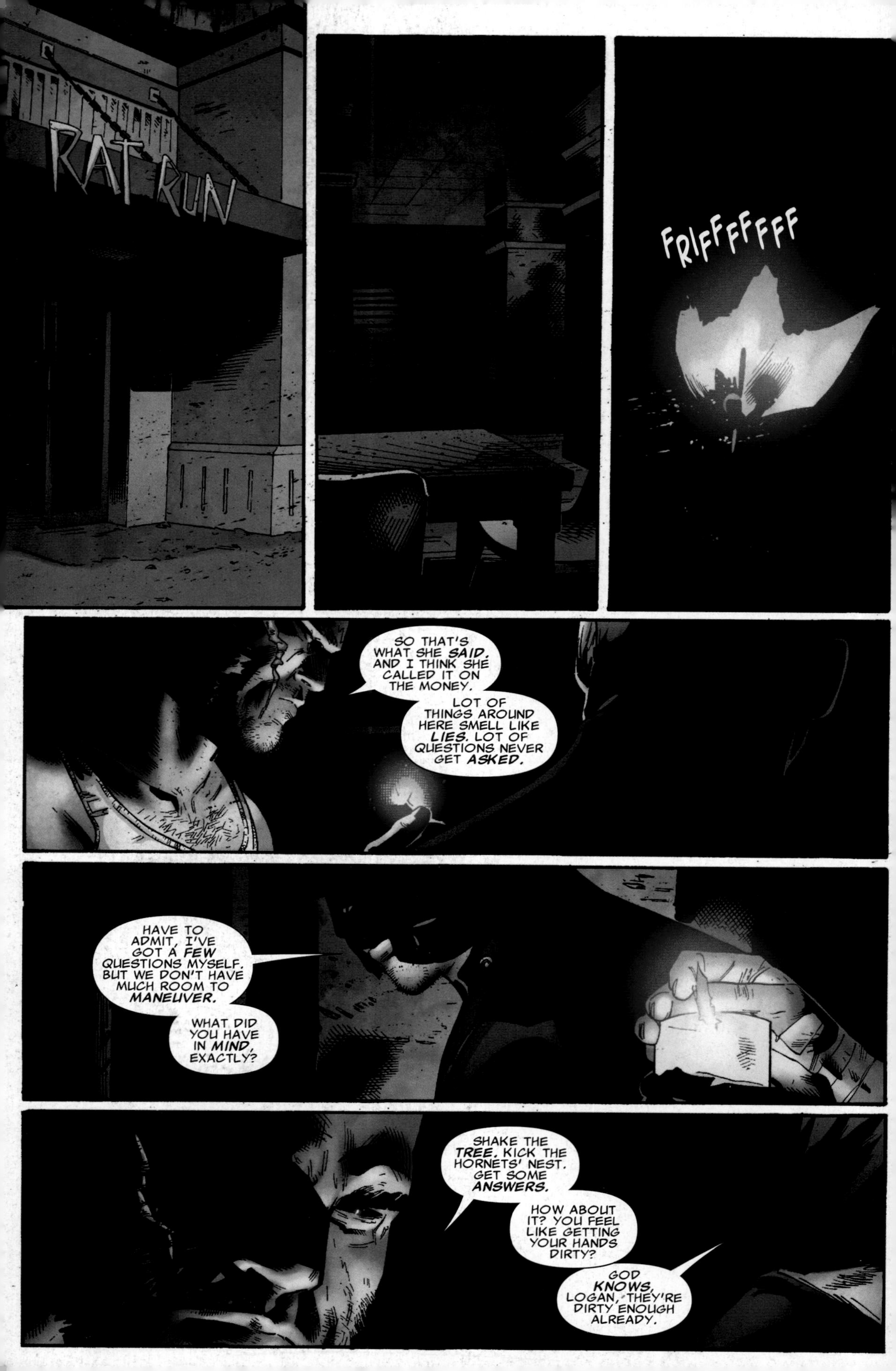
RAT RUN
FRIFFFFFFF
SO THAT'S WHAT SHE SAID. AND I THINK SHE CALLED IT ON THE MONEY.
LOT OF THINGS AROUND HERE SMELL LIKE LIES. LOT OF QUESTIONS NEVER GET ASKED.
HAVE TO ADMIT, I'VE GOT A FEW QUESTIONS MYSELF. BUT WE DON'T HAVE MUCH ROOM TO MANEUVER.
WHAT DID YOU HAVE IN MIND, EXACTLY?
SHAKE THE TREE. KICK THE HORNETS' NEST. GET SOME ANSWERS.
HOW ABOUT IT? YOU FEEL LIKE GETTING YOUR HANDS DIRTY?
GOD KNOWS, LOGAN, THEY'RE DIRTY ENOUGH ALREADY.

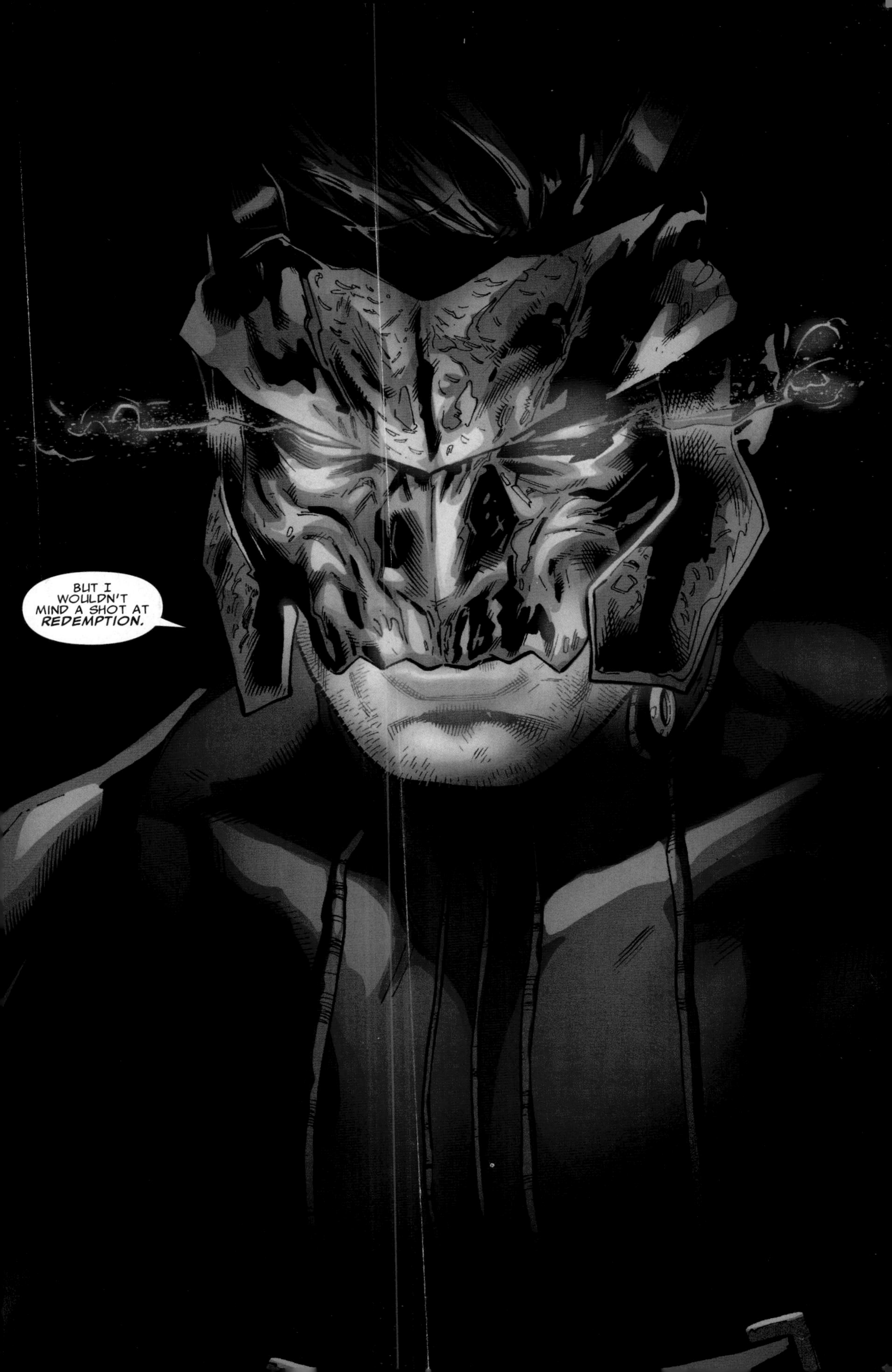
BUT I WOULDN'T MIND A SHOT AT *REDEMPTION.*

NEW MUTANTS #23

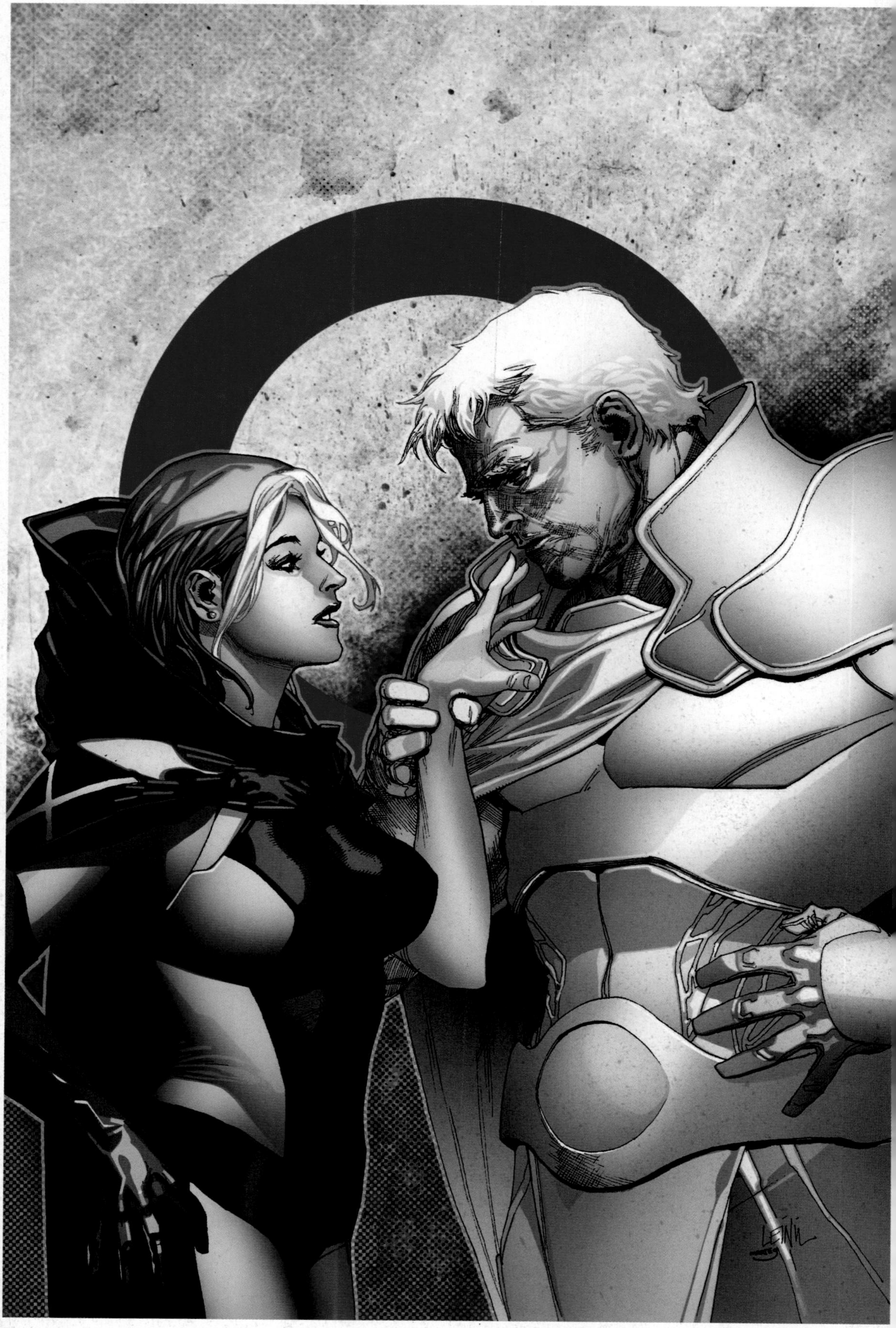

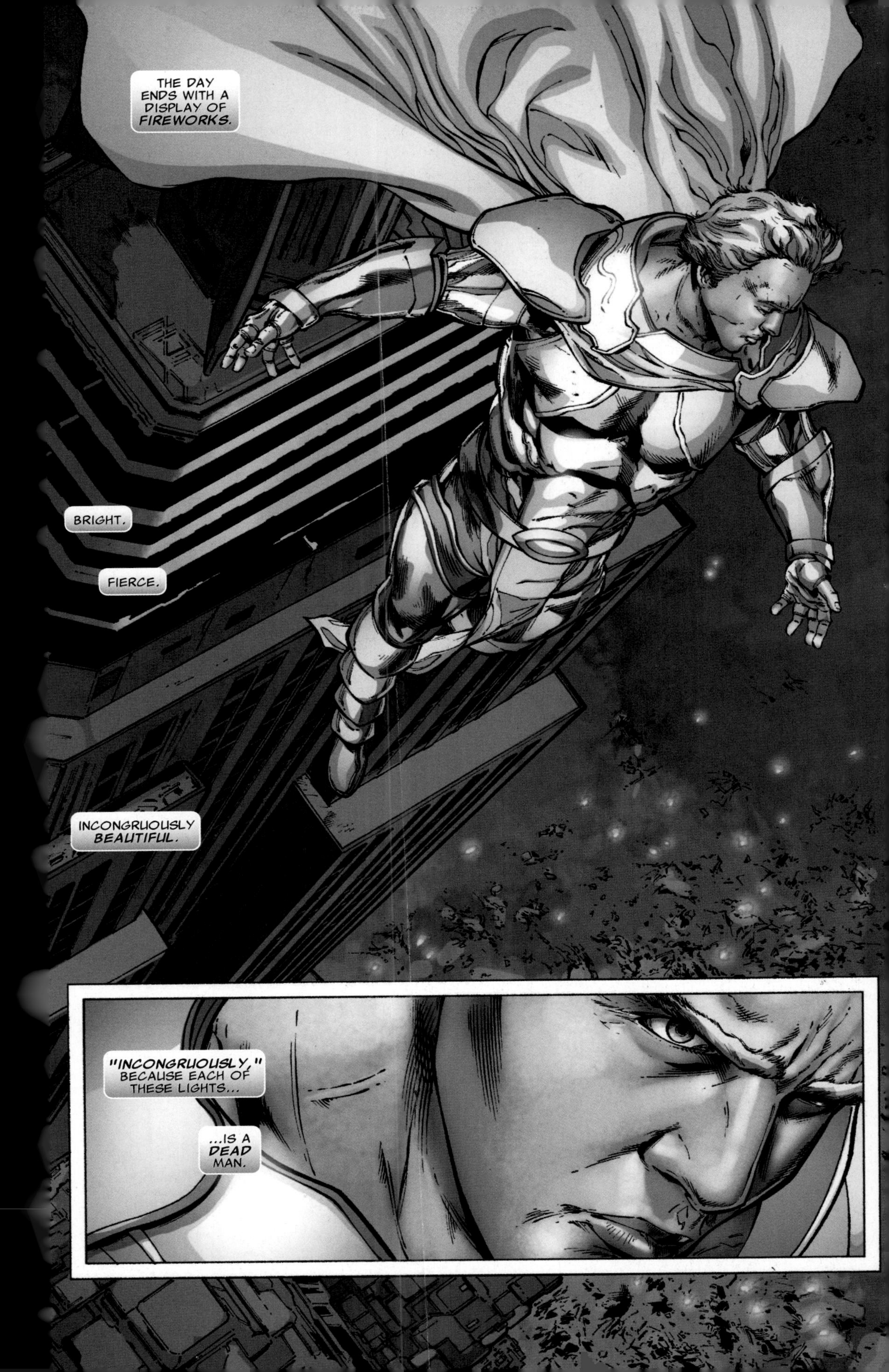

THE DAY ENDS WITH A DISPLAY OF FIREWORKS.
BRIGHT.
FIERCE.
INCONGRUOUSLY BEAUTIFUL.
"INCONGRUOUSLY," BECAUSE EACH OF THESE LIGHTS...
...IS A DEAD MAN.

OUR HUMAN **ENEMIES** ARE AFRAID THAT WE MIGHT SCAVENGE THEIR DISCARDED TECH.

PULL BACK! PULL BACK TO THE **FORCE WALLS!**

SO EVERY SUIT OF **ARMOR** CONTAINS A DIAGNOSTIC MONITOR AND A **SUICIDE CHIP.**

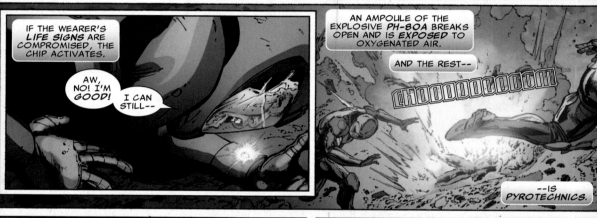

IF THE WEARER'S **LIFE SIGNS** ARE COMPROMISED, THE CHIP ACTIVATES.

AW, NO! I'M **GOOD!** I CAN STILL--

AN AMPOULE OF THE EXPLOSIVE **PH-80A** BREAKS OPEN AND IS **EXPOSED** TO OXYGENATED AIR.

AND THE REST--

CHOOOOOOOOOOM

--IS PYROTECHNICS.

EVEN IN WAR TIME-- **ESPECIALLY** IN WAR TIME--THE GOAL MUST BE TO KEEP SOME SMALL PORTION OF YOUR OWN **HUMANITY** UNTOUCHED AND INVIOLATE.

WOUNDED. GET THEM TO THE **HEALERS.**

EVEN IF THE REST OF YOUR SOUL IS A **BUTCHER'S** SHOP.

THERE MUST BE A **SHRINE** IN SOME REMOTE CORNER OF YOUR BEING. A PLACE OF **SANCTITY.**

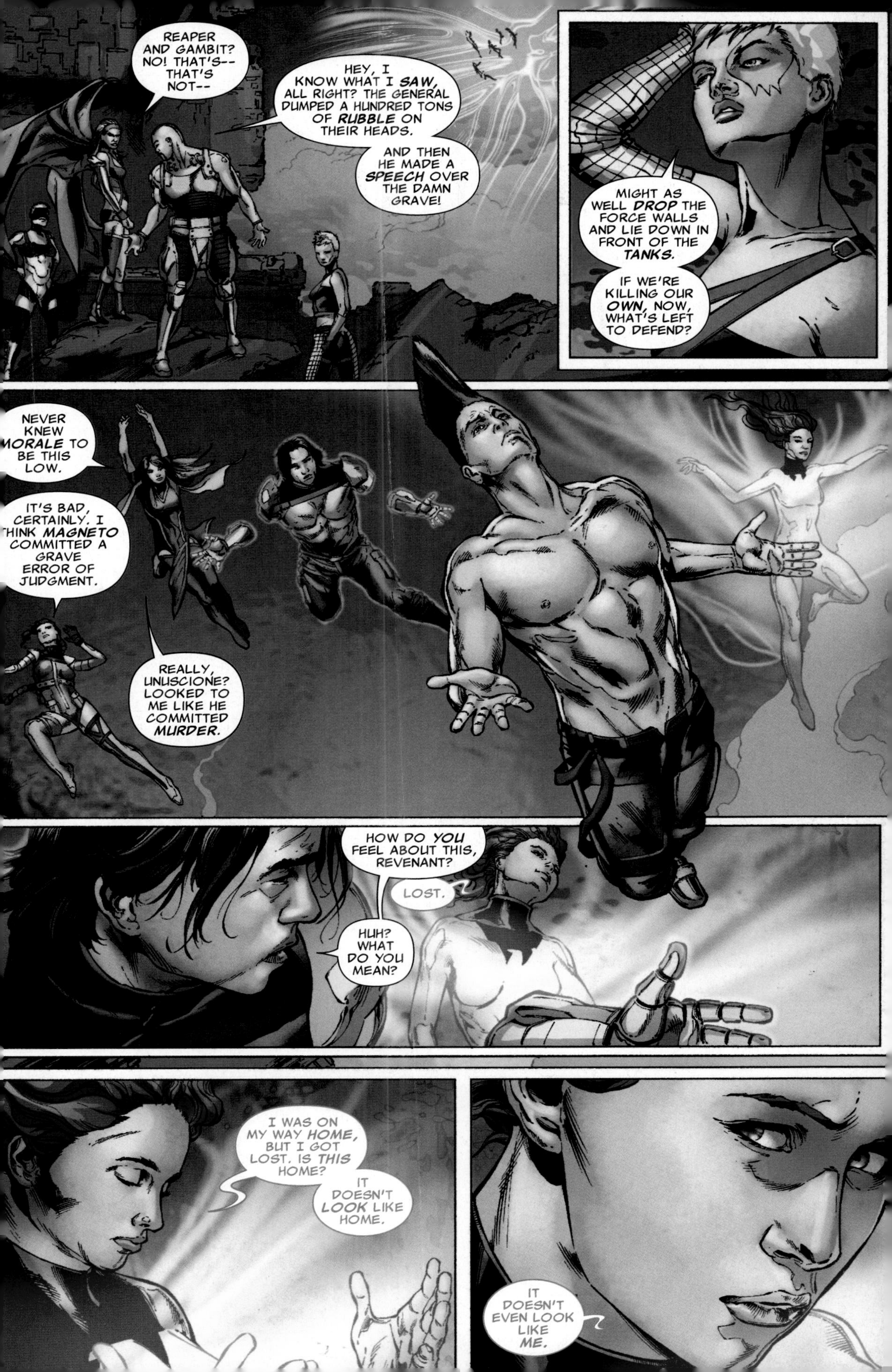
REAPER AND GAMBIT? NO! THAT'S-- THAT'S NOT--
HEY, I KNOW WHAT I SAW, ALL RIGHT? THE GENERAL DUMPED A HUNDRED TONS OF RUBBLE ON THEIR HEADS.
AND THEN HE MADE A SPEECH OVER THE DAMN GRAVE!
MIGHT AS WELL DROP THE FORCE WALLS AND LIE DOWN IN FRONT OF THE TANKS.
IF WE'RE KILLING OUR OWN, NOW, WHAT'S LEFT TO DEFEND?
NEVER KNEW MORALE TO BE THIS LOW.
IT'S BAD, CERTAINLY. I THINK MAGNETO COMMITTED A GRAVE ERROR OF JUDGMENT.
REALLY, UNUSCIONE? LOOKED TO ME LIKE HE COMMITTED MURDER.
HOW DO YOU FEEL ABOUT THIS, REVENANT?
LOST.
HUH? WHAT DO YOU MEAN?
I WAS ON MY WAY HOME, BUT I GOT LOST. IS THIS HOME?
IT DOESN'T LOOK LIKE HOME.
IT DOESN'T EVEN LOOK LIKE ME.

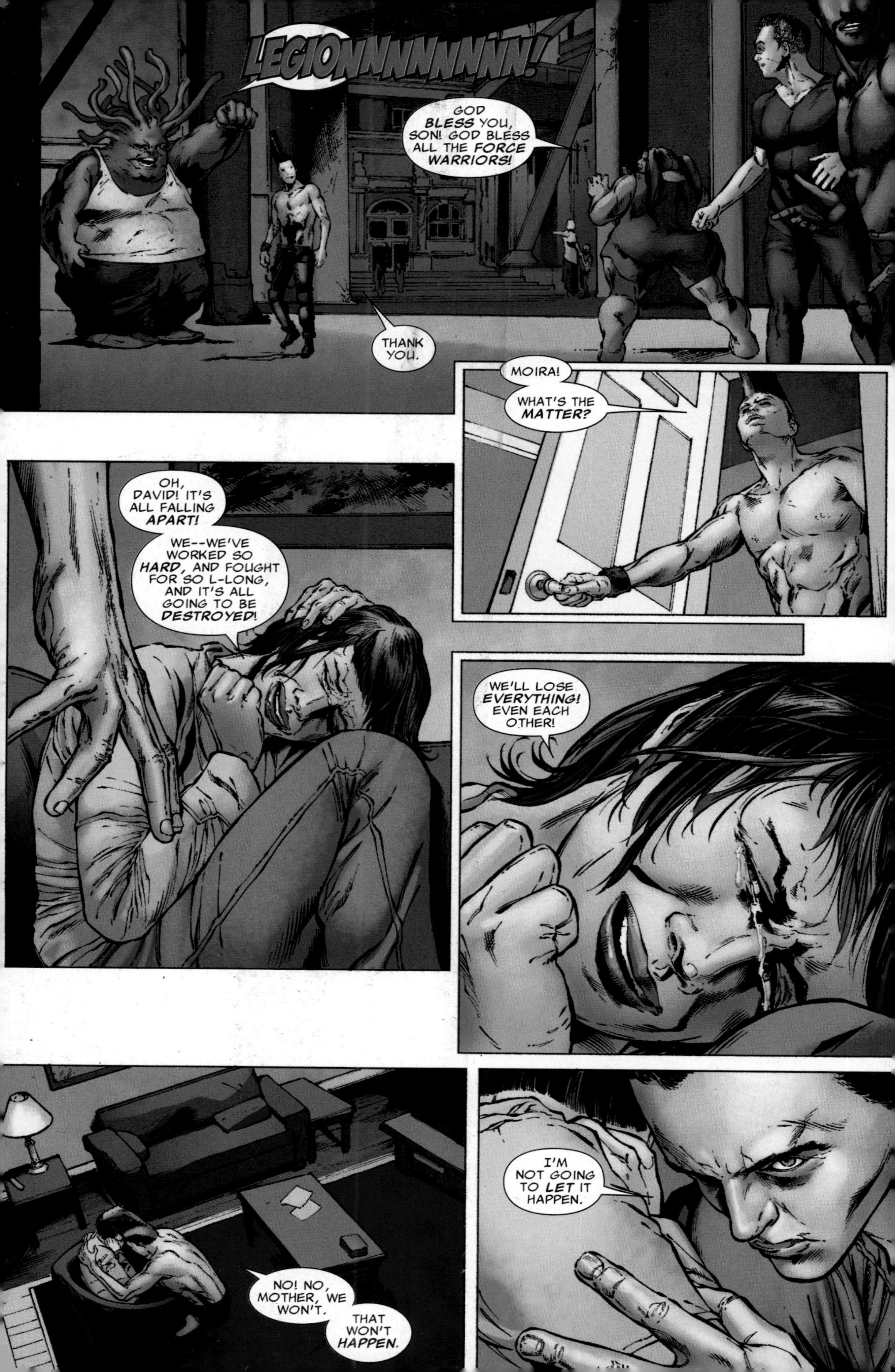

LEGIONNNNNNNN!
GOD BLESS YOU, SON! GOD BLESS ALL THE FORCE WARRIORS!
THANK YOU.
MOIRA!
WHAT'S THE MATTER?
OH, DAVID! IT'S ALL FALLING APART!
WE--WE'VE WORKED SO HARD, AND FOUGHT FOR SO L-LONG, AND IT'S ALL GOING TO BE DESTROYED!
WE'LL LOSE EVERYTHING! EVEN EACH OTHER!
NO! NO, MOTHER, WE WON'T.
THAT WON'T HAPPEN.
I'M NOT GOING TO LET IT HAPPEN.

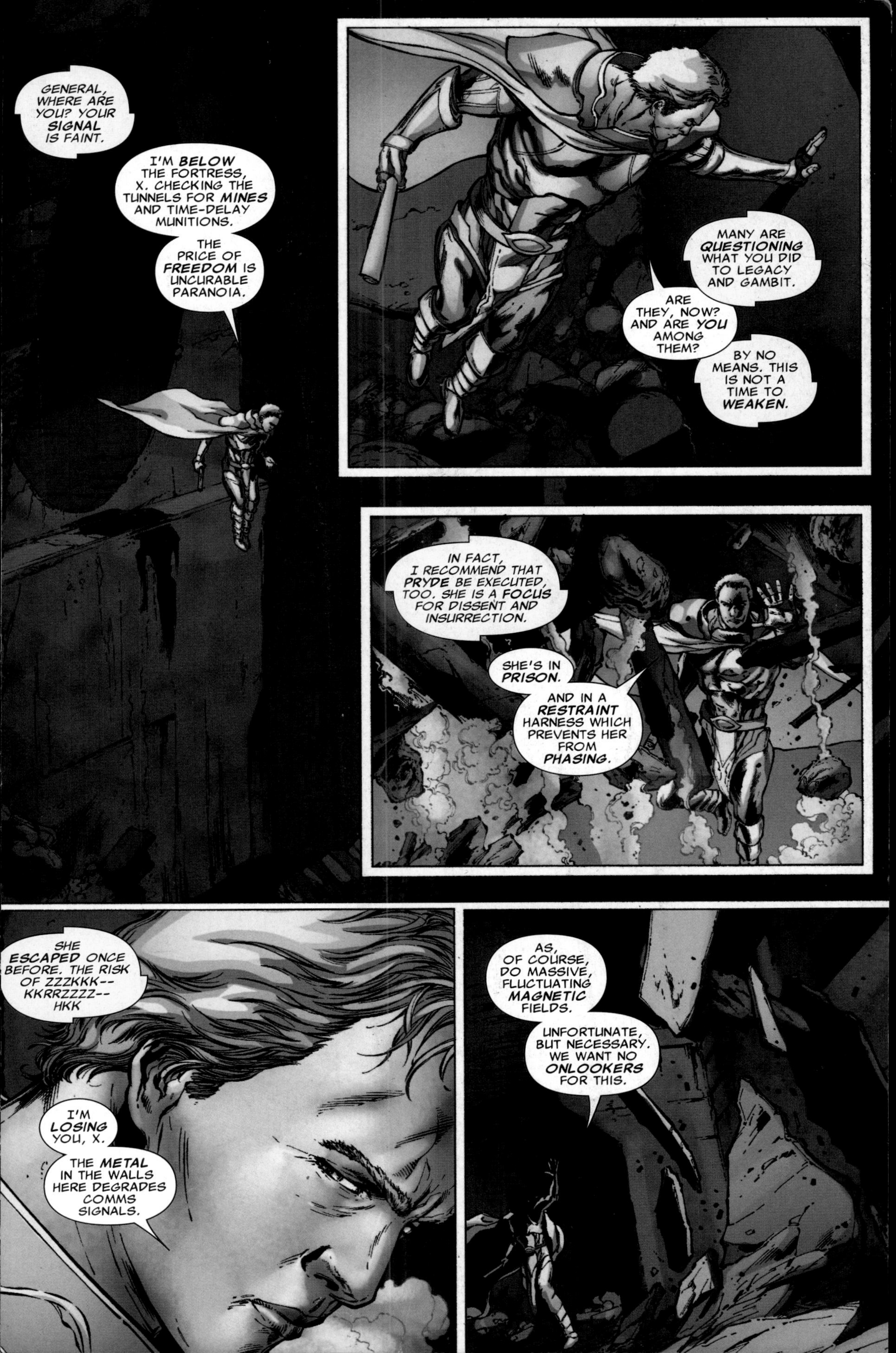
GENERAL, WHERE ARE YOU? YOUR SIGNAL IS FAINT.
I'M BELOW THE FORTRESS, X. CHECKING THE TUNNELS FOR MINES AND TIME-DELAY MUNITIONS.
THE PRICE OF FREEDOM IS UNCURABLE PARANOIA.
MANY ARE QUESTIONING WHAT YOU DID TO LEGACY AND GAMBIT.
ARE THEY, NOW? AND ARE YOU AMONG THEM?
BY NO MEANS. THIS IS NOT A TIME TO WEAKEN.
IN FACT, I RECOMMEND THAT PRYDE BE EXECUTED, TOO. SHE IS A FOCUS FOR DISSENT AND INSURRECTION.
SHE'S IN PRISON.
AND IN A RESTRAINT HARNESS WHICH PREVENTS HER FROM PHASING.
SHE ESCAPED ONCE BEFORE. THE RISK OF ZZZKKK--KKRRZZZZ--HKK
I'M LOSING YOU, X.
THE METAL IN THE WALLS HERE DEGRADES COMMS SIGNALS.
AS, OF COURSE, DO MASSIVE, FLUCTUATING MAGNETIC FIELDS.
UNFORTUNATE, BUT NECESSARY. WE WANT NO ONLOOKERS FOR THIS.

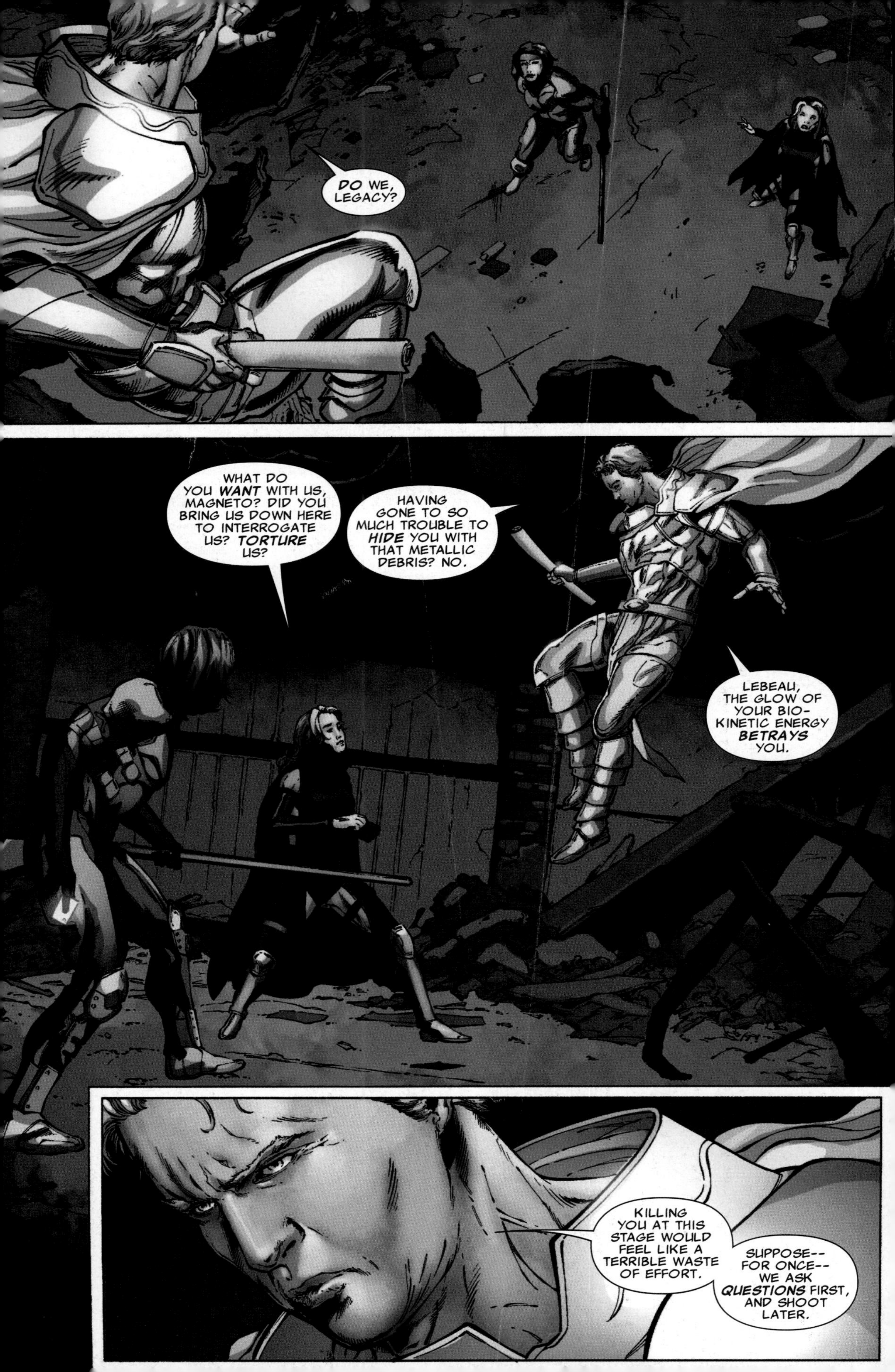

DO WE, LEGACY?
WHAT DO YOU WANT WITH US, MAGNETO? DID YOU BRING US DOWN HERE TO INTERROGATE US? TORTURE US?
HAVING GONE TO SO MUCH TROUBLE TO HIDE YOU WITH THAT METALLIC DEBRIS? NO.
LEBEAU, THE GLOW OF YOUR BIO-KINETIC ENERGY BETRAYS YOU.
KILLING YOU AT THIS STAGE WOULD FEEL LIKE A TERRIBLE WASTE OF EFFORT.
SUPPOSE--FOR ONCE--WE ASK QUESTIONS FIRST, AND SHOOT LATER.

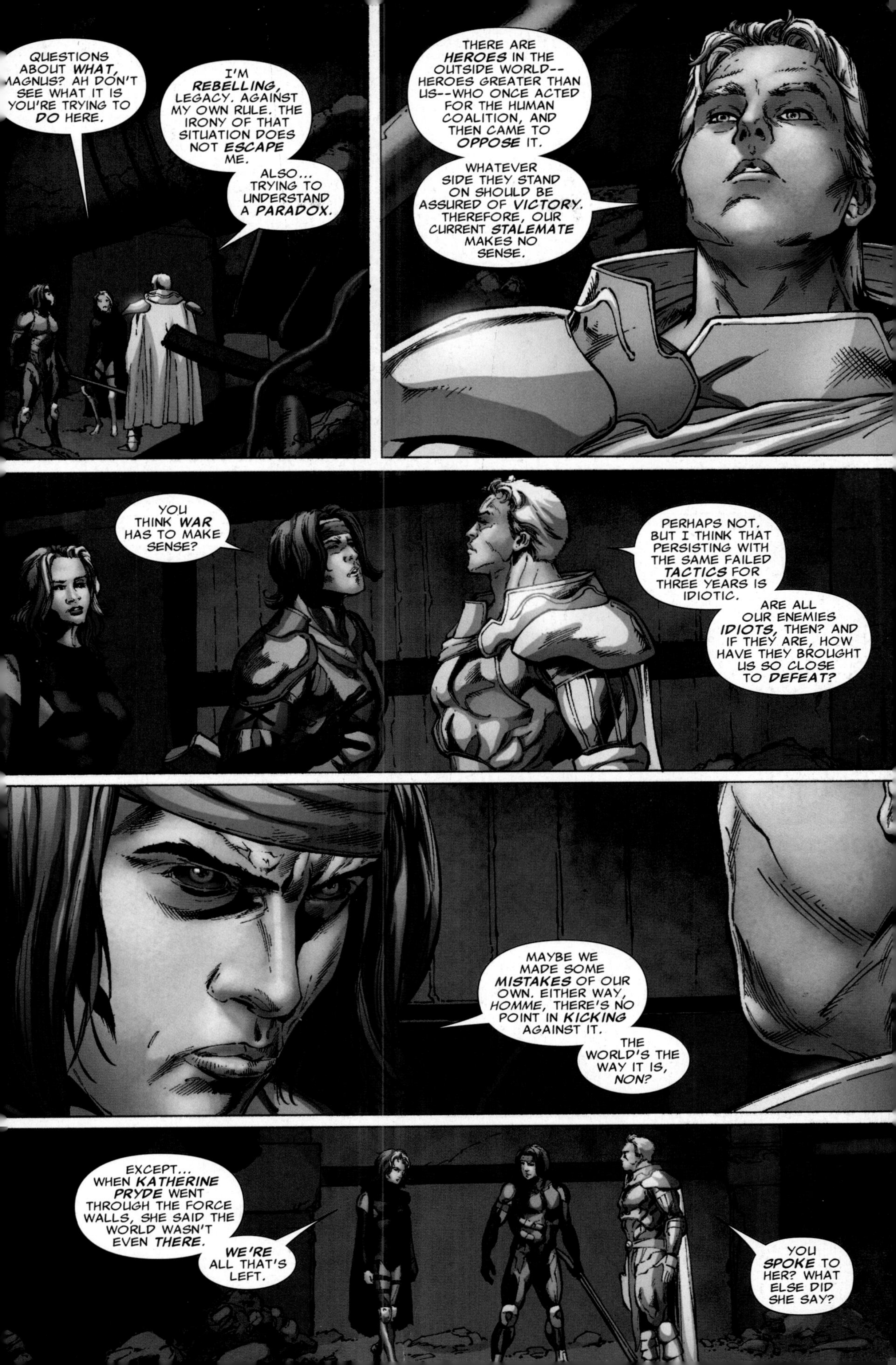
QUESTIONS ABOUT WHAT, MAGNUS? AH DON'T SEE WHAT IT IS YOU'RE TRYING TO DO HERE.
I'M REBELLING, LEGACY. AGAINST MY OWN RULE. THE IRONY OF THAT SITUATION DOES NOT ESCAPE ME.
ALSO... TRYING TO UNDERSTAND A PARADOX.
THERE ARE HEROES IN THE OUTSIDE WORLD-- HEROES GREATER THAN US--WHO ONCE ACTED FOR THE HUMAN COALITION, AND THEN CAME TO OPPOSE IT.
WHATEVER SIDE THEY STAND ON SHOULD BE ASSURED OF VICTORY. THEREFORE, OUR CURRENT STALEMATE MAKES NO SENSE.
YOU THINK WAR HAS TO MAKE SENSE?
PERHAPS NOT. BUT I THINK THAT PERSISTING WITH THE SAME FAILED TACTICS FOR THREE YEARS IS IDIOTIC.
ARE ALL OUR ENEMIES IDIOTS, THEN? AND IF THEY ARE, HOW HAVE THEY BROUGHT US SO CLOSE TO DEFEAT?
MAYBE WE MADE SOME MISTAKES OF OUR OWN. EITHER WAY, HOMME, THERE'S NO POINT IN KICKING AGAINST IT.
THE WORLD'S THE WAY IT IS, NON?
EXCEPT... WHEN KATHERINE PRYDE WENT THROUGH THE FORCE WALLS, SHE SAID THE WORLD WASN'T EVEN THERE.
WE'RE ALL THAT'S LEFT.
YOU SPOKE TO HER? WHAT ELSE DID SHE SAY?

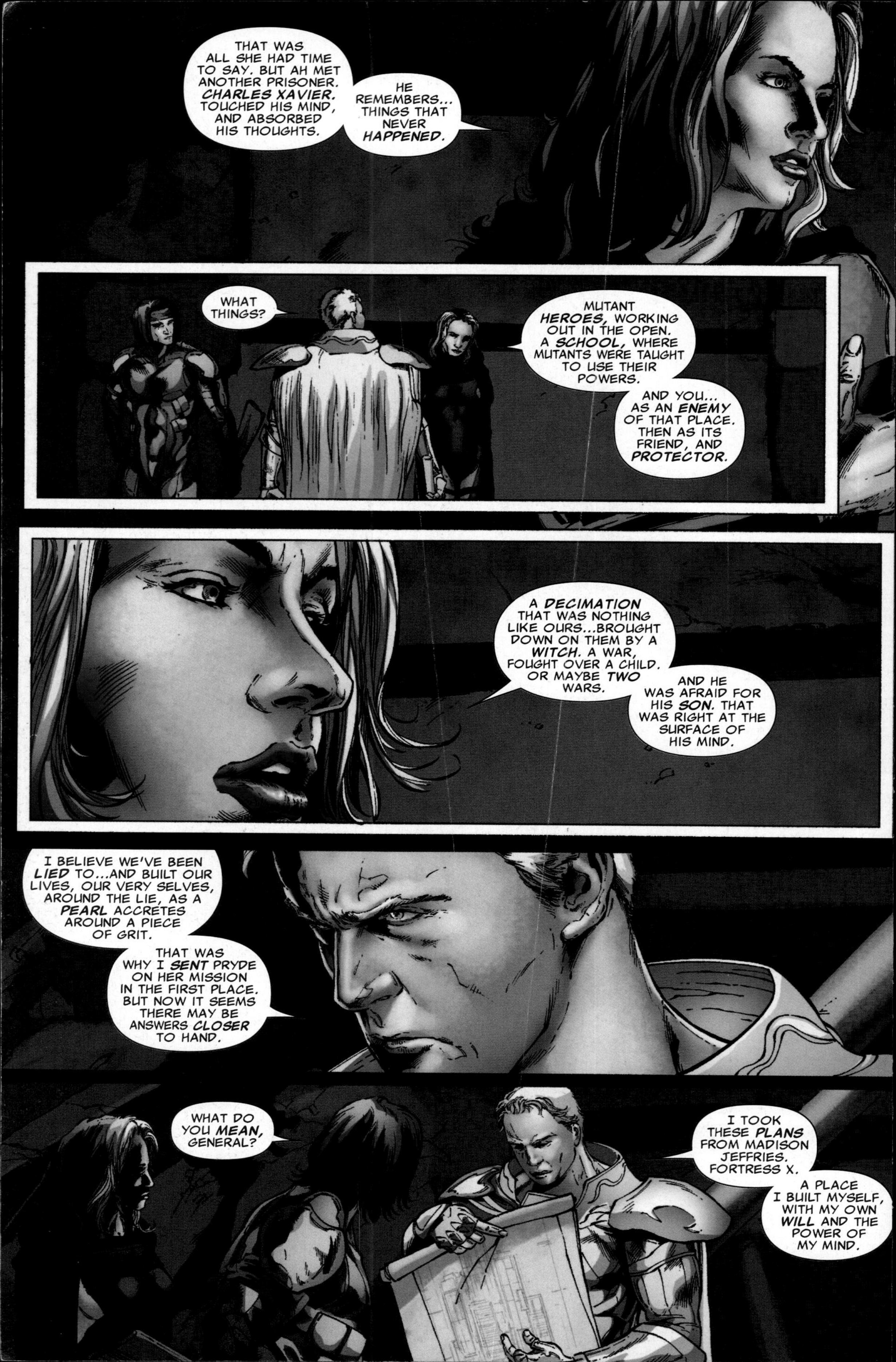

THAT WAS ALL SHE HAD TIME TO SAY. BUT AH MET ANOTHER PRISONER. CHARLES XAVIER. TOUCHED HIS MIND, AND ABSORBED HIS THOUGHTS.
HE REMEMBERS... THINGS THAT NEVER HAPPENED.
WHAT THINGS?
MUTANT HEROES, WORKING OUT IN THE OPEN. A SCHOOL, WHERE MUTANTS WERE TAUGHT TO USE THEIR POWERS.
AND YOU... AS AN ENEMY OF THAT PLACE. THEN AS ITS FRIEND, AND PROTECTOR.
A DECIMATION THAT WAS NOTHING LIKE OURS...BROUGHT DOWN ON THEM BY A WITCH. A WAR, FOUGHT OVER A CHILD. OR MAYBE TWO WARS.
AND HE WAS AFRAID FOR HIS SON. THAT WAS RIGHT AT THE SURFACE OF HIS MIND.
I BELIEVE WE'VE BEEN LIED TO...AND BUILT OUR LIVES, OUR VERY SELVES, AROUND THE LIE, AS A PEARL ACCRETES AROUND A PIECE OF GRIT.
THAT WAS WHY I SENT PRYDE ON HER MISSION IN THE FIRST PLACE. BUT NOW IT SEEMS THERE MAY BE ANSWERS CLOSER TO HAND.
WHAT DO YOU MEAN, GENERAL?
I TOOK THESE PLANS FROM MADISON JEFFRIES. FORTRESS X.
A PLACE I BUILT MYSELF, WITH MY OWN WILL AND THE POWER OF MY MIND.

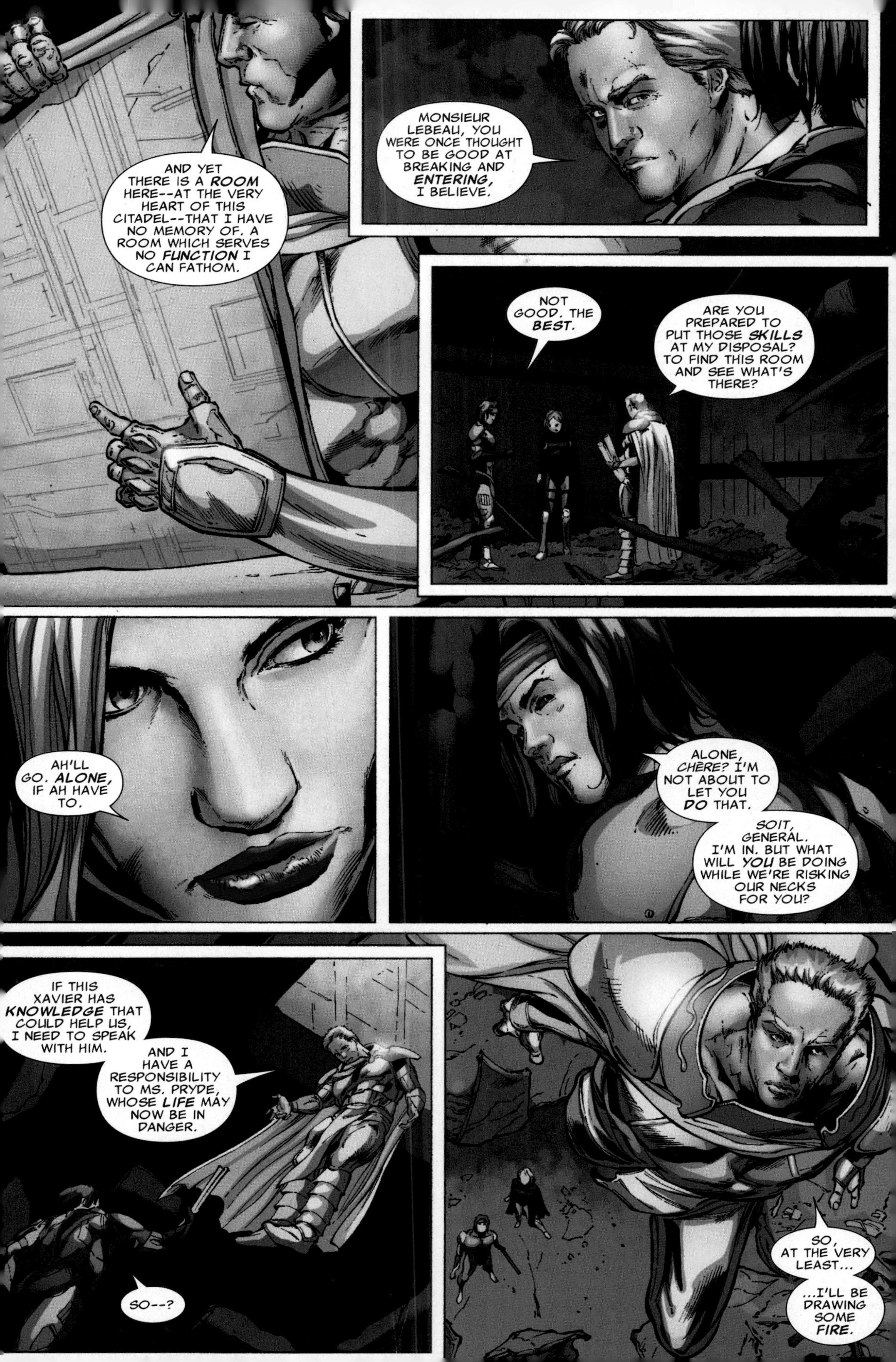
MONSIEUR LEBEAU, YOU WERE ONCE THOUGHT TO BE GOOD AT BREAKING AND ENTERING, I BELIEVE.
AND YET THERE IS A ROOM HERE--AT THE VERY HEART OF THIS CITADEL--THAT I HAVE NO MEMORY OF. A ROOM WHICH SERVES NO FUNCTION I CAN FATHOM.
NOT GOOD. THE BEST.
ARE YOU PREPARED TO PUT THOSE SKILLS AT MY DISPOSAL? TO FIND THIS ROOM AND SEE WHAT'S THERE?
AH'LL GO. ALONE, IF AH HAVE TO.
ALONE, CHÈRE? I'M NOT ABOUT TO LET YOU DO THAT.
SOIT, GENERAL. I'M IN. BUT WHAT WILL YOU BE DOING WHILE WE'RE RISKING OUR NECKS FOR YOU?
IF THIS XAVIER HAS KNOWLEDGE THAT COULD HELP US, I NEED TO SPEAK WITH HIM.
AND I HAVE A RESPONSIBILITY TO MS. PRYDE, WHOSE LIFE MAY NOW BE IN DANGER.
SO--?
SO, AT THE VERY LEAST...
...I'LL BE DRAWING SOME FIRE.

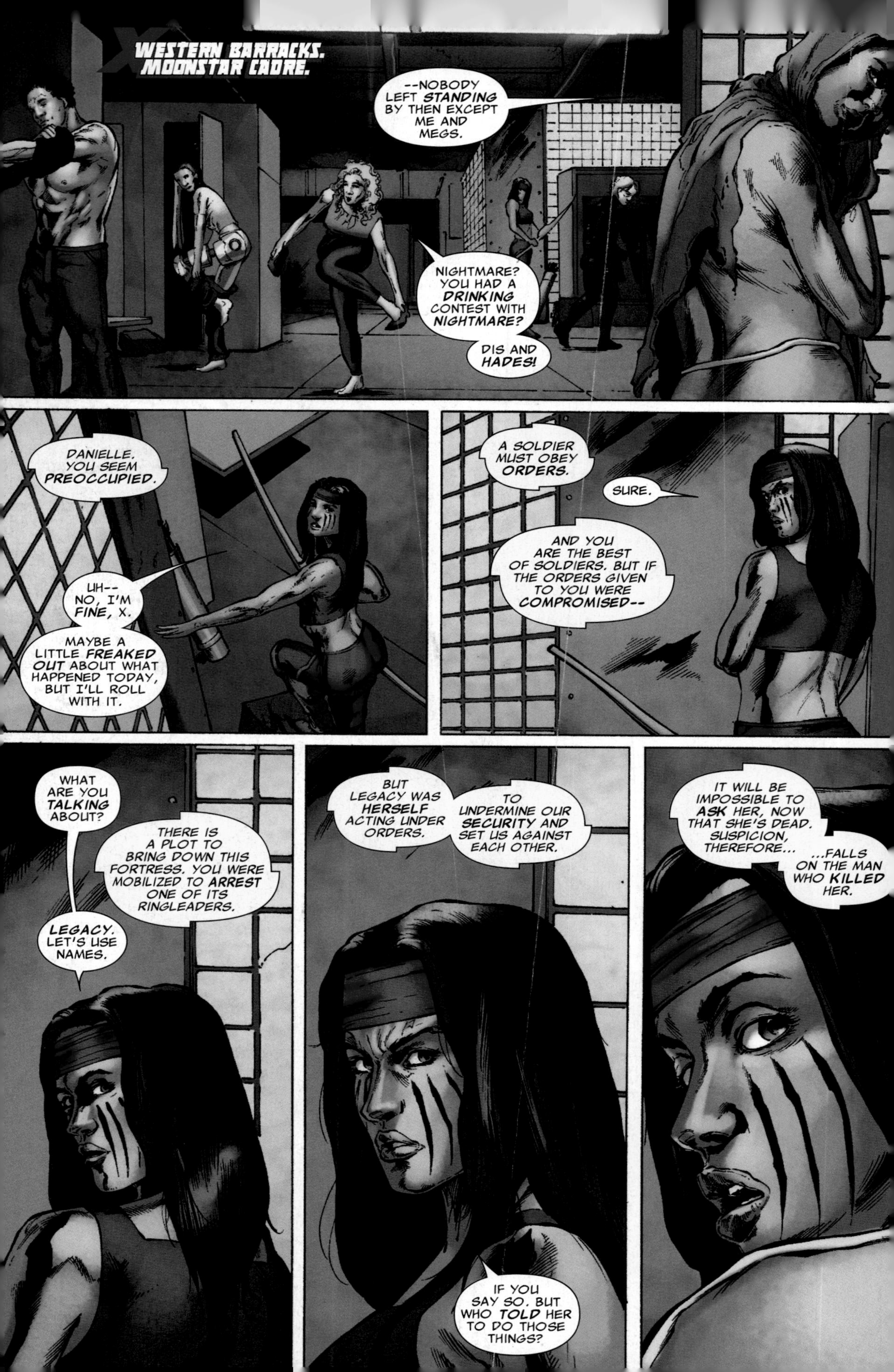
WESTERN BARRACKS. MOONSTAR CADRE.
--NOBODY LEFT STANDING BY THEN EXCEPT ME AND MEGS.
NIGHTMARE? YOU HAD A DRINKING CONTEST WITH NIGHTMARE?
DIS AND HADES!
DANIELLE. YOU SEEM PREOCCUPIED.
UH-- NO, I'M FINE, X.
MAYBE A LITTLE FREAKED OUT ABOUT WHAT HAPPENED TODAY, BUT I'LL ROLL WITH IT.
A SOLDIER MUST OBEY ORDERS.
SURE.
AND YOU ARE THE BEST OF SOLDIERS. BUT IF THE ORDERS GIVEN TO YOU WERE COMPROMISED--
WHAT ARE YOU TALKING ABOUT?
THERE IS A PLOT TO BRING DOWN THIS FORTRESS. YOU WERE MOBILIZED TO ARREST ONE OF ITS RINGLEADERS.
LEGACY. LET'S USE NAMES.
BUT LEGACY WAS HERSELF ACTING UNDER ORDERS.
TO UNDERMINE OUR SECURITY AND SET US AGAINST EACH OTHER.
IF YOU SAY SO. BUT WHO TOLD HER TO DO THOSE THINGS?
IT WILL BE IMPOSSIBLE TO ASK HER, NOW THAT SHE'S DEAD. SUSPICION, THEREFORE...
...FALLS ON THE MAN WHO KILLED HER.

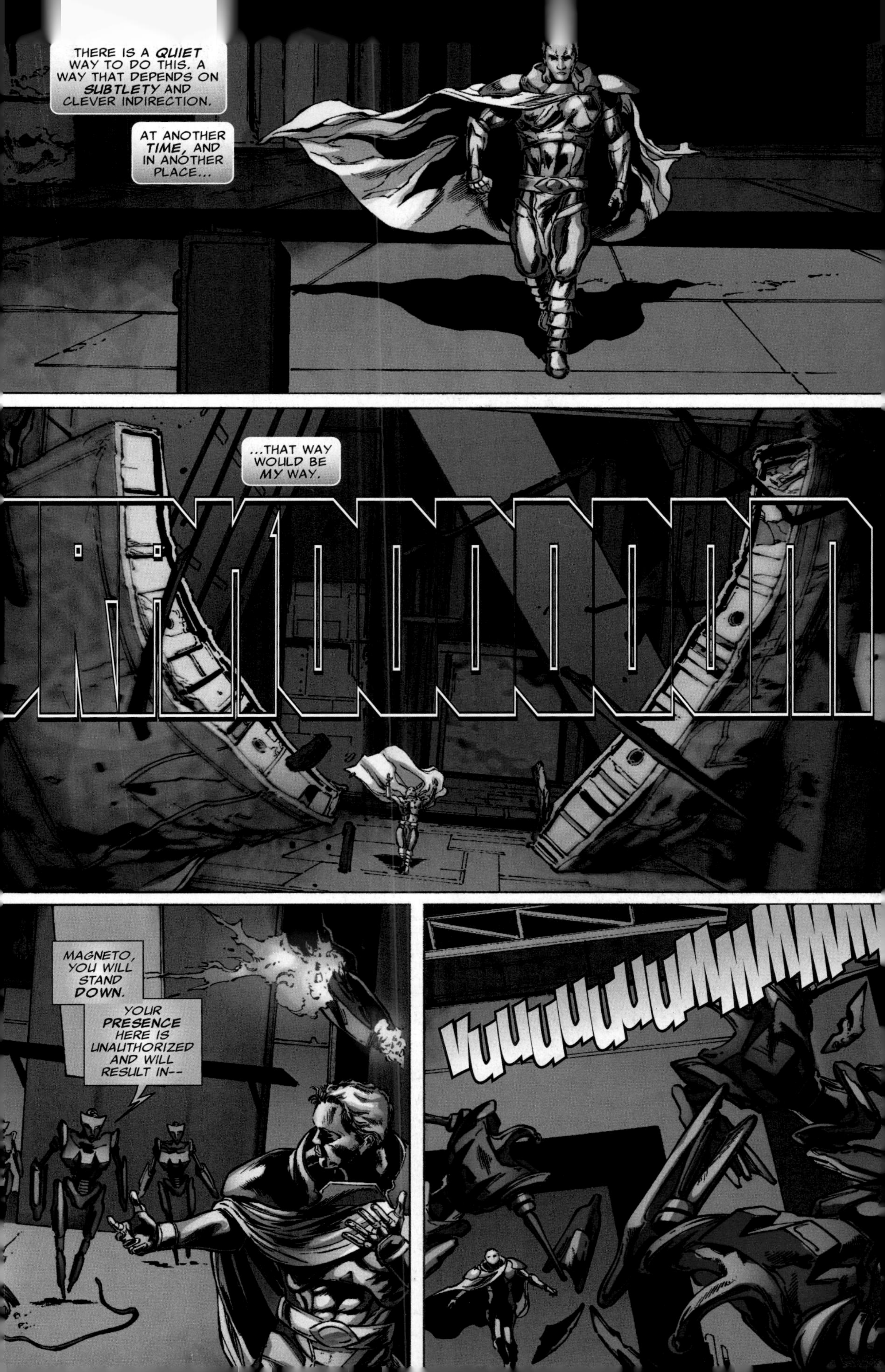
THERE IS A QUIET WAY TO DO THIS. A WAY THAT DEPENDS ON SUBTLETY AND CLEVER INDIRECTION.
AT ANOTHER TIME, AND IN ANOTHER PLACE...
...THAT WAY WOULD BE MY WAY.
MAGNETO, YOU WILL STAND DOWN.
YOUR PRESENCE HERE IS UNAUTHORIZED AND WILL RESULT IN--

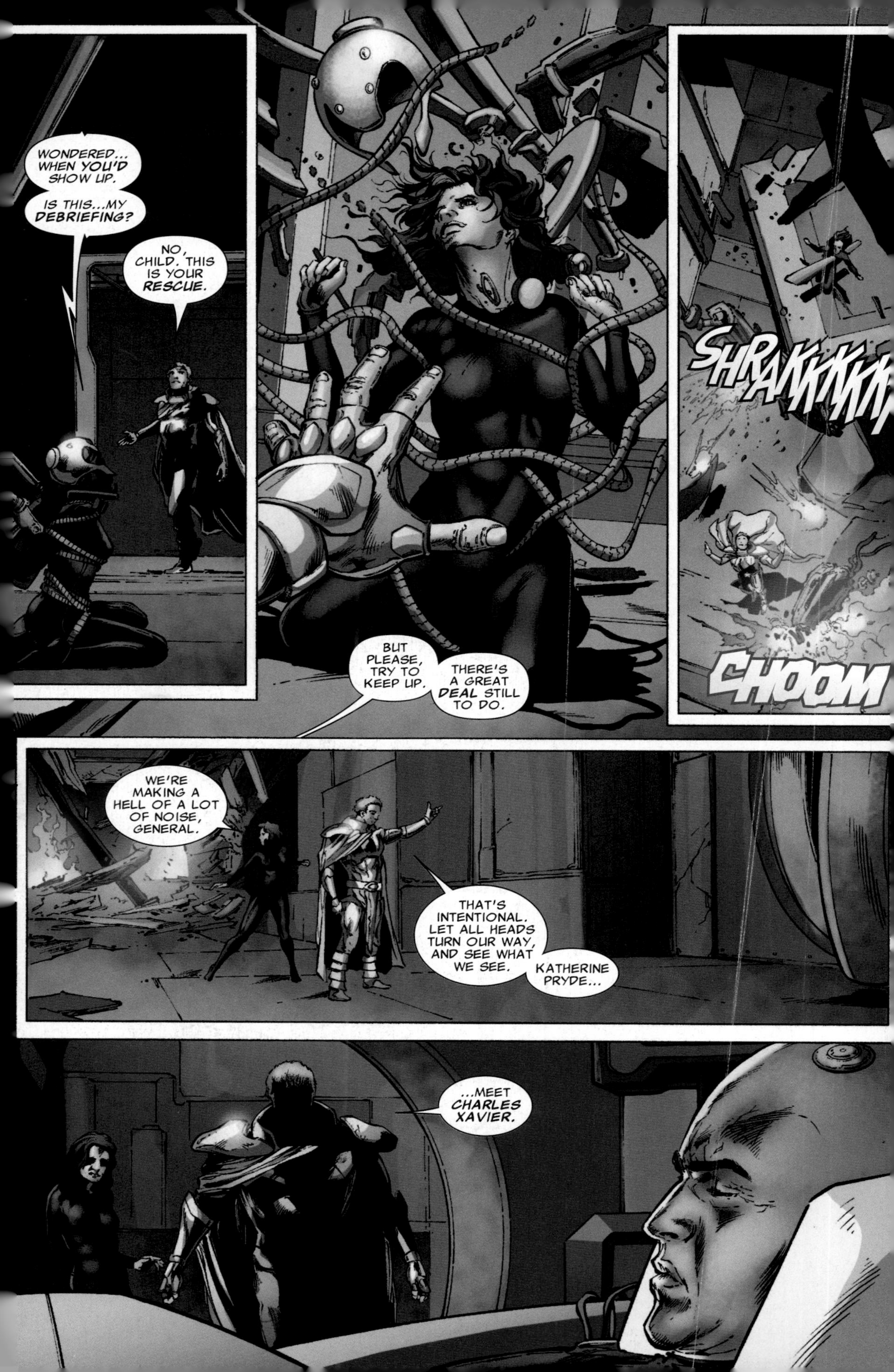
WONDERED... WHEN YOU'D SHOW UP.
IS THIS...MY DEBRIEFING?
NO, CHILD. THIS IS YOUR RESCUE.
SHRAKKKKK
CHOOM
BUT PLEASE, TRY TO KEEP UP.
THERE'S A GREAT DEAL STILL TO DO.
WE'RE MAKING A HELL OF A LOT OF NOISE, GENERAL.
THAT'S INTENTIONAL. LET ALL HEADS TURN OUR WAY, AND SEE WHAT WE SEE.
KATHERINE PRYDE...
...MEET CHARLES XAVIER.

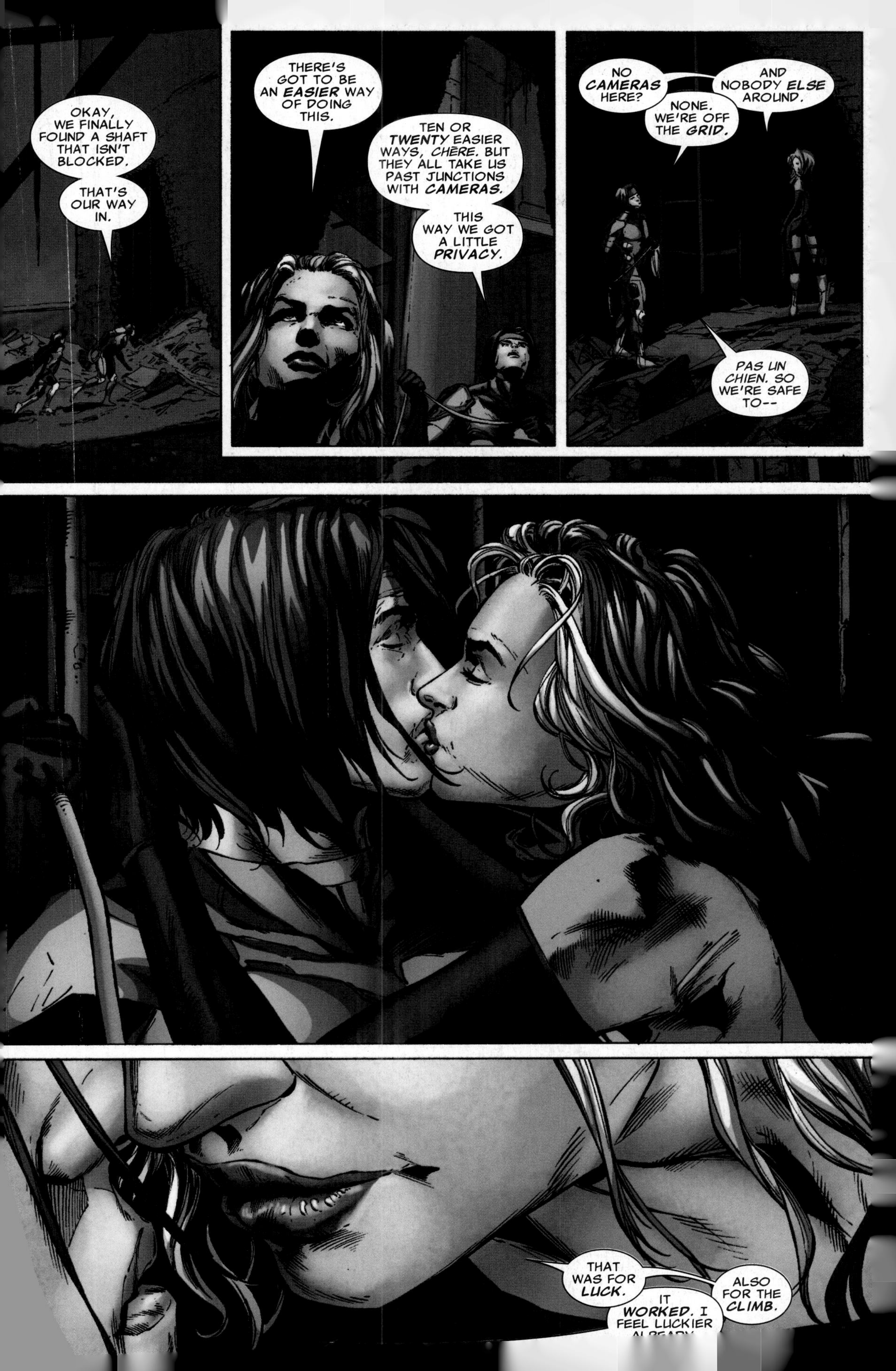
OKAY, WE FINALLY FOUND A SHAFT THAT ISN'T BLOCKED.
THAT'S OUR WAY IN.
THERE'S GOT TO BE AN EASIER WAY OF DOING THIS.
TEN OR TWENTY EASIER WAYS, CHÈRE. BUT THEY ALL TAKE US PAST JUNCTIONS WITH CAMERAS.
THIS WAY WE GOT A LITTLE PRIVACY.
NO CAMERAS HERE?
NONE. WE'RE OFF THE GRID.
AND NOBODY ELSE AROUND.
PAS UN CHIEN. SO WE'RE SAFE TO--
THAT WAS FOR LUCK.
ALSO FOR THE CLIMB.
IT WORKED. I FEEL LUCKIER

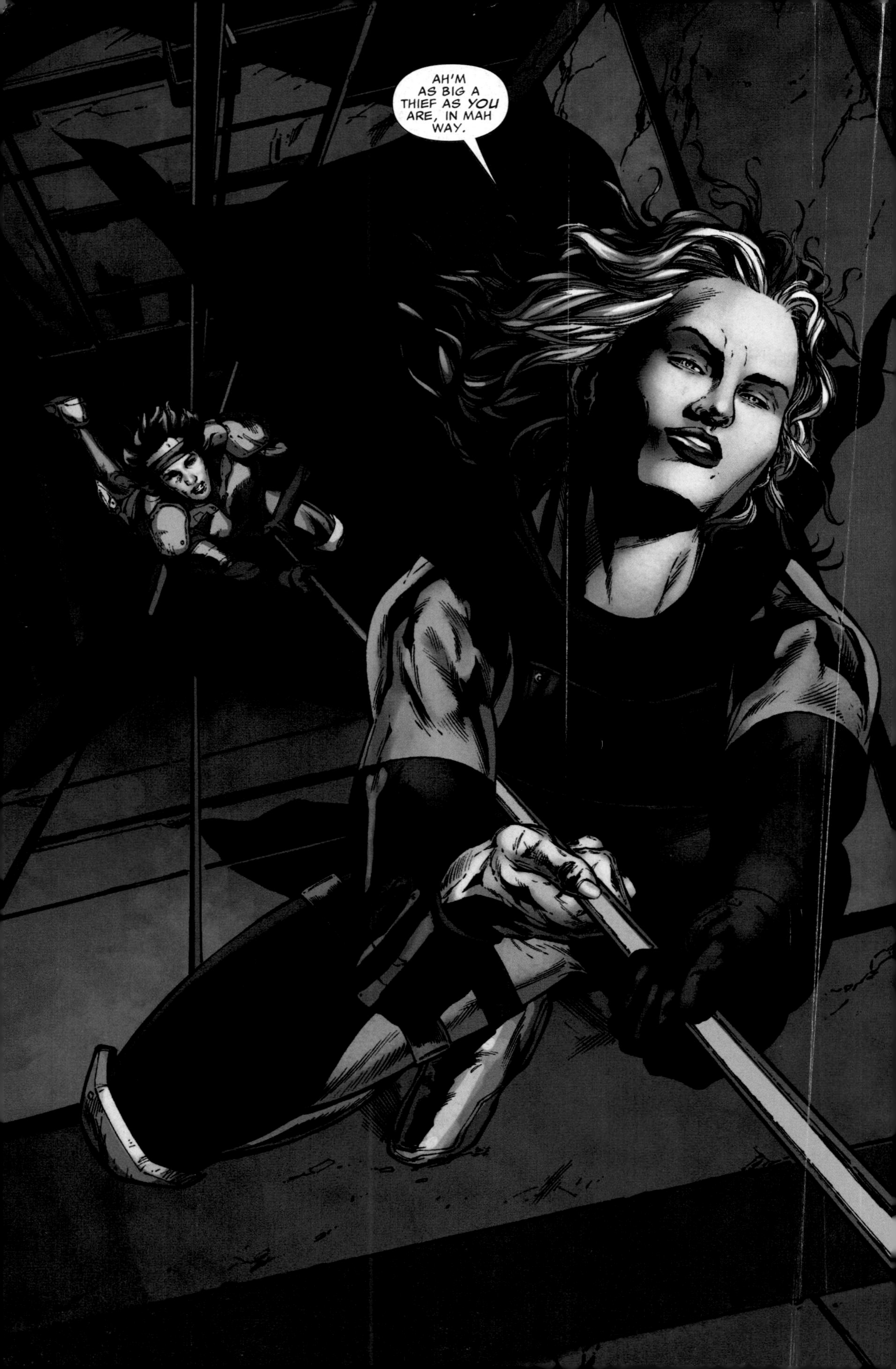
AH'M AS BIG A THIEF AS YOU ARE, IN MAH WAY.

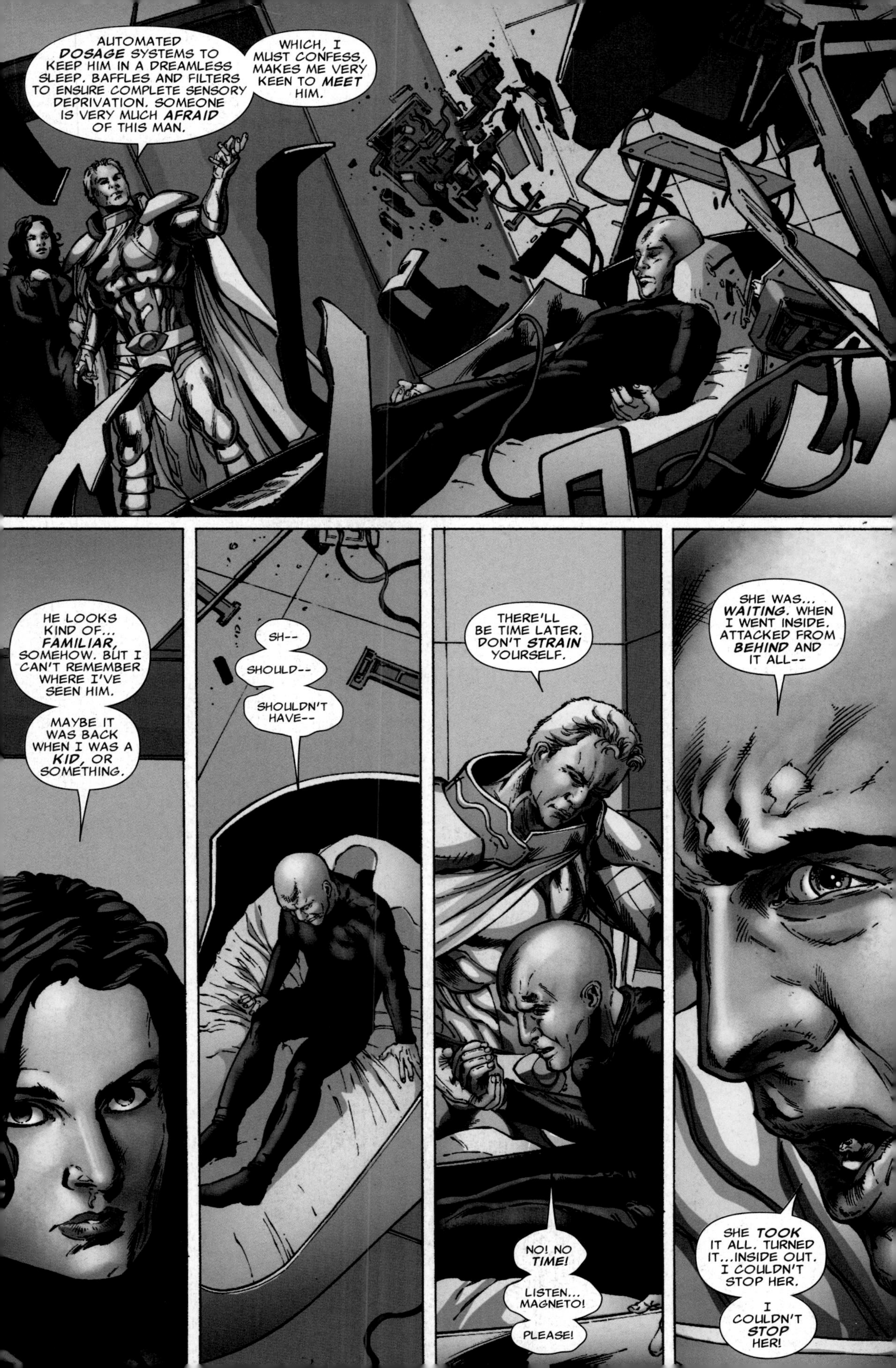
AUTOMATED DOSAGE SYSTEMS TO KEEP HIM IN A DREAMLESS SLEEP. BAFFLES AND FILTERS TO ENSURE COMPLETE SENSORY DEPRIVATION. SOMEONE IS VERY MUCH AFRAID OF THIS MAN.
WHICH, I MUST CONFESS, MAKES ME VERY KEEN TO MEET HIM.
HE LOOKS KIND OF... FAMILIAR, SOMEHOW. BUT I CAN'T REMEMBER WHERE I'VE SEEN HIM.
MAYBE IT WAS BACK WHEN I WAS A KID, OR SOMETHING.
SH--
SHOULD--
SHOULDN'T HAVE--
THERE'LL BE TIME LATER. DON'T STRAIN YOURSELF.
NO! NO TIME!
LISTEN... MAGNETO!
PLEASE!
SHE WAS... WAITING. WHEN I WENT INSIDE. ATTACKED FROM BEHIND AND IT ALL--
SHE TOOK IT ALL. TURNED IT...INSIDE OUT. I COULDN'T STOP HER.
I COULDN'T STOP HER!

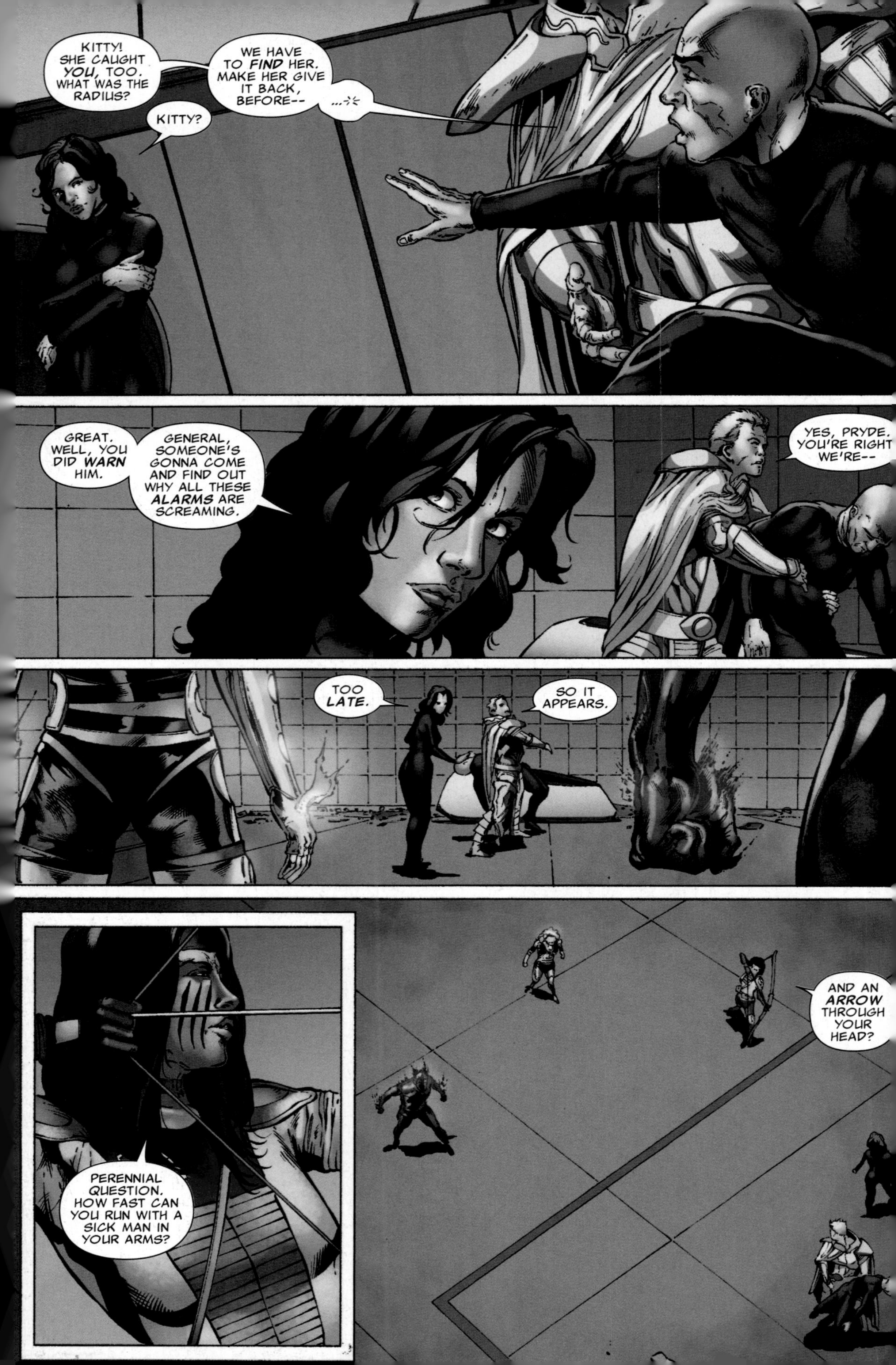
KITTY! SHE CAUGHT YOU, TOO. WHAT WAS THE RADIUS?
WE HAVE TO FIND HER. MAKE HER GIVE IT BACK, BEFORE--
KITTY?
GREAT. WELL, YOU DID WARN HIM.
GENERAL, SOMEONE'S GONNA COME AND FIND OUT WHY ALL THESE ALARMS ARE SCREAMING.
YES, PRYDE. YOU'RE RIGHT WE'RE--
TOO LATE.
SO IT APPEARS.
PERENNIAL QUESTION. HOW FAST CAN YOU RUN WITH A SICK MAN IN YOUR ARMS?
AND AN ARROW THROUGH YOUR HEAD?

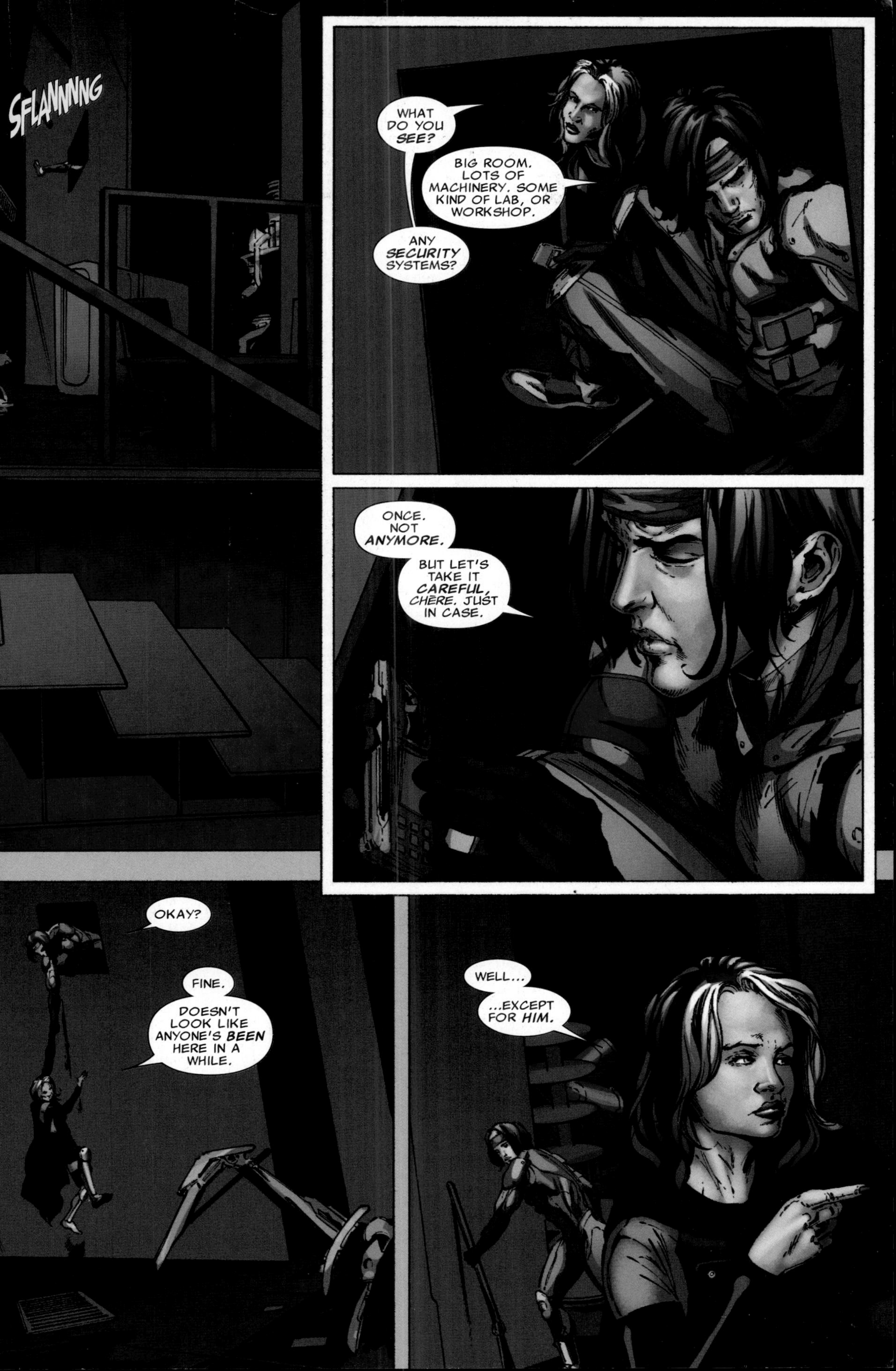
SFLANNNNG
WHAT DO YOU SEE?
BIG ROOM. LOTS OF MACHINERY. SOME KIND OF LAB, OR WORKSHOP.
ANY SECURITY SYSTEMS?
ONCE. NOT ANYMORE.
BUT LET'S TAKE IT CAREFUL, CHÈRE. JUST IN CASE.
OKAY?
FINE.
DOESN'T LOOK LIKE ANYONE'S BEEN HERE IN A WHILE.
WELL...
...EXCEPT FOR HIM.

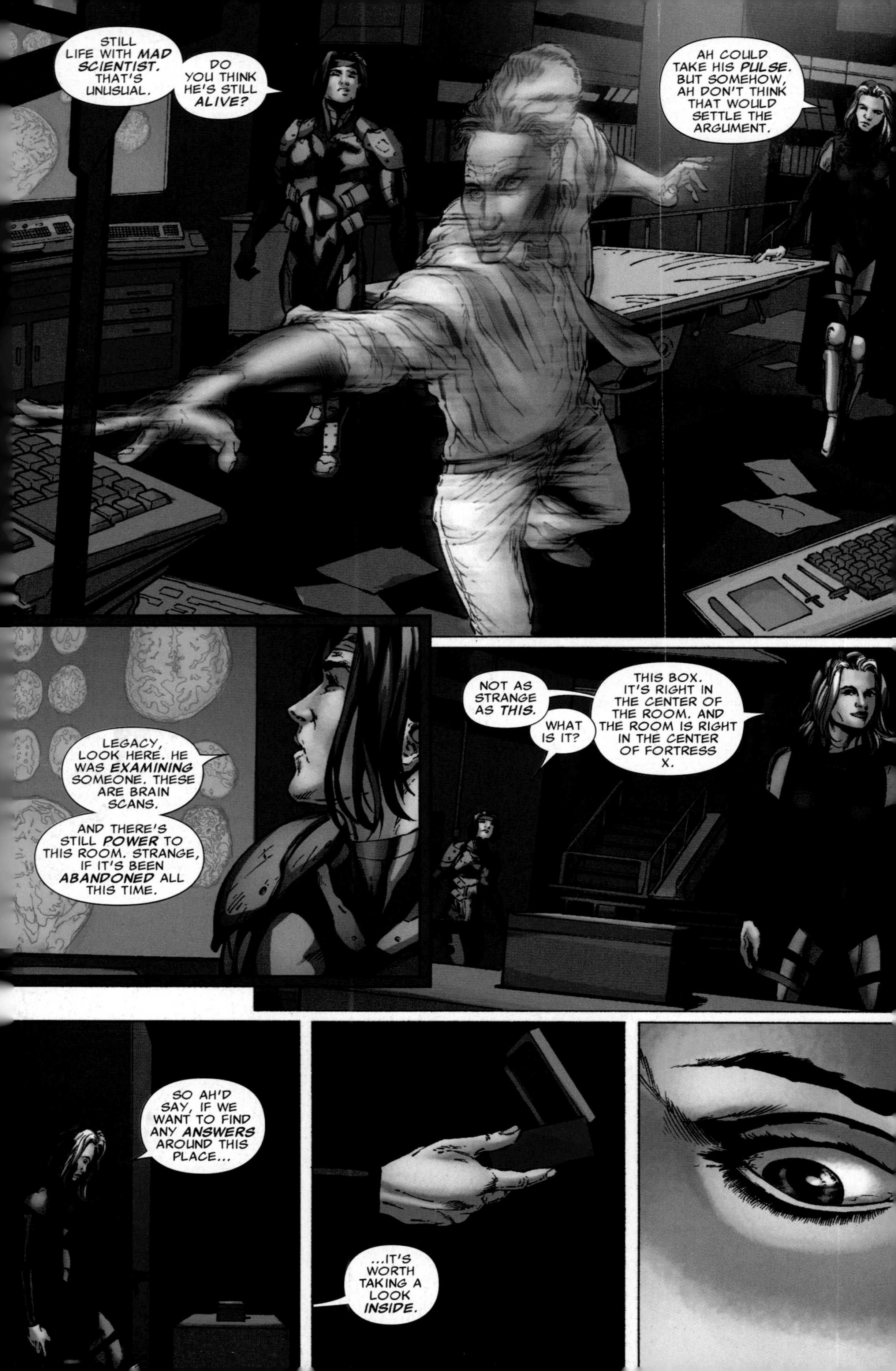
STILL LIFE WITH MAD SCIENTIST. THAT'S UNUSUAL.
DO YOU THINK HE'S STILL ALIVE?
AH COULD TAKE HIS PULSE. BUT SOMEHOW, AH DON'T THINK THAT WOULD SETTLE THE ARGUMENT.
LEGACY, LOOK HERE. HE WAS EXAMINING SOMEONE. THESE ARE BRAIN SCANS.
AND THERE'S STILL POWER TO THIS ROOM. STRANGE, IF IT'S BEEN ABANDONED ALL THIS TIME.
NOT AS STRANGE AS THIS.
WHAT IS IT?
THIS BOX. IT'S RIGHT IN THE CENTER OF THE ROOM. AND THE ROOM IS RIGHT IN THE CENTER OF FORTRESS X.
SO AH'D SAY, IF WE WANT TO FIND ANY ANSWERS AROUND THIS PLACE...
...IT'S WORTH TAKING A LOOK INSIDE.

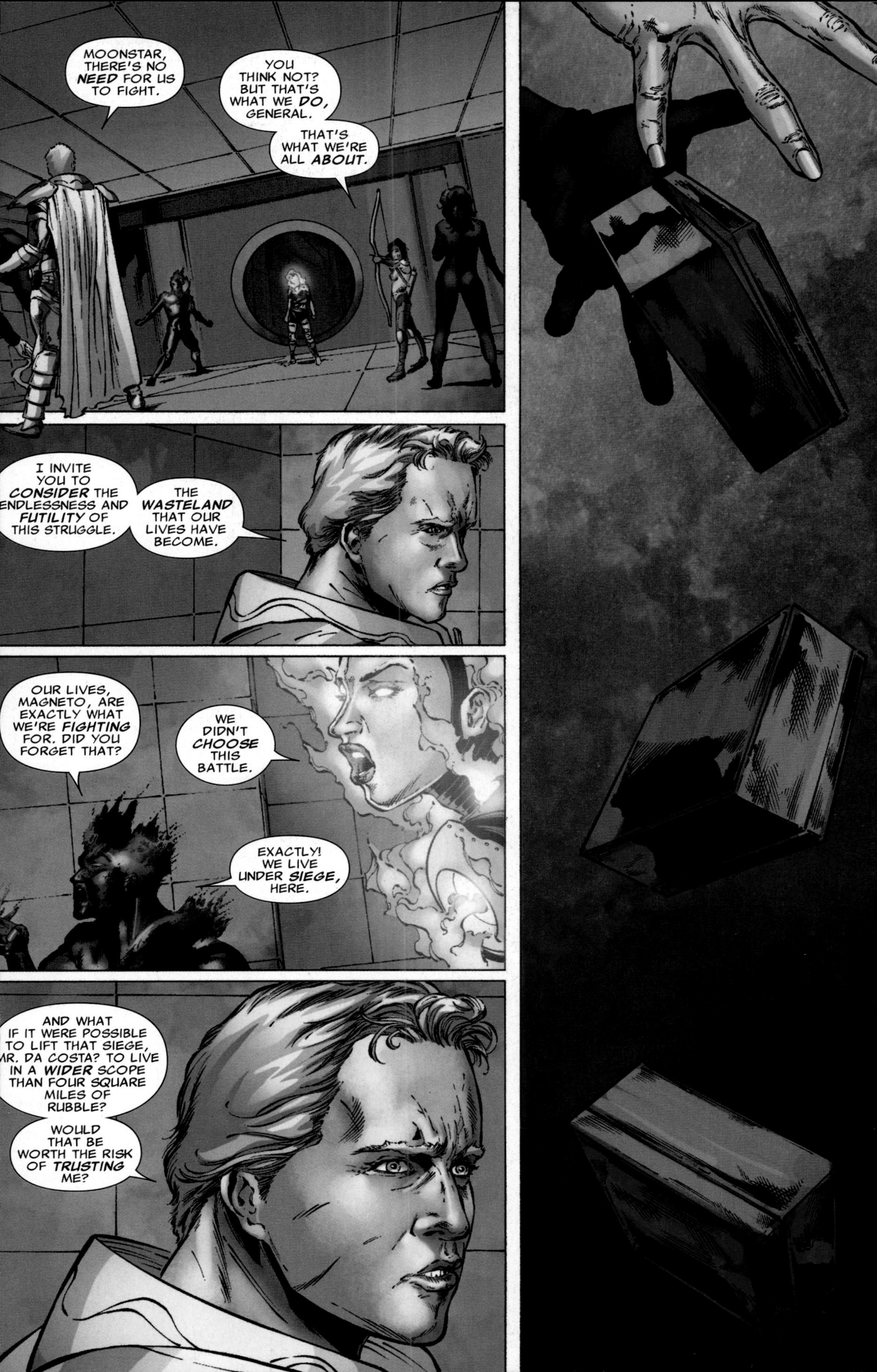

MOONSTAR, THERE'S NO NEED FOR US TO FIGHT.
YOU THINK NOT? BUT THAT'S WHAT WE DO, GENERAL.
THAT'S WHAT WE'RE ALL ABOUT.
I INVITE YOU TO CONSIDER THE ENDLESSNESS AND FUTILITY OF THIS STRUGGLE.
THE WASTELAND THAT OUR LIVES HAVE BECOME.
OUR LIVES, MAGNETO, ARE EXACTLY WHAT WE'RE FIGHTING FOR. DID YOU FORGET THAT?
WE DIDN'T CHOOSE THIS BATTLE.
EXACTLY! WE LIVE UNDER SIEGE, HERE.
AND WHAT IF IT WERE POSSIBLE TO LIFT THAT SIEGE, MR. DA COSTA? TO LIVE IN A WIDER SCOPE THAN FOUR SQUARE MILES OF RUBBLE?
WOULD THAT BE WORTH THE RISK OF TRUSTING ME?

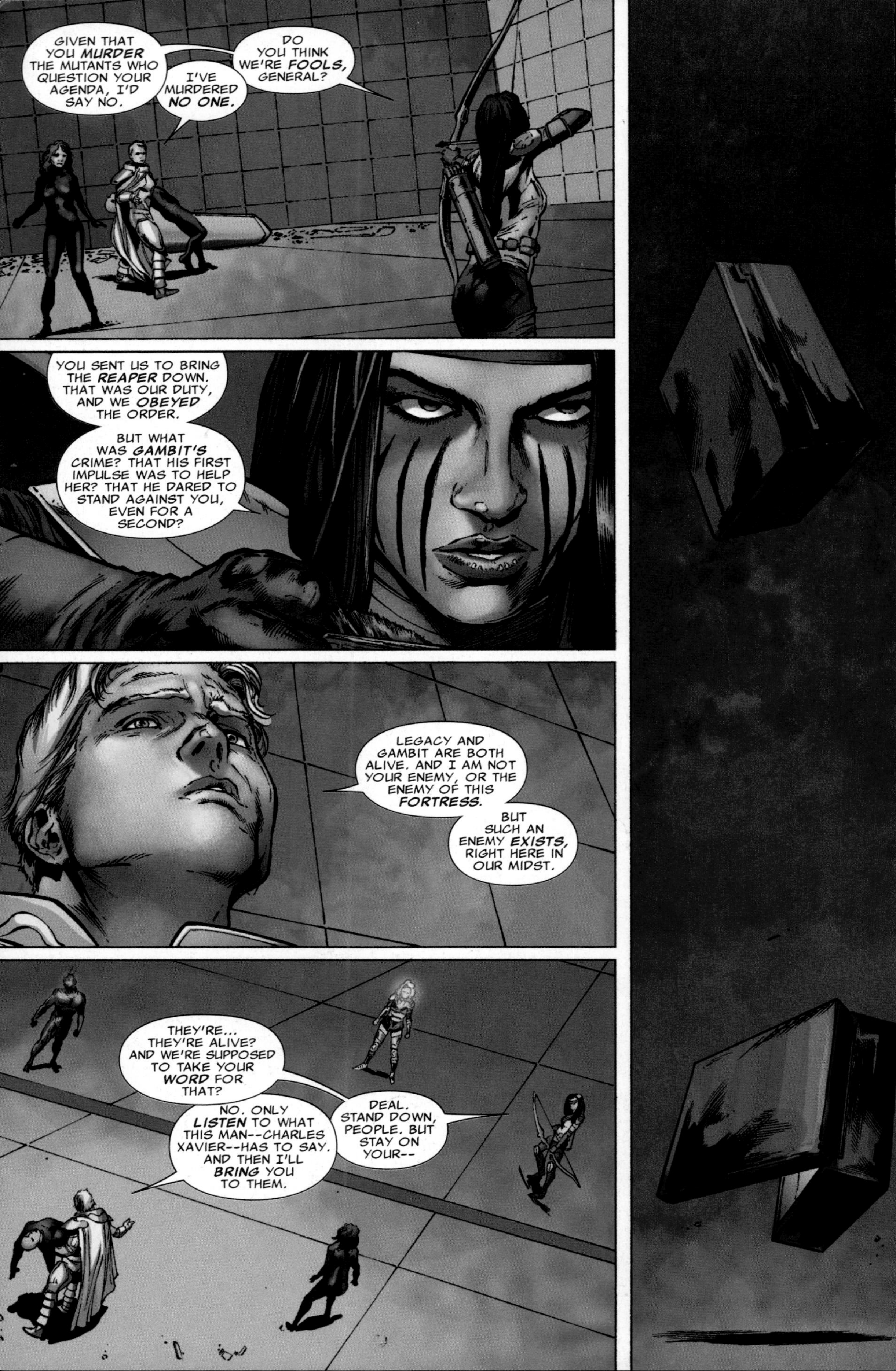
DO YOU THINK WE'RE FOOLS, GENERAL?
GIVEN THAT YOU MURDER THE MUTANTS WHO QUESTION YOUR AGENDA, I'D SAY NO.
I'VE MURDERED NO ONE.
YOU SENT US TO BRING THE REAPER DOWN. THAT WAS OUR DUTY, AND WE OBEYED THE ORDER.
BUT WHAT WAS GAMBIT'S CRIME? THAT HIS FIRST IMPULSE WAS TO HELP HER? THAT HE DARED TO STAND AGAINST YOU, EVEN FOR A SECOND?
LEGACY AND GAMBIT ARE BOTH ALIVE. AND I AM NOT YOUR ENEMY, OR THE ENEMY OF THIS FORTRESS.
BUT SUCH AN ENEMY EXISTS, RIGHT HERE IN OUR MIDST.
THEY'RE... THEY'RE ALIVE? AND WE'RE SUPPOSED TO TAKE YOUR WORD FOR THAT?
NO. ONLY LISTEN TO WHAT THIS MAN--CHARLES XAVIER--HAS TO SAY. AND THEN I'LL BRING YOU TO THEM.
DEAL. STAND DOWN, PEOPLE. BUT STAY ON YOUR--

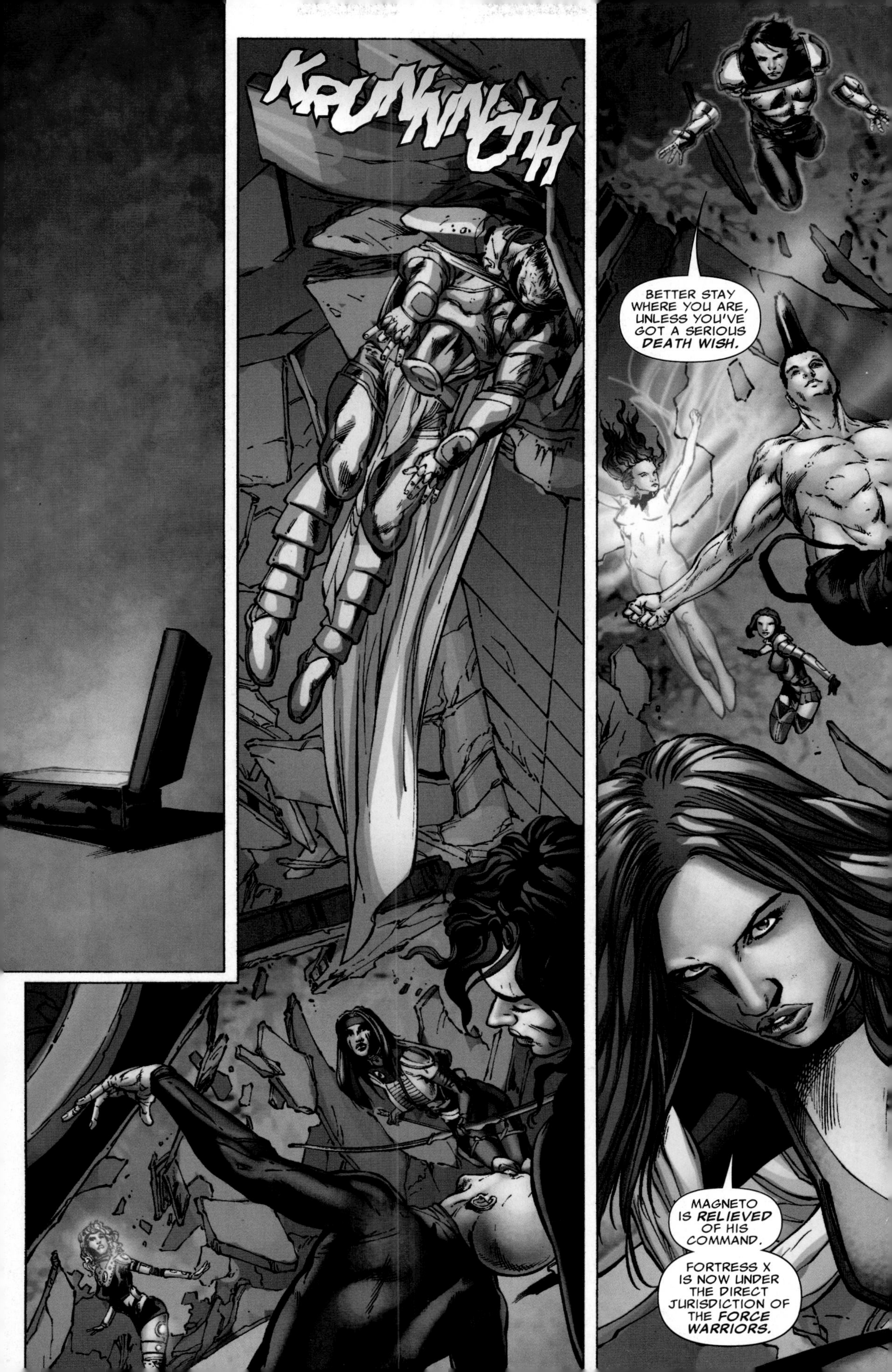
KRUNNNCHH
BETTER STAY WHERE YOU ARE, UNLESS YOU'VE GOT A SERIOUS DEATH WISH.
MAGNETO IS RELIEVED OF HIS COMMAND.
FORTRESS X IS NOW UNDER THE DIRECT JURISDICTION OF THE FORCE WARRIORS.

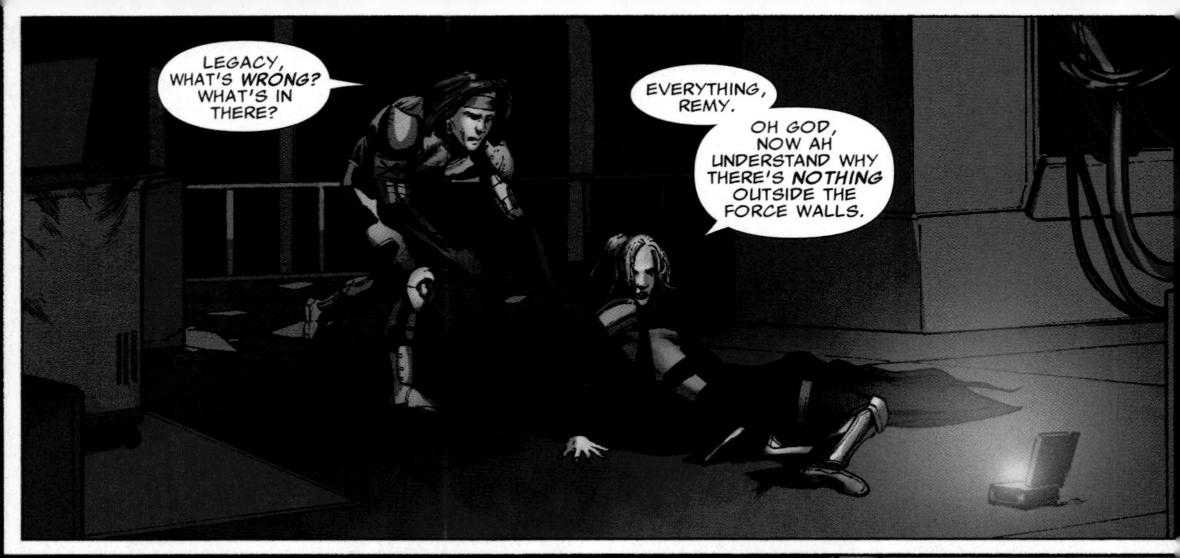
LEGACY, WHAT'S WRONG? WHAT'S IN THERE?
EVERYTHING, REMY.
OH GOD, NOW AH UNDERSTAND WHY THERE'S NOTHING OUTSIDE THE FORCE WALLS.

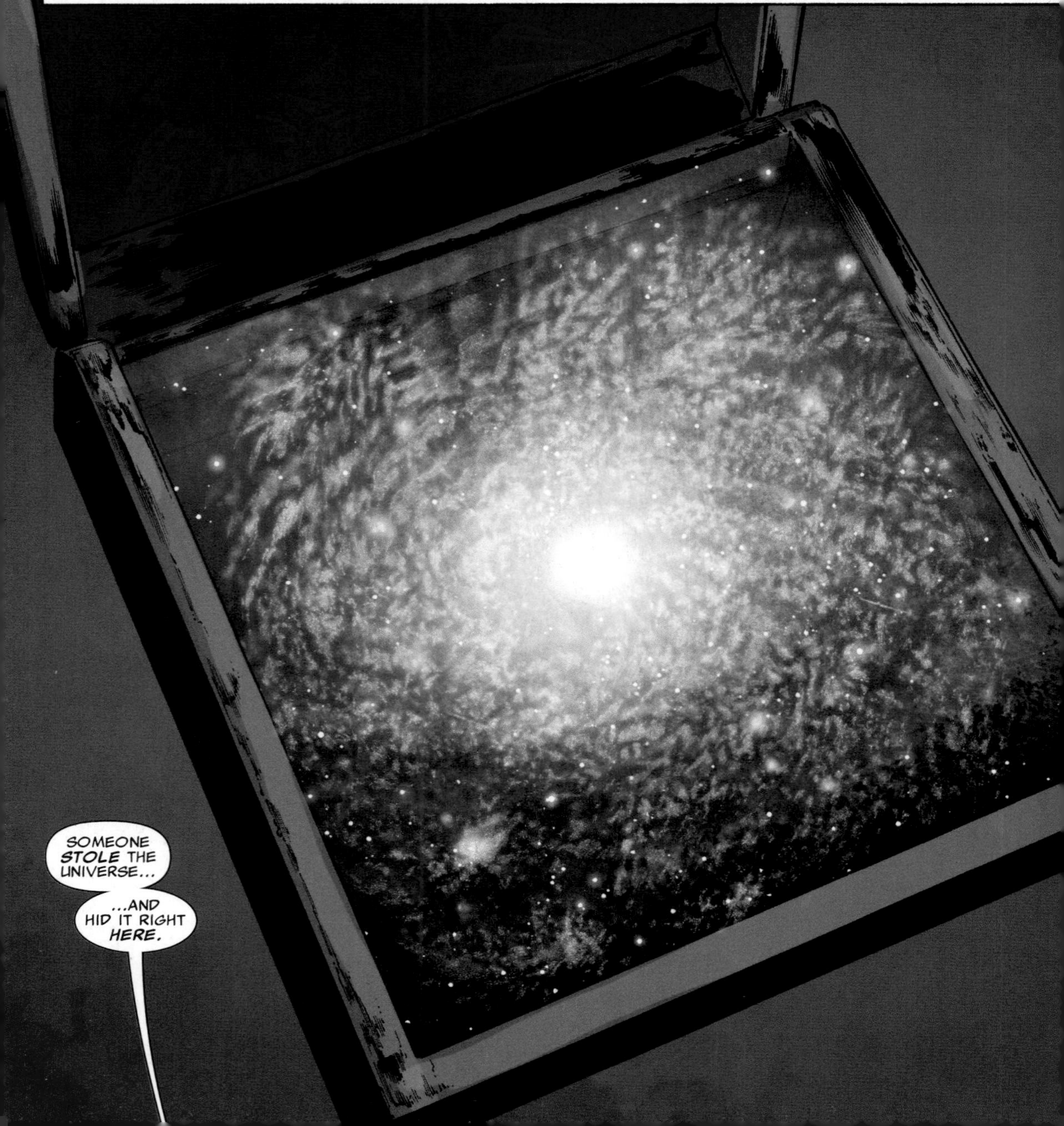
SOMEONE STOLE THE UNIVERSE...
...AND HID IT RIGHT HERE.

X-MEN LEGACY #247

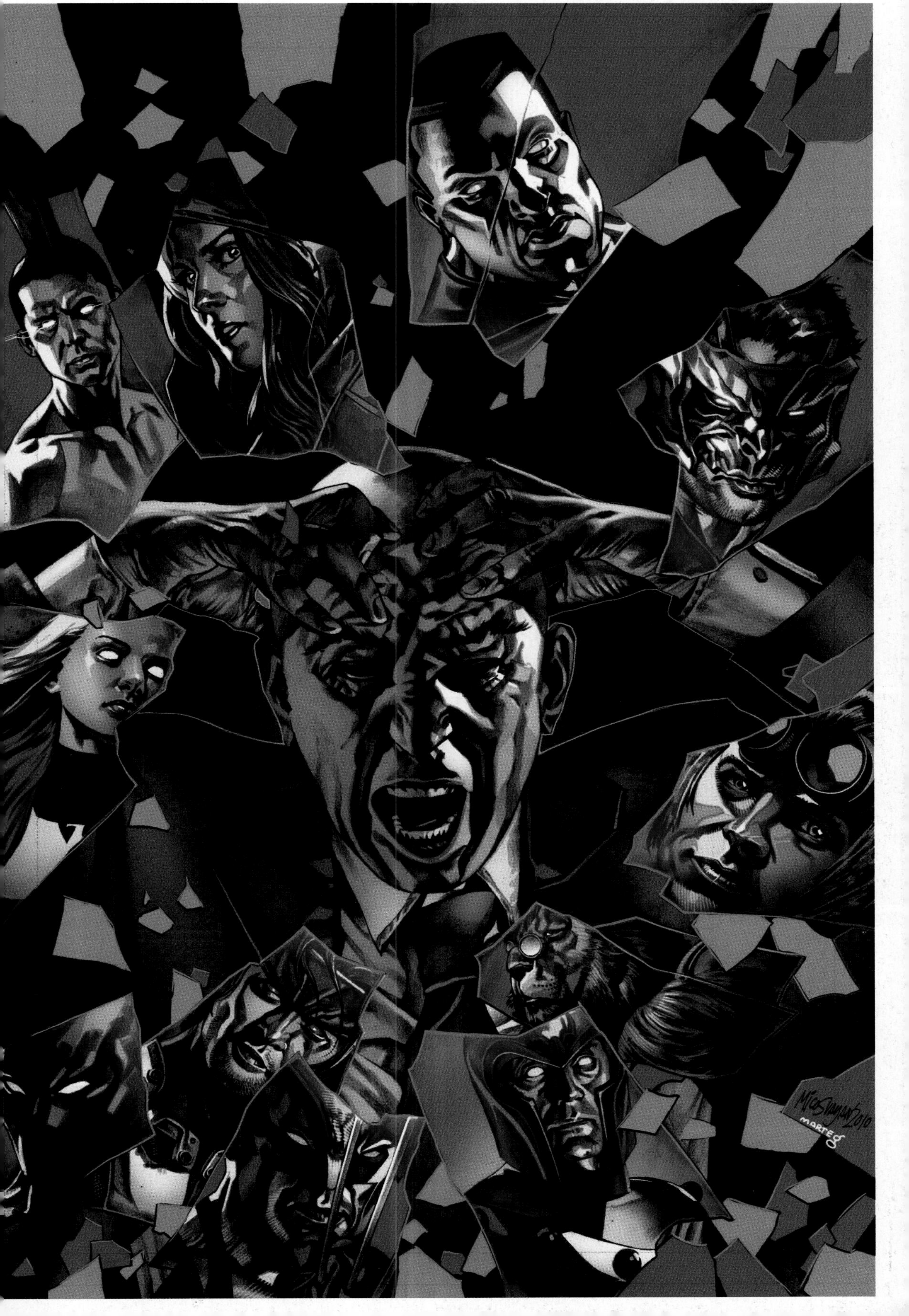

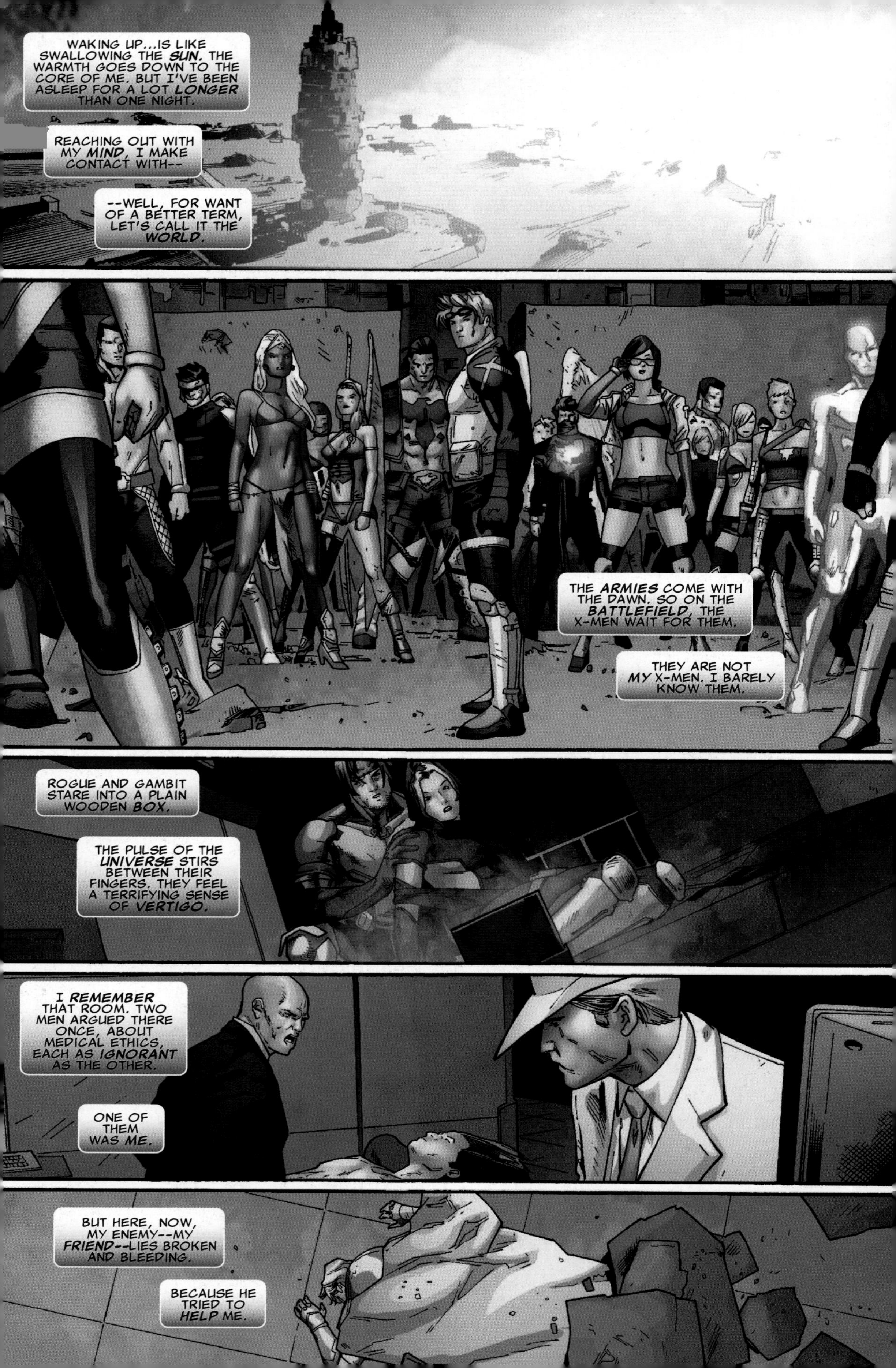
WAKING UP...IS LIKE SWALLOWING THE SUN. THE WARMTH GOES DOWN TO THE CORE OF ME. BUT I'VE BEEN ASLEEP FOR A LOT LONGER THAN ONE NIGHT.
REACHING OUT WITH MY MIND, I MAKE CONTACT WITH--
--WELL, FOR WANT OF A BETTER TERM, LET'S CALL IT THE WORLD.
THE ARMIES COME WITH THE DAWN. SO ON THE BATTLEFIELD, THE X-MEN WAIT FOR THEM.
THEY ARE NOT MY X-MEN. I BARELY KNOW THEM.
ROGUE AND GAMBIT STARE INTO A PLAIN WOODEN BOX.
THE PULSE OF THE UNIVERSE STIRS BETWEEN THEIR FINGERS. THEY FEEL A TERRIFYING SENSE OF VERTIGO.
I REMEMBER THAT ROOM. TWO MEN ARGUED THERE ONCE, ABOUT MEDICAL ETHICS, EACH AS IGNORANT AS THE OTHER.
ONE OF THEM WAS ME.
BUT HERE, NOW, MY ENEMY--MY FRIEND--LIES BROKEN AND BLEEDING.
BECAUSE HE TRIED TO HELP ME.

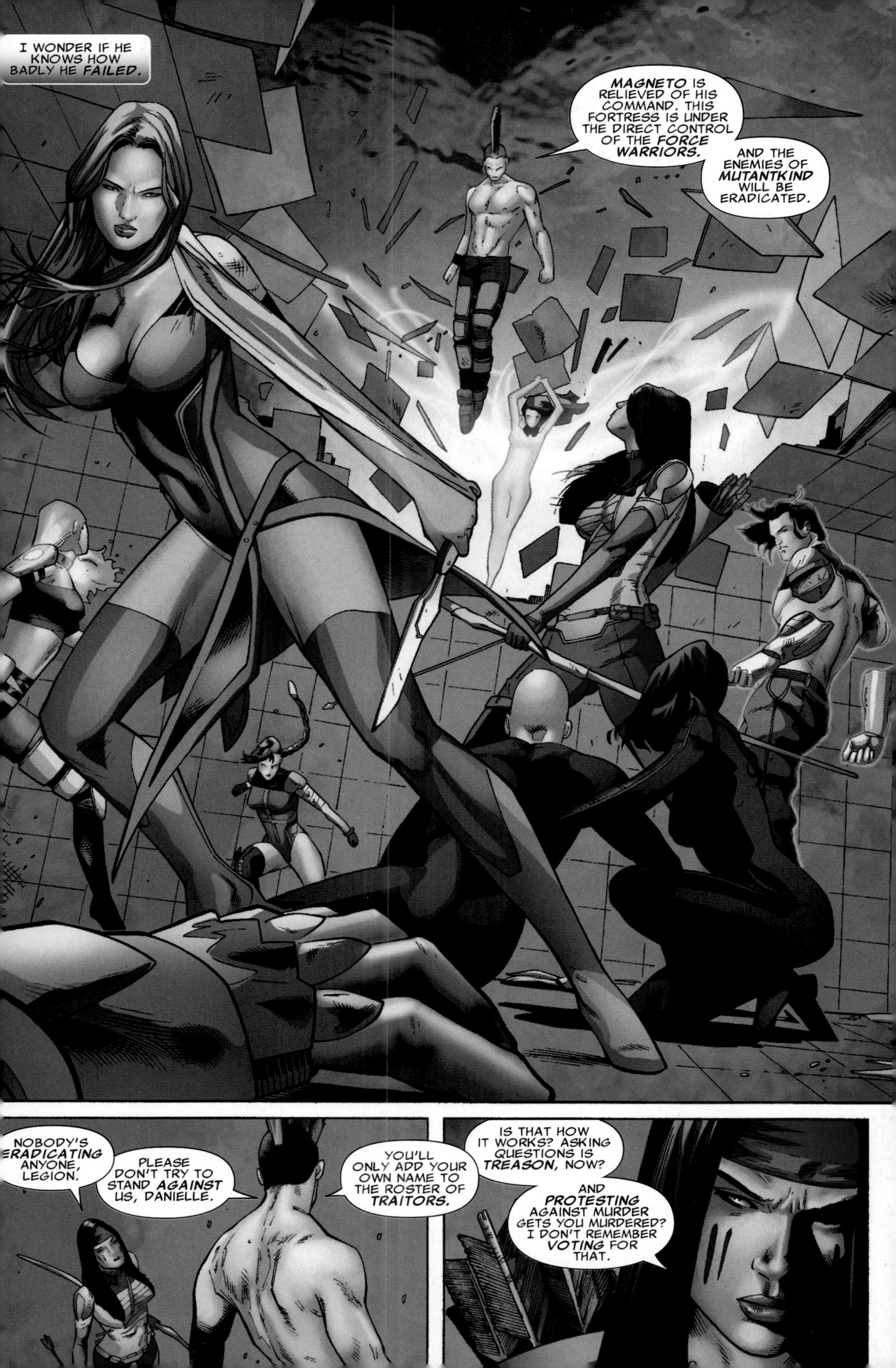
I WONDER IF HE KNOWS HOW BADLY HE FAILED.
MAGNETO IS RELIEVED OF HIS COMMAND. THIS FORTRESS IS UNDER THE DIRECT CONTROL OF THE FORCE WARRIORS.
AND THE ENEMIES OF MUTANTKIND WILL BE ERADICATED.
NOBODY'S ERADICATING ANYONE, LEGION.
PLEASE DON'T TRY TO STAND AGAINST US, DANIELLE.
YOU'LL ONLY ADD YOUR OWN NAME TO THE ROSTER OF TRAITORS.
IS THAT HOW IT WORKS? ASKING QUESTIONS IS TREASON, NOW?
AND PROTESTING AGAINST MURDER GETS YOU MURDERED? I DON'T REMEMBER VOTING FOR THAT.

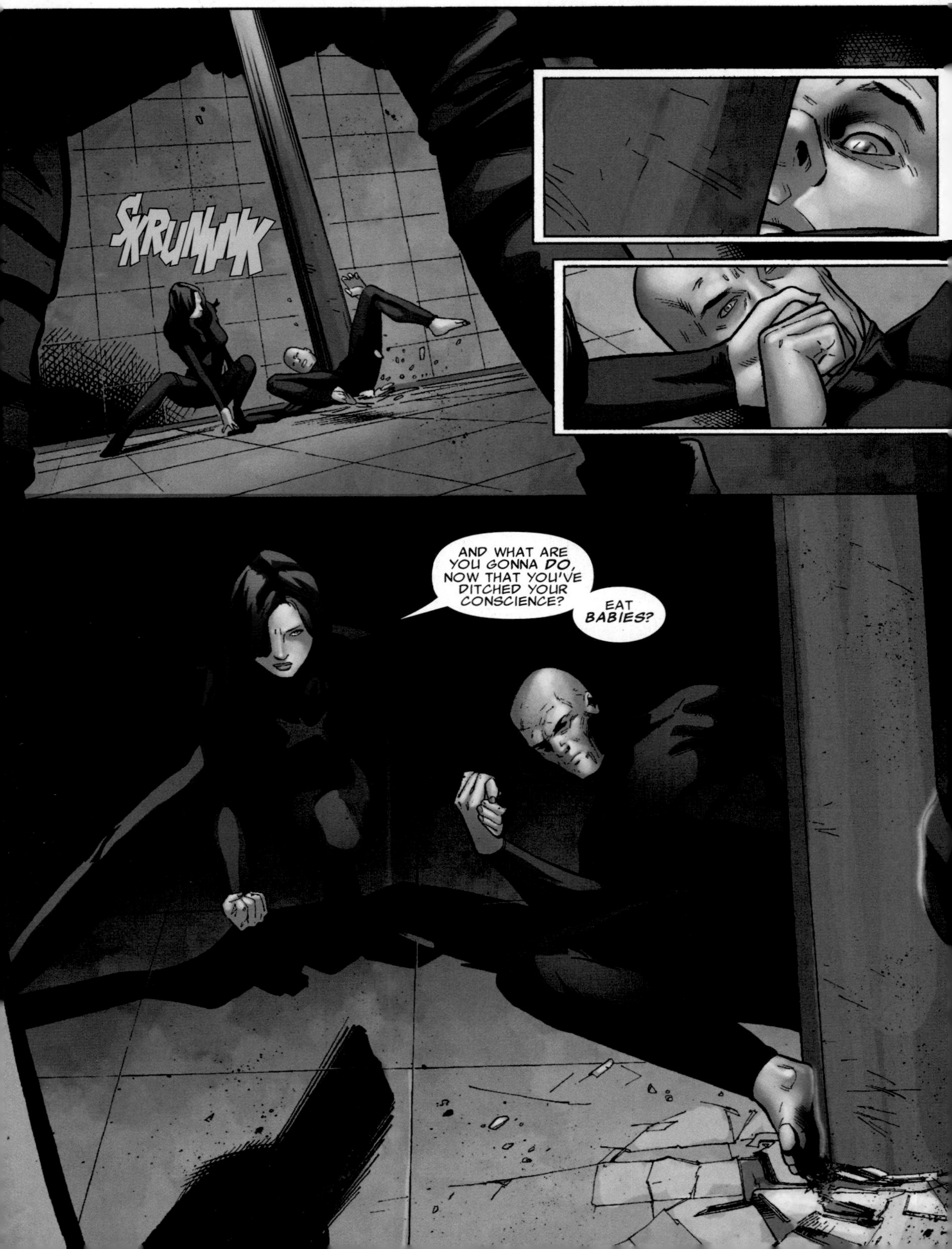
SKRUNNNK
AND WHAT ARE YOU GONNA DO, NOW THAT YOU'VE DITCHED YOUR CONSCIENCE?
EAT BABIES?

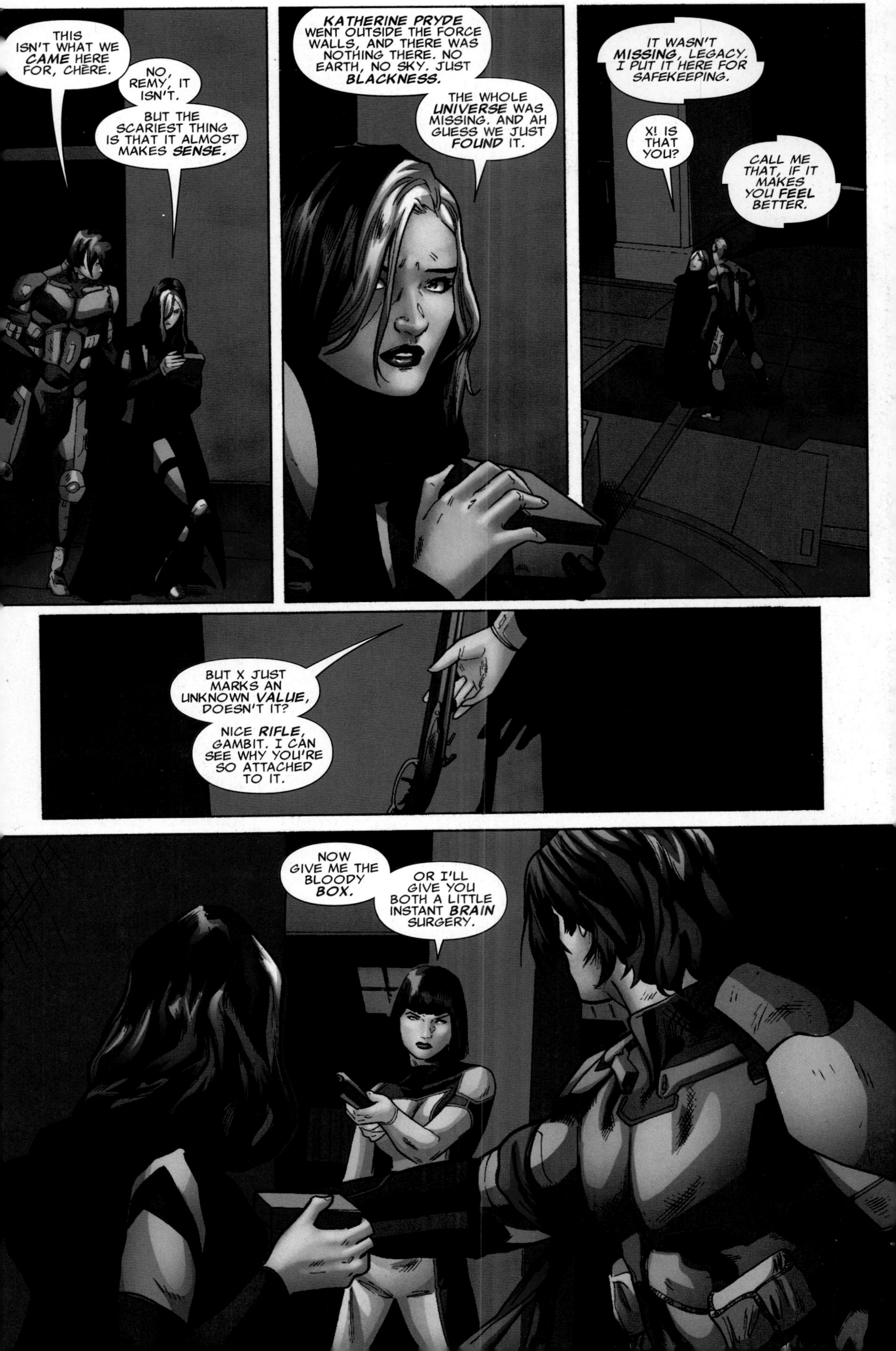

THIS ISN'T WHAT WE CAME HERE FOR, CHÈRE.
NO, REMY, IT ISN'T.
BUT THE SCARIEST THING IS THAT IT ALMOST MAKES SENSE.
KATHERINE PRYDE WENT OUTSIDE THE FORCE WALLS, AND THERE WAS NOTHING THERE. NO EARTH, NO SKY. JUST BLACKNESS.
THE WHOLE UNIVERSE WAS MISSING. AND AH GUESS WE JUST FOUND IT.
IT WASN'T MISSING, LEGACY. I PUT IT HERE FOR SAFEKEEPING.
X! IS THAT YOU?
CALL ME THAT, IF IT MAKES YOU FEEL BETTER.
BUT X JUST MARKS AN UNKNOWN VALUE, DOESN'T IT?
NICE RIFLE, GAMBIT. I CAN SEE WHY YOU'RE SO ATTACHED TO IT.
NOW GIVE ME THE BLOODY BOX.
OR I'LL GIVE YOU BOTH A LITTLE INSTANT BRAIN SURGERY.

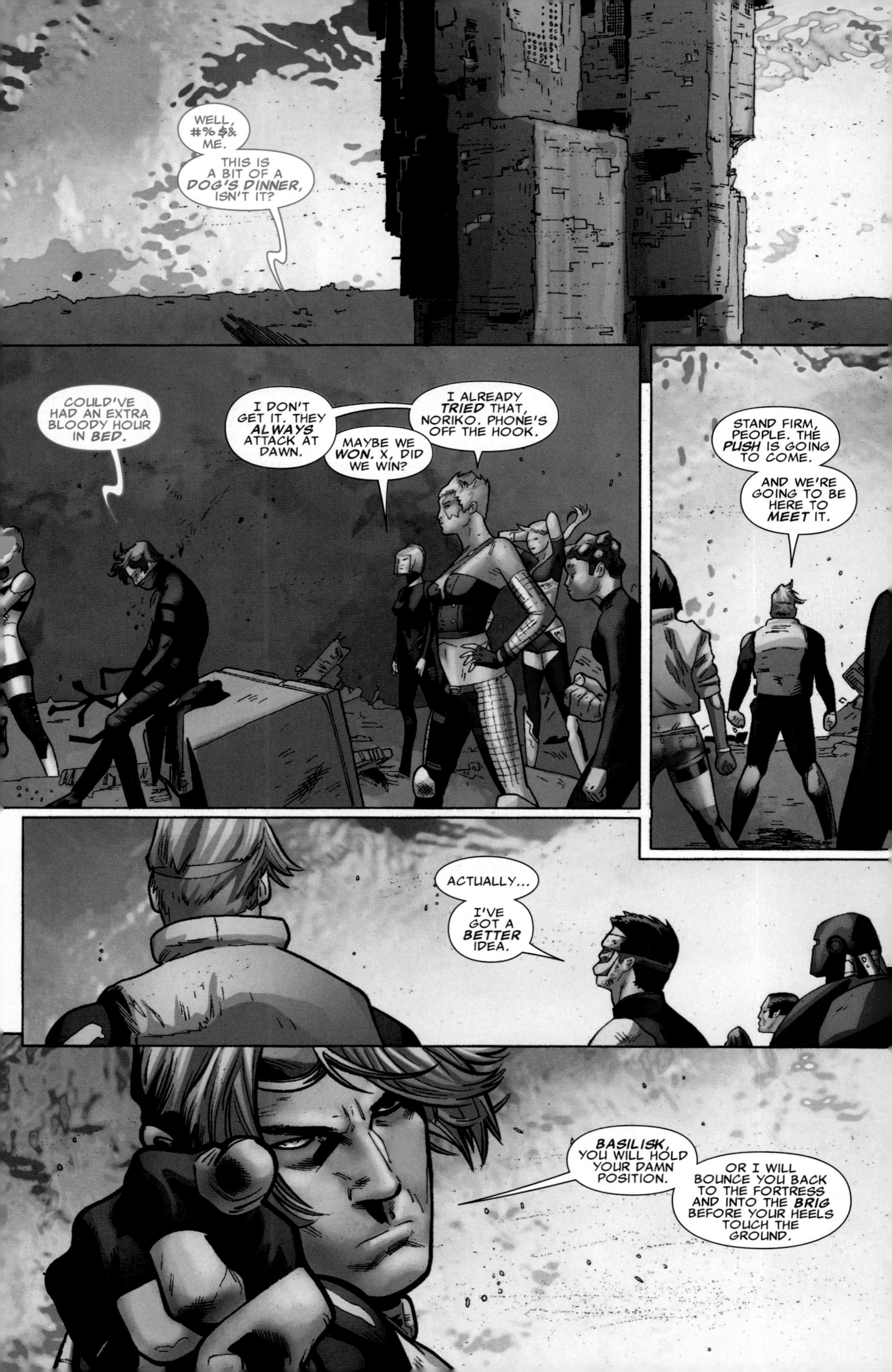
WELL, #%$& ME.
THIS IS A BIT OF A DOG'S DINNER, ISN'T IT?
COULD'VE HAD AN EXTRA BLOODY HOUR IN BED.
I DON'T GET IT. THEY ALWAYS ATTACK AT DAWN.
I ALREADY TRIED THAT, NORIKO. PHONE'S OFF THE HOOK.
MAYBE WE WON. X, DID WE WIN?
STAND FIRM, PEOPLE. THE PUSH IS GOING TO COME.
AND WE'RE GOING TO BE HERE TO MEET IT.
ACTUALLY...
I'VE GOT A BETTER IDEA.
BASILISK, YOU WILL HOLD YOUR DAMN POSITION.
OR I WILL BOUNCE YOU BACK TO THE FORTRESS AND INTO THE BRIG BEFORE YOUR HEELS TOUCH THE GROUND.

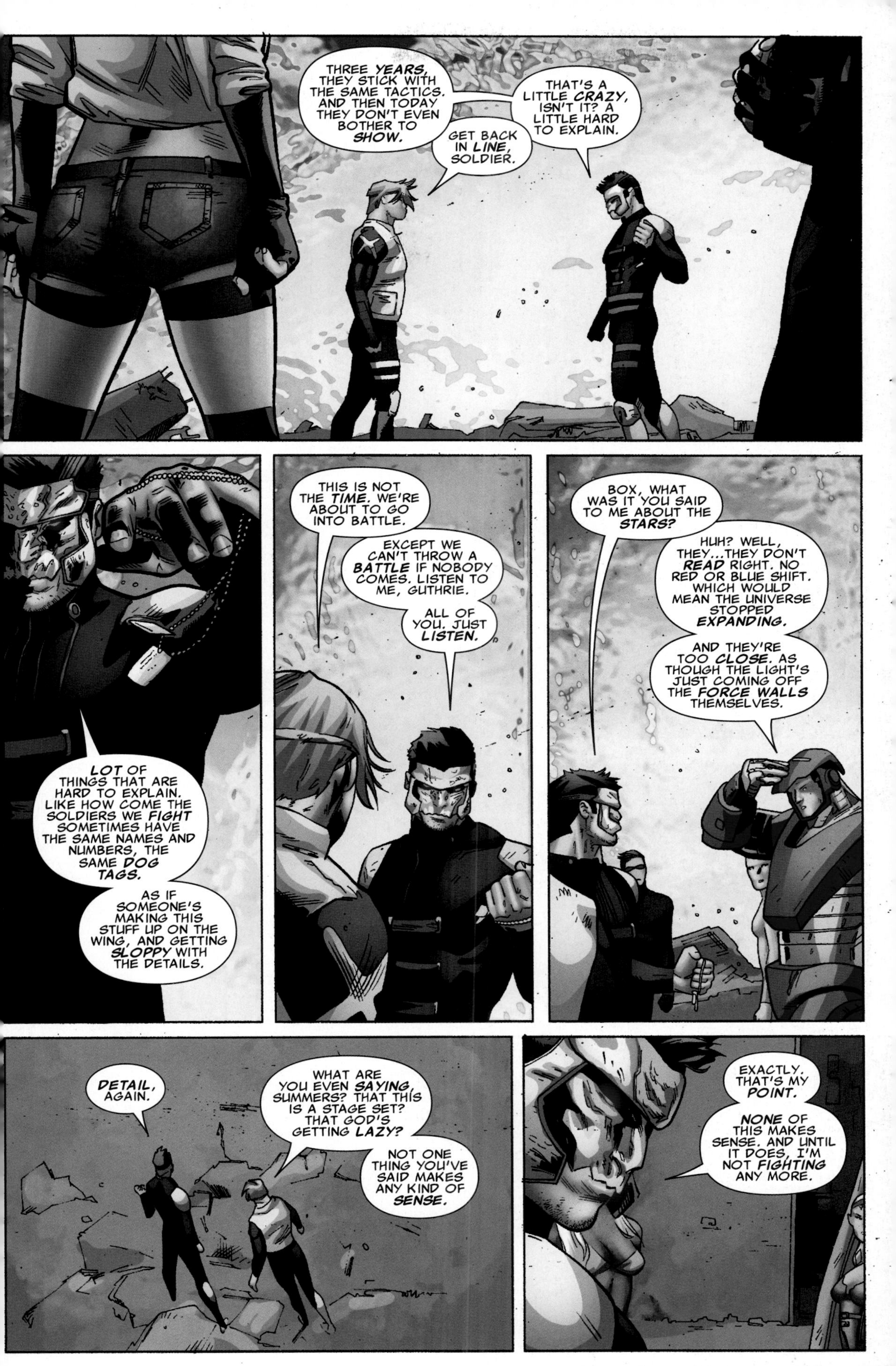
THREE YEARS, THEY STICK WITH THE SAME TACTICS. AND THEN TODAY THEY DON'T EVEN BOTHER TO SHOW.
THAT'S A LITTLE CRAZY, ISN'T IT? A LITTLE HARD TO EXPLAIN.
GET BACK IN LINE, SOLDIER.
LOT OF THINGS THAT ARE HARD TO EXPLAIN. LIKE HOW COME THE SOLDIERS WE FIGHT SOMETIMES HAVE THE SAME NAMES AND NUMBERS, THE SAME DOG TAGS.
AS IF SOMEONE'S MAKING THIS STUFF UP ON THE WING, AND GETTING SLOPPY WITH THE DETAILS.
THIS IS NOT THE TIME. WE'RE ABOUT TO GO INTO BATTLE.
EXCEPT WE CAN'T THROW A BATTLE IF NOBODY COMES. LISTEN TO ME, GUTHRIE.
ALL OF YOU. JUST LISTEN.
BOX, WHAT WAS IT YOU SAID TO ME ABOUT THE STARS?
HUH? WELL, THEY...THEY DON'T READ RIGHT. NO RED OR BLUE SHIFT. WHICH WOULD MEAN THE UNIVERSE STOPPED EXPANDING.
AND THEY'RE TOO CLOSE. AS THOUGH THE LIGHT'S JUST COMING OFF THE FORCE WALLS THEMSELVES.
DETAIL, AGAIN.
WHAT ARE YOU EVEN SAYING, SUMMERS? THAT THIS IS A STAGE SET? THAT GOD'S GETTING LAZY?
NOT ONE THING YOU'VE SAID MAKES ANY KIND OF SENSE.
EXACTLY. THAT'S MY POINT.
NONE OF THIS MAKES SENSE. AND UNTIL IT DOES, I'M NOT FIGHTING ANY MORE.

MY NEW JOB IS LOOKING FOR *ANSWERS*, AND I'M STARTING AT THE TOP.

ANYONE *ELSE* WHO'S INTERESTED CAN COME WITH ME.

YOU WILL HOLD *POSITION*.

EVERYONE WILL HOLD POSITION UNTIL THE *GENERAL* TELLS US OTHERWISE.

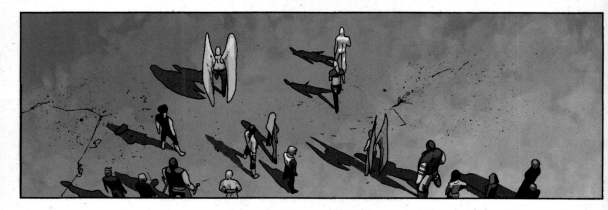

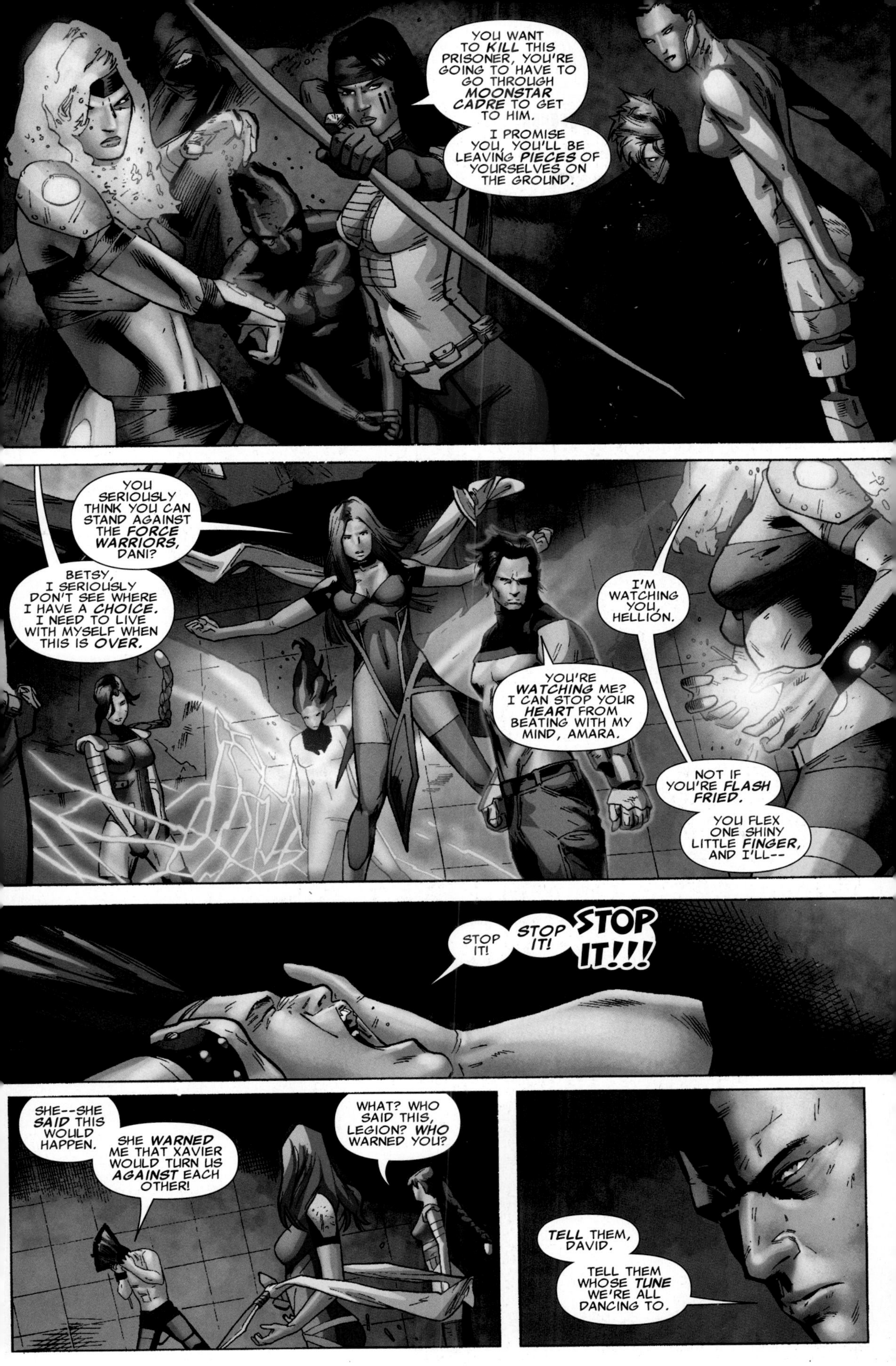
YOU WANT TO KILL THIS PRISONER, YOU'RE GOING TO HAVE TO GO THROUGH MOONSTAR CADRE TO GET TO HIM.
I PROMISE YOU, YOU'LL BE LEAVING PIECES OF YOURSELVES ON THE GROUND.
YOU SERIOUSLY THINK YOU CAN STAND AGAINST THE FORCE WARRIORS, DANI?
BETSY, I SERIOUSLY DON'T SEE WHERE I HAVE A CHOICE. I NEED TO LIVE WITH MYSELF WHEN THIS IS OVER.
I'M WATCHING YOU, HELLION.
YOU'RE WATCHING ME? I CAN STOP YOUR HEART FROM BEATING WITH MY MIND, AMARA.
NOT IF YOU'RE FLASH FRIED.
YOU FLEX ONE SHINY LITTLE FINGER, AND I'LL--
STOP IT!
STOP IT!
STOP IT!!!
SHE--SHE SAID THIS WOULD HAPPEN.
SHE WARNED ME THAT XAVIER WOULD TURN US AGAINST EACH OTHER!
WHAT? WHO SAID THIS, LEGION? WHO WARNED YOU?
TELL THEM, DAVID.
TELL THEM WHOSE TUNE WE'RE ALL DANCING TO.

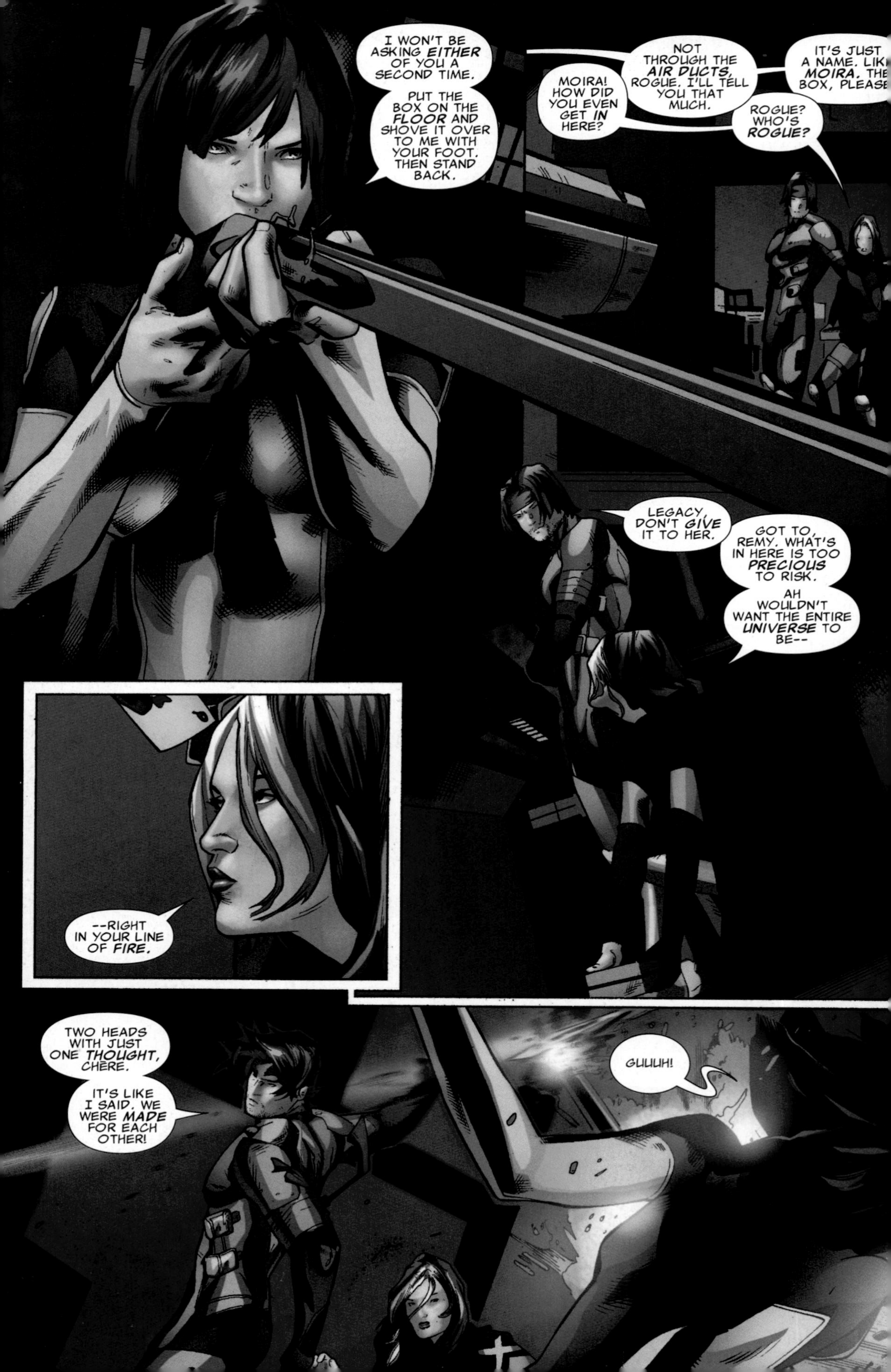

I WON'T BE ASKING EITHER OF YOU A SECOND TIME.
PUT THE BOX ON THE FLOOR AND SHOVE IT OVER TO ME WITH YOUR FOOT. THEN STAND BACK.
MOIRA! HOW DID YOU EVEN GET IN HERE?
NOT THROUGH THE AIR DUCTS, ROGUE. I'LL TELL YOU THAT MUCH.
IT'S JUST A NAME. LIK MOIRA. THE BOX, PLEASE
ROGUE? WHO'S ROGUE?
LEGACY, DON'T GIVE IT TO HER.
GOT TO, REMY. WHAT'S IN HERE IS TOO PRECIOUS TO RISK.
AH WOULDN'T WANT THE ENTIRE UNIVERSE TO BE--
--RIGHT IN YOUR LINE OF FIRE.
TWO HEADS WITH JUST ONE THOUGHT, CHÈRE.
IT'S LIKE I SAID. WE WERE MADE FOR EACH OTHER!
GUUUH!

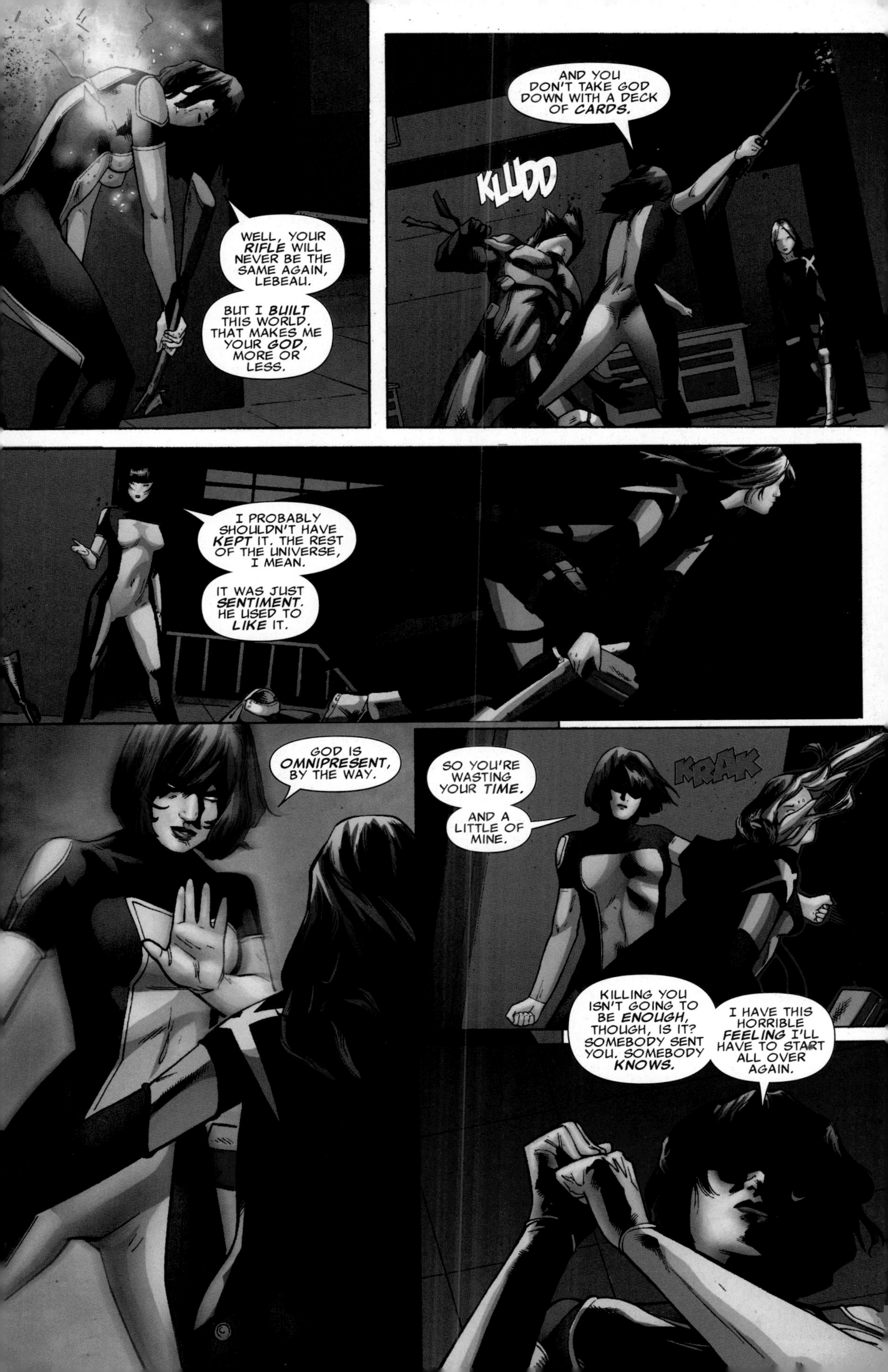
WELL, YOUR RIFLE WILL NEVER BE THE SAME AGAIN, LEBEAU.
BUT I BUILT THIS WORLD. THAT MAKES ME YOUR GOD, MORE OR LESS.
AND YOU DON'T TAKE GOD DOWN WITH A DECK OF CARDS.
KLUDD
I PROBABLY SHOULDN'T HAVE KEPT IT. THE REST OF THE UNIVERSE, I MEAN.
IT WAS JUST SENTIMENT. HE USED TO LIKE IT.
GOD IS OMNIPRESENT, BY THE WAY.
SO YOU'RE WASTING YOUR TIME.
AND A LITTLE OF MINE.
KRAK
KILLING YOU ISN'T GOING TO BE ENOUGH, THOUGH, IS IT? SOMEBODY SENT YOU. SOMEBODY KNOWS.
I HAVE THIS HORRIBLE FEELING I'LL HAVE TO START ALL OVER AGAIN.

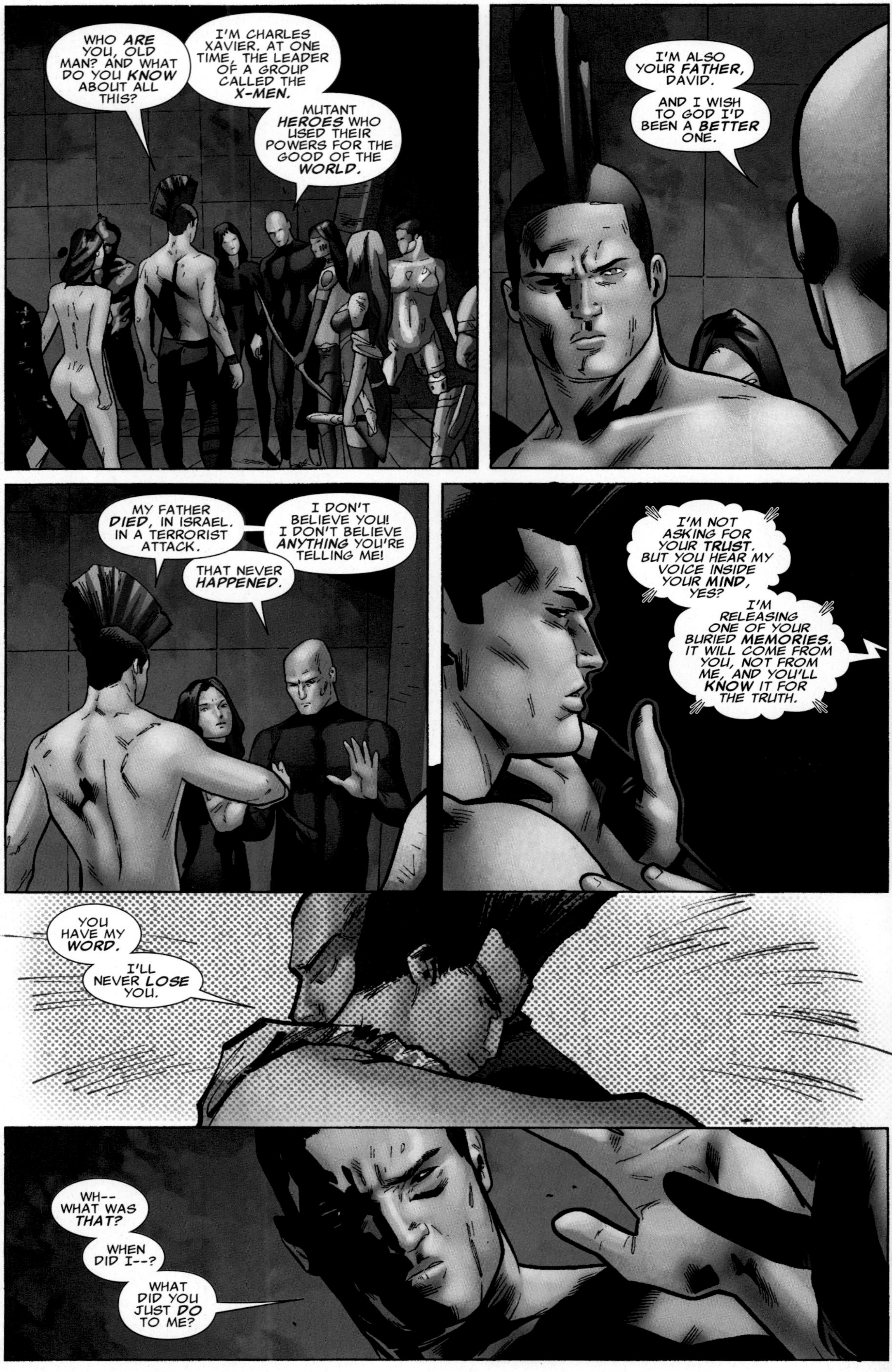
WHO ARE YOU, OLD MAN? AND WHAT DO YOU KNOW ABOUT ALL THIS?
I'M CHARLES XAVIER. AT ONE TIME, THE LEADER OF A GROUP CALLED THE X-MEN.
MUTANT HEROES WHO USED THEIR POWERS FOR THE GOOD OF THE WORLD.
I'M ALSO YOUR FATHER, DAVID.
AND I WISH TO GOD I'D BEEN A BETTER ONE.
MY FATHER DIED, IN ISRAEL. IN A TERRORIST ATTACK.
I DON'T BELIEVE YOU! I DON'T BELIEVE ANYTHING YOU'RE TELLING ME!
THAT NEVER HAPPENED.
I'M NOT ASKING FOR YOUR TRUST. BUT YOU HEAR MY VOICE INSIDE YOUR MIND, YES?
I'M RELEASING ONE OF YOUR BURIED MEMORIES. IT WILL COME FROM YOU, NOT FROM ME, AND YOU'LL KNOW IT FOR THE TRUTH.
YOU HAVE MY WORD.
I'LL NEVER LOSE YOU.
WH-- WHAT WAS THAT?
WHEN DID I--?
WHAT DID YOU JUST DO TO ME?

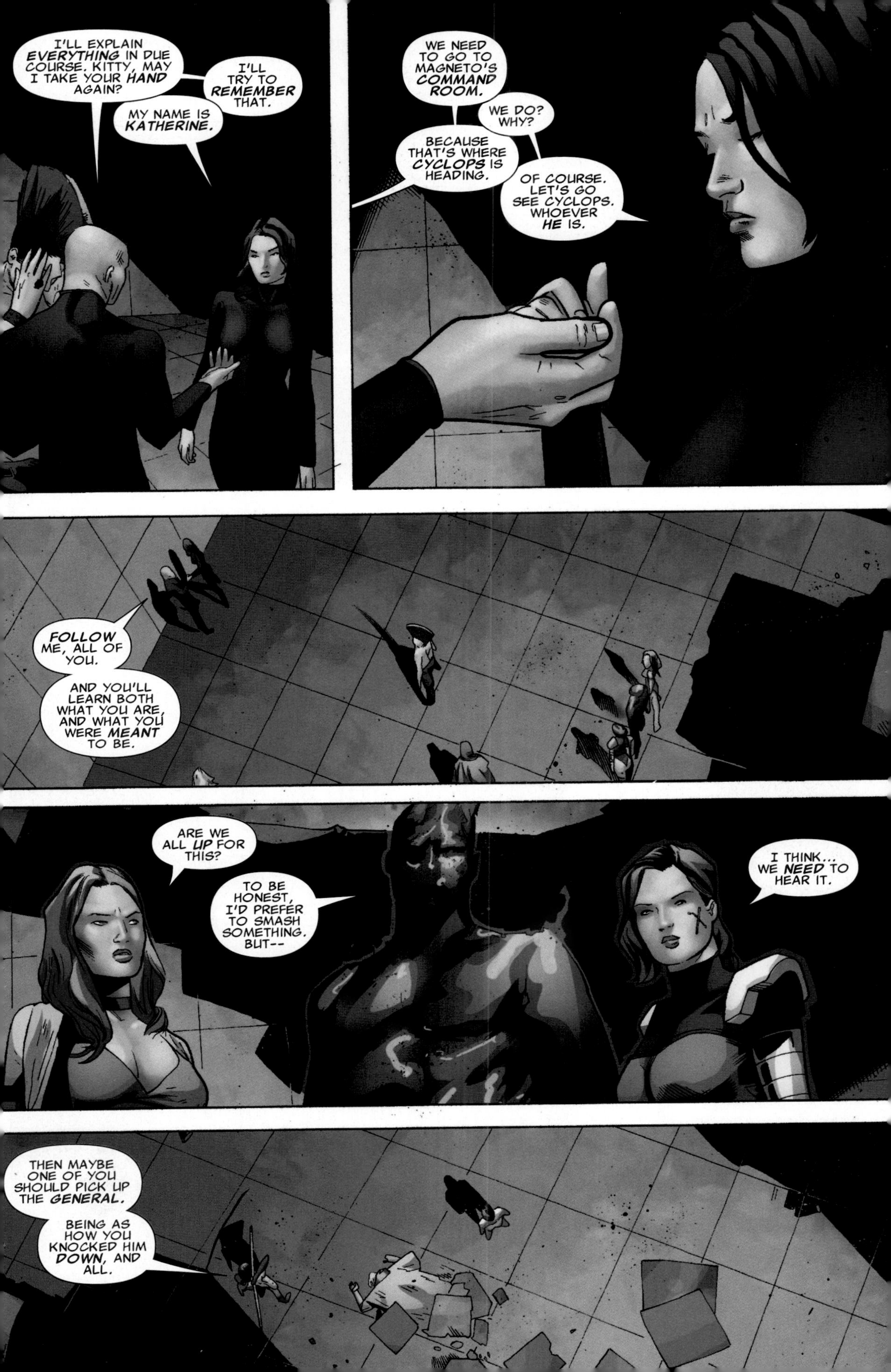
I'LL EXPLAIN EVERYTHING IN DUE COURSE. KITTY, MAY I TAKE YOUR HAND AGAIN?
MY NAME IS KATHERINE.
I'LL TRY TO REMEMBER THAT.
WE NEED TO GO TO MAGNETO'S COMMAND ROOM.
WE DO? WHY?
BECAUSE THAT'S WHERE CYCLOPS IS HEADING.
OF COURSE. LET'S GO SEE CYCLOPS. WHOEVER HE IS.
FOLLOW ME, ALL OF YOU.
AND YOU'LL LEARN BOTH WHAT YOU ARE, AND WHAT YOU WERE MEANT TO BE.
ARE WE ALL UP FOR THIS?
TO BE HONEST, I'D PREFER TO SMASH SOMETHING. BUT--
I THINK... WE NEED TO HEAR IT.
THEN MAYBE ONE OF YOU SHOULD PICK UP THE GENERAL.
BEING AS HOW YOU KNOCKED HIM DOWN, AND ALL.

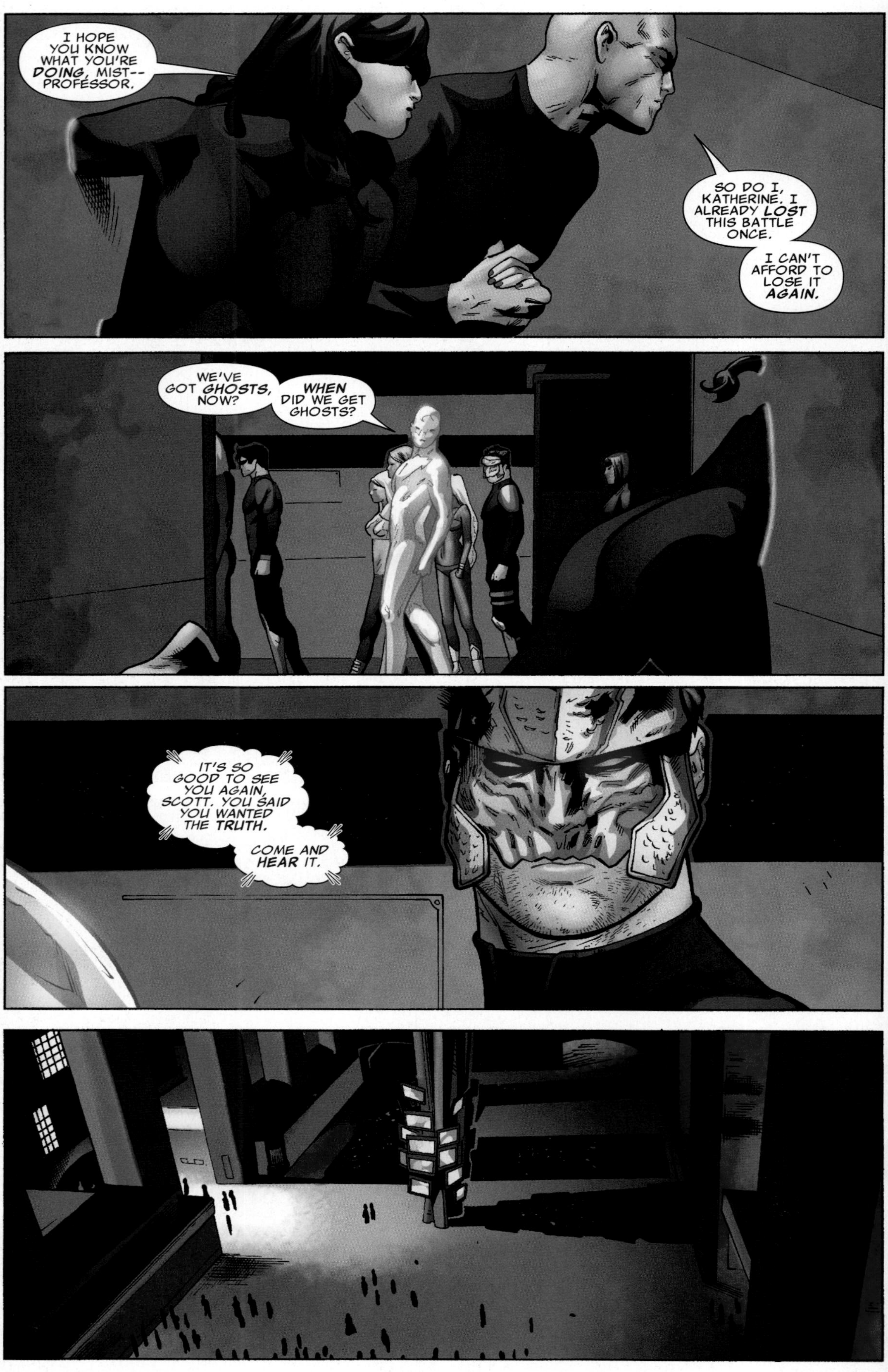
I HOPE YOU KNOW WHAT YOU'RE DOING, MIST-- PROFESSOR.
SO DO I, KATHERINE. I ALREADY LOST THIS BATTLE ONCE.
I CAN'T AFFORD TO LOSE IT AGAIN.
WE'VE GOT GHOSTS, NOW?
WHEN DID WE GET GHOSTS?
IT'S SO GOOD TO SEE YOU AGAIN, SCOTT. YOU SAID YOU WANTED THE TRUTH.
COME AND HEAR IT.

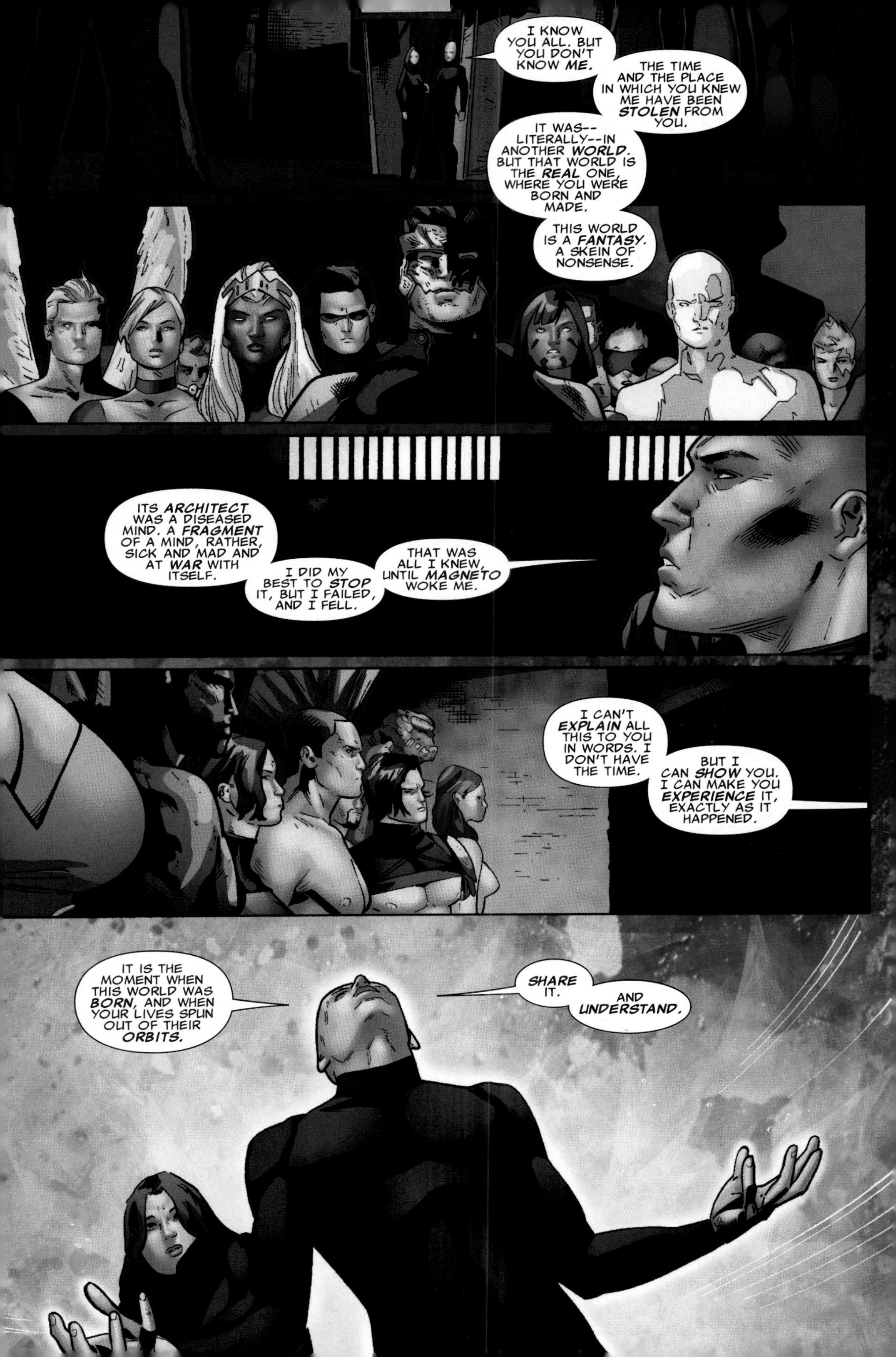
I KNOW YOU ALL. BUT YOU DON'T KNOW ME.
THE TIME AND THE PLACE IN WHICH YOU KNEW ME HAVE BEEN STOLEN FROM YOU.
IT WAS-- LITERALLY--IN ANOTHER WORLD. BUT THAT WORLD IS THE REAL ONE, WHERE YOU WERE BORN AND MADE.
THIS WORLD IS A FANTASY. A SKEIN OF NONSENSE.
ITS ARCHITECT WAS A DISEASED MIND. A FRAGMENT OF A MIND, RATHER, SICK AND MAD AND AT WAR WITH ITSELF.
I DID MY BEST TO STOP IT, BUT I FAILED, AND I FELL.
THAT WAS ALL I KNEW, UNTIL MAGNETO WOKE ME.
I CAN'T EXPLAIN ALL THIS TO YOU IN WORDS. I DON'T HAVE THE TIME.
BUT I CAN SHOW YOU. I CAN MAKE YOU EXPERIENCE IT, EXACTLY AS IT HAPPENED.
IT IS THE MOMENT WHEN THIS WORLD WAS BORN, AND WHEN YOUR LIVES SPUN OUT OF THEIR ORBITS.
SHARE IT.
AND UNDERSTAND.

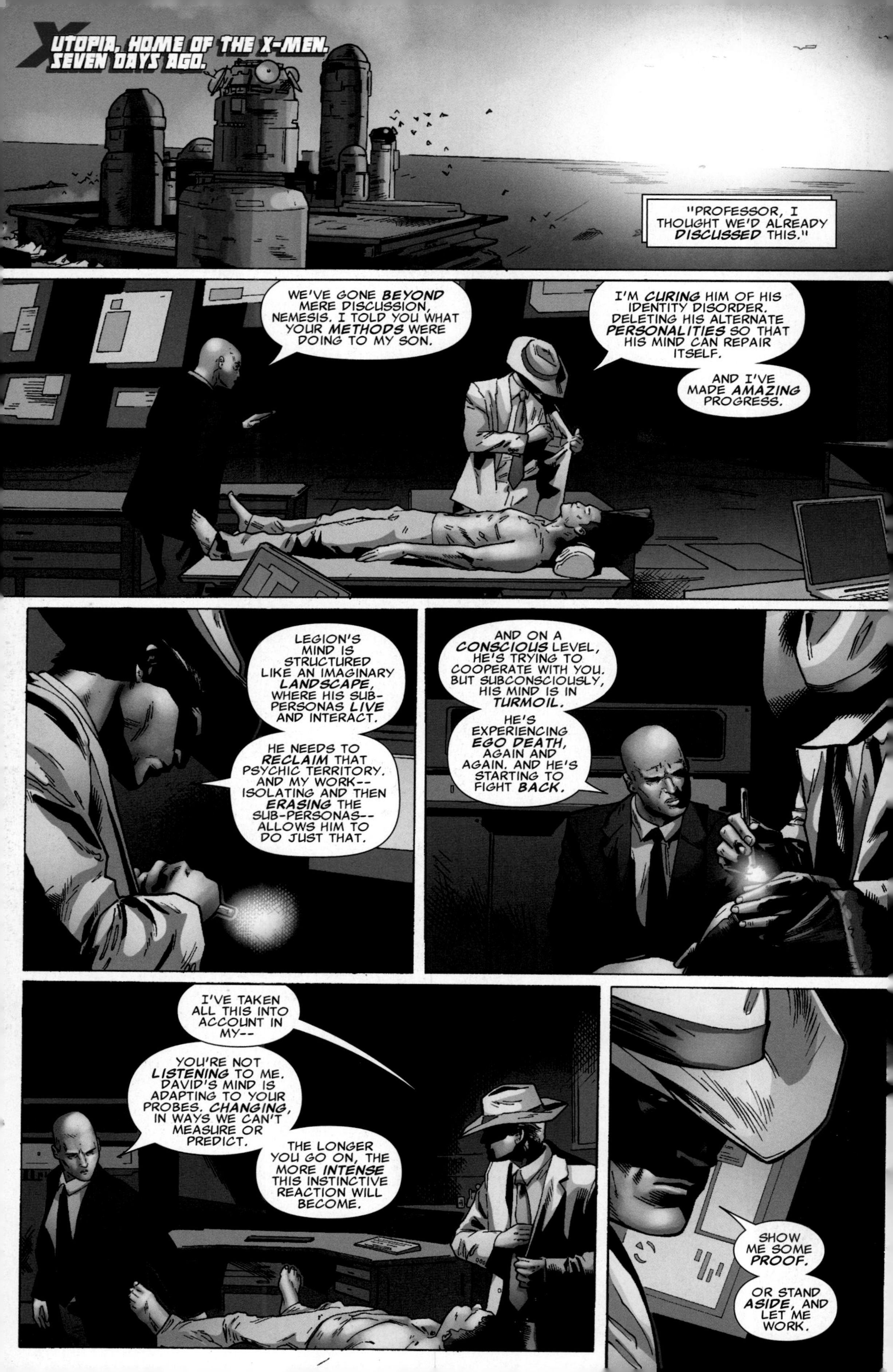
UTOPIA, HOME OF THE X-MEN. SEVEN DAYS AGO.
"PROFESSOR, I THOUGHT WE'D ALREADY DISCUSSED THIS."
WE'VE GONE BEYOND MERE DISCUSSION, NEMESIS. I TOLD YOU WHAT YOUR METHODS WERE DOING TO MY SON.
I'M CURING HIM OF HIS IDENTITY DISORDER. DELETING HIS ALTERNATE PERSONALITIES SO THAT HIS MIND CAN REPAIR ITSELF.
AND I'VE MADE AMAZING PROGRESS.
LEGION'S MIND IS STRUCTURED LIKE AN IMAGINARY LANDSCAPE, WHERE HIS SUB-PERSONAS LIVE AND INTERACT.
HE NEEDS TO RECLAIM THAT PSYCHIC TERRITORY. AND MY WORK--ISOLATING AND THEN ERASING THE SUB-PERSONAS--ALLOWS HIM TO DO JUST THAT.
AND ON A CONSCIOUS LEVEL, HE'S TRYING TO COOPERATE WITH YOU. BUT SUBCONSCIOUSLY, HIS MIND IS IN TURMOIL.
HE'S EXPERIENCING EGO DEATH, AGAIN AND AGAIN. AND HE'S STARTING TO FIGHT BACK.
I'VE TAKEN ALL THIS INTO ACCOUNT IN MY--
YOU'RE NOT LISTENING TO ME. DAVID'S MIND IS ADAPTING TO YOUR PROBES. CHANGING, IN WAYS WE CAN'T MEASURE OR PREDICT.
THE LONGER YOU GO ON, THE MORE INTENSE THIS INSTINCTIVE REACTION WILL BECOME.
SHOW ME SOME PROOF.
OR STAND ASIDE, AND LET ME WORK.

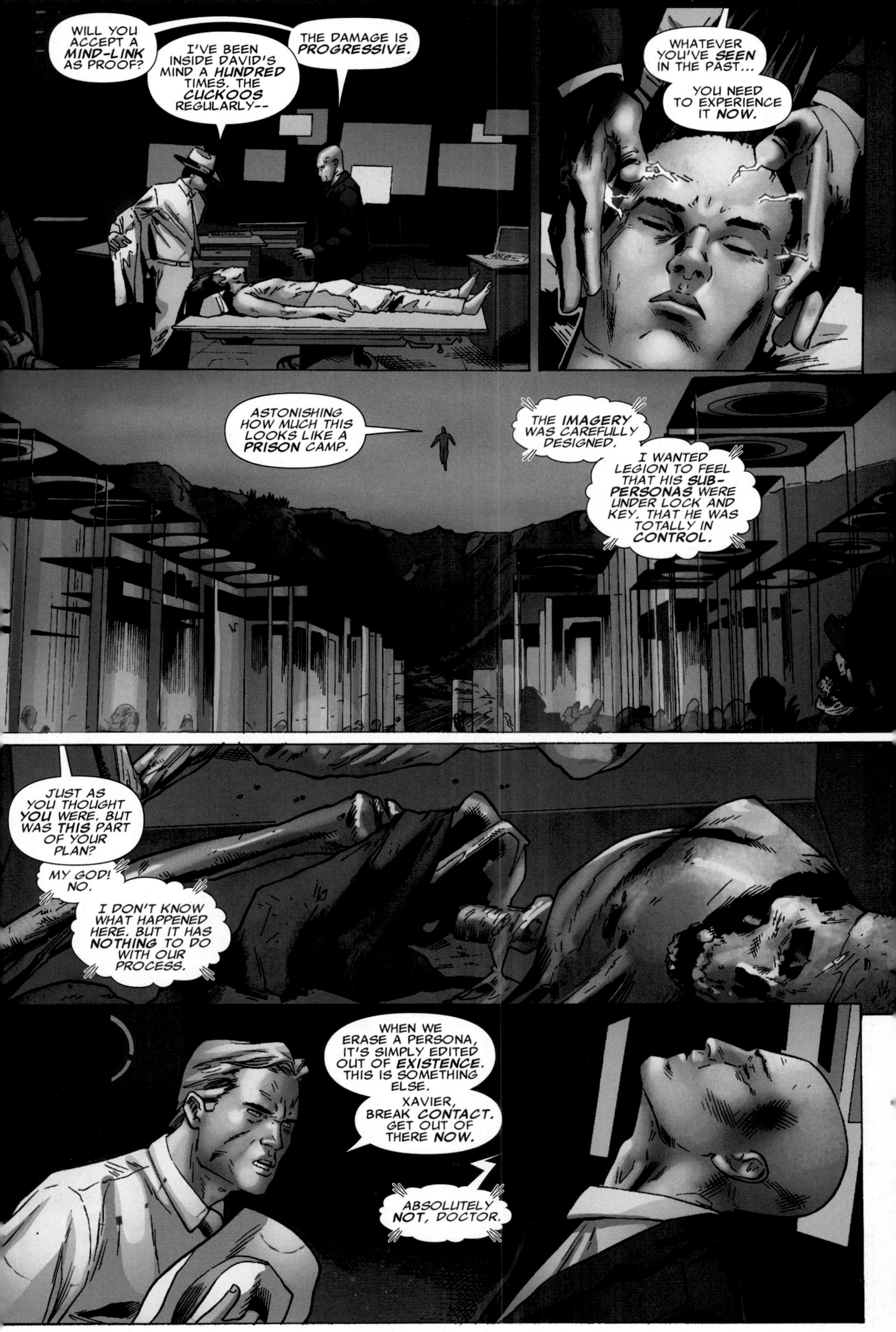

WILL YOU ACCEPT A MIND-LINK AS PROOF?
I'VE BEEN INSIDE DAVID'S MIND A HUNDRED TIMES. THE CUCKOOS REGULARLY--
THE DAMAGE IS PROGRESSIVE.
WHATEVER YOU'VE SEEN IN THE PAST...
YOU NEED TO EXPERIENCE IT NOW.
ASTONISHING HOW MUCH THIS LOOKS LIKE A PRISON CAMP.
THE IMAGERY WAS CAREFULLY DESIGNED.
I WANTED LEGION TO FEEL THAT HIS SUB-PERSONAS WERE UNDER LOCK AND KEY. THAT HE WAS TOTALLY IN CONTROL.
JUST AS YOU THOUGHT YOU WERE. BUT WAS THIS PART OF YOUR PLAN?
MY GOD! NO.
I DON'T KNOW WHAT HAPPENED HERE. BUT IT HAS NOTHING TO DO WITH OUR PROCESS.
WHEN WE ERASE A PERSONA, IT'S SIMPLY EDITED OUT OF EXISTENCE. THIS IS SOMETHING ELSE.
XAVIER, BREAK CONTACT. GET OUT OF THERE NOW.
ABSOLUTELY NOT, DOCTOR.

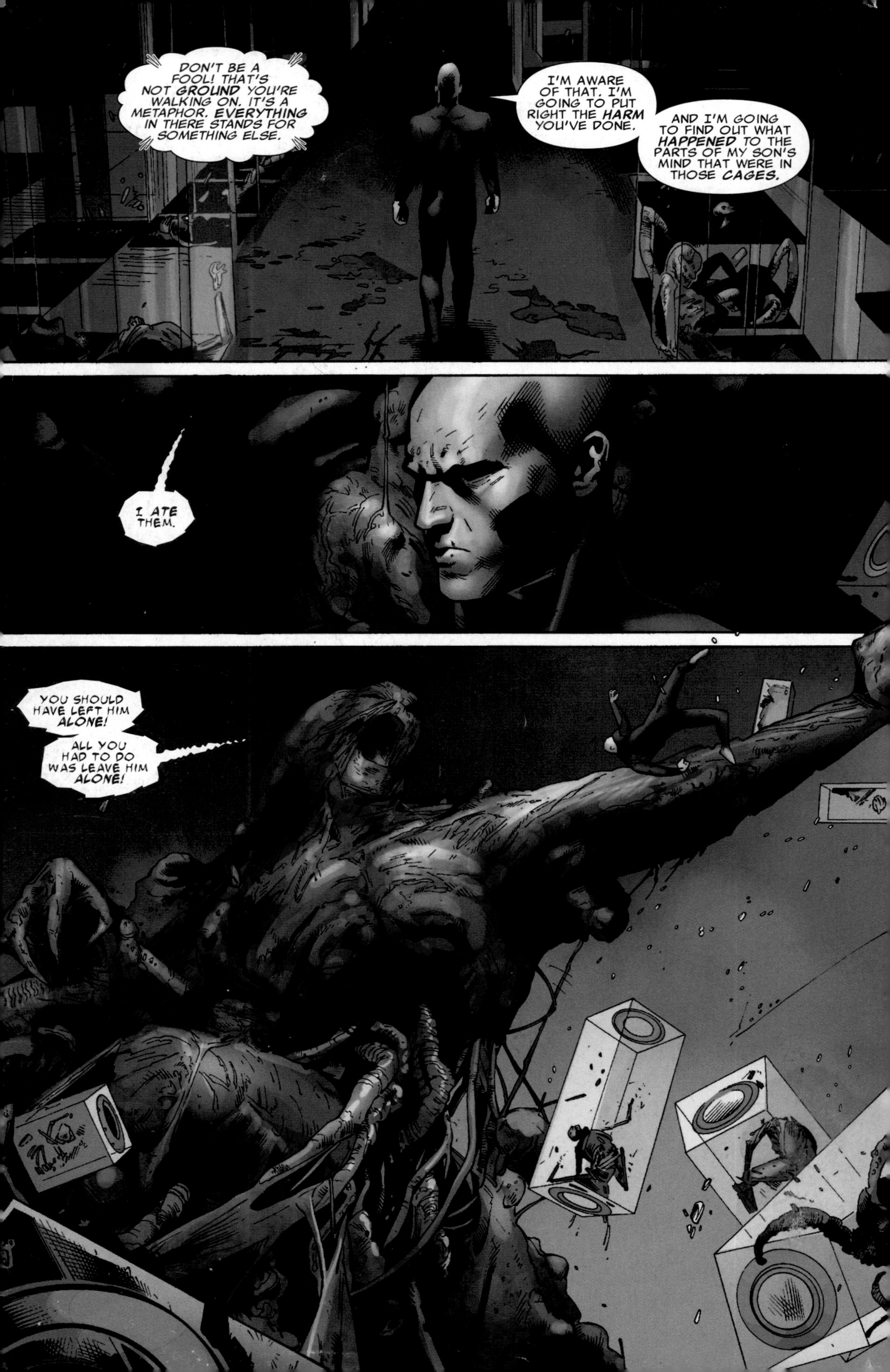
DON'T BE A FOOL! THAT'S NOT GROUND YOU'RE WALKING ON. IT'S A METAPHOR. EVERYTHING IN THERE STANDS FOR SOMETHING ELSE.
I'M AWARE OF THAT. I'M GOING TO PUT RIGHT THE HARM YOU'VE DONE.
AND I'M GOING TO FIND OUT WHAT HAPPENED TO THE PARTS OF MY SON'S MIND THAT WERE IN THOSE CAGES.
I ATE THEM.
YOU SHOULD HAVE LEFT HIM ALONE!
ALL YOU HAD TO DO WAS LEAVE HIM ALONE!

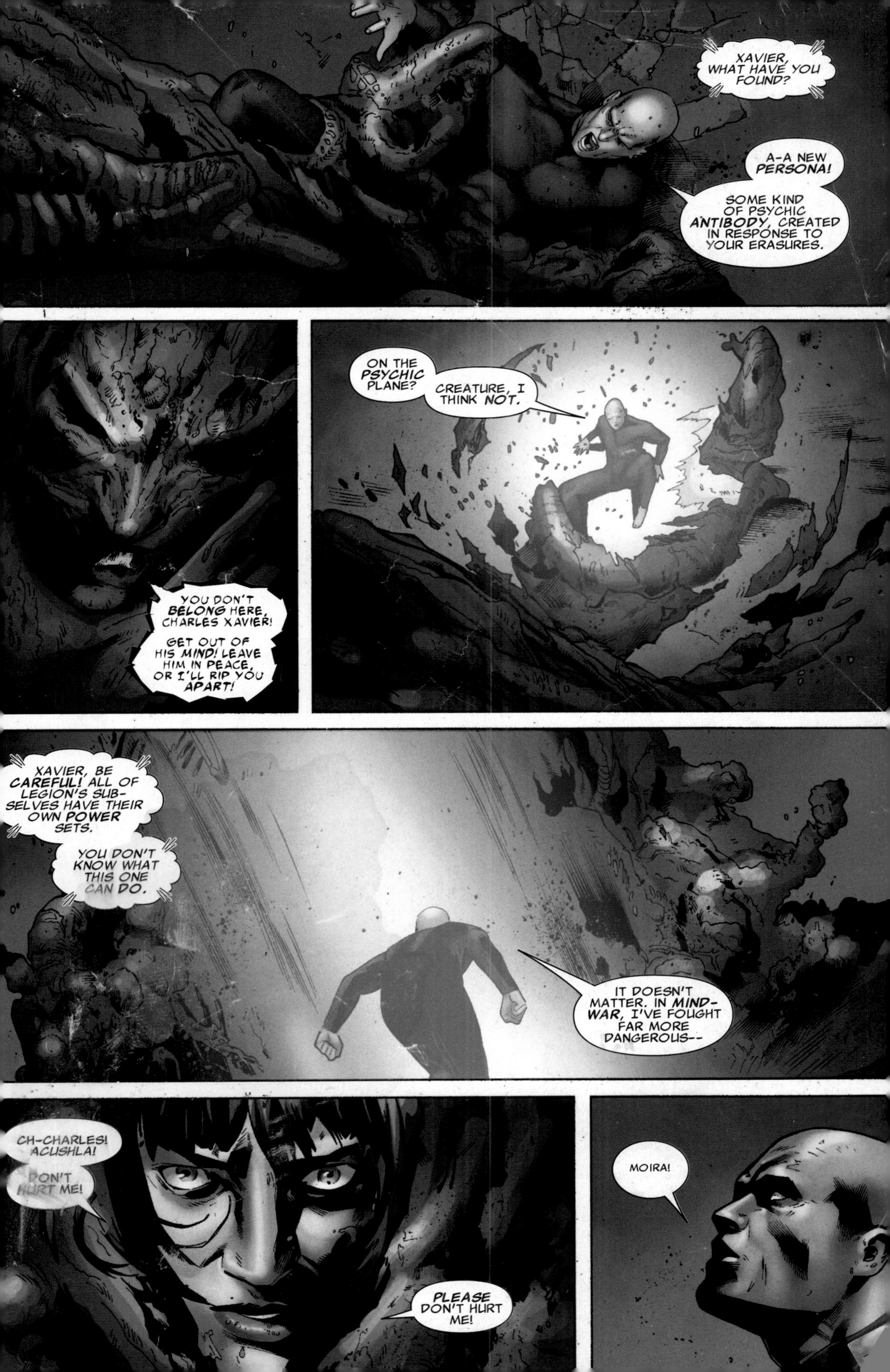
XAVIER, WHAT HAVE YOU FOUND?
A-A NEW PERSONA!
SOME KIND OF PSYCHIC ANTIBODY, CREATED IN RESPONSE TO YOUR ERASURES.
YOU DON'T BELONG HERE, CHARLES XAVIER!
GET OUT OF HIS MIND! LEAVE HIM IN PEACE, OR I'LL RIP YOU APART!
ON THE PSYCHIC PLANE?
CREATURE, I THINK NOT.
XAVIER, BE CAREFUL! ALL OF LEGION'S SUB-SELVES HAVE THEIR OWN POWER SETS.
YOU DON'T KNOW WHAT THIS ONE CAN DO.
IT DOESN'T MATTER. IN MIND-WAR, I'VE FOUGHT FAR MORE DANGEROUS--
CH-CHARLES! ACUSHLA!
DON'T HURT ME!
PLEASE DON'T HURT ME!
MOIRA!

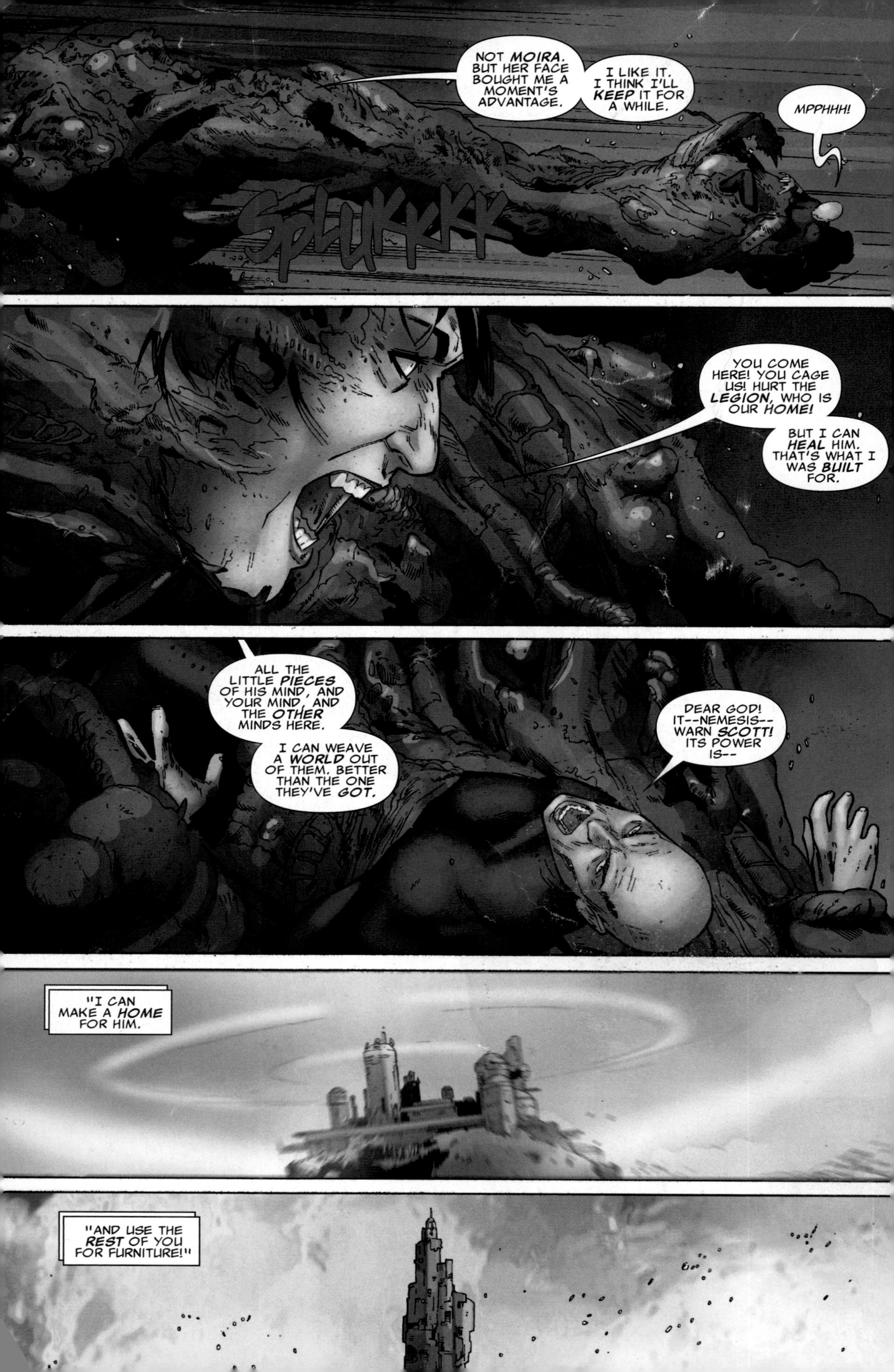
NOT MOIRA. BUT HER FACE BOUGHT ME A MOMENT'S ADVANTAGE.
I LIKE IT. I THINK I'LL KEEP IT FOR A WHILE.
MPPHHH!
SPLUKKKK
YOU COME HERE! YOU CAGE US! HURT THE LEGION, WHO IS OUR HOME!
BUT I CAN HEAL HIM. THAT'S WHAT I WAS BUILT FOR.
ALL THE LITTLE PIECES OF HIS MIND, AND YOUR MIND, AND THE OTHER MINDS HERE.
I CAN WEAVE A WORLD OUT OF THEM. BETTER THAN THE ONE THEY'VE GOT.
DEAR GOD! IT--NEMESIS--WARN SCOTT! ITS POWER IS--
"I CAN MAKE A HOME FOR HIM.
"AND USE THE REST OF YOU FOR FURNITURE!"

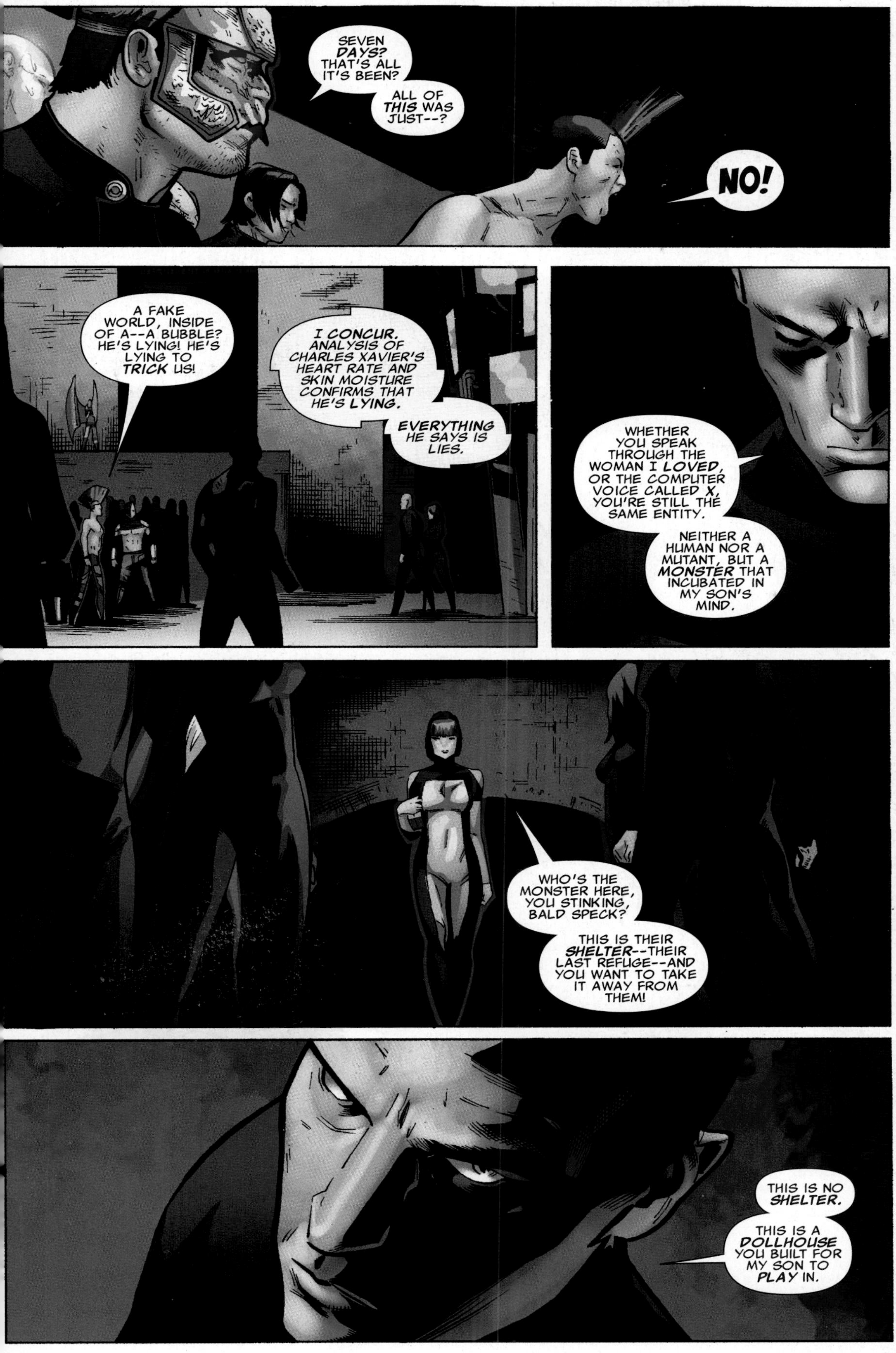
SEVEN DAYS? THAT'S ALL IT'S BEEN?
ALL OF THIS WAS JUST--?
NO!
A FAKE WORLD, INSIDE OF A--A BUBBLE? HE'S LYING! HE'S LYING TO TRICK US!
I CONCUR. ANALYSIS OF CHARLES XAVIER'S HEART RATE AND SKIN MOISTURE CONFIRMS THAT HE'S LYING.
EVERYTHING HE SAYS IS LIES.
WHETHER YOU SPEAK THROUGH THE WOMAN I LOVED, OR THE COMPUTER VOICE CALLED X, YOU'RE STILL THE SAME ENTITY.
NEITHER A HUMAN NOR A MUTANT, BUT A MONSTER THAT INCUBATED IN MY SON'S MIND.
WHO'S THE MONSTER HERE, YOU STINKING, BALD SPECK?
THIS IS THEIR SHELTER--THEIR LAST REFUGE--AND YOU WANT TO TAKE IT AWAY FROM THEM!
THIS IS NO SHELTER.
THIS IS A DOLLHOUSE YOU BUILT FOR MY SON TO PLAY IN.

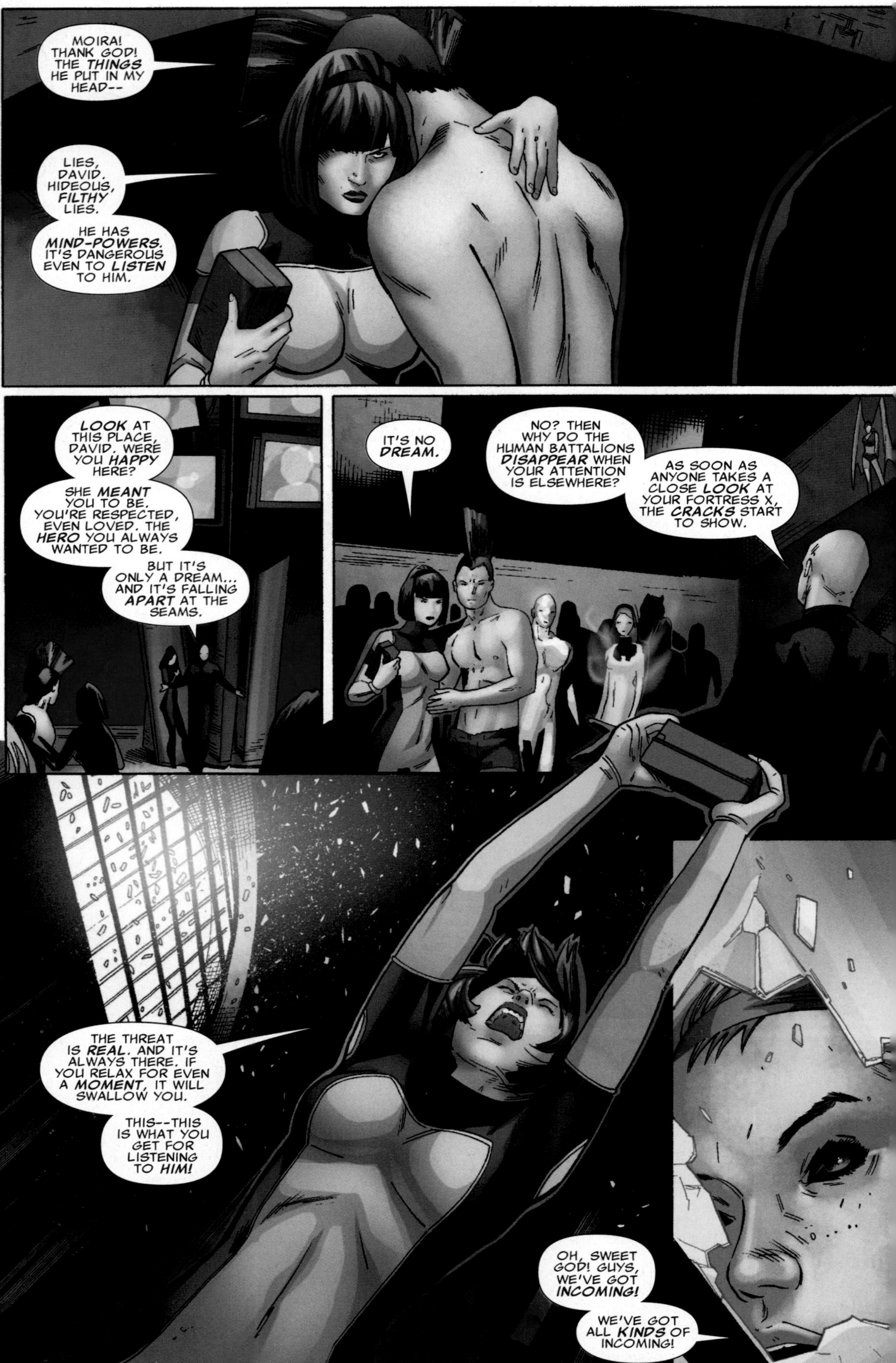
MOIRA! THANK GOD! THE THINGS HE PUT IN MY HEAD--
LIES, DAVID. HIDEOUS, FILTHY LIES.
HE HAS MIND-POWERS. IT'S DANGEROUS EVEN TO LISTEN TO HIM.
LOOK AT THIS PLACE, DAVID. WERE YOU HAPPY HERE?
SHE MEANT YOU TO BE. YOU'RE RESPECTED, EVEN LOVED. THE HERO YOU ALWAYS WANTED TO BE.
BUT IT'S ONLY A DREAM... AND IT'S FALLING APART AT THE SEAMS.
IT'S NO DREAM.
NO? THEN WHY DO THE HUMAN BATTALIONS DISAPPEAR WHEN YOUR ATTENTION IS ELSEWHERE?
AS SOON AS ANYONE TAKES A CLOSE LOOK AT YOUR FORTRESS X, THE CRACKS START TO SHOW.
THE THREAT IS REAL. AND IT'S ALWAYS THERE. IF YOU RELAX FOR EVEN A MOMENT, IT WILL SWALLOW YOU.
THIS--THIS IS WHAT YOU GET FOR LISTENING TO HIM!
OH, SWEET GOD! GUYS, WE'VE GOT INCOMING!
WE'VE GOT ALL KINDS OF INCOMING!

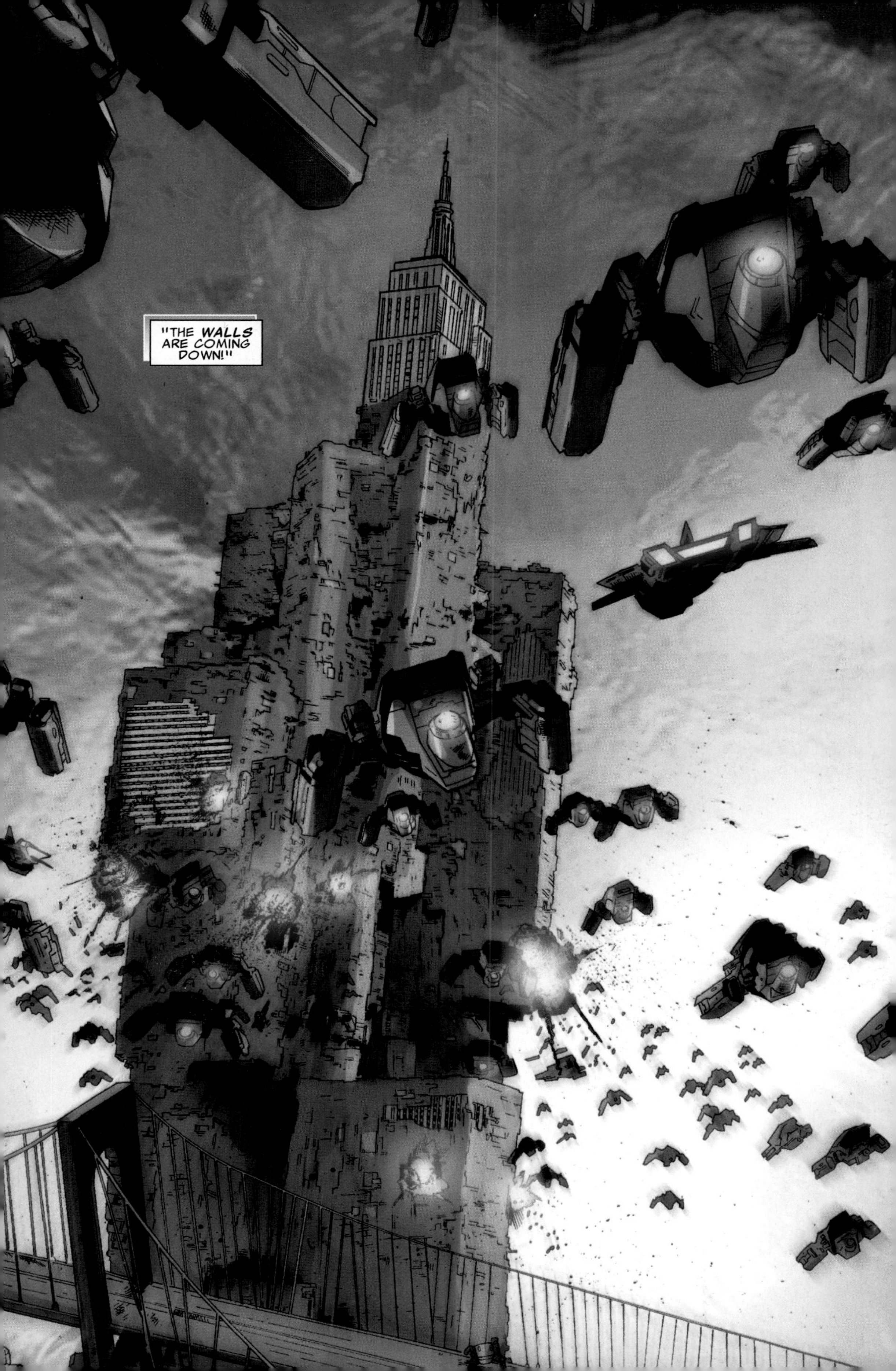
"THE WALLS ARE COMING DOWN!"

NEW MUTANTS #24

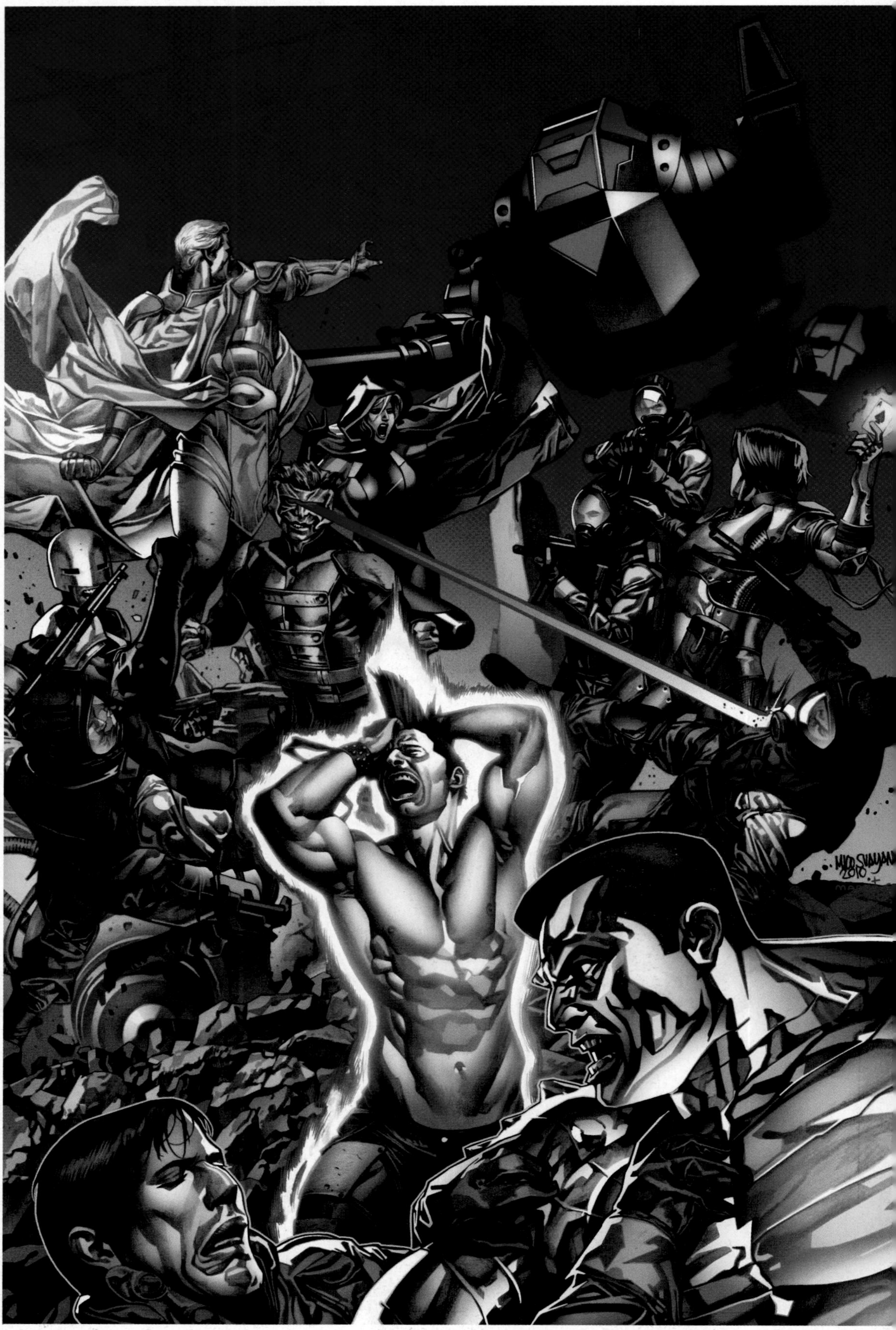

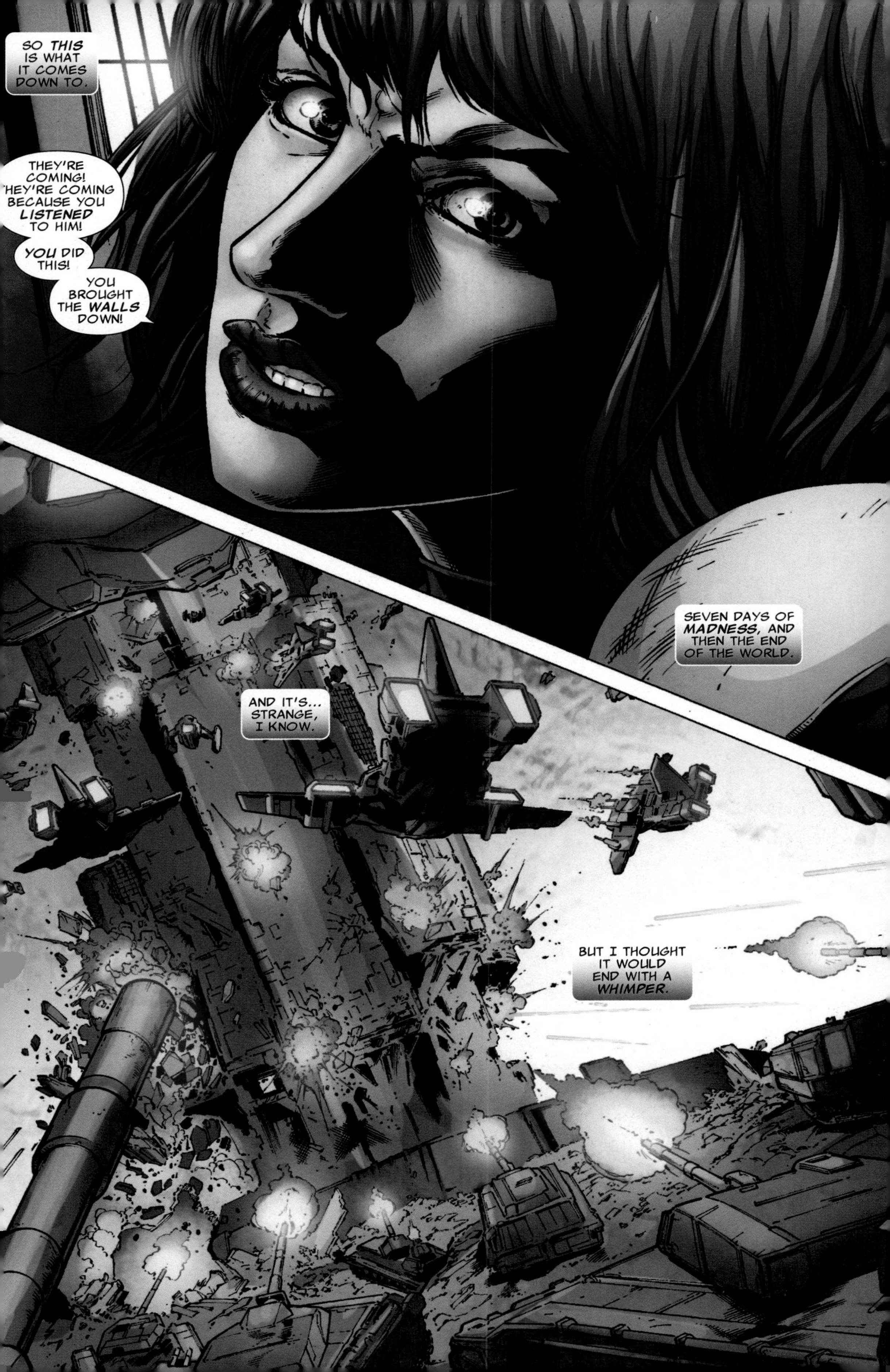
SO THIS IS WHAT IT COMES DOWN TO.
THEY'RE COMING! THEY'RE COMING BECAUSE YOU LISTENED TO HIM!
YOU DID THIS!
YOU BROUGHT THE WALLS DOWN!
SEVEN DAYS OF MADNESS, AND THEN THE END OF THE WORLD.
AND IT'S... STRANGE, I KNOW.
BUT I THOUGHT IT WOULD END WITH A WHIMPER.

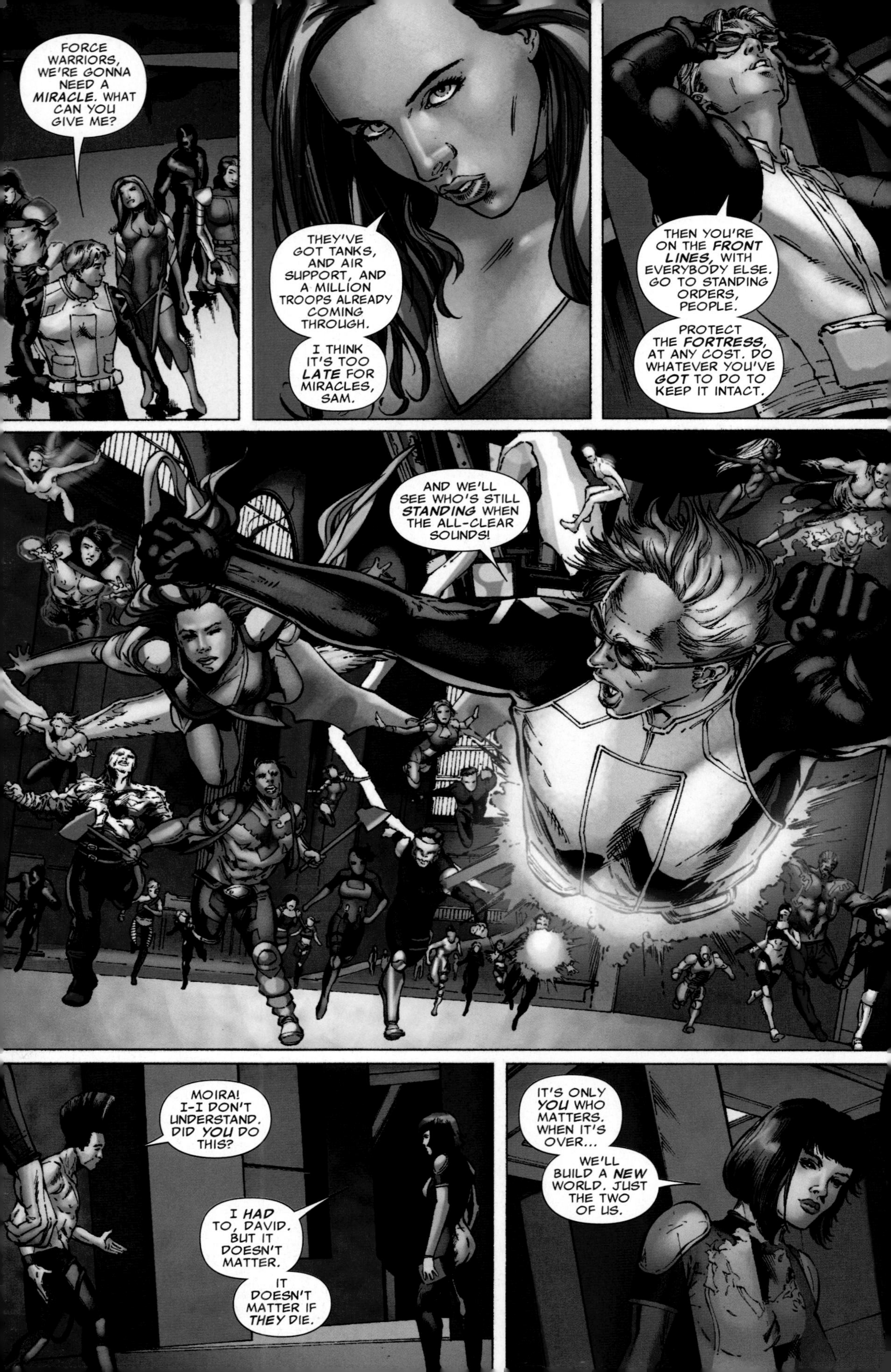
FORCE WARRIORS, WE'RE GONNA NEED A MIRACLE. WHAT CAN YOU GIVE ME?
THEY'VE GOT TANKS, AND AIR SUPPORT, AND A MILLION TROOPS ALREADY COMING THROUGH.
I THINK IT'S TOO LATE FOR MIRACLES, SAM.
THEN YOU'RE ON THE FRONT LINES, WITH EVERYBODY ELSE. GO TO STANDING ORDERS, PEOPLE.
PROTECT THE FORTRESS, AT ANY COST. DO WHATEVER YOU'VE GOT TO DO TO KEEP IT INTACT.
AND WE'LL SEE WHO'S STILL STANDING WHEN THE ALL-CLEAR SOUNDS!
MOIRA! I-I DON'T UNDERSTAND. DID YOU DO THIS?
I HAD TO, DAVID. BUT IT DOESN'T MATTER.
IT DOESN'T MATTER IF THEY DIE.
IT'S ONLY YOU WHO MATTERS. WHEN IT'S OVER...
WE'LL BUILD A NEW WORLD. JUST THE TWO OF US.

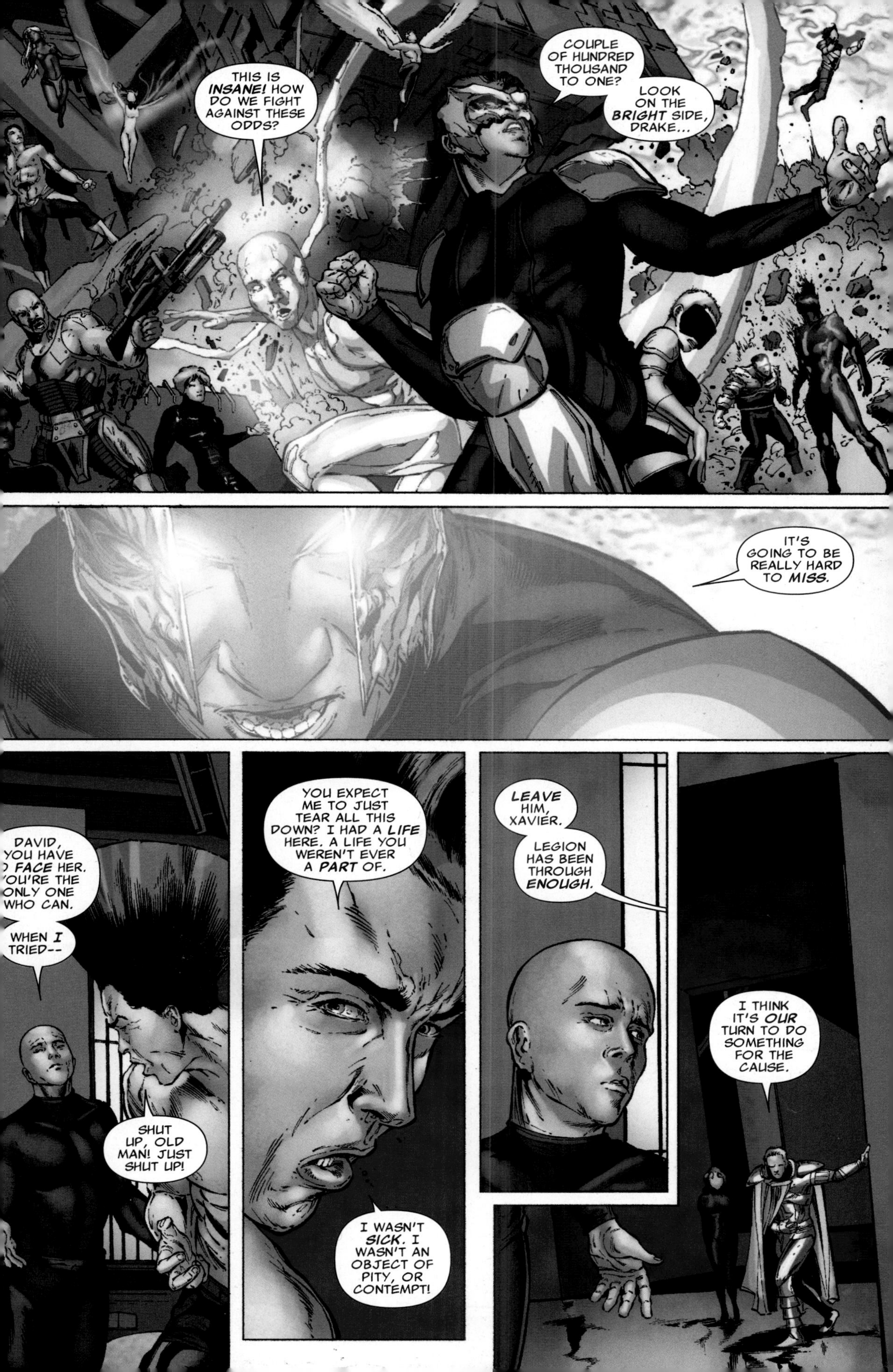
THIS IS INSANE! HOW DO WE FIGHT AGAINST THESE ODDS?
COUPLE OF HUNDRED THOUSAND TO ONE?
LOOK ON THE BRIGHT SIDE, DRAKE...
IT'S GOING TO BE REALLY HARD TO MISS.
DAVID, YOU HAVE TO FACE HER. YOU'RE THE ONLY ONE WHO CAN.
WHEN I TRIED--
SHUT UP, OLD MAN! JUST SHUT UP!
YOU EXPECT ME TO JUST TEAR ALL THIS DOWN? I HAD A LIFE HERE. A LIFE YOU WEREN'T EVER A PART OF.
I WASN'T SICK. I WASN'T AN OBJECT OF PITY, OR CONTEMPT!
LEAVE HIM, XAVIER.
LEGION HAS BEEN THROUGH ENOUGH.
I THINK IT'S OUR TURN TO DO SOMETHING FOR THE CAUSE.

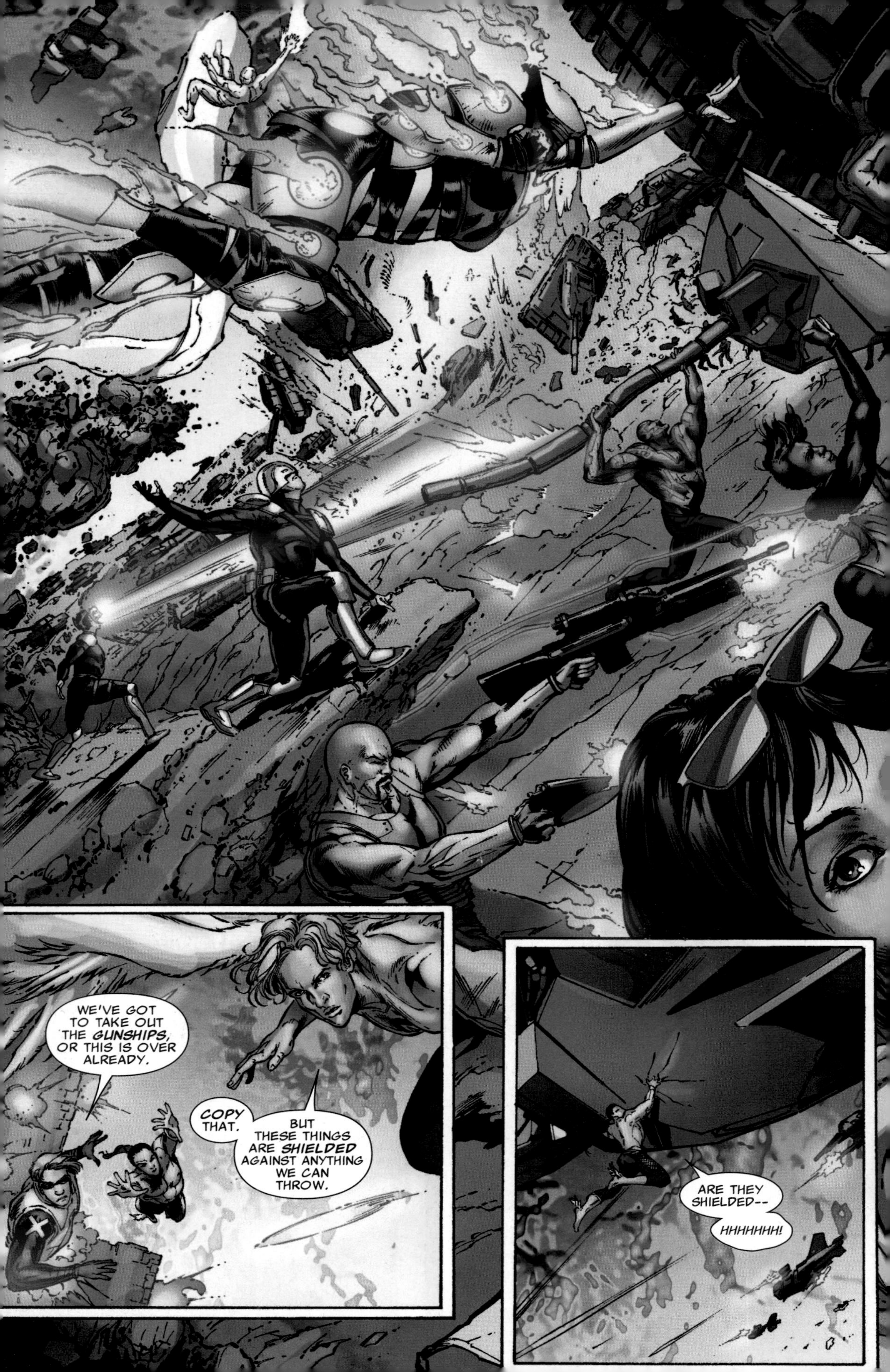
WE'VE GOT TO TAKE OUT THE *GUNSHIPS*, OR THIS IS OVER ALREADY.
COPY THAT.
BUT THESE THINGS ARE *SHIELDED* AGAINST ANYTHING WE CAN THROW.
ARE THEY SHIELDED--
HHHHHHH!

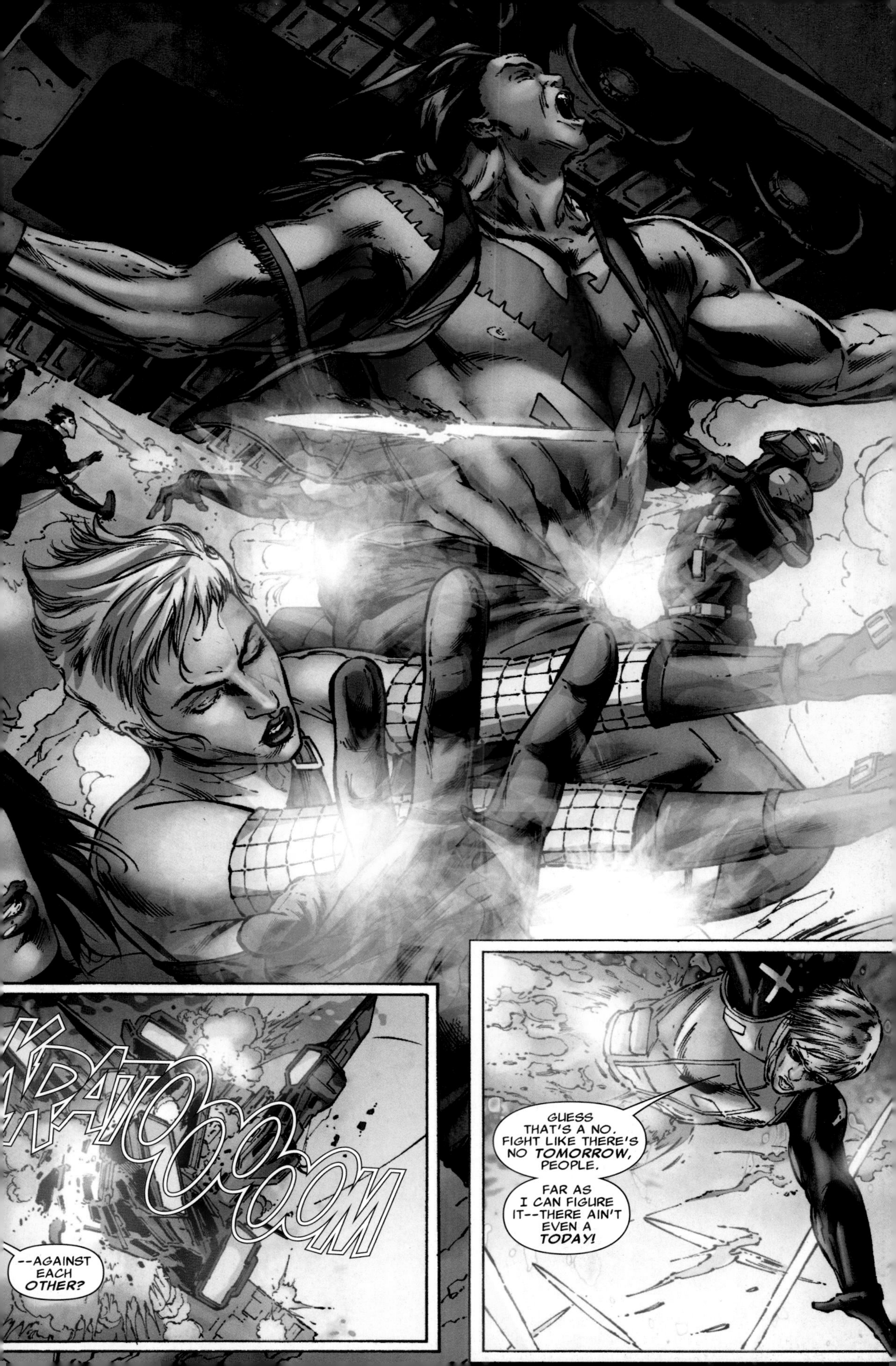
KRATOOOOOM
--AGAINST EACH OTHER?
GUESS THAT'S A NO. FIGHT LIKE THERE'S NO TOMORROW, PEOPLE.
FAR AS I CAN FIGURE IT--THERE AIN'T EVEN A TODAY!

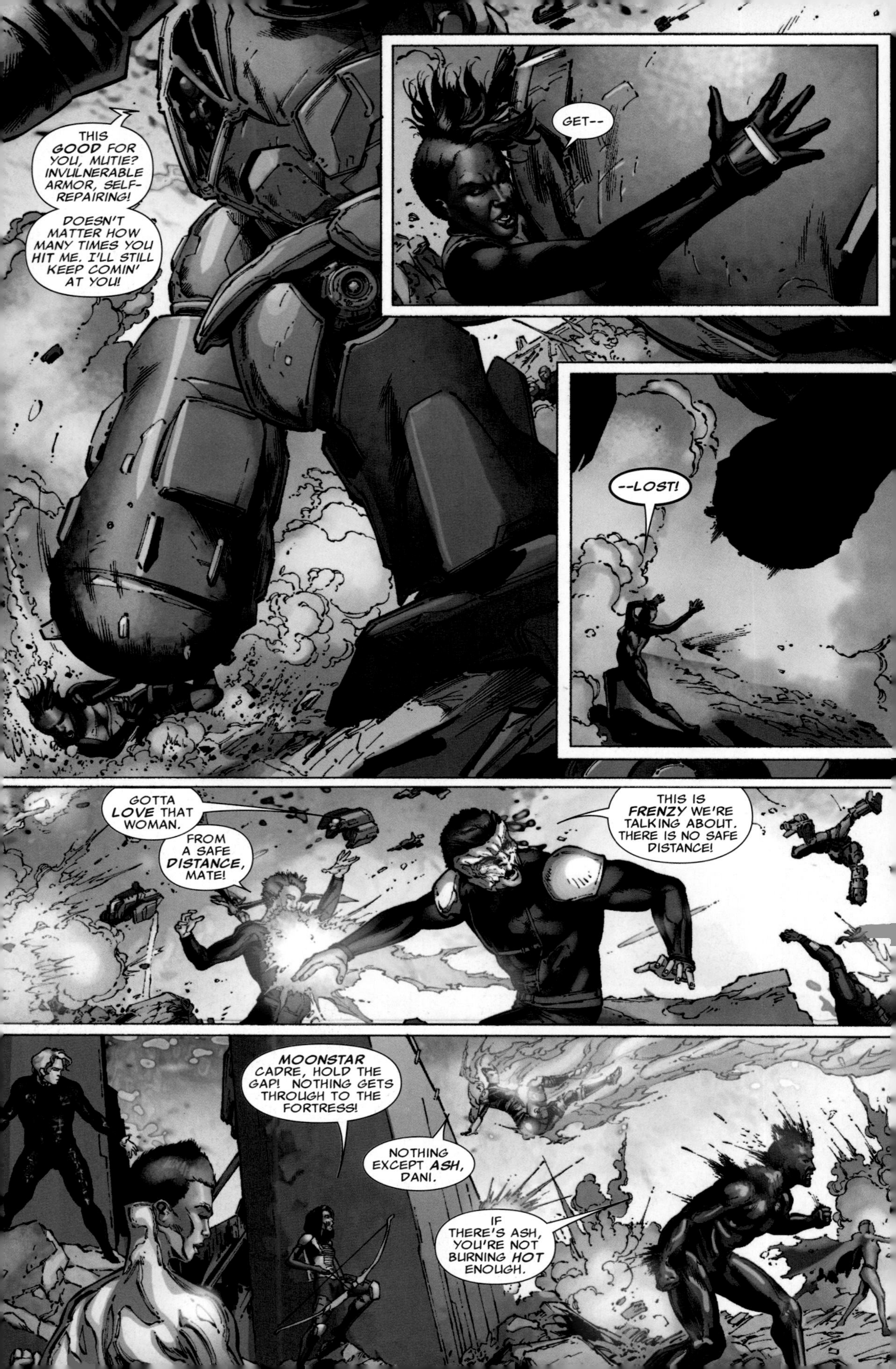
THIS **GOOD** FOR YOU, MUTIE? INVULNERABLE ARMOR, SELF-REPAIRING!
DOESN'T MATTER HOW MANY TIMES YOU HIT ME. I'LL STILL KEEP COMIN' AT YOU!
GET--
--LOST!
GOTTA **LOVE** THAT WOMAN.
FROM A SAFE **DISTANCE**, MATE!
THIS IS **FRENZY** WE'RE TALKING ABOUT. THERE IS NO SAFE DISTANCE!
MOONSTAR CADRE, HOLD THE GAP! NOTHING GETS THROUGH TO THE FORTRESS!
NOTHING EXCEPT **ASH**, DANI.
IF THERE'S ASH, YOU'RE NOT BURNING **HOT** ENOUGH.

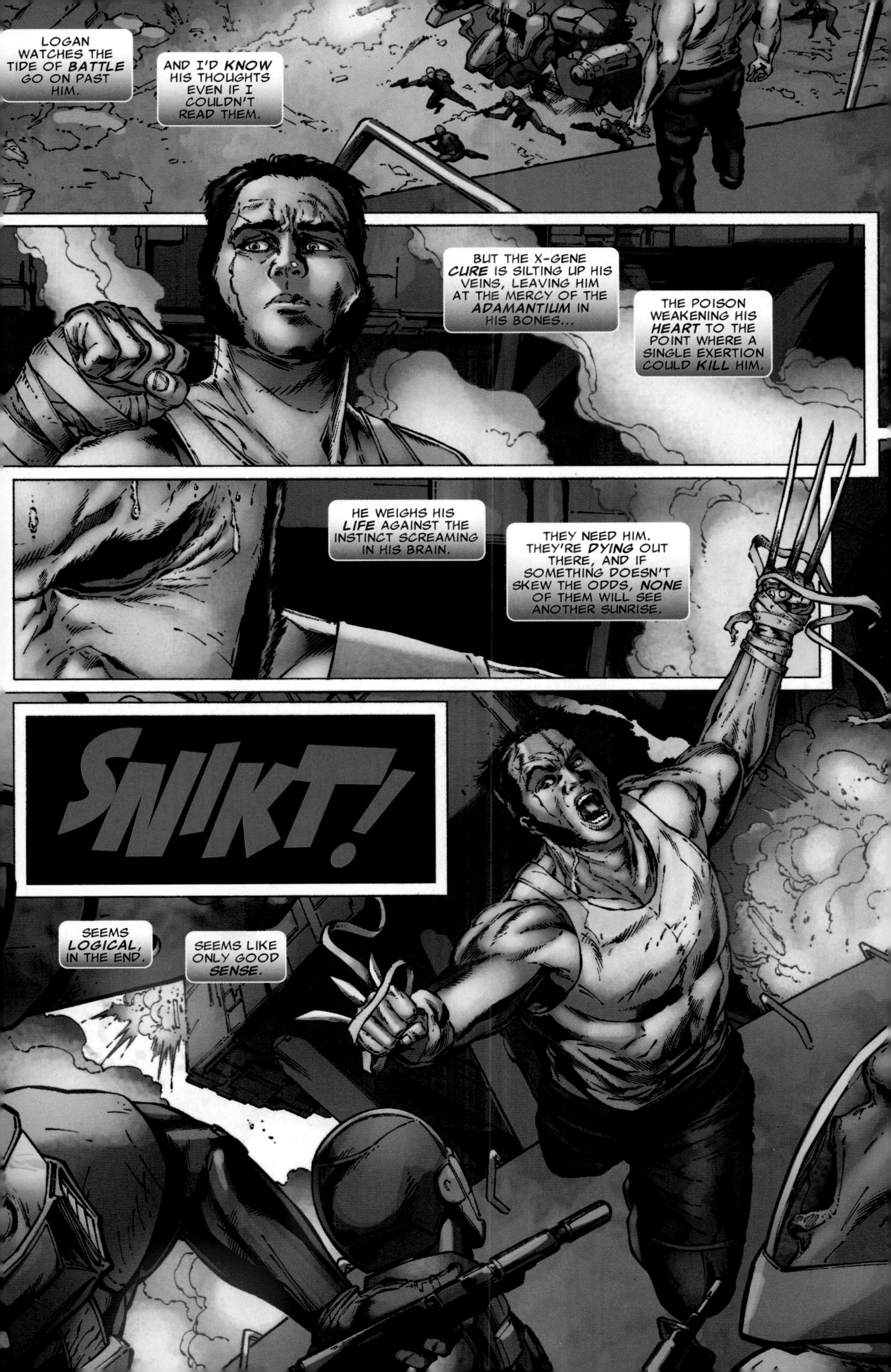

LOGAN WATCHES THE TIDE OF BATTLE GO ON PAST HIM.
AND I'D KNOW HIS THOUGHTS EVEN IF I COULDN'T READ THEM.
BUT THE X-GENE CURE IS SILTING UP HIS VEINS, LEAVING HIM AT THE MERCY OF THE ADAMANTIUM IN HIS BONES...
THE POISON WEAKENING HIS HEART TO THE POINT WHERE A SINGLE EXERTION COULD KILL HIM.
HE WEIGHS HIS LIFE AGAINST THE INSTINCT SCREAMING IN HIS BRAIN.
THEY NEED HIM. THEY'RE DYING OUT THERE, AND IF SOMETHING DOESN'T SKEW THE ODDS, NONE OF THEM WILL SEE ANOTHER SUNRISE.
SNIKT!
SEEMS LOGICAL, IN THE END.
SEEMS LIKE ONLY GOOD SENSE.

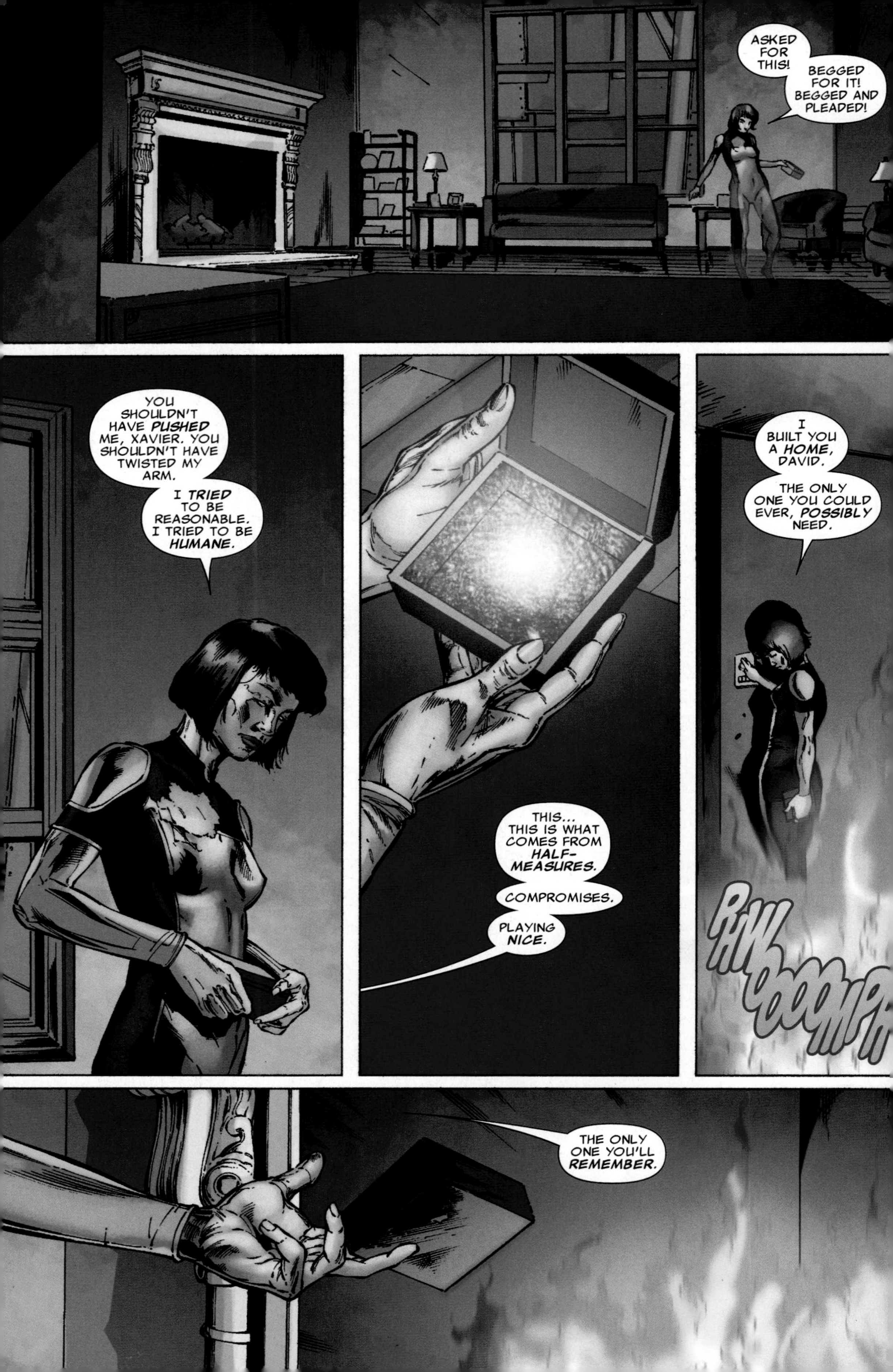
ASKED FOR THIS!
BEGGED FOR IT! BEGGED AND PLEADED!
YOU SHOULDN'T HAVE PUSHED ME, XAVIER. YOU SHOULDN'T HAVE TWISTED MY ARM.
I TRIED TO BE REASONABLE. I TRIED TO BE HUMANE.
THIS... THIS IS WHAT COMES FROM HALF-MEASURES.
COMPROMISES.
PLAYING NICE.
I BUILT YOU A HOME, DAVID.
THE ONLY ONE YOU COULD EVER, POSSIBLY NEED.
PHWOOOMPH
THE ONLY ONE YOU'LL REMEMBER.

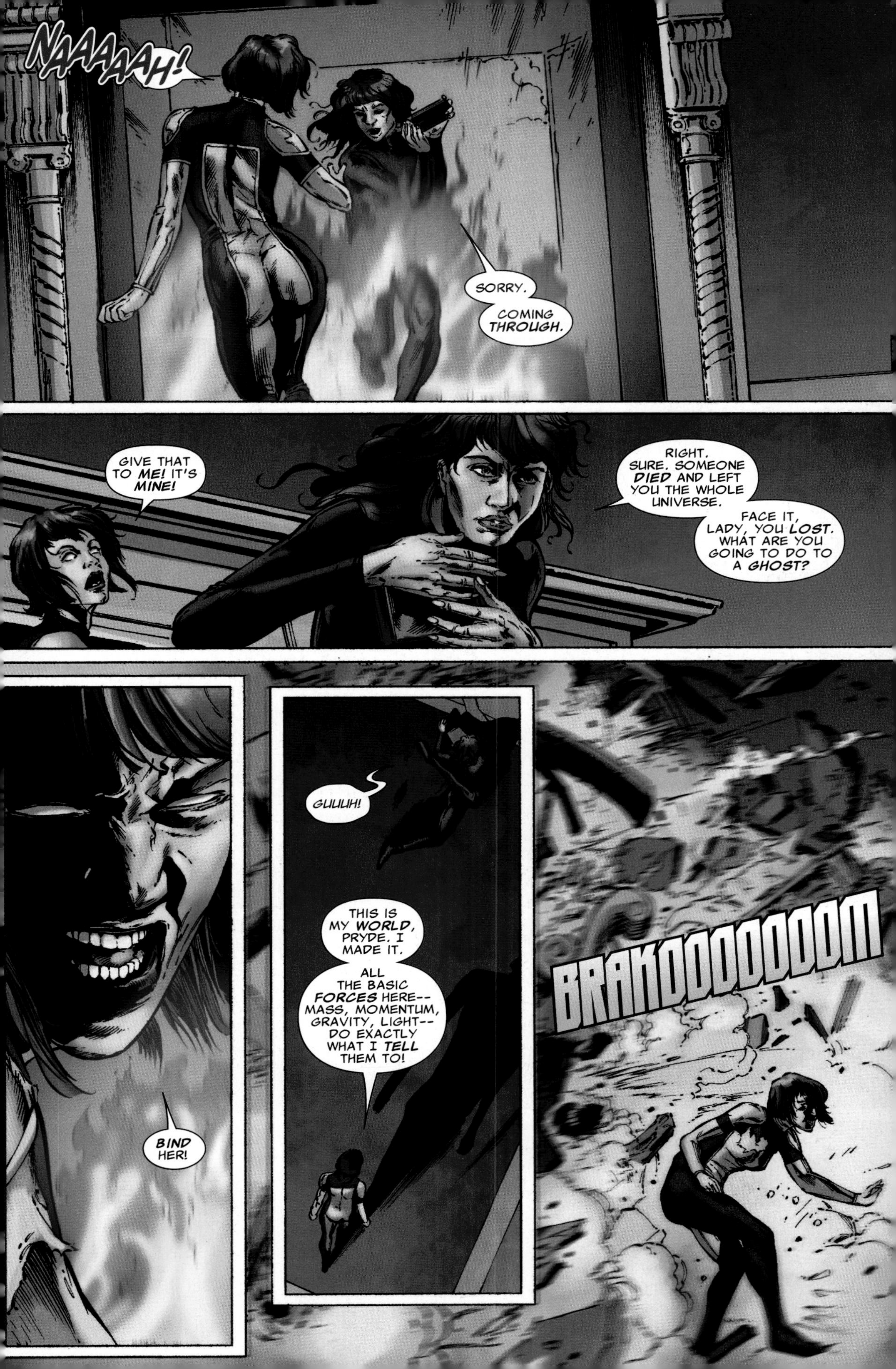

NAAAAAAH!
SORRY.
COMING THROUGH.
GIVE THAT TO ME! IT'S MINE!
RIGHT. SURE. SOMEONE DIED AND LEFT YOU THE WHOLE UNIVERSE.
FACE IT, LADY, YOU LOST. WHAT ARE YOU GOING TO DO TO A GHOST?
BIND HER!
GUUUH!
THIS IS MY WORLD, PRYDE. I MADE IT.
ALL THE BASIC FORCES HERE-- MASS, MOMENTUM, GRAVITY, LIGHT-- DO EXACTLY WHAT I TELL THEM TO!
BRAKOOOOOOOOM

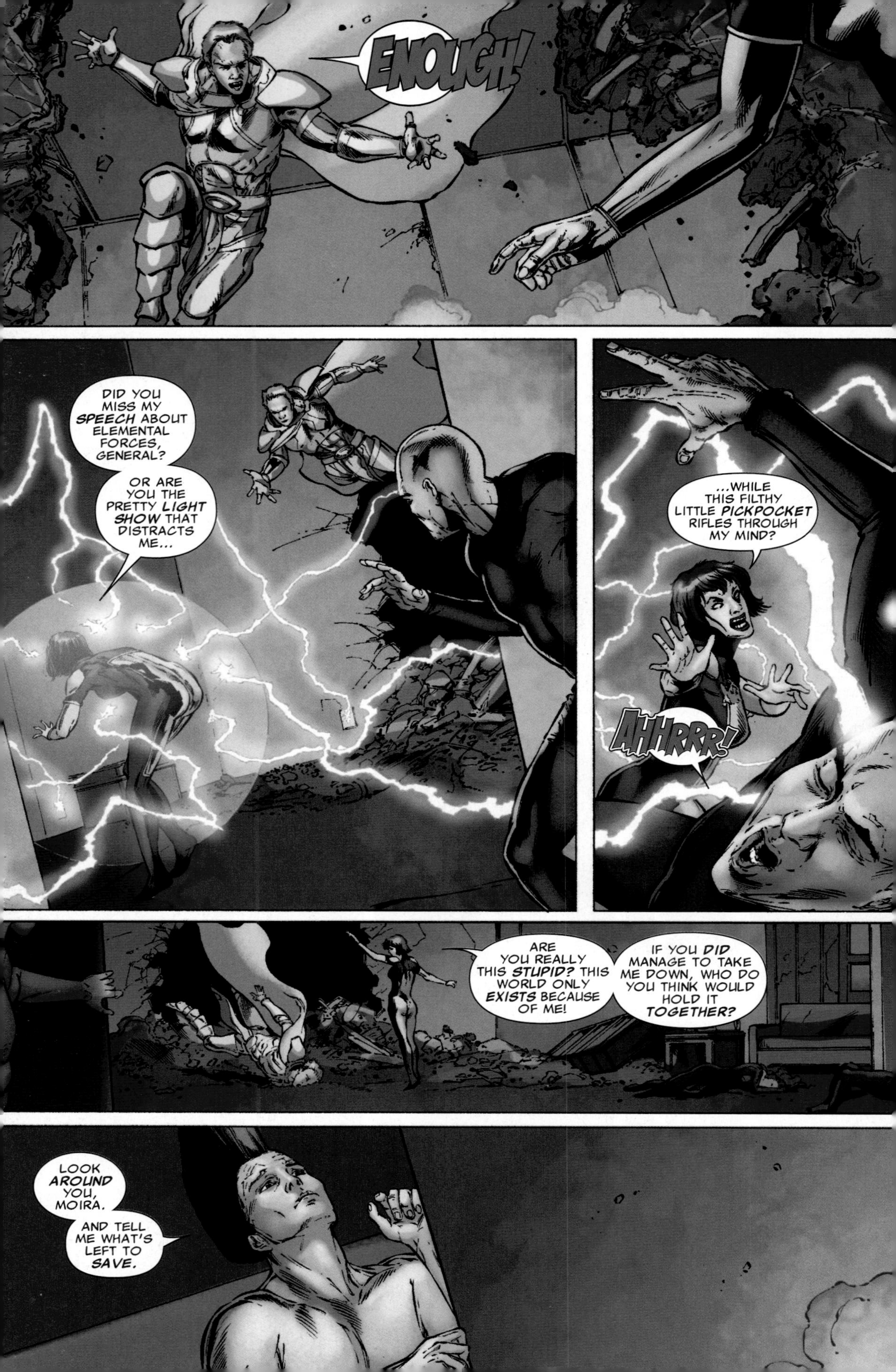
ENOUGH!
DID YOU MISS MY SPEECH ABOUT ELEMENTAL FORCES, GENERAL?
OR ARE YOU THE PRETTY LIGHT SHOW THAT DISTRACTS ME...
...WHILE THIS FILTHY LITTLE PICKPOCKET RIFLES THROUGH MY MIND?
AHHRRR!
ARE YOU REALLY THIS STUPID? THIS WORLD ONLY EXISTS BECAUSE OF ME!
IF YOU DID MANAGE TO TAKE ME DOWN, WHO DO YOU THINK WOULD HOLD IT TOGETHER?
LOOK AROUND YOU, MOIRA.
AND TELL ME WHAT'S LEFT TO SAVE.

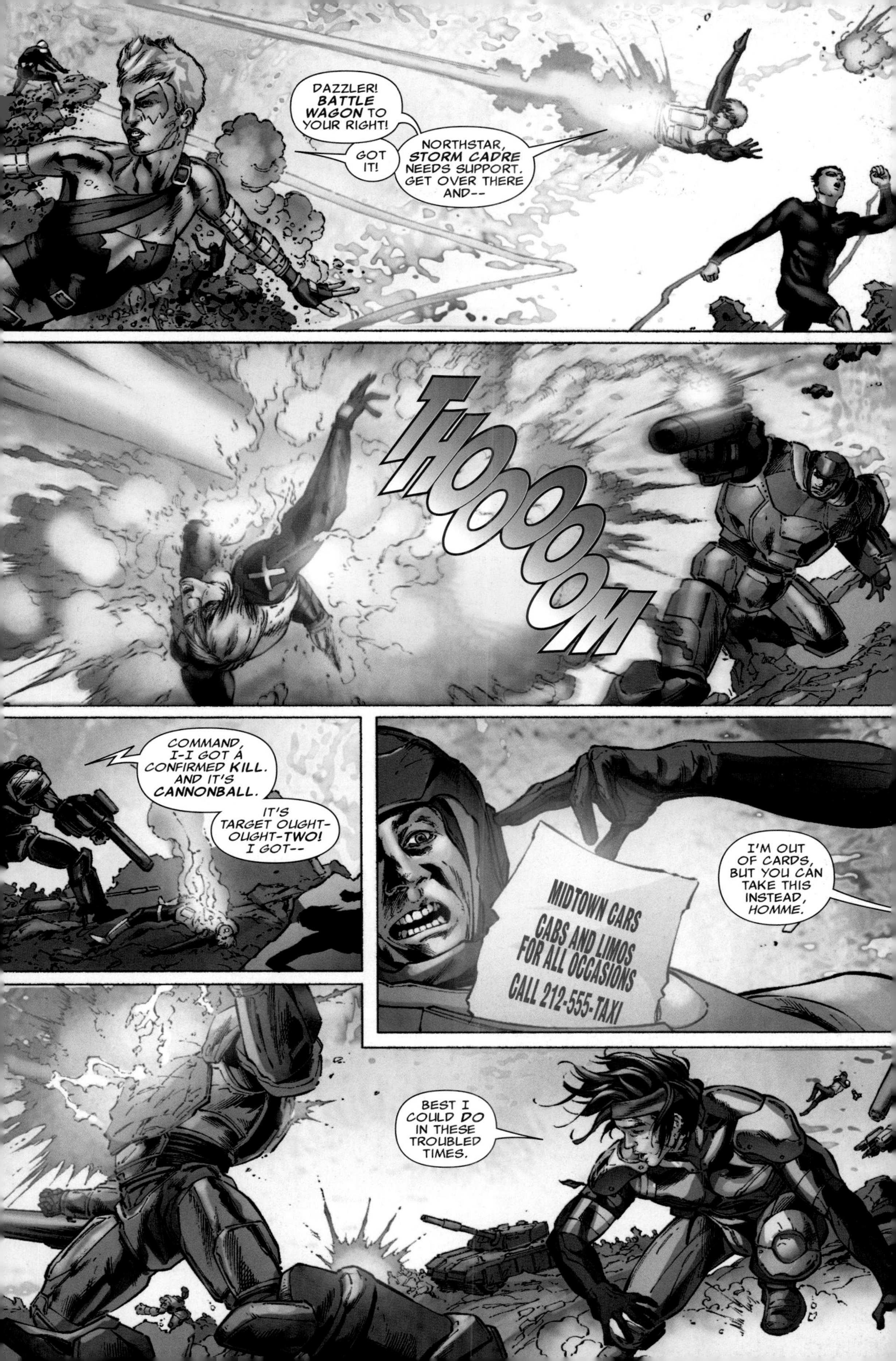
DAZZLER! BATTLE WAGON TO YOUR RIGHT!
GOT IT!
NORTHSTAR, STORM CADRE NEEDS SUPPORT. GET OVER THERE AND--
THOOOOOM
COMMAND, I-I GOT A CONFIRMED KILL. AND IT'S CANNONBALL.
IT'S TARGET OUGHT-OUGHT-TWO! I GOT--
MIDTOWN CARS
CABS AND LIMOS FOR ALL OCCASIONS
CALL 212-555-TAXI
I'M OUT OF CARDS, BUT YOU CAN TAKE THIS INSTEAD, HOMME.
BEST I COULD DO IN THESE TROUBLED TIMES.

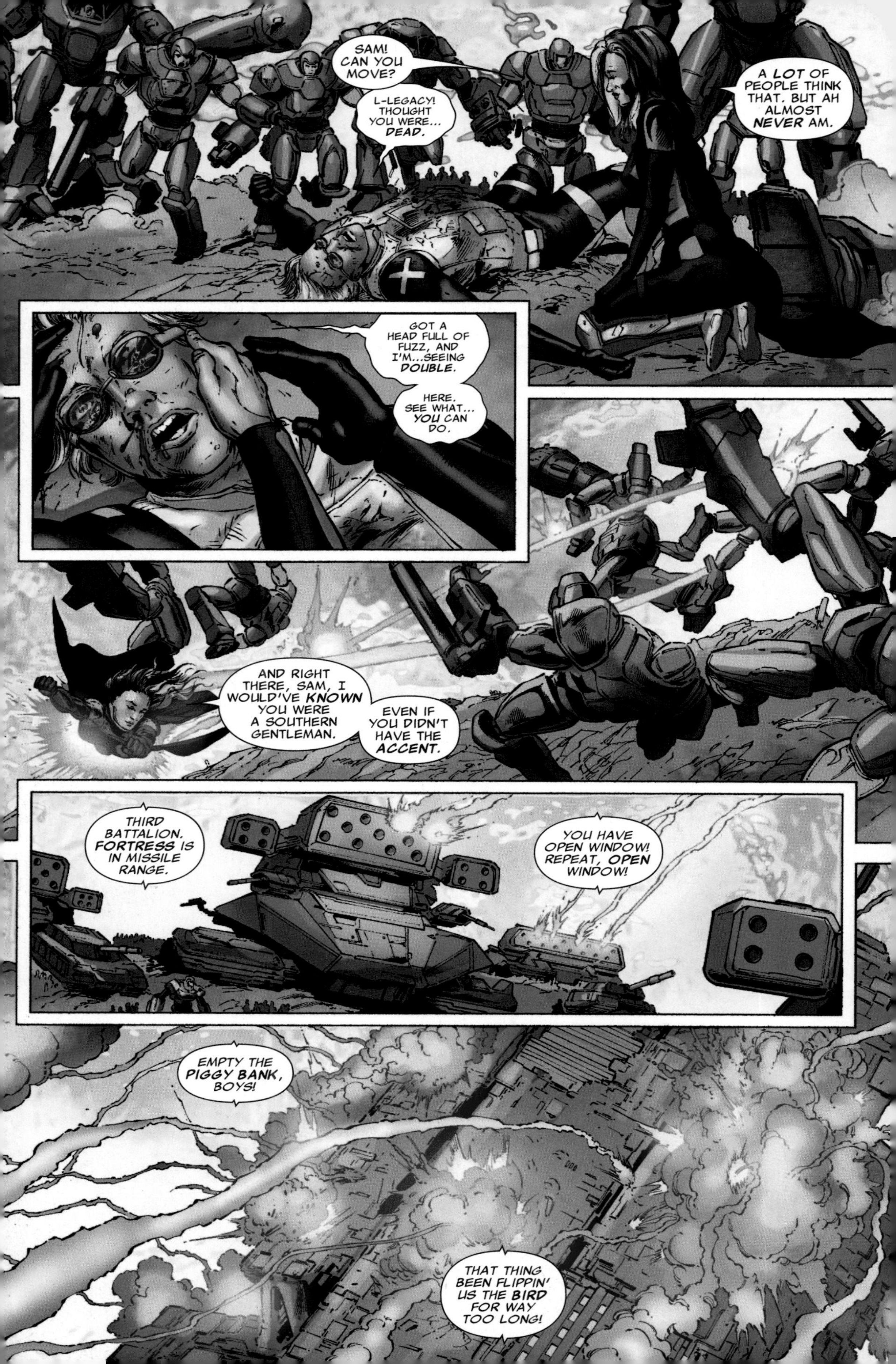
SAM! CAN YOU MOVE?
L-LEGACY! THOUGHT YOU WERE... DEAD.
A LOT OF PEOPLE THINK THAT. BUT AH ALMOST NEVER AM.
GOT A HEAD FULL OF FUZZ, AND I'M...SEEING DOUBLE.
HERE. SEE WHAT... YOU CAN DO.
AND RIGHT THERE, SAM, I WOULD'VE KNOWN YOU WERE A SOUTHERN GENTLEMAN.
EVEN IF YOU DIDN'T HAVE THE ACCENT.
THIRD BATTALION. FORTRESS IS IN MISSILE RANGE.
YOU HAVE OPEN WINDOW! REPEAT, OPEN WINDOW!
EMPTY THE PIGGY BANK, BOYS!
THAT THING BEEN FLIPPIN' US THE BIRD FOR WAY TOO LONG!

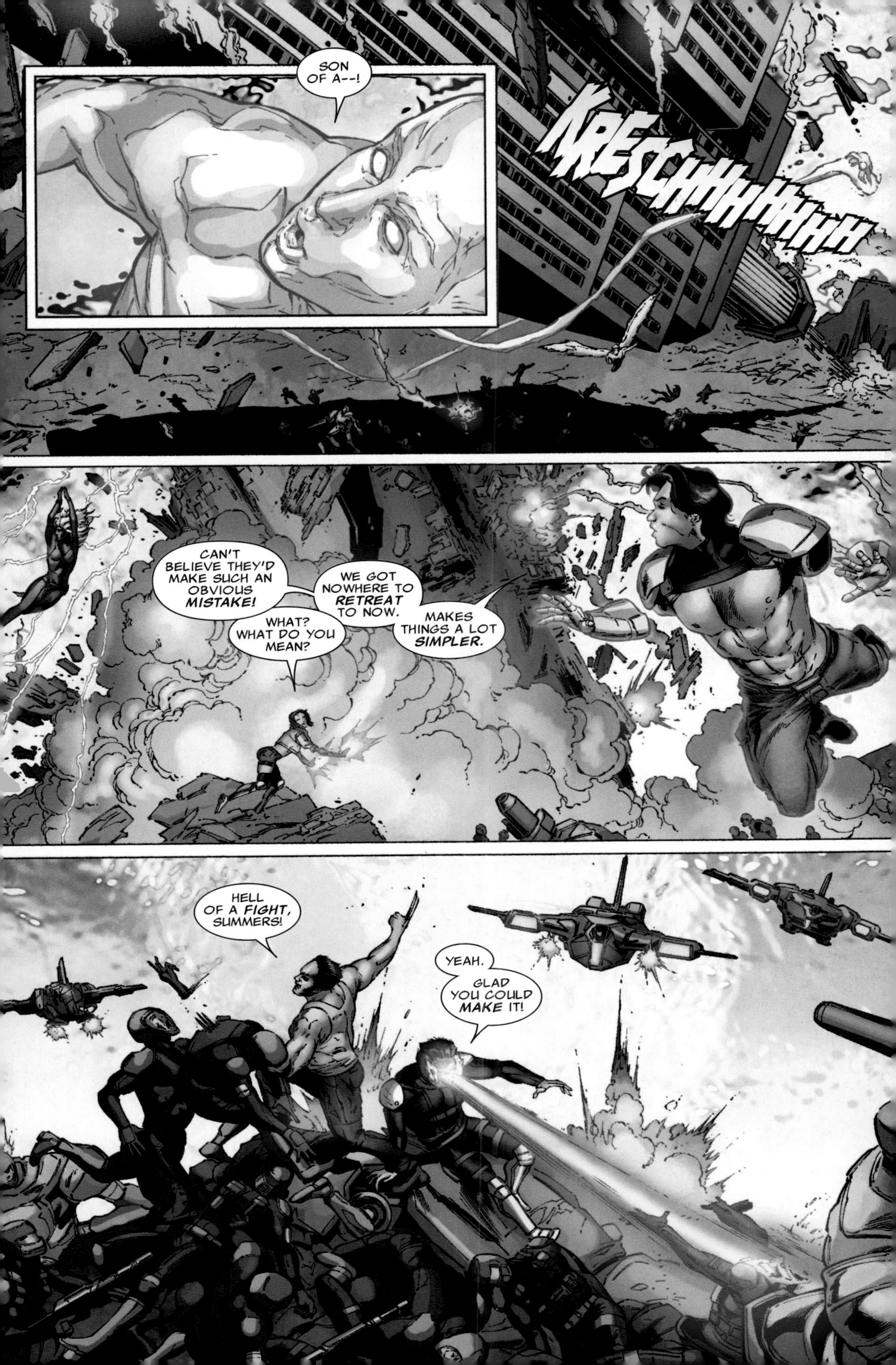
SON OF A--!
KRESCHHHHHHHHH
CAN'T BELIEVE THEY'D MAKE SUCH AN OBVIOUS MISTAKE!
WHAT? WHAT DO YOU MEAN?
WE GOT NOWHERE TO RETREAT TO NOW.
MAKES THINGS A LOT SIMPLER.
HELL OF A FIGHT, SUMMERS!
YEAH.
GLAD YOU COULD MAKE IT!

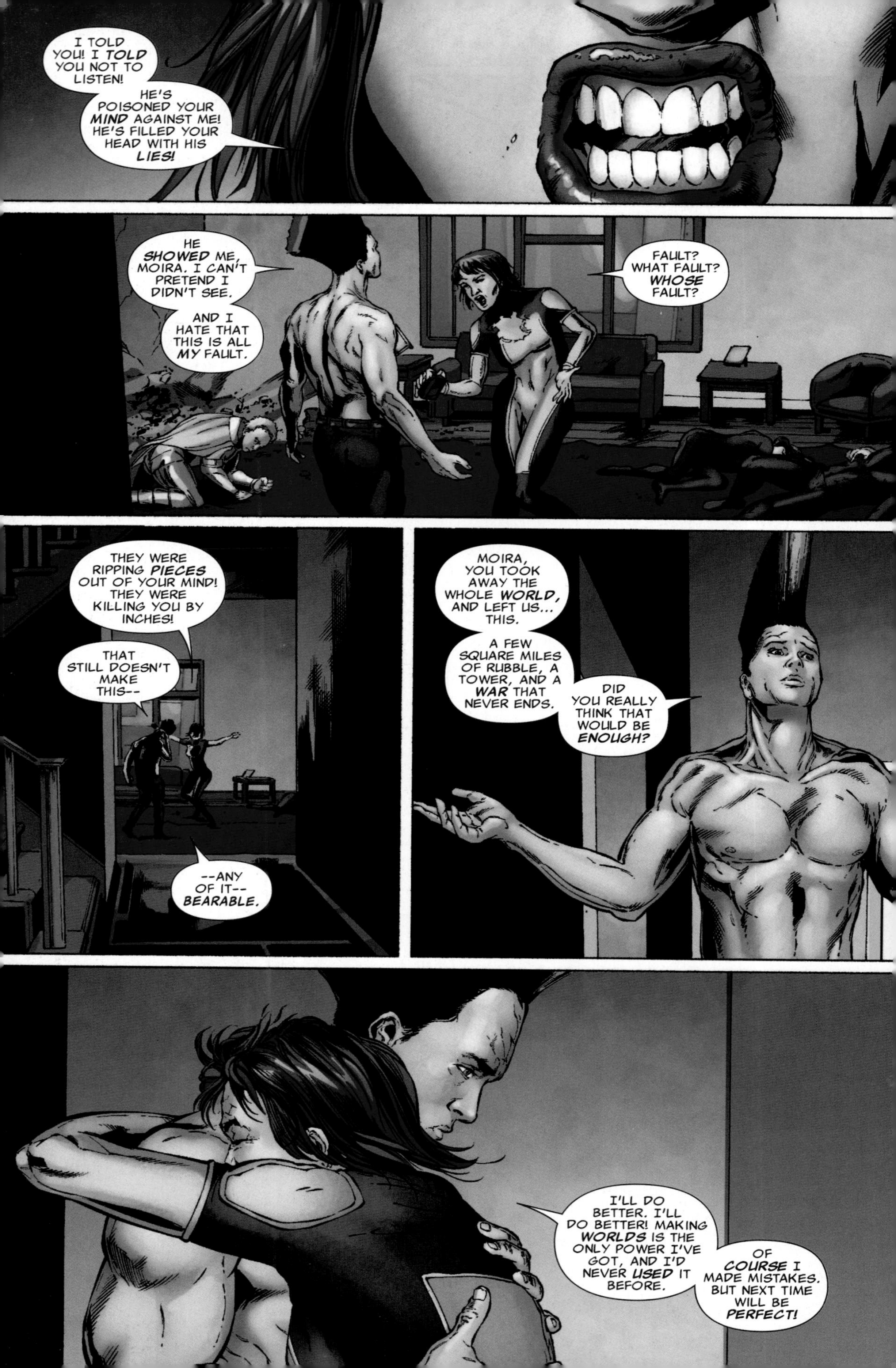
I TOLD YOU! I TOLD YOU NOT TO LISTEN!
HE'S POISONED YOUR MIND AGAINST ME! HE'S FILLED YOUR HEAD WITH HIS LIES!
HE SHOWED ME, MOIRA. I CAN'T PRETEND I DIDN'T SEE.
AND I HATE THAT THIS IS ALL MY FAULT.
FAULT? WHAT FAULT? WHOSE FAULT?
THEY WERE RIPPING PIECES OUT OF YOUR MIND! THEY WERE KILLING YOU BY INCHES!
THAT STILL DOESN'T MAKE THIS--
--ANY OF IT--BEARABLE.
MOIRA, YOU TOOK AWAY THE WHOLE WORLD, AND LEFT US... THIS.
A FEW SQUARE MILES OF RUBBLE, A TOWER, AND A WAR THAT NEVER ENDS.
DID YOU REALLY THINK THAT WOULD BE ENOUGH?
I'LL DO BETTER. I'LL DO BETTER! MAKING WORLDS IS THE ONLY POWER I'VE GOT, AND I'D NEVER USED IT BEFORE.
OF COURSE I MADE MISTAKES. BUT NEXT TIME WILL BE PERFECT!

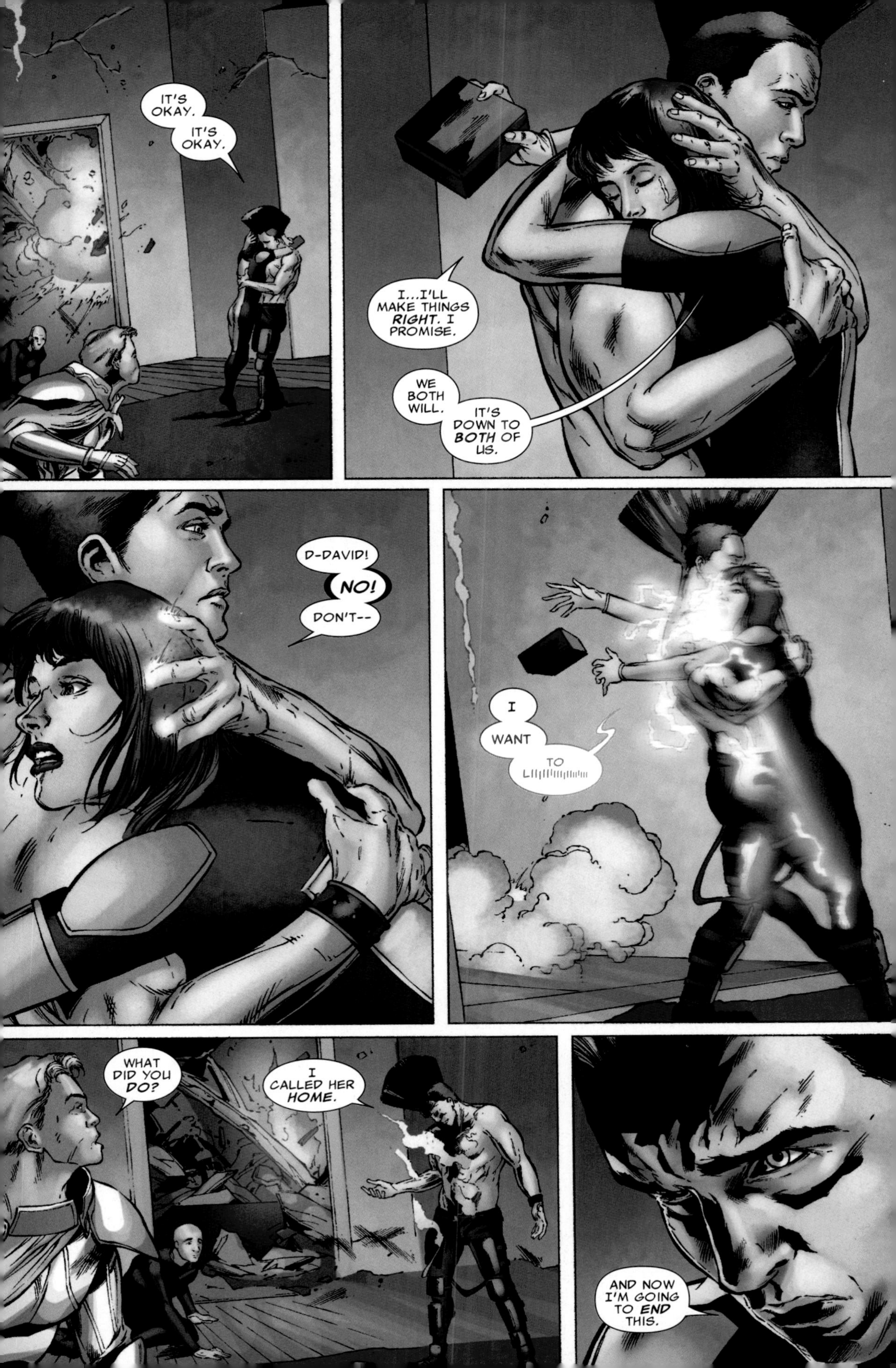
IT'S OKAY.
IT'S OKAY.
I...I'LL MAKE THINGS RIGHT. I PROMISE.
WE BOTH WILL.
IT'S DOWN TO BOTH OF US.
D-DAVID!
NO!
DON'T--
I
WANT
TO
WHAT DID YOU DO?
I CALLED HER HOME.
AND NOW I'M GOING TO END THIS.

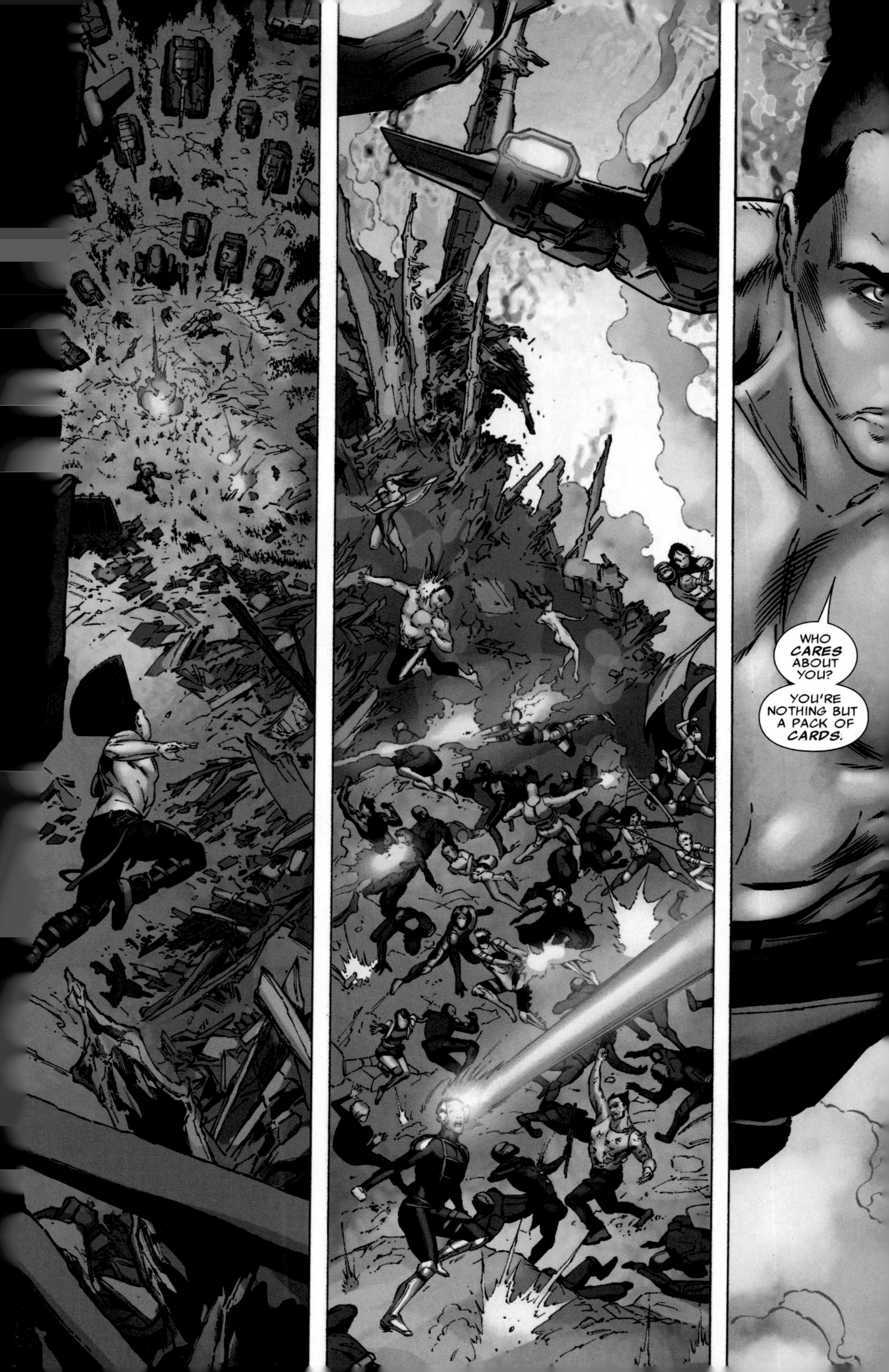
WHO CARES ABOUT YOU?
YOU'RE NOTHING BUT A PACK OF CARDS.

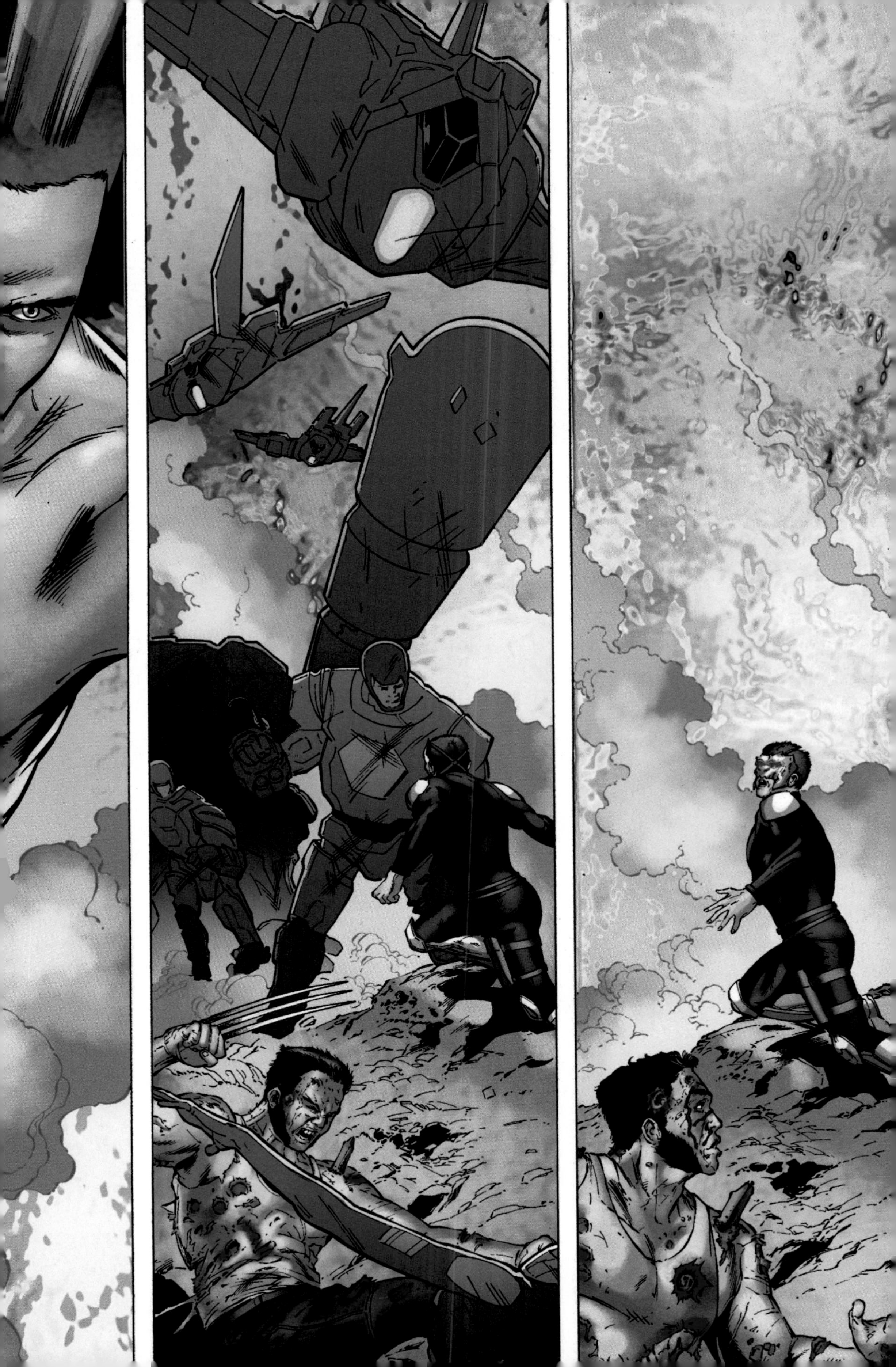

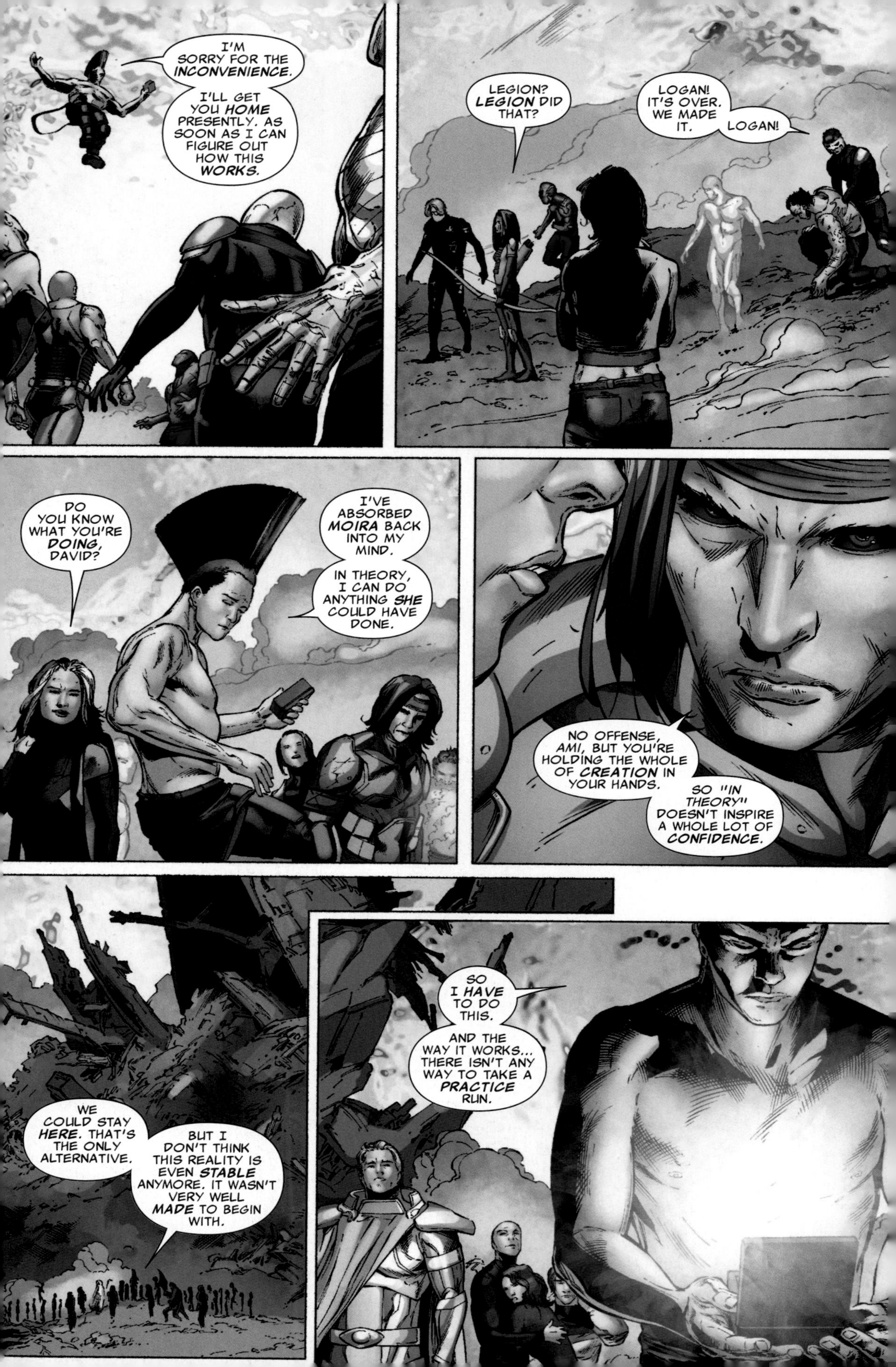
I'M SORRY FOR THE INCONVENIENCE.
I'LL GET YOU HOME PRESENTLY. AS SOON AS I CAN FIGURE OUT HOW THIS WORKS.
LEGION? LEGION DID THAT?
LOGAN! IT'S OVER. WE MADE IT.
LOGAN!
DO YOU KNOW WHAT YOU'RE DOING, DAVID?
I'VE ABSORBED MOIRA BACK INTO MY MIND.
IN THEORY, I CAN DO ANYTHING SHE COULD HAVE DONE.
NO OFFENSE, AMI, BUT YOU'RE HOLDING THE WHOLE OF CREATION IN YOUR HANDS.
SO "IN THEORY" DOESN'T INSPIRE A WHOLE LOT OF CONFIDENCE.
WE COULD STAY HERE. THAT'S THE ONLY ALTERNATIVE.
BUT I DON'T THINK THIS REALITY IS EVEN STABLE ANYMORE. IT WASN'T VERY WELL MADE TO BEGIN WITH.
SO I HAVE TO DO THIS.
AND THE WAY IT WORKS... THERE ISN'T ANY WAY TO TAKE A PRACTICE RUN.

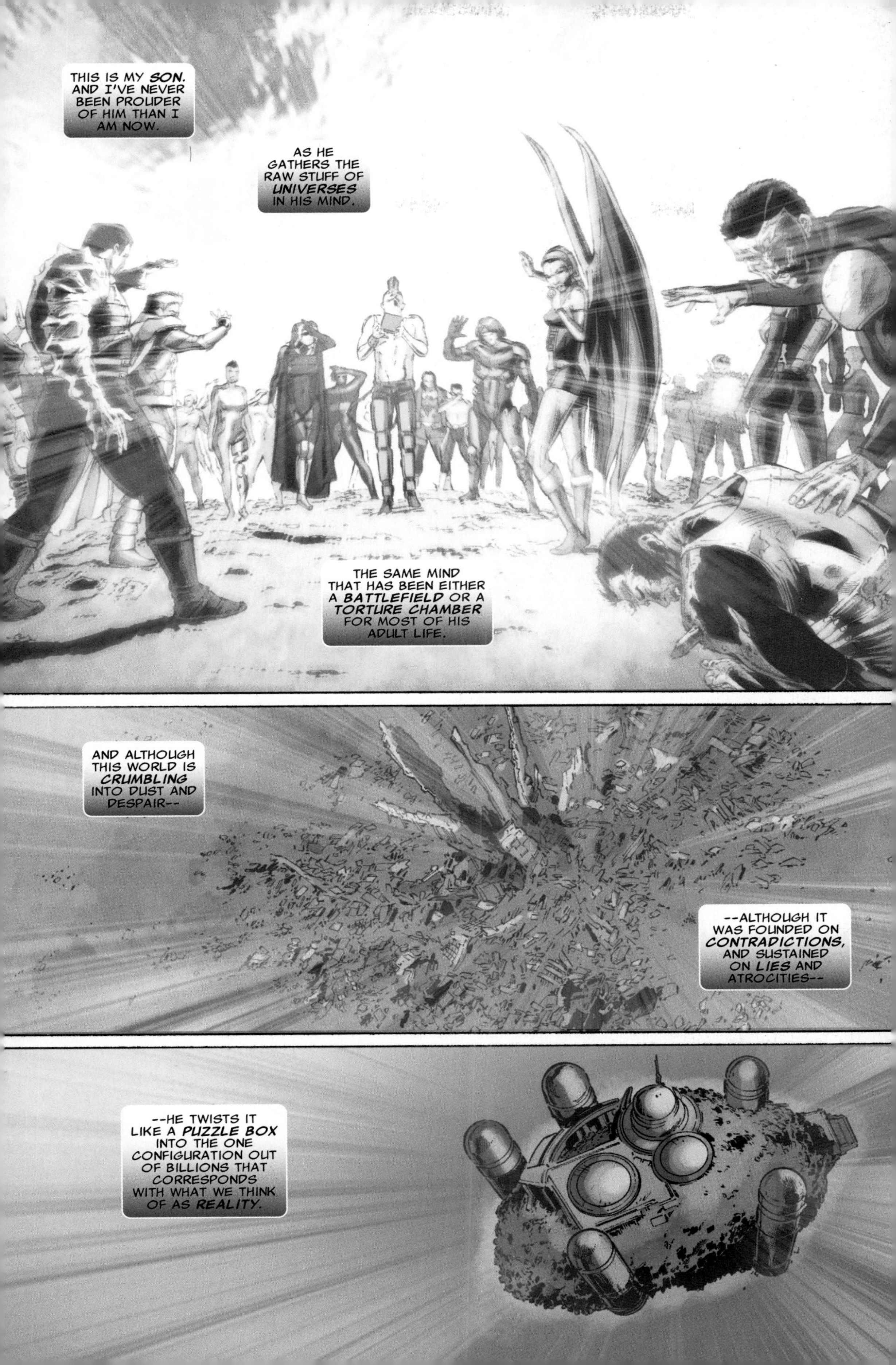
THIS IS MY SON. AND I'VE NEVER BEEN PROUDER OF HIM THAN I AM NOW.
AS HE GATHERS THE RAW STUFF OF UNIVERSES IN HIS MIND.
THE SAME MIND THAT HAS BEEN EITHER A BATTLEFIELD OR A TORTURE CHAMBER FOR MOST OF HIS ADULT LIFE.
AND ALTHOUGH THIS WORLD IS CRUMBLING INTO DUST AND DESPAIR--
--ALTHOUGH IT WAS FOUNDED ON CONTRADICTIONS, AND SUSTAINED ON LIES AND ATROCITIES--
--HE TWISTS IT LIKE A PUZZLE BOX INTO THE ONE CONFIGURATION OUT OF BILLIONS THAT CORRESPONDS WITH WHAT WE THINK OF AS REALITY.

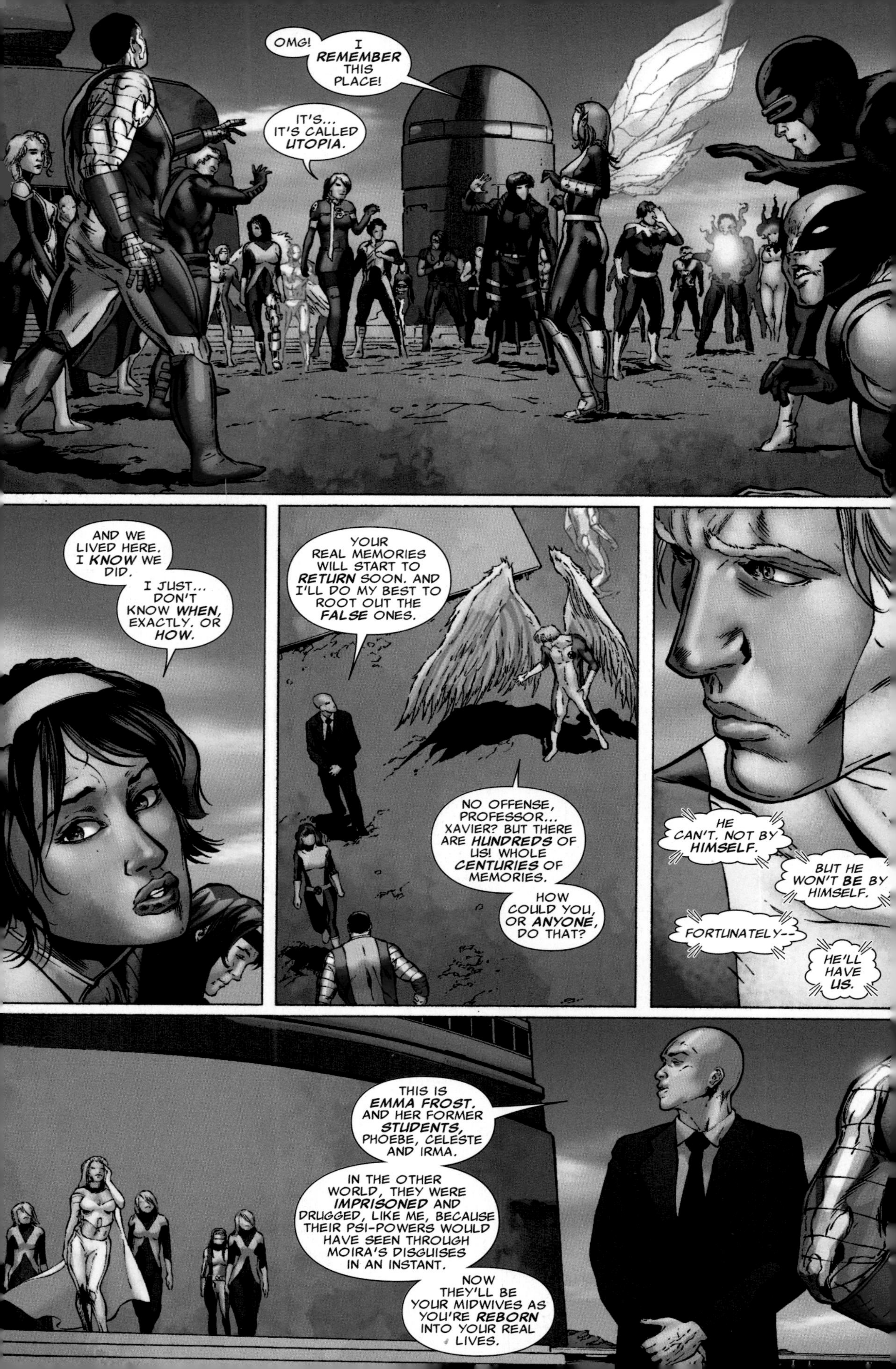
OMG!
I REMEMBER THIS PLACE!
IT'S... IT'S CALLED UTOPIA.
AND WE LIVED HERE. I KNOW WE DID.
I JUST... DON'T KNOW WHEN, EXACTLY. OR HOW.
YOUR REAL MEMORIES WILL START TO RETURN SOON. AND I'LL DO MY BEST TO ROOT OUT THE FALSE ONES.
NO OFFENSE, PROFESSOR... XAVIER? BUT THERE ARE HUNDREDS OF US! WHOLE CENTURIES OF MEMORIES.
HOW COULD YOU, OR ANYONE, DO THAT?
HE CAN'T. NOT BY HIMSELF.
BUT HE WON'T BE BY HIMSELF.
FORTUNATELY--
HE'LL HAVE US.
THIS IS EMMA FROST, AND HER FORMER STUDENTS, PHOEBE, CELESTE AND IRMA.
IN THE OTHER WORLD, THEY WERE IMPRISONED AND DRUGGED, LIKE ME, BECAUSE THEIR PSI-POWERS WOULD HAVE SEEN THROUGH MOIRA'S DISGUISES IN AN INSTANT.
NOW THEY'LL BE YOUR MIDWIVES AS YOU'RE REBORN INTO YOUR REAL LIVES.

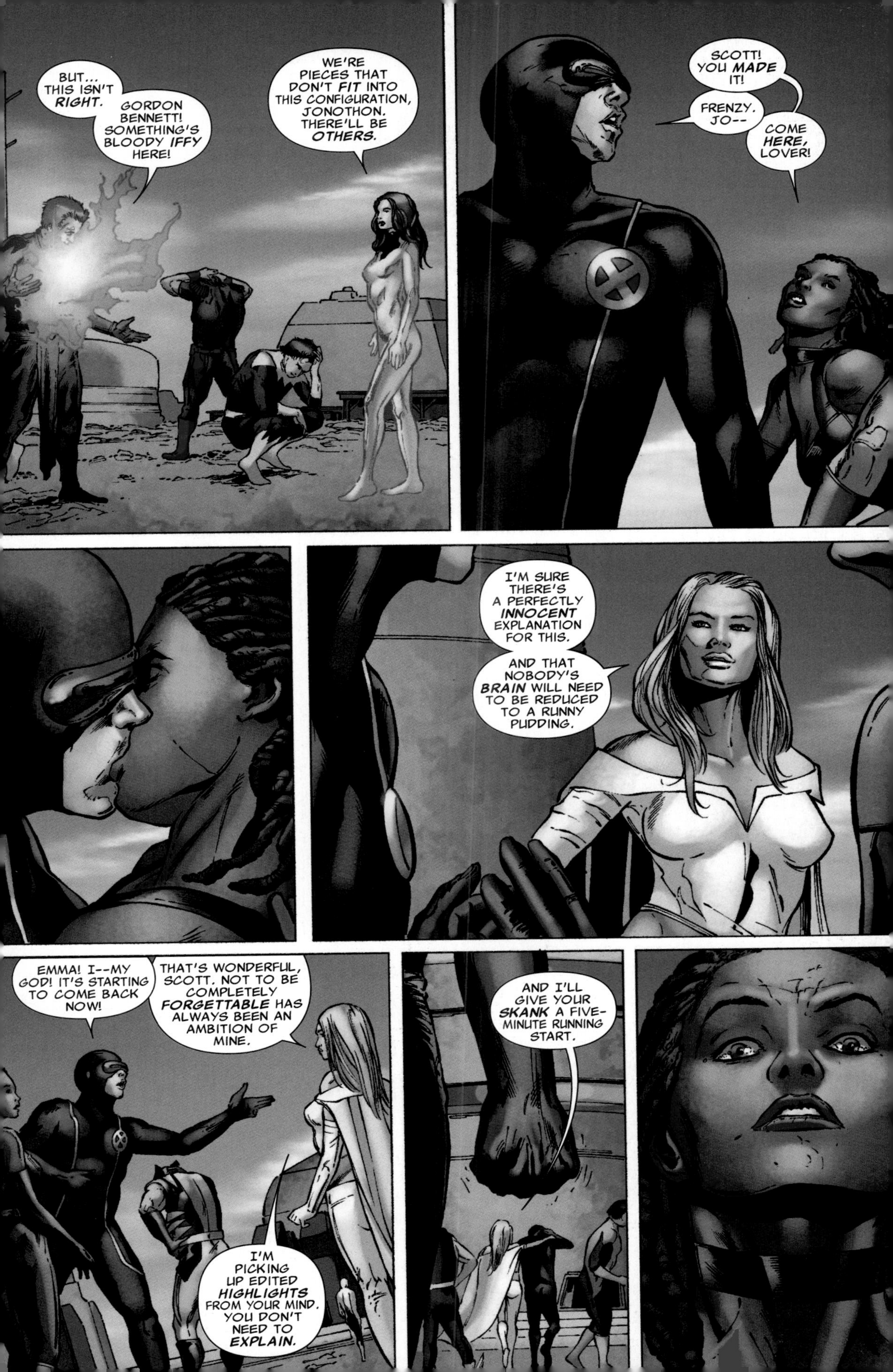

BUT... THIS ISN'T RIGHT.
GORDON BENNETT! SOMETHING'S BLOODY IFFY HERE!
WE'RE PIECES THAT DON'T FIT INTO THIS CONFIGURATION, JONOTHON. THERE'LL BE OTHERS.
SCOTT! YOU MADE IT!
FRENZY. JO--
COME HERE, LOVER!
I'M SURE THERE'S A PERFECTLY INNOCENT EXPLANATION FOR THIS.
AND THAT NOBODY'S BRAIN WILL NEED TO BE REDUCED TO A RUNNY PUDDING.
EMMA! I--MY GOD! IT'S STARTING TO COME BACK NOW!
THAT'S WONDERFUL, SCOTT. NOT TO BE COMPLETELY FORGETTABLE HAS ALWAYS BEEN AN AMBITION OF MINE.
I'M PICKING UP EDITED HIGHLIGHTS FROM YOUR MIND. YOU DON'T NEED TO EXPLAIN.
AND I'LL GIVE YOUR SKANK A FIVE-MINUTE RUNNING START.

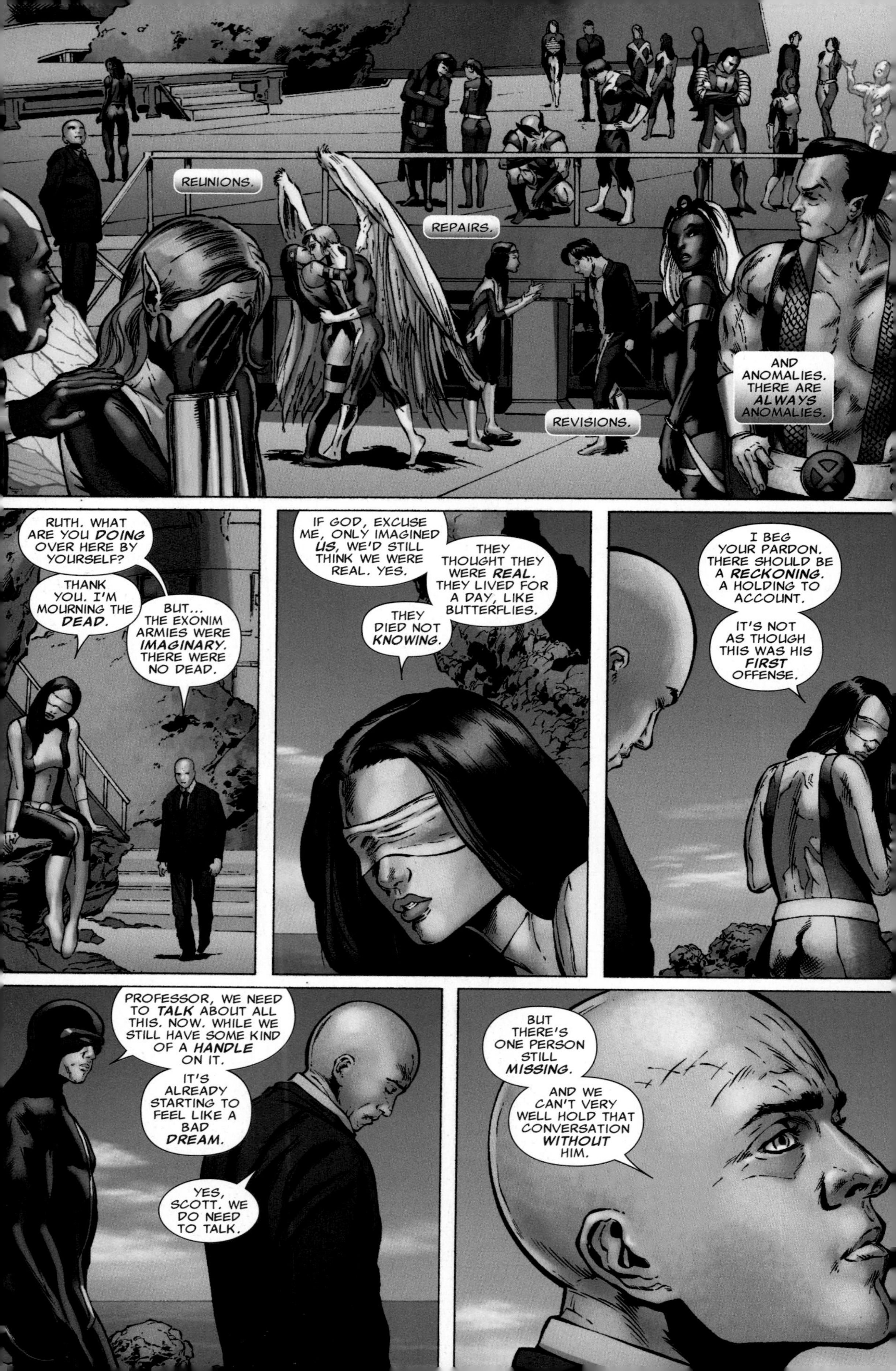
REUNIONS.
REPAIRS.
REVISIONS.
AND ANOMALIES. THERE ARE ALWAYS ANOMALIES.
RUTH. WHAT ARE YOU DOING OVER HERE BY YOURSELF?
THANK YOU. I'M MOURNING THE DEAD.
BUT... THE EXONIM ARMIES WERE IMAGINARY. THERE WERE NO DEAD.
IF GOD, EXCUSE ME, ONLY IMAGINED US, WE'D STILL THINK WE WERE REAL. YES.
THEY THOUGHT THEY WERE REAL. THEY LIVED FOR A DAY, LIKE BUTTERFLIES.
THEY DIED NOT KNOWING.
I BEG YOUR PARDON. THERE SHOULD BE A RECKONING. A HOLDING TO ACCOUNT.
IT'S NOT AS THOUGH THIS WAS HIS FIRST OFFENSE.
PROFESSOR, WE NEED TO TALK ABOUT ALL THIS. NOW. WHILE WE STILL HAVE SOME KIND OF A HANDLE ON IT.
IT'S ALREADY STARTING TO FEEL LIKE A BAD DREAM.
YES, SCOTT. WE DO NEED TO TALK.
BUT THERE'S ONE PERSON STILL MISSING.
AND WE CAN'T VERY WELL HOLD THAT CONVERSATION WITHOUT HIM.

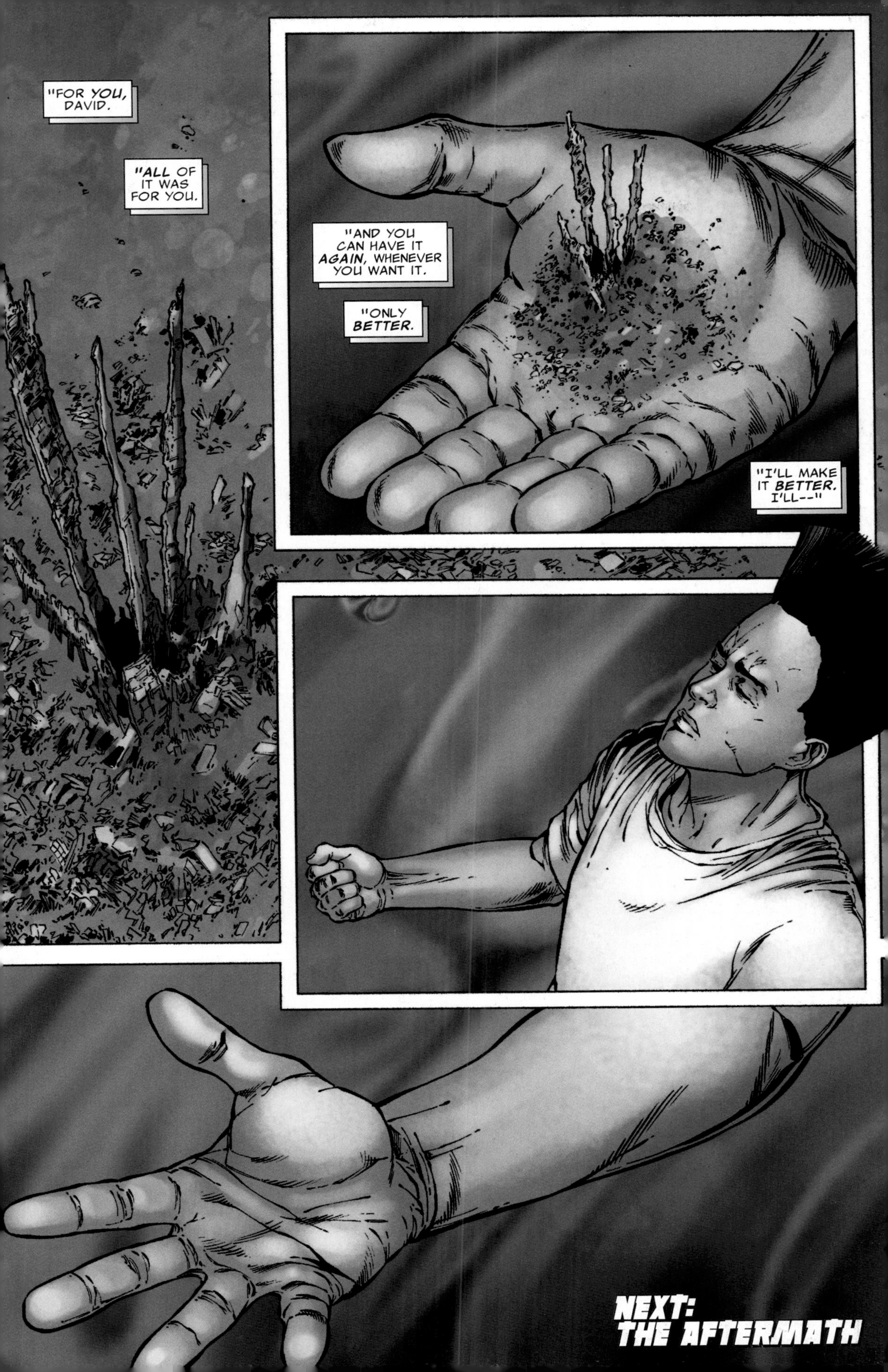
"FOR YOU, DAVID.
"ALL OF IT WAS FOR YOU.
"AND YOU CAN HAVE IT AGAIN, WHENEVER YOU WANT IT.
"ONLY BETTER.
"I'LL MAKE IT BETTER. I'LL--"
NEXT: THE AFTERMATH

AGE OF X: UNIVERSE #1

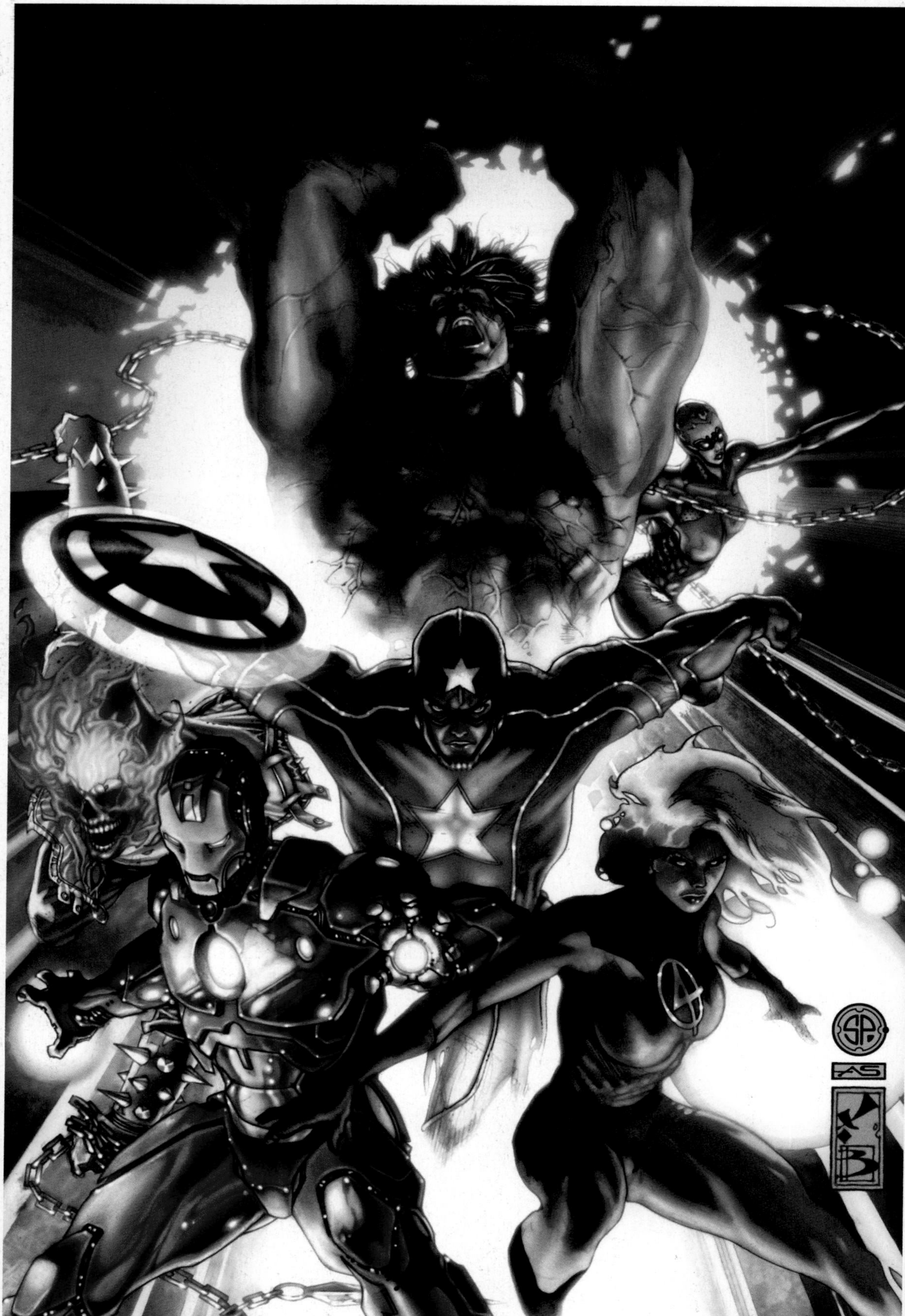

In a world where the X-Men never existed and mutantkind has been hunted to extinction, the few remaining mutants band together to make their last stand.

But they're not the only ones who have banded together. Those who would see mutantkind eliminated have plans of their own...

AGE OF X UNIVERSE

CHAPTER 1

AVENGERS

WRITTEN BY SIMON SPURRIER
PENCILED BY KHOI PHAM
INKED BY TOM PALMER
COLORED BY SONIA OBACK

SPIDER-MAN

WRITTEN BY JIM MCCANN
ART BY PAUL DAVIDSON
COLORED BY ANTONIO FABELA

LETTERED BY VC'S JOE SABINO
COVER ART BY SIMONE BIANCHI & SIMONE PERUZZI

EDITOR: DANIEL KETCHUM
X-MEN GROUP EDITOR: NICK LOWE
EDITOR IN CHIEF: AXEL ALONSO
CHIEF CREATIVE OFFICER: JOE QUESADA
PUBLISHER: DAN BUCKLEY
EXECUTIVE PRODUCER: ALAN FINE

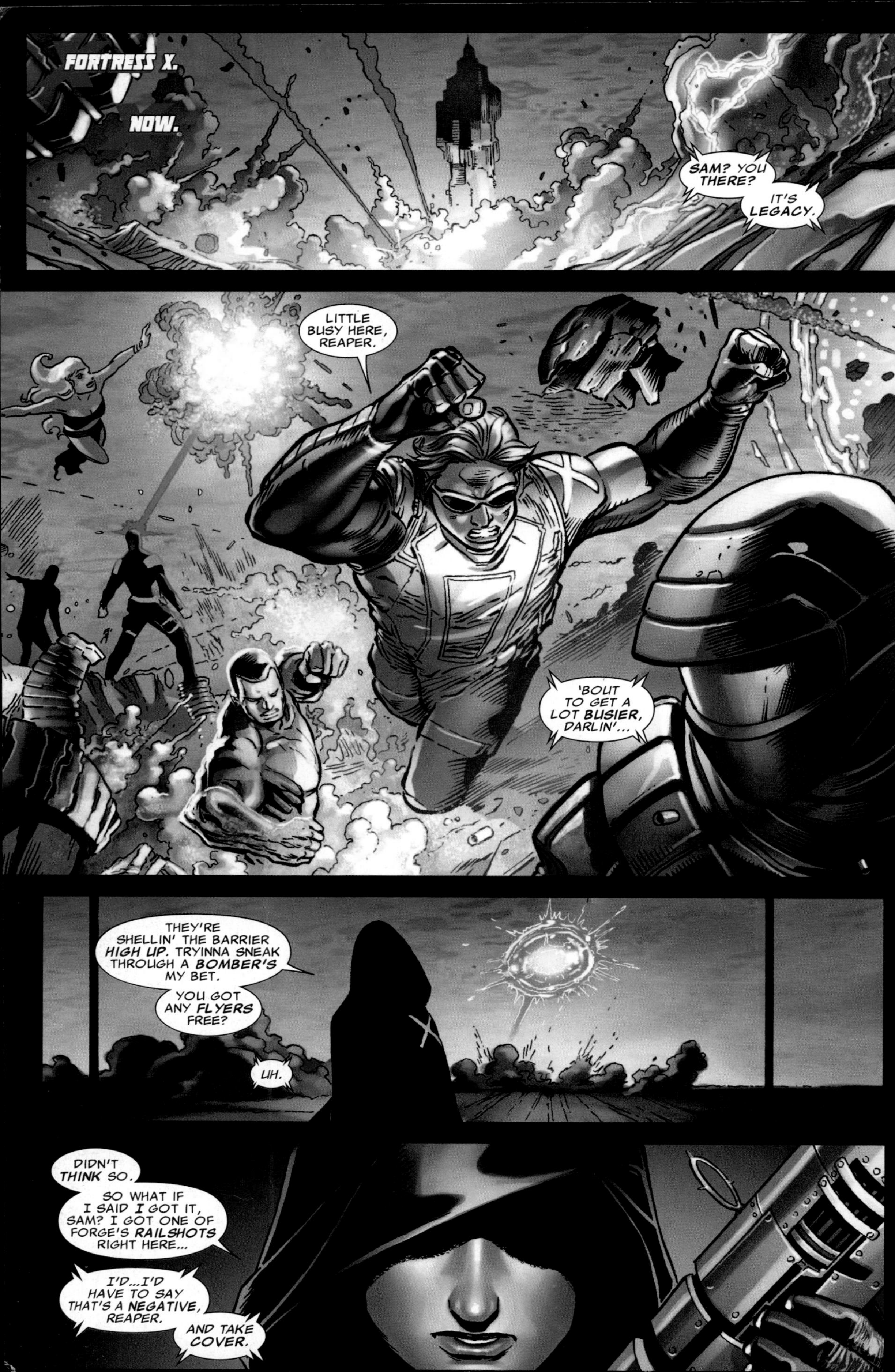
FORTRESS X.
NOW.
SAM? YOU THERE?
IT'S LEGACY.
LITTLE BUSY HERE, REAPER.
'BOUT TO GET A LOT BUSIER, DARLIN'...
THEY'RE SHELLIN' THE BARRIER HIGH UP. TRYINNA SNEAK THROUGH A BOMBER'S MY BET.
YOU GOT ANY FLYERS FREE?
UH.
DIDN'T THINK SO.
SO WHAT IF I SAID I GOT IT, SAM? I GOT ONE OF FORGE'S RAILSHOTS RIGHT HERE...
I'D...I'D HAVE TO SAY THAT'S A NEGATIVE, REAPER.
AND TAKE COVER.

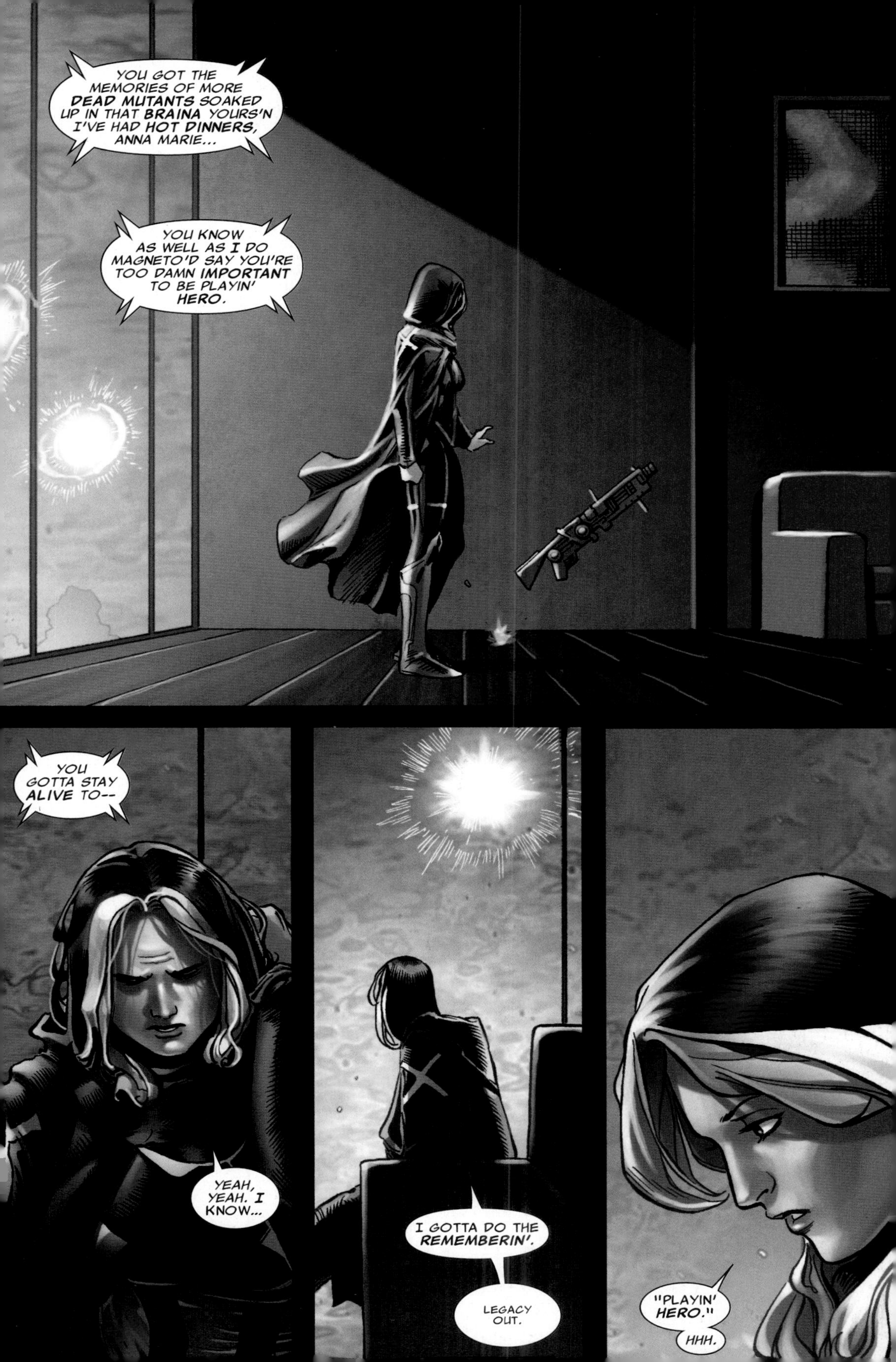
YOU GOT THE MEMORIES OF MORE DEAD MUTANTS SOAKED UP IN THAT BRAINA YOURS'N I'VE HAD HOT DINNERS, ANNA MARIE...
YOU KNOW AS WELL AS I DO MAGNETO'D SAY YOU'RE TOO DAMN IMPORTANT TO BE PLAYIN' HERO.
YOU GOTTA STAY ALIVE TO--
YEAH, YEAH. I KNOW...
I GOTTA DO THE REMEMBERIN'.
LEGACY OUT.
"PLAYIN' HERO."
HHH.

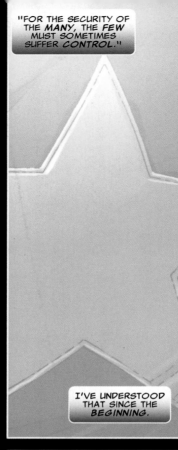

"FOR THE SECURITY OF THE *MANY,* THE *FEW* MUST SOMETIMES SUFFER *CONTROL.*"

I'VE UNDERSTOOD THAT SINCE THE *BEGINNING.*

SINCE THE *INTERMARRIAGE LAWS* PASSED AND MUTANTS MARCHED OUTSIDE CONGRESS.

SINCE *ONE RIOT COP* RAISED HIS *BATON* AND *HUNDREDS DIED* IN *UNEARTHLY RETALIATION.*

SINCE THE *STERILIZATIONS* AND *DEPORTATIONS* BRED ONLY *DISASTER.*

SINCE EVERY ATTEMPT TO *PURIFY* OR *PACIFY* THE MUTANTS WAS MET WITH *DISPROPORTIONATE DEFENSE.*

SINCE THE *PHOENIX* SNUBBED *SURRENDER* AND RAZED ALBANY IN AN INSTANT OF COSMIC *RAGE...*

...AND TOOK *WITH* HER TWO THOUSAND OF MY FELLOW *SOLDIERS.*

SINCE I CAN *REMEMBER,* I'VE BEEN FIGHTING THE *MUTANTS.*

ALONE.

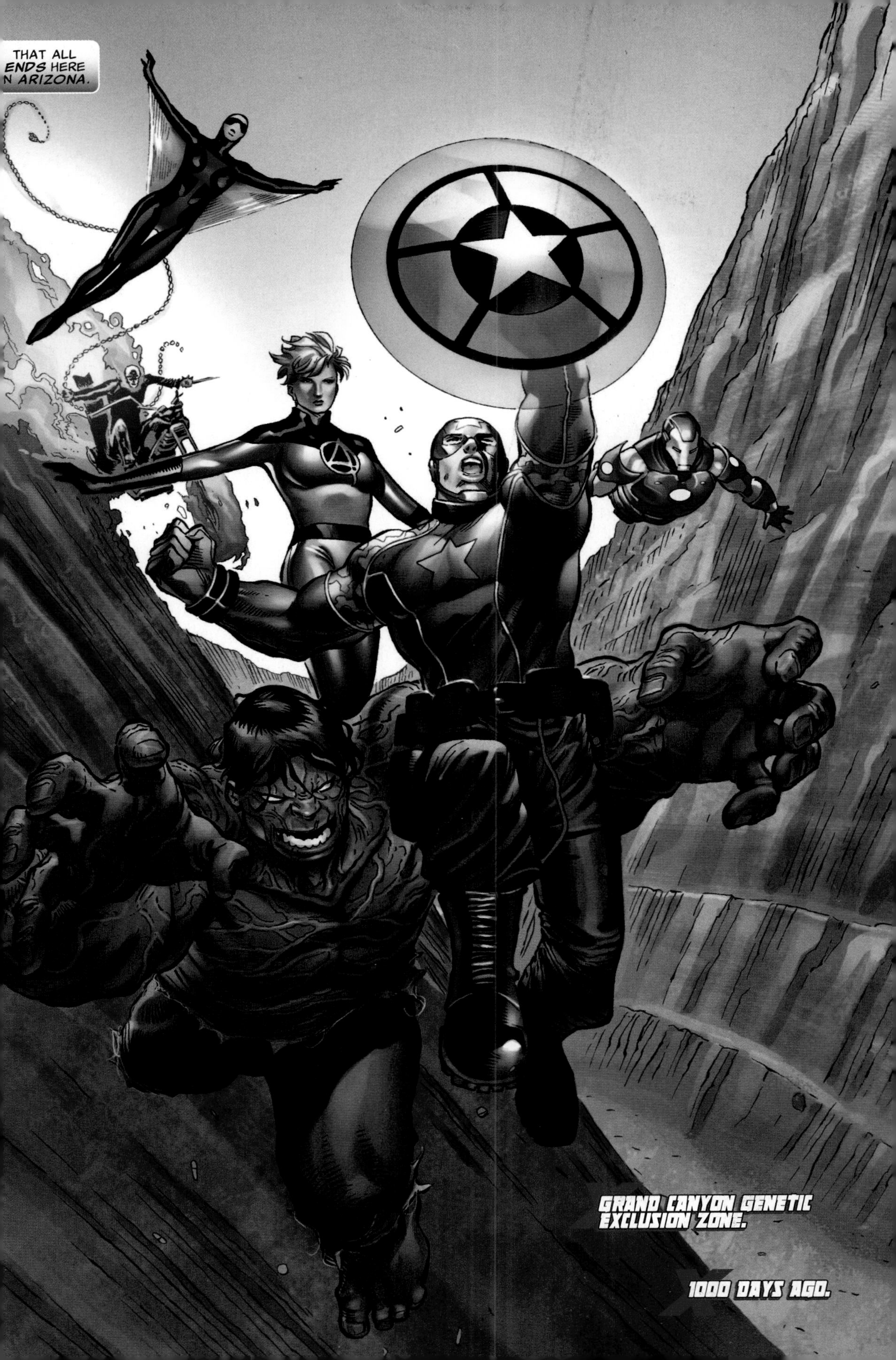
THAT ALL ENDS HERE N ARIZONA.
GRAND CANYON GENETIC EXCLUSION ZONE.
1000 DAYS AGO.

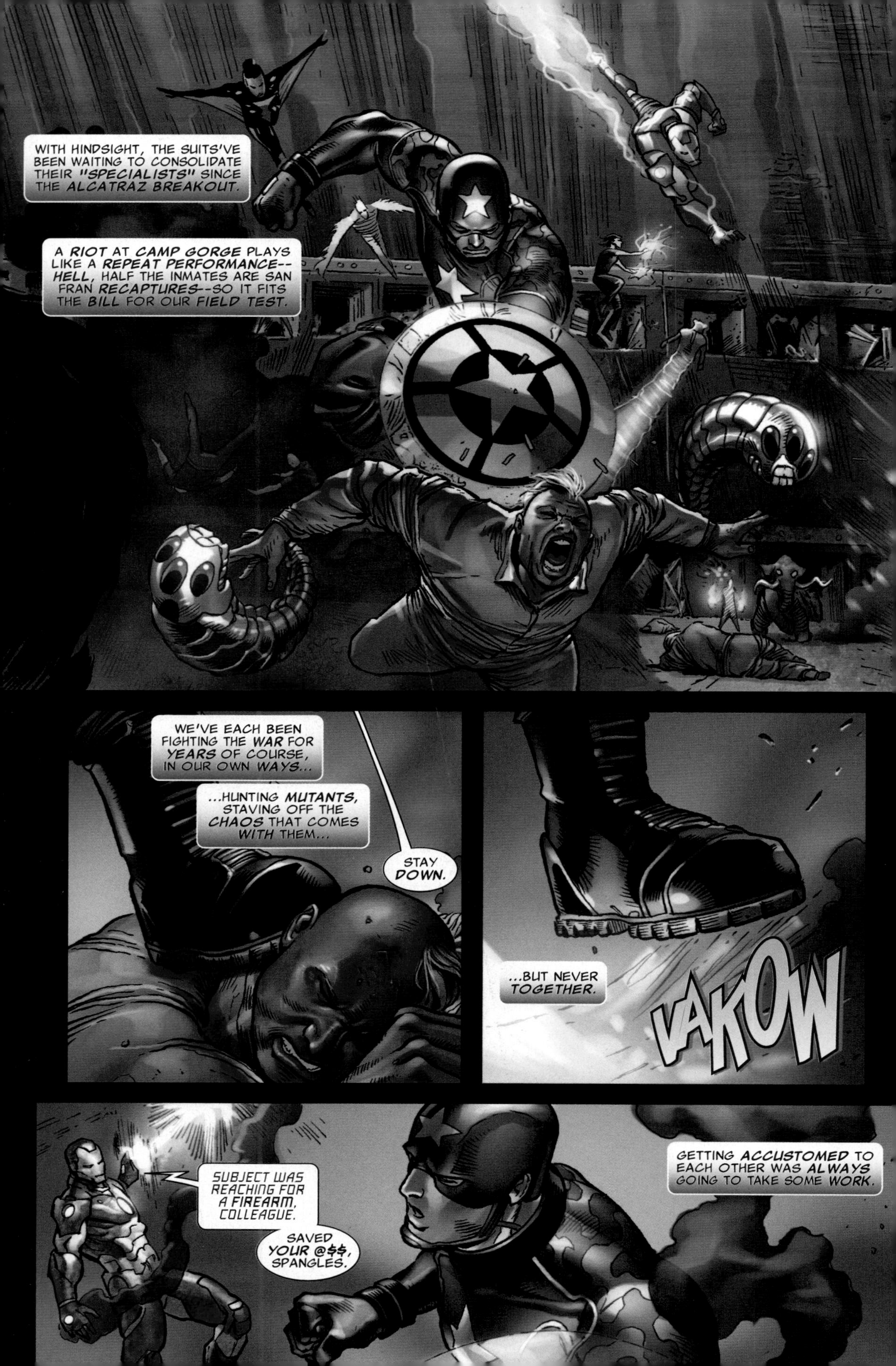
WITH HINDSIGHT, THE SUITS'VE BEEN WAITING TO CONSOLIDATE THEIR "SPECIALISTS" SINCE THE ALCATRAZ BREAKOUT.
A RIOT AT CAMP GORGE PLAYS LIKE A REPEAT PERFORMANCE--HELL, HALF THE INMATES ARE SAN FRAN RECAPTURES--SO IT FITS THE BILL FOR OUR FIELD TEST.
WE'VE EACH BEEN FIGHTING THE WAR FOR YEARS OF COURSE, IN OUR OWN WAYS...
...HUNTING MUTANTS, STAVING OFF THE CHAOS THAT COMES WITH THEM...
STAY DOWN.
...BUT NEVER TOGETHER.
VAKOW
SUBJECT WAS REACHING FOR A FIREARM, COLLEAGUE.
SAVED YOUR @$$, SPANGLES.
GETTING ACCUSTOMED TO EACH OTHER WAS ALWAYS GOING TO TAKE SOME WORK.

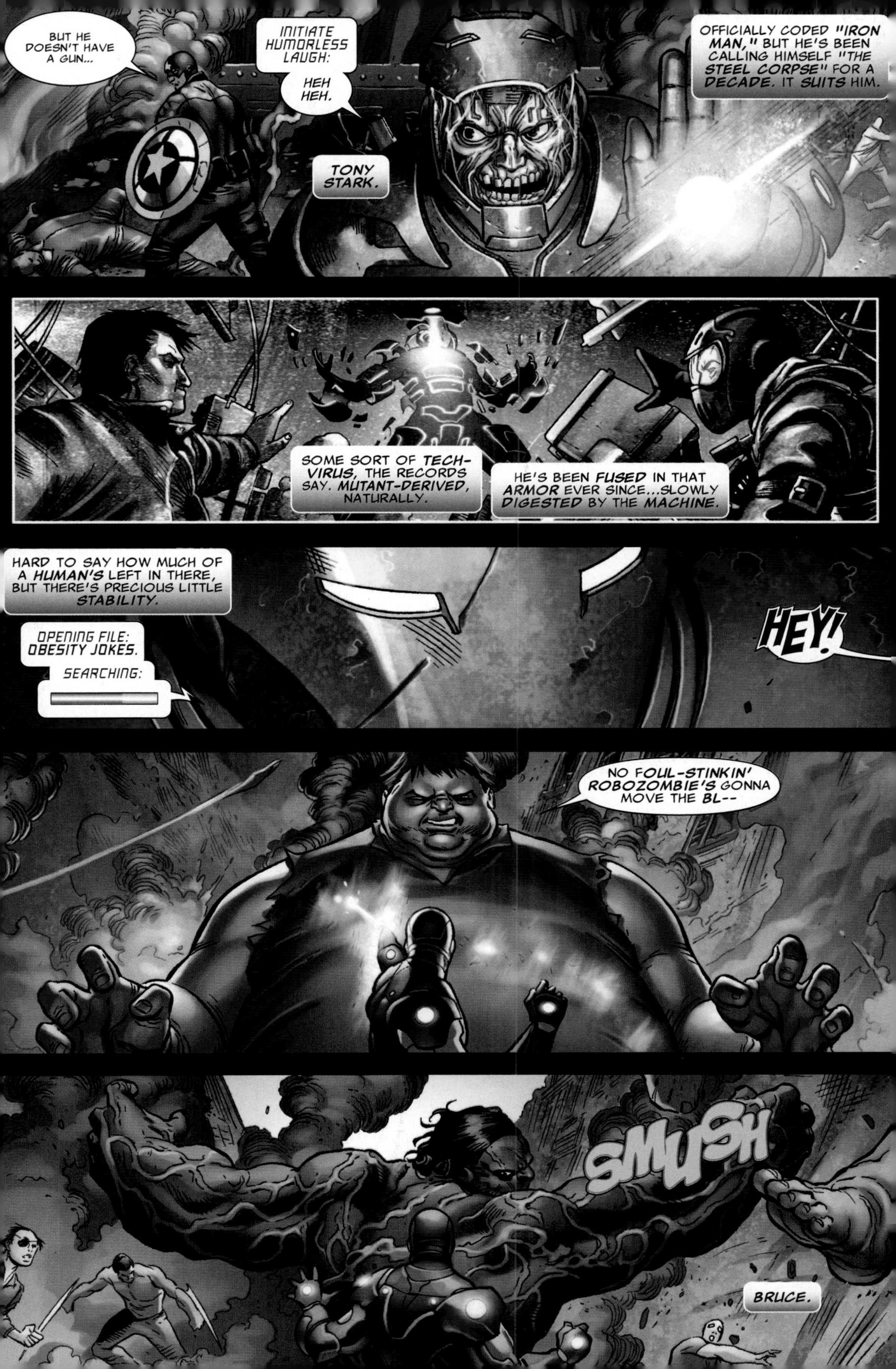
BUT HE DOESN'T HAVE A GUN...
INITIATE HUMORLESS LAUGH:
HEH HEH.
TONY STARK.
OFFICIALLY CODED "IRON MAN," BUT HE'S BEEN CALLING HIMSELF "THE STEEL CORPSE" FOR A DECADE. IT SUITS HIM.
SOME SORT OF TECH-VIRUS, THE RECORDS SAY. MUTANT-DERIVED, NATURALLY.
HE'S BEEN FUSED IN THAT ARMOR EVER SINCE...SLOWLY DIGESTED BY THE MACHINE.
HARD TO SAY HOW MUCH OF A HUMAN'S LEFT IN THERE, BUT THERE'S PRECIOUS LITTLE STABILITY.
OPENING FILE: OBESITY JOKES.
SEARCHING:
HEY!
NO FOUL-STINKIN' ROBOZOMBIE'S GONNA MOVE THE BL--
SMUSH
BRUCE.

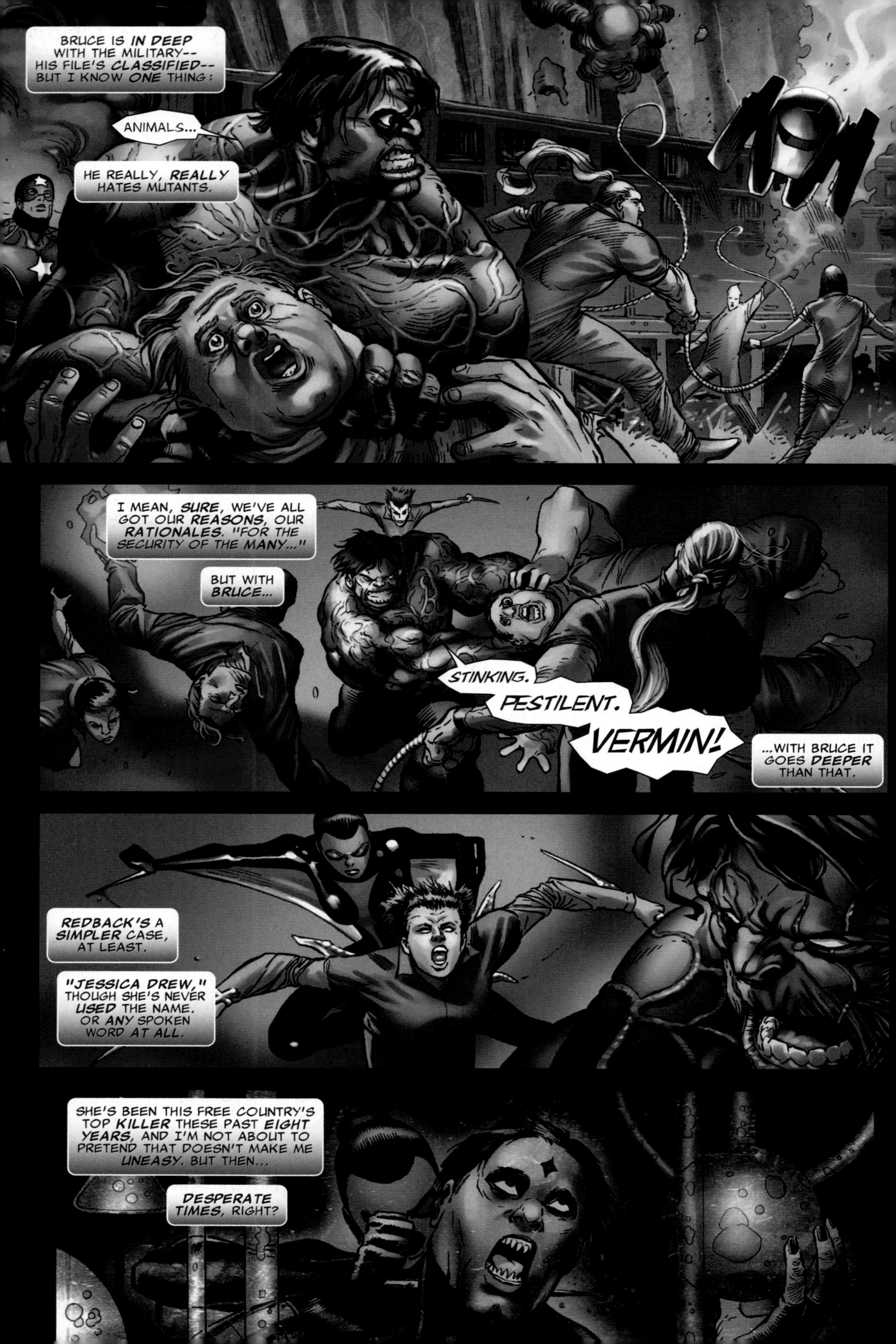
BRUCE IS IN DEEP WITH THE MILITARY-- HIS FILE'S CLASSIFIED-- BUT I KNOW ONE THING:
ANIMALS...
HE REALLY, REALLY HATES MUTANTS.
I MEAN, SURE, WE'VE ALL GOT OUR REASONS, OUR RATIONALES. "FOR THE SECURITY OF THE MANY..."
BUT WITH BRUCE...
STINKING.
PESTILENT.
VERMIN!
...WITH BRUCE IT GOES DEEPER THAN THAT.
REDBACK'S A SIMPLER CASE, AT LEAST.
"JESSICA DREW," THOUGH SHE'S NEVER USED THE NAME. OR ANY SPOKEN WORD AT ALL.
SHE'S BEEN THIS FREE COUNTRY'S TOP KILLER THESE PAST EIGHT YEARS, AND I'M NOT ABOUT TO PRETEND THAT DOESN'T MAKE ME UNEASY. BUT THEN...
DESPERATE TIMES, RIGHT?

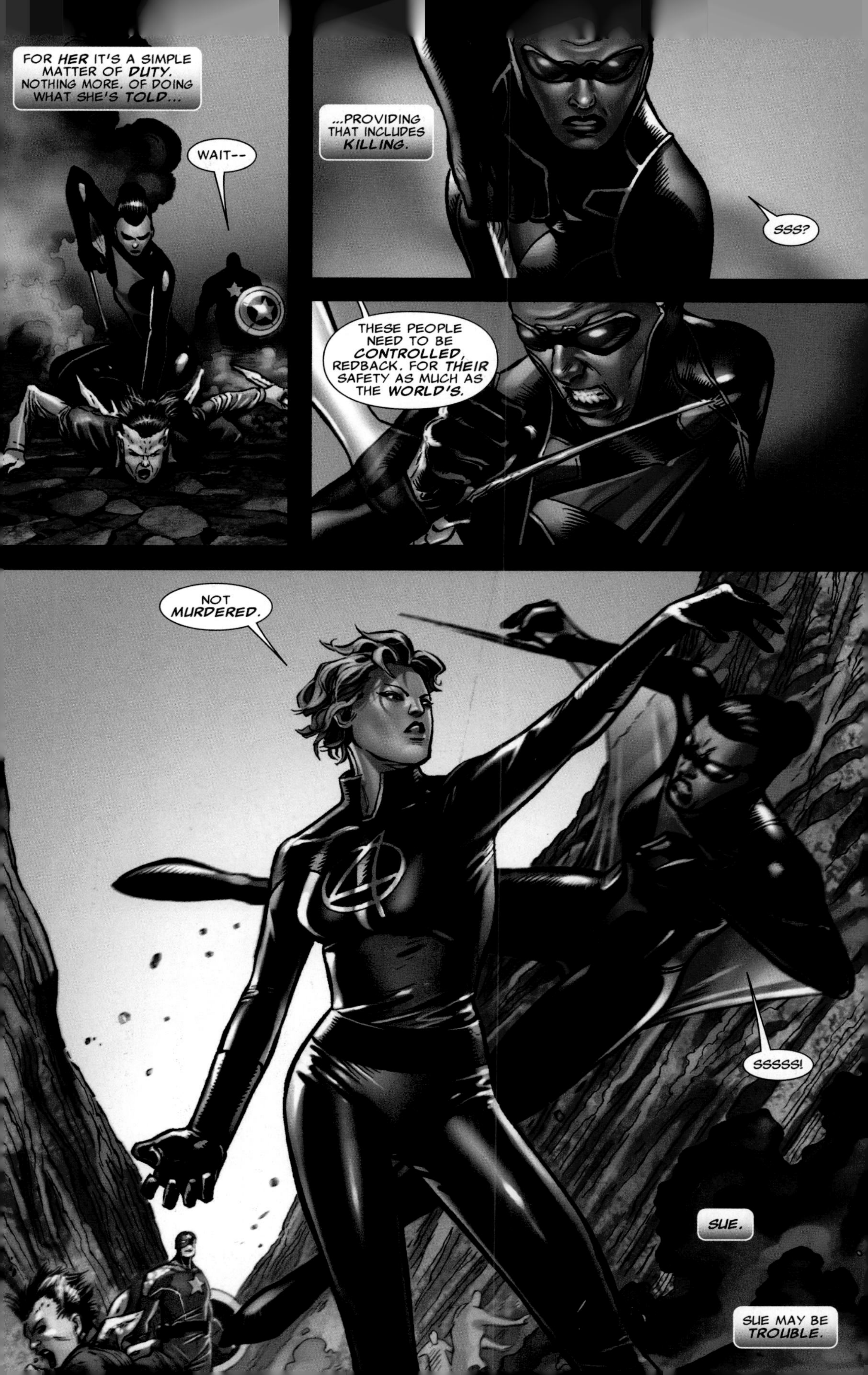
FOR HER IT'S A SIMPLE MATTER OF DUTY. NOTHING MORE. OF DOING WHAT SHE'S TOLD...
WAIT--
...PROVIDING THAT INCLUDES KILLING.
SSS?
THESE PEOPLE NEED TO BE CONTROLLED, REDBACK. FOR THEIR SAFETY AS MUCH AS THE WORLD'S.
NOT MURDERED.
SSSSS!
SUE.
SUE MAY BE TROUBLE.

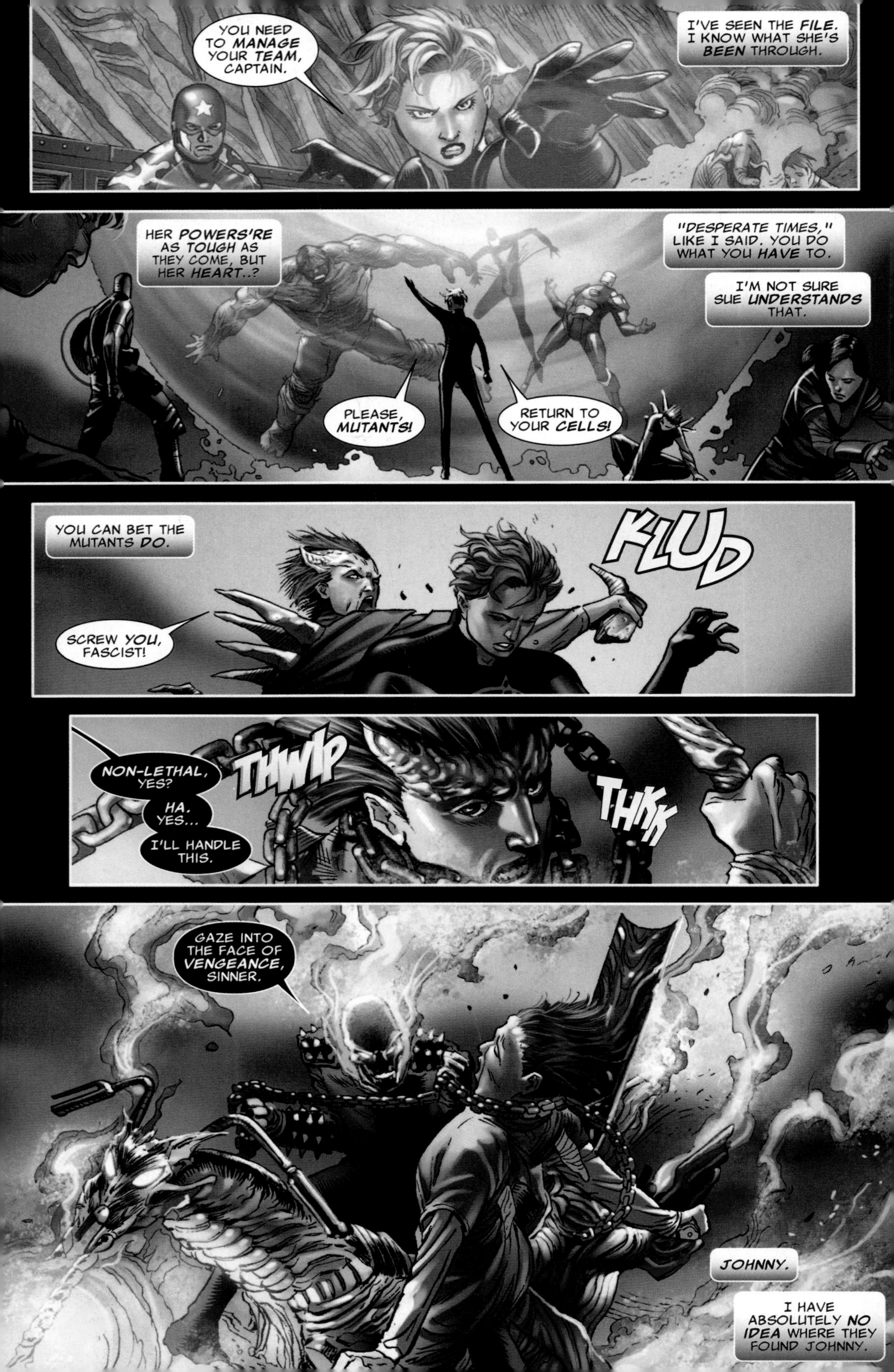

YOU NEED TO MANAGE YOUR TEAM, CAPTAIN.
I'VE SEEN THE FILE. I KNOW WHAT SHE'S BEEN THROUGH.
HER POWERS'RE AS TOUGH AS THEY COME, BUT HER HEART..?
"DESPERATE TIMES," LIKE I SAID. YOU DO WHAT YOU HAVE TO.
I'M NOT SURE SUE UNDERSTANDS THAT.
PLEASE, MUTANTS!
RETURN TO YOUR CELLS!
YOU CAN BET THE MUTANTS DO.
KLUD
SCREW YOU, FASCIST!
NON-LETHAL, YES?
HA. YES...
I'LL HANDLE THIS.
THWIP
THKK
GAZE INTO THE FACE OF VENGEANCE, SINNER.
JOHNNY.
I HAVE ABSOLUTELY NO IDEA WHERE THEY FOUND JOHNNY.

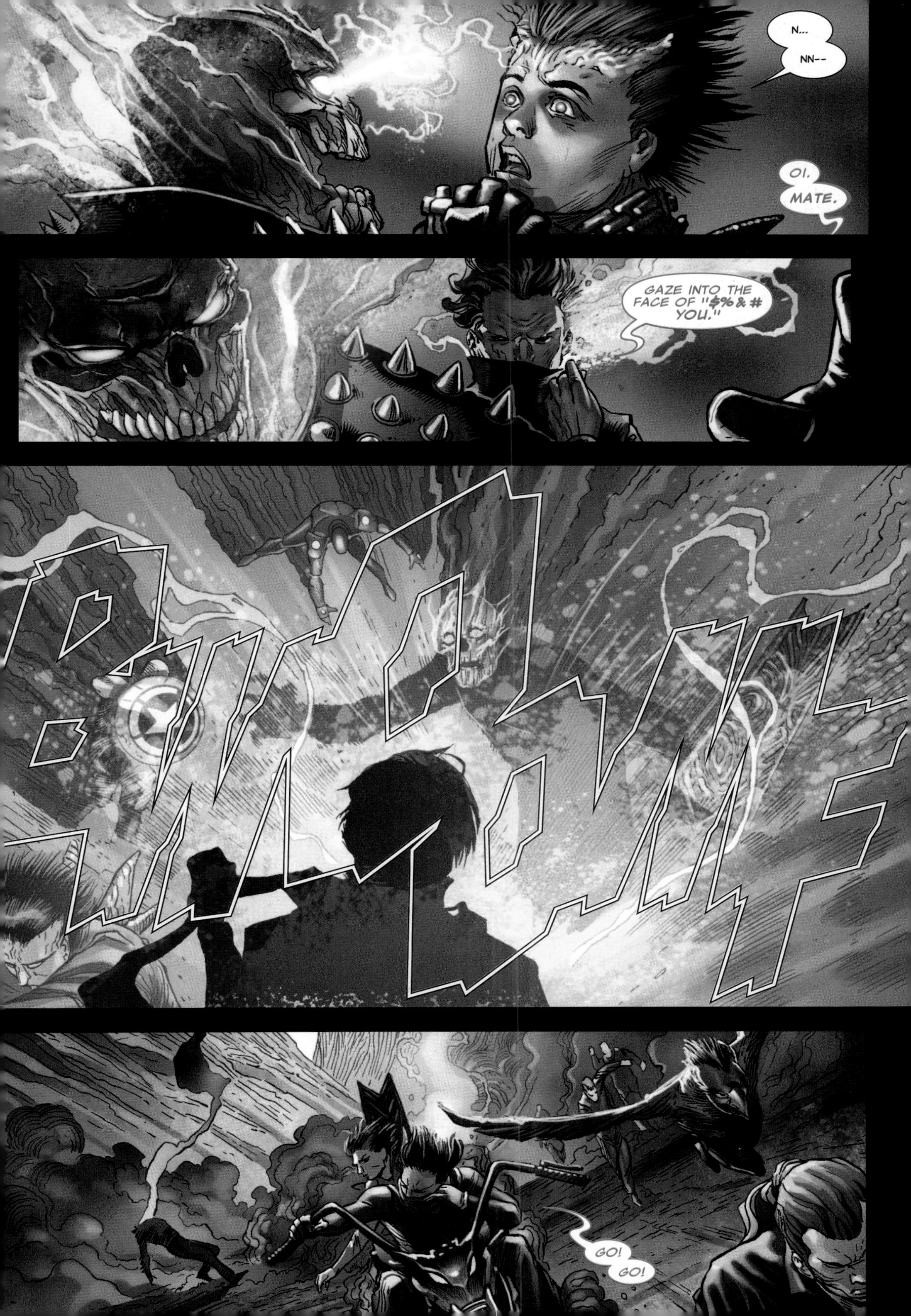
N...
NN--
OI. MATE.
GAZE INTO THE FACE OF "$%&# YOU."
GO! GO!

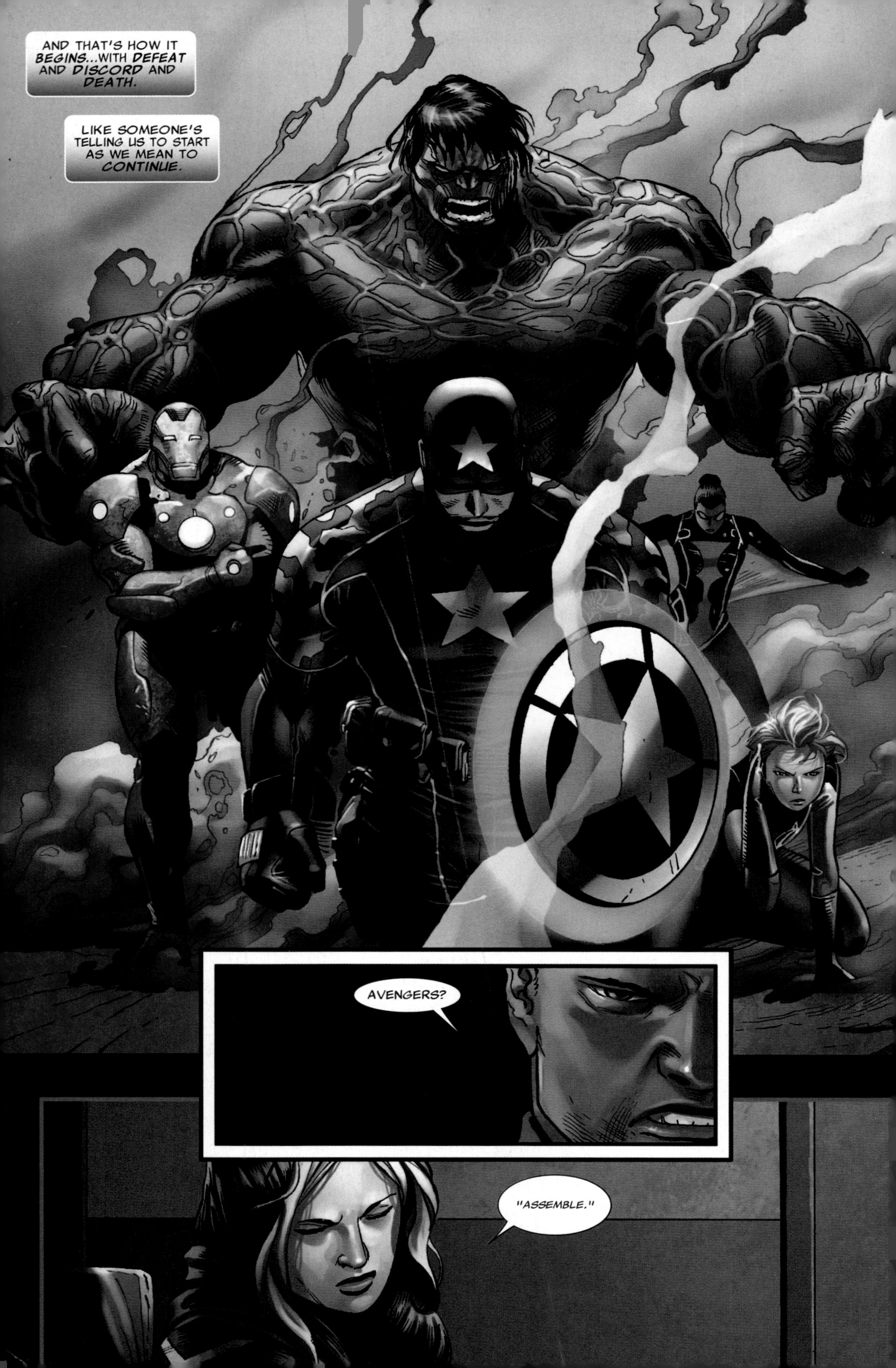
AND THAT'S HOW IT BEGINS...WITH DEFEAT AND DISCORD AND DEATH.
LIKE SOMEONE'S TELLING US TO START AS WE MEAN TO CONTINUE.
AVENGERS?
"ASSEMBLE."

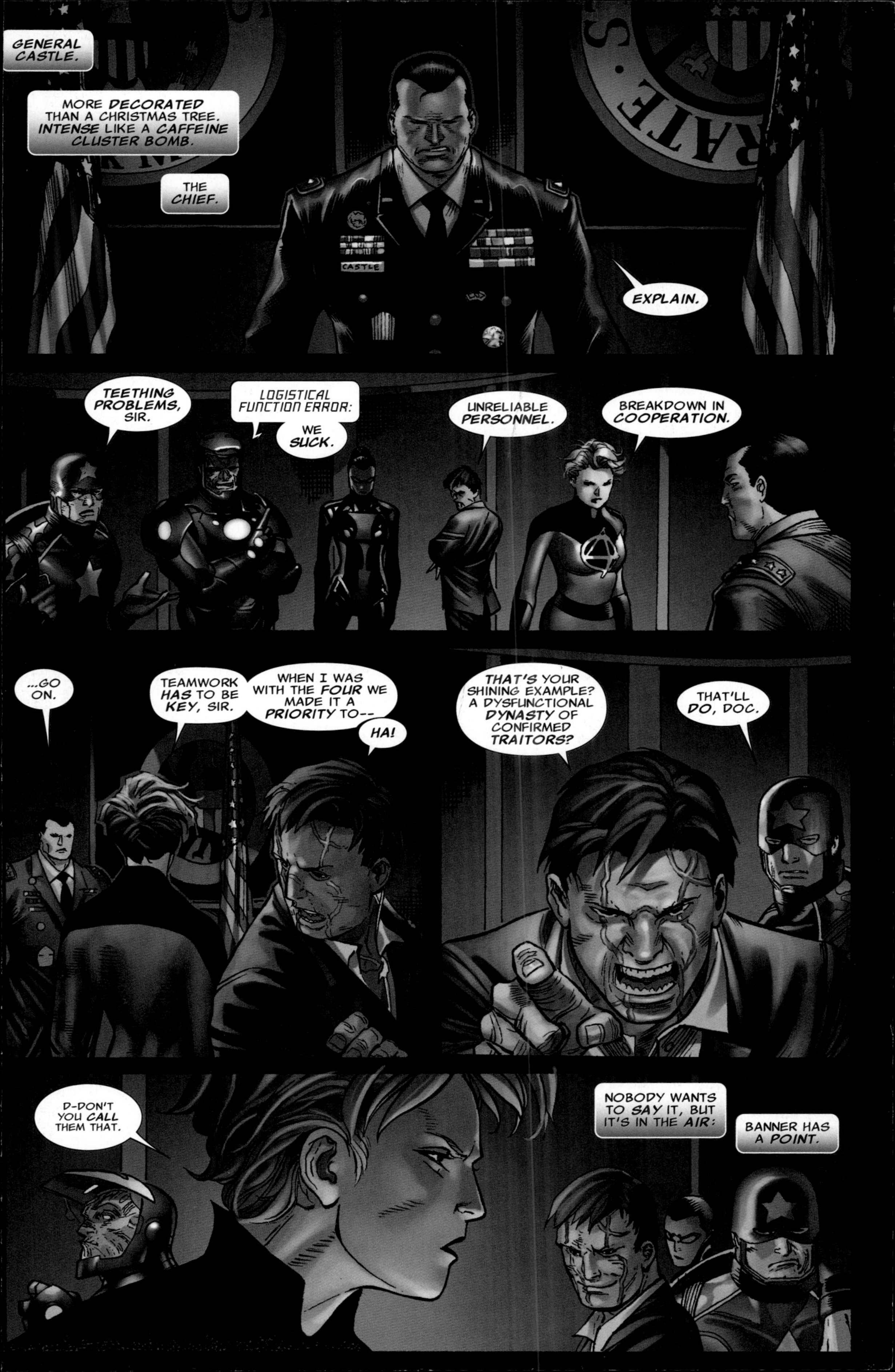
GENERAL CASTLE.
MORE DECORATED THAN A CHRISTMAS TREE. INTENSE LIKE A CAFFEINE CLUSTER BOMB.
THE CHIEF.
CASTLE
EXPLAIN.
TEETHING PROBLEMS, SIR.
LOGISTICAL FUNCTION ERROR:
WE SUCK.
UNRELIABLE PERSONNEL.
BREAKDOWN IN COOPERATION.
...GO ON.
TEAMWORK HAS TO BE KEY, SIR.
WHEN I WAS WITH THE FOUR WE MADE IT A PRIORITY TO--
HA!
THAT'S YOUR SHINING EXAMPLE? A DYSFUNCTIONAL DYNASTY OF CONFIRMED TRAITORS?
THAT'LL DO, DOC.
D-DON'T YOU CALL THEM THAT.
NOBODY WANTS TO SAY IT, BUT IT'S IN THE AIR:
BANNER HAS A POINT.

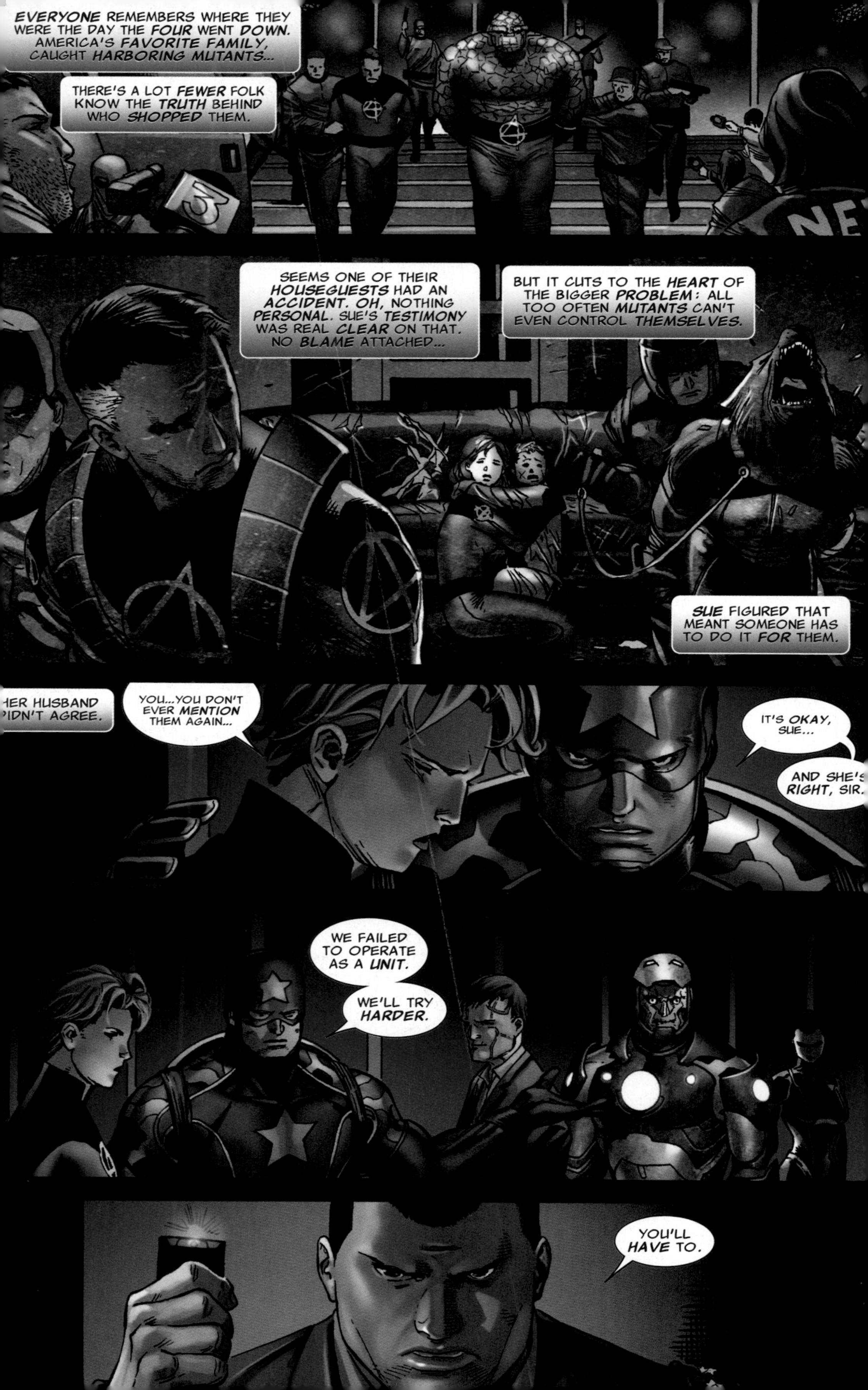
EVERYONE REMEMBERS WHERE THEY WERE THE DAY THE FOUR WENT DOWN. AMERICA'S FAVORITE FAMILY, CAUGHT HARBORING MUTANTS...
THERE'S A LOT FEWER FOLK KNOW THE TRUTH BEHIND WHO SHOPPED THEM.
SEEMS ONE OF THEIR HOUSEGUESTS HAD AN ACCIDENT. OH, NOTHING PERSONAL. SUE'S TESTIMONY WAS REAL CLEAR ON THAT. NO BLAME ATTACHED...
BUT IT CUTS TO THE HEART OF THE BIGGER PROBLEM: ALL TOO OFTEN MUTANTS CAN'T EVEN CONTROL THEMSELVES.
SUE FIGURED THAT MEANT SOMEONE HAS TO DO IT FOR THEM.
HER HUSBAND DIDN'T AGREE.
YOU...YOU DON'T EVER MENTION THEM AGAIN...
IT'S OKAY, SUE...
AND SHE'S RIGHT, SIR.
WE FAILED TO OPERATE AS A UNIT.
WE'LL TRY HARDER.
YOU'LL HAVE TO.

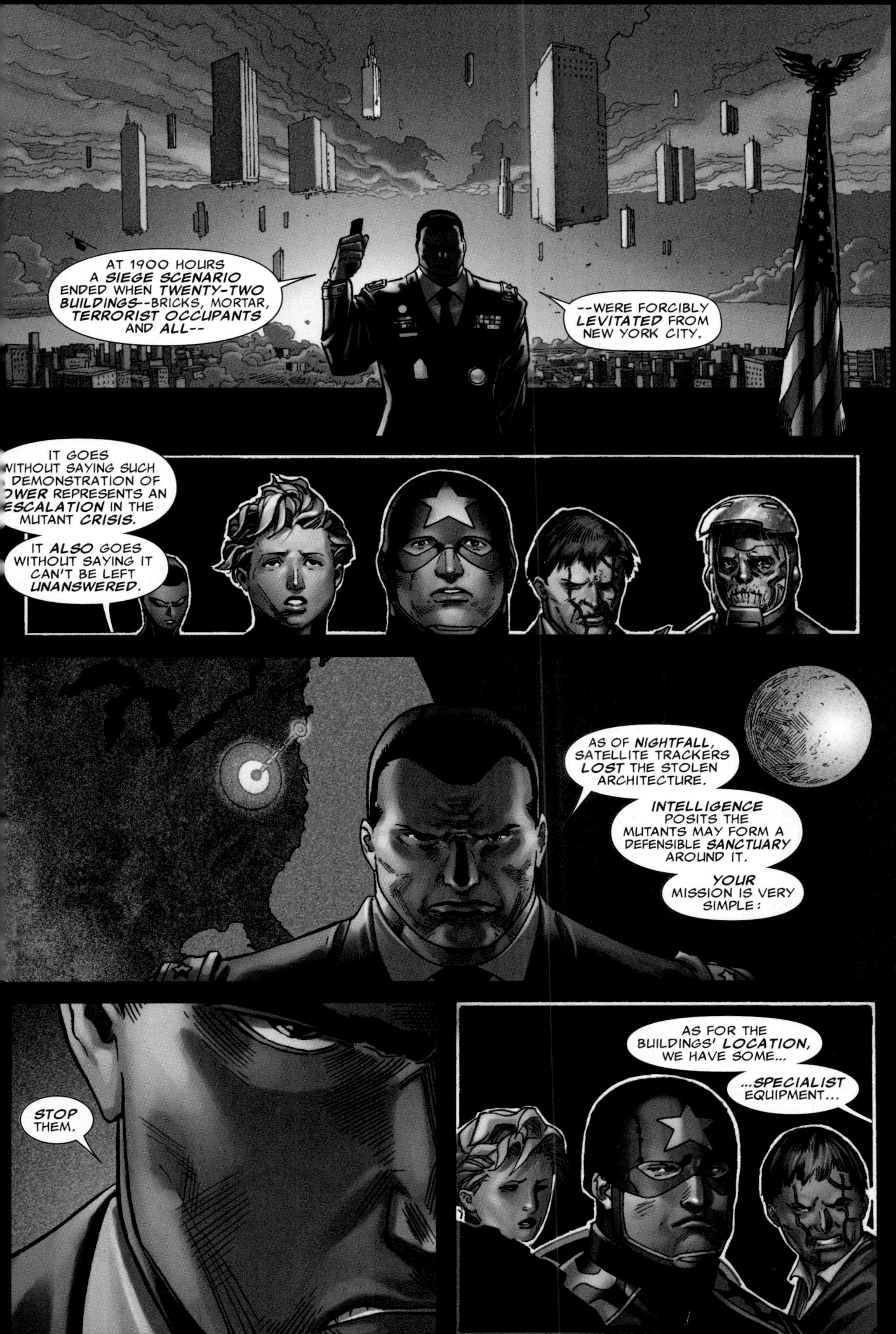
AT 1900 HOURS A SIEGE SCENARIO ENDED WHEN TWENTY-TWO BUILDINGS--BRICKS, MORTAR, TERRORIST OCCUPANTS AND ALL--
--WERE FORCIBLY LEVITATED FROM NEW YORK CITY.
IT GOES WITHOUT SAYING SUCH A DEMONSTRATION OF POWER REPRESENTS AN ESCALATION IN THE MUTANT CRISIS.
IT ALSO GOES WITHOUT SAYING IT CAN'T BE LEFT UNANSWERED.
AS OF NIGHTFALL, SATELLITE TRACKERS LOST THE STOLEN ARCHITECTURE.
INTELLIGENCE POSITS THE MUTANTS MAY FORM A DEFENSIBLE SANCTUARY AROUND IT.
YOUR MISSION IS VERY SIMPLE:
STOP THEM.
AS FOR THE BUILDINGS' LOCATION, WE HAVE SOME...
...SPECIALIST EQUIPMENT...

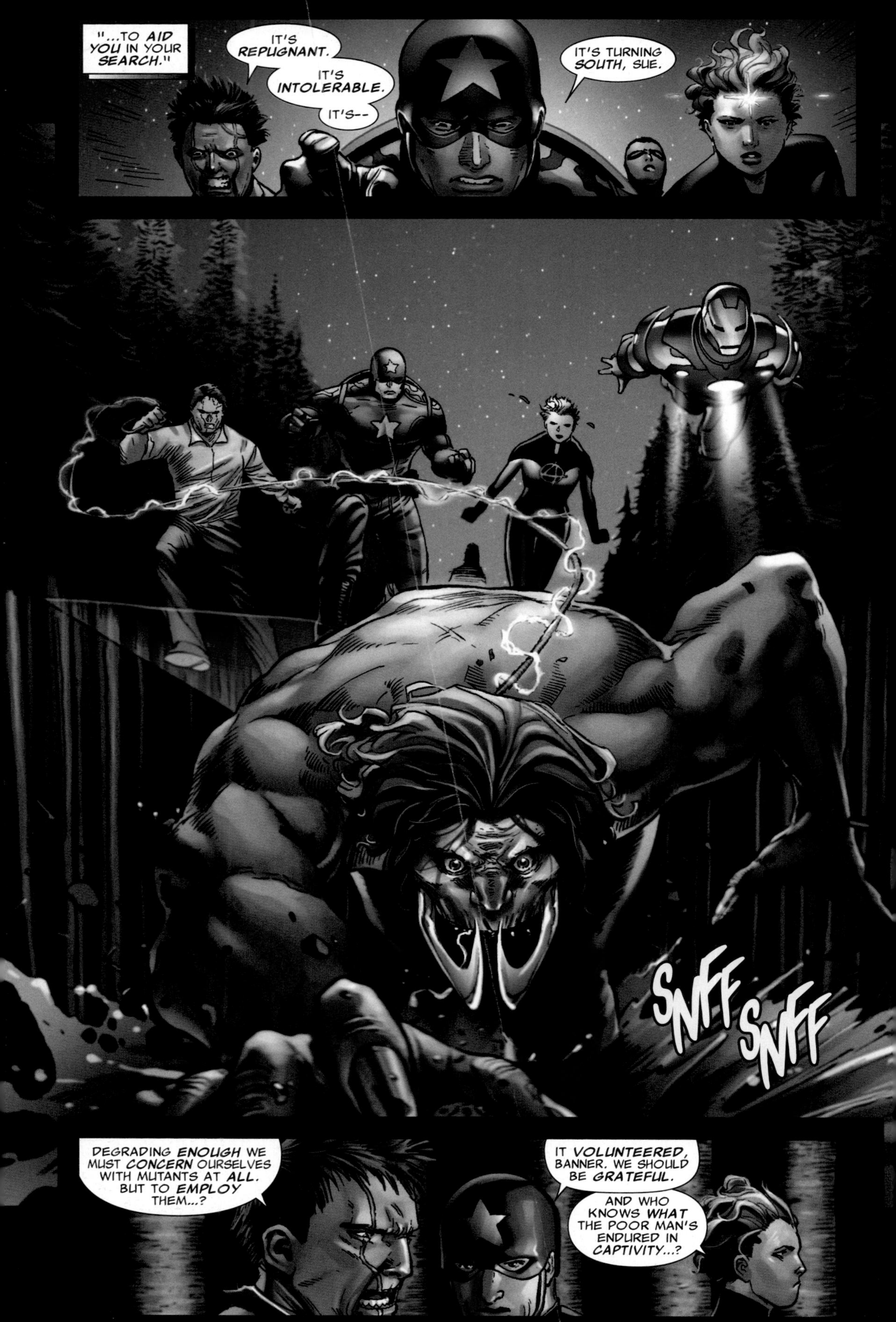
"...TO AID YOU IN YOUR SEARCH."
IT'S REPUGNANT.
IT'S INTOLERABLE.
IT'S--
IT'S TURNING SOUTH, SUE.
SNIFF SNIFF
DEGRADING ENOUGH WE MUST CONCERN OURSELVES WITH MUTANTS AT ALL. BUT TO EMPLOY THEM...?
IT VOLUNTEERED, BANNER. WE SHOULD BE GRATEFUL.
AND WHO KNOWS WHAT THE POOR MAN'S ENDURED IN CAPTIVITY...?

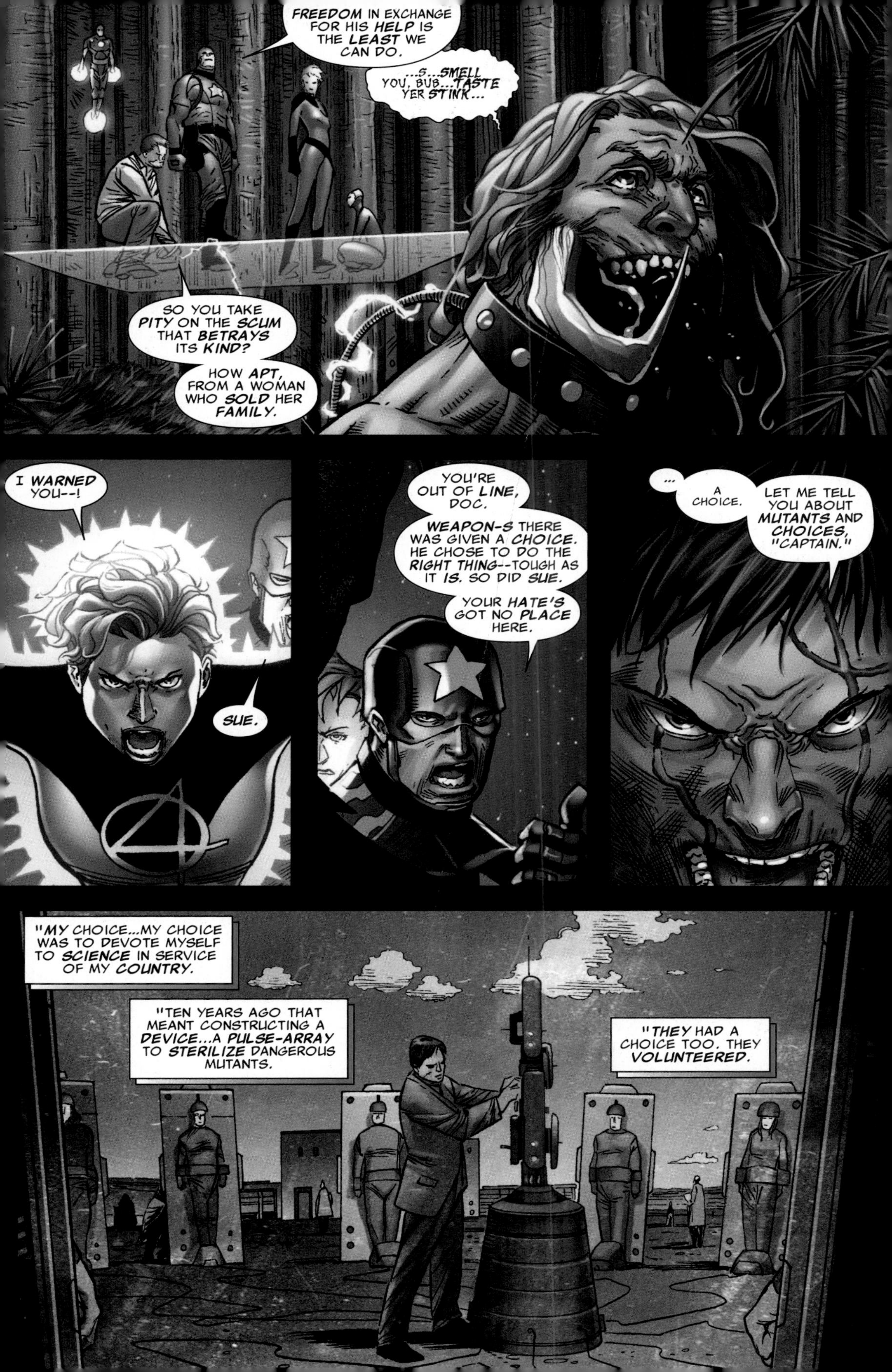
FREEDOM IN EXCHANGE FOR HIS HELP IS THE LEAST WE CAN DO.
...S...SMELL YOU, BUB...TASTE YER STINK...
SO YOU TAKE PITY ON THE SCUM THAT BETRAYS ITS KIND?
HOW APT, FROM A WOMAN WHO SOLD HER FAMILY.
I WARNED YOU--!
SUE.
YOU'RE OUT OF LINE, DOC.
WEAPON-S THERE WAS GIVEN A CHOICE. HE CHOSE TO DO THE RIGHT THING--TOUGH AS IT IS. SO DID SUE.
YOUR HATE'S GOT NO PLACE HERE.
...
A CHOICE.
LET ME TELL YOU ABOUT MUTANTS AND CHOICES, "CAPTAIN."
"MY CHOICE...MY CHOICE WAS TO DEVOTE MYSELF TO SCIENCE IN SERVICE OF MY COUNTRY.
"TEN YEARS AGO THAT MEANT CONSTRUCTING A DEVICE...A PULSE-ARRAY TO STERILIZE DANGEROUS MUTANTS.
"THEY HAD A CHOICE TOO. THEY VOLUNTEERED.

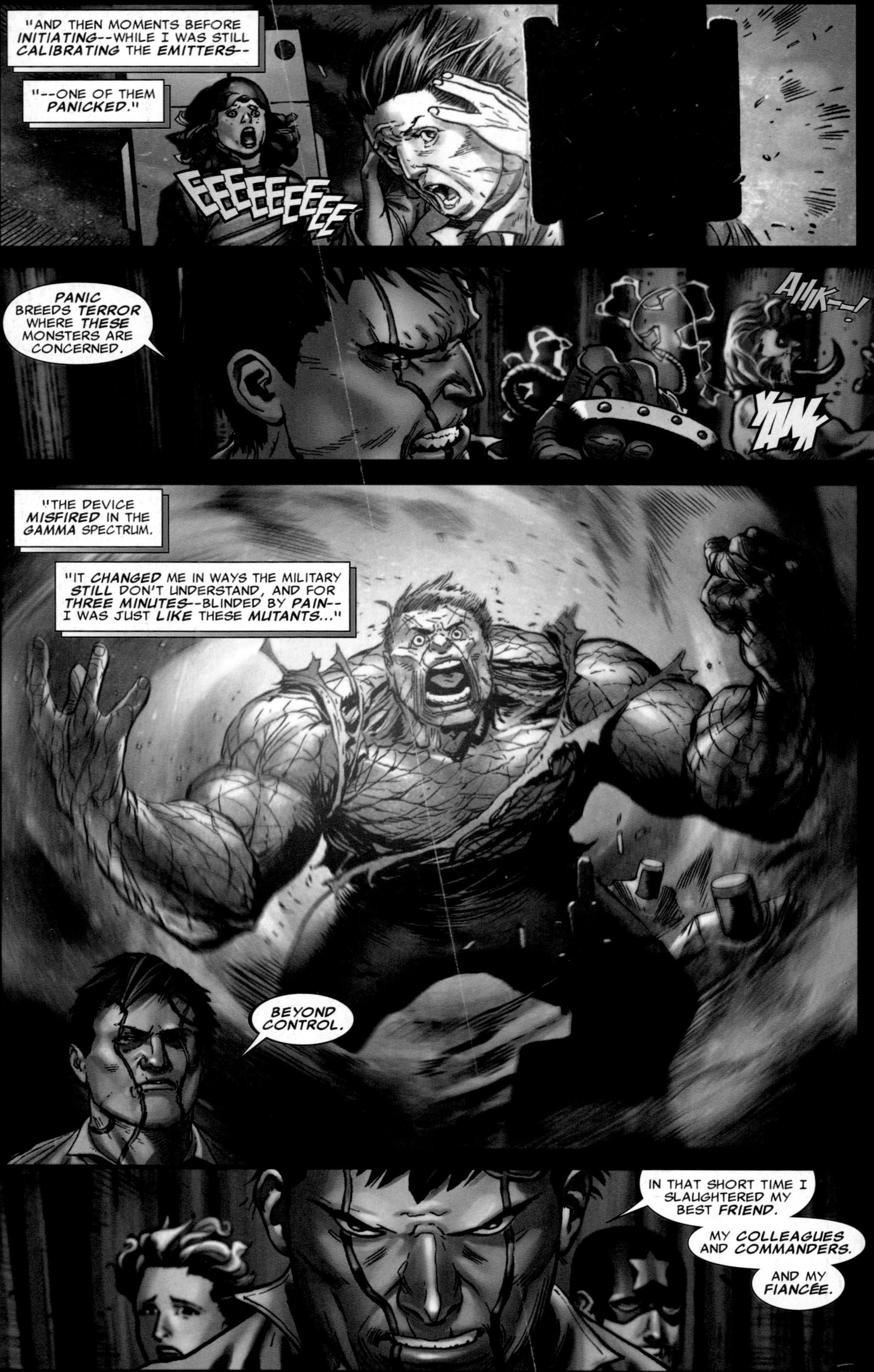
"AND THEN MOMENTS BEFORE INITIATING--WHILE I WAS STILL CALIBRATING THE EMITTERS--
"--ONE OF THEM PANICKED."
EEEEEEEEE
PANIC BREEDS TERROR WHERE THESE MONSTERS ARE CONCERNED.
AIIIK--!
YANK
"THE DEVICE MISFIRED IN THE GAMMA SPECTRUM.
"IT CHANGED ME IN WAYS THE MILITARY STILL DON'T UNDERSTAND, AND FOR THREE MINUTES--BLINDED BY PAIN--I WAS JUST LIKE THESE MUTANTS..."
BEYOND CONTROL.
IN THAT SHORT TIME I SLAUGHTERED MY BEST FRIEND.
MY COLLEAGUES AND COMMANDERS.
AND MY FIANCÉE.

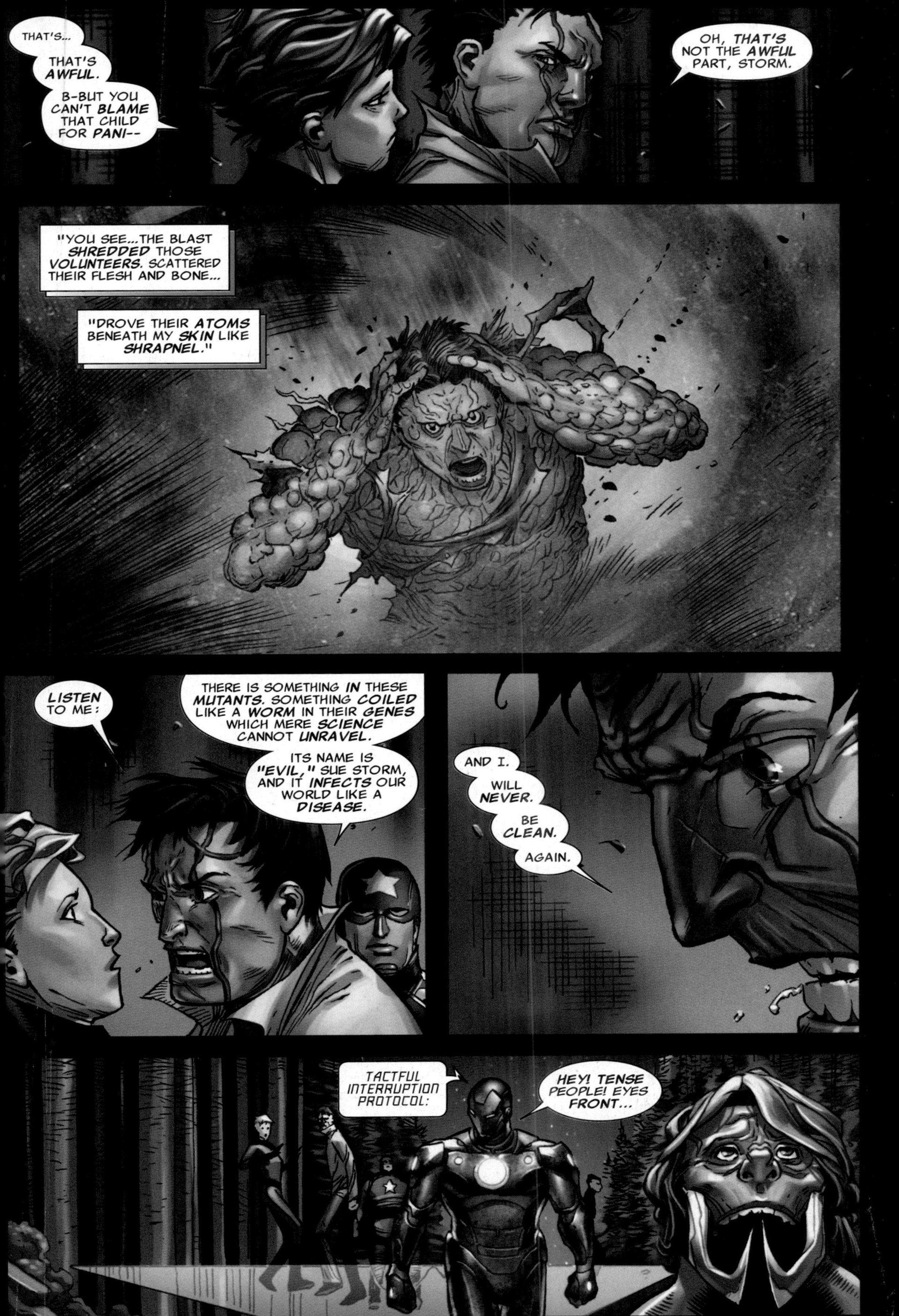
THAT'S...
THAT'S AWFUL.
B-BUT YOU CAN'T BLAME THAT CHILD FOR PANI--
OH, THAT'S NOT THE AWFUL PART, STORM.
"YOU SEE...THE BLAST SHREDDED THOSE VOLUNTEERS. SCATTERED THEIR FLESH AND BONE...
"DROVE THEIR ATOMS BENEATH MY SKIN LIKE SHRAPNEL."
LISTEN TO ME:
THERE IS SOMETHING IN THESE MUTANTS. SOMETHING COILED LIKE A WORM IN THEIR GENES WHICH MERE SCIENCE CANNOT UNRAVEL.
ITS NAME IS "EVIL," SUE STORM, AND IT INFECTS OUR WORLD LIKE A DISEASE.
AND I.
WILL NEVER.
BE CLEAN.
AGAIN.
TACTFUL INTERRUPTION PROTOCOL:
HEY! TENSE PEOPLE! EYES FRONT...

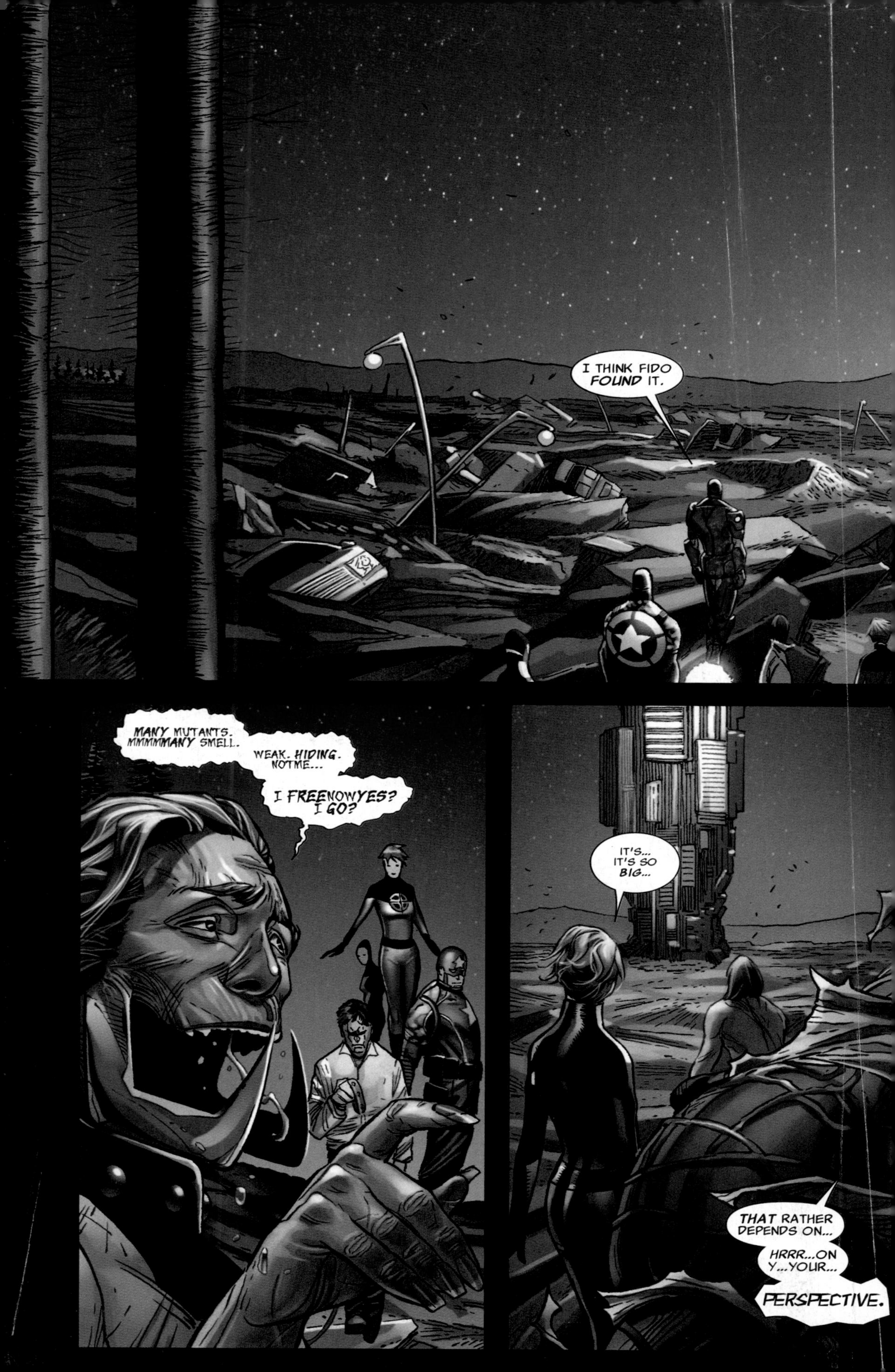
I THINK FIDO FOUND IT.
MANY MUTANTS. MMMMMANY SMELL.
WEAK. HIDING. NOTME...
I FREENOWYES? I GO?
IT'S... IT'S SO BIG...
THAT RATHER DEPENDS ON...
HRRR...ON Y...YOUR...
PERSPECTIVE.

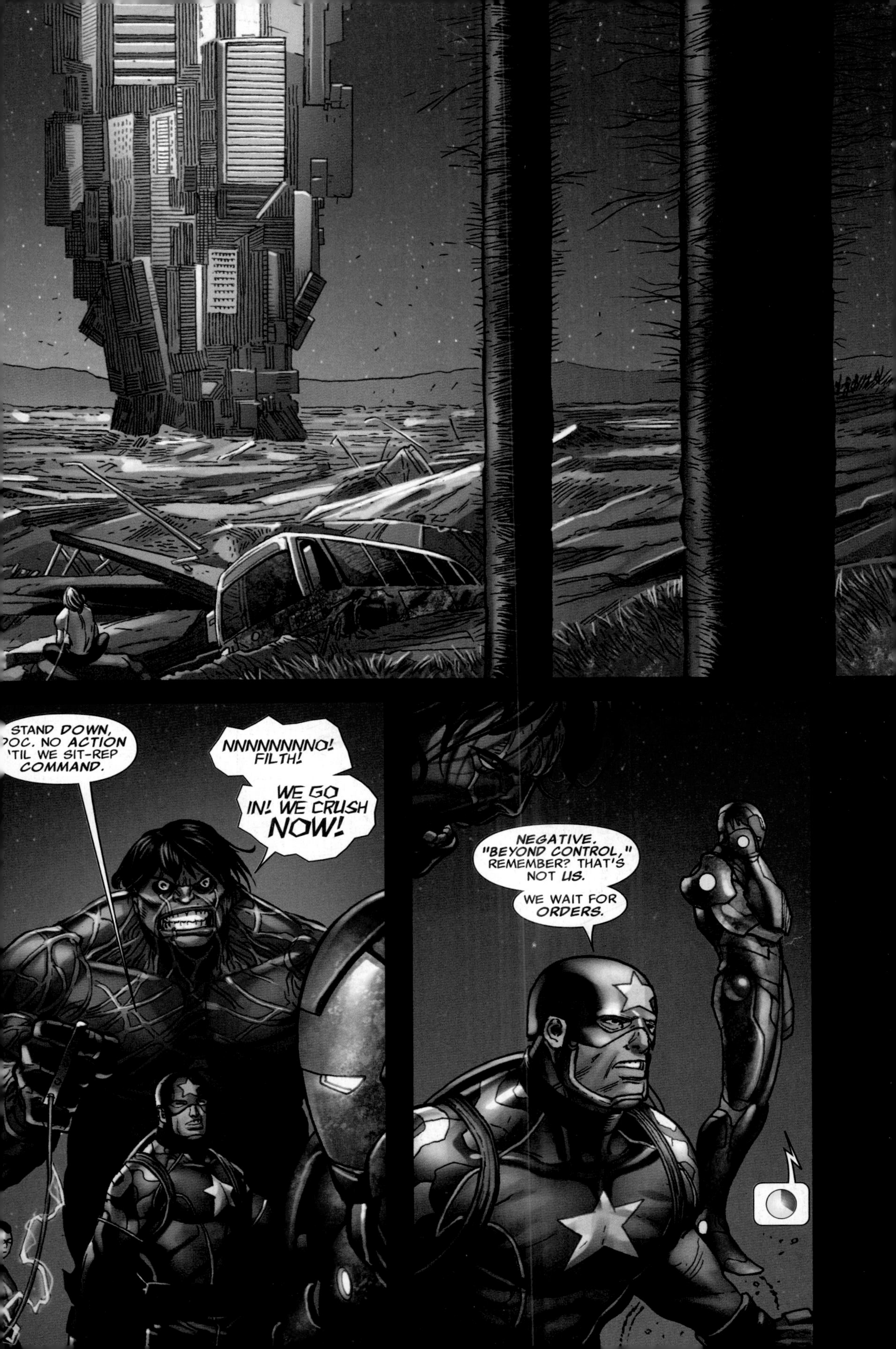
STAND DOWN, DOC. NO ACTION 'TIL WE SIT-REP COMMAND.
NNNNNNNNO! FILTH!
WE GO IN! WE CRUSH NOW!
NEGATIVE. "BEYOND CONTROL," REMEMBER? THAT'S NOT US.
WE WAIT FOR ORDERS.

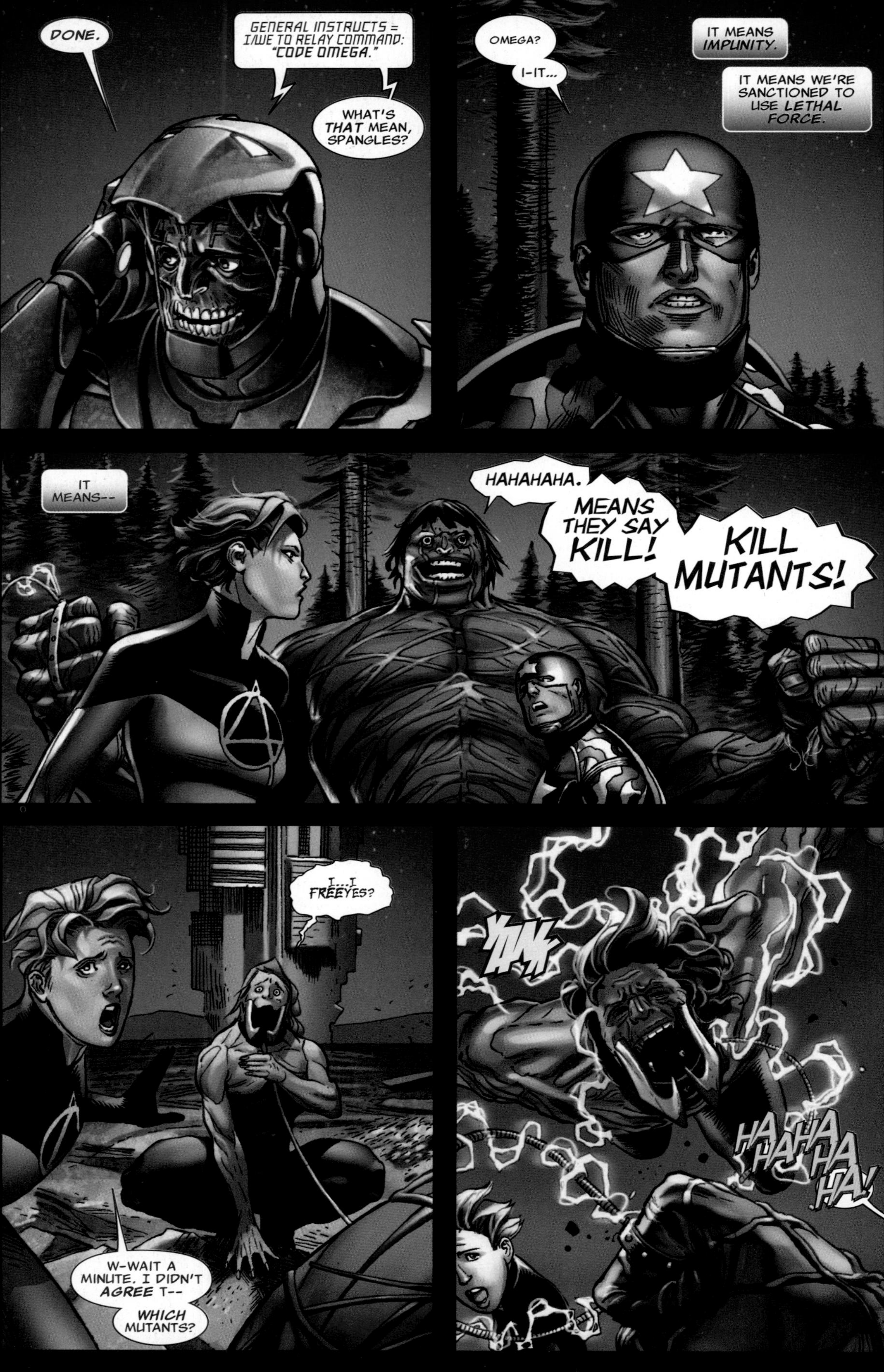
DONE.
GENERAL INSTRUCTS = I/WE TO RELAY COMMAND: "CODE OMEGA."
WHAT'S THAT MEAN, SPANGLES?
OMEGA?
I-IT...
IT MEANS IMPUNITY.
IT MEANS WE'RE SANCTIONED TO USE LETHAL FORCE.
IT MEANS--
HAHAHAHA.
MEANS THEY SAY KILL!
KILL MUTANTS!
I...I FREEYES?
W-WAIT A MINUTE. I DIDN'T AGREE T--
WHICH MUTANTS?
HA HA HA HA HA HA HA!

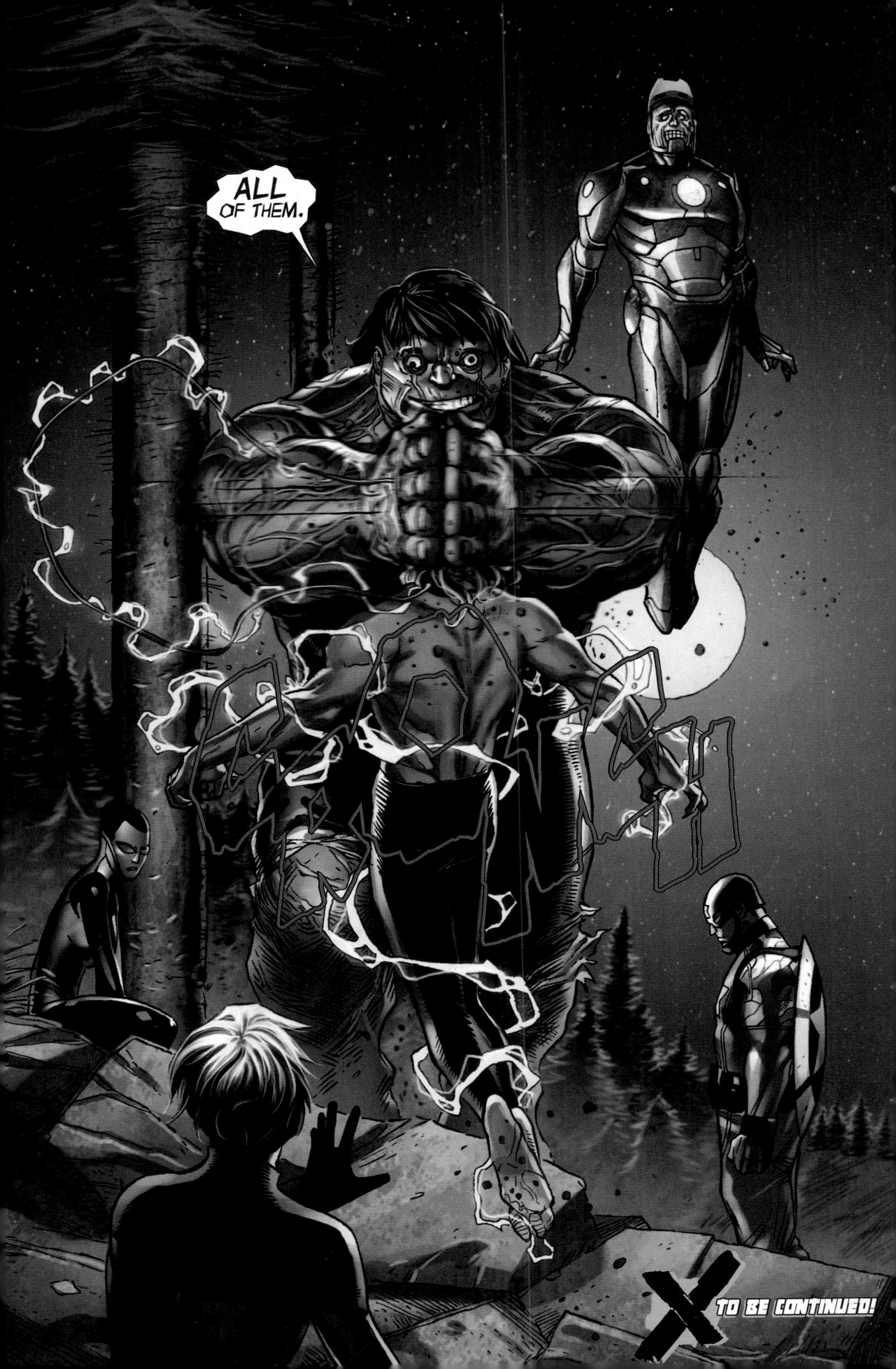
ALL OF THEM.
TO BE CONTINUED!

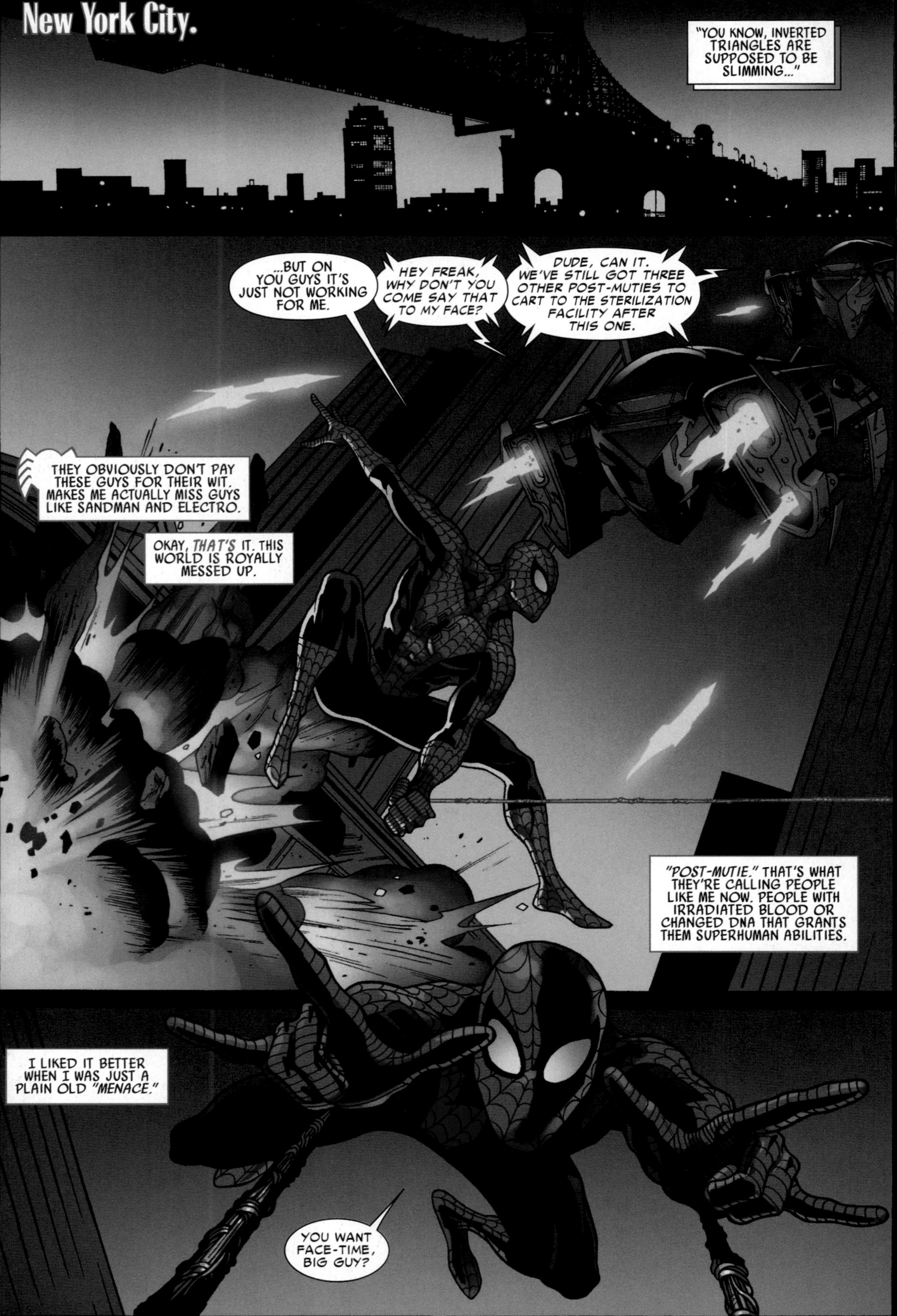
New York City.
"YOU KNOW, INVERTED TRIANGLES ARE SUPPOSED TO BE SLIMMING..."
...BUT ON YOU GUYS IT'S JUST NOT WORKING FOR ME.
HEY FREAK, WHY DON'T YOU COME SAY THAT TO MY FACE?
DUDE, CAN IT. WE'VE STILL GOT THREE OTHER POST-MUTIES TO CART TO THE STERILIZATION FACILITY AFTER THIS ONE.
THEY OBVIOUSLY DON'T PAY THESE GUYS FOR THEIR WIT. MAKES ME ACTUALLY MISS GUYS LIKE SANDMAN AND ELECTRO.
OKAY, THAT'S IT. THIS WORLD IS ROYALLY MESSED UP.
"POST-MUTIE." THAT'S WHAT THEY'RE CALLING PEOPLE LIKE ME NOW. PEOPLE WITH IRRADIATED BLOOD OR CHANGED DNA THAT GRANTS THEM SUPERHUMAN ABILITIES.
I LIKED IT BETTER WHEN I WAS JUST A PLAIN OLD "MENACE."
YOU WANT FACE-TIME, BIG GUY?

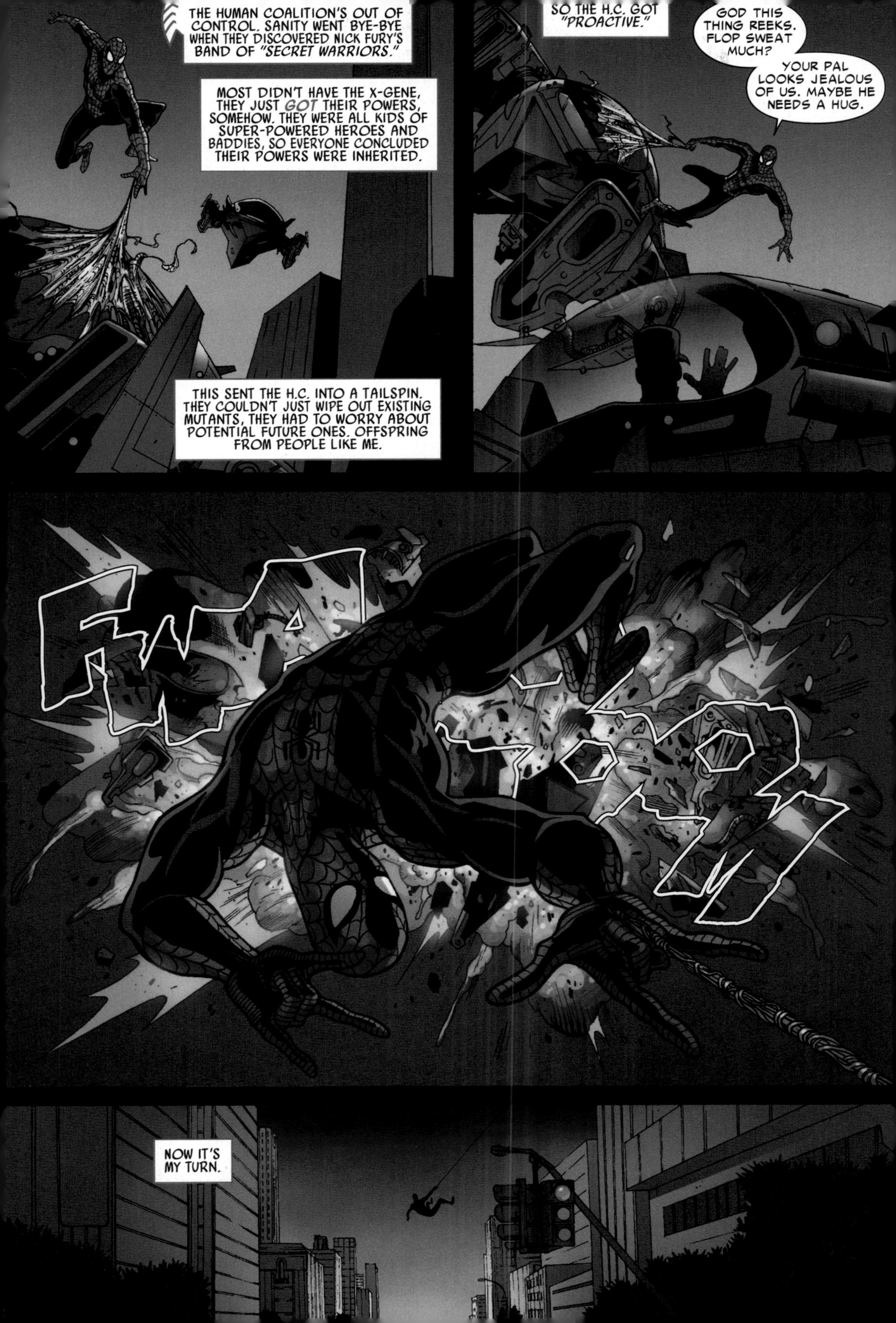
THE HUMAN COALITION'S OUT OF CONTROL. SANITY WENT BYE-BYE WHEN THEY DISCOVERED NICK FURY'S BAND OF "SECRET WARRIORS."
MOST DIDN'T HAVE THE X-GENE, THEY JUST GOT THEIR POWERS, SOMEHOW. THEY WERE ALL KIDS OF SUPER-POWERED HEROES AND BADDIES, SO EVERYONE CONCLUDED THEIR POWERS WERE INHERITED.
THIS SENT THE H.C. INTO A TAILSPIN. THEY COULDN'T JUST WIPE OUT EXISTING MUTANTS, THEY HAD TO WORRY ABOUT POTENTIAL FUTURE ONES. OFFSPRING FROM PEOPLE LIKE ME.
SO THE H.C. GOT "PROACTIVE."
GOD THIS THING REEKS. FLOP SWEAT MUCH?
YOUR PAL LOOKS JEALOUS OF US. MAYBE HE NEEDS A HUG.
FWA-KOOM
NOW IT'S MY TURN.

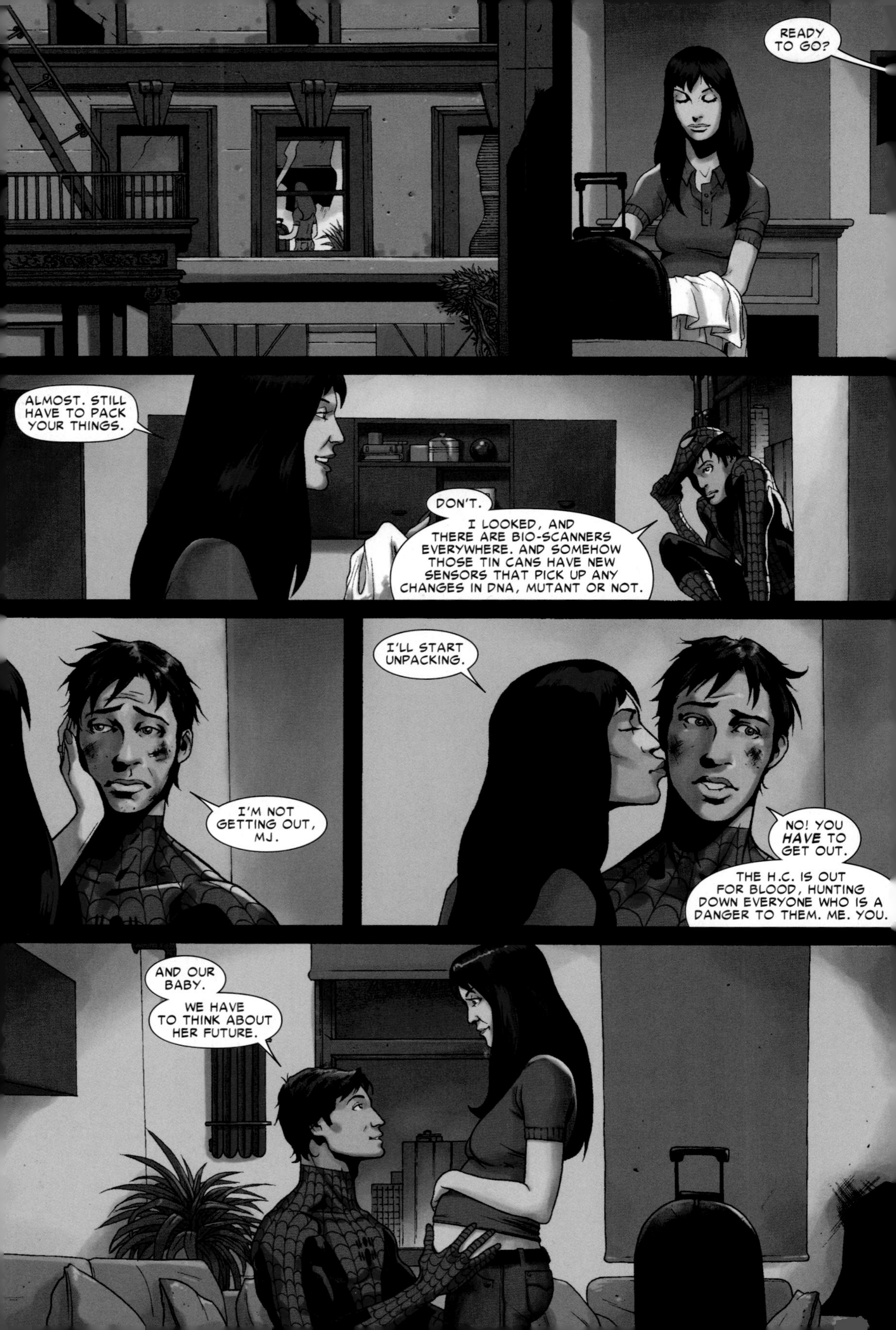
READY TO GO?
ALMOST. STILL HAVE TO PACK YOUR THINGS.
DON'T.
I LOOKED, AND THERE ARE BIO-SCANNERS EVERYWHERE. AND SOMEHOW THOSE TIN CANS HAVE NEW SENSORS THAT PICK UP ANY CHANGES IN DNA, MUTANT OR NOT.
I'M NOT GETTING OUT, MJ.
I'LL START UNPACKING.
NO! YOU *HAVE* TO GET OUT.
THE H.C. IS OUT FOR BLOOD, HUNTING DOWN EVERYONE WHO IS A DANGER TO THEM. ME. YOU.
AND OUR BABY.
WE HAVE TO THINK ABOUT HER FUTURE.

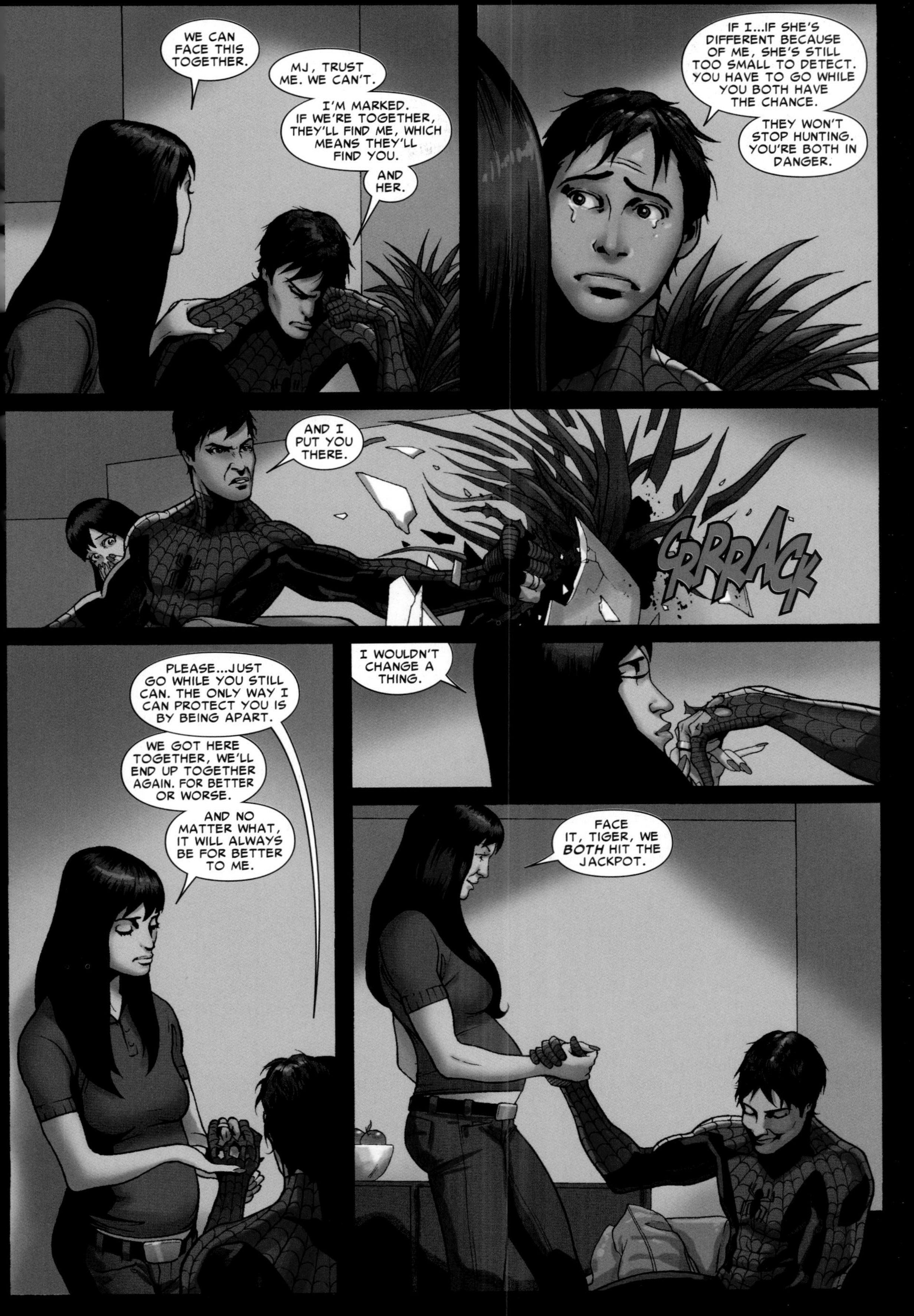

WE CAN FACE THIS TOGETHER.
MJ, TRUST ME. WE CAN'T.
I'M MARKED. IF WE'RE TOGETHER, THEY'LL FIND ME, WHICH MEANS THEY'LL FIND YOU.
AND HER.
IF I...IF SHE'S DIFFERENT BECAUSE OF ME, SHE'S STILL TOO SMALL TO DETECT. YOU HAVE TO GO WHILE YOU BOTH HAVE THE CHANCE.
THEY WON'T STOP HUNTING. YOU'RE BOTH IN DANGER.
AND I PUT YOU THERE.
CRRRACK
PLEASE...JUST GO WHILE YOU STILL CAN. THE ONLY WAY I CAN PROTECT YOU IS BY BEING APART.
WE GOT HERE TOGETHER, WE'LL END UP TOGETHER AGAIN. FOR BETTER OR WORSE.
AND NO MATTER WHAT, IT WILL ALWAYS BE FOR BETTER TO ME.
I WOULDN'T CHANGE A THING.
FACE IT, TIGER, WE *BOTH* HIT THE JACKPOT.

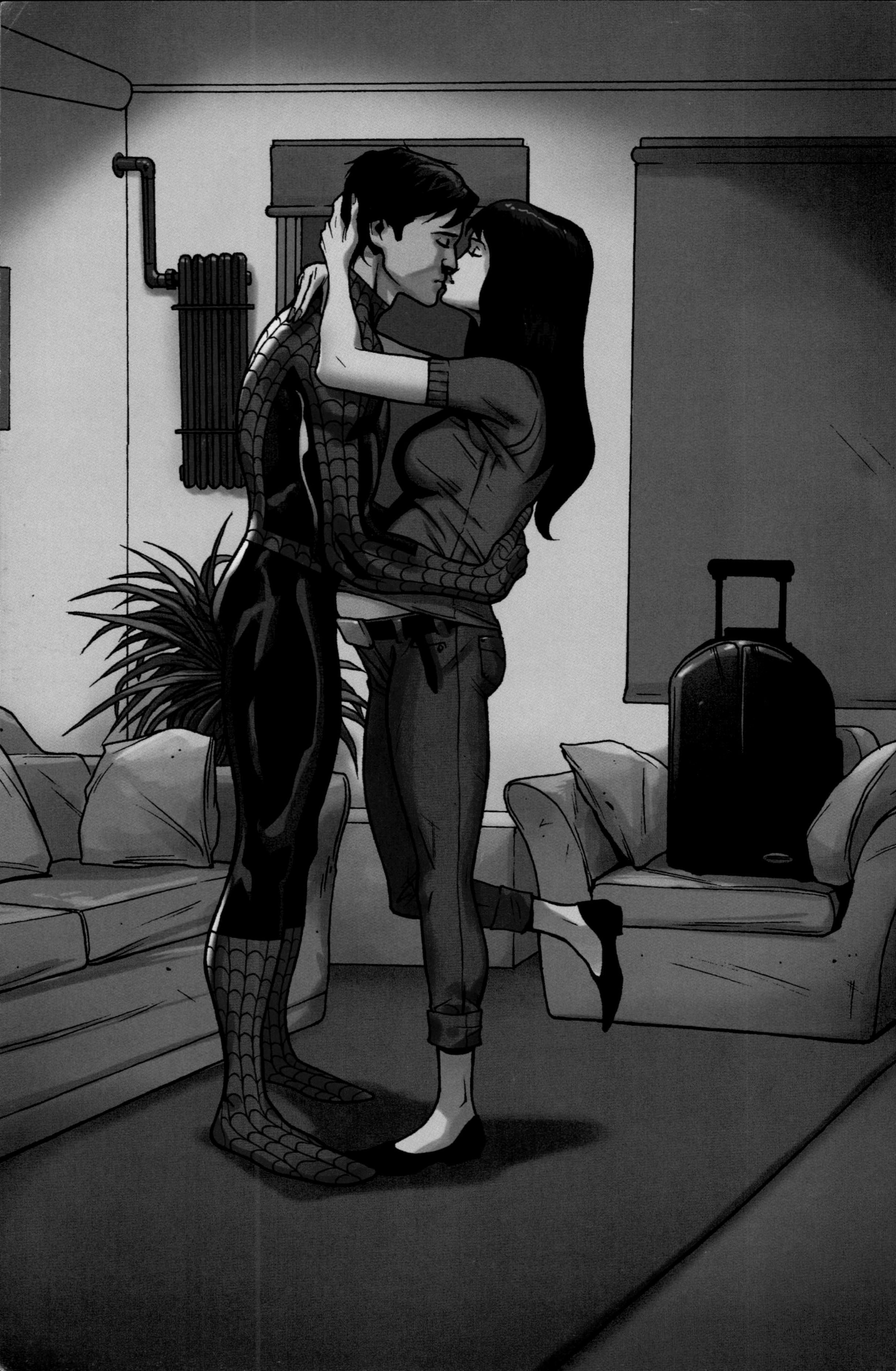

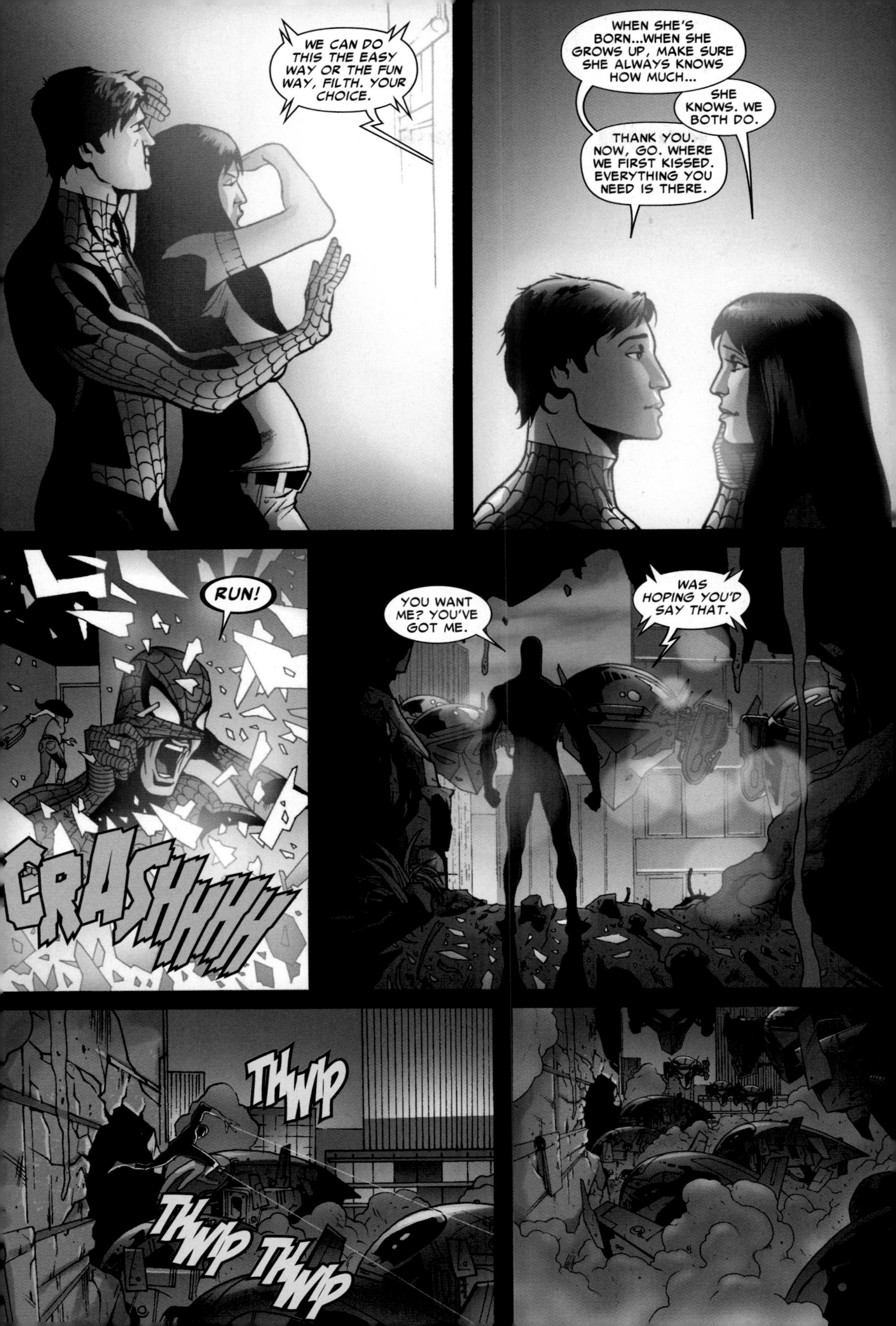
WE CAN DO THIS THE EASY WAY OR THE FUN WAY, FILTH. YOUR CHOICE.
WHEN SHE'S BORN...WHEN SHE GROWS UP, MAKE SURE SHE ALWAYS KNOWS HOW MUCH...
SHE KNOWS. WE BOTH DO.
THANK YOU. NOW, GO. WHERE WE FIRST KISSED. EVERYTHING YOU NEED IS THERE.
RUN!
CRASHHHH
YOU WANT ME? YOU'VE GOT ME.
WAS HOPING YOU'D SAY THAT.
THWIP
THWIP
THWIP

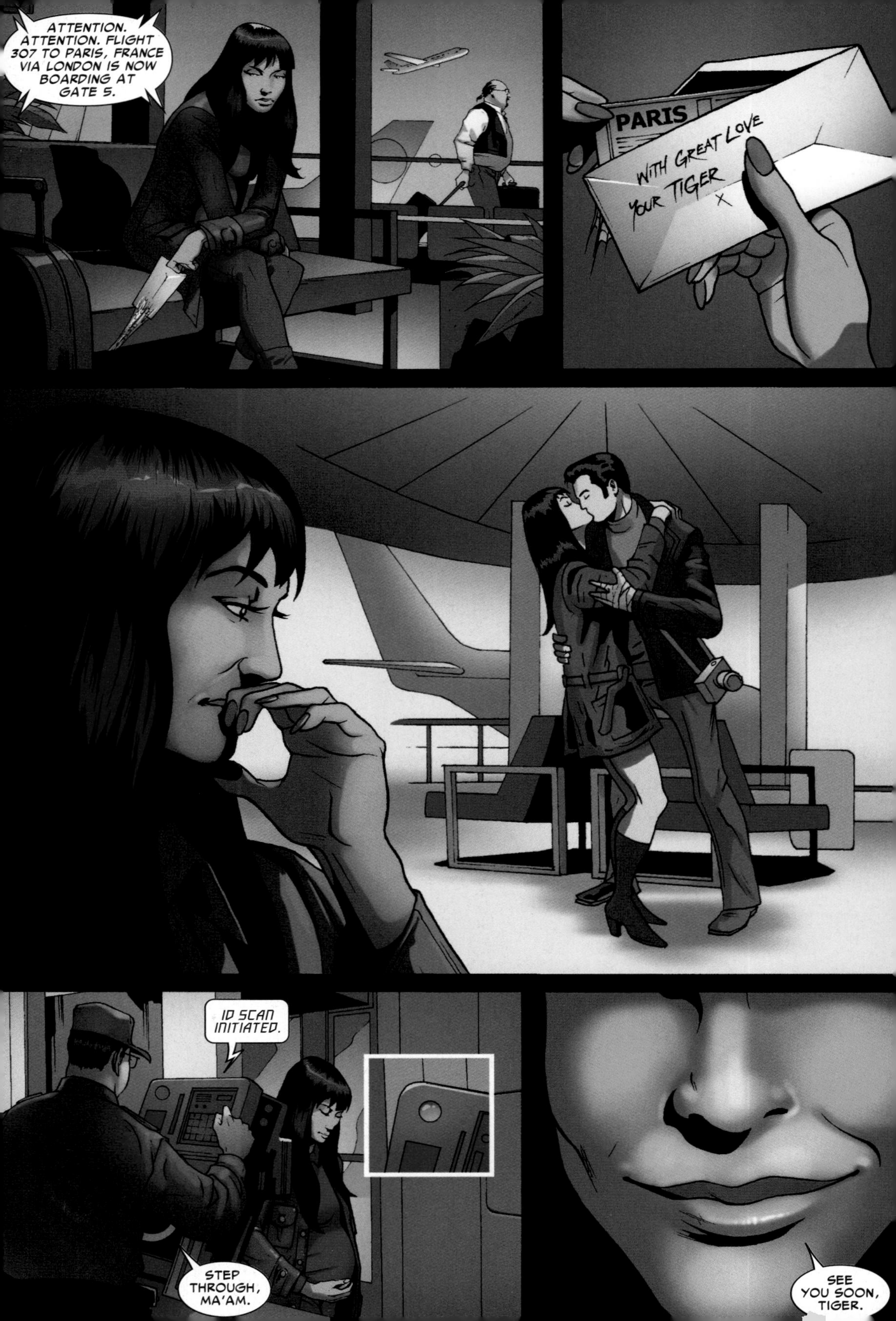
ATTENTION. ATTENTION. FLIGHT 307 TO PARIS, FRANCE VIA LONDON IS NOW BOARDING AT GATE 5.
PARIS
WITH GREAT LOVE YOUR TIGER X
ID SCAN INITIATED.
STEP THROUGH, MA'AM.
SEE YOU SOON, TIGER.

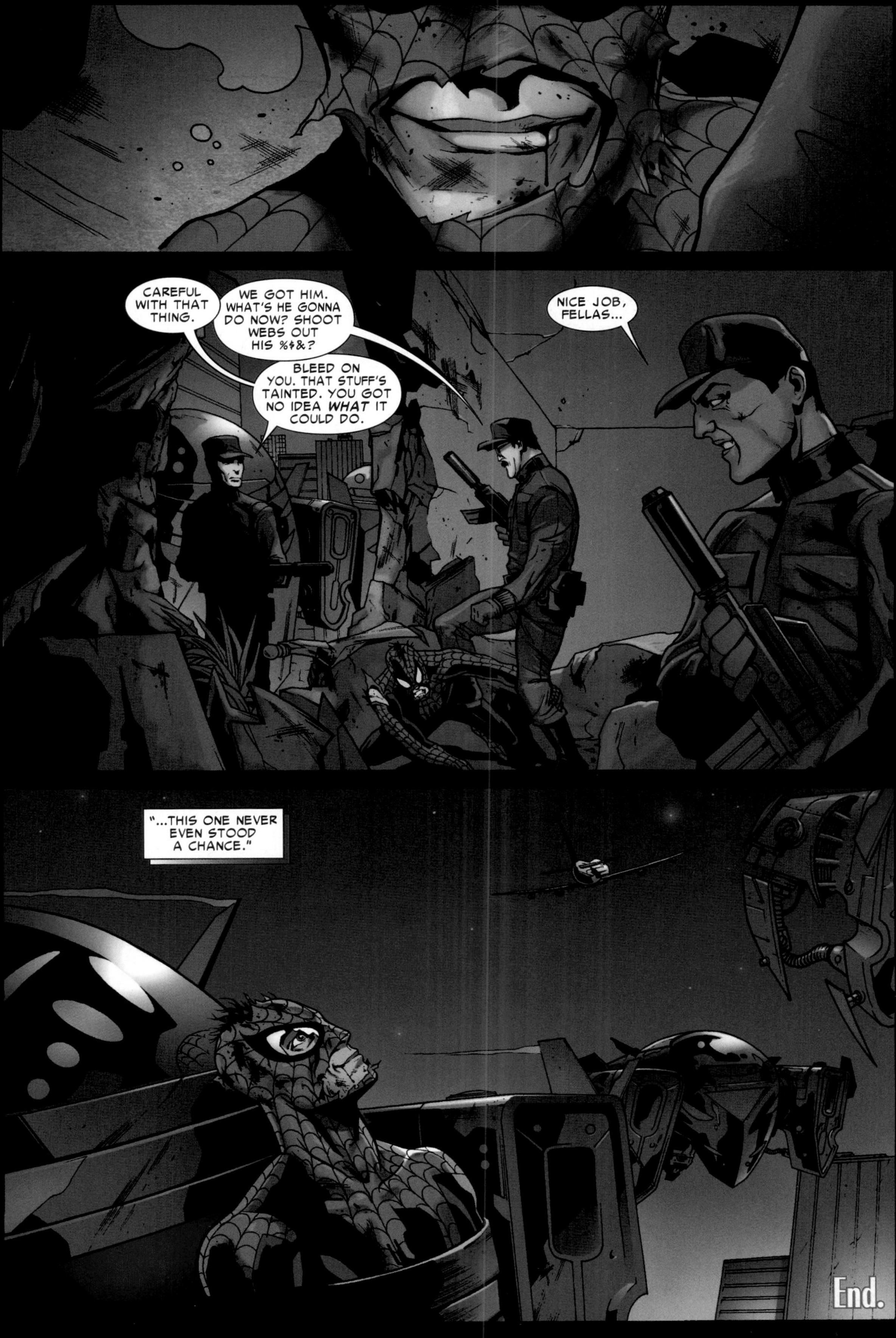

CAREFUL WITH THAT THING.
WE GOT HIM. WHAT'S HE GONNA DO NOW? SHOOT WEBS OUT HIS %$&?
BLEED ON YOU. THAT STUFF'S TAINTED. YOU GOT NO IDEA *WHAT* IT COULD DO.
NICE JOB, FELLAS...
"...THIS ONE NEVER EVEN STOOD A CHANCE."
End.

AGE OF X: UNIVERSE #2

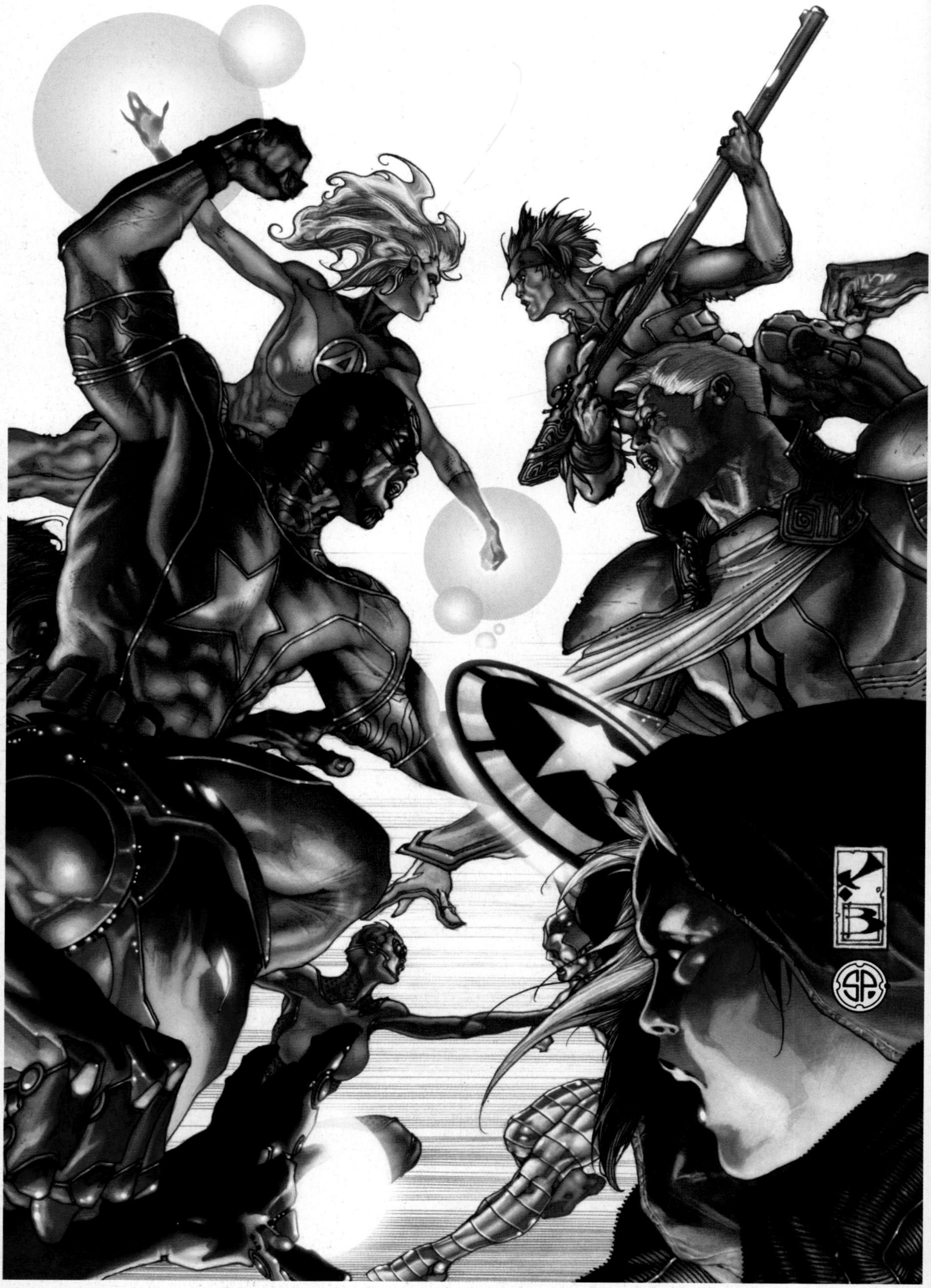

Captain America. Iron Man. Redback. The Hulk. Sue Storm. They are THE AVENGERS--human super heroes who have been handpicked by the United States government to apprehend fugitive mutants. Under orders from General Frank Castle, the Avengers pursue the few remaining mutants to their last bastion, FORTRESS X. But upon arriving, the Avengers learn the true nature of their mission: they have not been sent to arrest the mutants, but to exterminate them.

AGE OF X

UNIVERSE

CHAPTER 2

AVENGERS

WRITTEN BY SIMON SPURRIER
PENCILED BY KHOI PHAM
INKED BY TOM PALMER
COLORED BY SONIA OBACK

DAZZLER

WRITTEN BY CHUCK KIM
ART BY GABRIEL HERNANDEZ WALTA

LETTERED BY VC'S JOE SABINO
COVER ART BY SIMONE BIANCHI & SIMONE PERUZZI

ASSISTANT EDITORS: SEBASTIAN GIRNER & JORDAN D. WHITE
EDITOR: DANIEL KETCHUM
X-MEN GROUP EDITOR: NICK LOWE
EDITOR IN CHIEF: AXEL ALONSO
CHIEF CREATIVE OFFICER: JOE QUESADA
PUBLISHER: DAN BUCKLEY
EXECUTIVE PRODUCER: ALAN FINE

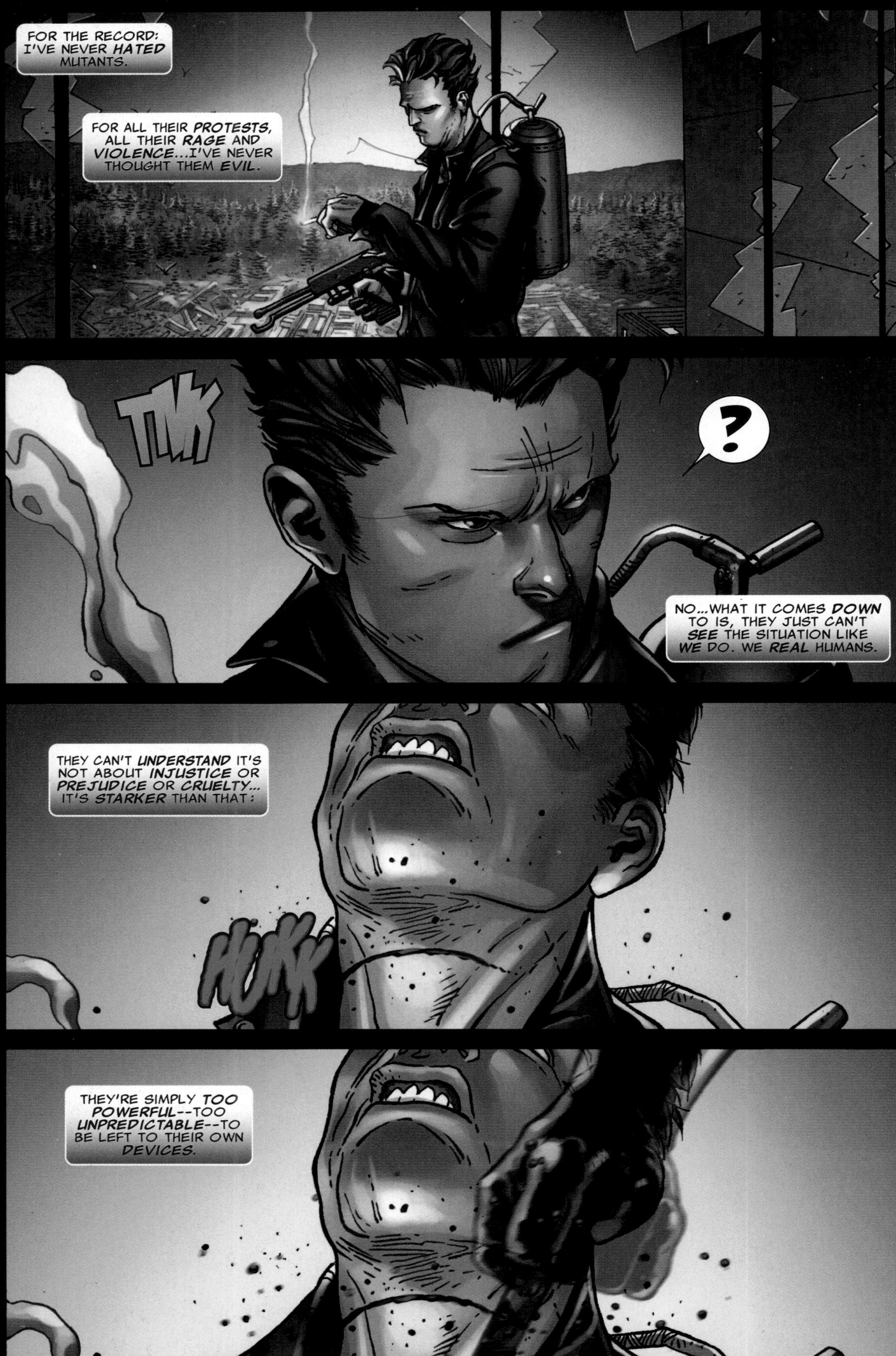

FOR THE RECORD: I'VE NEVER HATED MUTANTS.
FOR ALL THEIR PROTESTS, ALL THEIR RAGE AND VIOLENCE...I'VE NEVER THOUGHT THEM EVIL.
TINK
?
NO...WHAT IT COMES DOWN TO IS, THEY JUST CAN'T SEE THE SITUATION LIKE WE DO. WE REAL HUMANS.
THEY CAN'T UNDERSTAND IT'S NOT ABOUT INJUSTICE OR PREJUDICE OR CRUELTY... IT'S STARKER THAN THAT:
HUKK
THEY'RE SIMPLY TOO POWERFUL--TOO UNPREDICTABLE--TO BE LEFT TO THEIR OWN DEVICES.

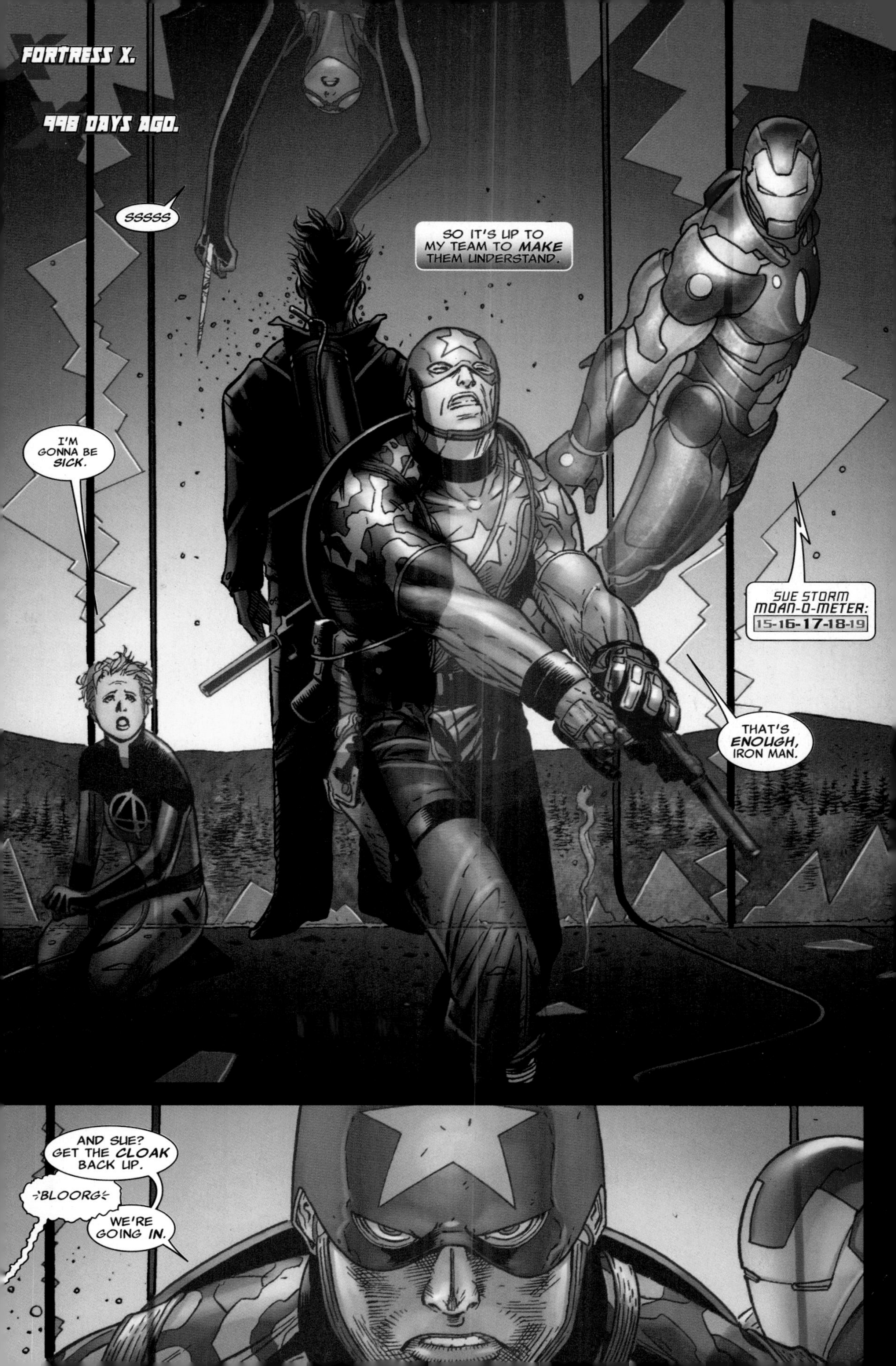
FORTRESS X.
998 DAYS AGO.
SSSSS
SO IT'S UP TO MY TEAM TO MAKE THEM UNDERSTAND.
I'M GONNA BE SICK.
SUE STORM MOAN-O-METER: 15-16-17-18-19
THAT'S ENOUGH, IRON MAN.
AND SUE? GET THE CLOAK BACK UP.
BLOORG
WE'RE GOING IN.

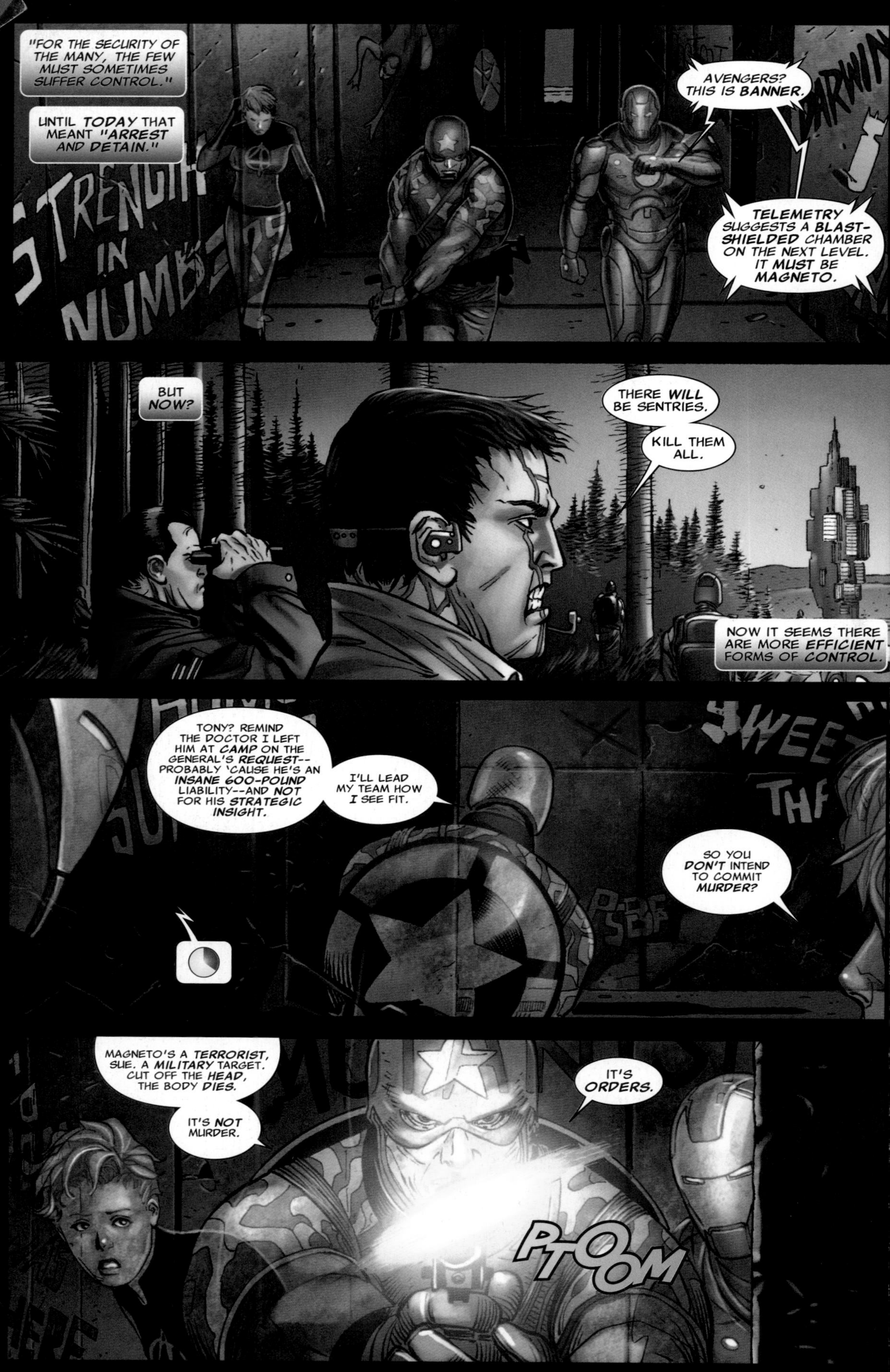
"FOR THE SECURITY OF THE MANY, THE FEW MUST SOMETIMES SUFFER CONTROL."
UNTIL TODAY THAT MEANT "ARREST AND DETAIN."
STRENGTH IN NUMBERS
AVENGERS? THIS IS BANNER.
TELEMETRY SUGGESTS A BLAST-SHIELDED CHAMBER ON THE NEXT LEVEL. IT MUST BE MAGNETO.
BUT NOW?
THERE WILL BE SENTRIES.
KILL THEM ALL.
NOW IT SEEMS THERE ARE MORE EFFICIENT FORMS OF CONTROL.
TONY? REMIND THE DOCTOR I LEFT HIM AT CAMP ON THE GENERAL'S REQUEST--PROBABLY 'CAUSE HE'S AN INSANE 600-POUND LIABILITY--AND NOT FOR HIS STRATEGIC INSIGHT.
I'LL LEAD MY TEAM HOW I SEE FIT.
SO YOU DON'T INTEND TO COMMIT MURDER?
MAGNETO'S A TERRORIST, SUE. A MILITARY TARGET. CUT OFF THE HEAD, THE BODY DIES.
IT'S NOT MURDER.
IT'S ORDERS.
PTOOOM

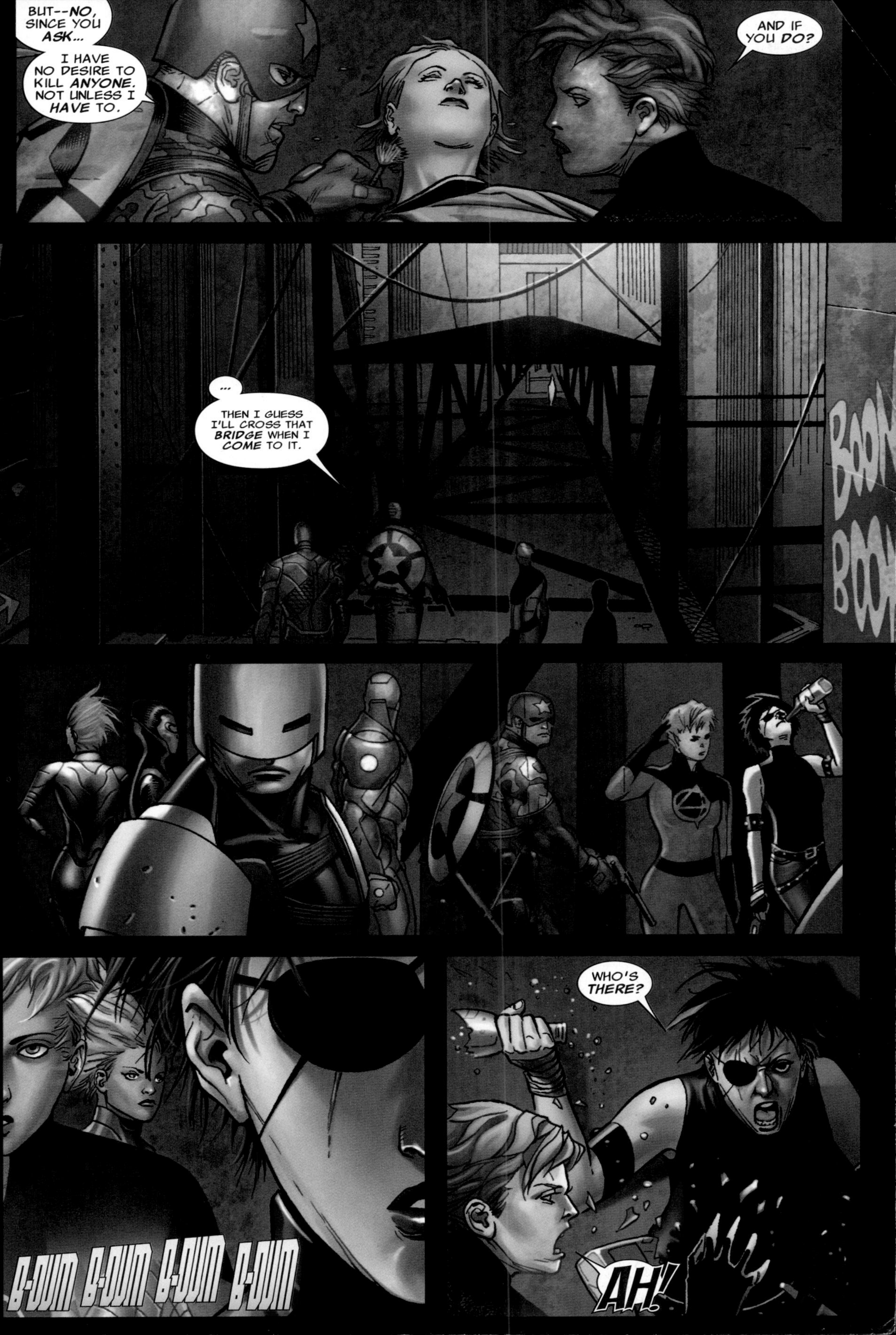

BUT--NO, SINCE YOU ASK...
I HAVE NO DESIRE TO KILL ANYONE. NOT UNLESS I HAVE TO.
AND IF YOU DO?
...
THEN I GUESS I'LL CROSS THAT BRIDGE WHEN I COME TO IT.
B-DUM B-DUM B-DUM B-DUM
WHO'S THERE?
AH!

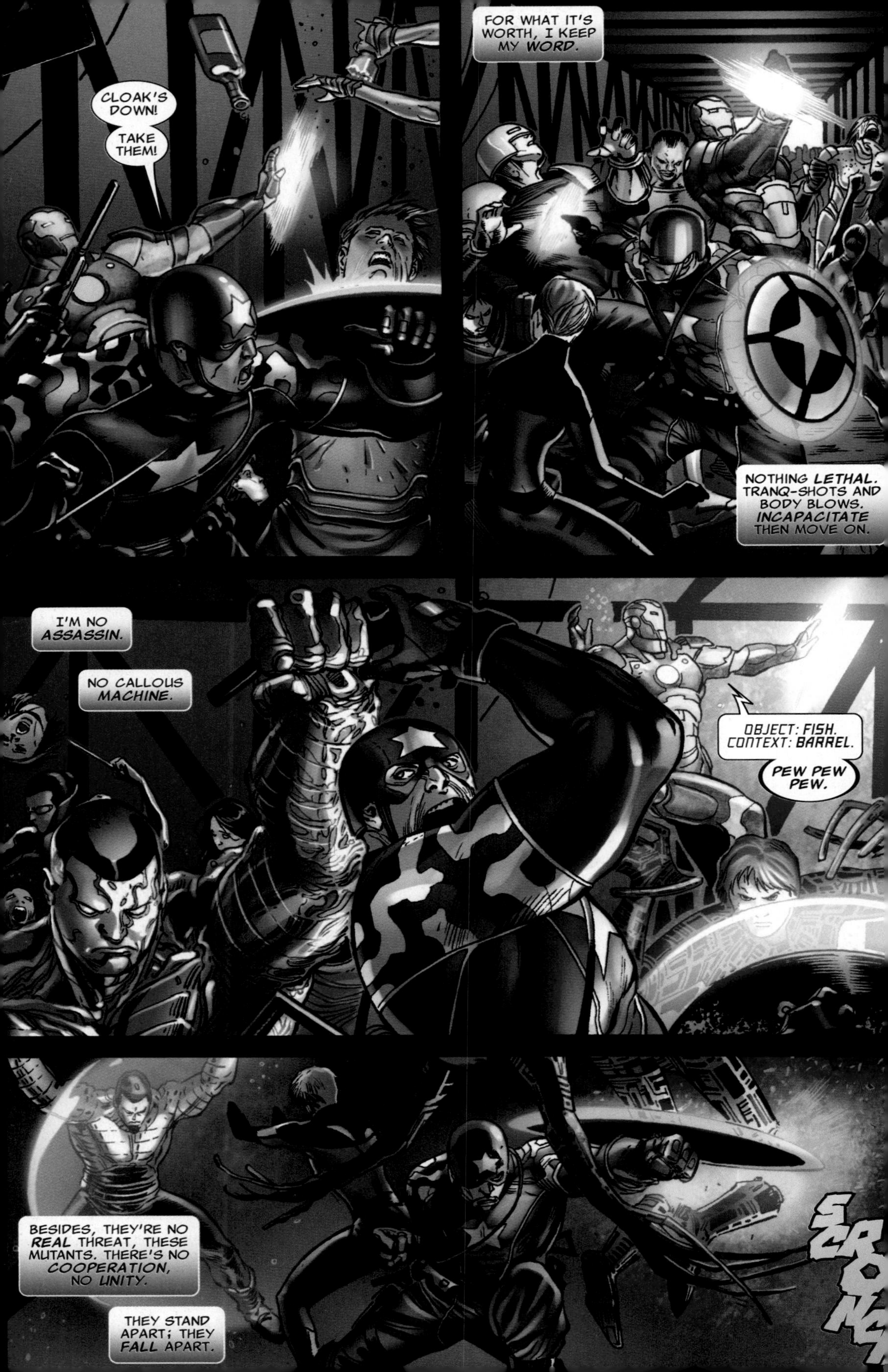
CLOAK'S DOWN!
TAKE THEM!
FOR WHAT IT'S WORTH, I KEEP MY WORD.
NOTHING LETHAL. TRANQ-SHOTS AND BODY BLOWS. INCAPACITATE THEN MOVE ON.
I'M NO ASSASSIN.
NO CALLOUS MACHINE.
OBJECT: FISH. CONTEXT: BARREL.
PEW PEW PEW.
BESIDES, THEY'RE NO REAL THREAT, THESE MUTANTS. THERE'S NO COOPERATION, NO UNITY.
THEY STAND APART; THEY FALL APART.
SCRONCH

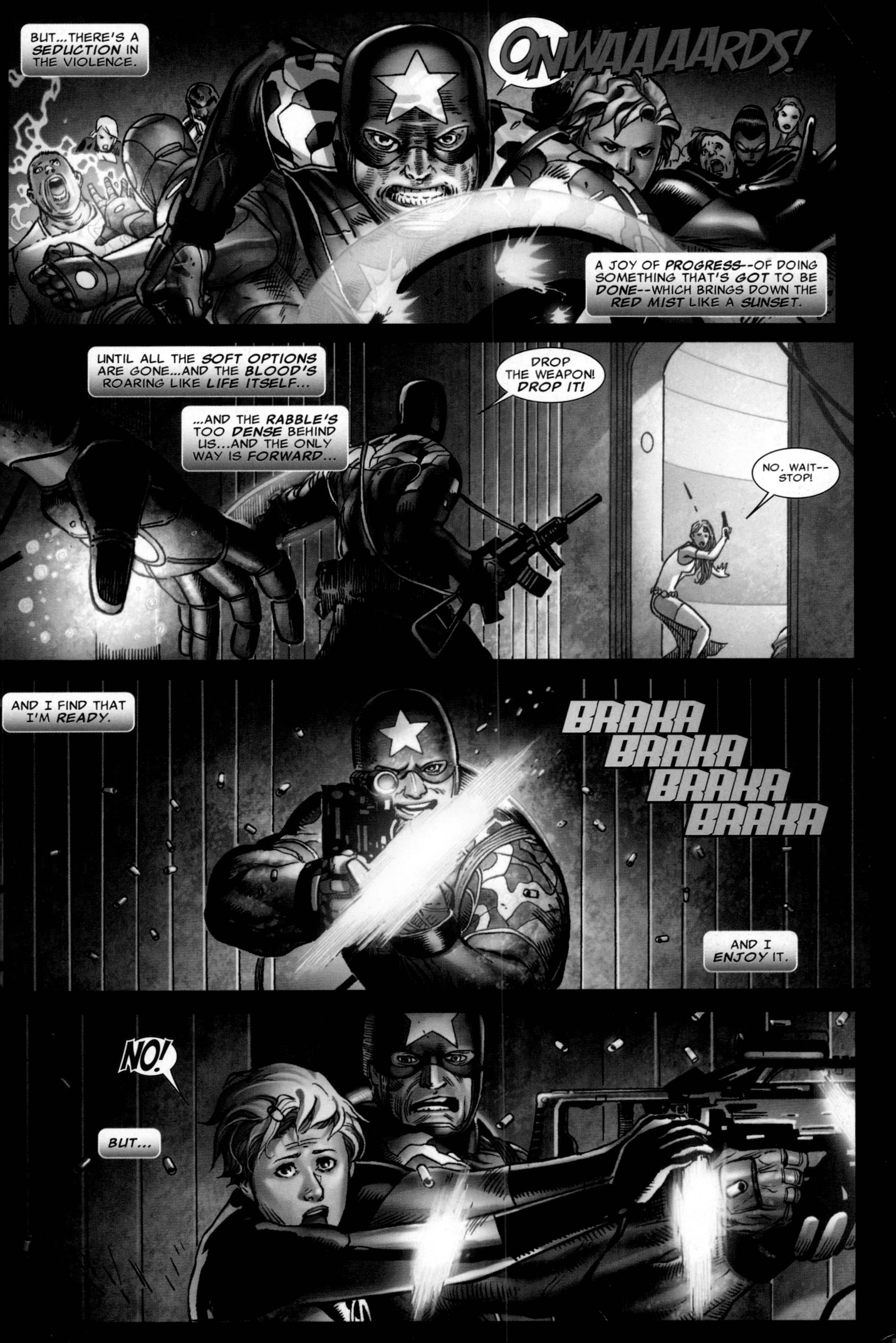

BUT...THERE'S A SEDUCTION IN THE VIOLENCE.
ONWAAAARDS!
A JOY OF PROGRESS--OF DOING SOMETHING THAT'S GOT TO BE DONE--WHICH BRINGS DOWN THE RED MIST LIKE A SUNSET.
UNTIL ALL THE SOFT OPTIONS ARE GONE...AND THE BLOOD'S ROARING LIKE LIFE ITSELF...
...AND THE RABBLE'S TOO DENSE BEHIND US...AND THE ONLY WAY IS FORWARD...
DROP THE WEAPON! DROP IT!
NO. WAIT-- STOP!
AND I FIND THAT I'M READY.
BRAKA BRAKA BRAKA BRAKA
AND I ENJOY IT.
NO!
BUT...

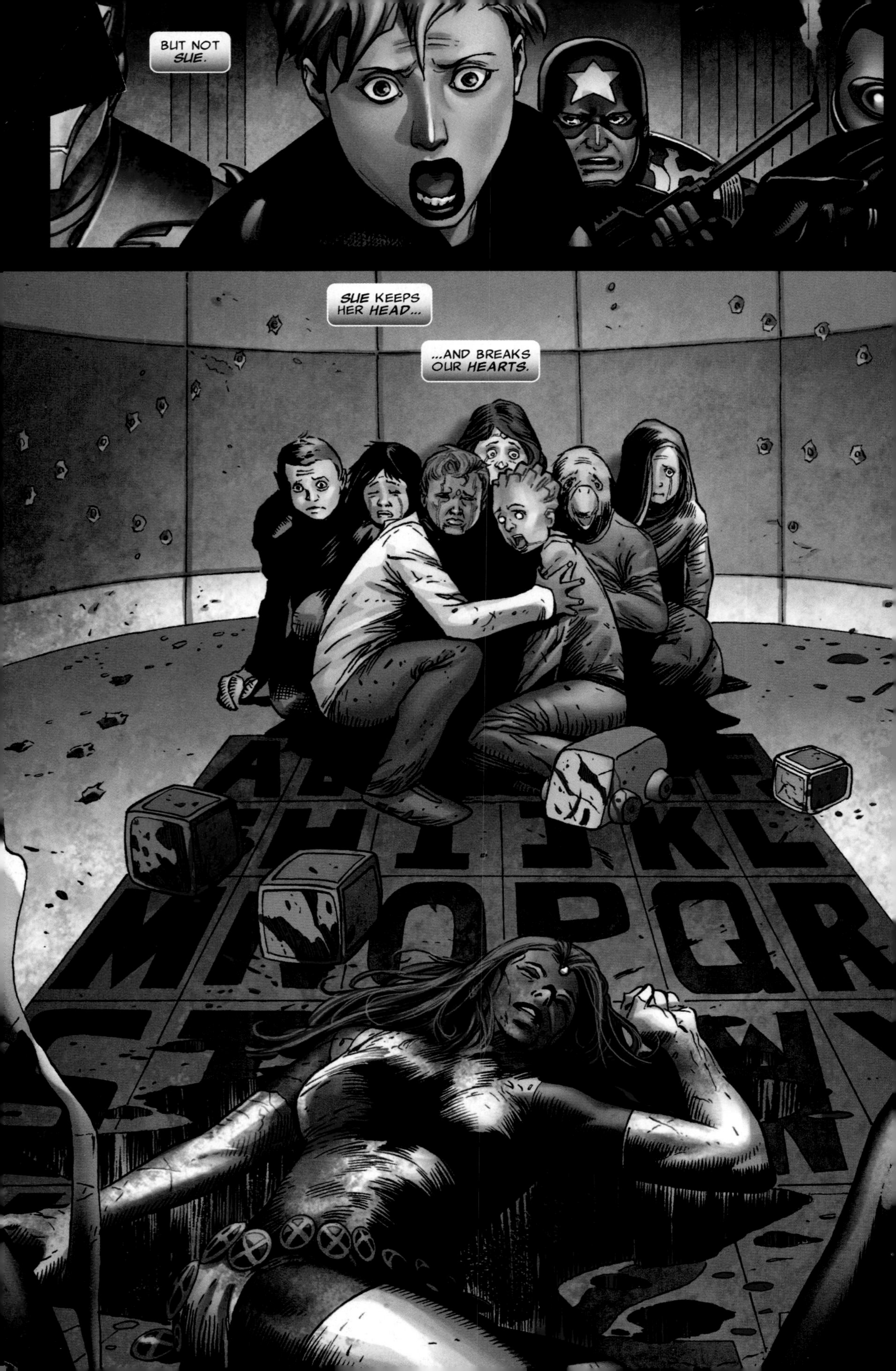
BUT NOT SUE.
SUE KEEPS HER HEAD...
...AND BREAKS OUR HEARTS.

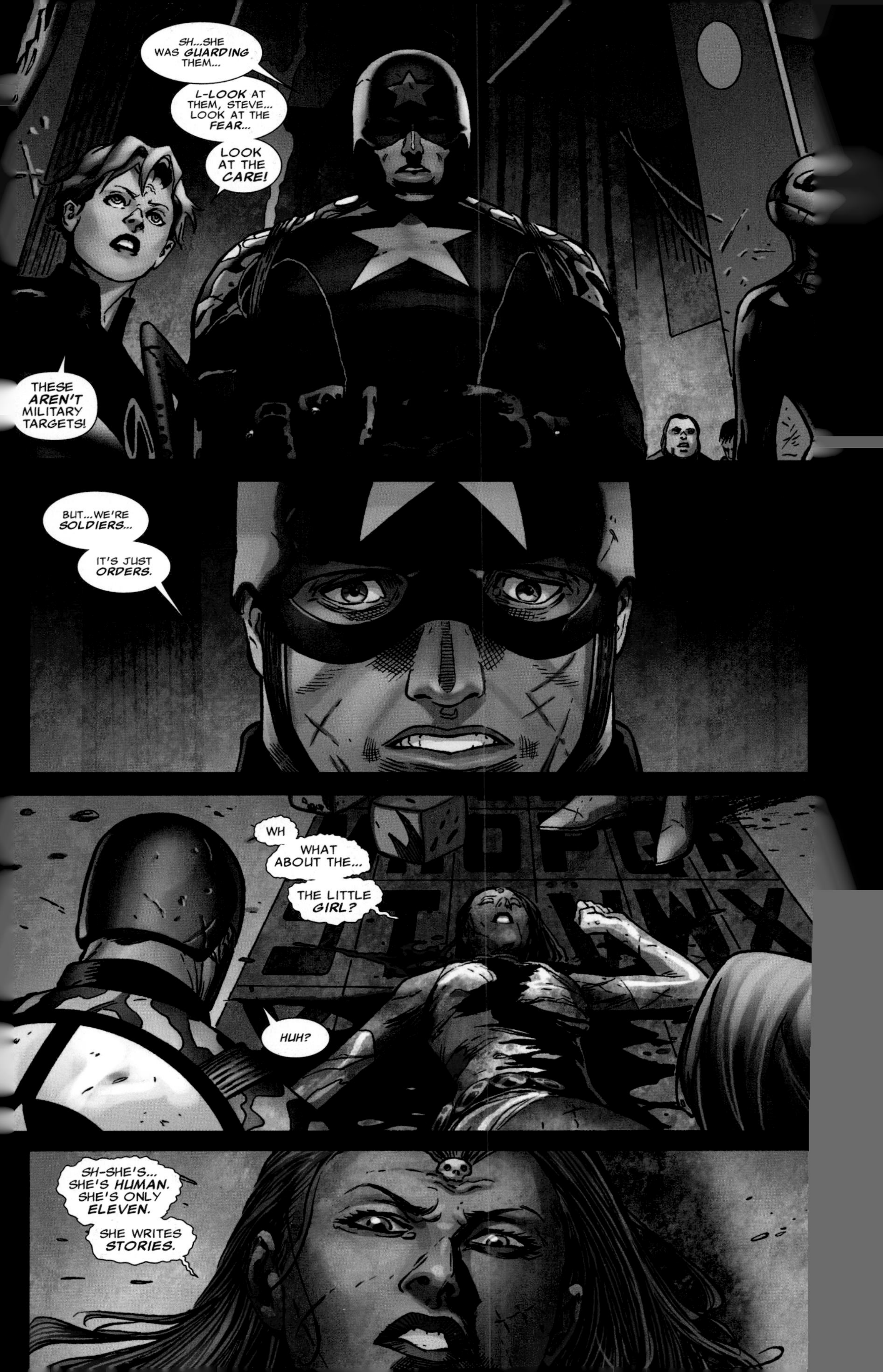

SH...SHE WAS GUARDING THEM...
L-LOOK AT THEM, STEVE... LOOK AT THE FEAR...
LOOK AT THE CARE!
THESE AREN'T MILITARY TARGETS!
BUT...WE'RE SOLDIERS...
IT'S JUST ORDERS.
WH
WHAT ABOUT THE...
THE LITTLE GIRL?
HUH?
SH-SHE'S... SHE'S HUMAN. SHE'S ONLY ELEVEN.
SHE WRITES STORIES.

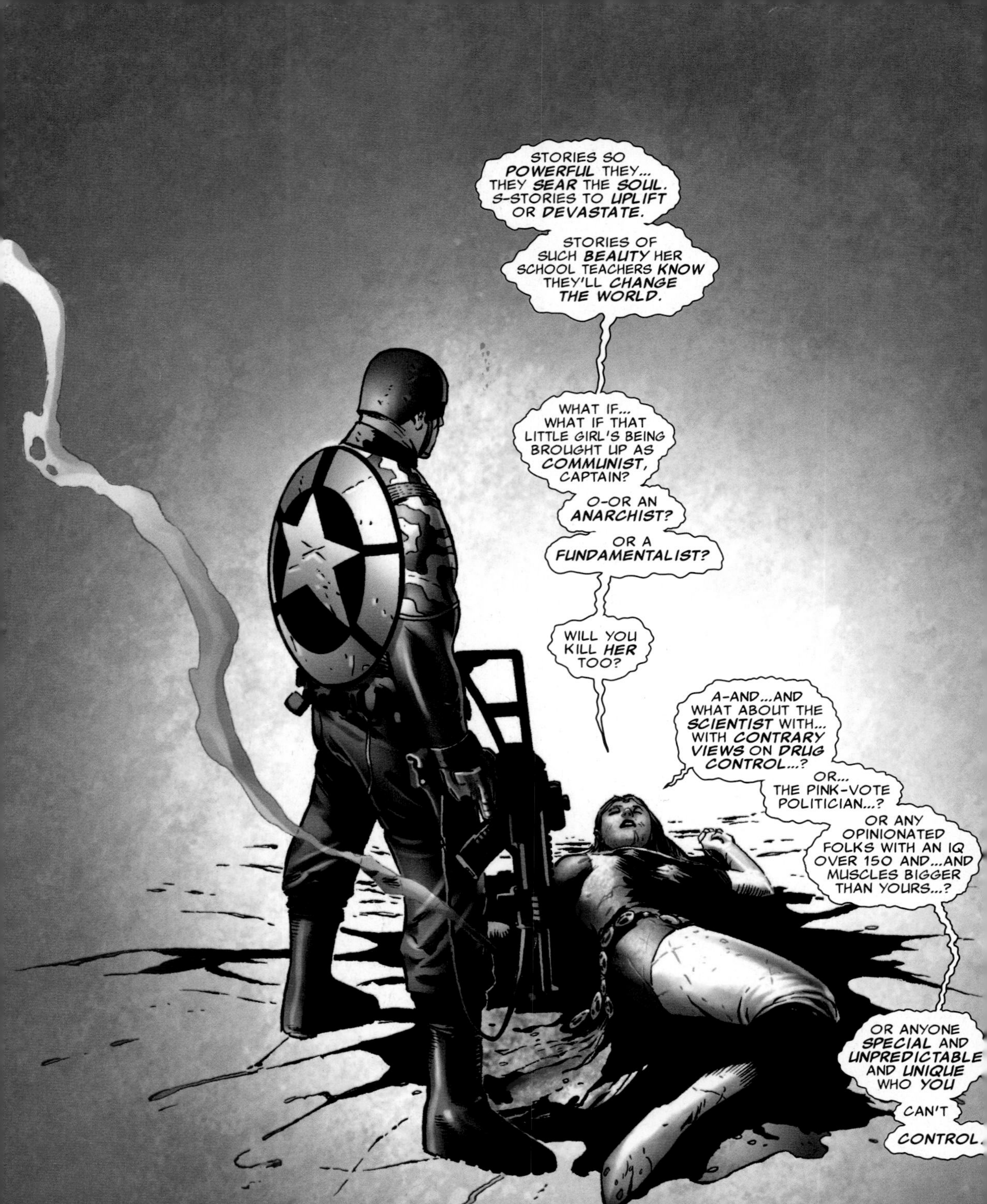
STORIES SO POWERFUL THEY... THEY SEAR THE SOUL. S-STORIES TO UPLIFT OR DEVASTATE.
STORIES OF SUCH BEAUTY HER SCHOOL TEACHERS KNOW THEY'LL CHANGE THE WORLD.
WHAT IF... WHAT IF THAT LITTLE GIRL'S BEING BROUGHT UP AS COMMUNIST, CAPTAIN?
O-OR AN ANARCHIST?
OR A FUNDAMENTALIST?
WILL YOU KILL HER TOO?
A-AND...AND WHAT ABOUT THE SCIENTIST WITH... WITH CONTRARY VIEWS ON DRUG CONTROL...?
OR... THE PINK-VOTE POLITICIAN...?
OR ANY OPINIONATED FOLKS WITH AN IQ OVER 150 AND...AND MUSCLES BIGGER THAN YOURS...?
OR ANYONE SPECIAL AND UNPREDICTABLE AND UNIQUE WHO YOU
CAN'T
CONTROL.
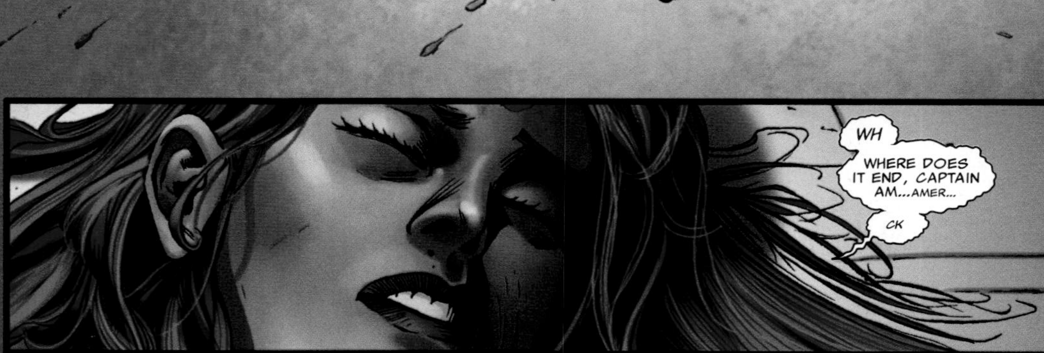
WH
WHERE DOES IT END, CAPTAIN AM...AMER...
CK

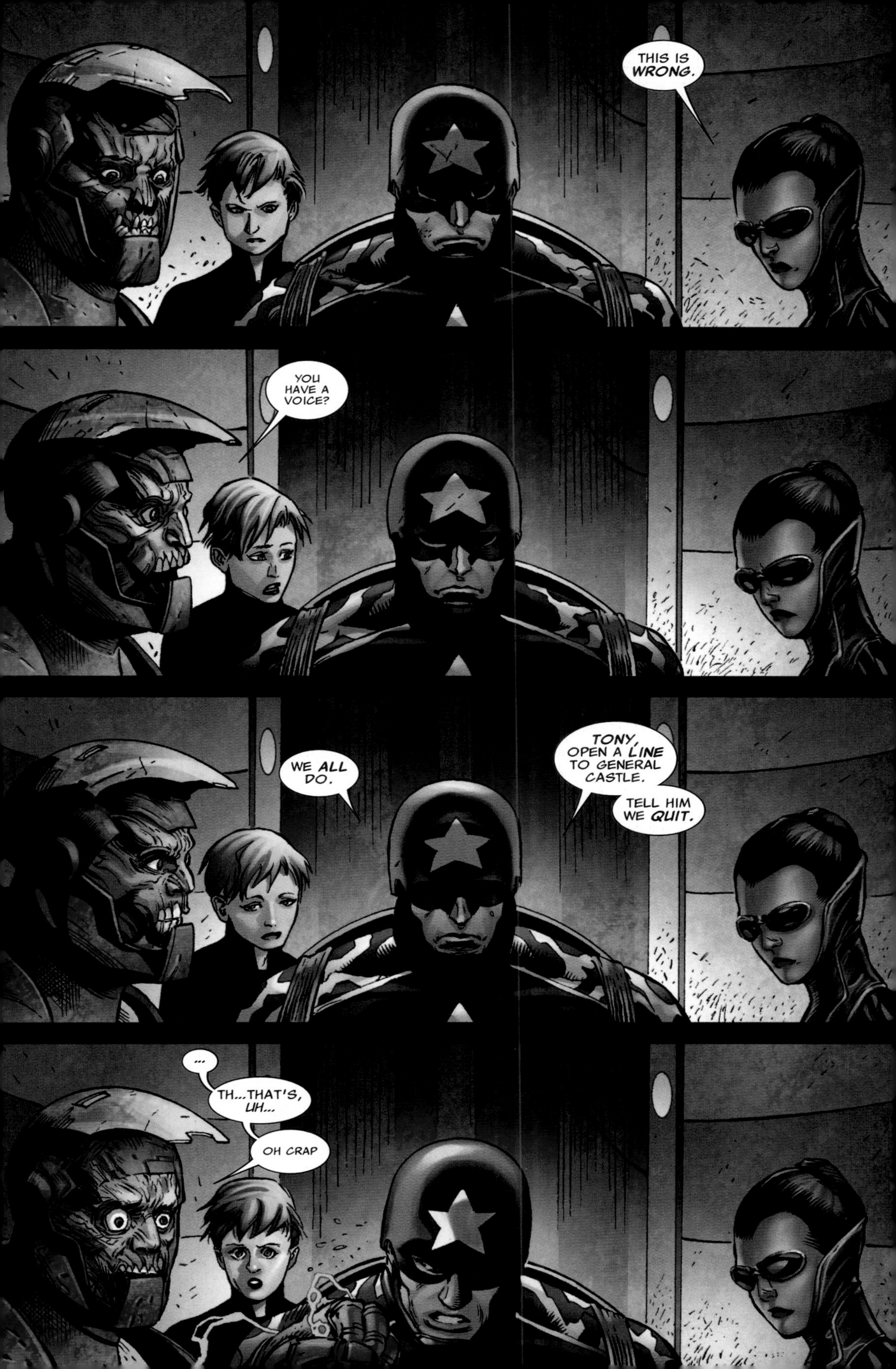
THIS IS WRONG.
YOU HAVE A VOICE?
WE ALL DO.
TONY, OPEN A LINE TO GENERAL CASTLE.
TELL HIM WE QUIT.
...
TH...THAT'S, UH...
OH CRAP

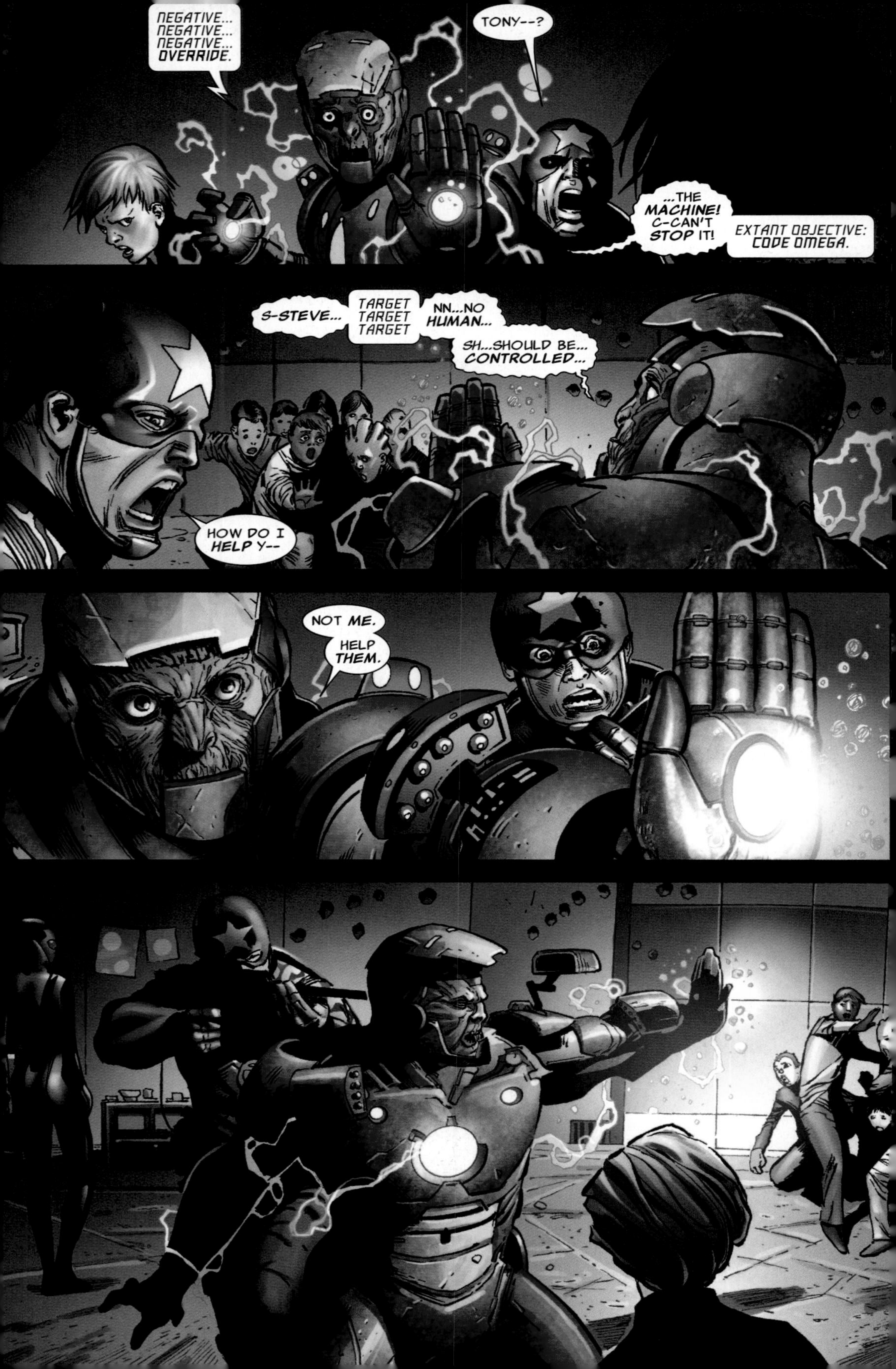
NEGATIVE... NEGATIVE... NEGATIVE... OVERRIDE.
TONY--?
...THE MACHINE! C-CAN'T STOP IT!
EXTANT OBJECTIVE: CODE OMEGA.
S-STEVE...
TARGET TARGET TARGET
NN...NO HUMAN...
SH...SHOULD BE... CONTROLLED...
HOW DO I HELP Y--
NOT ME. HELP THEM.

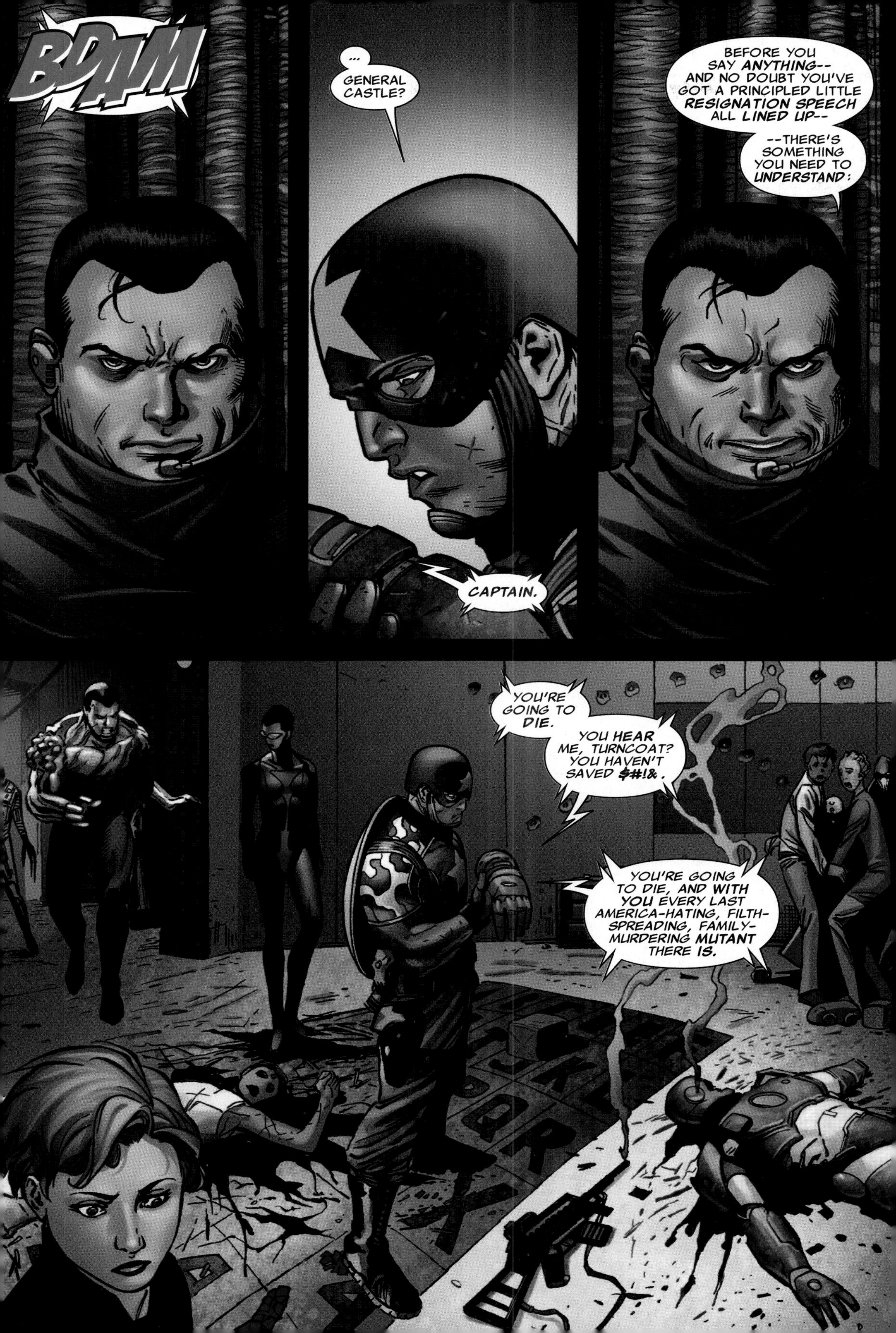
BDAM
... GENERAL CASTLE?
CAPTAIN.
BEFORE YOU SAY ANYTHING-- AND NO DOUBT YOU'VE GOT A PRINCIPLED LITTLE RESIGNATION SPEECH ALL LINED UP--
--THERE'S SOMETHING YOU NEED TO UNDERSTAND:
YOU'RE GOING TO DIE.
YOU HEAR ME, TURNCOAT? YOU HAVEN'T SAVED $#!&.
YOU'RE GOING TO DIE, AND WITH YOU EVERY LAST AMERICA-HATING, FILTH-SPREADING, FAMILY-MURDERING MUTANT THERE IS.

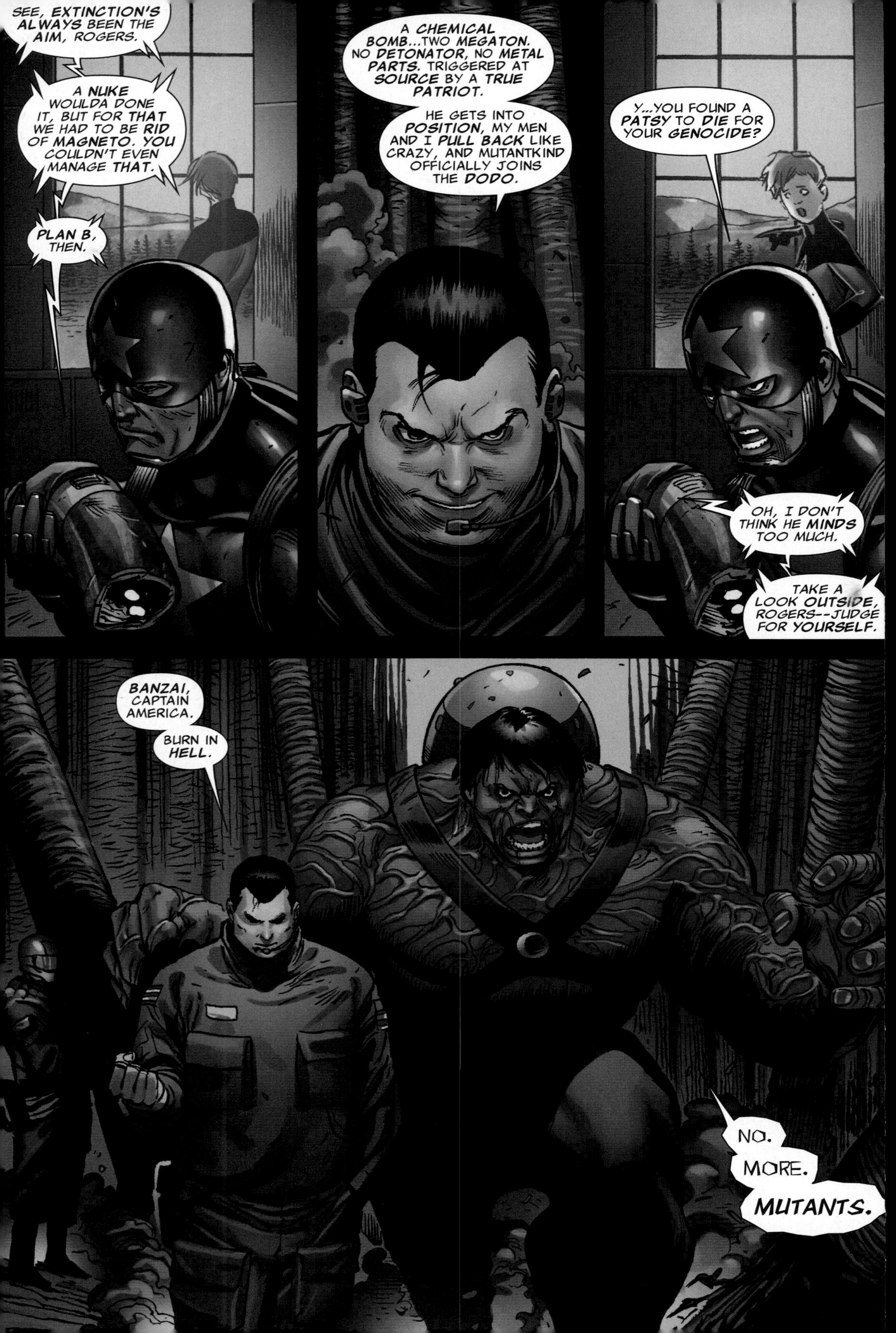

SEE, EXTINCTION'S ALWAYS BEEN THE AIM, ROGERS.
A NUKE WOULDA DONE IT, BUT FOR THAT WE HAD TO BE RID OF MAGNETO. YOU COULDN'T EVEN MANAGE THAT.
PLAN B, THEN.
A CHEMICAL BOMB...TWO MEGATON. NO DETONATOR, NO METAL PARTS. TRIGGERED AT SOURCE BY A TRUE PATRIOT.
HE GETS INTO POSITION, MY MEN AND I PULL BACK LIKE CRAZY, AND MUTANTKIND OFFICIALLY JOINS THE DODO.
Y...YOU FOUND A PATSY TO DIE FOR YOUR GENOCIDE?
OH, I DON'T THINK HE MINDS TOO MUCH.
TAKE A LOOK OUTSIDE, ROGERS--JUDGE FOR YOURSELF.
BANZAI, CAPTAIN AMERICA.
BURN IN HELL.
NO.
MORE.
MUTANTS.

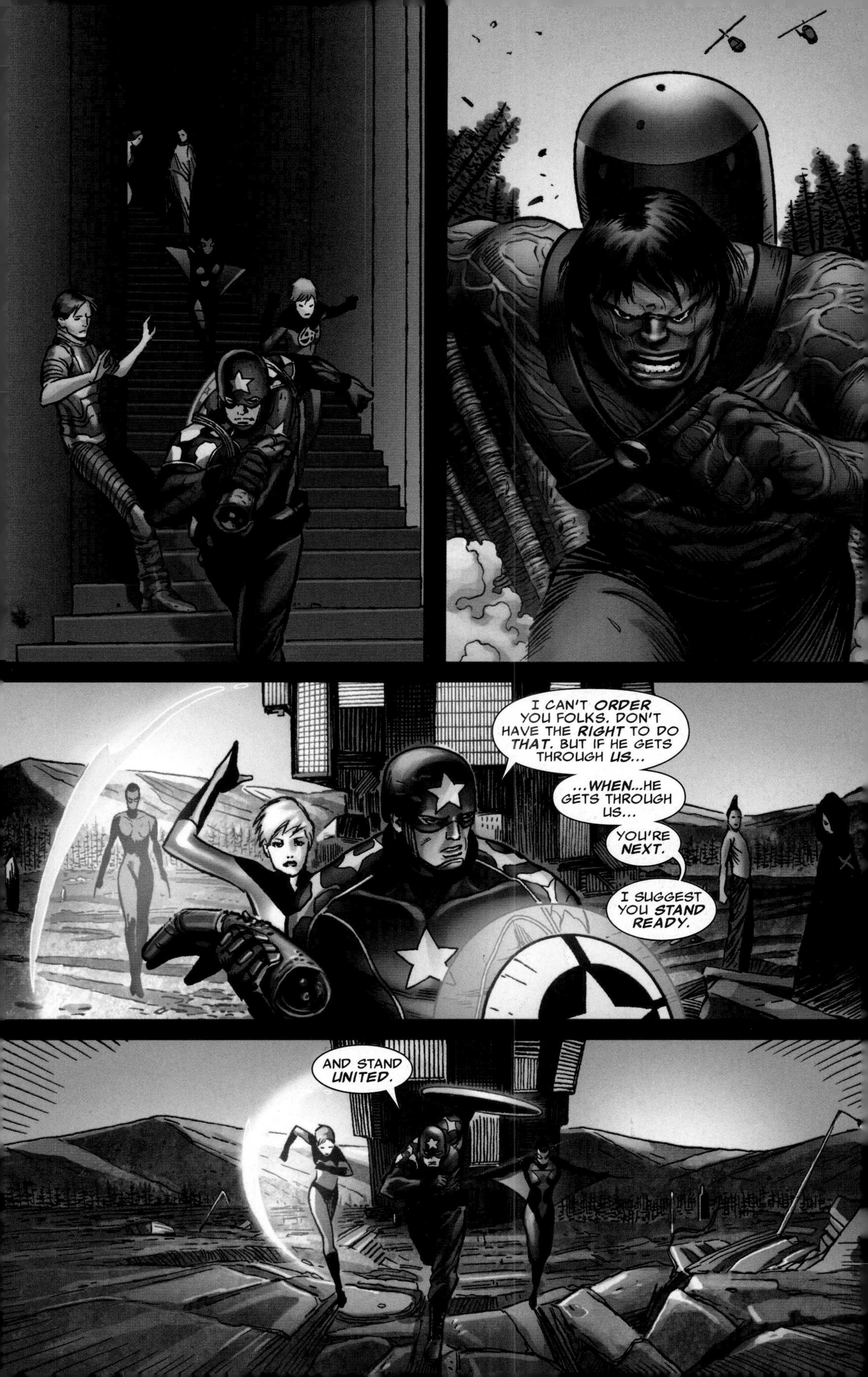
I CAN'T ORDER YOU FOLKS. DON'T HAVE THE RIGHT TO DO THAT. BUT IF HE GETS THROUGH US...
...WHEN...HE GETS THROUGH US...
YOU'RE NEXT.
I SUGGEST YOU STAND READY.
AND STAND UNITED.

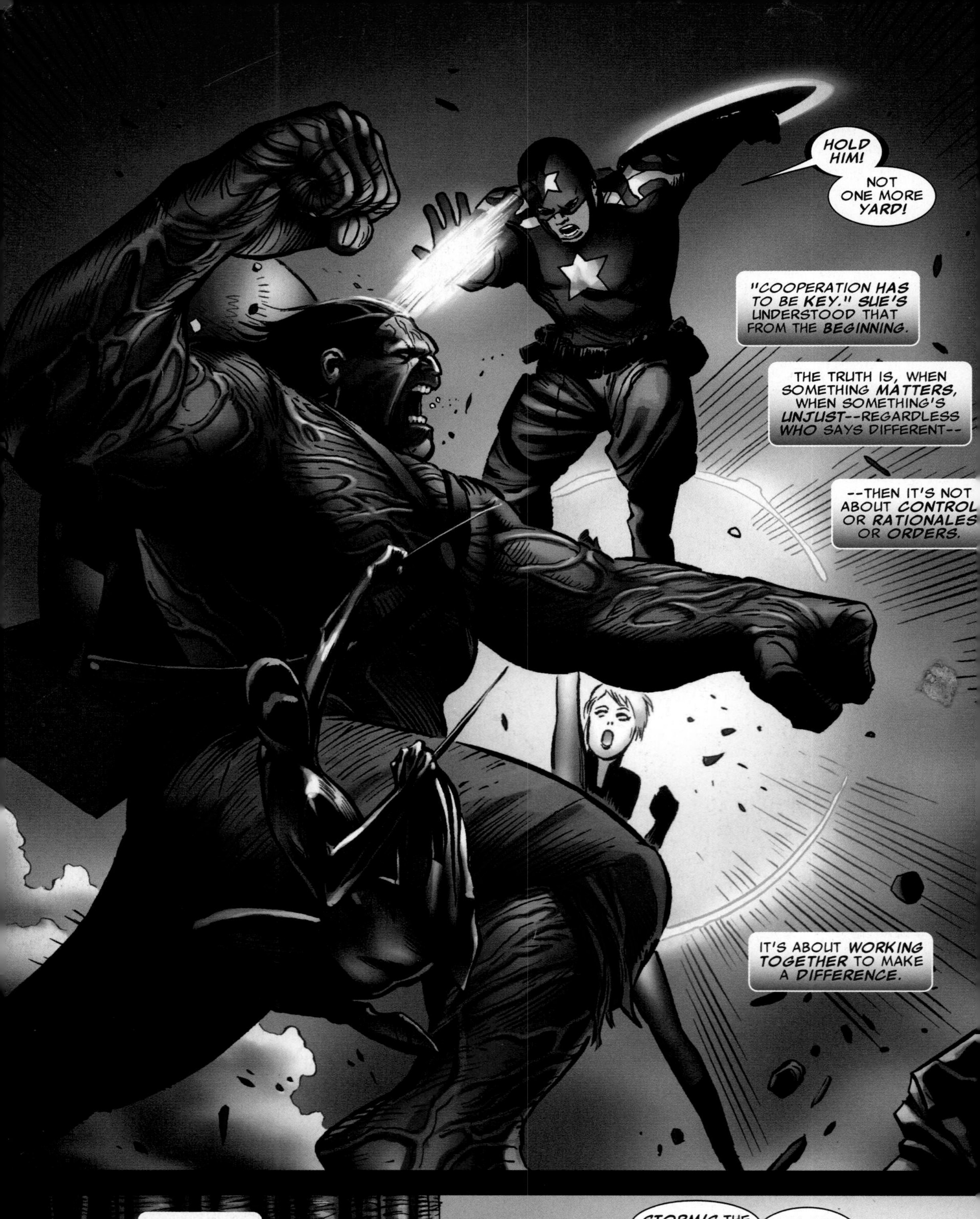
HOLD HIM!
NOT ONE MORE YARD!
"COOPERATION HAS TO BE KEY." SUE'S UNDERSTOOD THAT FROM THE BEGINNING.
THE TRUTH IS, WHEN SOMETHING MATTERS, WHEN SOMETHING'S UNJUST--REGARDLESS WHO SAYS DIFFERENT--
--THEN IT'S NOT ABOUT CONTROL OR RATIONALES OR ORDERS.
IT'S ABOUT WORKING TOGETHER TO MAKE A DIFFERENCE.

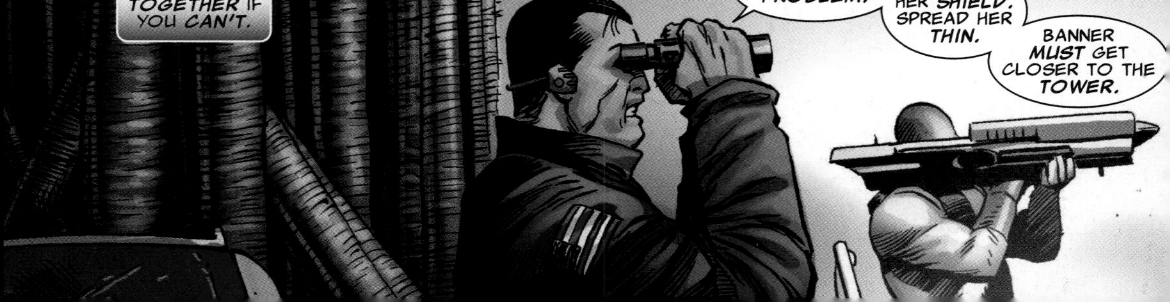
OR DYING TOGETHER IF YOU CAN'T.
STORM'S THE PROBLEM.
AIM FOR HER SHIELD. SPREAD HER THIN.
BANNER MUST GET CLOSER TO THE TOWER.

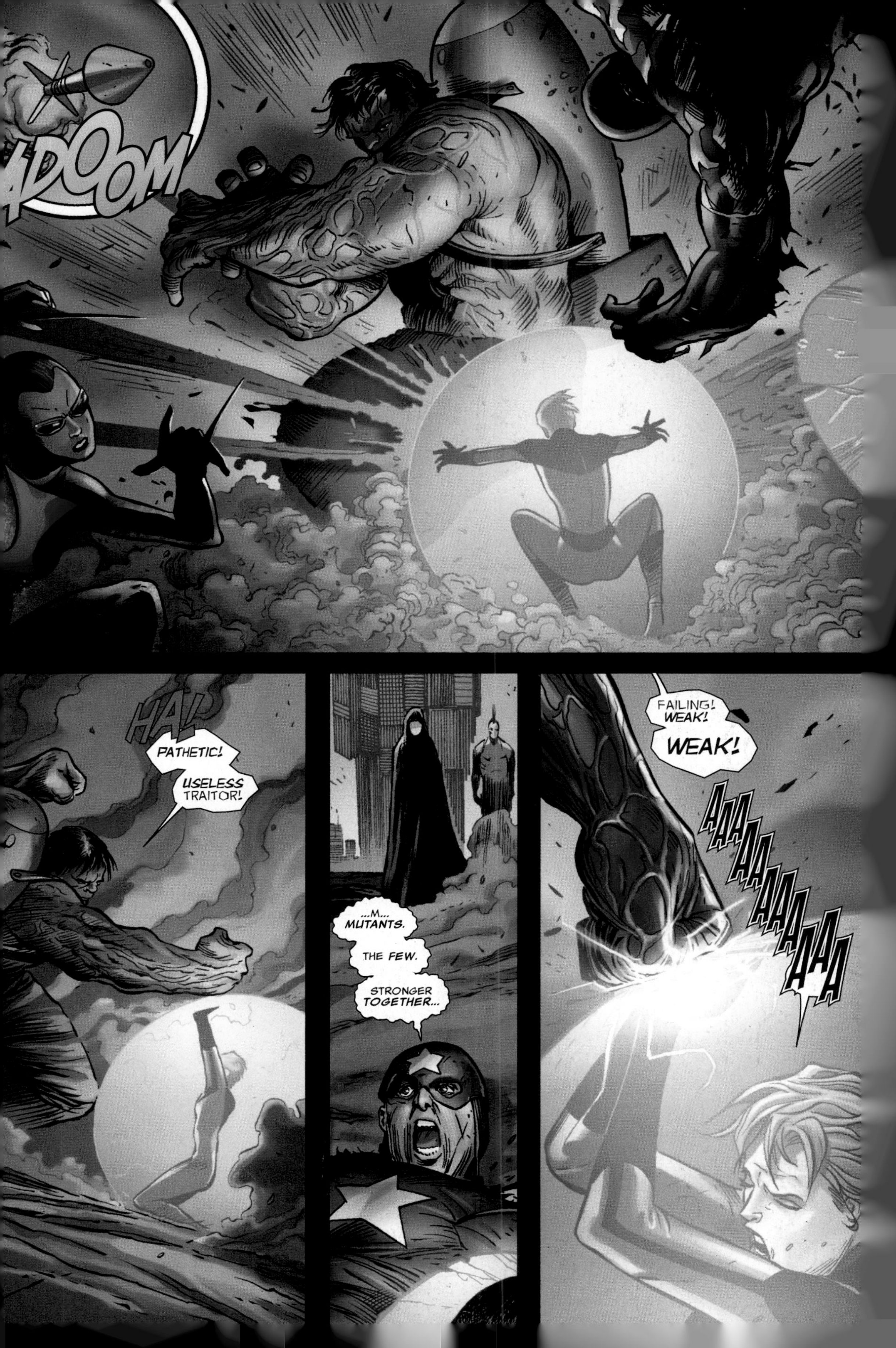
BADOOM
HA!
PATHETIC!
USELESS TRAITOR!
...M... MUTANTS.
THE FEW.
STRONGER TOGETHER...
FAILING! WEAK!
WEAK!
AAAAAAAAAAAAA

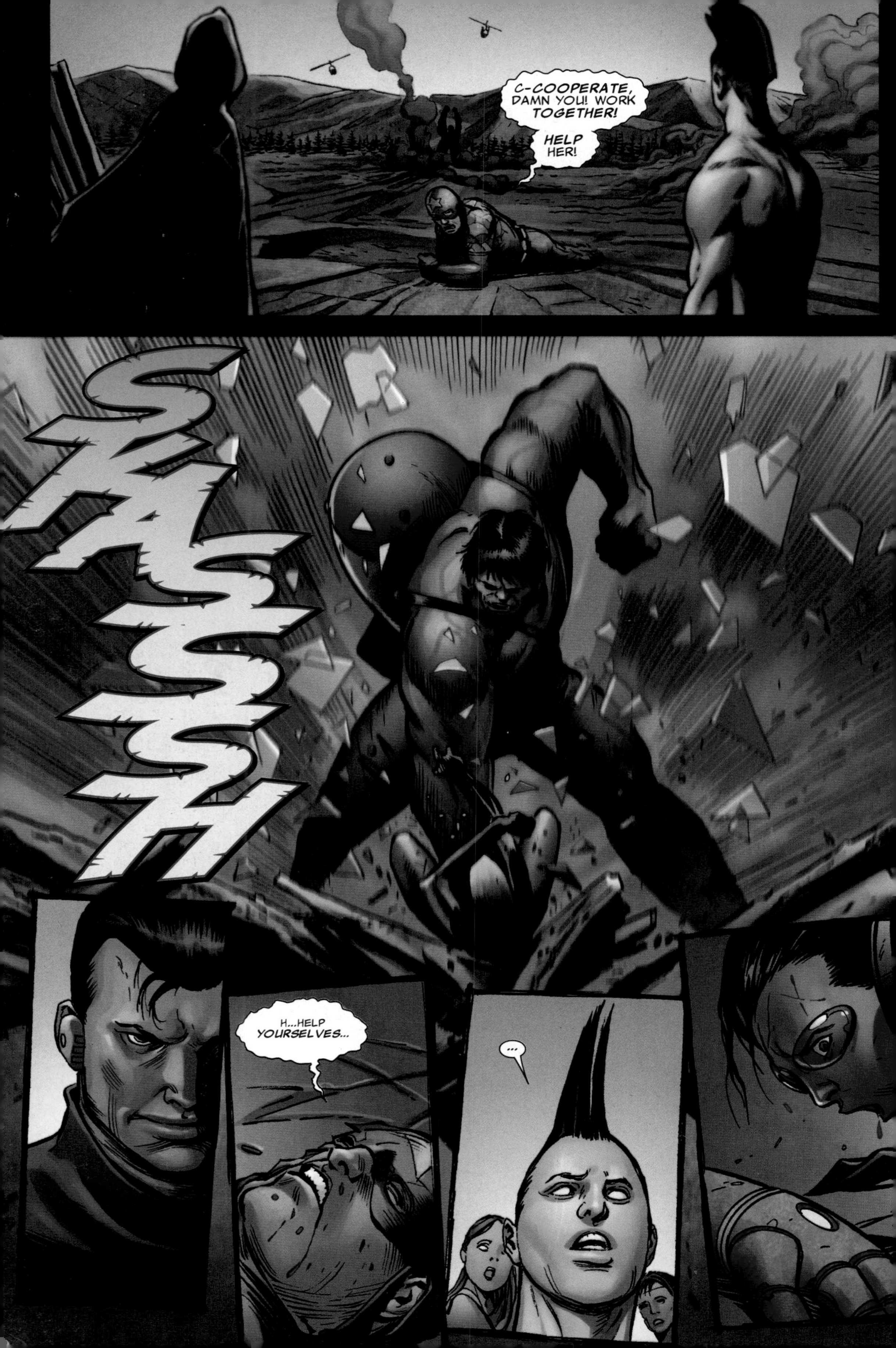
C-COOPERATE, DAMN YOU! WORK TOGETHER!
HELP HER!
SHASSHH
H...HELP YOURSELVES...
...

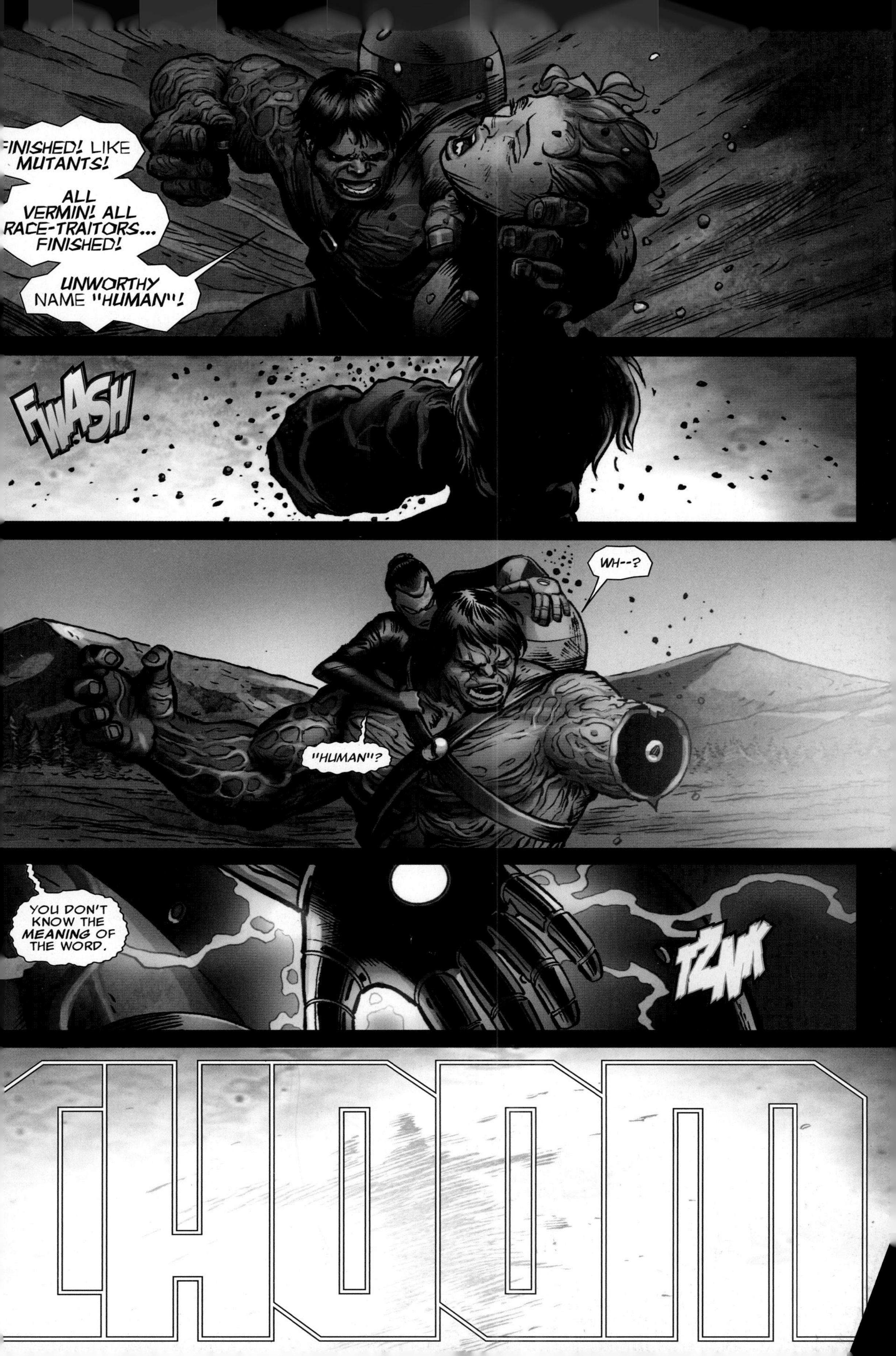
FINISHED! LIKE MUTANTS!
ALL VERMIN! ALL RACE-TRAITORS... FINISHED!
UNWORTHY NAME "HUMAN"!
FWASH
WH--?
"HUMAN"?
YOU DON'T KNOW THE MEANING OF THE WORD.
TZNK
THOOM

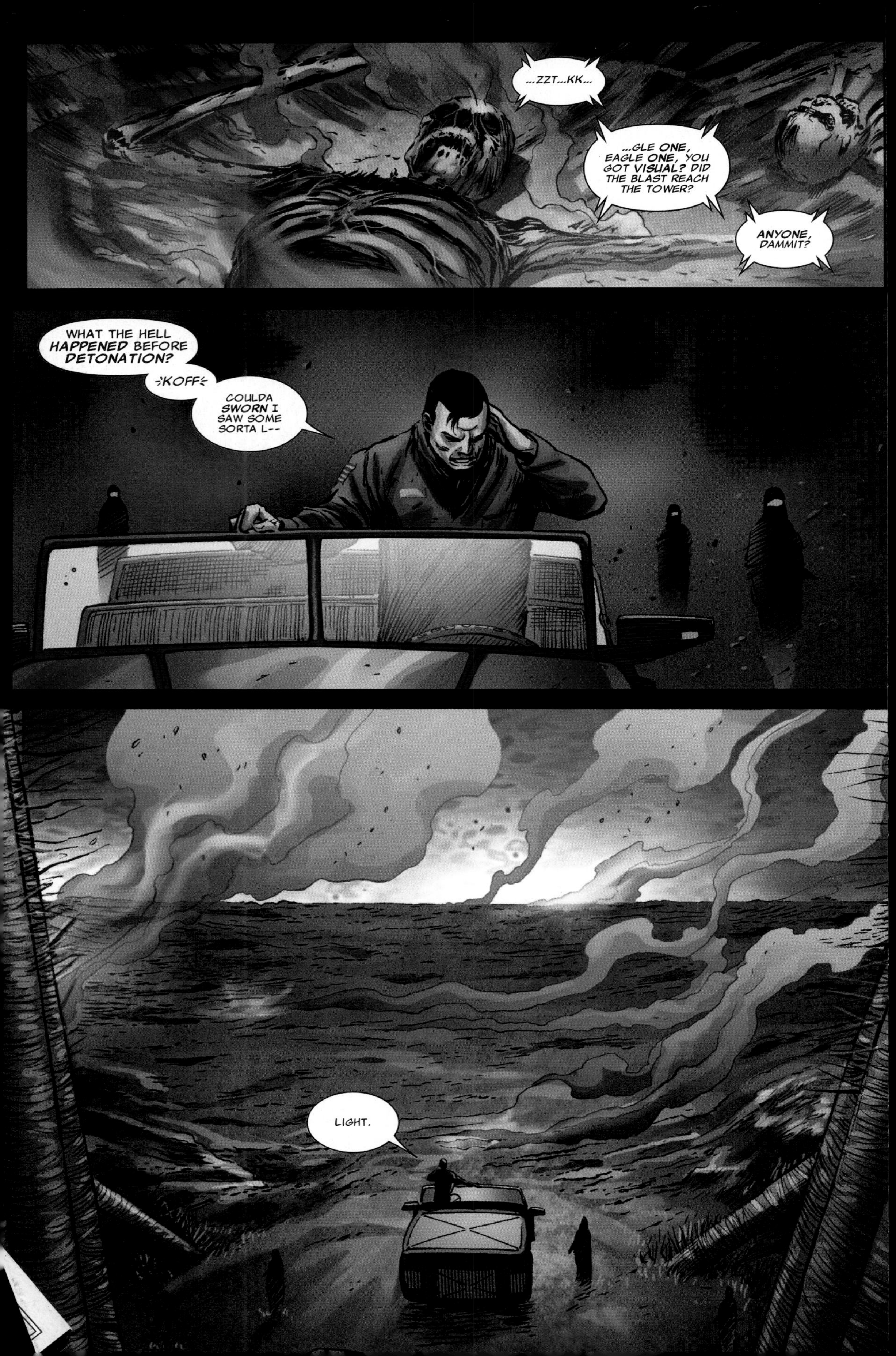
...ZZT...KK...
...GLE ONE, EAGLE ONE, YOU GOT VISUAL? DID THE BLAST REACH THE TOWER?
ANYONE, DAMMIT?
WHAT THE HELL HAPPENED BEFORE DETONATION?
KOFF
COULDA SWORN I SAW SOME SORTA L--
LIGHT.

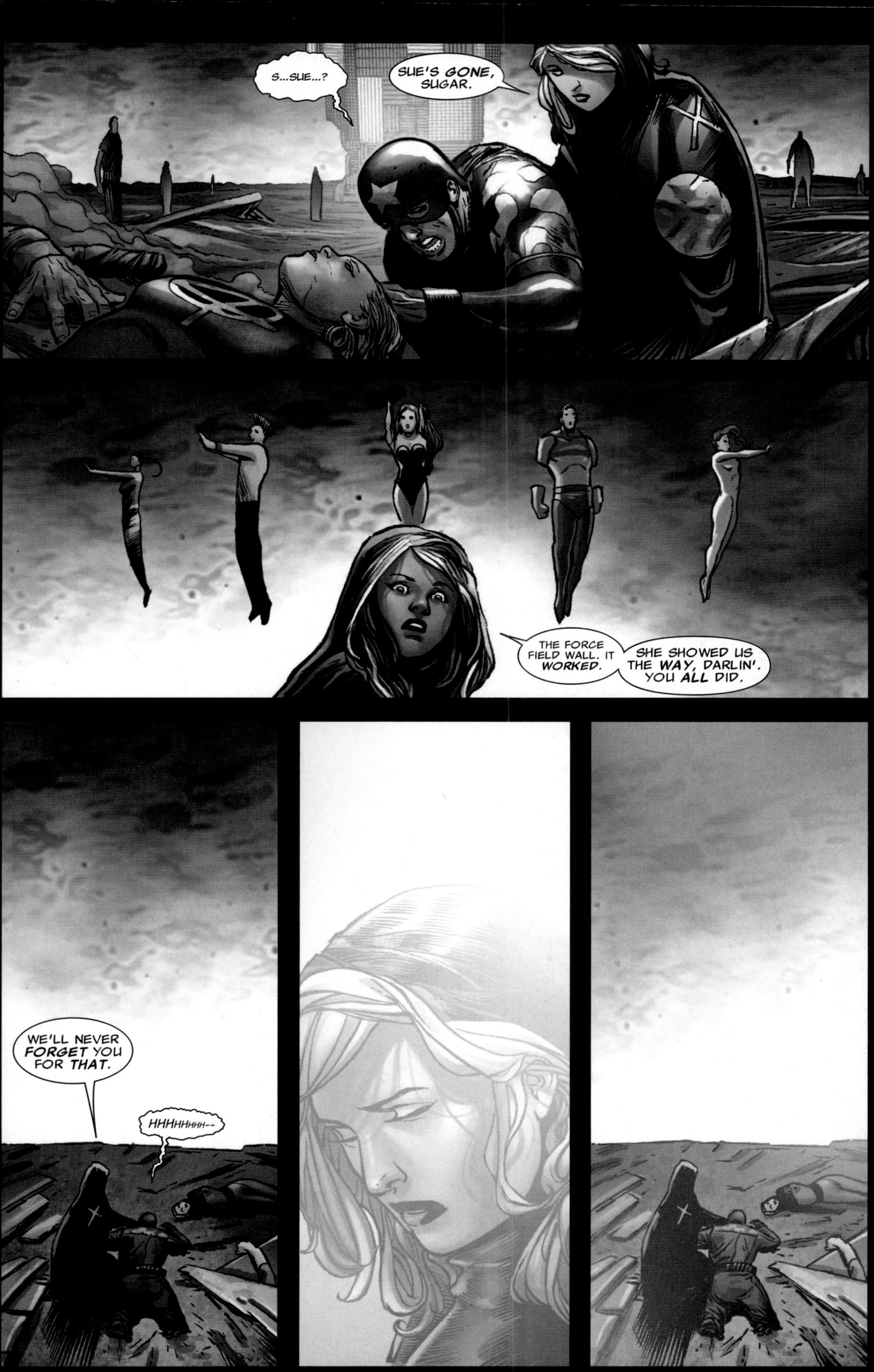
S...SUE...?
SUE'S GONE, SUGAR.
THE FORCE FIELD WALL. IT WORKED.
SHE SHOWED US THE WAY, DARLIN'. YOU ALL DID.
WE'LL NEVER FORGET YOU FOR THAT.
HHHHHHHH--

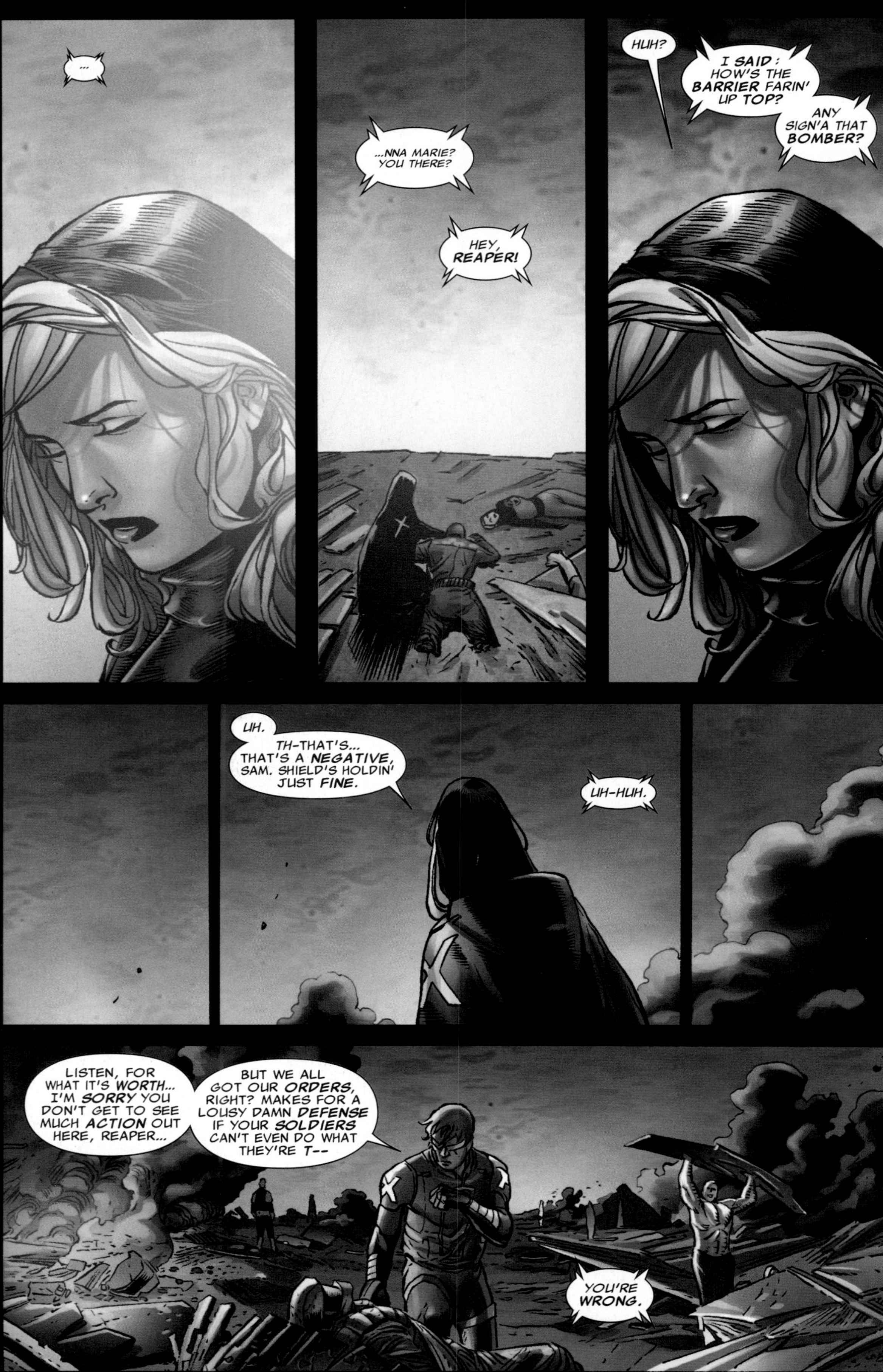
...
...NNA MARIE? YOU THERE?
HEY, REAPER!
HUH?
I SAID: HOW'S THE BARRIER FARIN' UP TOP?
ANY SIGN'A THAT BOMBER?
UH.
TH-THAT'S... THAT'S A NEGATIVE, SAM. SHIELD'S HOLDIN' JUST FINE.
UH-HUH.
LISTEN, FOR WHAT IT'S WORTH... I'M SORRY YOU DON'T GET TO SEE MUCH ACTION OUT HERE, REAPER...
BUT WE ALL GOT OUR ORDERS, RIGHT? MAKES FOR A LOUSY DAMN DEFENSE IF YOUR SOLDIERS CAN'T EVEN DO WHAT THEY'RE T--
YOU'RE WRONG.

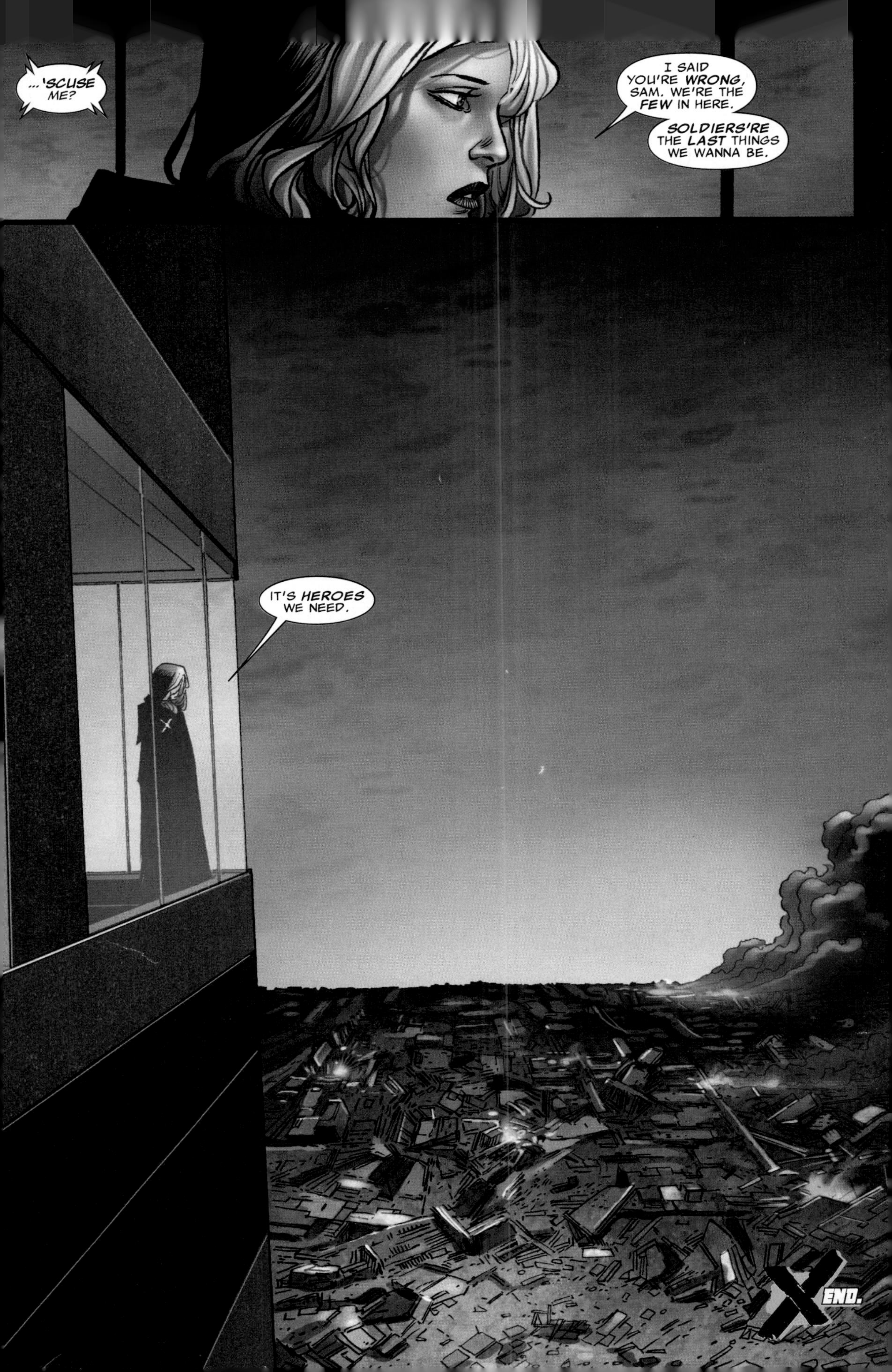
...'SCUSE ME?
I SAID YOU'RE WRONG, SAM. WE'RE THE FEW IN HERE.
SOLDIERS'RE THE LAST THINGS WE WANNA BE.
IT'S HEROES WE NEED.
END.

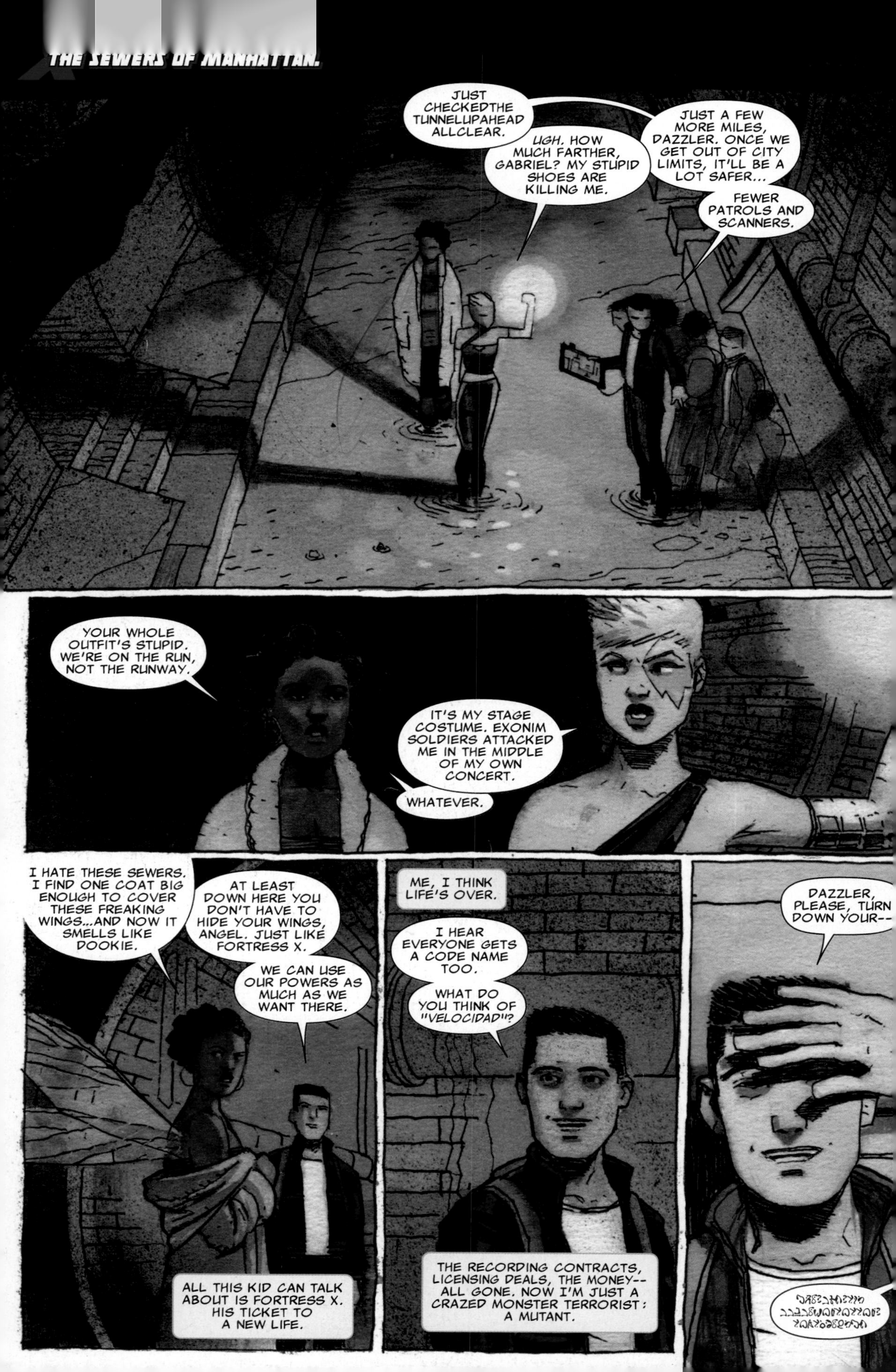
THE SEWERS OF MANHATTAN.
JUST CHECKEDTHE TUNNELUPAHEAD ALLCLEAR.
UGH. HOW MUCH FARTHER, GABRIEL? MY STUPID SHOES ARE KILLING ME.
JUST A FEW MORE MILES, DAZZLER. ONCE WE GET OUT OF CITY LIMITS, IT'LL BE A LOT SAFER...
FEWER PATROLS AND SCANNERS.
YOUR WHOLE OUTFIT'S STUPID. WE'RE ON THE RUN, NOT THE RUNWAY.
IT'S MY STAGE COSTUME. EXONIM SOLDIERS ATTACKED ME IN THE MIDDLE OF MY OWN CONCERT.
WHATEVER.
I HATE THESE SEWERS. I FIND ONE COAT BIG ENOUGH TO COVER THESE FREAKING WINGS...AND NOW IT SMELLS LIKE DOOKIE.
AT LEAST DOWN HERE YOU DON'T HAVE TO HIDE YOUR WINGS, ANGEL. JUST LIKE FORTRESS X.
WE CAN USE OUR POWERS AS MUCH AS WE WANT THERE.
ALL THIS KID CAN TALK ABOUT IS FORTRESS X. HIS TICKET TO A NEW LIFE.
ME, I THINK LIFE'S OVER.
I HEAR EVERYONE GETS A CODE NAME TOO.
WHAT DO YOU THINK OF "VELOCIDAD"?
THE RECORDING CONTRACTS, LICENSING DEALS, THE MONEY-- ALL GONE. NOW I'M JUST A CRAZED MONSTER TERRORIST: A MUTANT.
DAZZLER, PLEASE, TURN DOWN YOUR--

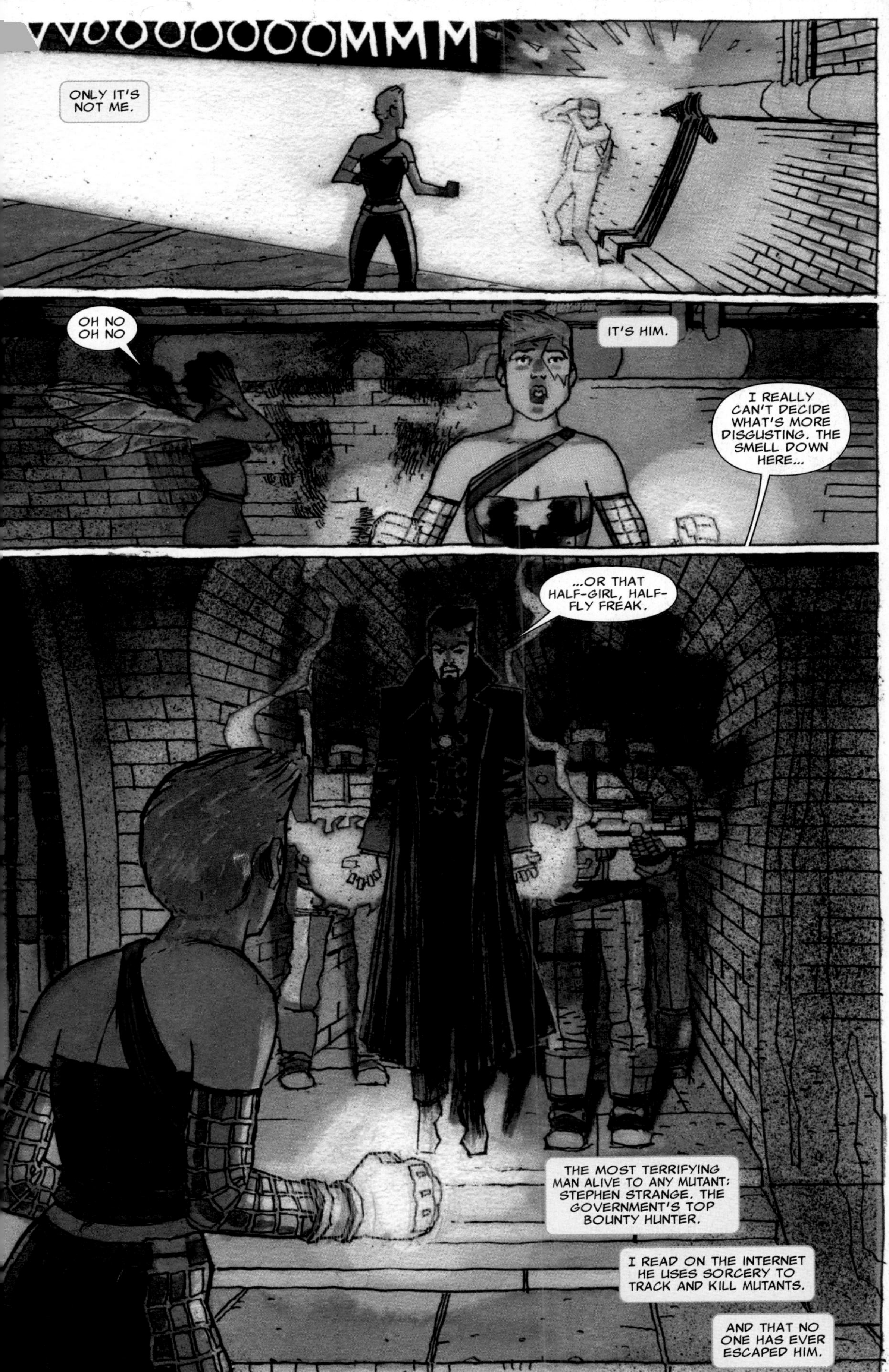
VVOOOOOOOMMM
ONLY IT'S NOT ME.
OH NO OH NO
IT'S HIM.
I REALLY CAN'T DECIDE WHAT'S MORE DISGUSTING. THE SMELL DOWN HERE...
...OR THAT HALF-GIRL, HALF-FLY FREAK.
THE MOST TERRIFYING MAN ALIVE TO ANY MUTANT: STEPHEN STRANGE. THE GOVERNMENT'S TOP BOUNTY HUNTER.
I READ ON THE INTERNET HE USES SORCERY TO TRACK AND KILL MUTANTS.
AND THAT NO ONE HAS EVER ESCAPED HIM.

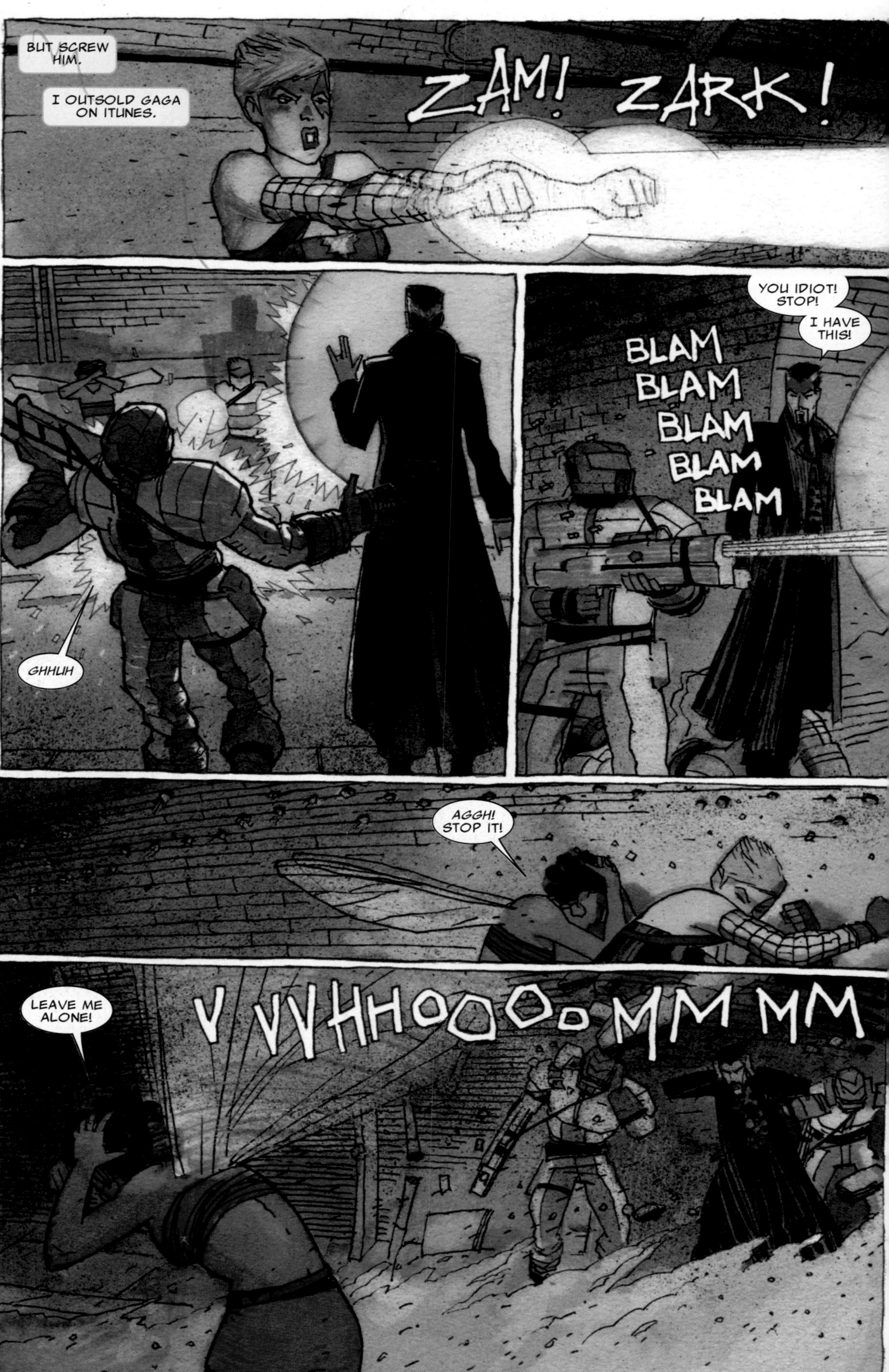
BUT SCREW HIM.
I OUTSOLD GAGA ON ITUNES.
ZAM! ZARK!
GHHUH
YOU IDIOT! STOP!
I HAVE THIS!
BLAM BLAM BLAM BLAM BLAM
AGGH! STOP IT!
LEAVE ME ALONE!
V VVHHOOOoMM MM

VOOOOoMMMM

IDIOT! YOUR RICOCHET FIRE COULD HAVE KILLED US ALL!

SIR, THE OTHER MUTANT MUST HAVE ESCAPED.

OF COURSE SHE DID. FIND HER. BUT BE WARNED, IF I HEAR ONE GUNSHOT I'LL TURN YOUR SKINS INSIDE OUT.

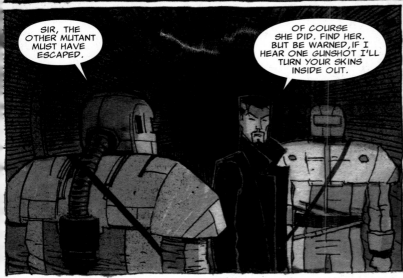

THE GIRL IS MINE.

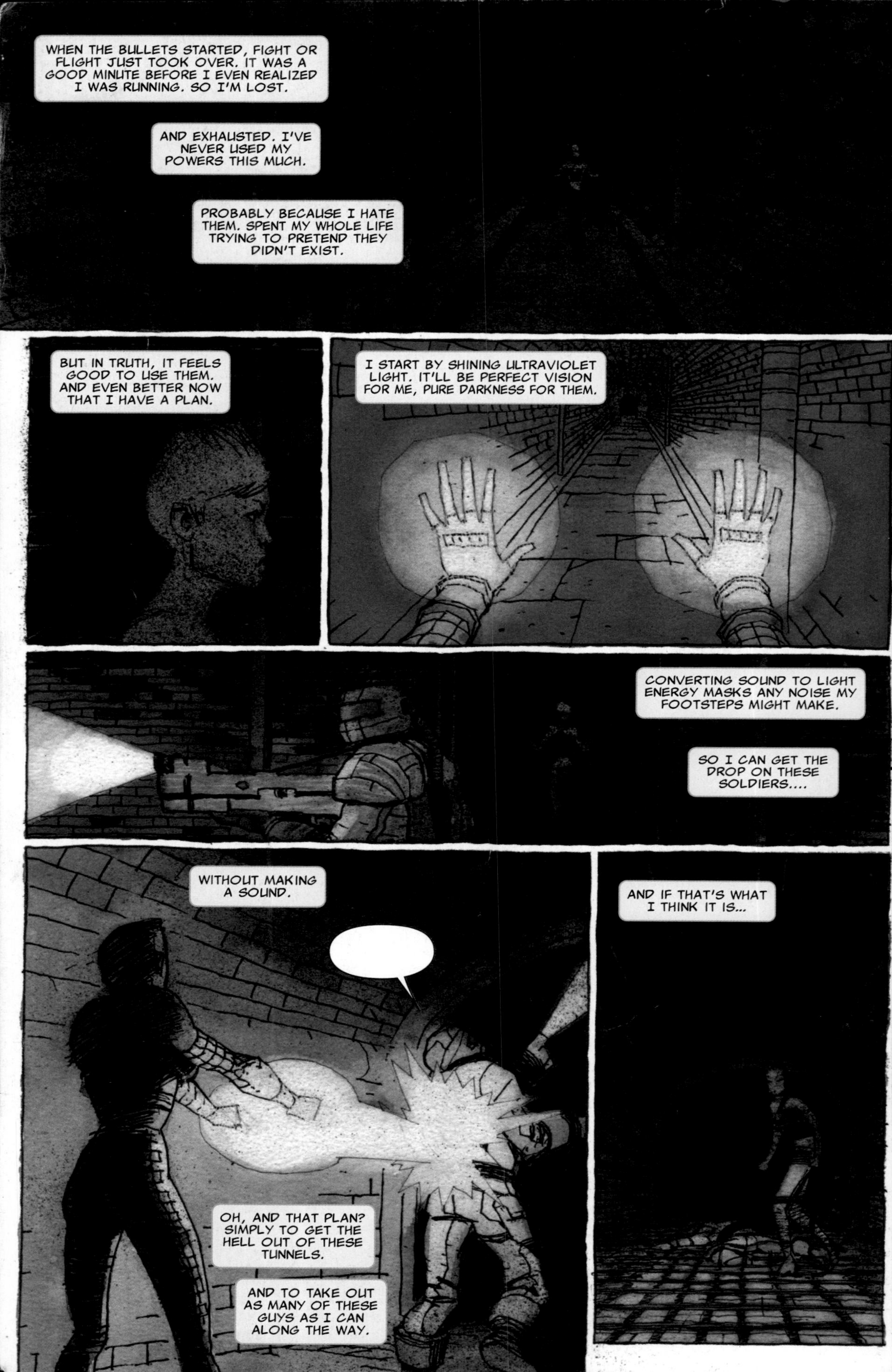

WHEN THE BULLETS STARTED, FIGHT OR FLIGHT JUST TOOK OVER. IT WAS A GOOD MINUTE BEFORE I EVEN REALIZED I WAS RUNNING. SO I'M LOST.

AND EXHAUSTED. I'VE NEVER USED MY POWERS THIS MUCH.

PROBABLY BECAUSE I HATE THEM. SPENT MY WHOLE LIFE TRYING TO PRETEND THEY DIDN'T EXIST.

BUT IN TRUTH, IT FEELS GOOD TO USE THEM. AND EVEN BETTER NOW THAT I HAVE A PLAN.

I START BY SHINING ULTRAVIOLET LIGHT. IT'LL BE PERFECT VISION FOR ME, PURE DARKNESS FOR THEM.

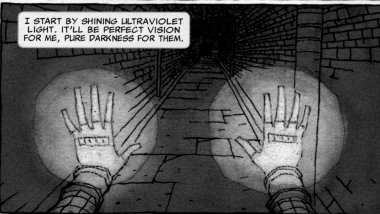

CONVERTING SOUND TO LIGHT ENERGY MASKS ANY NOISE MY FOOTSTEPS MIGHT MAKE.

SO I CAN GET THE DROP ON THESE SOLDIERS....

WITHOUT MAKING A SOUND.

AND IF THAT'S WHAT I THINK IT IS...

OH, AND THAT PLAN? SIMPLY TO GET THE HELL OUT OF THESE TUNNELS.

AND TO TAKE OUT AS MANY OF THESE GUYS AS I CAN ALONG THE WAY.

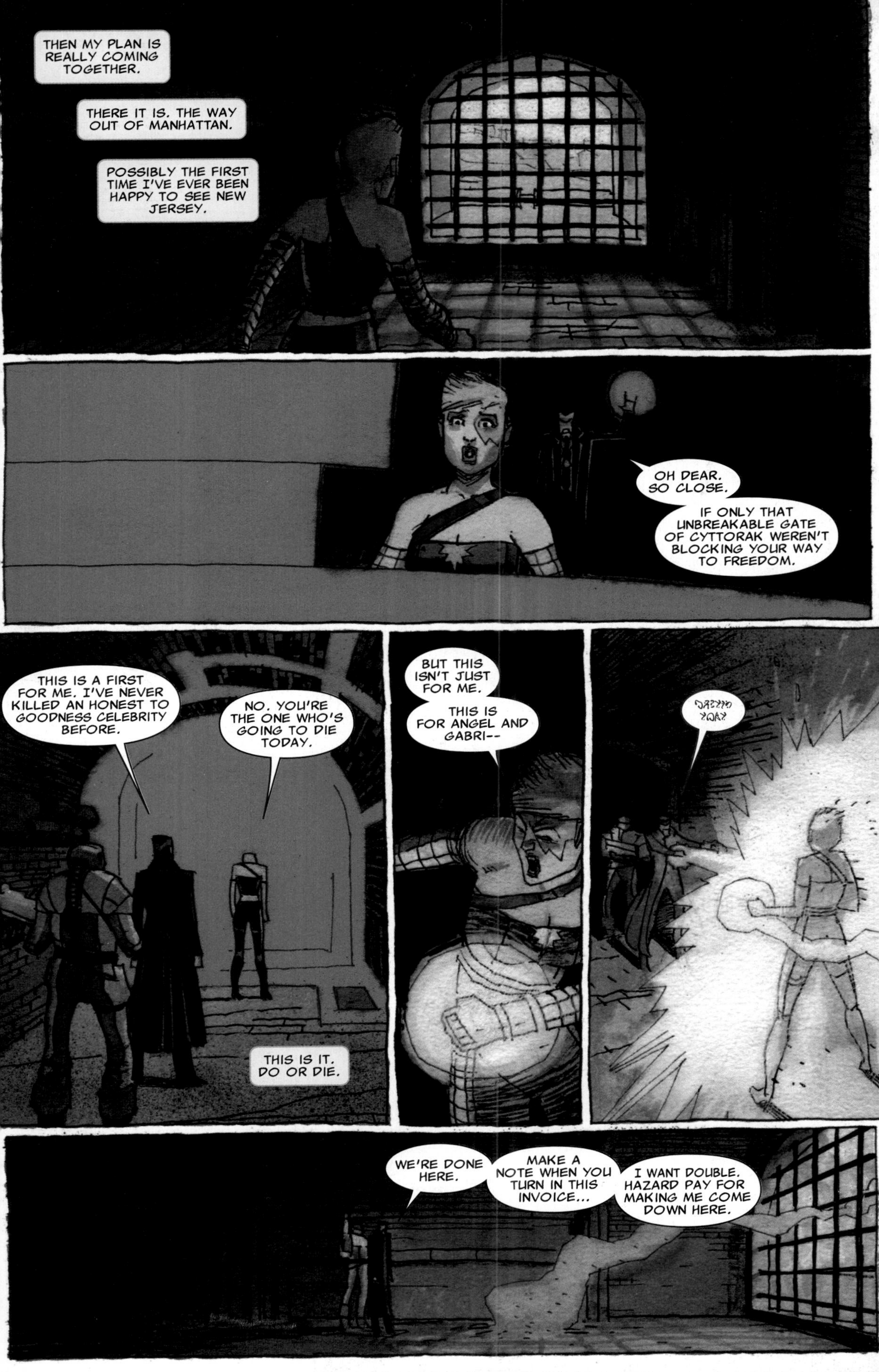
THEN MY PLAN IS REALLY COMING TOGETHER.
THERE IT IS. THE WAY OUT OF MANHATTAN.
POSSIBLY THE FIRST TIME I'VE EVER BEEN HAPPY TO SEE NEW JERSEY.
OH DEAR. SO CLOSE.
IF ONLY THAT UNBREAKABLE GATE OF CYTTORAK WEREN'T BLOCKING YOUR WAY TO FREEDOM.
THIS IS A FIRST FOR ME. I'VE NEVER KILLED AN HONEST TO GOODNESS CELEBRITY BEFORE.
NO. YOU'RE THE ONE WHO'S GOING TO DIE TODAY.
THIS IS IT. DO OR DIE.
BUT THIS ISN'T JUST FOR ME.
THIS IS FOR ANGEL AND GABRI--
WE'RE DONE HERE.
MAKE A NOTE WHEN YOU TURN IN THIS INVOICE...
I WANT DOUBLE. HAZARD PAY FOR MAKING ME COME DOWN HERE.

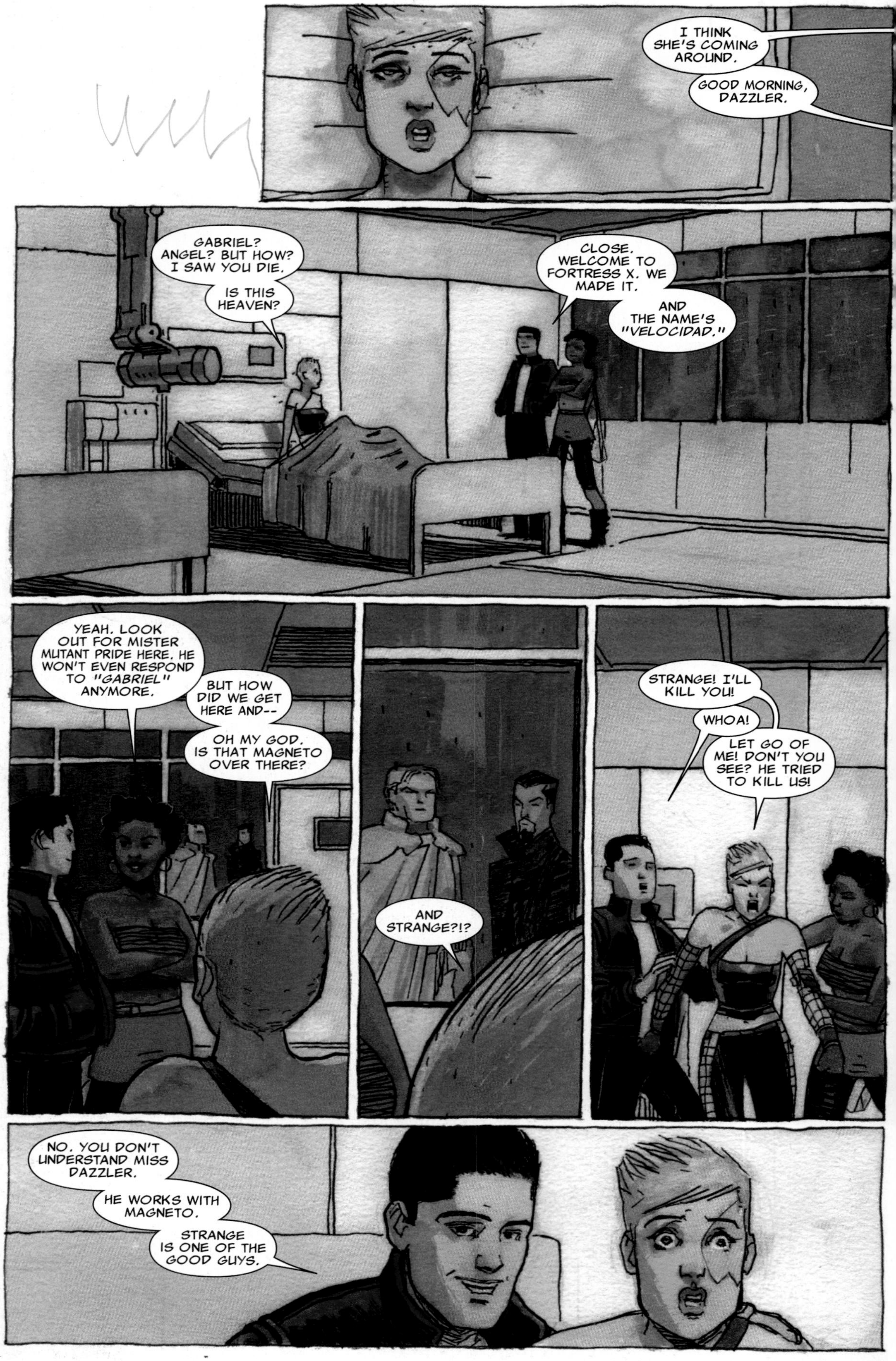
I THINK SHE'S COMING AROUND.
GOOD MORNING, DAZZLER.
GABRIEL? ANGEL? BUT HOW? I SAW YOU DIE.
IS THIS HEAVEN?
CLOSE. WELCOME TO FORTRESS X. WE MADE IT.
AND THE NAME'S "VELOCIDAD."
YEAH. LOOK OUT FOR MISTER MUTANT PRIDE HERE. HE WON'T EVEN RESPOND TO "GABRIEL" ANYMORE.
BUT HOW DID WE GET HERE AND--
OH MY GOD. IS THAT MAGNETO OVER THERE?
AND STRANGE?!?
STRANGE! I'LL KILL YOU!
WHOA!
LET GO OF ME! DON'T YOU SEE? HE TRIED TO KILL US!
NO. YOU DON'T UNDERSTAND MISS DAZZLER.
HE WORKS WITH MAGNETO.
STRANGE IS ONE OF THE GOOD GUYS.

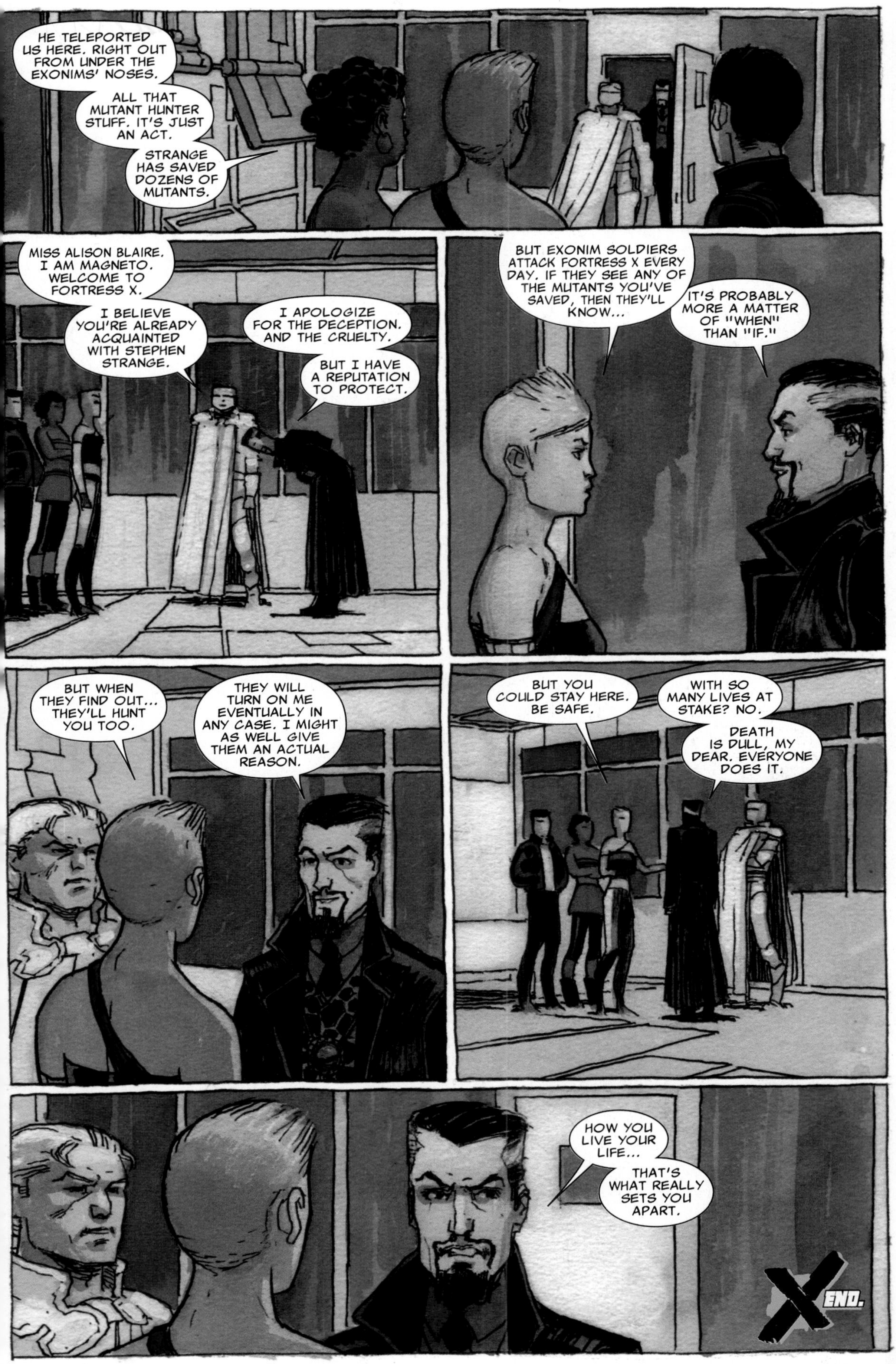
HE TELEPORTED US HERE. RIGHT OUT FROM UNDER THE EXONIMS' NOSES.
ALL THAT MUTANT HUNTER STUFF. IT'S JUST AN ACT.
STRANGE HAS SAVED DOZENS OF MUTANTS.
MISS ALISON BLAIRE. I AM MAGNETO. WELCOME TO FORTRESS X.
I BELIEVE YOU'RE ALREADY ACQUAINTED WITH STEPHEN STRANGE.
I APOLOGIZE FOR THE DECEPTION. AND THE CRUELTY.
BUT I HAVE A REPUTATION TO PROTECT.
BUT EXONIM SOLDIERS ATTACK FORTRESS X EVERY DAY. IF THEY SEE ANY OF THE MUTANTS YOU'VE SAVED, THEN THEY'LL KNOW...
IT'S PROBABLY MORE A MATTER OF "WHEN" THAN "IF."
BUT WHEN THEY FIND OUT... THEY'LL HUNT YOU TOO.
THEY WILL TURN ON ME EVENTUALLY IN ANY CASE. I MIGHT AS WELL GIVE THEM AN ACTUAL REASON.
BUT YOU COULD STAY HERE. BE SAFE.
WITH SO MANY LIVES AT STAKE? NO.
DEATH IS DULL, MY DEAR. EVERYONE DOES IT.
HOW YOU LIVE YOUR LIFE...
THAT'S WHAT REALLY SETS YOU APART.
END.

AGE OF X: ALPHA VARIANT

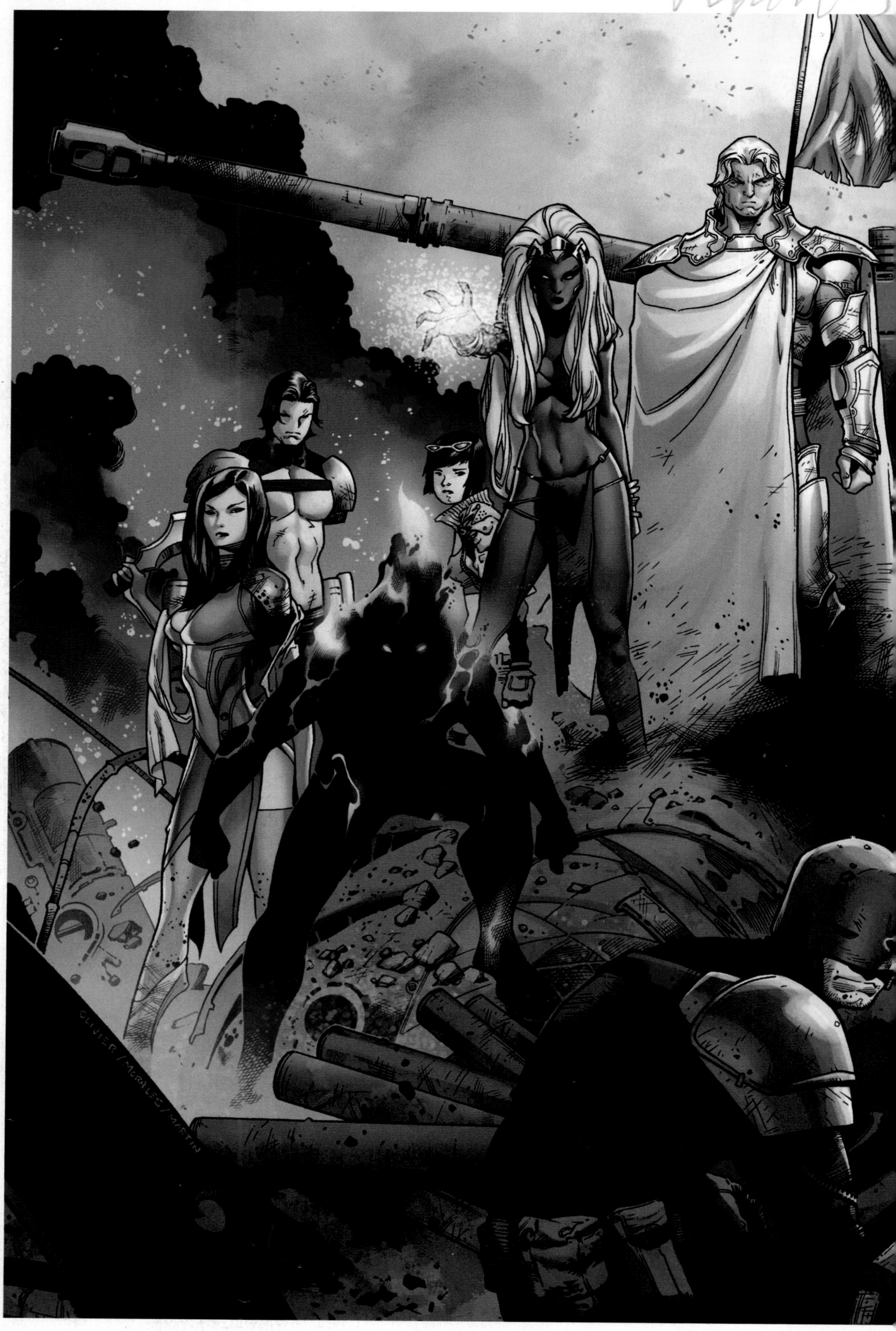

BY OLIVIER COIPEL, MARK MORALES & LAURA MARTIN

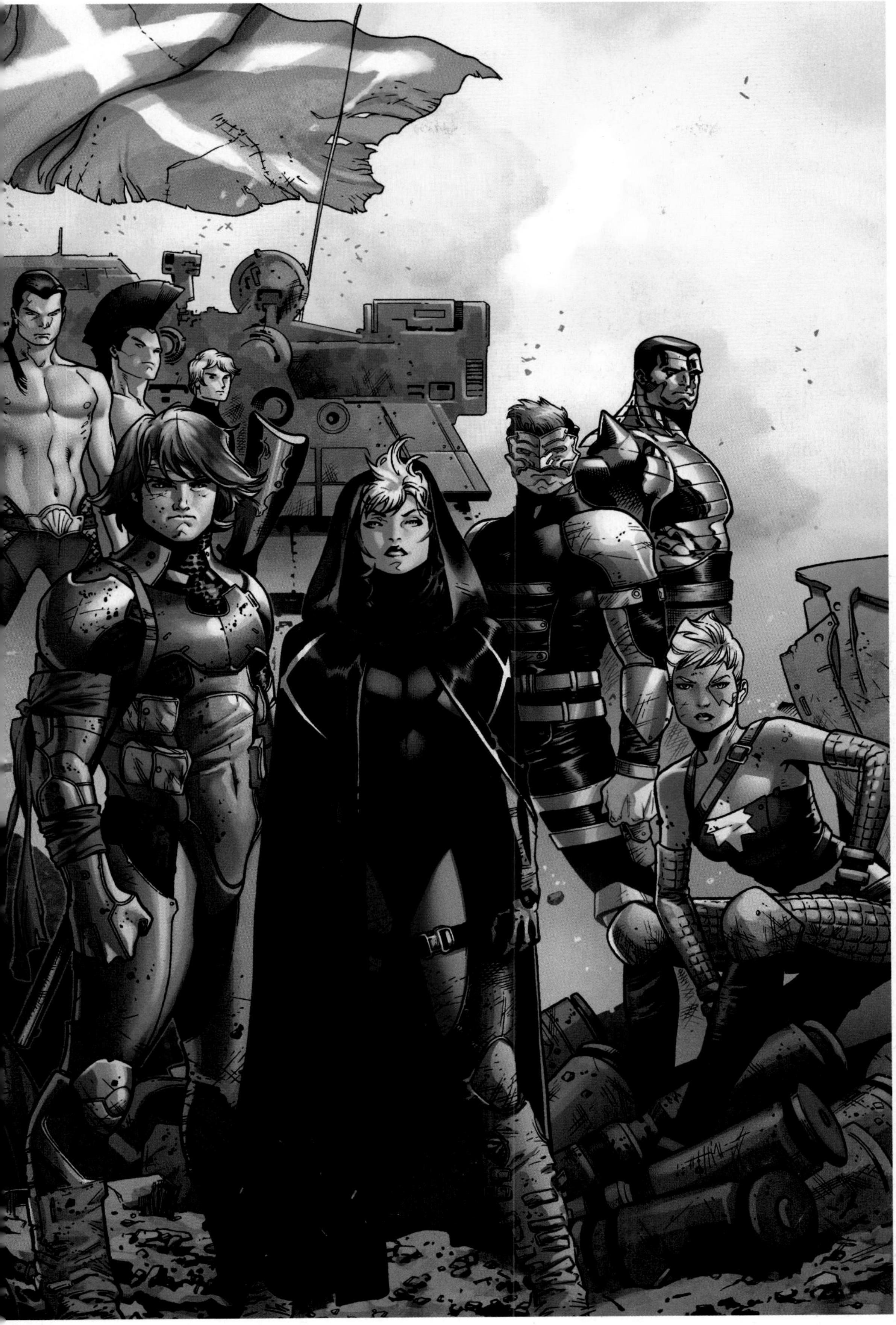

X-MEN LEGACY #245 AND NEW MUTANTS #22 VARIANTS

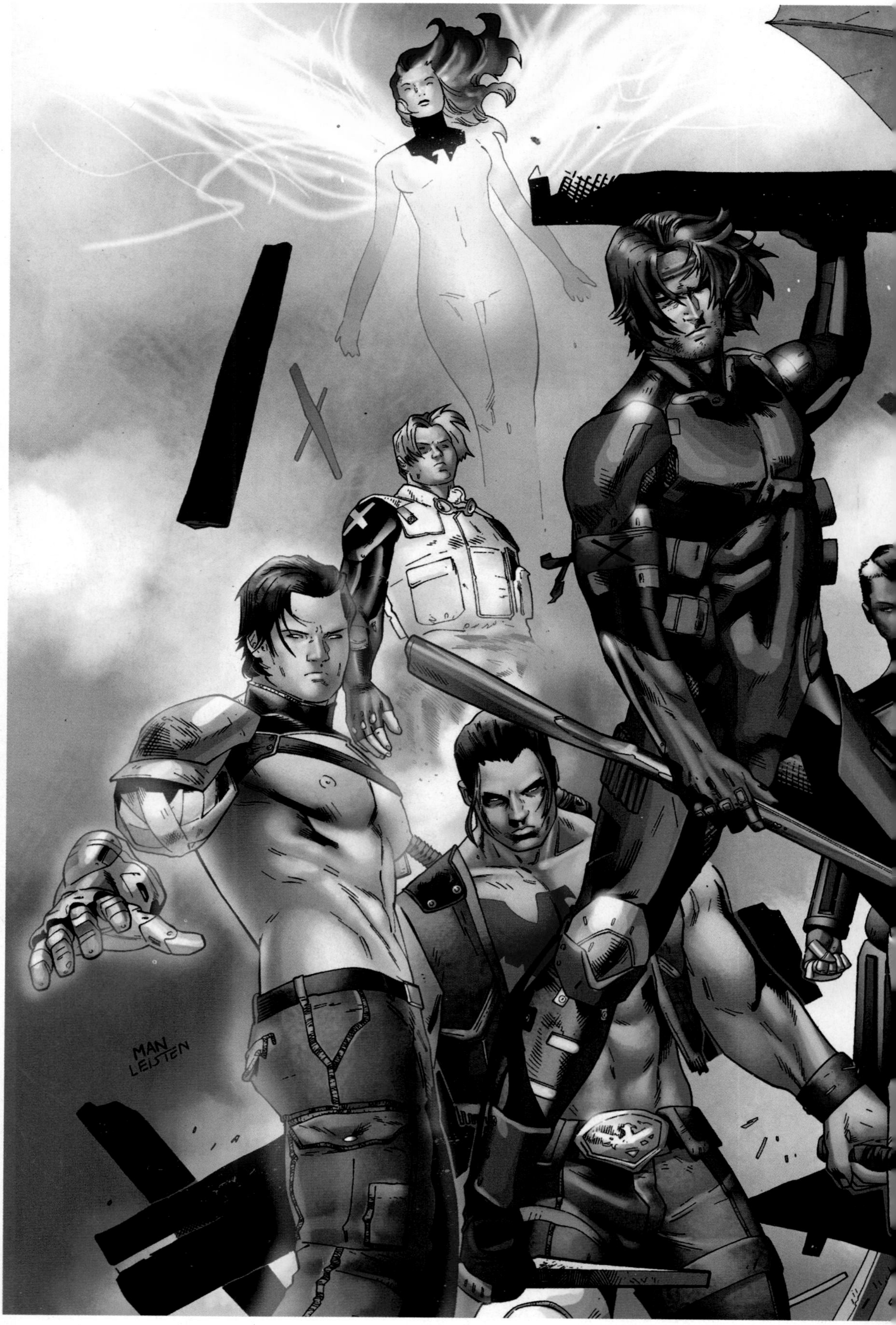

BY CLAY MANN, JAY LEISTEN & BRIAN REBER

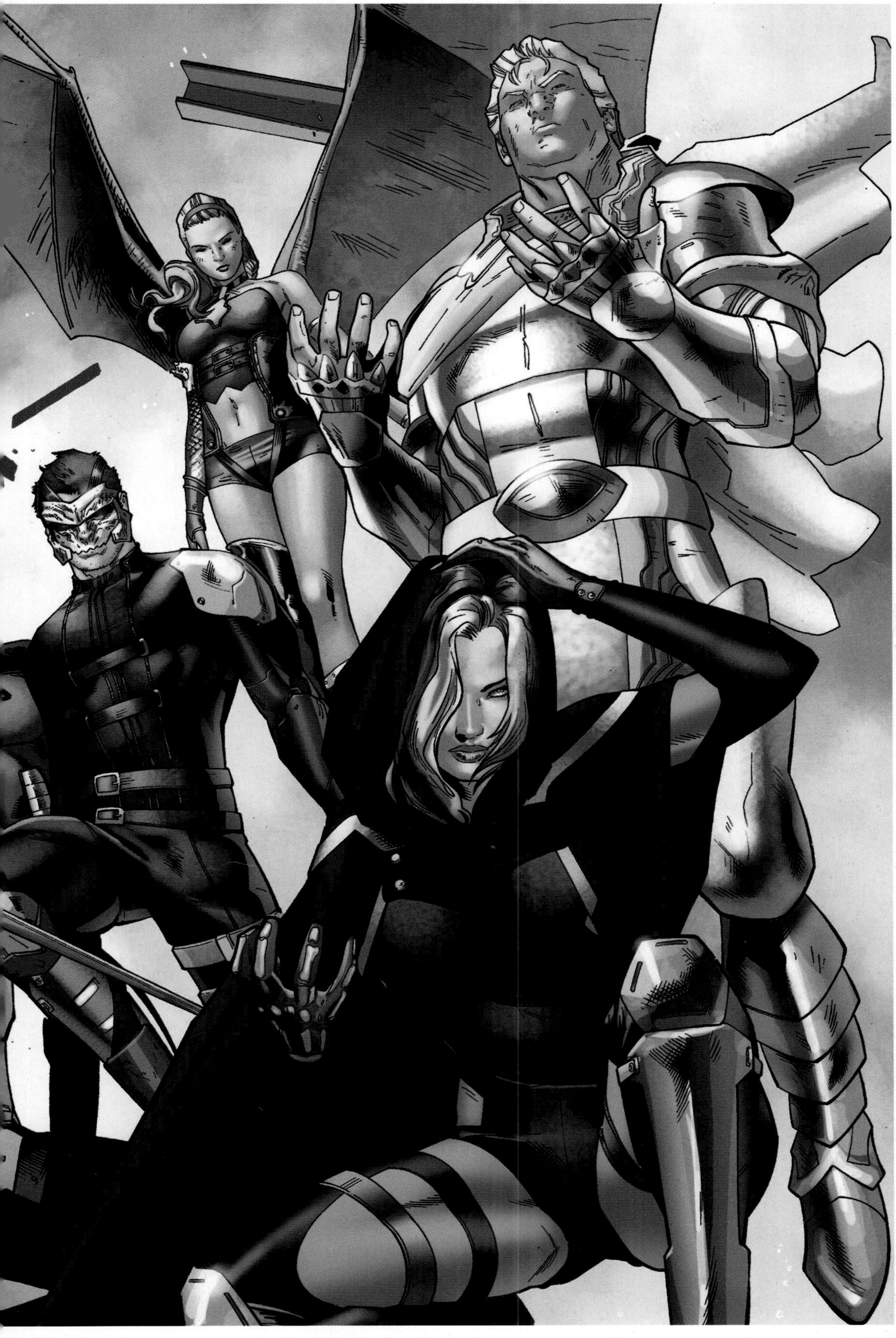

AGE OF X HISTORICAL LOGS

HISTORICAL LOG 1A: THE MARCH FOR PURITY

USER ACCESS GRANTED
SECURITY CLEARANCE: OMEGA

No Freaks!!!!

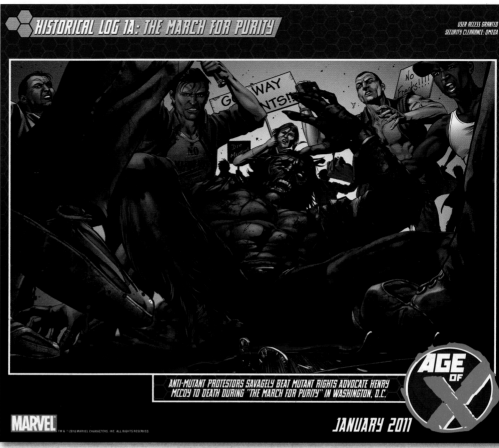

ANTI-MUTANT PROTESTORS SAVAGELY BEAT MUTANT RIGHTS ADVOCATE HENRY MCCOY TO DEATH DURING "THE MARCH FOR PURITY" IN WASHINGTON, D.C.

AGE OF X

MARVEL

JANUARY 2011

HISTORICAL LOG 2B: THE PHOENIX DESTROYS ALBANY

USER ACCESS GRANTED
SECURITY CLEARANCE: OMEGA

THE MUTANT ABILITIES OF A YOUNG WOMAN NAMED JEAN GREY MANIFEST IN THE FORM OF AN EXPLOSIVE, FIERY PHOENIX THAT IMMOLATES EVERYTHING IN ITS PATH. THE CITY OF ALBANY, NEW YORK IS DECIMATED, LEAVING 600,000 DEAD.

AGE OF X

MARVEL

JANUARY 2011

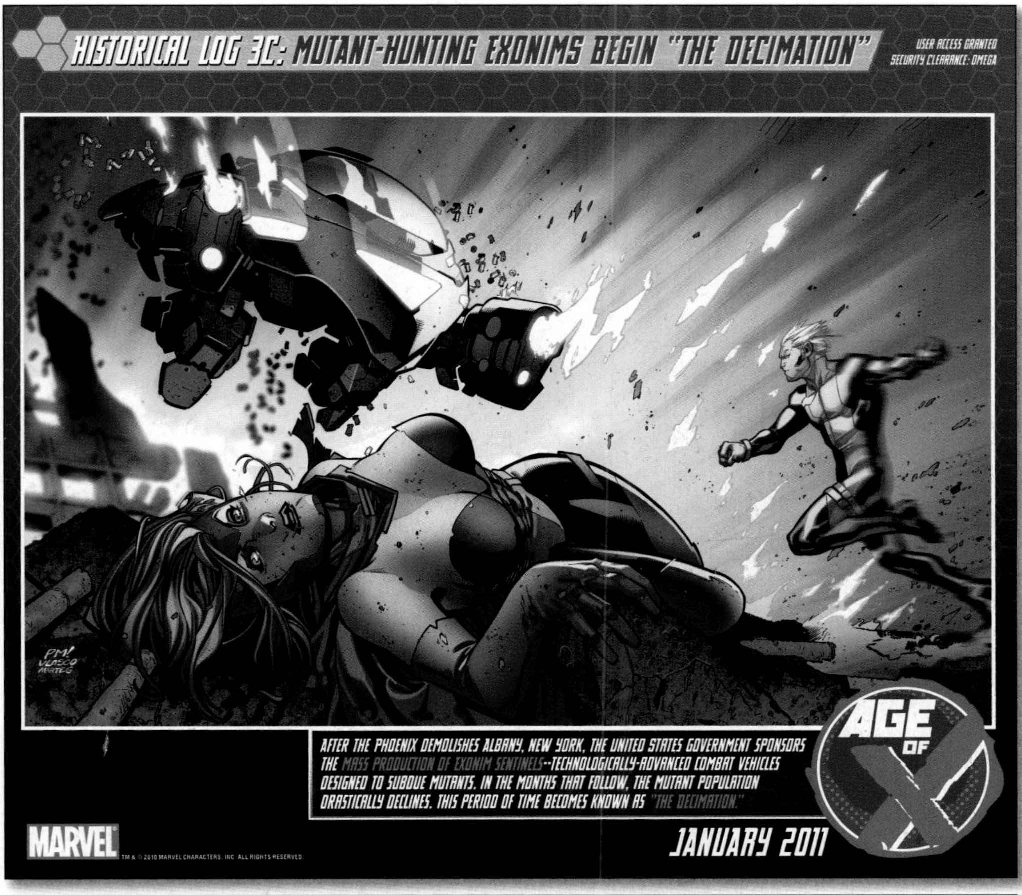
HISTORICAL LOG 3C: MUTANT-HUNTING EXONIMS BEGIN "THE DECIMATION"
USER ACCESS GRANTED
SECURITY CLEARANCE: OMEGA
AFTER THE PHOENIX DEMOLISHES ALBANY, NEW YORK, THE UNITED STATES GOVERNMENT SPONSORS THE MASS PRODUCTION OF EXONIM SENTINELS--TECHNOLOGICALLY-ADVANCED COMBAT VEHICLES DESIGNED TO SUBDUE MUTANTS. IN THE MONTHS THAT FOLLOW, THE MUTANT POPULATION DRASTICALLY DECLINES. THIS PERIOD OF TIME BECOMES KNOWN AS "THE DECIMATION."
AGE OF X
MARVEL
TM & © 2010 MARVEL CHARACTERS, INC. ALL RIGHTS RESERVED.
JANUARY 2011

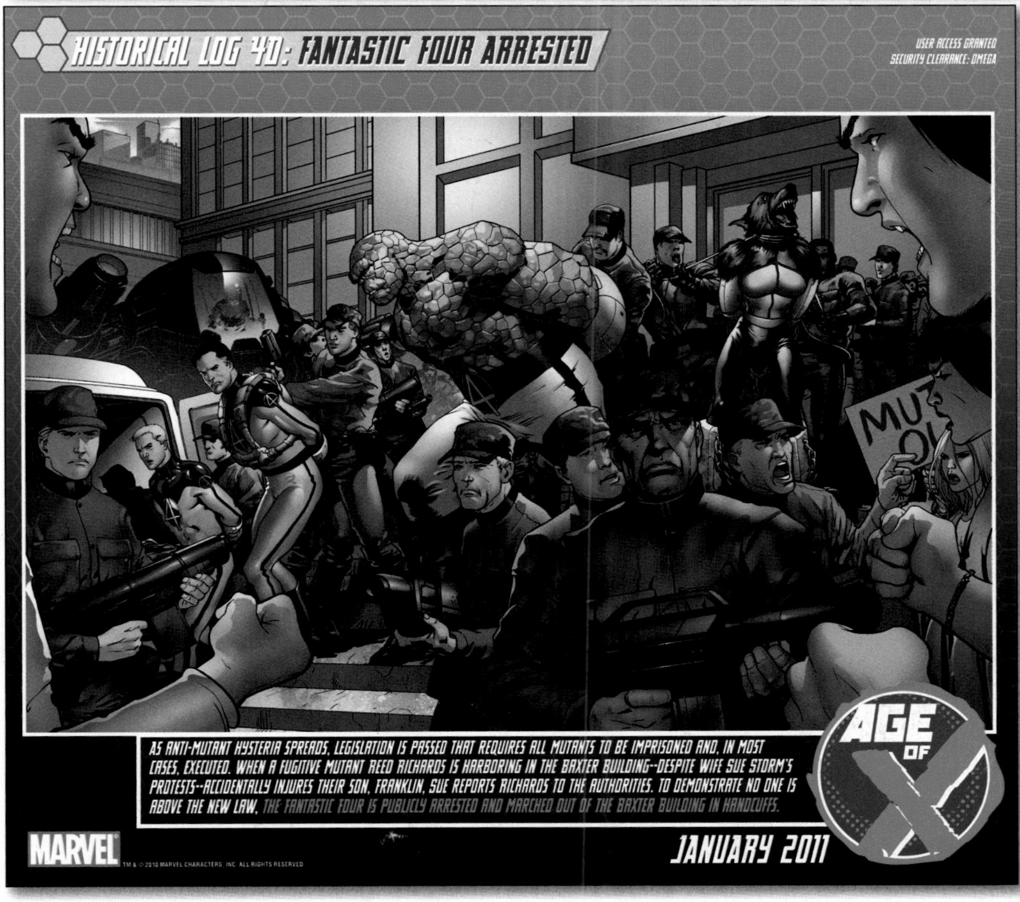
HISTORICAL LOG 4D: FANTASTIC FOUR ARRESTED
USER ACCESS GRANTED
SECURITY CLEARANCE: OMEGA
MUT
AS ANTI-MUTANT HYSTERIA SPREADS, LEGISLATION IS PASSED THAT REQUIRES ALL MUTANTS TO BE IMPRISONED AND, IN MOST CASES, EXECUTED. WHEN A FUGITIVE MUTANT REED RICHARDS IS HARBORING IN THE BAXTER BUILDING--DESPITE WIFE SUE STORM'S PROTESTS--ACCIDENTALLY INJURES THEIR SON, FRANKLIN, SUE REPORTS RICHARDS TO THE AUTHORITIES. TO DEMONSTRATE NO ONE IS ABOVE THE NEW LAW, THE FANTASTIC FOUR IS PUBLICLY ARRESTED AND MARCHED OUT OF THE BAXTER BUILDING IN HANDCUFFS.
AGE OF X
MARVEL
TM & © 2010 MARVEL CHARACTERS, INC. ALL RIGHTS RESERVED.
JANUARY 2011

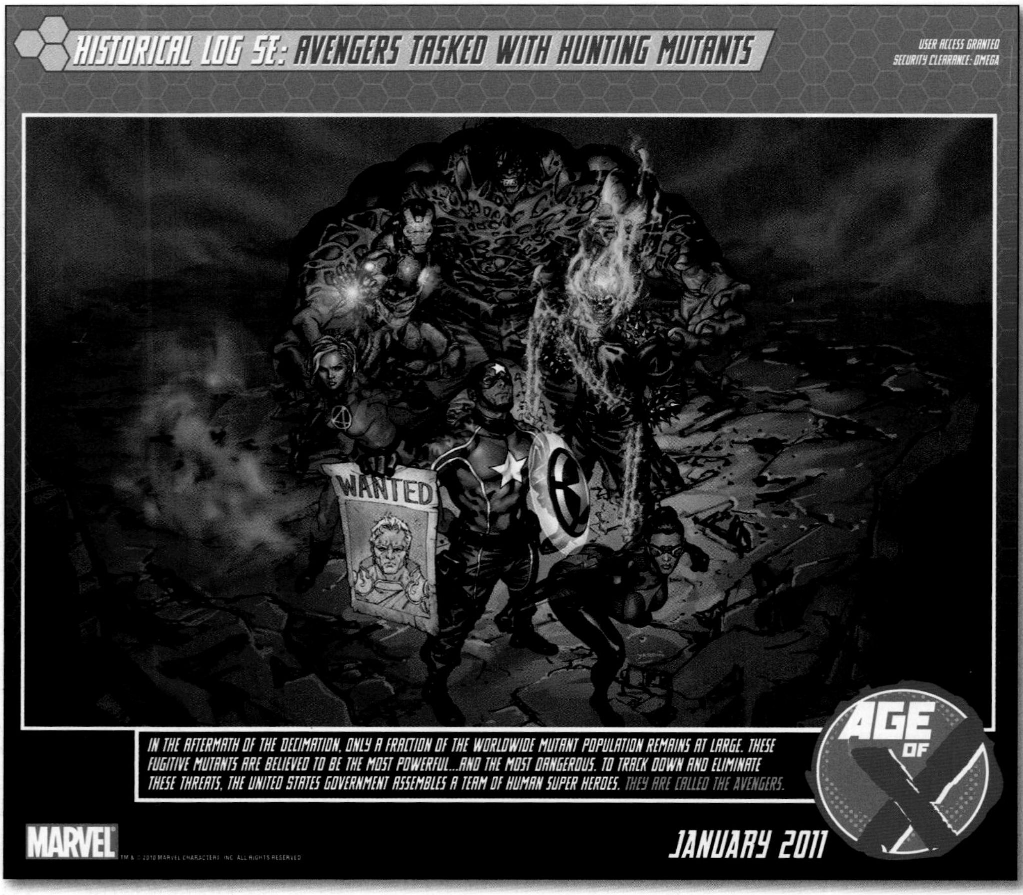
HISTORICAL LOG 5E: AVENGERS TASKED WITH HUNTING MUTANTS
USER ACCESS GRANTED
SECURITY CLEARANCE: OMEGA
WANTED
IN THE AFTERMATH OF THE DECIMATION, ONLY A FRACTION OF THE WORLDWIDE MUTANT POPULATION REMAINS AT LARGE. THESE FUGITIVE MUTANTS ARE BELIEVED TO BE THE MOST POWERFUL...AND THE MOST DANGEROUS. TO TRACK DOWN AND ELIMINATE THESE THREATS, THE UNITED STATES GOVERNMENT ASSEMBLES A TEAM OF HUMAN SUPER HEROES. THEY ARE CALLED THE AVENGERS.
AGE OF X
MARVEL
TM & © 2010 MARVEL CHARACTERS, INC. ALL RIGHTS RESERVED
JANUARY 2011

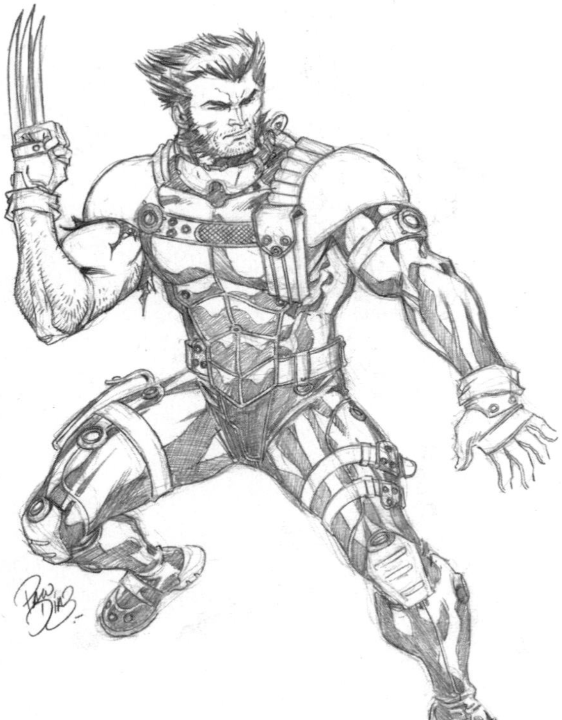
PACO DIAZ

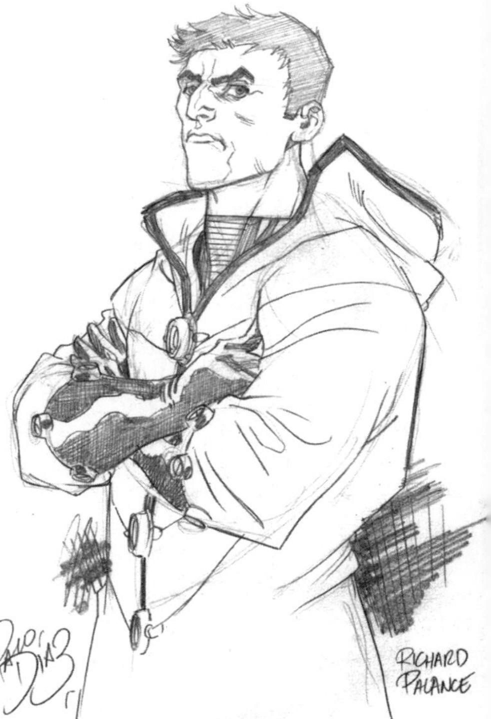
PACO DIAZ
RICHARD PALANCE

BY PACO DIAZ

AGE OF X SKETCHES

BY CARLO BARBERI

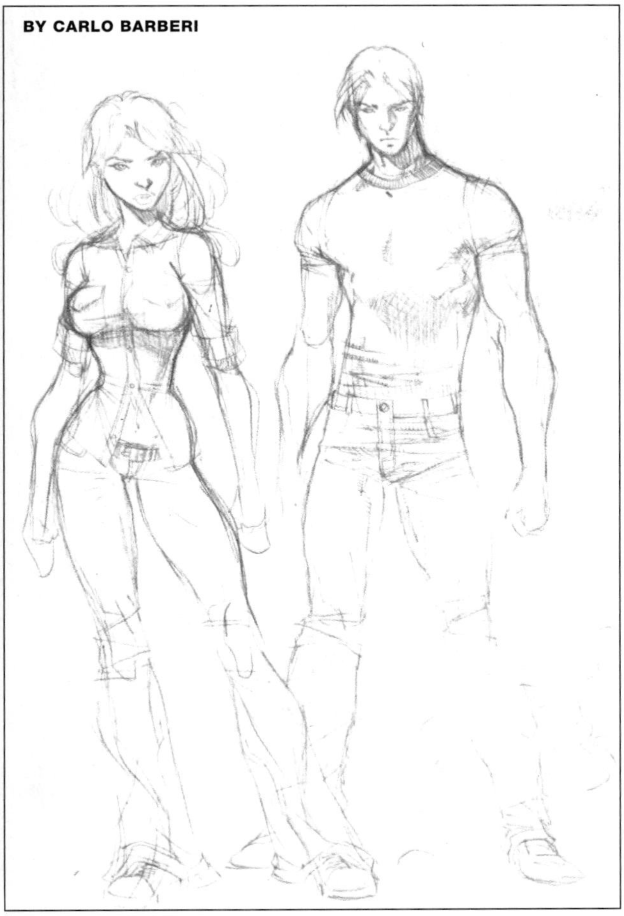

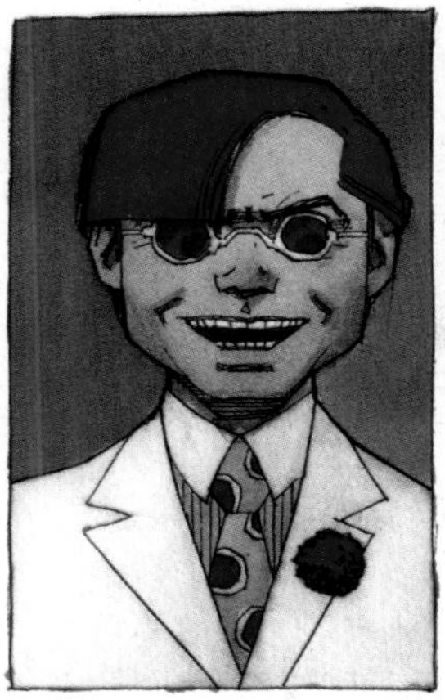

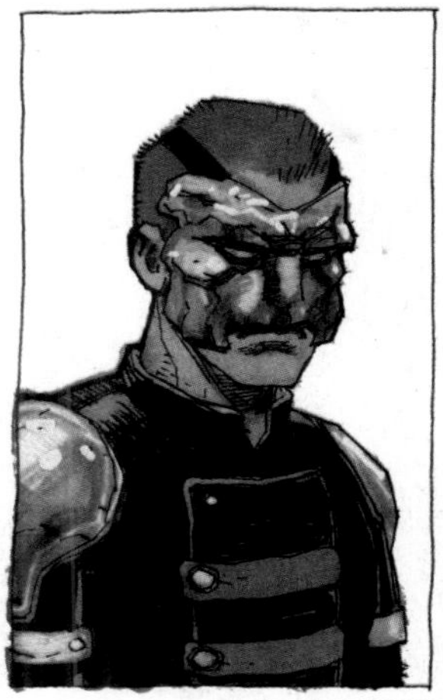

BY GABRIEL HERNANDEZ WALTA

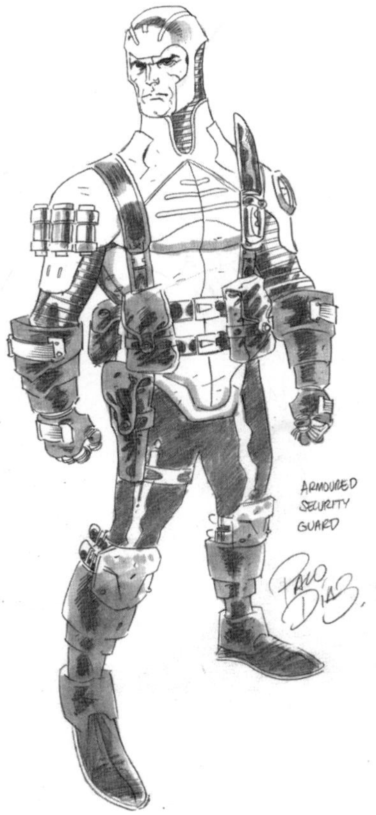
ARMOURED
SECURITY
GUARD

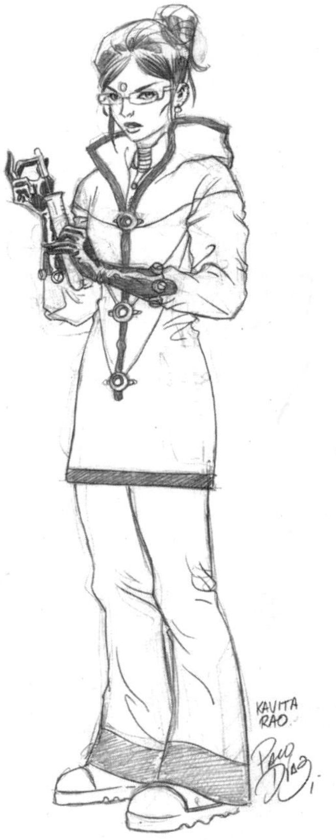
KAVITA
RAO

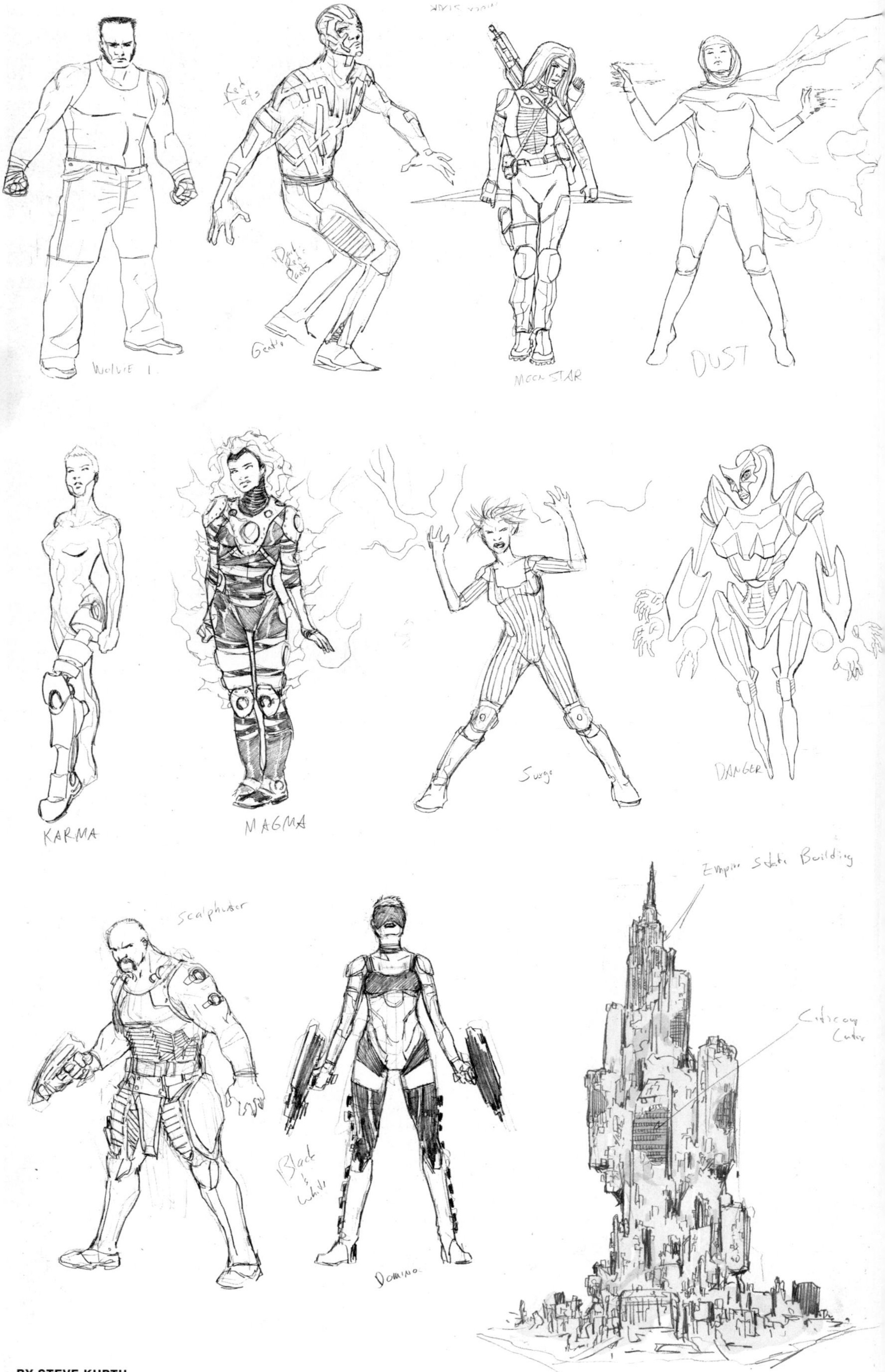
Wolvie 1
Red Tats
Dark Red Pants
Genetic
MOON STAR
DUST
KARMA
MAGMA
Surge
DANGER
Scalphunter
Black & White
Domino
Empire State Building

BY STEVE KURTH

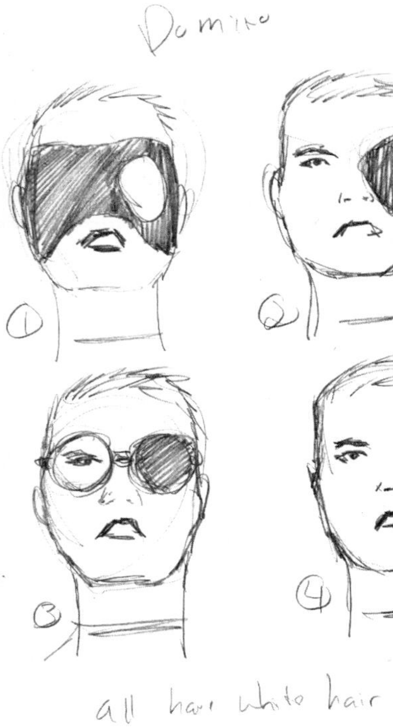
Domino
1
2
3
4
all have white hair

BY MIRCO PIERFEDERICI

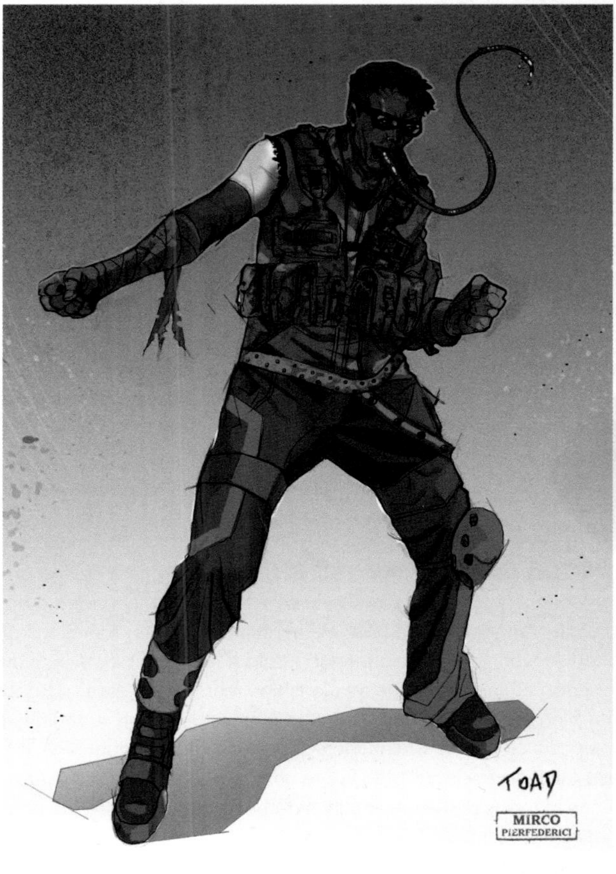
TOAD
MIRCO PIERFEDERICI

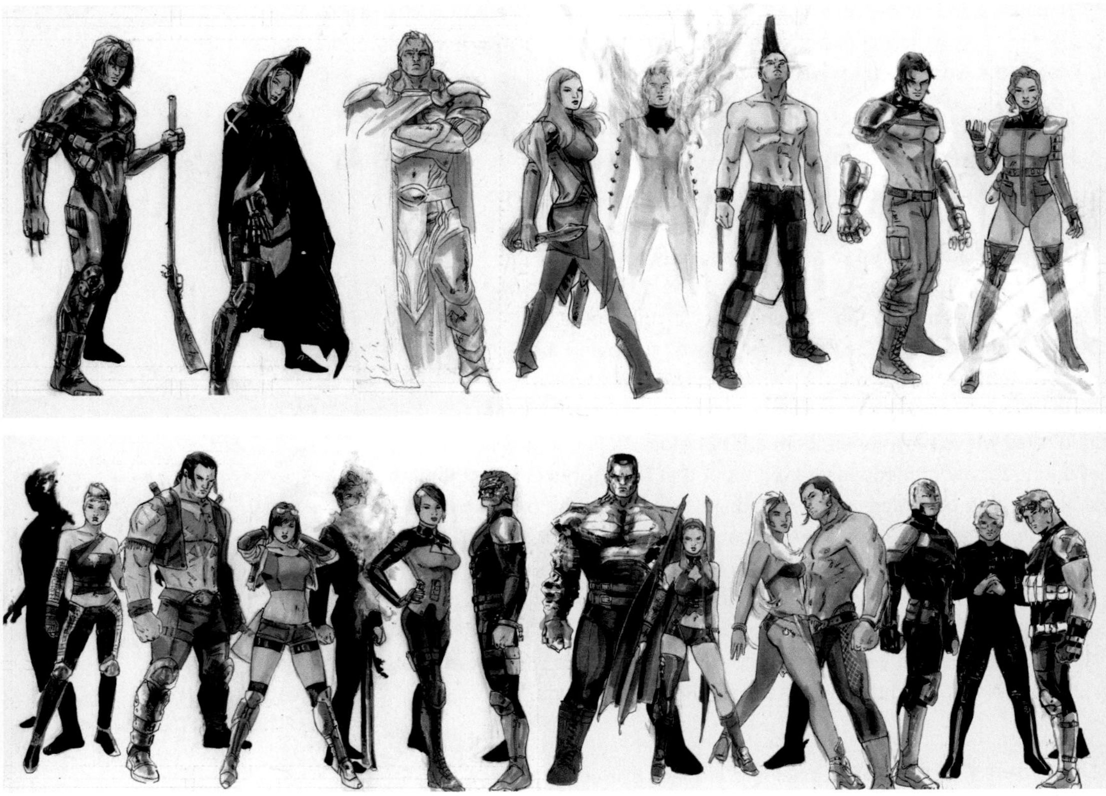

BY CLAY MANN

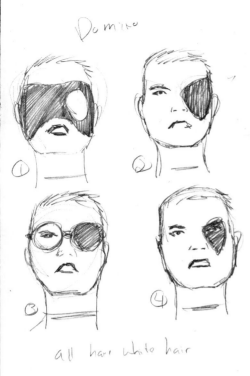

LETTERS FROM THE
CREATIVE TEAM

OUR GOAL WITH THE six monthly chapters of Age of X — beginning with *X-Men: Legacy #245* — has been to throw the reader right in at the deep end: to present an incredible and inexplicable situation without really explaining it, and then to make the unravelling of that explanation proceed alongside the events of the series. No exposition up front: you just have to roll with it while the extraordinary events that created the Age of X are gradually unveiled.

But as some of our core characters took shape in our minds, we came to feel that their individual backstories — not thei origins, so much, but the stories of how they came to be in Fortress X and what each of them is fighting for — were interesting and compelling enough that they added up to a kind of prelude to the event as a whole. That was the thinking behind this Alpha issue: that it should be, in a way, what an overture is to a musical or a symphony. It hits some of our key themes, and it sets the tone for what's to follow. But believe us, you ain't seen nothing yet.

Next: the death of a mutant, the grim task of the Reaper, and a camera that never lies...

— MIKE CAREY

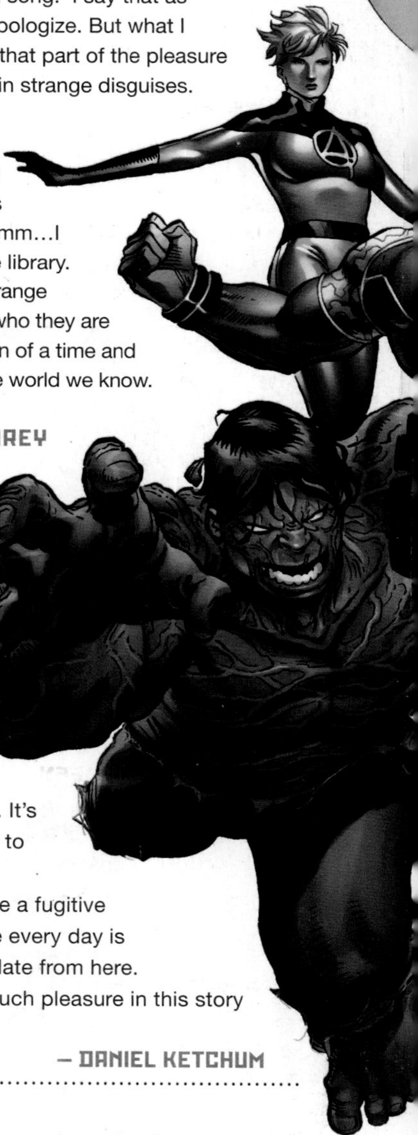

WRITING A STORY LIKE THIS is a bit like playing a jazz riff on an existing song. I say that as someone who's not that into jazz, so if the comparison feels a bit forced, I apologize. But what I mean is that you take familiar elements and you play variations on them, so that part of the pleasure is rediscovering those old friends — old notes, old melodies, old themes — in strange disguises.

I don't think any of the relationships that we see here — Scott Summers and Frenzy, Psylocke and Iceman, Storm and Namor — are inherently implausible. In fact, I think there's a clear logical through-line in each case. I also think that what all of the core characters become in the Age of X makes sense in terms of their essential natures. But if you disagree, come at me. Umm...I mean on a message board or at a Con, obviously, not with a lead pipe in the library.

So yeah, that was one of the themes in this opening issue: old friends in strange disguises. I hope you enjoy measuring the distances and the angles between who they are and who they were. I know you'll enjoy Clay's spectacular whole-cloth invention of a time and a place that — for all its weirdness — is just one turn of the road away from the world we know.

That is, the world we think we know.

— MIKE CAREY

AS A STORYTELLER, I'VE ALWAYS believed in the principle that if you go out telling a story that you would want to read, an audience will follow.

When Mike Carey came to me with the ideas that would eventually come to be Age of X, I knew he was on to something special. Here was a story that featured the full complement of X-Men, their backs to the wall, the only way out being their fantastic mutant abilities and their unfailing determination to persevere. It's our favorite X-Men characters in new relationships, and in roles we've never seen them adopt before, acting in ways that might appear immediately foreign, but that have roots in the essential. It's exactly the kind of X-Men story I would like to read. So I'm only too happy to have it told in the pages of *X-Men: Legacy* and *New Mutants*.

This month, you've seen Rogue — in the guise of the Reaper — become a fugitive in an effort to uncover the dark secret hidden at the heart of a world where every day is mutantkind's last stand. We're off to a running start...and things only escalate from here.

I can only hope that you are a member of our audience who takes as much pleasure in this story as we do. Enjoy it. As much as it is for us, this one's for you.

— DANIEL KETCHUM

IN A SIX-PART STORY ARC, pacing is a quadruple-edged sword.

Firstly, you have to worry about the dramatic impact and impetus of your opening episode. We had a lot of pieces, and we had to put them all into play in the first chapter so that the stuff they were given to do later

PASSOVER

MADE Easy

PHOTOGRAPHY DANIEL LAILAH

FOOD STYLIST AMIT FARBER

PUBLISHER MESORAH PUBLICATIONS, LTD.

DESIGN RACHELADLERDESIGN.COM

Leah Schapira & Victoria Dwek

First Edition — First Impression / Febuary 2013

Published by **ARTSCROLL / SHAAR PRESS**
4401 Second Avenue / Brooklyn, NY 11232 / (718) 921-9000
www.artscroll.com

Distributed in Israel by **SIFRIATI / A. GITLER**
6 Hayarkon Street / Bnei Brak 51127 / Israel

Distributed in Europe by **LEHMANNS**
Unit E, Viking Business Park, Rolling Mill Road
Jarrow, Tyne and Wear, NE32 3DP / England

Distributed in Australia and New Zealand by **GOLDS WORLD OF JUDAICA**
3-13 William Street / Balaclava, Melbourne 3183, Victoria / Australia

Distributed in South Africa by **KOLLEL BOOKSHOP**
Northfield Centre / 17 Northfield Avenue / Glenhazel 2192 / Johannesburg, South Africa

ISBN-10: 1-4226-1353-4 / ISBN-13: 978-1-4226-1353-5

Printed in Canada by Noble Book Press

Acknowledgments

We always say that our ideas aren't ours. We can be totally stumped, but then **Hashem** inserts something brilliant into our heads out of nowhere. We owe Him credit for every little teaspoon in this book.

Thank you to our chief taste testers, our **husbands** and **children**, our encouraging **parents**, and the rest of our **families**. You helped cook, taste, babysit, and give valuable feedback. We wish we could promise you there'll be an ice cream book in the future!

Rachel Adler, our graphic artist, reads our minds. No one else could have produced our pages with so much personality. We think the design of this book is unparalleled. Thanks also to the man behind the scenes, **Zalman Roth**.

The **ArtScroll** team's dedication and enthusiasm are invigorating. Thanks to the leader, **Gedaliah Zlotowitz**, and to editor **Felice Eisner**, who finds editing recipes as exciting as eating them. Thanks to **Gavriel Sanders**, to **Goldy Helfgott**, who named our book, and to the rest of the staff who kept things moving so it would come out as scheduled. They made sure Passover arrives on time!

To our talented team, **Daniel Lailah** and **Amit Farber**, our photographer and stylist. You brought our vision to life in such a beautiful and delicious way.

Over the years, many of my recipes have been inspired by my friends and family. Every food idea I hear provides fertile ground for new recipes to grow.

The role our communities play in inspiring our cooking motivated me to co-found the recipe-sharing website, CookKosher.com. Through CookKosher, I have been introduced to many more amazing home cooks. In creating parts of this cookbook, Victoria and I were stimulated by many CookKosher members. You will find their member names on the pages where they've either shared or inspired a recipe. In appreciation, they'll each be receiving a copy of this cookbook.

We hope you enjoy these delicious tried-and-true recipes, and that they inspire you to have fun creating delicious meals for your families. And we hope we've made it easy, too.

Leah

Introduction

VICTORIA: You thought you were smart to buy extra potato starch and ground nuts last Passover to develop recipes throughout the year. But it wasn't nearly enough.

LEAH: We're an unlikely pair to write a Passover cookbook.

VICTORIA: For sure. I like vegetables and dessert. And you like pizza and pastrami (but not together).

LEAH: True. I soon ran out and ended up collecting potato starch from all the neighbors. They agreed on one condition: I let them taste the food.

VICTORIA: I found three full containers in my mother-in-law's pantry. But then I hit the real jackpot: she went down to her basement freezer and came up carrying a shopping bag full of ground nuts.

LEAH: No, not because of that. We come from different backgrounds and have very different Passover customs.

VICTORIA: But that wasn't the biggest challenge.

LEAH: You're right. The biggest challenge was tracking down potato starch in August.

LEAH: Do you think it's time to tell our families that they've been eating Passover food for the past six months?

VICTORIA: They might've been onto something when I served Matzaroni and Cheese for dinner.

LEAH: Or when I made egg noodles from scratch for the lo mein.

VICTORIA: I actually think my husband caught on when I served six different types of fish at one meal and asked him to rate them. For every recipe that made it into this book, there were three that didn't.

LEAH: That's what's great about a cookbook with 60 recipes. For a recipe to earn a spot, we really had to love it. And it had to be easy enough, too. There are lots of recipes we liked that didn't make it. Remember the chicken with the root vegetable coating? It was good, but man, was it ugly!

VICTORIA: My freezer is full of runner-ups. If a dish made it into the freezer, it didn't make it into the book.

LEAH: That's because the winning recipes were all eaten up.

VICTORIA: Back to our differences. I come from a Syrian-Jewish background, so we eat plenty of rice on Passover. We also have peas and green beans, which many consider kitniot and don't eat. And, of course, we enjoy *gebrokts*. It isn't Passover without matzah pancakes every morning (though this year, it'll be Banana French Toast, page 94).

LEAH: Eating rice on Passover would be amazing! My grandparents came from Hungry ... I mean Hungary. Over there, in der heim, Passover meant potatoes, potatoes, and potatoes. So now, in America, it's potatoes, potatoes, and potato starch. And since I don't brok, no matzah pizza for me.

VICTORIA: So you're left with potatoes ... and pastrami? But seriously, after all these months, I think we could say we've gathered a whole bunch of fabulous and diverse ideas that would be savored in any Jewish household.

LEAH: And I think we can agree on one more thing.

VICTORIA: That we love lemon desserts?

LEAH: That too. This Passover, we're both making all THESE recipes.

VICTORIA: No question. And this Passover will be more delicious and easy than it's ever been.

In the Glass and On Your Plate

A Food & Wine Pairing Guide

VICTORIA: **Whenever Shabbat begins and I** realize that I've forgotten the wine, I always feel a little sad. It's not just the wine itself that we enjoy. Sipping a glass of wine while enjoying a Shabbat or Yom Tov meal just makes everything taste better. As a host, I know that my guests really get excited when I bring one of their favorite bottles to the table.

What do we love? When we're serving meat for a holiday meal, it's usually a Cabernet Sauvignon or Merlot that we're pouring. But we're never limited to those. We also love a spicy Shiraz/Syrah, or a California Zinfandel.

Big Reds
Enjoy them with rich proteins such as braised ribs, hearty beef dishes, and anything you've thrown on the BBQ. Bitter veggies like eggplant or arugula, or a meaty fish, like grilled tuna steak, will also work with these reds. Chocolate doesn't pair well with the dry reds, but rather one that has some sweetness, like the Jeunesse Cabernet.

Lighter Reds
Enjoy them with poultry such as chicken, turkey, and duck. Lamb and veal are also great with a light red. Post-Passover, pasta in a creamy pink sauce or pesto, wild rice, quinoa, and veggies like spinach and kale will go well with a light red. A light red's versatility allows it to still pair well with filet mignon, short ribs, and roast beef. You can also pair it with tuna, salmon, and gourmet cheeses.

Whites
Enjoy them with fresh crisp salads, soups, grilled vegetables, and fish dishes. Whites will complement rich buttery dishes and those that use lots of fresh herbs or are salty, spicy, or hot.

Whites with some sweetness, such as Moscato, are nice when enjoyed with fruity desserts.

Big Reds

Cabernet Sauvignon is the most robust of the medium-to-full-bodied wines. Other varietals include Merlot, Zinfandel, Syrah/Shiraz, and Malbec.

Our picks Carmel Kayoumi Cabernet Sauvignon, Weinstock Cellar Select Zinfandel, Flam Reserve Syrah, Herzog Reserve Alexander Valley Cabernet Sauvignon, and Psagot Merlot.

Lighter Reds

Pinot Noir is a light-bodied red. Some blends and many Italian wines, such as Chianti, are also light.

Our picks Domaine Netofa Red, Barkan Classic Pinot Noir, Ovadia Estates Chianti, and Weinstock Red by W.

Whites

This category includes Sauvignon Blanc, Rieslings, and Chardonnay.

Our picks Baron Herzog Chenin Blanc, Carmel Kayoumi Riesling, Goose Bay Sauvignon Blanc, Herzog Reserve Russian River Chardonnay, and of course the blue bottle, Bartenura Moscato.

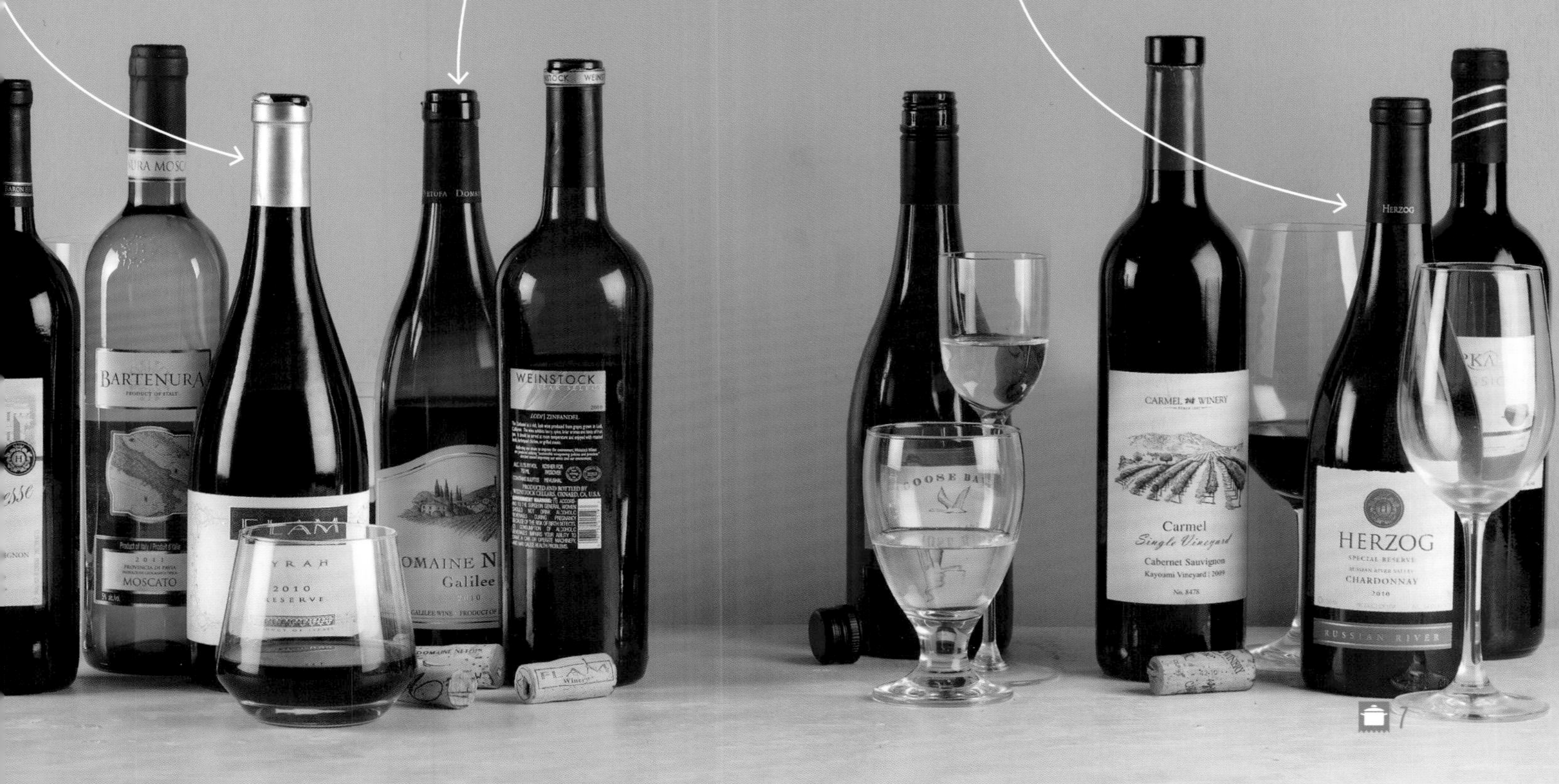

BARTENURA
MOSCATO
FLAM
SYRAH
2010
RESERVE
WEINSTOCK
Galilee
CARMEL WINERY
Carmel
Single Vineyard
Cabernet Sauvignon
HERZOG
SPECIAL RESERVE
CHARDONNAY
2010
RUSSIAN RIVER

Seder Night *The Four Cups and Charoset*

Is now the time to break out "the good stuff" I've been saving?

That's what we're doing. It's definitely appropriate to honor the night by enjoying one of your favorite wines — but not necessarily for the four cups, which are downed quickly. I know it's hard to wait to open up that Castel or Chalk Hill and we can't say that we're patient either — but save the best for the meal, when you can sip slowly and savor it with food.

The bright side of being patient is that the wine will have time to "open up" if you decant your prized bottle before the Seder begins (if you don't have a decanter, you can let the wine breathe in a glass pitcher. Simply uncorking doesn't really expose the wine to the oxygen it needs). This "breathing" time can be anywhere from 30 minutes to 3 to 4 hours.

How much wine should I purchase?

The minimum required amount to drink is 3.5 oz for each of the four cups. Since the glasses need to be filled to the top, it's best to invest in mini wine glasses that are the right size (and since mini things are in style, they shouldn't be hard to find). That's 14 oz per person per Seder night. Play it safe with three 750-ml. bottles for every 4 people so you have ample supply. Divide your guests into three categories: 1) Dry wine drinkers 2) Sweet wine drinkers 3) Grape juice drinkers. Then do the math.

Should I chill my bottles of wines?

There's room in your fridge? Seriously, though, reds are best served at room temperature, as chilling will hide their aromatics. Back in the day, though, room temperature was a cool 60°F vs. today's 70°F. If you do not have a wine refrigerator (which will keep the wine between 55°F and 60°F), you can chill Seder wine for a short 30 minutes. Drinking wine at 60°F will help you during the Seder, as it will help hide the alcohol taste a bit.

White wine and rosés, however, should be either stored in the refrigerator or chilled for at least 1 hour before serving. They should be crisp and refreshing.

Are there specific wines that are ideal for Seder night drinking, perhaps with lower alcohol content?

Red wine should be used. As far as alcohol, when you see that the alcohol listed on the bottle is 12% instead of 14%, it may not sound like a big difference, but it is. Wines with 12% alcohol won't go to your head nearly as fast. Barkan's Pinot Noir and Weinstock Red by W are both low-alcohol choices that appeal to a wide range of wine drinkers. They're also budget-friendly, which is great if you're expecting a big crowd. Their fruitiness may even convert sweet-wine drinkers over to the other side.

Charoses

WHEN we first discussed including *charoses* recipes, I didn't think we should. But then I realized that I need a recipe myself. This year is the first time I won't rely on my mother or mother-in-law to make it for me. —L.

YIELD *2 LBS*

- 2 sweet red apples, peeled and grated
- 2 Granny Smith apples, peeled and grated
- 2½ cups chopped, peeled hazelnuts, toasted
- 2 cups sweet red wine
- 1 tsp ground fresh ginger, or to taste

1. In a medium bowl, combine apples, hazelnuts, wine, and ginger to taste.

> Use hazelnuts without the peel. If you cannot find peeled hazelnuts, simply toast whole hazelnuts. Rub the nuts between your palms or in a dish towel and the peels will come off. Then, chop coarsely and measure the correct quantity.

> Syrian charoset is meant to resemble the mortar used by the Jews while working in Egypt. And even though it reminds us of affliction, it tastes sweet as a reminder that all our difficulties are still blessings from G-d. The dates for charoset are traditionally ground to a paste using a food mill (and many still do it that way), but modern conveniences work just as well.

Syrian Charoset [GEBROKTS]

I'M being honest. The *Korech* step of the Seder, when we combine matzah, Romaine lettuce, and this *charoset*, is the culinary highlight of my year. I express that every year at the table and lots of people always nod in agreement. We also enjoy *charoset* as a spread all throughout the week of Passover. —V.

YIELD *2 LBS*

- 1½ lbs large pitted dates
- ½ cup ground walnuts
- ¼ cup sweet wine
- ¼ tsp ground cinnamon
- ½-1 Tbsp matzah meal

1. Place dates into a medium saucepan. Add water to just cover. Bring to a boil over medium-high heat and boil for 15 minutes, stirring occasionally. Drain well.

2. In the bowl of a food processor, process dates until smooth. Transfer dates to a medium bowl. Stir in walnuts, wine, and cinnamon. Add matzah meal as needed to bind.

9

Building Blocks

Pass the Mayo

LEAH: **My grandmother** in Brazil makes mayonnaise every single week. My kids still talk about the mayonnaise they smeared on their matzah when we spent one Passover there a few years ago. The greatest misconception about mayonnaise is that it's complicated to make. With our promise to make Passover easy, we believe it's easy and we'll show you how it's done.

1

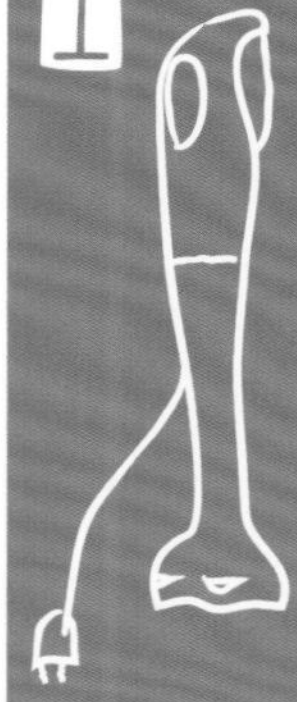

There are two basic methods. One uses a food processor or blender. The second, quicker version uses an immersion blender. You can use our fresh mayo in the Lemon-Mayonnaise Dipping Sauce on page 76.

2

Or you can make the most delicious Roasted Red Pepper Mayo. Preheat your oven to 475°F. Roast a red pepper until it's blistered, about 25 minutes. Seal it in a plastic bag for 15 minutes. Remove and discard the peel and add the pepper to the food processor along with the ingredients listed in our mayo recipe.

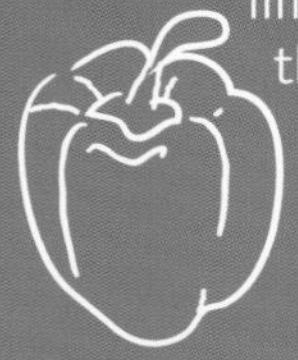

3

How about trying the freshest Eggplant Babaganoush you've ever tasted? Just roast a whole eggplant, scoop out the flesh, and blend along with the ingredients in our mayo recipe, below. Enjoy the babaganoush with matzah or with our Crispy Crackers on page 18.

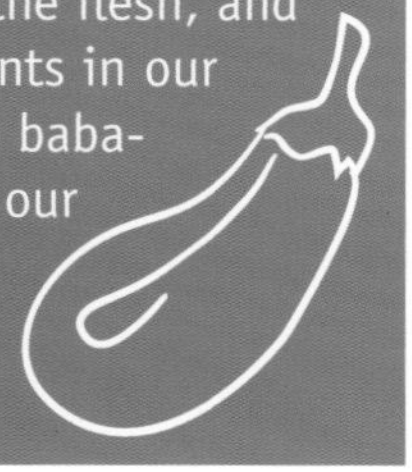

4

You can also lighten it up a bit by replacing each yolk with an egg white. Whichever way you do it, try it!

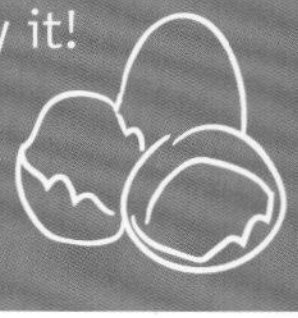

Homemade Mayonnaise

INGREDIENTS

- 3   garlic cloves
      or
- ¼   onion
- •   juice of 1½ lemons
- 2   eggs
- ½   tsp salt
- 1   pinch black pepper
- 3 cups   oil

INSTRUCTIONS

1. In the bowl of a food processor or in a blender, blend garlic, lemon juice, and eggs.

2. With the machine running, slowly pour in the oil in a thin stream.

3. Blend until thoroughly combined and mayonnaise is emulsified. Do not over-mix. When the mayonnaise is thick and holds together, it's done. Store in refrigerator for up to one week.

THE IMMERSION BLENDER METHOD

Add oil to a tall jar (you can use the one that comes with the immersion blender). Add garlic, lemon juice, eggs, salt, and pepper. Insert the immersion blender and blend, without moving the blender, for 2 minutes. When the mixture begins to thicken, move the immersion blender up and down until mayonnaise is emulsified.

Building Blocks the Passover Crunch

YOU WON'T MISS YOUR BREADCRUMBS for the next eight days. And you won't have to keep chomping on more matzah to satisfy the craving for crunch.

1 What should you use instead? Use **ground nuts** such as filberts or pecans in place of breadcrumbs to coat eggplant slices for an authentic *eggplant parmesan*. Dip your eggplant slices in potato starch, then egg, then nuts, and fry as usual.

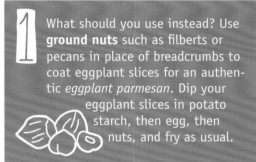

2 Process **yellow soup croutons** (aka soup mandel) for a great crumb you can use to coat *shake n' bake chicken*. Coat the chicken in a mixture of equal parts mayo, honey, and imitation mustard. Coat with the crushed croutons. Spread a few tablespoons of oil on the bottom of your baking pan, add the chicken, spray with nonstick cooking spray or drizzle with oil, and bake.

3 Mix and match! You can also fry or bake nut-coated chicken. Or try different flavors of **crushed potato chips** on chicken cutlets too, just as we did on our crispy baked *Zucchini Sticks* (check them out on page 76).

4 We even made a creamy and healthy *Cauliflower Gratin* dish (page 82) with a dusting of crumbs on top. If you can't find Passover crumbs in your grocery, you can try our easy crushed crouton idea or make a batch of our **homemade Passover Crumbs**.

Passover Crumbs

YIELD *2½ cups*

INGREDIENTS

⅔ cup	water
4 Tbsp	oil
1	pinch salt
1¼ cups	potato starch
3	eggs
•	dash of paprika (optional)

INSTRUCTIONS

1. Preheat oven to 400°F. Grease a baking sheet.

2. In a small saucepan, bring water, oil, and salt to a boil. Remove from heat and use a fork to whisk in potato starch. Quickly add eggs, one at a time, mixing well.

3. Drop at least 8 rounds of batter onto prepared baking sheet. Bake for 30 minutes. Remove from oven. Wearing gloves, shred baked batter. Return to oven and turn off heat. Keep the door closed and leave pan in the oven for 30 minutes until batter has dried. Place in a food processor and blend until coarse crumbs form. If some of the crumbs are still moist, return them to the baking sheet and continue drying in an oven that has been preheated and turned off.

What to do with your batch of homemade Passover crumbs?

Make *classic fried chicken nuggets*. Rub a little oil, salt, and pepper onto the chicken. Dip in beaten egg and coat in crumbs. Heat oil in a skillet and pan-fry for 5-6 minutes per side until coating is golden and crispy and chicken is cooked through.

Building Blocks — The Crepe

LEAH: Crepes may look difficult to achieve, but they're an easy-to-master art. Once you have 'em down pat, you'll be whipping them out on automatic. All you need is a wide offset or slotted spatula (the wide one with the long slots).

VICTORIA: Tell the truth. You flip them with your fingers. But go with the spatula. It makes flipping easy.

LEAH: They'll freeze really well too. When you have a freezer full of crepes, there are lots of things you can make with them.

1
Fill them with almost anything. Fold them into an eggroll, like in our Brisket Eggrolls (page 22). Stuff them with sautéed mushrooms or potatoes and fold them into a purse. You can fry or bake those little crepe packages.

2
How about some Passover pasta? We made our crepes into noodles in the Vegetable Lo Mein (page 88). Just stack them, roll them up, and slice. You can also use those noodles to make a noodle kugel (spread out the sliced noodles and let dry for a few hours, then just substitute them in your all year round recipe).

3
Enjoy a savory crepe for breakfast with veggies and cheese. Or a sweet crepe for breakfast with yogurt and fresh fruit.

4
Make an easy dessert. Serve crepes with berry sauce or chocolate sauce (try ours, on page 113) and whipped cream. Sauté sliced apples or pears with cinnamon. Serve the hot fruit over crepes and drizzle with caramel.

Basic Passover Crepe

YIELD *20 to 24 (10-inch) or 32 (6-inch) crepes*

INGREDIENTS

12	large eggs
¾ cup	potato starch
1 cup	water
1 tsp	salt

INSTRUCTIONS

1. In a blender (or using an immersion blender), beat eggs. Add potato starch, water, and salt. Blend until smooth.

2. Lightly grease a crepe pan or skillet. Heat over medium-high heat. Add 3-4 tablespoons batter and swirl the pan to coat the bottom with a thin layer. Let cook until crepe is firm and edges appear golden, about 1 minute. Flip crepe, using a slotted spatula. Cook for 15 seconds and flip over onto plate. Repeat with remaining batter, re-greasing pan as necessary. Stack crepes as they are completed.

PLATE IT!

Serve your Meatballs in Blueberry Sauce (page 20) just like we did.

1 [Begin by adding finely diced tomatoes and scallions to a shot glass.

2 [Top with a single meatball.

3 [Drop a spoonful of blueberry sauce over the meatball.

4 [Top with curly scallions and serve with little skewers. To make curly scallions, soak scallion strips in ice water for at least 20 minutes.

Starters

Crispy Crackers and Mock Techineh

INGREDIENTS

CRACKERS

1 lb	potato starch (about 2½ cups)
8 oz	ground almonds
½ cup	olive oil
1 cup	water
2 tsp	salt

TECHINEH

¼ cup	walnut oil
½ cup	ground almonds
6-8	garlic cloves
½ cup	fresh lemon juice
1–2 tsp	salt
•	handful fresh parsley
•	up to 1 cup cold water

INSTRUCTIONS

1. Preheat oven to 350°F. In a large bowl, combine potato starch, almonds, olive oil, water, and salt. Knead until a dough forms.

2. Divide dough into 4-6 balls. Using a rolling pin, roll each ball as thinly as possible between two pieces of parchment paper. Remove top piece of parchment paper. Cut dough into squares or triangles (you will not be able to move the crackers apart before baking, but that is fine, as they will not spread). Transfer parchment paper with the crackers to a baking sheet and bake 15 minutes, until crispy.

3. Meanwhile, prepare the techineh: In the bowl of a food processor, combine oil, almonds, garlic, lemon juice, salt, and parsley. Pulse until smooth. With the motor running, slowly add water, thinning the mixture to desired consistency. Serve alongside crackers as a dip.

YIELD

80 crackers and 2 cups tec.

INSPIRED BY COOKKOSHER MEMBER *Cook7*

Don't own a Passover rolling pin? Use an unopened soda bottle as a stand-in.

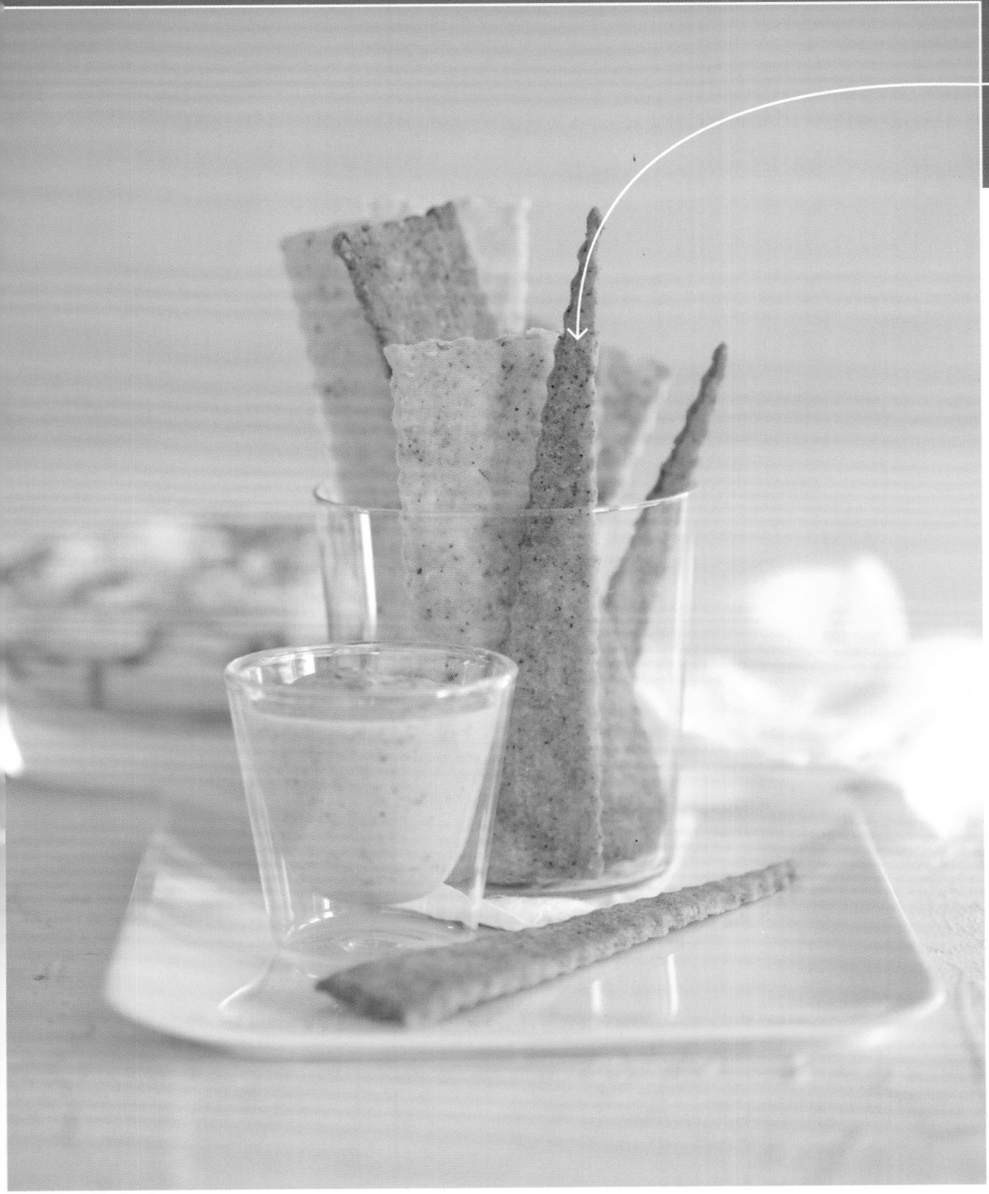

You can make different flavors by adding seasoning. Check out our paprika-flavored and basil-flavored crackers.

As we were wrapping up our first cookbook meeting, Leah quickly pulled out potato starch and almonds and said, "Let's make the crackers right now." Soon after, when we pulled these from the oven, we were surprised to find them pleasantly addictive. They bake evenly, so you can slice them into any shape. We love them with this Mock Techineh, but you can also serve these crackers with guacamole, fried eggplant (or fried eggplant and techineh), or any of your favorite dips. –V.

Meatballs in Blueberry Sauce

INGREDIENTS

1 lb	ground meat
1 Tbsp	paprika
1 tsp	brown sugar
½ tsp	salt
½ tsp	coarse black pepper
•	dash cinnamon
3 Tbsp	Passover crumbs
1	small onion, finely diced
1 Tbsp	oil
1	egg

SAUCE

½ cup	ketchup
½ cup	blueberry preserves
¼ cup	water
2 Tbsp	sugar

INSTRUCTIONS

1. In a large bowl, combine meat, paprika, brown sugar, salt, black pepper, cinnamon, crumbs, onion, oil, and egg. Form mixture into ping-pong-size balls.

2. In a medium saucepan over medium heat, combine ketchup, blueberry preserves, water, and sugar. Bring to a boil. Drop in meatballs. Lower heat and cover. Cook for 1 hour, checking periodically. If mixture seems to be burning, lower heat further. Serve warm or at room temperature.

YIELD
30 meatballs

TIDBIT:
Jews from Iran and Afghanistan have a tradition of whipping themselves with scallions, symbolizing the whips the Egyptian slave drivers used on the Jews in Egypt.

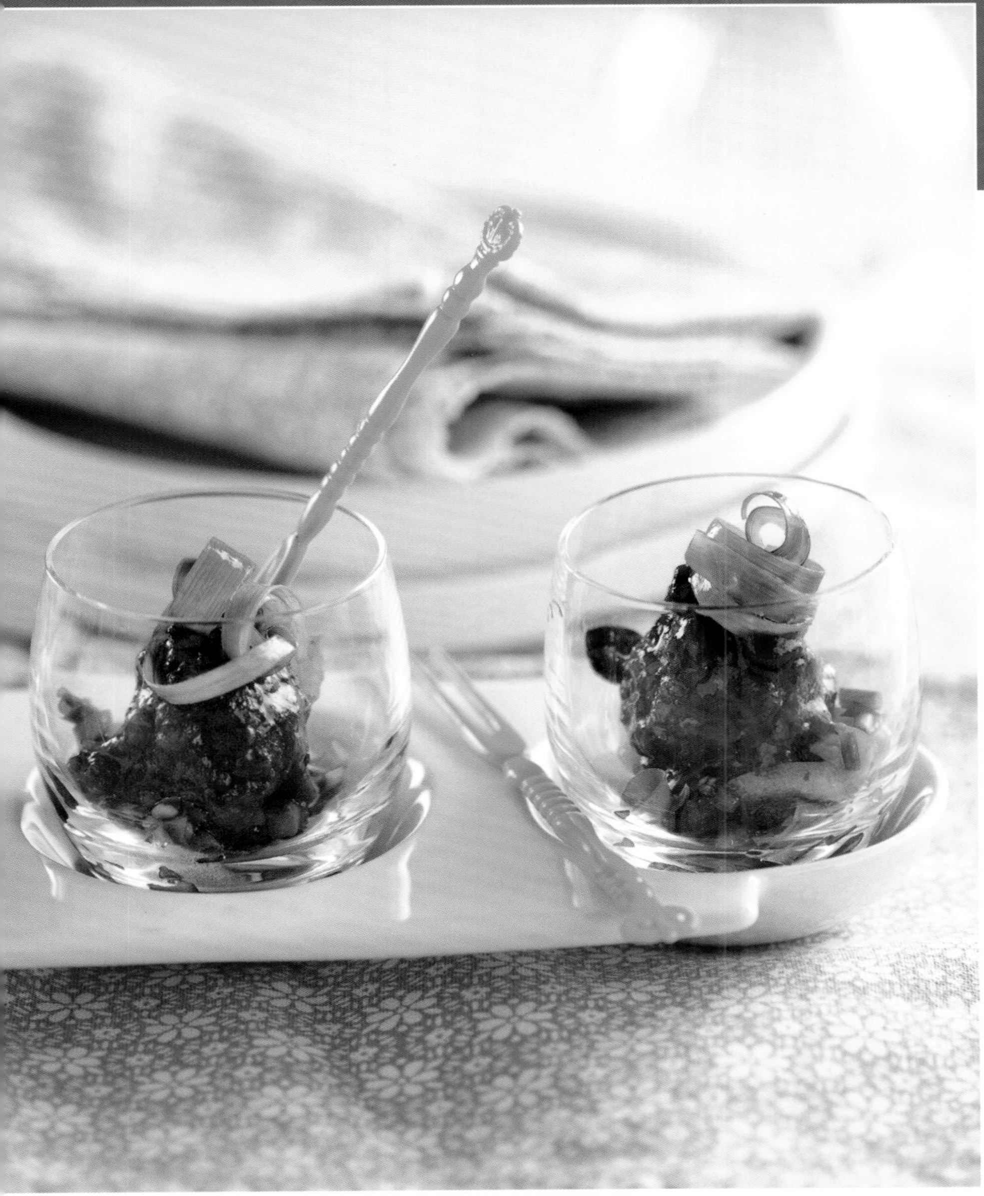

AFTER I made the meatballs, I thought maybe we shouldn't include them. They were too good to enjoy only on Passover and should be saved for a book we'd use all year round. But then I realized that's the case with all the recipes! –L.

Brisket Eggrolls

INGREDIENTS

½ lb	brisket (2½ cups cooked shredded meat)
•	salt, to taste
•	coarse black pepper, to taste
¼ cup	oil, divided, plus more for frying
1	medium onion, diced
1	medium red onion, diced
1½ Tbsp	sugar
1½ Tbsp	lemon juice
¼ tsp	salt
•	pinch coarse black pepper
3 Tbsp	orange juice
10	(6-inch) crepes (see Building Blocks, page 14)

INSTRUCTIONS

1. You may skip the first step if you are using leftover meat. Season brisket with salt and pepper. Heat 2 tablespoons oil in a sauté pan over medium heat. Sear brisket for 3 minutes on each side. Lower heat, cover, and cook brisket for 1-1½ hours, checking periodically. If meat seems to be burning, lower heat further.

2. Shred meat. Set aside.

3. Heat 2 tablespoons oil in a sauté pan over medium heat. Add onions and sauté 10-12 minutes, stirring occasionally. Add sugar, lemon juice, salt, and black pepper. Sauté 5 additional minutes. Stir in orange juice; taste to adjust seasoning. Remove from heat and stir in shredded meat.

4. Place 2 tablespoons onion-meat filling towards the bottom-center of each crepe. Roll, eggroll-style: fold up bottom to cover filling. Fold in sides, then roll upward to close.

5. Heat 1 inch oil in a sauté pan over medium-high heat. When hot (eggrolls should sizzle when slipped into the pan), fry eggrolls until golden, about 3-4 minutes per side.

YIELD
10 eggrolls

There are a couple of dipping sauces in this book you can serve alongside these eggrolls. See pages 52 and 60.

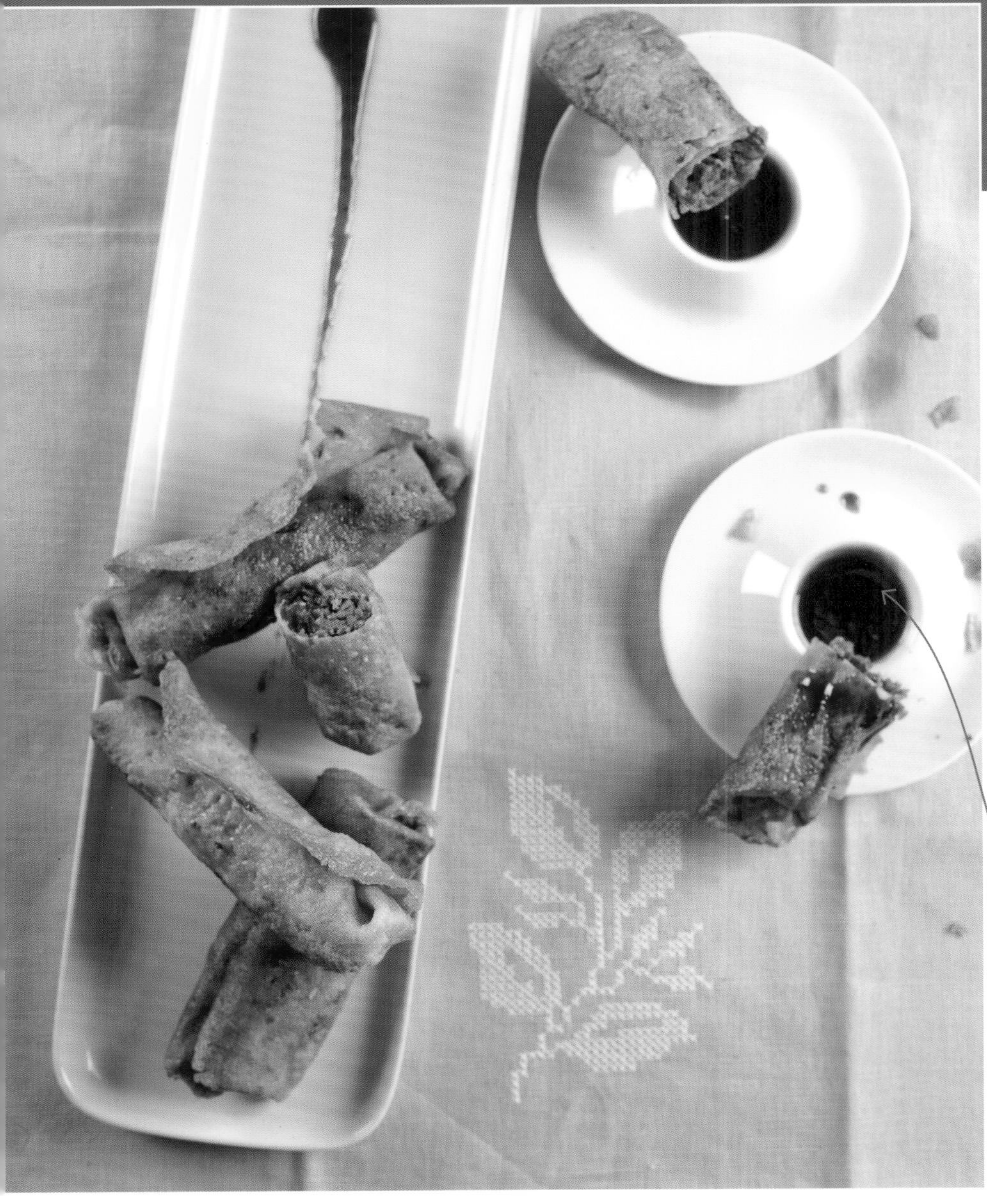

I love eggrolls all year, and especially on Passover, when we can fill a crepe with any veggies, like sautéed shredded cabbage, kohlrabi, and carrots, and fry. This one, though, is an eggroll the men will especially love. –L.

C'mon Leah. There's more to say. These are awesome. –V.

Oh, yeah. And they're awesome. You can use any leftover meat you want and turn them into this great appetizer. –L.

Make your own Passover teriyaki sauce. Combine 1 cup water, 1/4 cup imitation soy sauce, 3 Tbsp brown sugar, and 1 minced garlic clove in a saucepan over medium-high heat. Bring to a boil. Add 2 tablespoons potato starch dissolved in cold water. Add to mixture and cook until thickened.

Chips and Dip

INGREDIENTS

1 sweet potato
3 blue potatoes
1 yucca, peeled
1 large parsnip, peeled
4 large beets (golden or red), peeled
• oil for frying
• salt for sprinkling

ROASTED PEPPER DIP

1 red pepper
1 yellow pepper
1 Tbsp chopped walnuts
1 Tbsp olive oil
2 garlic cloves
1 tsp chopped fresh basil
¼ tsp salt, or to taste

INSTRUCTIONS

1. Using a mandoline, slice vegetables $\frac{1}{16}$-inch thick (or on the 1.3mm setting).
2. Heat 1-2 inches oil in a medium saucepan until hot (a chip should sizzle when dropped in). Fry chips in batches, about 2 minutes, until beginning to turn golden at the edges. Remove chips to a paper-towel-lined plate. Sprinkle with salt.
3. Prepare the dip: Preheat oven to 375°F. Place peppers into a baking pan and roast until skin is blistered, about 40 minutes. Let cool and remove stem and seeds.
4. In the bowl of a food processor, combine roasted peppers, walnuts, olive oil, garlic, basil, and salt. Pulse to combine. Serve alongside chips.

THE BAKING METHOD

Preheat oven to 400°F. Spread chips on a greased baking sheet. Spray generously with nonstick cooking spray and sprinkle with salt. Bake for 6 minutes, then flip chips. Some chips are more in a rush to be ready than others, so you'll have to remove the chips that are already browned around the edges. Bake an additional 6 minutes, checking halfway through to remove chips that have browned. Beets will take longer than the other vegetables. Chips should crisp up when cooled. If they are still soft when cool, return to the oven for 2 more minutes.

YIELD

8 servings

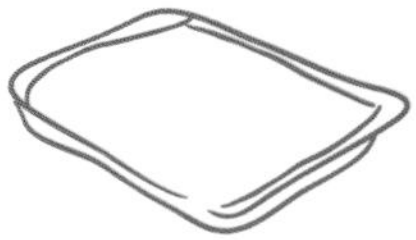

To retain crispness, store chips in a metal or aluminum pan only, covered with foil. No plastic! No paper towels! If the chips become slightly soft, crisp in the oven for 1 to 2 minutes at 350°F.

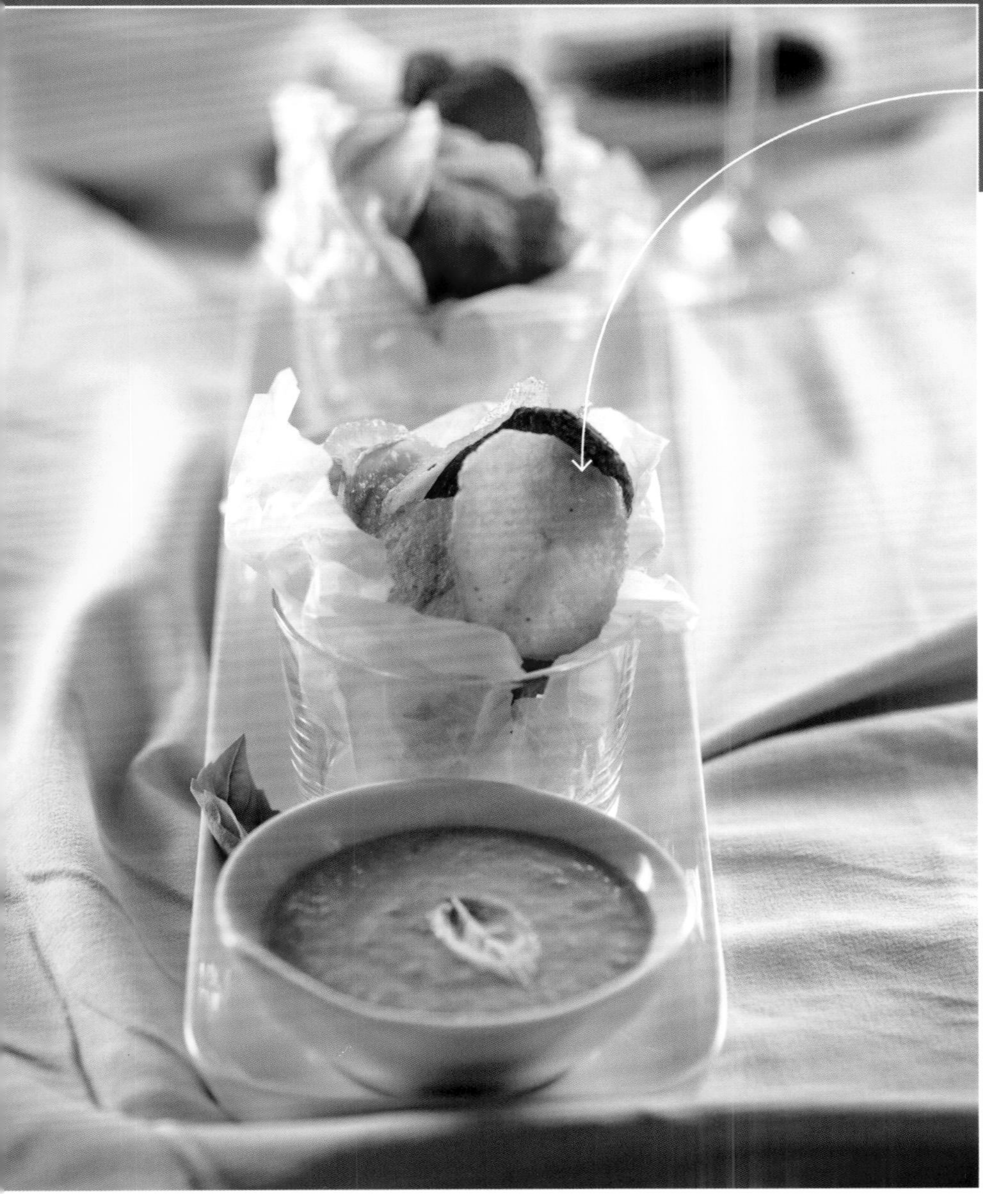

Sweet potatoes, blue potatoes, and yucca will remain nice and crisp for days. Parsnips and beets are better the same day.

AFTER spending two Sundays burning oven-baked sweet potato chips, Leah asked, "Why don't you just fry them?" I was planning on frying them too, but thought we should give you a healthy option. Here are the baking tricks I learned: 1) Flip 'em halfway through. 2) They don't become crispy in the oven, so don't keep baking until they do. They become crispy when they cool.

A mandoline makes these veggies into beautiful company-worthy chips in seconds. A vegetable peeler will work as well; they just won't be as pretty. –V.

Antipasti Rolls

INGREDIENTS

CARAMELIZED-ONION PESTO

½ cup	water
2 Tbsp	olive oil
2 Tbsp	sugar
2	large onions, cut into very thin strips
2	garlic cloves, minced
¼ tsp	salt
1 Tbsp	chopped fresh basil
1	eggplant, cut vertically into ¼-inch-thick strips
2	zucchinis, cut vertically into ¼-inch-thick strips
•	olive oil, for brushing
•	salt to taste

INSTRUCTIONS

1. Prepare the caramelized-onion pesto: In a sauté pan over medium-high heat, bring water, oil, and sugar to a boil. Add onions and garlic. Cover, lower heat, and cook until water has evaporated and onions are golden, about 30 minutes. Season with salt. Drain well; stir in basil.

2. Preheat oven to broil. Place eggplant slices on a greased baking sheet. Brush with olive oil and sprinkle with salt. Broil for 4-5 minutes per side, watching that they don't blister (overcooked vegetables will fall apart). Repeat with zucchini.

3. Place a heaping teaspoon of onions at the edge of each vegetable strip and roll up. Serve warm, cold, or at room temperature.

YIELD
4-6 servings

TIDBIT:
Although Sephardim eat kitniot, they do not eat chummus. This is because the word "chametz" sounds like "chummus."

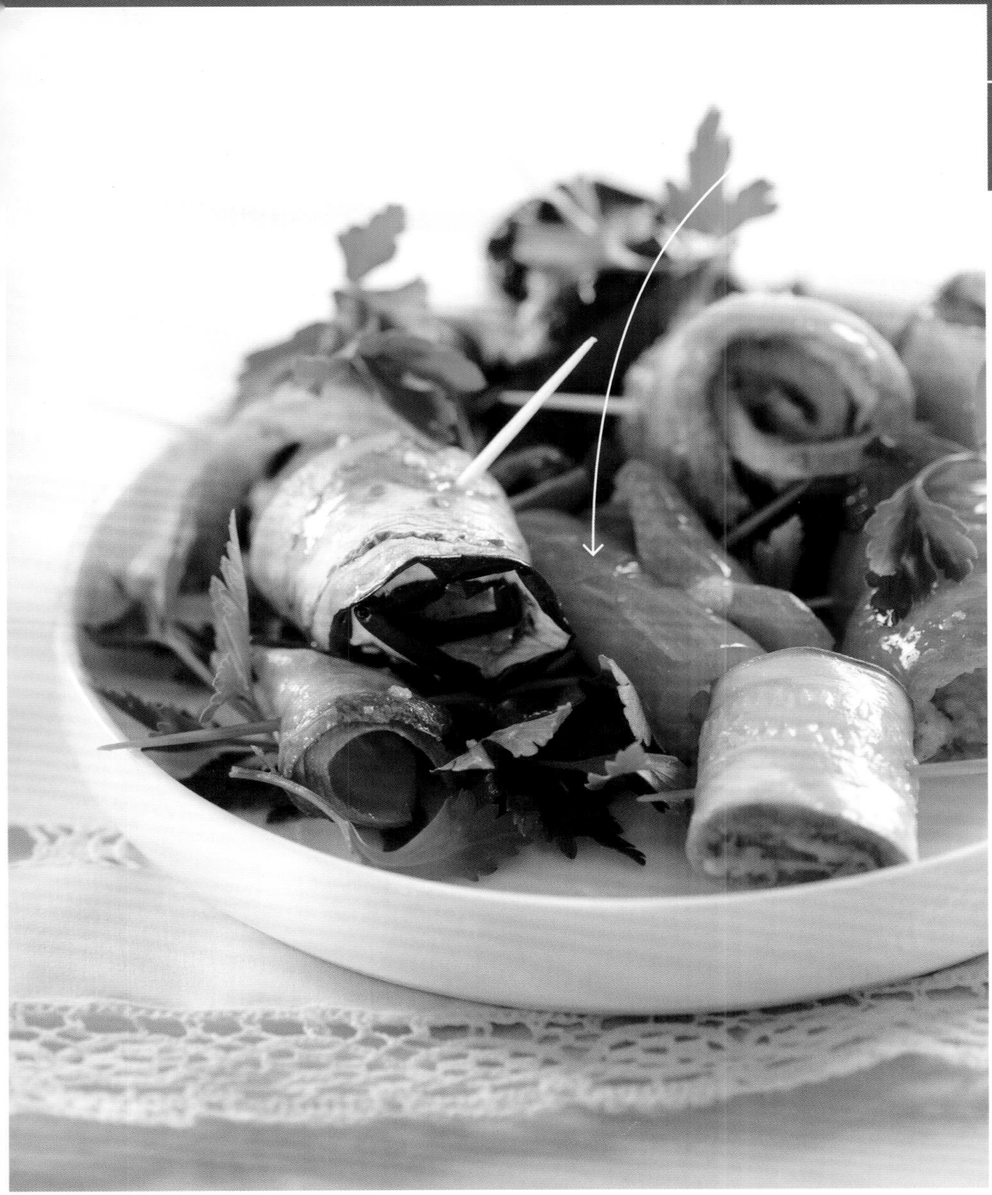

You can also use red, orange, or yellow roasted peppers to add variety to this dish.

THROUGHOUT the year, I love these caramelized onions on top of mini pizza doughs. We even enjoy them straight out of the pan. Your guests will think they're eating plain ol' grilled vegetables until they take a bite and discover that these rolls are packed with loads of flavor. –V.

PLATE IT!

Did you think Turnip and Beet Pickles (page 42) could look so beautiful?

1 [The turnips take on a pretty pinkish-red hue when marinating with the beets.

2 [Use a vegetable peeler to create thin carrot strips and insert them into ice-cold water. Carrots will take a few hours to curl up.

3 [Place a piece of lettuce on the plate as a base. Top with a handful of turnip and beet pickles.

4 [Repeat with a second layer of lettuce, turnips, and beets.

5 [Finish with curly carrots.

Soups and Salads

Orange Soup

INGREDIENTS

3 Tbsp	olive oil
2	large onions, diced
3	garlic cloves, minced
1	large (approximately 4-lb) butternut squash, peeled, seeded, and cubed
2	large carrots, peeled and chopped
2	sweet potatoes, peeled and chopped
4 cups	chicken or vegetable stock
6-7 cups	water, divided
4	marrow bones (optional)
1 Tbsp	salt, or to taste
¼ tsp	black pepper, or to taste

INSTRUCTIONS

1. Heat oil in a large stockpot over medium heat. Add onions and garlic and fry until onions are soft, about 5 minutes. Add butternut squash, carrots, and sweet potatoes. Stir to combine. Sauté until vegetables soften a bit, about 20 minutes.

2. Add stock, 4 cups water, marrow bones (optional), salt, and pepper. Bring to a boil over high heat. Lower heat and simmer 2-3 hours, until vegetables are tender. Remove from heat and let cool slightly.

3. Using a slotted spoon, remove the marrow bones. Purée soup in the pot using an immersion blender (you can also purée soup in batches in a standard blender). Add additional 2-3 cups water until soup is desired consistency. Taste; adjust seasoning. Return soup to heat to rewarm. Serve hot.

YIELD

10-12 servings

INSPIRED BY COOKKOSHER MEMBER
Overtimecook

As the marrow bones cook in the soup, they add great flavor and creaminess. You can place the bones in a net bag for a cleaner soup. Omit if you prefer a pareve version.

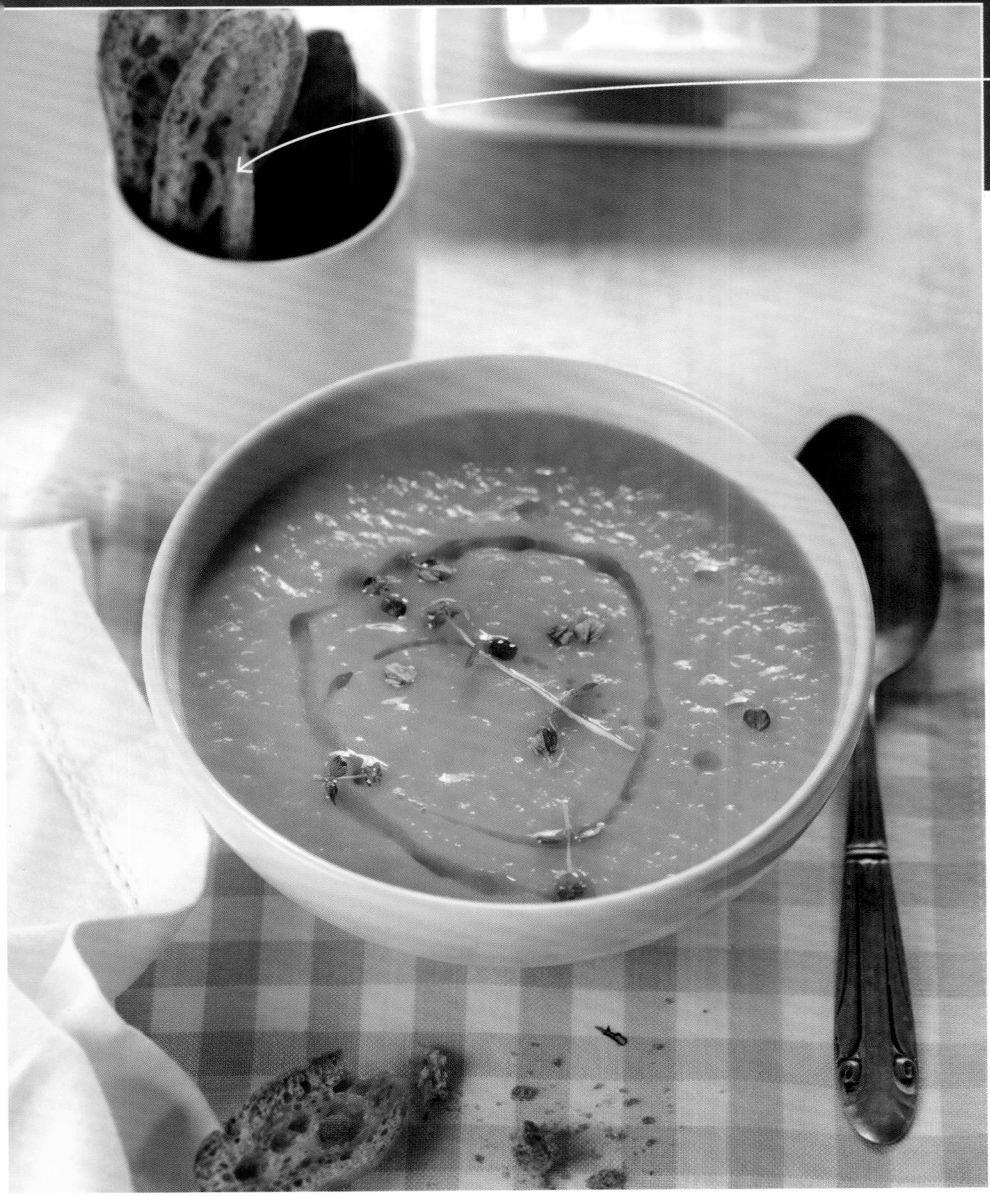

Make these bagel chips by slicing and toasting our Bubbe's Egg Bagels on page 96.

WE tried lots of "orange" vegetable soups using either acorn or butternut squash but none had that finish-the-bowl-and-want-seconds factor that would make it worthy of inclusion in this book. Then, our friend and fellow food writer Miriam Pascal told us about her version. It makes a big batch, but that's no problem because it freezes beautifully. And with this one, we didn't mind having leftovers for lunch the next day. –V.

Roasted Tomato and Eggplant Soup

INGREDIENTS

3	large beef tomatoes
1	large eggplant, sliced in half
4-5 Tbsp	olive oil, divided
1 Tbsp	lemon juice
1	large onion, chopped
3	garlic cloves, minced
4 cups	chicken stock
½ tsp	dried basil
1 tsp	salt
¼ tsp	black pepper

INSTRUCTIONS

1. Place a rack in the top third of the oven. Preheat oven to 400°F. Line a baking sheet with parchment paper.

2. Using a paring knife, make a small x incision on the base of each tomato. Place tomatoes and eggplant halves, cut side up, on the prepared baking sheet. Drizzle 2-3 tablespoons olive oil and the lemon juice over tomatoes and eggplant. Place baking sheet on prepared rack and bake for 45 minutes.

3. Heat remaining oil in a 5-quart pot over medium heat. Add onion and garlic and sauté until soft and beginning to turn golden, about 5-7 minutes.

4. Remove tomatoes and eggplant from oven. Peel the tomatoes; discard peel and add tomatoes to the pot.

5. Scoop out the eggplant flesh and add to a medium bowl. Using a fork, mash eggplants and add to the pot. Sauté for 1 to 2 minutes. Add chicken stock, basil, salt, and pepper. Cover and cook 45 minutes. Remove from heat and let cool slightly.

6. Purée soup using an immersion blender in the pot (you can also purée soup in batches in a standard blender). Taste; adjust seasoning. Return soup to heat to re-warm. Serve hot.

YIELD

4-6 servings

TIDBIT:
Some have a custom to use only bottled water on Passover, because they feared that chamatz was in the water supply.

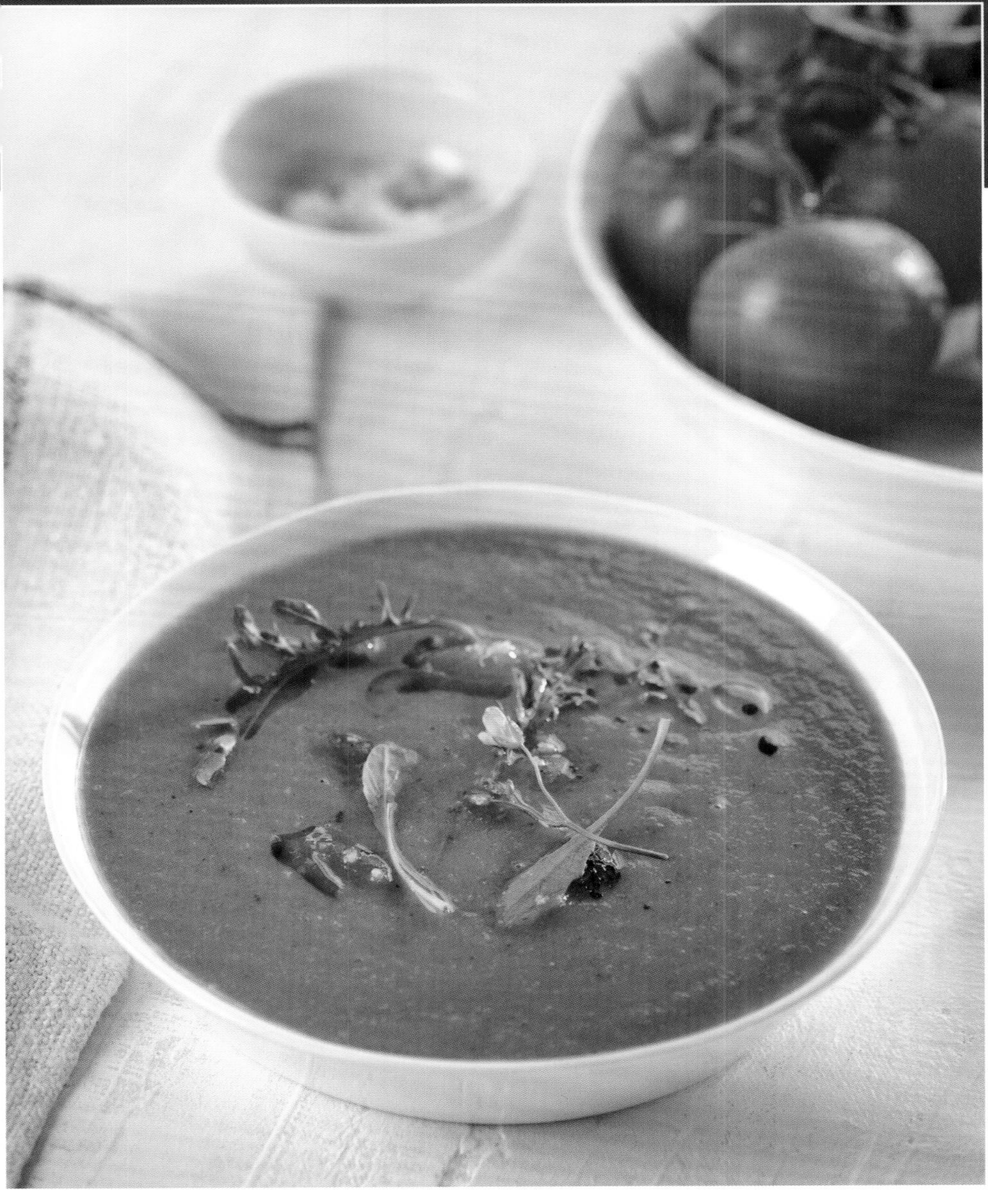

ROASTED tomato soup is one of my favorite soups. To give it a new twist, I paired it with roasted eggplant, which has a light smokiness. I think it's a perfect match. –L.

Butternut Squash Salad *with* Sugar n' Spice Nuts

INGREDIENTS

1	butternut squash, peeled, cut into ¾-inch cubes
2 Tbsp	oil
½ tsp	sugar
¼ tsp	salt
⅛ tsp	coarse black pepper
1	head Romaine lettuce, chopped
1	green apple, diced

SUGAR N' SPICE NUTS

½ cup	sliced almonds
2 tsp	sugar
⅛ tsp	cinnamon
¼ tsp	salt
¼ tsp	paprika
1 tsp	oil

SHALLOT DRESSING

1-2	shallots
¼ cup	oil
1 Tbsp	lemon juice
½ tsp	salt
¼ tsp	coarse black pepper

INSTRUCTIONS

1. Preheat oven to 475°F. Line a baking sheet with aluminum foil. Spread butternut squash on prepared baking sheet and toss with oil, sugar, salt, and pepper. Bake for 35-40 minutes until tender. Let cool.

2. Prepare the nuts: Preheat oven to 300°F. Line a baking sheet with parchment paper. Spread almonds on prepared baking sheet and toss with sugar, cinnamon, salt, and paprika. Drizzle oil over spiced nuts. Bake for 10 minutes.

3. Prepare the dressing: In the bowl of a food processor, combine shallots, oil, lemon juice, salt, and pepper. Process until shallots are completely minced and dressing is uniform. Adjust seasoning to taste.

4. In a large salad bowl, combine lettuce, butternut squash, green apple, and almonds. Toss with shallot dressing and serve.

YIELD

4 servings

Shallots will almost disappear when processed, resulting in a smooth and mild dressing. You can substitute 1/3 red or white onion. The dressing will have a bit more bite.

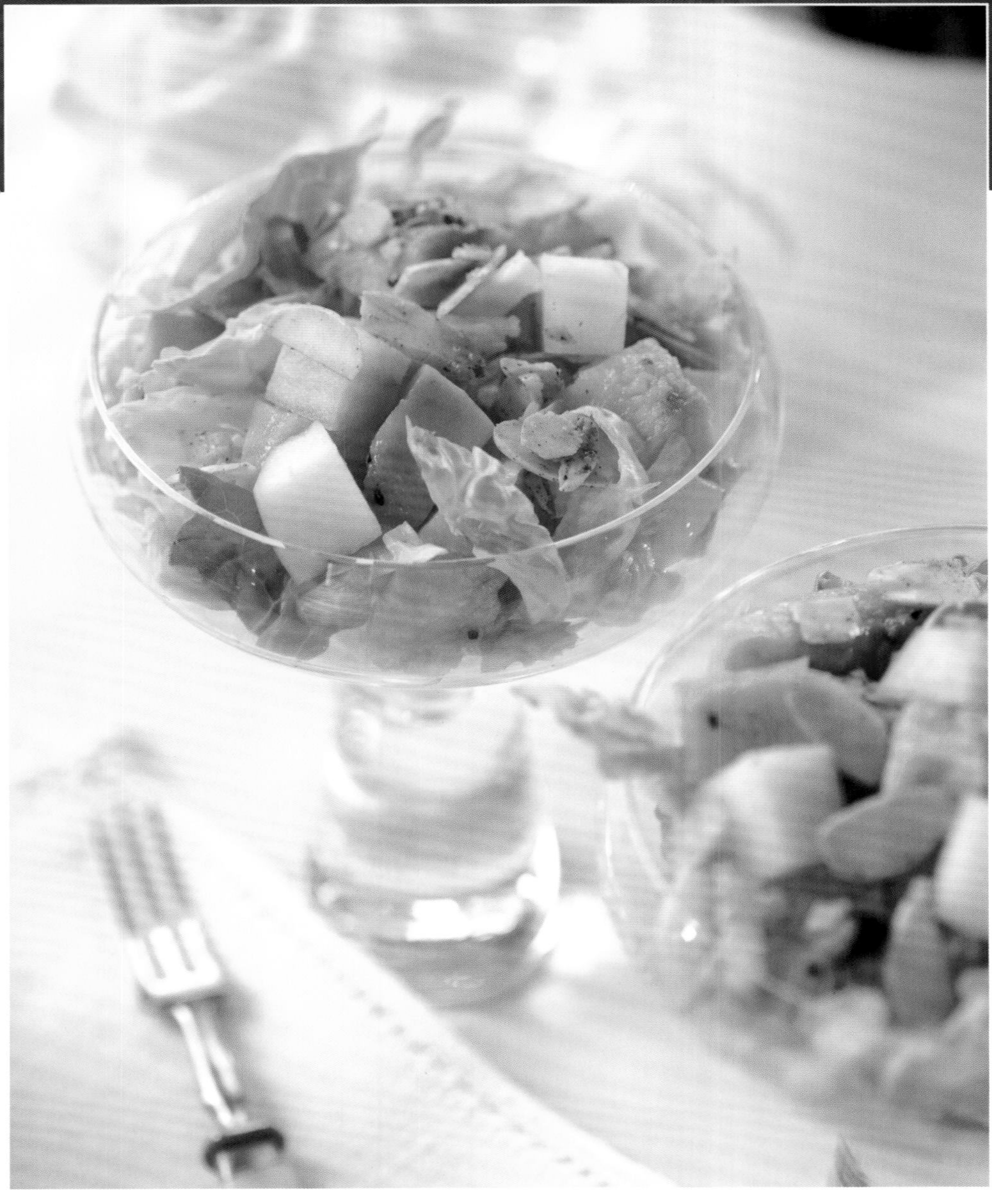

THEY say that the best way to get your family to eat vegetables is to cut up the veggies and leave them on the counter. Well, the roasted butternut squash in this salad was definitely sitting on the counter before I had a chance to finish preparing the salad, but I didn't intend for it to be eaten that way. Every few minutes, a little hand would come and sneak some off the tray. But hey, they're eating vegetables! I wasn't going to complain. One more roasted butternut squash later, this salad was done. –L.

Citrus Beet Salad *with* Honey–Balsamic Vinaigrette

INGREDIENTS

4	large beets, peeled and cubed
1 Tbsp	olive oil
•	salt to taste
•	coarse black pepper to taste
2	oranges
1	ripe, firm avocado, diced
1 cup	diced jicama
½ cup	slivered almonds, toasted

DRESSING

2 Tbsp	olive oil
2 Tbsp	balsamic vinegar
3 tsp	honey
1 tsp	imitation mustard
1 Tbsp	chopped fresh dill
•	pinch salt
•	pinch coarse black pepper

INSTRUCTIONS

1. Preheat oven to 400°F. In a medium roasting pan, toss beet cubes with olive oil, salt, and pepper. Spread in a single layer. Bake until fork tender, about 30-45 minutes. Let cool.

2. Meanwhile, using a paring knife, peel oranges and remove the supremes. (See sidebar, facing page.)

3. In a medium bowl, combine orange supremes, avocado, and jicama.

4. Prepare the dressing: In a small bowl, whisk together oil, balsamic vinegar, honey, imitation mustard, dill, salt, and pepper.

5. Toss salad with dressing. Top with cooled beets. Sprinkle with almonds.

YIELD

4 servings

INSPIRED BY COOKKOSHER MEMBER
elineli07

After you've supremed your oranges, squeeze the membranes and save the juice to prepare refreshing Citrus-Ade (page 124).

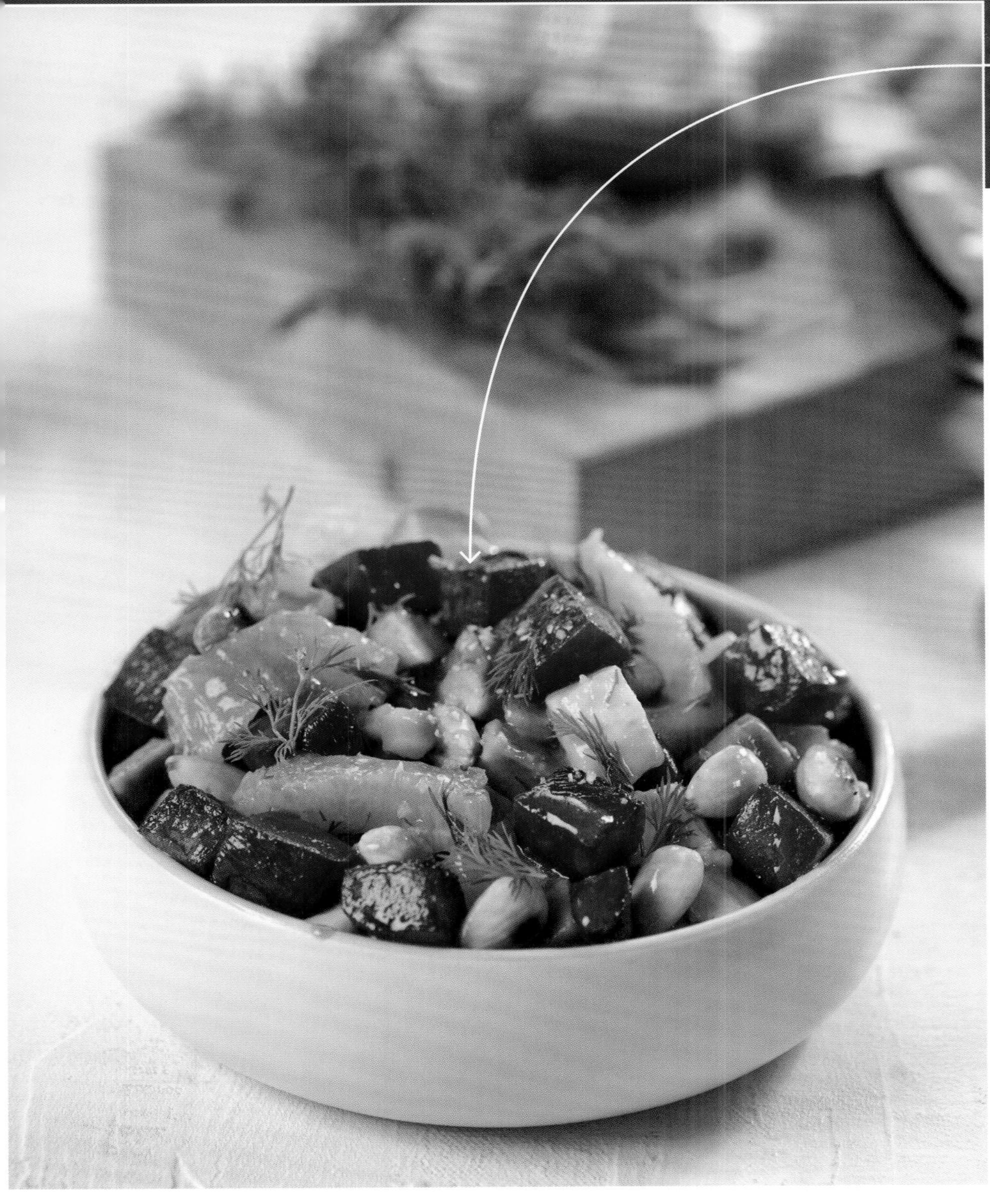

To keep this salad from turning pink, don't add the beets until the end.

WHENEVER I used to prepare a salad that contained oranges or grapefruit, I didn't know that you're not supposed to include the membranes. I'd peel and separate the segments, just as we do when eating a whole orange. The recipes, though, would never turn out right.

Then, I learned how to supreme citrus correctly, by removing the peel using a paring knife, exposing the fruit inside the membranes. The next step is extracting the pretty fruit, or "supremes" from between the membranes. Citrus suddenly became a very welcome addition to bright and fresh-tasting salads, like this one.

–V.

Lime-Infused Pear Salad *with Toasted Walnuts*

INGREDIENTS

1 Tbsp	olive oil
2	pears (Bosc or Anjou), diced
1	head Romaine lettuce, chopped
½	red onion, finely diced
½	cucumber, finely diced
1	small kohlrabi, finely diced
⅓ cup	chopped walnuts, toasted

DAIRY OPTION

⅓ cup	crumbled feta cheese

DRESSING

•	juice of 1½ limes (about 3 Tbsp)
½ tsp	sugar
¼ tsp	salt
⅛ tsp	coarse black pepper
2 Tbsp	olive oil

INSTRUCTIONS

1. Heat olive oil in a sauté pan over medium heat. Add pears and sauté until they begin to turn soft and golden, about 10-15 minutes. Remove from heat and let cool.

2. Prepare the dressing: In a small bowl, whisk together lime juice, sugar, salt, and pepper. Drizzle in olive oil.

3. In a large bowl, combine lettuce, red onion, cucumber, kohlrabi, and toasted walnuts. Add feta cheese if for a dairy meal. Top with cooled pears. Drizzle dressing over salad and toss to combine.

YIELD
4 servings

TIDBIT:
Many have a custom to peel all fruits and vegetables on Passover.

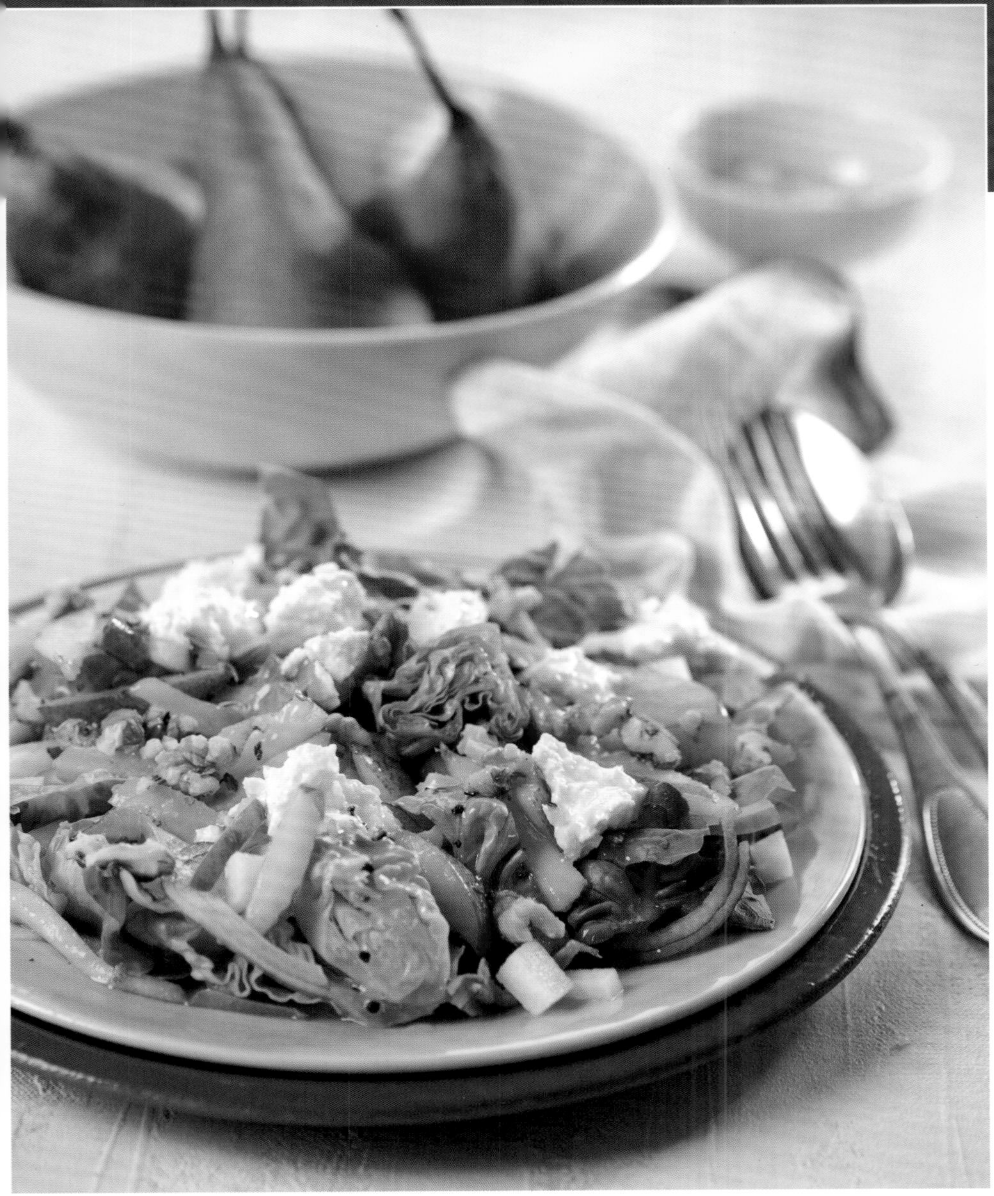

ONE night in December, I was testing this recipe while the rest of my family was sitting down for dinner. My kids had already eaten and had run off by the time I arrived at the table with the salad. I put a small portion on my husband's plate, then put the serving bowl in front of me to enjoy the rest by myself. There was no other dinner left for me, but I really didn't mind. –V.

Russian Coleslaw

INGREDIENTS

½ cup	mayonnaise
½ cup	vinegar
5 Tbsp	sugar
1 Tbsp	dried dill weed
•	dash coarse black pepper
8	Kirby cucumbers, peeled and finely diced
1	red onion, finely diced

INSTRUCTIONS

1. Prepare the dressing: In a medium bowl, whisk together mayonnaise, vinegar, sugar, dill, and black pepper.

2. Add cucumbers, a little at a time, tossing each addition in the dressing.

3. Add red onion and toss to combine. Allow slaw to marinate in the refrigerator overnight.

YIELD

4 servings

TIDBIT:
Yemenite Jews use soft matzah that resembles a large, spongy pita. This was the common custom among most Sephardic Jews until recently.

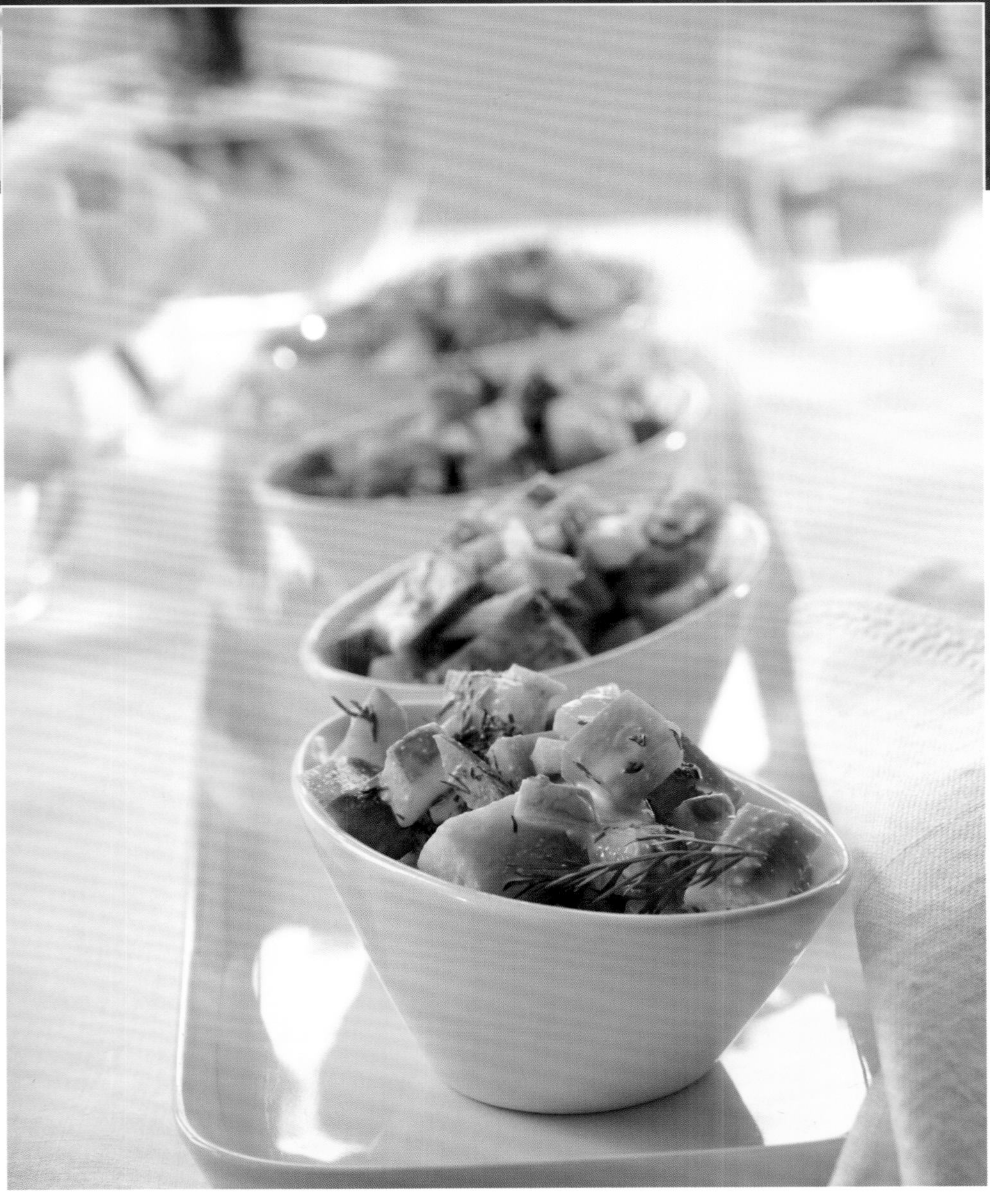

COLESLAW is one salad that many argue is better store-bought rather than homemade. Everyone's always trying to recreate their favorite deli version. I've tried many times too, but something just wasn't right. Thanks to Yussi of Yussi's Deli in Lakewood for helping us tweak our recipe so we can love the homemade version just as much as the one we buy.

What? No cabbage? That's right. I think you'll agree that not every slaw is about cabbage. -L.

Turnip and Beet Pickles

INGREDIENTS

2	large turnips, peeled and thinly sliced into half-moons
1	beet, peeled and thinly sliced into half-moons
8	garlic cloves
1	jalapeño, sliced into rings (do not remove seeds)
1 cup	water
½ Tbsp	salt
1 tsp	vinegar

INSTRUCTIONS

1. Combine turnips, beet, garlic, and jalapeño in a jar.
2. Pour water, salt, and vinegar over vegetables. Cover and shake to combine.
3. Note: Best if made at least 2 days ahead. This salad will keep in the refrigerator for 10-14 days.

Don't have a jar? You can make this in a bowl; just make sure the water is covering the veggies.

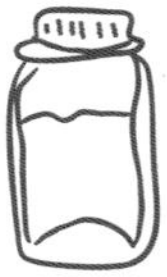

YIELD

3 lbs

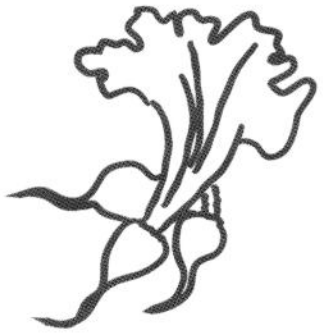

TIDBIT:

Borscht is a common Passover food staple in Askhanazi homes. Since the Karaites interpreted the verse "All chametz, you shall not eat," to include all sour food, not only leavened bread, we distance ourselves from them by drinking soured beetroot, borscht.

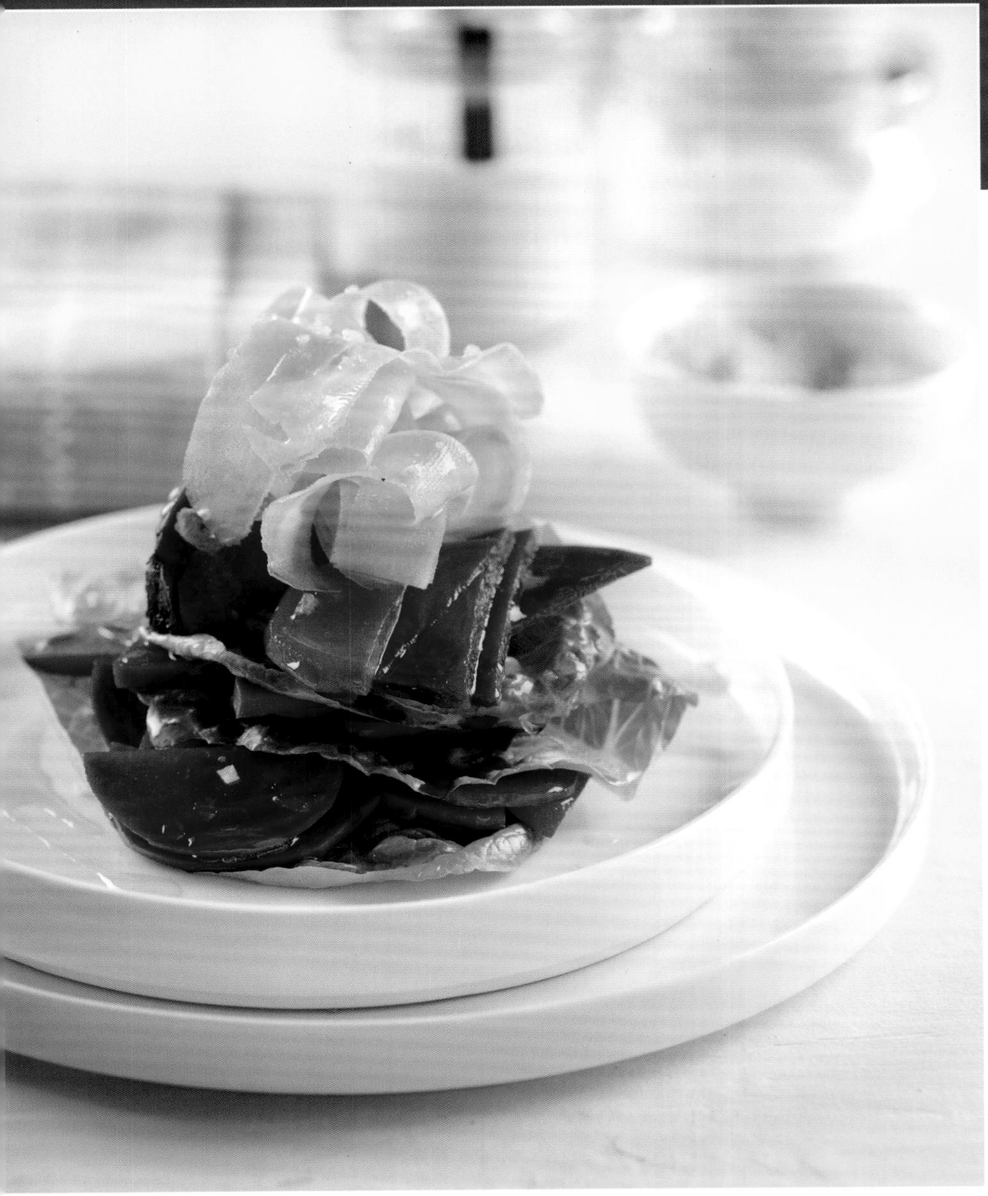

MRS. Weiss is famous for her salads and dips. This is the latest popular addition to her Shabbos table, as regular pickles can become boring. Can't wait 'til Shabbos? Keep a jar in the fridge for a virtually calorie-free snack.

–L

Grilled Vegetable Salad *with* Creamy Dressing

INGREDIENTS

1	sweet potato, sliced into half-moons
1	zucchini, peeled and sliced into ½ inch rounds
1	eggplant, peeled and cubed
1	red pepper, cubed
1	yellow pepper, cubed
8 oz	mushrooms
•	olive oil, for brushing
•	garlic powder, to taste
1	head Romaine lettuce, chopped

DRESSING

⅓ cup	brown sugar
3 Tbsp	mayonnaise
½ tsp	crushed garlic
½ tsp	imitation mustard
⅓ cup	vinegar or lemon juice
1 tsp	salt
¼ cup	oil

INSTRUCTIONS

1. Preheat oven to 425°F. Line a baking sheet with aluminum foil. Spread sweet potato on baking sheet and brush with olive oil. Bake for 15 minutes. Remove from oven and add zucchini, eggplant, peppers, and mushrooms. Brush all vegetables with olive oil and season with garlic powder. Bake until tender, about 30-40 minutes.

2. Prepare the dressing: Using an immersion blender or in the bowl of a food processor, blend brown sugar, mayonnaise, garlic, imitation mustard, vinegar, and salt. Drizzle in olive oil and blend until combined.

3. In a large bowl, combine lettuce and grilled vegetables. Toss with a few tablespoons of dressing just before serving. You will have extra dressing.

YIELD
6-8 servings

INSPIRED BY COOKKOSHER MEMBER
Doctor

TIDBIT:
In some families, the leftover marror lettuce is used during the Yom Tov meals so that one mitzvah can be used in another mitzvah.

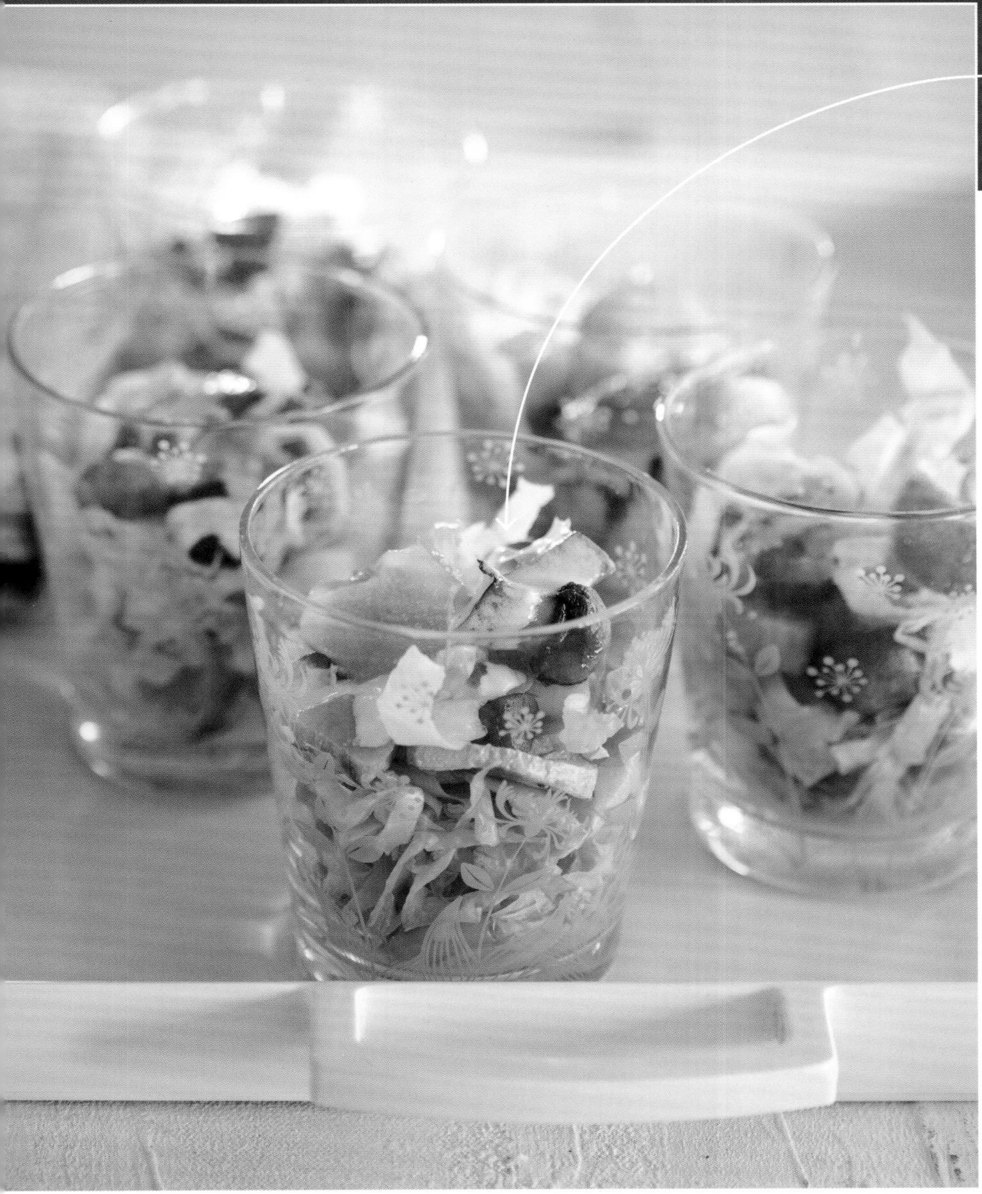

During the year, this salad tastes great with croutons or chow mein noodles added on top.

EVERY time I attend a potluck party, the host requests that I bring this salad. I've made it so many times, I can prepare it in my sleep. There's something about the warm roasted vegetables that makes this very filling and comforting to eat.

You can roast all the veggies and prepare the dressing in advance. Then, when you're ready to serve it, simply toss them all together.

—L.

PLATE IT!

Love chicken but don't love how it looks on the plate? Here's how to make your Apple-Jam Drumettes (page 48) as enticing as the photo.

1 We plated our drumettes with mashed potatoes and sweet potatoes. Make your own ring mold by removing the top and bottom of a can.

2 Begin by adding the mashed potatoes into a ring mold. The mashed potatoes were made by mashing boiled potatoes with oil and salt.

3 Layer mashed sweet potatoes on top. Remove ring. For smooth sweet potatoes like these, send them through a strainer after mashing.

4 Place one drumette in the center of the potato stack.

5 Place a second drumstick on the plate beside the potatoes. Top with a few spoons of Apple-Jam sauce.

6 Finish by topping with curly scallions (see page 16).

Main Dishes

Apple-Jam Chicken Drumettes

INGREDIENTS

12	chicken drumsticks or 20 drumettes
3 Tbsp	oil
1	small onion, finely diced
1	garlic clove, crushed
¼ tsp	salt
½ cup	apricot jam or home-made orange jam (recipe below)
½ cup	apple juice ←
2 Tbsp	red wine
1 Tbsp	sugar
1 tsp	potato starch dissolved in 1 Tbsp water
½ tsp	black pepper

HOMEMADE ORANGE JAM

2	large oranges
1 cup	sugar
¼ cup	water

INSTRUCTIONS

1. Preheat oven to 350°F. Place chicken into a 9 x 13-inch baking pan.

2. Heat oil in a saucepan over medium heat. Add onion and garlic and sauté until onion is soft and beginning to turn golden, 5-7 minutes.

3. Season with salt. Add jam, apple juice, wine, and sugar. Raise heat and bring to a boil. Boil for 3-4 minutes.

4. Add dissolved potato starch. Cook until mixture thickens, about 1 minute. Season with pepper.

5. Pour sauce over chicken. Cover tightly and bake for 3-3½ hours.

HOMEMADE ORANGE JAM INSTRUCTIONS   YIELD 1 CUP

1. Using a paring knife, peel oranges, leaving some white pith. Cut oranges into quarters. In the bowl of a food processor, process oranges until almost smooth.

2. In a small saucepan over high heat, combine processed oranges, sugar, and water. Bring to a boil and let cook for 15 minutes, stirring frequently, until thickened.

Ran out of apple juice? See replacement index, page 126.

YIELD
4-6 servings

TIDBIT:
The largest Seder in the world is celebrated in Katmandu, Nepal whose 1,800 participants collectively consume 1,100 lbs of matzah.

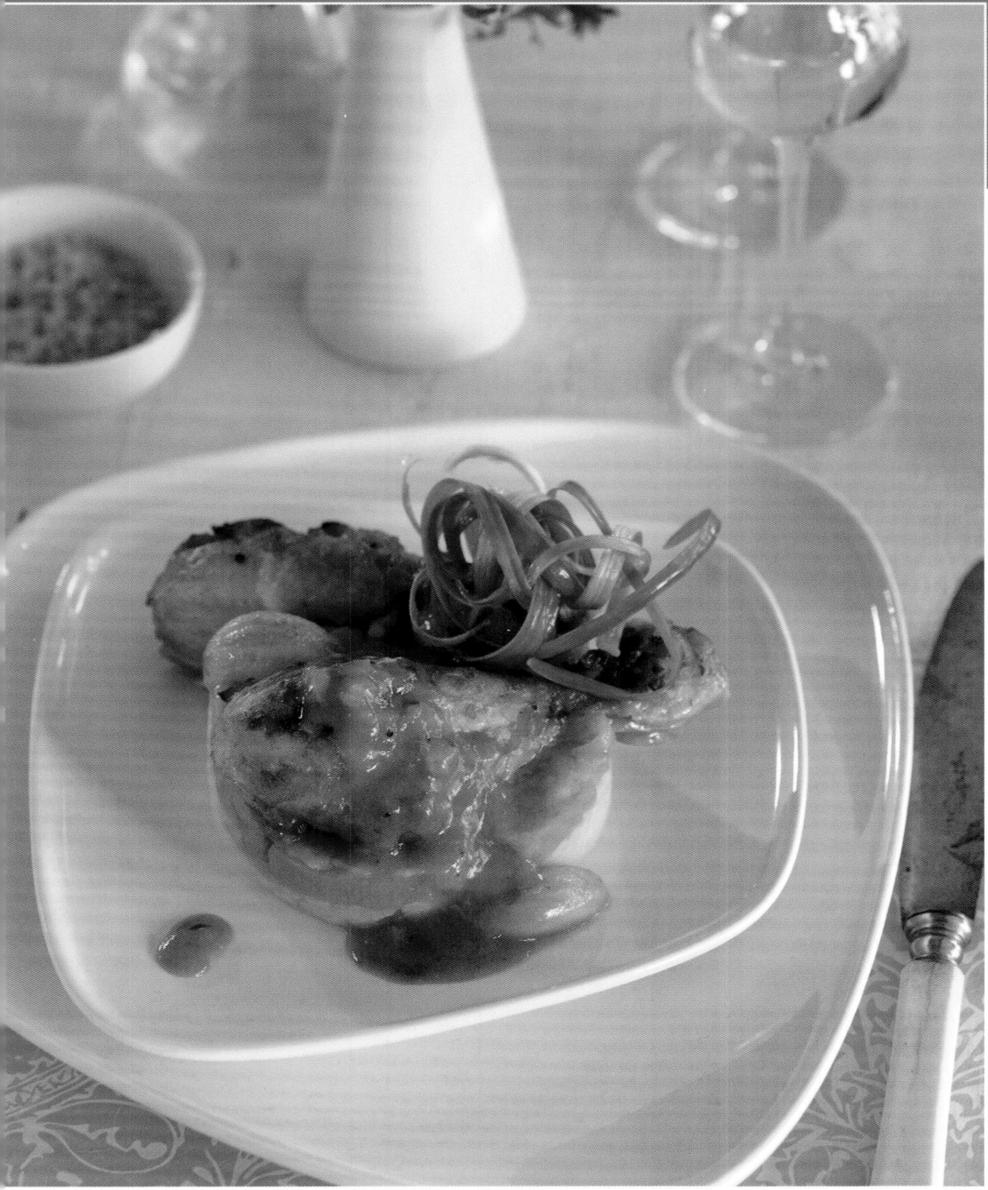

THIS is one of those dishes you can prepare quickly early in the day, then forget about it in the oven while you go out. The long cooking time will result in the succulent, soft-as-anything, falling-off-the-bone kind of chicken that the kids (and adults) love.

The sauce will freeze well, so you can prepare it in advance, then simply defrost and pour over the chicken — and dinner is done.

–L.

Seder Night Chicken

INGREDIENTS

1	chicken, quartered
•	salt
•	coarse black pepper
3 Tbsp	oil
1 cup	orange juice
2 Tbsp	honey
2 Tbsp	potato starch
¼ tsp	ground ginger
¼ tsp	cinnamon (optional)
2	sweet potatoes, peeled and sliced (optional)
2	oranges, supremed

INSTRUCTIONS

1. Heat oil in a sauté pan over medium heat. Pat chicken dry and season with salt and pepper. Add chicken, skin side down, to sauté pan and cook for 6-10 minutes, until chicken is beginning to brown. Turn chicken skin side up and cook additional 5 minutes. Remove chicken from pan and set aside.
2. Add orange juice and honey to the pan. Stir in potato starch, ginger, and cinnamon (optional). Return chicken pieces to the pan. Place sweet potato slices beside and over the chicken. Cover and cook over medium-low heat for 75-90 minutes. Check the chicken periodically to ensure there is plenty of liquid in the pan to avoid burning.
3. Before serving, add orange supremes and cook for 2-3 minutes. Serve hot.

If you're not a fan of ginger, replace it with garlic.

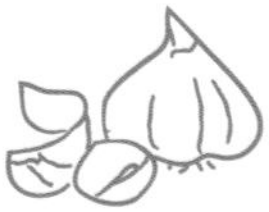

YIELD

4 servings

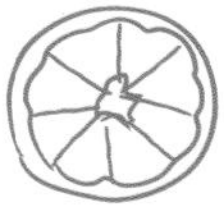

Never supremed an orange before? *See page 37 for more about this technique.*

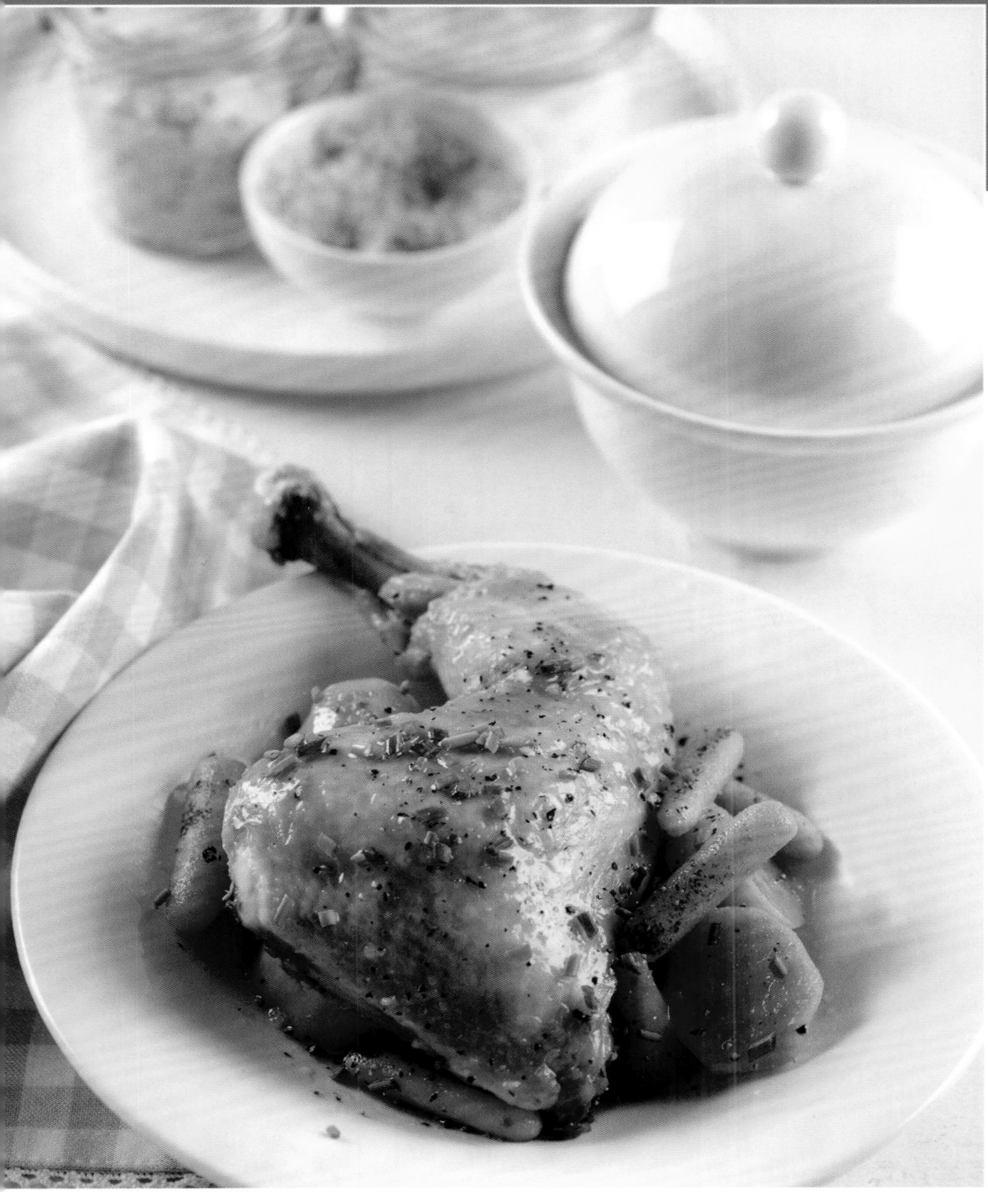

IT'S a widespread custom to avoid serving broiled or roasted meat or chicken during the Seder meal. That's the reason so many people turn to the stovetop to prepare their main dish. On one side of my family, they like the chicken from the soup, or as we call it, "Chicken of the Sea." But for the other side, who prefer a formal main, we now have this dish that also makes a great one-pot meal any night of the year.

–L.

Schnitzel Nuggets *with Apricot Dipping Sauce*

INGREDIENTS

1½ lbs	chicken cutlets, cut into nuggets
•	oil for frying

BATTER

1 cup	potato starch
1 tsp	salt
1 Tbsp	paprika
½ cup	water
2 tsp	oil
2	eggs
1 tsp	baking powder

SAUCE

½ cup	apricot jam
¼ cup	brown sugar
¼ cup	ketchup
1 Tbsp	lemon juice or vinegar
1	garlic clove, crushed
•	pinch salt
•	pinch coarse black pepper

INSTRUCTIONS

1. In a medium bowl, combine potato starch, salt, paprika, water, oil, eggs, and baking powder. Add chicken nuggets to batter.

2. Heat oil in a small saucepan over medium-high heat. When oil is hot, add chicken nuggets, a few at a time, and fry until golden, about 5-6 minutes.

3. Prepare the dipping sauce: In a small saucepan over medium heat, combine jam, brown sugar, ketchup, lemon juice, garlic, salt, and pepper. Cook, stirring occasionally, until sugar is dissolved.

4. Serve dipping sauce alongside chicken, or toss with chicken in a heated skillet. Alternatively, for softer nuggets, you can drizzle the sauce over the chicken and bake for 10 to 15 minutes.

You can also use this batter to make fried fish or onion rings.

YIELD
4 servings

Prefer a made-from-scratch sauce? Use the Homemade Duck Sauce in the Braised Short Ribs recipe on page 60.

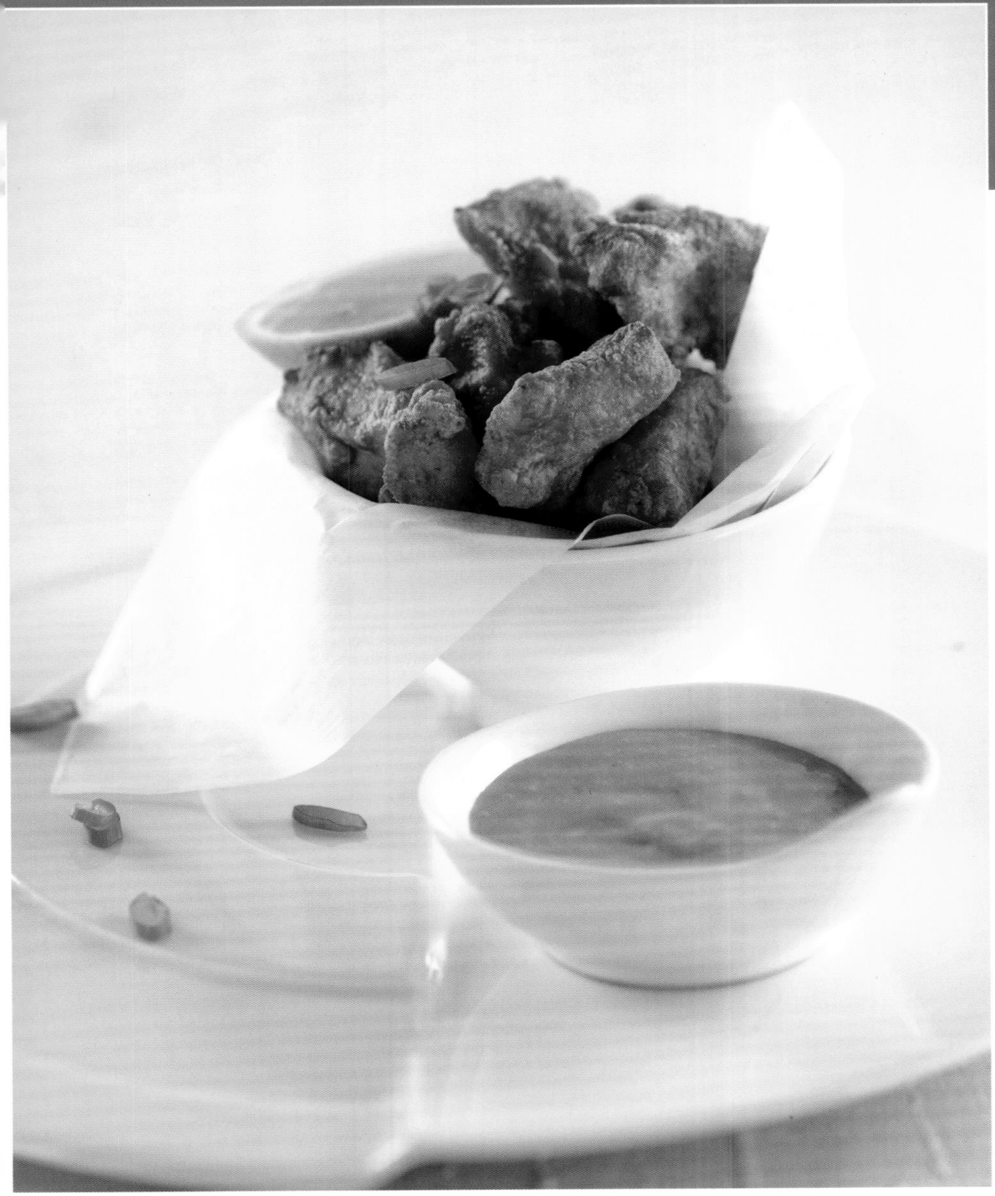

WHEN it comes to a kid-friendly dish, a fried chicken cutlet is a top contender, and we couldn't leave a Passover version out of this book. When my previous cookbook was published, I heard that many kids were requesting dinners based on the photos. So, kids, if you're reading this, point this one out to mom to prepare for dinner at least once during Passover.

You can also enjoy this dish sesame chicken-style by tossing it with the sauce. -L.

Eggplant-Wrapped Chicken

INGREDIENTS

EGGPLANT

1	tall eggplant
½ cup	oil
¼ tsp	salt
•	pinch coarse black pepper

MEAT MIXTURE

3 Tbsp	oil
1	onion, diced
2	garlic cloves, minced
½ lb	ground meat
½ tsp	salt
½ tsp	garlic powder

CHICKEN

6	boneless skinless chicken thighs
¼ tsp	salt
•	pinch coarse black pepper

INSTRUCTIONS

1. Preheat oven to broil. Grease a baking sheet. Cut eggplant lengthwise, ¼-inch thick, to get 6 or 7 slices. Reserve remaining eggplant scraps. Place eggplant slices on prepared baking sheet. Brush slices with oil and season with salt and pepper. Broil 5 minutes per side, until second side is beginning to brown. The slices should appear as if they were fried. Remove and set aside.

2. Preheat oven to 350°F.

3. Peel and finely dice remaining eggplant to obtain ½ cup diced eggplant. Heat oil in a sauté pan over medium heat. Add onion, garlic, and diced eggplant and sauté until soft, about 5-7 minutes.

4. In a small bowl, combine onion mixture with ground meat. Season with salt and garlic powder.

5. Season chicken thighs with salt and pepper. Place a tablespoon of the meat mixture into each thigh and roll up to close. Roll a eggplant slice around each stuffed chicken thigh. Place, seam side down and close together, in a baking pan. Cover and bake for 2½ hours.

YIELD
4-6 servings

TIDBIT:
Sephardic Jews re-enact the Exodu from Egypt following the Seder step of Yachatz. They take turns slinging the afikomon bag over their shoulder and responding to questions.
Q: "Where are you coming from?"
A: "From Egypt."
Q: "Where are you going?"
A: "To Yerusha-layim."
Q: "What are you carrying?"
A: "Matzah and marror."

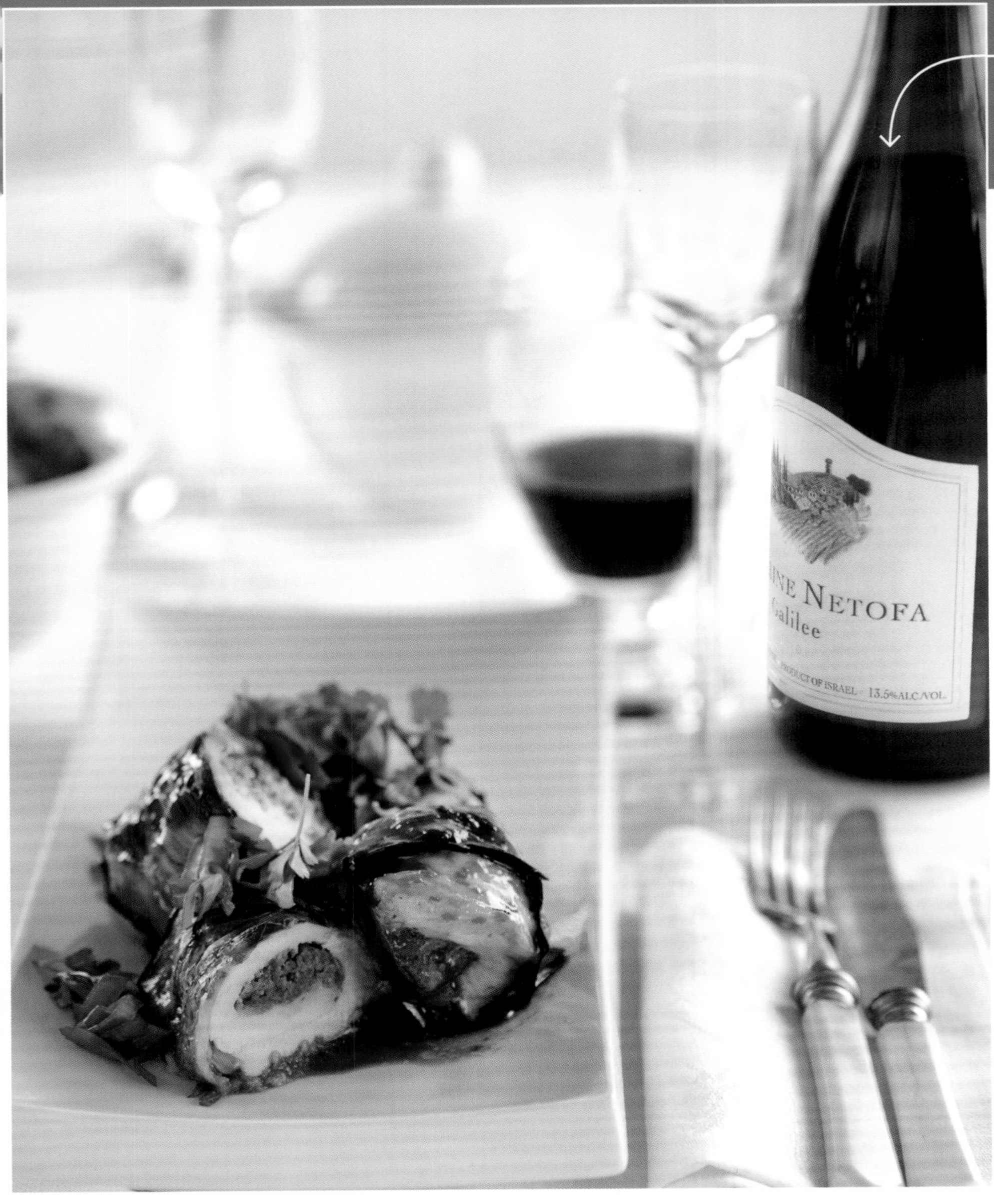
Netofa
Galilee
Product of Israel · 13.5%Alc./Vol.

Wine Pairing:
Domaine
Netofa Red

WHEN Shaya was eating this dish in his mother-in-law Rachel's house, he asked his wife Raizel, "Why don't you make this as good as your mom does?"

Raizel answered, "Because you told me you're on a diet, and I listened!"

Raizel had attempted a low-fat version of this dish. A good wife does as her husband asks. And a good mother-in-law keeps her son-in-law spoiled with good food. –V.

Veal Chops in White Wine Sauce

INGREDIENTS

6	veal chops
•	salt to taste
•	coarse black pepper to taste
3-4 Tbsp	oil
1	large onion, diced
8 oz	mushrooms, sliced (optional)
½ cup	white wine
½ cup	chicken stock
1 tsp	potato starch, dissolved in 2-3 Tbsp water
2 Tbsp	chopped fresh parsley

INSTRUCTIONS

1. Preheat oven to 350°F.

2. Season both sides of each veal chop with salt and pepper. Heat oil in a sauté pan over medium heat. Sear veal for 3-4 minutes on each side. Remove and place into a baking pan.

3. Add onion to the sauté pan over medium heat and sauté until soft and golden, about 7 minutes. Add mushrooms, if using, and cook additional 5 minutes. Add white wine and chicken stock, deglazing the pan, and cook additional 5 minutes. Stir in dissolved potato starch. Lower heat and cook until sauce thickens. Pour sauce over veal. Sprinkle with parsley. Cover and bake for 1½-2 hours. (Veal can be frozen at this point.) Uncover and bake for 20 minutes.

"Deglazing" describes the act of pouring liquid into a very hot pan, stirring to dislodge the delicious brown bits stuck to the bottom of the pan.

YIELD

6 servings

INSPIRED BY COOKKOSHER MEMBER
CookMama

Second cut veal chops have more fat that will render during the cooking, resulting in very tender and tasty meat. First cut veal chops will be leaner and prettier.

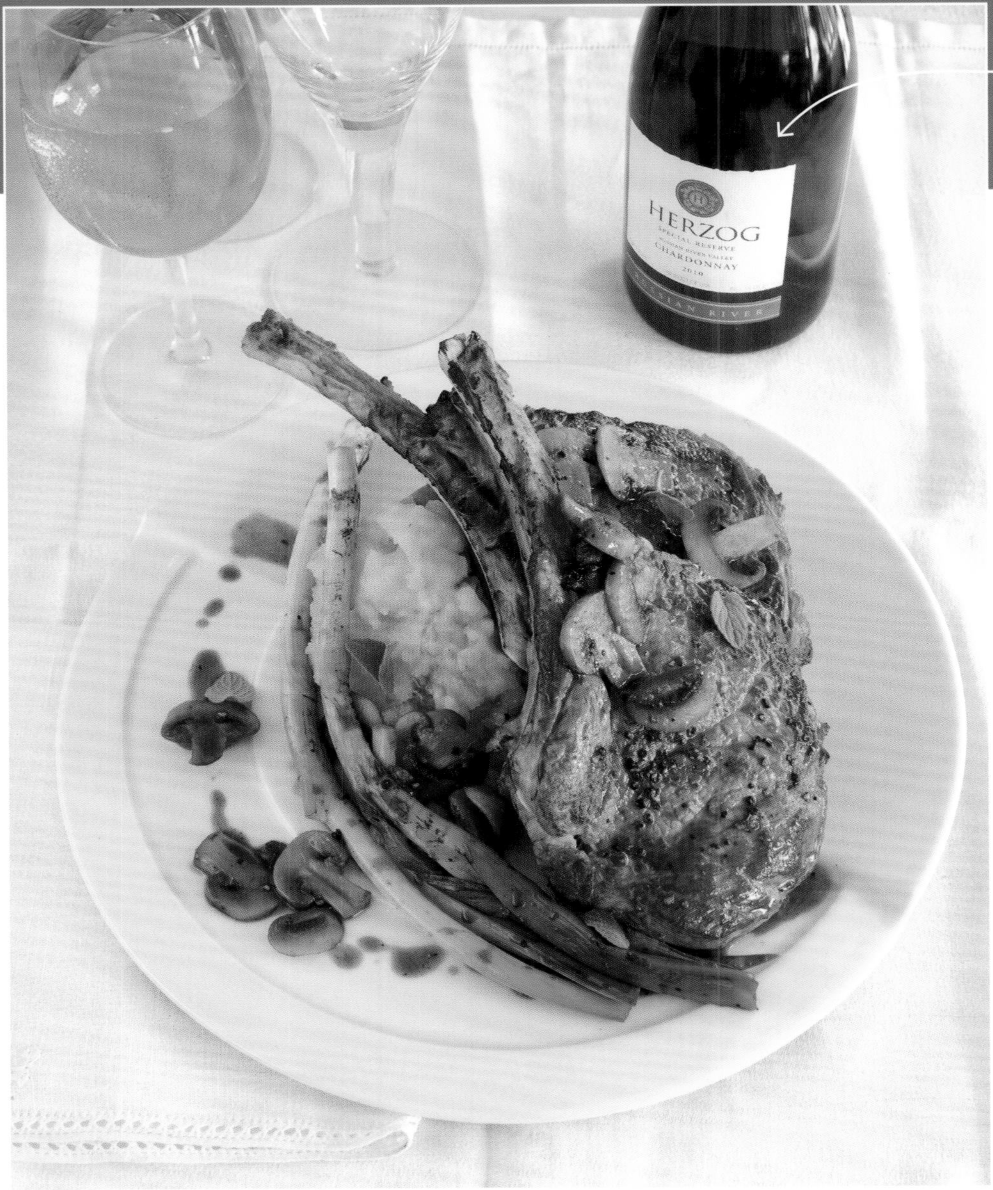
HERZOG
SPECIAL RESERVE
CHARDONNAY
2010

Wine Pairing:
Herzon Reserve
Russian River
Chardonnay

I save this recipe for holidays and special occasions. You can also use veal cutlets or veal spare ribs, but I prefer veal chops. They just look more elegant and special, and my family and guests love them. I've even made this recipe using chicken cutlets. Just reduce the amount of cooking time. This veal also freezes very well, so it's a great entrée to prepare in advance and check off your list. –L.

French Roast *with* Fresh Spice Rub

INGREDIENTS

1	small onion, cut into chunks
1	firm plum tomato, halved, seeds and juice removed
1½ tsp	salt
¼ tsp	black pepper
1 (3-lb)	French roast
¼ cup	oil

INSTRUCTIONS

1. In the bowl of a food processor, combine onion and tomato. Pulse until coarse. Add salt and pepper and pulse until smooth.

2. Place the roast into a 9 x 13-inch baking pan. Rub tomato-onion mixture all over roast. Drizzle oil over roast.

3. Preheat oven to broil. Place the baking pan on a baking sheet to catch any splatters during broiling. Broil roast for 15 minutes. Flip roast and broil additional 15 minutes. Remove from oven.

4. Preheat oven to 300°F. Cover roast and bake for 2 hours. Slice and serve with pan juices.

Make it ahead! After slicing, freeze this roast with the pan juices.

YIELD
4-6 servings

TIDBIT:
Hungarian Jews had the custom of eating broiled meat the night before the Seder night. Since we are not permitted to eat broiled meat at the Seder, they wished to show that we refrain only because of the prohibition.

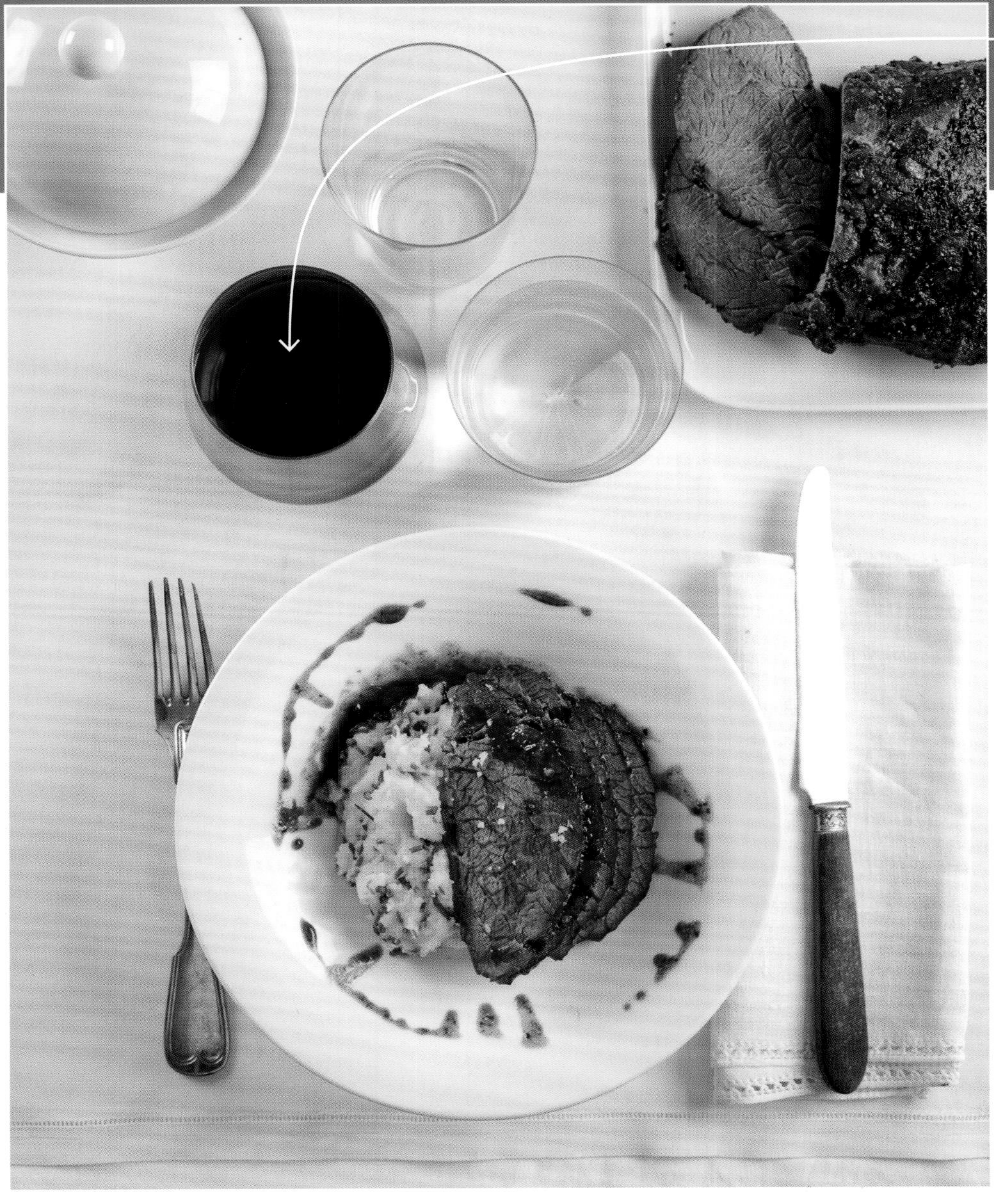

Wine Pairing:
Psagot Merlot

FINALLY! A roast that doesn't call for loads of processed ingredients poured over it. Our wet rub, made of fresh ingredients, combined with the initial broiling step, creates a savory and delectable crust around the roast. When the roast is then covered and cooked at a low temperature, the meat inside cooks to a soft, buttery texture. *–L.*

Braised Short Ribs *in* Homemade Duck Sauce

INGREDIENTS

1 Tbsp	oil
1	red onion, diced
6 Tbsp	sugar
½ tsp	chopped fresh ginger
•	juice of ½ lemon (about 1½ Tbsp)
2 tsp	potato starch
1 cup	orange juice
•	salt to taste
•	coarse black pepper to taste
3 lbs	short spare ribs

INSTRUCTIONS

1. Preheat oven to 300°F.

2. Heat oil in a sauté pan over medium heat. Add onion and sugar and cook, stirring constantly, for 10 minutes, until mixture is syrupy. Add ginger and lemon juice.

3. Dissolve potato starch in orange juice and add to the pot. Season with salt and pepper. Continue to cook until sauce thickens, about 3-4 minutes.

4. Place ribs into a 9 x 13-inch baking pan. Season with salt and pepper. Pour sauce over ribs. Cover tightly and bake for 2 hours. When serving, pour sauce over ribs.

YIELD
4-6 servings

You can also use this sauce over flanken, chicken, or fish.

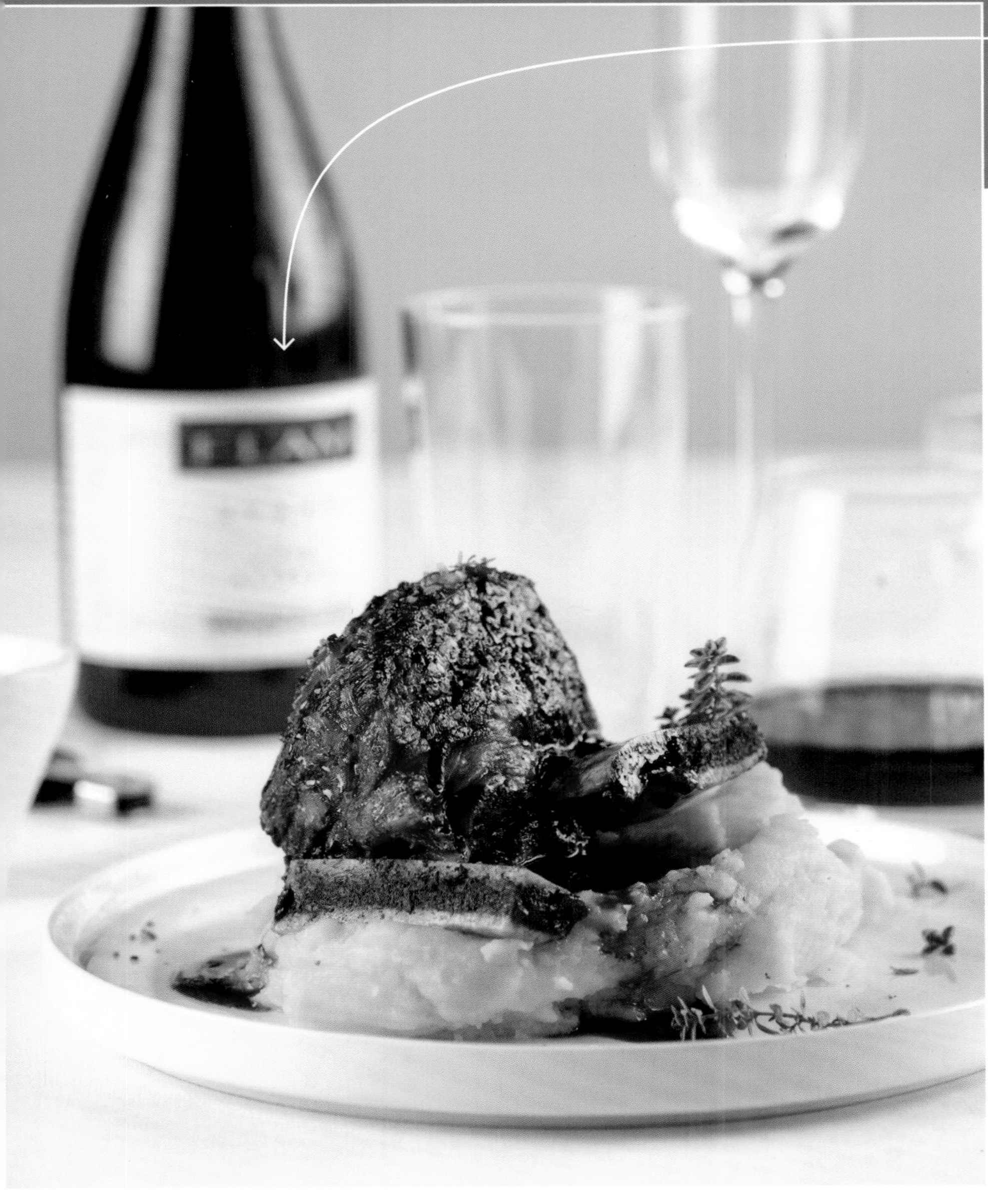
FLAM

Wine Pairing: Flam Reserve Syrah

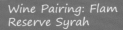

THIS is one that I know I'm going to be making all year round. When I first served Leah's sauce over short ribs, it took a few moments until I received a reaction from the men around the table. That's because they were busy enjoying the meat and didn't want to be disturbed. After they swallowed and verbalized their impression with an "A+," I knew we had a keeper. And I'm so happy it's a recipe I can make with real ingredients from my fridge and pantry and not another bottle of processed sauce.

Though ribs can be baked at 350°F, I like to cook them lower and slower to yield even softer meat. –V.

Sweet Potato Pepper Steak

INGREDIENTS

1½ lbs	pepper steak
•	salt to taste
•	coarse black pepper to taste
1–2 Tbsp	oil
1	medium onion, sliced into half moons
1	medium red onion, sliced into half moons
3¼ cups	chicken stock, divided (or more to cover)
1	sweet potato, peeled and grated
2 Tbsp	potato starch

INSTRUCTIONS

1. Season the pepper steak with salt and pepper. Heat oil in a sauté pan over medium-high heat. Add steak and sear in batches until browned, about 3 minutes per side. Remove meat and set aside.

2. Add onions to the pan and sauté until soft, about 5 minutes. Add more oil if necessary. Return meat to the pan, lower heat, and cook for 15-20 minutes (watch carefully so that it doesn't burn).

3. Add 2½ cups chicken stock. Add additional chicken stock if necessary to cover the meat. Add sweet potato. Cover and cook over low heat for 1 hour and 45 minutes. Check periodically to see if additional chicken stock is needed. (If the mixture is burning, lower heat further.)

4. In a small bowl, combine remaining ¾ cup cold chicken stock and potato starch. Add to pot. Raise heat to medium and continue to cook for 30 minutes, until sauce thickens. Taste and adjust seasoning.

Use beef stew, cubed chuck, or sliced cooked tongue in place of the pepper steak.

YIELD
4 servings

Serve with mashed potatoes or sweet potatoes. See Plate It! on page 46 for a great technique.

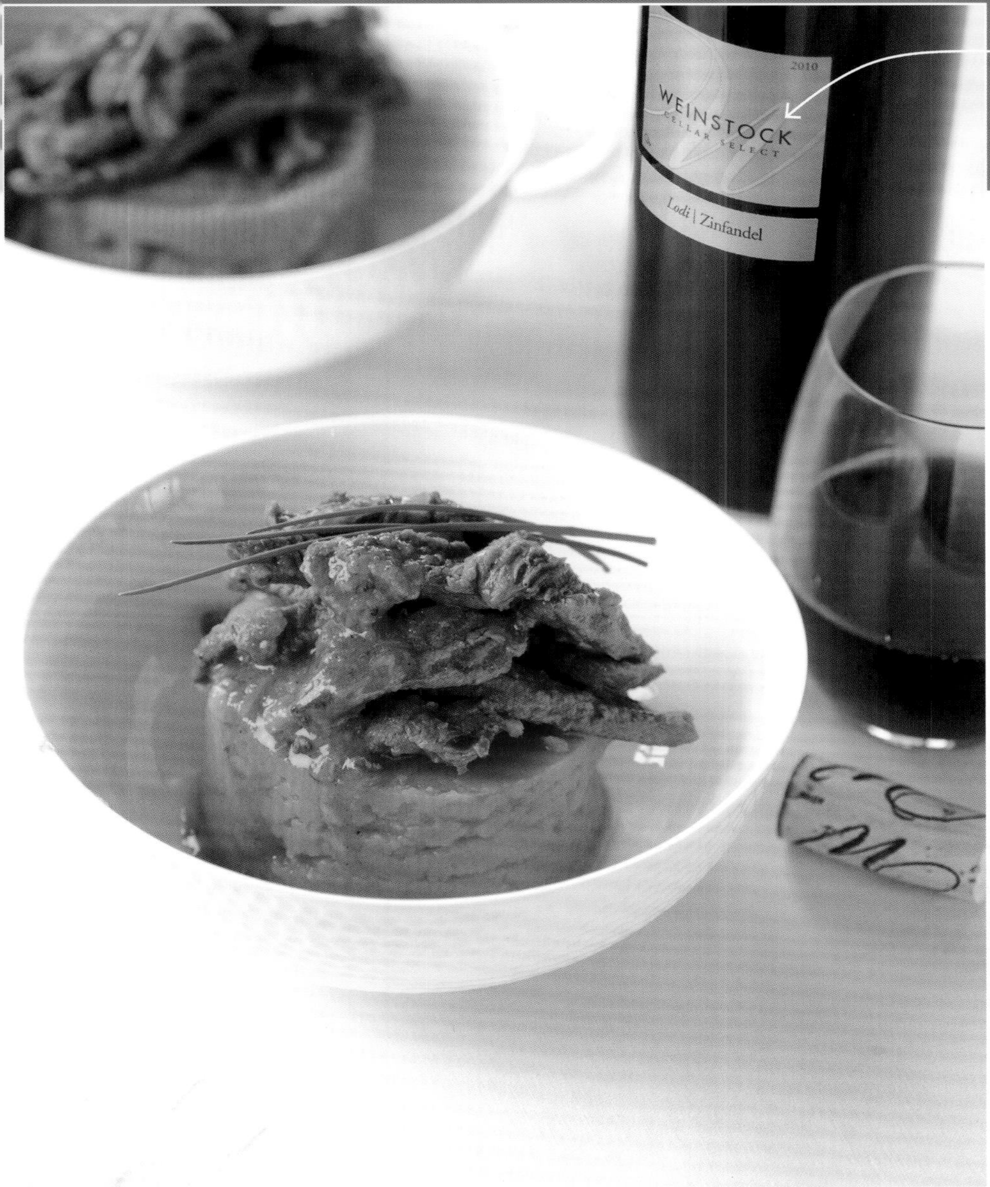
WEINSTOCK
CELLAR SELECT
2010
Lodi | Zinfandel

Wine Pairing:
Weinstock Cellar
Select Zinfandel

WHOEVER named pepper steak didn't consider the fact that not everyone likes peppers with their steak. Sans peppers, this is a recipe for those who want to enjoy a fresh flavor with this tender cut of meat. It's true comfort food in every sense of the word. The pepper steak also freezes very well. –L.

Tortillas *with* Tomato-Mint Salsa & Guacamole [GEBROKTS]

INGREDIENTS

TORTILLAS

1 cup	matzah meal or cake meal
½ tsp	salt
1 Tbsp	olive oil
1	egg
1 cup	water

MEAT FILLING

2 Tbsp	oil
1	onion, finely diced
1 lb	ground meat
2 tsp	chili powder
1 tsp	garlic powder
1 tsp	salt

TOMATO-MINT SALSA

2 cups	grape tomatoes, halved
1 Tbsp	fresh chopped mint leaves
1	jalapeño pepper, seeded, and minced

Ingredients continue on the next page →

INSTRUCTIONS

1. Prepare the tortillas: In a small bowl, combine matzah meal, salt, oil, egg, and water until thoroughly combined. Let batter rest for 5 minutes.

2. Grease a nonstick frying pan and heat over medium heat. Scoop ½ cup batter and drop it into frying pan. Using the greased bottom of a measuring cup, press the batter down to flatten into a round tortilla shape. Cook 3-4 minutes. Flip and cook additional 2-3 minutes. Repeat with remaining batter.

3. Prepare the meat filling: Heat oil in a sauté pan over medium heat. Add onion and sauté until soft, about 5 minutes. Add meat and cook until completely browned, stirring constantly. Season with chili powder, garlic powder, and salt.

4. Prepare the tomato-mint salsa: In a small bowl, stir together tomatoes, mint, jalapeño, onion, vinegar, salt, and pepper. Set aside.

5. Prepare the guacamole: In a small bowl, combine avocado, lime juice, red onion, olive oil, vinegar, garlic powder, and salt. Mash until guacamole is desired texture.

6. To serve, spread guacamole in the center of one tortilla. Top with meat and tomato-mint salsa. Top each tortilla with 2 tablespoons coleslaw (this adds great crunch and sweetness) and fold up.

YIELD

4 servings

INSPIRED BY COOKKOSHER MEMBER
AbbyPires and markowitzfam

TIDBIT:
Romaine lettuce, according to many, is the preferred vegetable to use for marror. Horseradish was commonly used for marror in Europe because Romaine lettuce was not widely cultivated there.

ALL year long, my kids beg me to make their favorite taco dinner, and this year, I can please them on Passover too. Place all the components of this dish on the table, and let everyone assemble their own sandwiches. It's a complete dinner in one recipe that's also refreshing, filling, and bursting with flavor.

Adjust the amount of jalapeño pepper in the tomato-mint salsa according to your heat tolerance. If you don't eat *gebrokts* on Passover, use a crepe to hold the filling together. –V.

INGREDIENTS CONTINUED

¼	red onion, finely chopped
1 Tbsp	white wine vinegar
¼ tsp	salt, divided
¼ tsp	fresh black pepper

LIME GUACAMOLE

1	avocado
•	juice of 1 lime

¼	red onion, finely diced
½ Tbsp	olive oil
½ Tbsp	vinegar
•	garlic powder to taste
•	salt to taste
½ cup	prepared coleslaw, for serving

Barbecue Rib Steak *with* Honey-Horseradish Glaze

INGREDIENTS

½ cup	honey
2 Tbsp	olive oil
¼ cup	grated horseradish
3	garlic cloves, minced
1 tsp	salt
1 tsp	coarse black pepper
4	rib steaks

INSTRUCTIONS

1. In a small bowl, combine honey, oil, horseradish, garlic, salt, and pepper. Baste onto rib steaks, reserving ¼ of the glaze. Marinate at room temperature for 15 minutes.
2. Preheat the BBQ grill or grease a grill pan. Cook steaks, about 6 minutes per side, depending on desired doneness. When cooking is complete, brush steaks with reserved glaze. Let rest for 5 minutes and serve.

YIELD

4 servings

INSPIRED BY COOKKOSHER MEMBER

Chanee

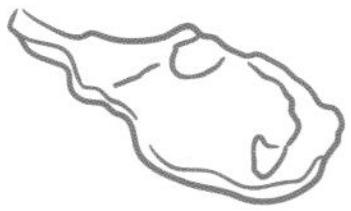

If you're preparing these steaks in advance, grill only 3 minutes per side; then refrigerate. Allow steaks to come to room temperature before rewarming and bake at 375°F for about 8 minutes, depending on thickness and desired doneness. Brush with reserved glaze.

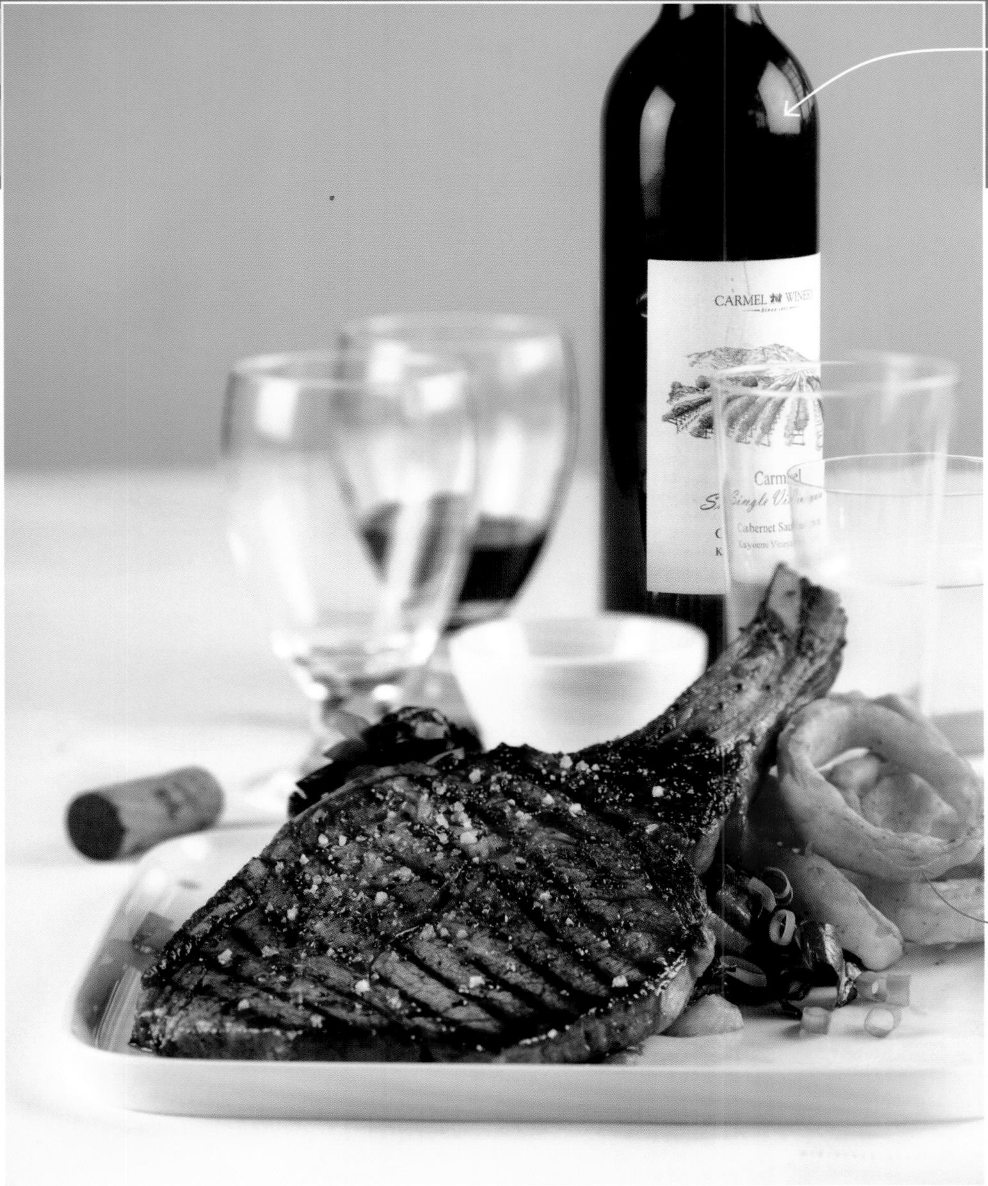
CARMEL

Wine Pairing:
Carmel Kayoumi
Cabernet Sauvignon

RIB steaks are my go-to dinner when I don't have time to cook, but I don't want my family to think I'm neglecting them. To the contrary, they think it's a special treat. They're worthy of gracing the table at a holiday meal, but still easy enough for a weekday when I ... um ... yeah ... don't want to cook. If your BBQ grill is in commission during Passover, this is the time to use it.

–V.

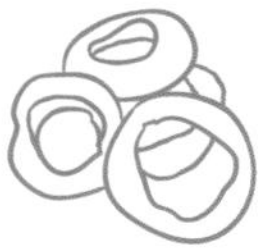

We used the shnitzel batter on page 52 to make these onion rings. Slice onions, separate rings, dip in batter, and deep fry.

Jalapeño–Lime–and–Ginger Salmon

INGREDIENTS

1 tsp	finely grated lime rind
¼ cup	lime juice (from about 2 large limes)
2 tsp	vegetable oil
1 tsp	minced fresh ginger
1	jalapeño pepper, seeded and finely minced
2 (6-oz)	salmon steaks or 4 salmon fillets

INSTRUCTIONS

1. Preheat oven to 350°F. Prepare the marinade: Whisk together the lime rind, lime juice, oil, ginger, and jalapeño. Set aside a teaspoon of the mixture. Place salmon steaks into a dish just large enough to hold them. Pour remaining marinade over salmon and turn to coat.

2. Marinate at room temperature for 15 minutes, turning once. (Do not marinate longer than 30 minutes or salmon will become mushy.)

3. Bake for 15 minutes. Turn oven to broil and broil 3-4 minutes. Fish should flake easily with a fork.

4. Remove to platter and spoon reserved marinade over salmon. Serve immediately.

YIELD

4 servings

INSPIRED BY COOKKOSHER MEMBER

rebecca2011

The seeds and membranes in your jalapeño pepper contain capsaicin, which leaves a burning sensation in your mouth when eaten. Wearing gloves, remove them carefully and discard, or save them to add heat to salsa.

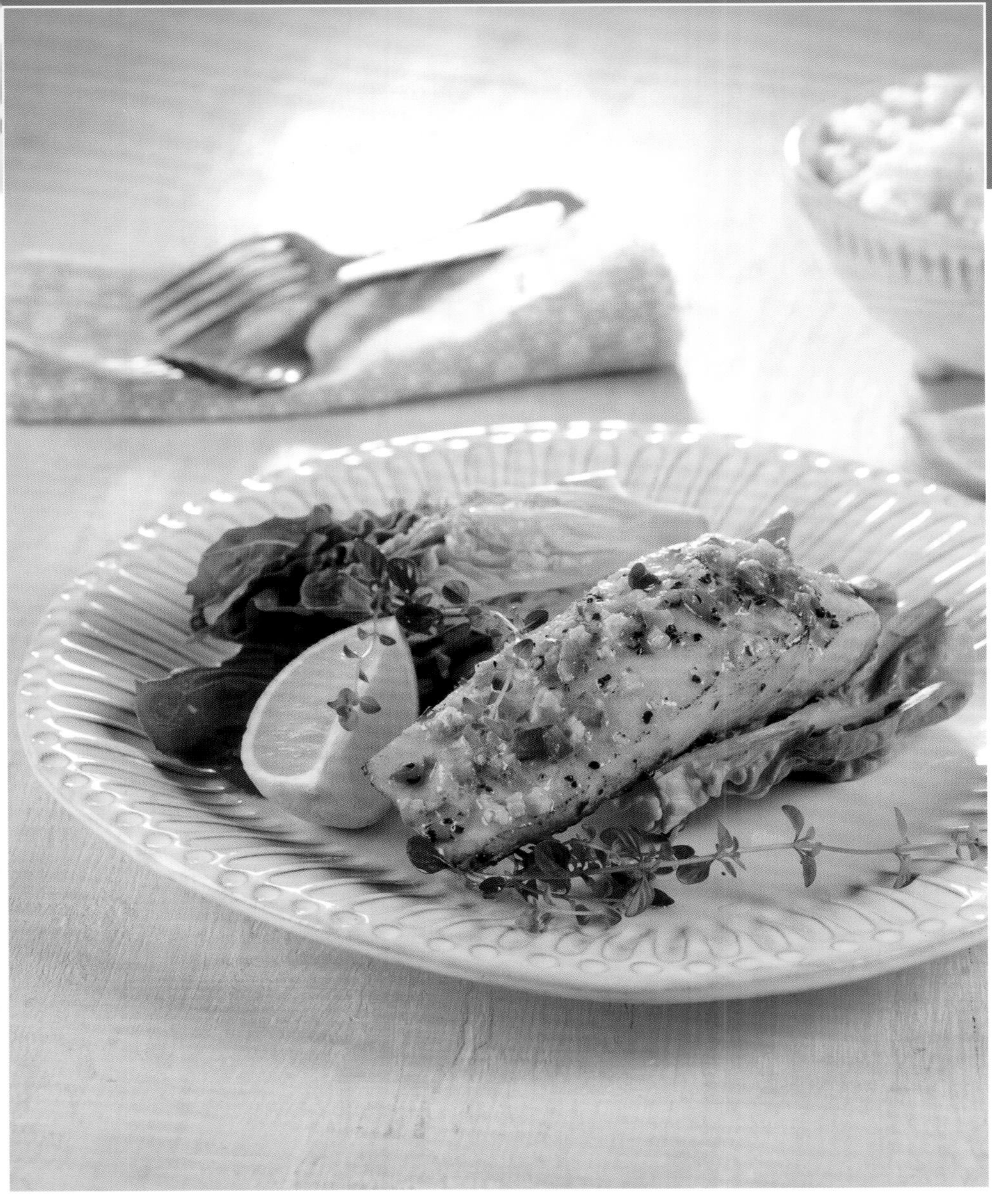

SALMON is very versatile fish that can be dressed with almost anything. Honey mustard, dill, teriyaki ... but after awhile every one of them becomes boring. Jalapeño, though, is exciting. It's a great way to add lots of flavor to your food without fat. —L.

Pesto Lemon Sole *with* Plum Tomatoes

INGREDIENTS

2 cups	fresh basil leaves, loosely packed
4	garlic cloves
½ cup	chopped walnuts
¼ tsp	salt
•	coarse black pepper to taste
4 Tbsp	olive oil
2	plum tomatoes, sliced
4	lemon sole, flounder, or tilapia fillets

INSTRUCTIONS

1. Preheat oven to 350°F.
2. In the bowl of a food processor, combine basil, garlic, walnuts, salt, and pepper. Pulse to combine. Add oil and pulse again to form the pesto.
3. Place fish into a baking pan. Spread pesto mixture over each fillet. Place plum tomato slices over the pesto. Bake, uncovered, until fish flakes easily with a fork, about 15 minutes.

The pesto works perfectly paired with salmon, too.

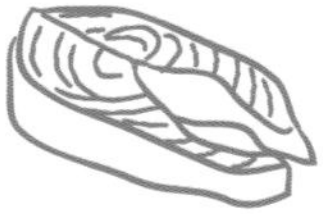

YIELD

4 servings

INSPIRED BY COOKKOSHER MEMBER
mkracoff

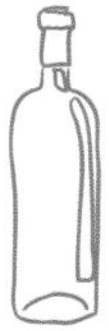

TIDBIT:

A man approached the Beis HaLevi and asked, "Can milk be substituted for the four cups at the Seder?" He answered it could not and gave him money for wine, then added more money to buy meat. He later explained, "If he had meat for his Seder, he wouldn't have thought to ask to use milk for his four cups."

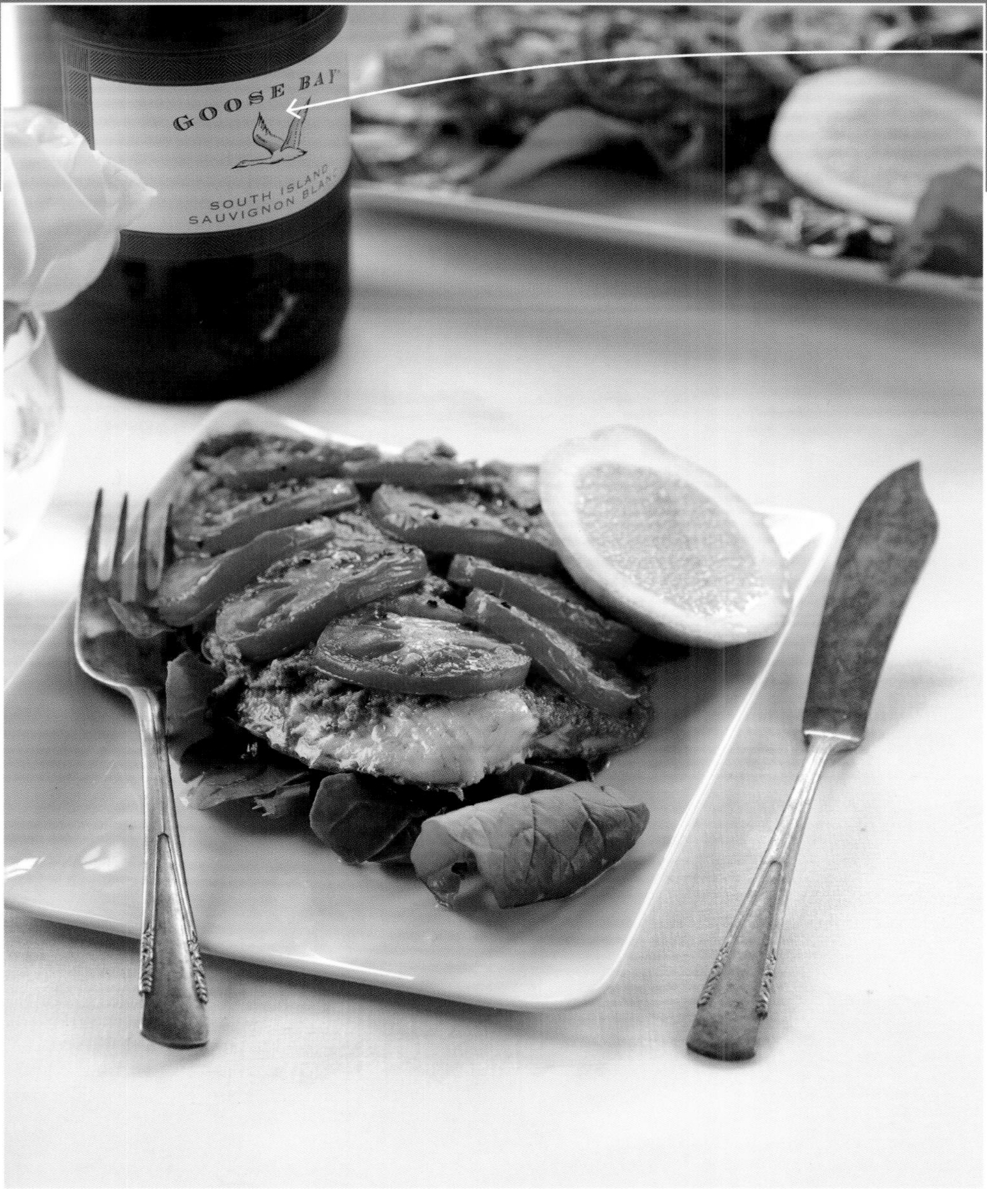
GOOSE BAY
SOUTH ISLAND
SAUVIGNON BLANC

Wine Pairing:
Goose Bay
Sauvignon Blanc

THE night I served this dish for dinner, I had also prepared the Yellow Squash Quiche on page 98. I was very full and satisfied after having my quiche with sour cream, so I relied on my husband's opinion to judge whether the fish was a contender for this book. Later on that evening, when I was clearing the table, I grabbed a fork and took a taste of the left-over fish. Then, I sat down to en-joy more. It was fresh, flavorful, and kept me reaching for anoth-er bite. The oils in the pesto and the plum tomatoes make sure that the fish stays moist. And since I ate this well after dinner was first served, I also know now that it's good served hot or cold. –V.

Honey-Pecan Salmon

INGREDIENTS

1 cup	mayonnaise
3 Tbsp	imitation mustard
3 Tbsp	honey
6	salmon fillets
1 cup	crushed honey-glazed pecans

INSTRUCTIONS

1. Preheat oven to 350°F.
2. In a small bowl, combine mayonnaise, mustard, and honey.
3. Place fillets onto a baking pan.
4. Smear dressing over salmon fillets. Press on pecans to form a crust.
5. Bake until fish flakes easily with a fork, 20-25 minutes.

For a more healthful version, use plain pecans for a dish that's a little less sweet, but still moist and fragrant.

YIELD

6 servings

INSPIRED BY COOKKOSHER MEMBER
Mindeeyounger

TIDBIT:

Some communities have the custom to eat falshe (false) fish, a gefilte-style dish made of ground meat, instead of fish. In those European communities, imported fish was preserved in alcohol, so it couldn't be used on Passover.

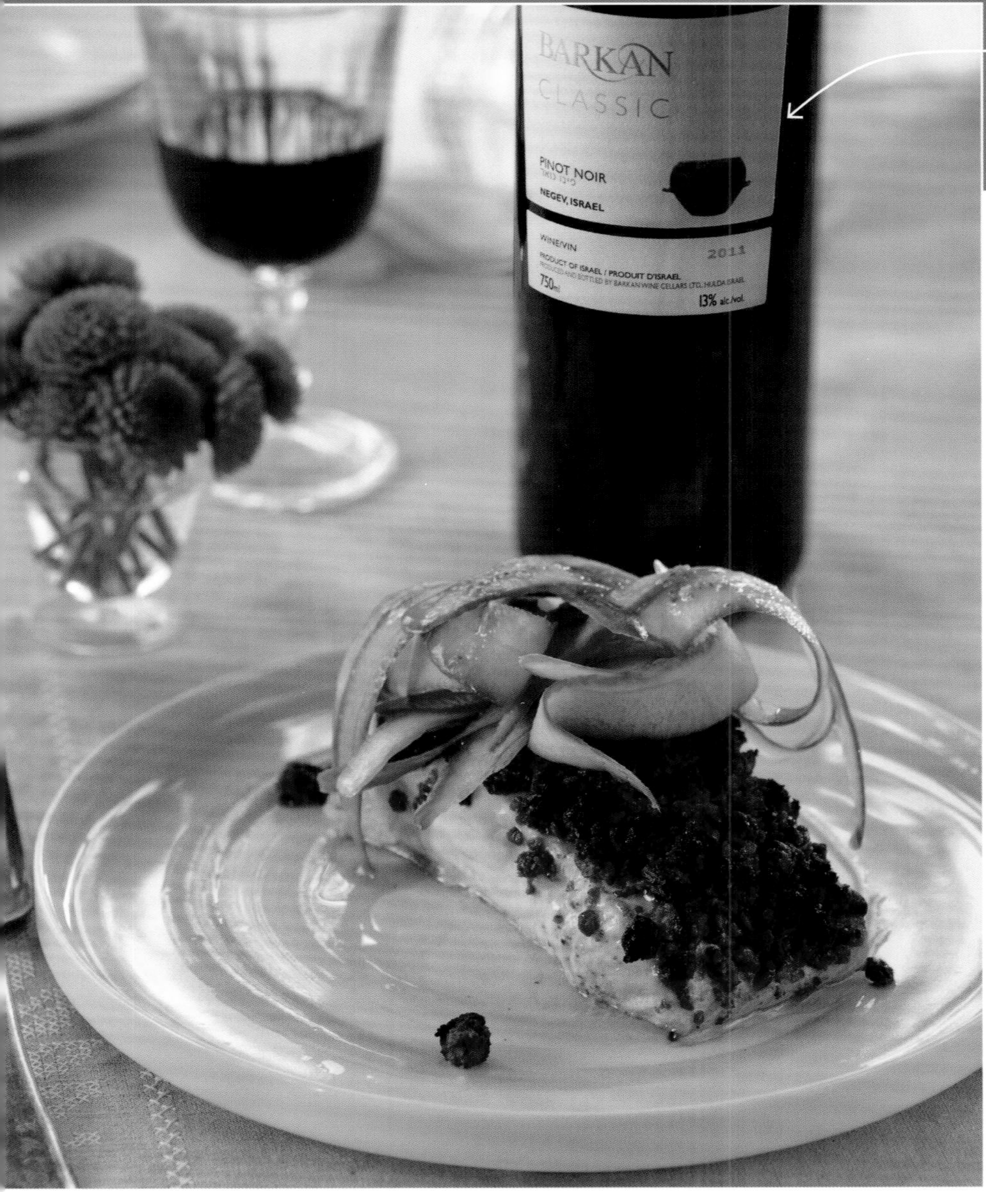
BARKAN
CLASSIC
PINOT NOIR
NEGEV, ISRAEL
WINE/VIN
2011
PRODUCT OF ISRAEL / PRODUIT D'ISRAEL
750ml
13% alc./vol.

*Wine Pairing:
Barkan Classic
Pinot Noir*

EVERY Passover, I look forward to making my easy honey-pecan chicken, where the chicken nuggets are coated in a honey-mayo mixture, and then in a mixture of crushed pecans and Passover crumbs. The nuggets are then baked at 400°F for 10-12 minutes per side. I love the aromatic pecans, and usually end up eating the stray nuts that have fallen into the pan.

The same goes for this salmon. It's foolproof, delicious, and the type of salmon that will please even the non-fish lovers. *–V.*

PLATE IT!

Kugel? Pretty? Impossible. Nope, it's possible. You can do it too. Here's how we plated our Potato and Flanken Kugel (page 86).

1 Slice kugel into two rectangular pieces. Place one piece on top of the other on an angle.

2 Top kugel with some of the shallots from the shallot-wine sauce (see below). Some shallots should fall to the plate.

3 Using a spoon, drizzle with the liquid of the shallot-wine sauce, encircling the kugel.

4 Finally, scatter chopped scallions on the dish.

Shallot-Wine Sauce

Heat oil in a frying pan. Add thinly sliced shallots and saute for 1-2 minutes. Add ¼ cup red wine and 2 tablespoons sugar. Let simmer until liquid is reduced by half.

Side Dishes

Potato-Chip Zucchini Sticks *with* Lemon-Mayo Dipping Sauce

INGREDIENTS

3-4 Tbsp	oil
2	large zucchini
¼ cup	potato starch
2	eggs
¾ tsp	salt
½ tsp	paprika
½ tsp	garlic powder
1 cup	crushed plain potato chips
1 cup	crushed barbecue potato chips

LEMON-MAYO DIPPING SAUCE

½ cup	mayonnaise
1 Tbsp	fresh lemon juice
1	scallion, white and light green parts, finely chopped
¼ tsp	salt
⅛ tsp	coarse black pepper

INSTRUCTIONS

1. Preheat oven to 400°F. Line 2 baking sheets with parchment paper. Brush each sheet with 1-2 tablespoons oil.
2. Slice each zucchini in half lengthwise and then widthwise to form quarters. Slice each quarter lengthwise into about 6 sticks.
3. Place zucchini sticks into a resealable plastic bag. Add potato starch to bag. Seal and shake to coat zucchini sticks in potato starch.
4. In a shallow dish, combine eggs, salt, paprika, and garlic powder. Place each type of crushed chips into a separate shallow dish.
5. Remove zucchini sticks from bag and dip into egg mixture, a few at time, then dip in either flavor of crushed potato chips. Repeat until all zucchini sticks are coated. Place on prepared baking sheets. Bake for 30 minutes.
6. Meanwhile, prepare the dipping sauce: In a small bowl, combine mayonnaise, lemon juice, scallion, salt, and pepper. Serve alongside zucchini sticks.

YIELD

6 servings

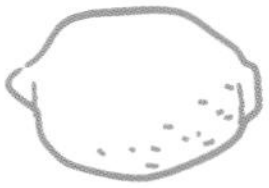

It's important to use freshly squeezed juice when lemon is the main flavor. Roll the lemon, at room temperature, on the counter for easier squeezing.

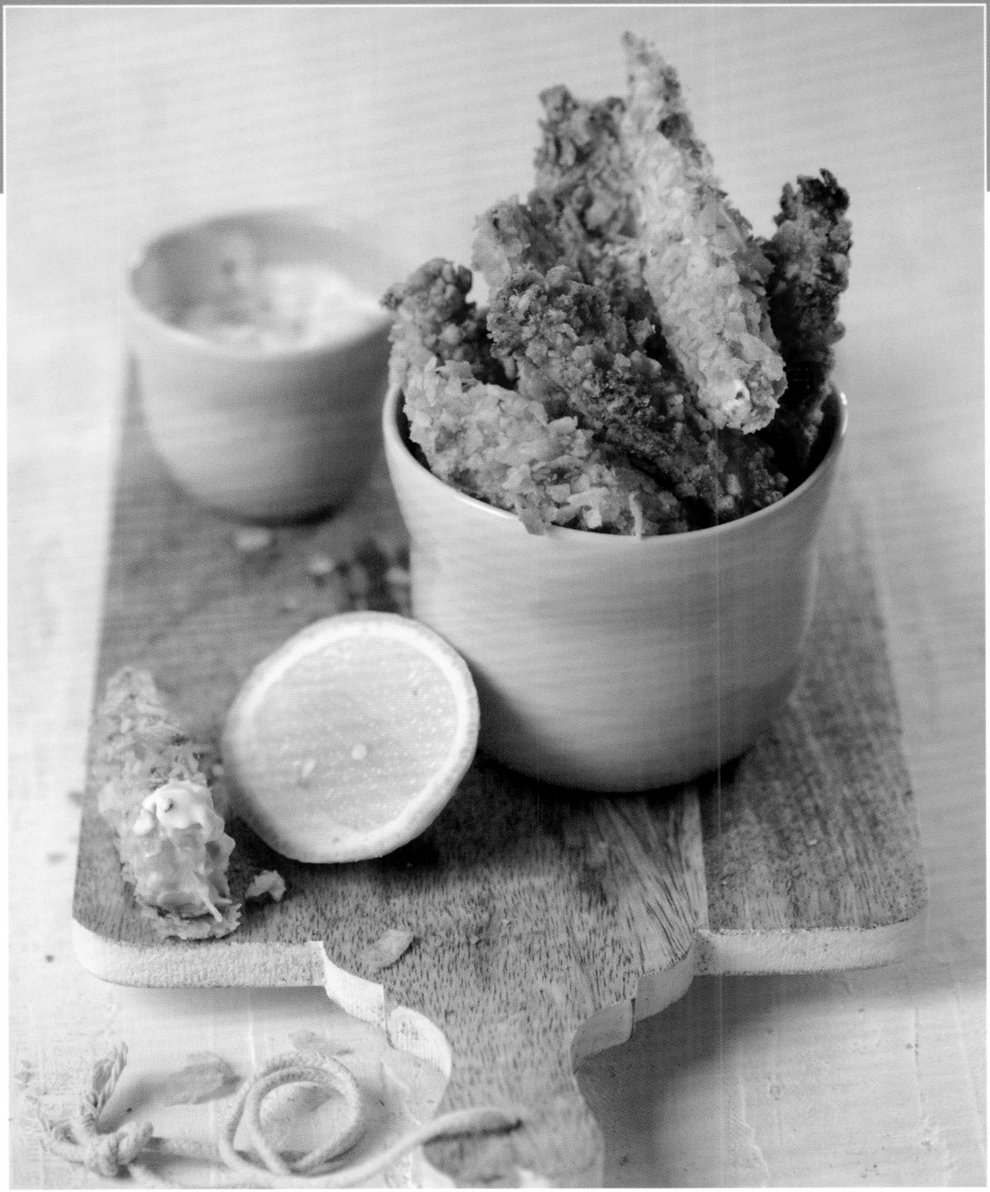

DURING the year, we coat anything we want with bread crumbs, or, my favorite, cornflake crumbs. For Passover, potato chips are the perfect replacement. Have fun playing with different flavors, including ketchup, honey BBQ, and onion and garlic chips — but use chips, not potato sticks.

Don't skip the dipping sauce! You'll love how the tanginess of the lemon complements the zucchini. –L.

Stuffed Onions

INGREDIENTS

8	small onions
1 Tbsp	olive oil

STUFFING

2 Tbsp	olive oil
1	large onion, finely diced
1	sweet potato, peeled and finely diced
1	zucchini, finely diced
1	small eggplant, peeled and finely diced
•	pinch coarse black pepper
1 tsp	onion powder
1-2 tsp	salt
1 cup	ground almonds

INSTRUCTIONS

1. Preheat oven to 350°F. Cutting off as little as possible, remove the two ends of each onion; peel onions. Make a slit through one side of each onion to the center, so that each ring is sliced halfway through.

2. In a large saucepan, bring water to boil. Add onions and boil 15 minutes. Strain and let cool. At this point, it should be easy to peel apart each onion layer. Separate onion layers.

3. Prepare the stuffing: Heat oil in a sauté pan over medium-high heat. Add onion and sweet potato; sauté, stirring occasionally, for 12 minutes. Add zucchini and eggplant. Cover, lower heat, and cook, stirring occasionally, until vegetables are soft and cooked through, about 20-30 minutes. Stir in seasoning and almonds. Remove from heat.

4. Place a spoonful of stuffing into each onion layer. Roll up and seal each layer. (Onions can be frozen at this point.)

5. Place stuffed onions into a baking pan just large enough to hold them. Sprinkle with oil. Cover and bake 20 minutes. Uncover and bake additional 10 minutes.

YIELD
24 stuffed onions

You can use red onions or a combination of red and white to give this dish a different look.

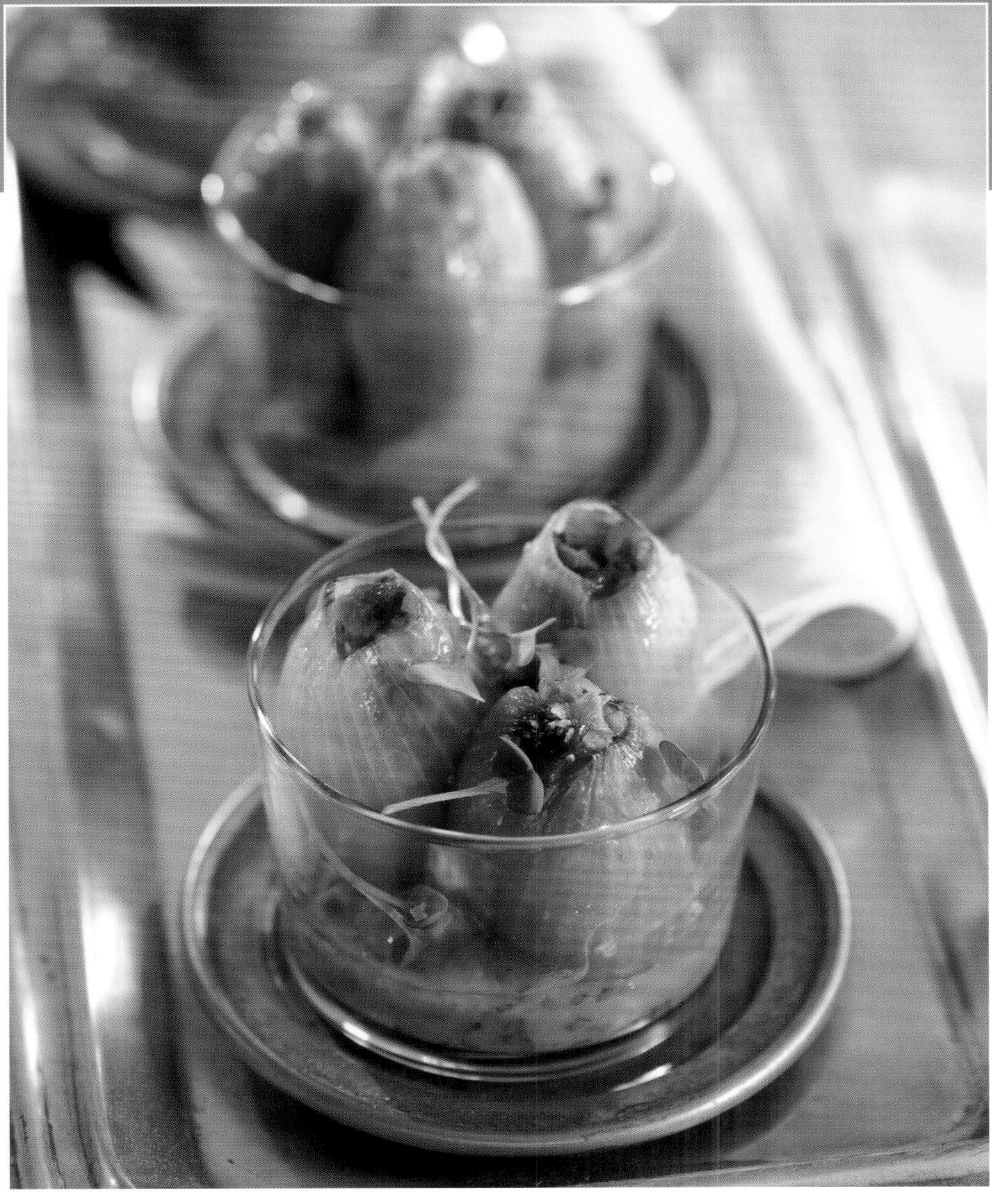

I had fun making these because onions are among the easiest vegetables to stuff. They're also freezer-friendly, so you can prepare this pretty side dish in advance and rewarm before the meal. The ground almonds in the recipe don't only do a great job of binding the stuffing together — they also taste way better than bread crumbs. The end result is a dainty and flavorful little bite. For a prettier presentation, be sure to select round onions. –V.

Spaghetti Squash Kugel

INGREDIENTS

1	spaghetti squash
1 Tbsp	oil
2	onions, finely diced
1	garlic clove, minced
4	eggs, lightly beaten
½ tsp	salt
1 tsp	coarse black pepper

INSTRUCTIONS

1. Preheat oven to 350°F. Wash spaghetti squash and place into a loaf pan. Bake for 1 hour. Remove from oven and let cool. Raise oven heat to 400°F.
2. Slice squash in half and remove seeds. Using a fork, scrape the strands of squash into a large bowl.
3. Heat oil in a sauté pan over medium heat. Add onions and garlic. Sauté until onions are soft, 5-7 minutes. Add onions to spaghetti squash. Add eggs, salt, and pepper. Pour mixture into a 9 x 13-inch baking pan. Bake until kugel is crispy on top, about 1 hour.

Nuke it! For quicker preparation, microwave a whole spaghetti squash for 1 minute to soften. Slice in half and remove seeds. Place cut side down in a dish with ½ inch of water. Microwave for 8-10 minutes. Continue with Step 2.

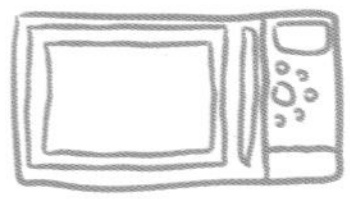

YIELD

6 servings

INSPIRED BY COOKKOSHER MEMBER

Estee

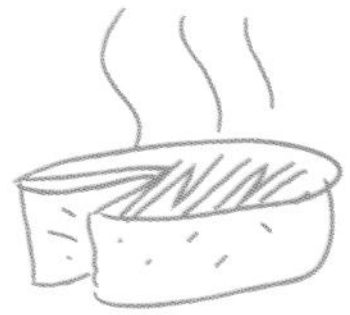

TIDBIT:

Even though we often bake it in square pans nowadays, the word kugel may stem from the Hebrew k'iygul ("as a circle"), referring to its traditionally round shape.

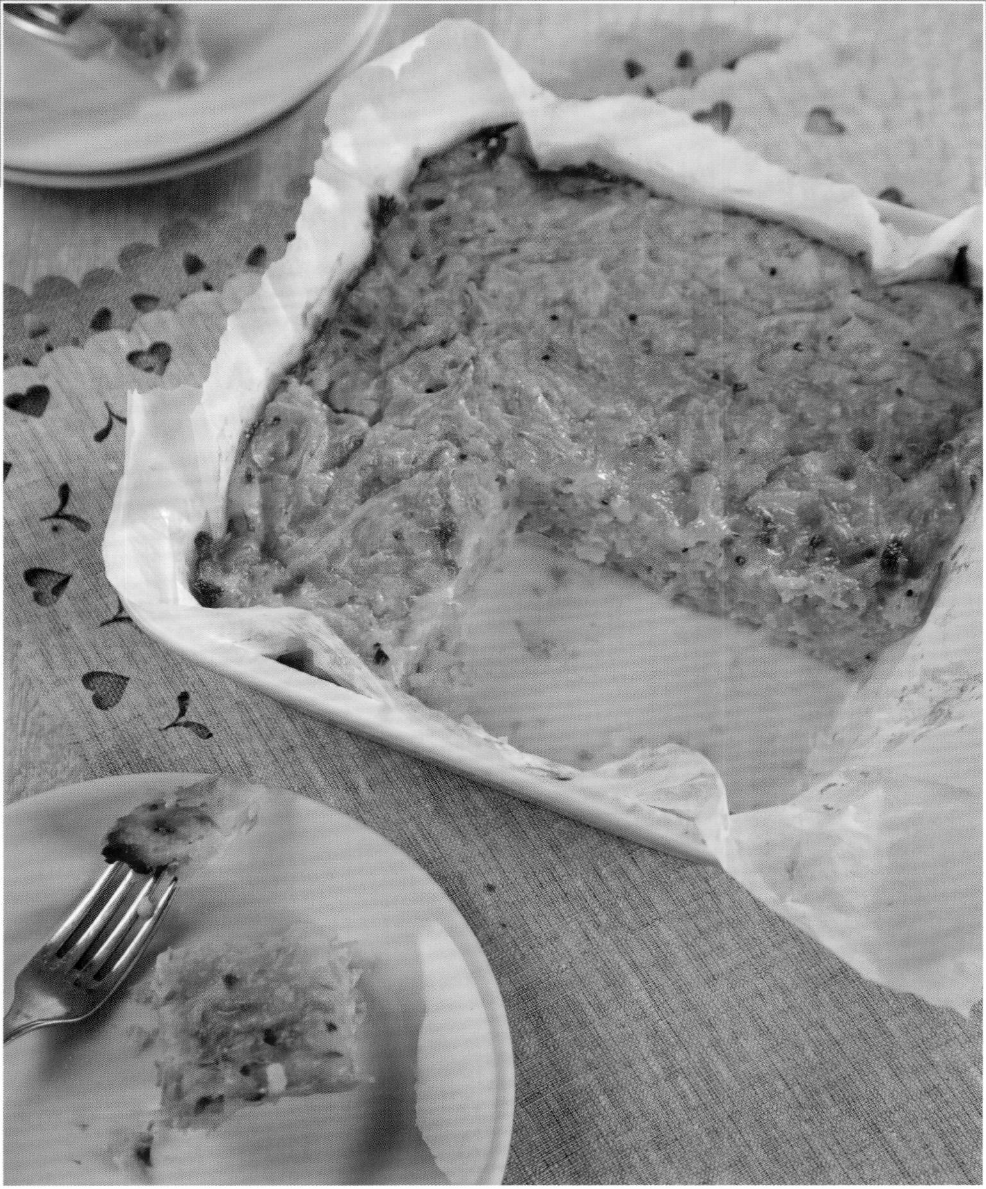

FOR member Estee, this recipe redeemed spaghetti squash. She had tried a few recipes using this unique squash before but had never really loved how they came out. She almost gave up before this kugel emerged from the oven. Spaghetti squash kugel is cool because it looks like noodle kugel, but is actually very low in calories. You can make it even lighter by replacing some of the yolks with whites. –L.

Cauliflower Gratin

INGREDIENTS

3 Tbsp	oil
1	onion, finely diced
1 (24-oz)	bag frozen cauliflower florets, completely thawed, divided
2 Tbsp	mayonnaise
¾ cup	chicken stock
1 tsp	salt
¼ cup	Passover crumbs

INSTRUCTIONS

4. Preheat oven to 375°F. Grease an 8-inch round baking dish. You can also prepare this dish using individual ramekins.

5. Heat oil in a medium saucepan over medium heat. Sauté onion until soft and just beginning to turn golden, 5-7 minutes.

6. Line the bottom of prepared baking pan or ramekins with ⅔ of the cauliflower florets.

7. In the bowl of a food processor, process remaining thawed cauliflower and sautéed onion until smooth. Return mixture to the saucepan. Add 2 tablespoons mayonnaise and chicken stock; bring to a boil over medium-high heat. Stir until mixture thickens, about 1 minute. Season with salt and remove from heat. Pour mixture over cauliflower florets. Sprinkle with Passover crumbs. Bake until top is firm and golden, about 1 hour. Serve hot.

YIELD
4 servings

Passover crumbs can be found on grocery store shelves, or make a batch of our homemade version on page 12. Both versions are not gebrokts.

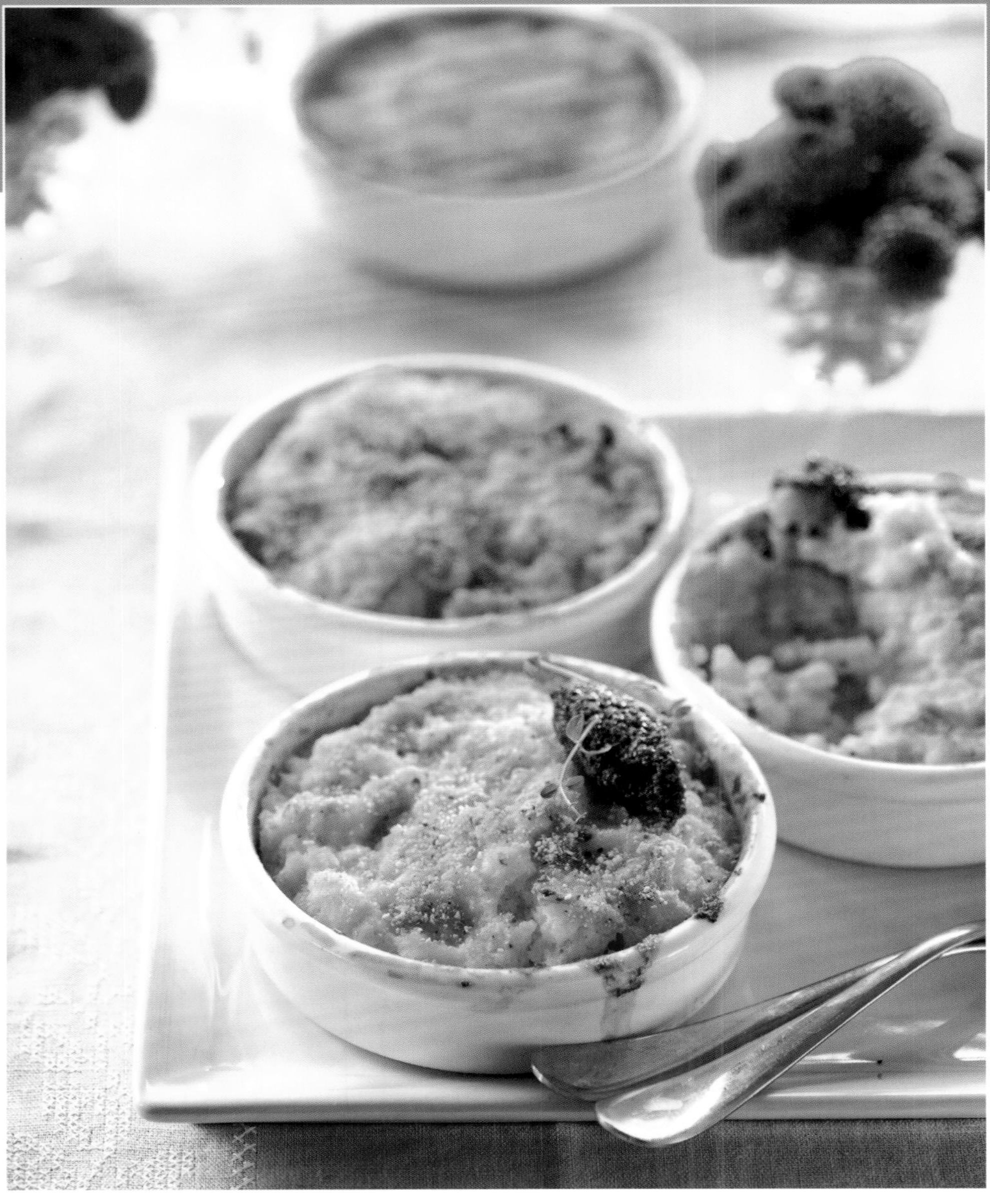

GRATIN dishes always look so yummy. But often, when I want to try one, I stop after I read the ingredient list, which usually includes lots of butter or margarine, cream, and/or cheese. And my next thought is that I'd rather roast my veggies and save all those calories for dessert. This pareve cauliflower version has all the creaminess without the cream, so I can have my cauliflower and plenty of dessert too. –V.

Extra-Crispy Spiced Potato Wedges

INGREDIENTS

6	yellow-skinned potatoes (such as Yukon Gold), cut into wedges
2 Tbsp	potato starch
2	egg whites
2 tsp	water
½ tsp	paprika
½ tsp	onion powder
1 tsp	salt
⅛ tsp	coarse black pepper
3-4 Tbsp	oil

INSTRUCTIONS

1. Preheat oven to 350°F. Line a baking sheet with parchment paper.
2. Add potatoes to a large stockpot. Add salted water to cover and bring to a boil over high heat. Let boil for 20 minutes. Drain completely.
3. In a large bowl, toss potatoes with potato starch. In a small bowl, combine egg whites and water. Beat with a fork until foamy. Add paprika, onion powder, salt, and pepper. Toss potatoes with spiced egg-white mixture.
4. Add oil to prepared baking sheet. Add potatoes and toss to coat. Spread potatoes in an even layer. Bake 90 minutes, or until potatoes reach desired crispness.

Do you like crispy sweet potatoes too? The parboiling-then-roasting technique will work great with any spud.

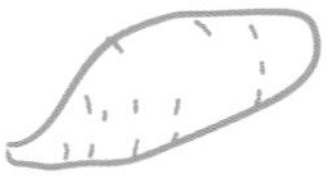

YIELD

4–6 servings

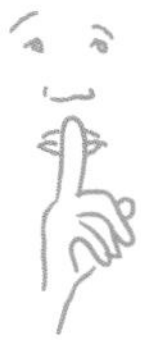

TIDBIT:
Jews in Djerba (Tunisia), whose ancestors came to North Africa after the expulsion from Spain in 1492, do not invite strangers for the Seder night. This may be a remnant of the secrecy of the Conversos.

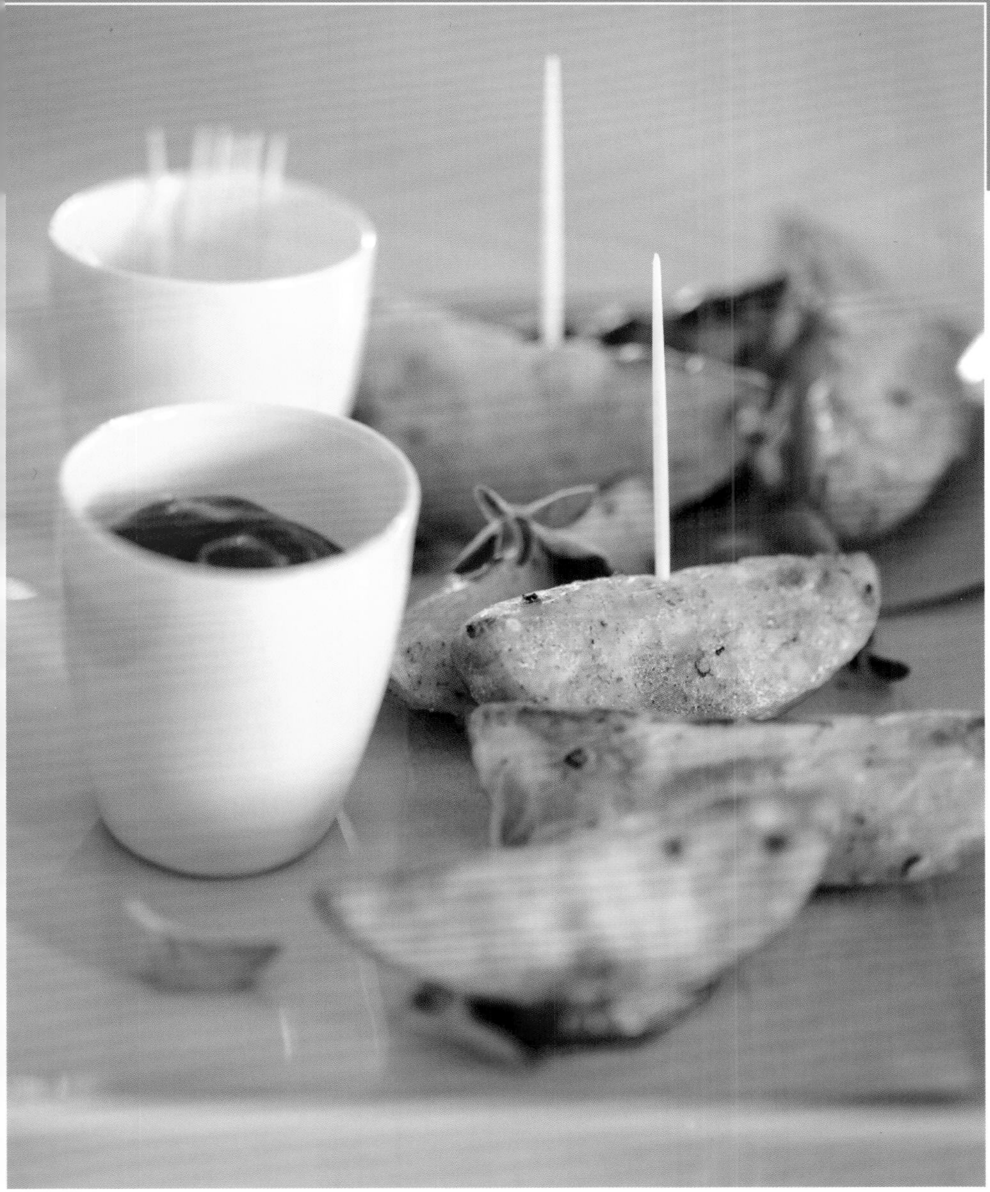

I didn't think there was a new way under the sun to make roasted potatoes, but this fresh technique is actually quite brilliant. The same potatoes we love are coated with potato starch and an egg-white mixture, forming an extra crispy and crunchy exterior. –L.

Potato and Flanken Kugel (Yapchik)

INGREDIENTS

1 lb	boneless flanken
½ tsp	paprika
•	salt, to taste
•	coarse black pepper, to taste
3 Tbsp	oil
	POTATO MIXTURE
5 lbs	yellow-skinned potatoes (such as Yukon Gold), peeled and cut into chunks
2	onions
1	zucchini, peeled
8	eggs
1 Tbsp	salt
⅛ tsp	coarse black pepper
½ cup	oil

INSTRUCTIONS

1. Season flanken with paprika, salt to taste, and pepper to taste. Heat 3 tablespoons oil in a sauté pan over medium heat. Add flanken and sear for 3 minutes on each side. Lower heat, cover, and cook 30-40 minutes, until meat is soft. The flanken will release its own cooking juices so there is no need to add other liquid. Remove from heat and let cool.
2. When cool, chop flanken into small pieces. Reserve the pan juices (there should be about ½ cup liquid in the pan).
3. Preheat oven to 350°F. Using the grating blade of the food processor, grate potatoes, onions, and zucchini.
4. In a large bowl, beat eggs with a fork. Add potato mixture and season with salt and pepper. Add oil; stir until all ingredients are combined.
5. Pour half the potato mixture into 1 (9 x 13-inch) baking pan or 2 (9 x 6-inch) loaf pans. Spread meat over potato mixture. Pour reserved pan juices over meat. Top with remaining potato mixture.
6. Bake, uncovered, for 30-40 minutes until potatoes are golden. Cover tightly and reduce heat to 200°F. Bake a minimum of 6 hours, up to overnight.

YIELD

12 servings

INSPIRED BY COOKKOSHER MEMBER

csg

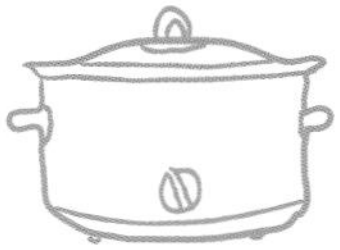

You can also make this in a slow cooker. Pour in the raw mixture and cook on high for 2-3 hours, then on low overnight.

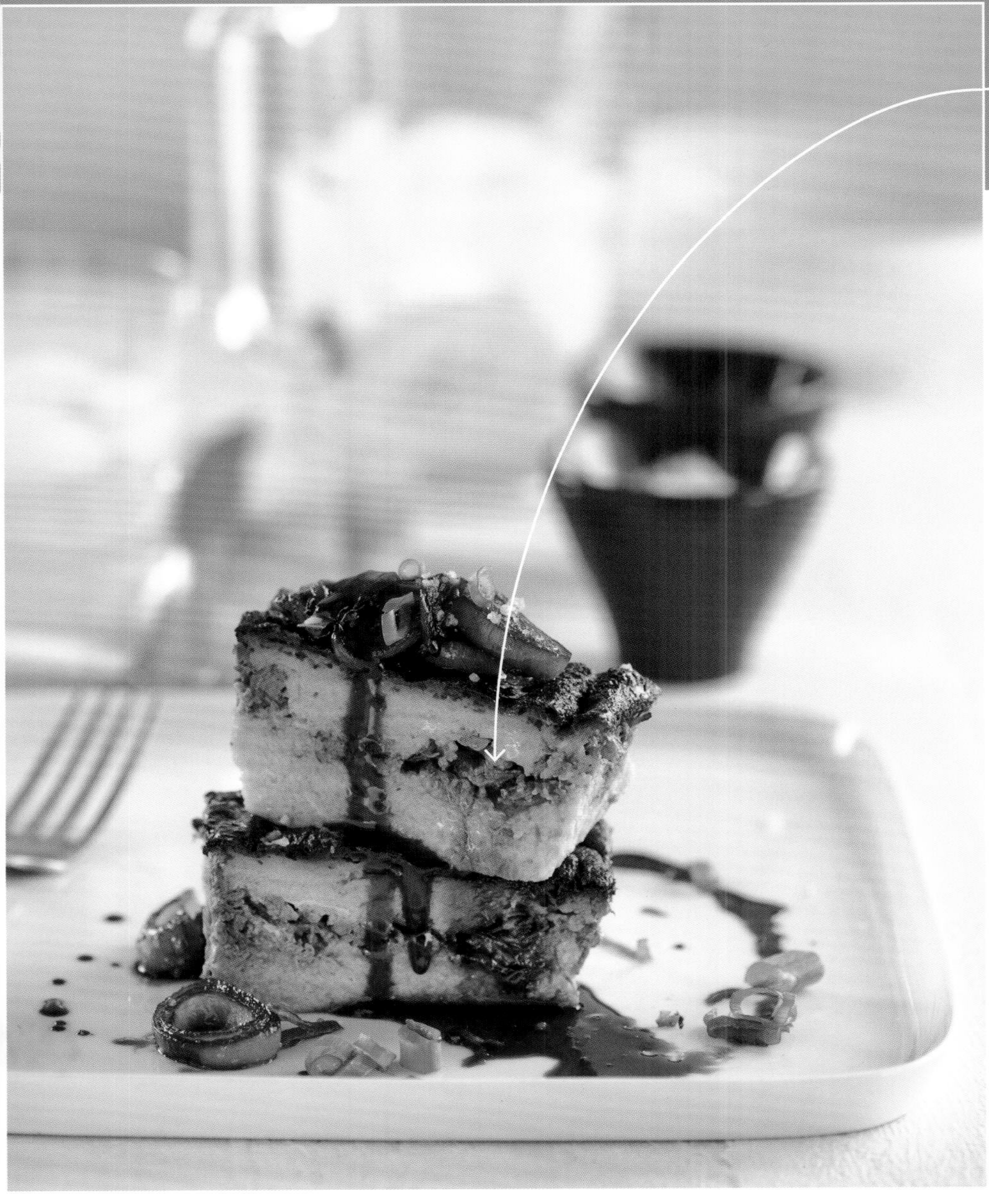

For a piece of meat in every bite, some mix the meat and potato mixture before adding to the pan.

WHENEVER we want to know about the history of a dish, we call food historian and author Gil Marks. When we asked him about Yapchik, we were surprised to hear that it wasn't a venerable, traditional food that had been enjoyed back in Eastern Europe. Instead, it was a modern-day invention, first becoming popular in the U.S. in the last decade. Then, I had a second call to make. To learn some Yapchik secrets, I contacted one caterer I know whose version is especially good. With his tips, I perfected our recipe. So even if it's not totally traditional—I bet it soon will be. *–L.*

Vegetable Lo Mein

INGREDIENTS

- **5** (10-in) crepes (see Building Blocks, page 14)

STIR FRY

- **3 Tbsp** oil, divided
- **1** large onion, cut into thin wedges
- **1** red pepper, cut into very thin strips
- **1** zucchini, cut into half-moons
- **1½ Tbsp** imitation soy sauce
- **1 Tbsp** honey
- **1** garlic clove, crushed
- • coarse black pepper to taste

INSTRUCTIONS

1. Stack crepes.
2. Roll up the crepe stack, jellyroll style. Slice the roll into ¼-inch thick slices to form the noodles. In a medium bowl, toss noodles with 1 tablespoon oil.
3. Heat ½ tablespoon oil in a skillet over medium-high heat. Add noodles and cook for 3-4 minutes, until noodles crisp up slightly. Flip noodles and cook for an additional 30 seconds or so on the other side. Remove to a platter.
4. Prepare the stir-fry: Heat remaining oil in a skillet or sauté pan over high heat. Add onion and sauté 4 minutes. Add red pepper and sauté additional 3-4 minutes. Add zucchini and cook until all vegetables have softened, 4-5 minutes.
5. Push vegetables to the side of the pan. Combine imitation soy sauce, honey, and garlic. Add to pan. Bring to a boil. Add noodles to the pan. Stir to combine sauce, vegetables, and noodles. Season with pepper to taste.

YIELD

4 servings

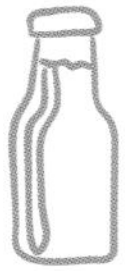

Can't find imitation soy sauce for Passover? See replacement index on page 126. Anything goes with a stir-fry. That includes adding your other stir-fry favorites, such as mushrooms and carrots.

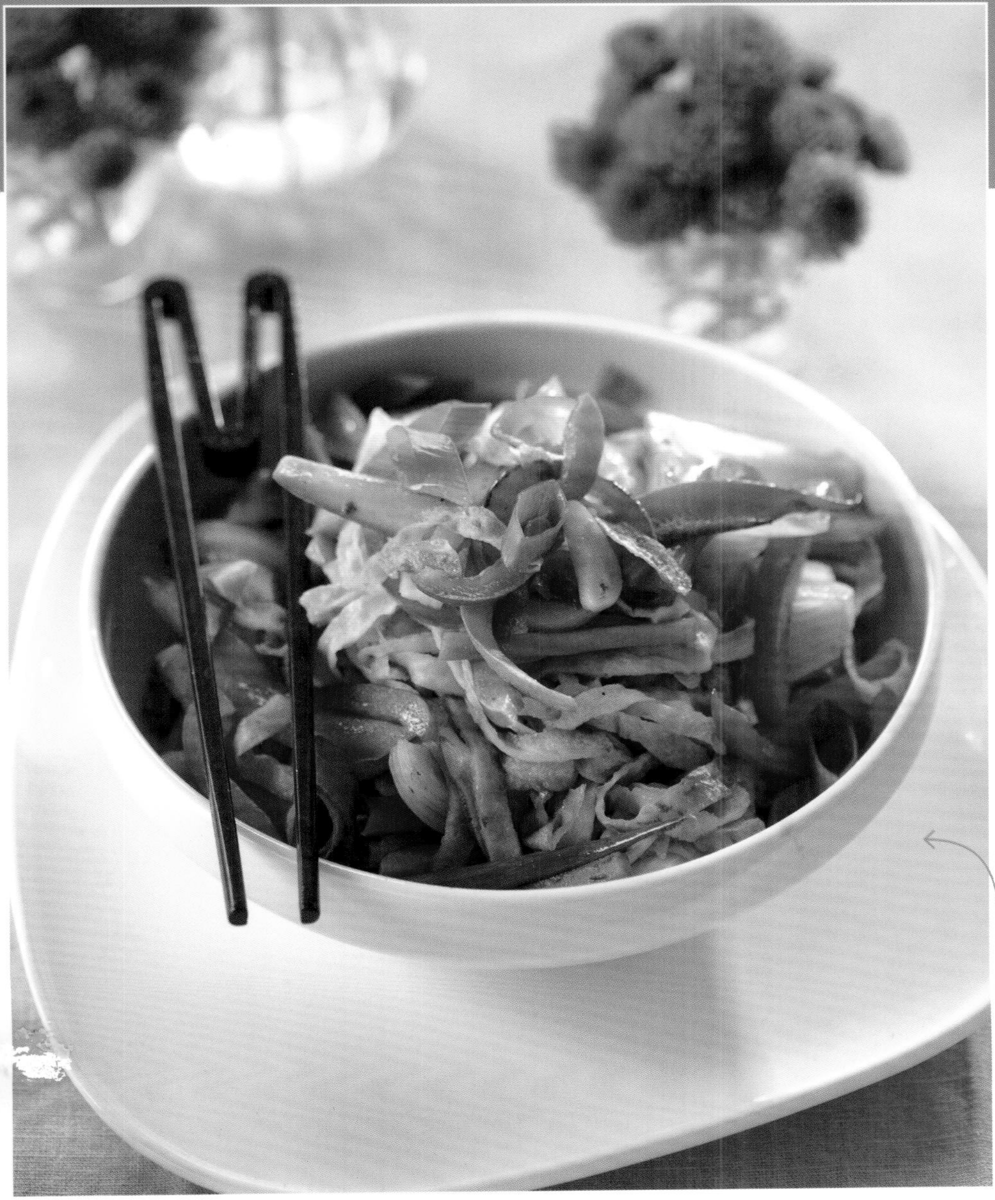

YOU don't have to miss your favorite Chinese takeout this Passover. I may or may have not finished the entire bowl of this Lo Mein by myself.

Sometimes, when I prepare a stir-fry dish with pasta and vegetables during the year, I save some plain noodles on the side for the pickier eaters in the family. The same goes on Passover. When I served this stir-fry, the little kids enjoyed the plain noodles while the adults really enjoyed the complete dish. -L.

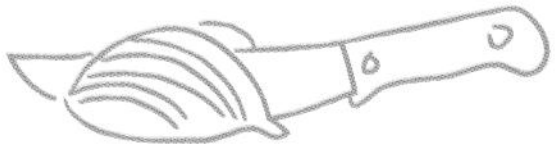

This method of cutting an onion is called "Frenching." Halve the onion and lay each half flat on the cutting board. Starting at one end, make thin angled cuts, slicing from stem end to root end.

Sweet Potato and Beet Terrine *with* Balsamic Glaze

INGREDIENTS

4	large beets
1 tsp	salt, divided
•	coarse black pepper to taste
2-3	sweet potatoes, peeled and sliced into ¼-inch rounds
6	Portobello mushroom caps, gills removed, sliced
•	olive oil for brushing

BALSAMIC GLAZE

½ cup	dry red wine
½ cup	balsamic vinegar
1 Tbsp	sugar

INSTRUCTIONS

1. Preheat oven to 375°F. Place beets into a baking dish and cover with foil. Bake for 90 minutes, or until beets are tender and peel comes off easily.

2. Peel beets and slice into ¼-inch rounds. Season with ¼ teaspoon salt and pepper. Set aside.

3. Prepare the balsamic glaze: Combine red wine, balsamic vinegar, and sugar in a small saucepan over high heat. Bring to a boil, then lower heat and simmer until wine is reduced to the consistency of syrup, about 30 minutes. The time will vary depending on the size of your pot.

4. Grease 3 baking sheets. Spread sweet potato slices on 2 sheets and brush with olive oil. Sprinkle each sheet of sweet potatoes with ¼ teaspoon salt and pepper. Bake until soft, about 25-30 minutes.

5. Spread Portobello mushroom slices on the third baking sheet. Brush liberally with oil and sprinkle with remaining ¼ teaspoon salt. Bake until soft, about 15 minutes.

6. Assemble the terrine: Grease a 9 x 5-inch loaf pan. Line the bottom and two sides of the loaf pan with parchment paper, letting some paper hang over the sides (this is so the terrine will release easily from the pan). Cover the bottom of the pan with overlapping sweet potato slices. There should be no seams. Brush

YIELD

6 servings

If you like a stronger wine flavor, or you just have loads of extra Seder wine to use up, sub it for the balsamic vinegar for an all-wine glaze. See replacement index, page 126.

Wine Pairing:
Carmel Kayoumi
Riesling

THIS is one of those beautiful side dishes that looks impressive when you bring it to the table to slice. But really, it's as simple as roasted vegetables layered in a loaf pan. Be sure to roast extra vegetables if using a baking dish that is larger than the standard 9 x 5-inch Pyrex loaf pan. Using a springform pan will yield a pretty result, but you will need much more to fill it up.   —V.

with balsamic glaze and olive oil. Add additional layers in the following order: beets, sweet potatoes, mushrooms, sweet potatoes, beets, sweet potatoes, brushing each layer with balsamic glaze and olive oil.

7. Place a piece of parchment paper or aluminum foil directly over the terrine. Place a heavy, similarly sized object, such as canned goods or a second loaf pan filled with water, over the terrine to weigh it down and compress the layers. Refrigerate for 24-48 hours.

8. To serve, allow to come to room temperature or bake at 350°F until warmed through, about 20 minutes, and let rest. Carefully flip onto a serving dish and remove parchment paper. Using a very sharp or serrated knife, cut into slices and serve.

PLATE IT!

If our Banana French Toast (page 94) wasn't already the most tempting Passover breakfast ever, here's how to make it look even better.

1 Begin by placing 2 pieces of Banana French Toast on a plate.

2 In a frying pan, sauté sliced bananas with 2 tablespoons sugar until golden, about 5 minutes.

3 Garnish with bananas and fresh orange supremes.

4 Pour on the Cinnamon Breakfast Syrup.

Brunch and Dairy

Banana French Toast *with* Cinnamon Breakfast Syrup

INGREDIENTS

BANANA TOAST

7	eggs, separated
1 cup	sugar
1 cup	mashed bananas (2-3 bananas)
¾ cup	potato starch

FRENCH TOAST BATTER

3	eggs
¾ cup	milk
¼ tsp	cinnamon
•	oil or butter for frying

CINNAMON BREAKFAST SYRUP

1 cup	sugar
1 tsp	vanilla sugar
•	scant ½ cup water
¼ tsp	cinnamon

INSTRUCTIONS

1. Preheat oven to 350°F. Line a jellyroll pan with parchment paper.

2. In the bowl of a mixer, whip egg whites. When foamy, slowly add sugar and whip until stiff. Reduce speed; slowly add yolks, bananas, and potato starch; mix to combine. Pour batter into pan and use a spatula to level the surface.

3. Bake for 15 minutes. Remove from oven and let cool. Cut into 12 squares. The banana toasts can be made ahead of time and frozen.

4. Prepare the batter: In a shallow dish, whisk together eggs, milk, and cinnamon.

5. Heat oil in a frying pan over medium heat (we found that 1 tablespoon of oil was sufficient to fry 4 to 5 squares).

6. Dredge squares in batter on both sides; add to frying pan. Fry until golden, about 1 minute per side.

7. Prepare the syrup: In a small saucepan, combine sugars and water. Bring to a boil over high heat (this will take about 4 minutes). Boil for 40-60 seconds, until syrup reaches desired consistency. Remove from heat and stir in cinnamon. Allow to cool. Serve over French toast.

YIELD
6 servings

Make it easy by preparing batches of banana toasts ahead of time.

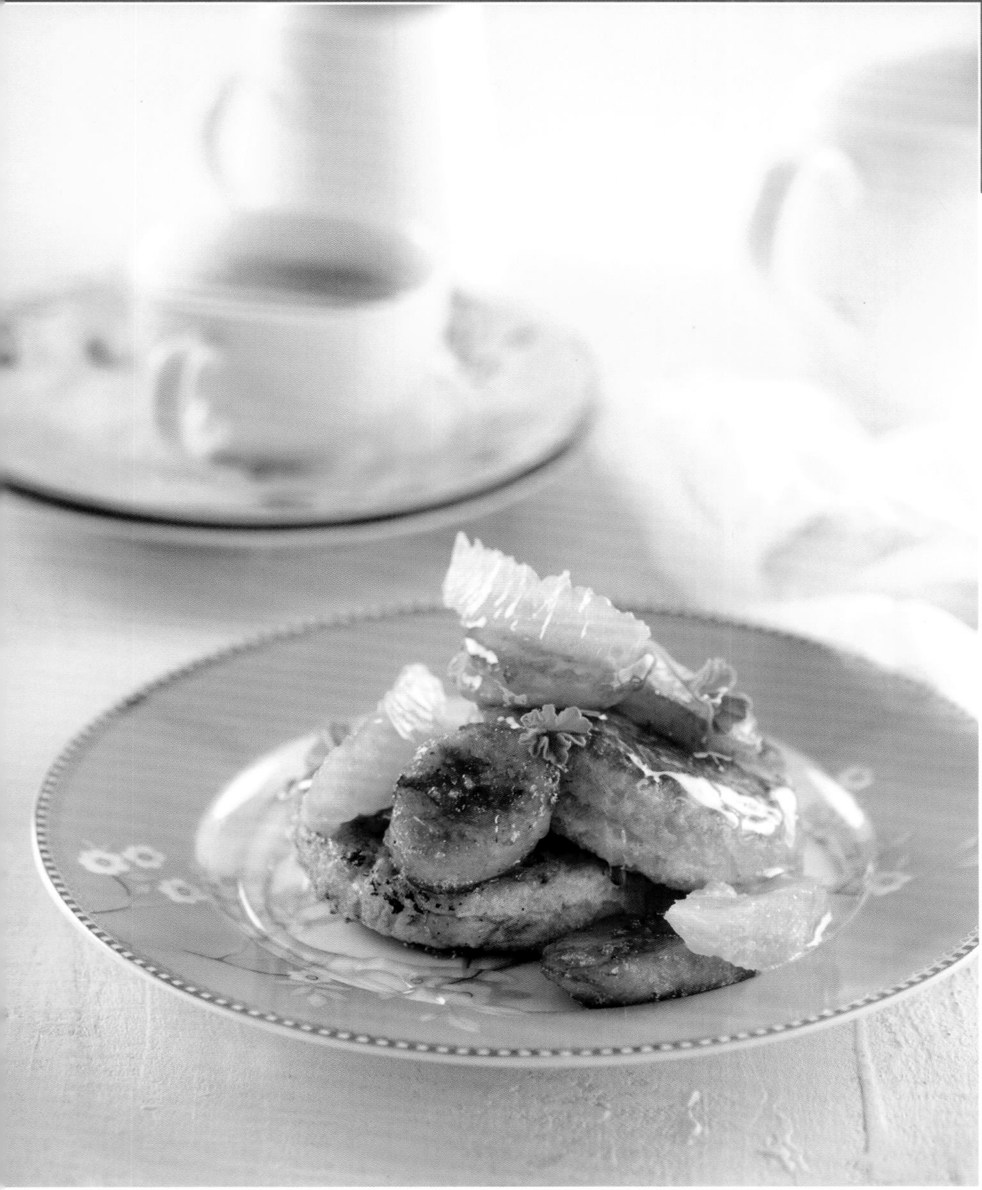

WE'RE really excited about this recipe. That's because we know that your family will also be super excited when they see this dish for breakfast. Hey, during the second round of recipe testing, my family was even excited to learn that this was for dinner.

Come Passover, this dish is going to bump matzah pancakes off their throne and take over as the favorite morning meal. I already know that's going to happen in my house. –V.

Bubbe's Egg Bagels [GEBROKTS]

INGREDIENTS

1¼ cups	water
½ cup	oil
2 cups	matzah meal
•	pinch salt
⅓ cup	sugar
6	eggs

INSTRUCTIONS

1. Preheat oven to 400°F. Grease a baking sheet.

2. In a medium saucepan, combine water and oil. Bring to a boil over high heat. Remove from heat and quickly add matzah meal, salt, and sugar. Let mixture stand for 10 minutes.

3. Add eggs, one at a time, beating to combine. With wet hands, shape mixture into balls and place on prepared sheet. Optional: Make a hole in the center to create the bagel shape.

4. Bake for 30 minutes. Reduce temperature to 350°F and bake for an additional 30 minutes.

YIELD
16 rolls

INSPIRED BY COOKKOSHER MEMBER
eralbert706

TIDBIT:
There is an ancient custom not to mention to word "bread" on Passover. Instead, all bread products are referred to as "chametz."

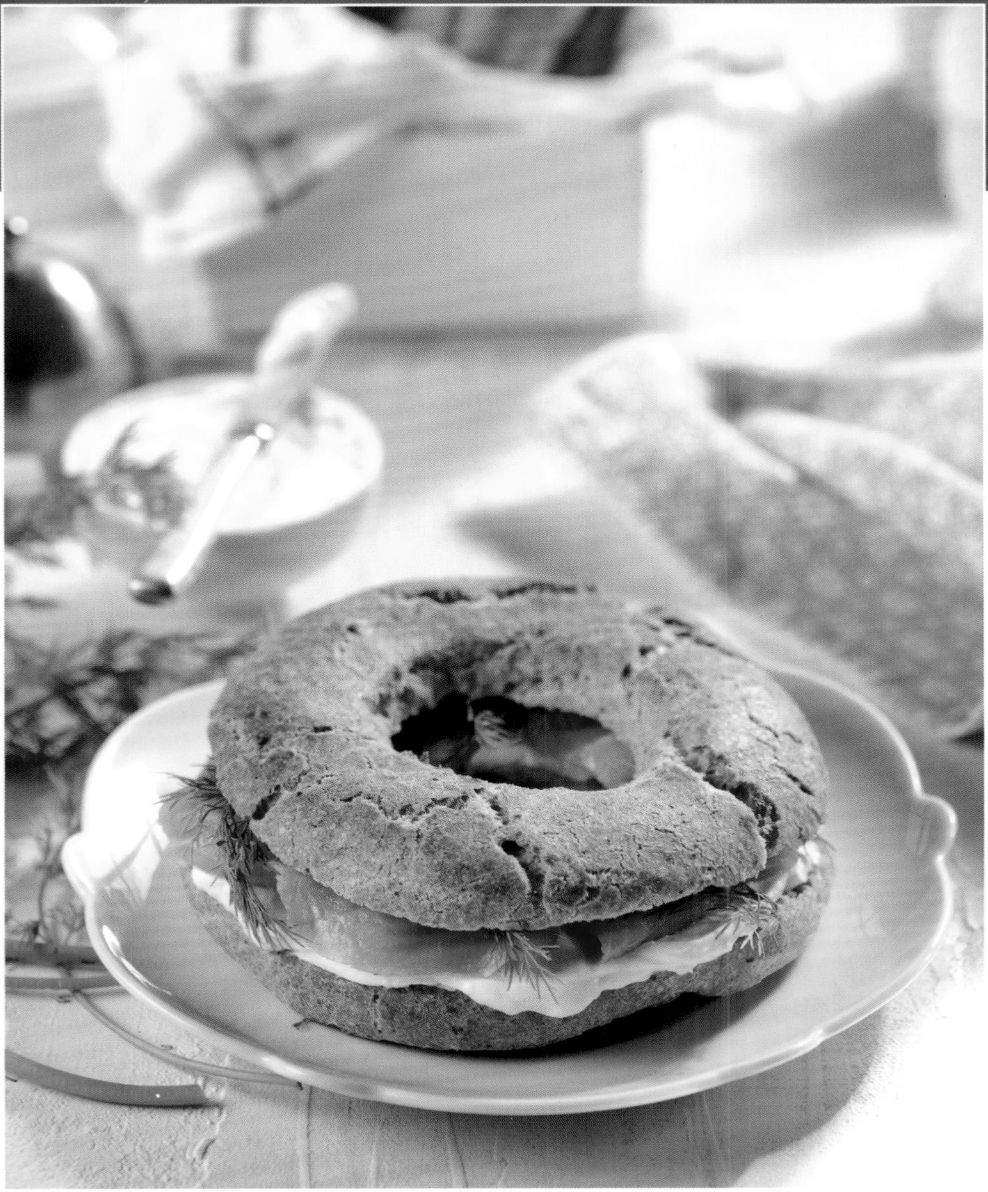

In one of my earliest memories, I'm sitting on the steps of the Javits Center, eating Passover rolls with cream cheese while on a Chol HaMoed outing. For this book, we tested lots of versions of those rolls. My mom was a little skeptical when I told her that we found a roll that was even better than hers. And though all the recipes we tried had the same exact ingredients, it was the technique that set them apart. Some came out like hockey pucks, and others were passable, but these were fluffy and tempted us until the batch was finished (even though it was October). –V.

Yellow Squash Quiche (Kusa Jiben)

INGREDIENTS

3 Tbsp	oil
1	large sweet onion, finely diced
6	yellow squash (about 3 lbs)
1¼ tsp	salt
2	eggs
2 cups	shredded mozzarella or muenster cheese
½ cup	sour cream or yogurt

INSTRUCTIONS

1. Preheat oven to 350°F. Grease a 9 x 13-inch baking pan.

2. Heat oil in a large skillet over medium heat. Add onion and fry, stirring occasionally, until onion is soft and just beginning to turn golden, about 7 minutes.

3. Meanwhile, cut squash into large chunks. In the bowl of a food processor, shred or grate squash until coarse. Add squash to skillet and stir to combine. Lower heat to medium-low and cook, stirring occasionally, until squash is completely wilted, liquid is bubbling at the sides, and mixture is mushy, about 20 minutes.

4. Drain squash mixture in a colander to remove liquid; discard liquid.

5. In a large mixing bowl, combine squash mixture and salt. Taste and adjust seasoning if necessary. Add eggs and cheese; stir to combine. Pour mixture into prepared baking pan. Bake 45 minutes.

6. Turn oven to broil. Broil 2 to 3 minutes, until brown caramelized spots form on the top. Top each serving with a tablespoon of sour cream.

YIELD

8 servings

TIDBIT:
In some communities, milk products were eaten the morning of the Seder, because milk brings on sleep and they wanted to sleep during the day in order to be awake and clear-headed during the long Seder.

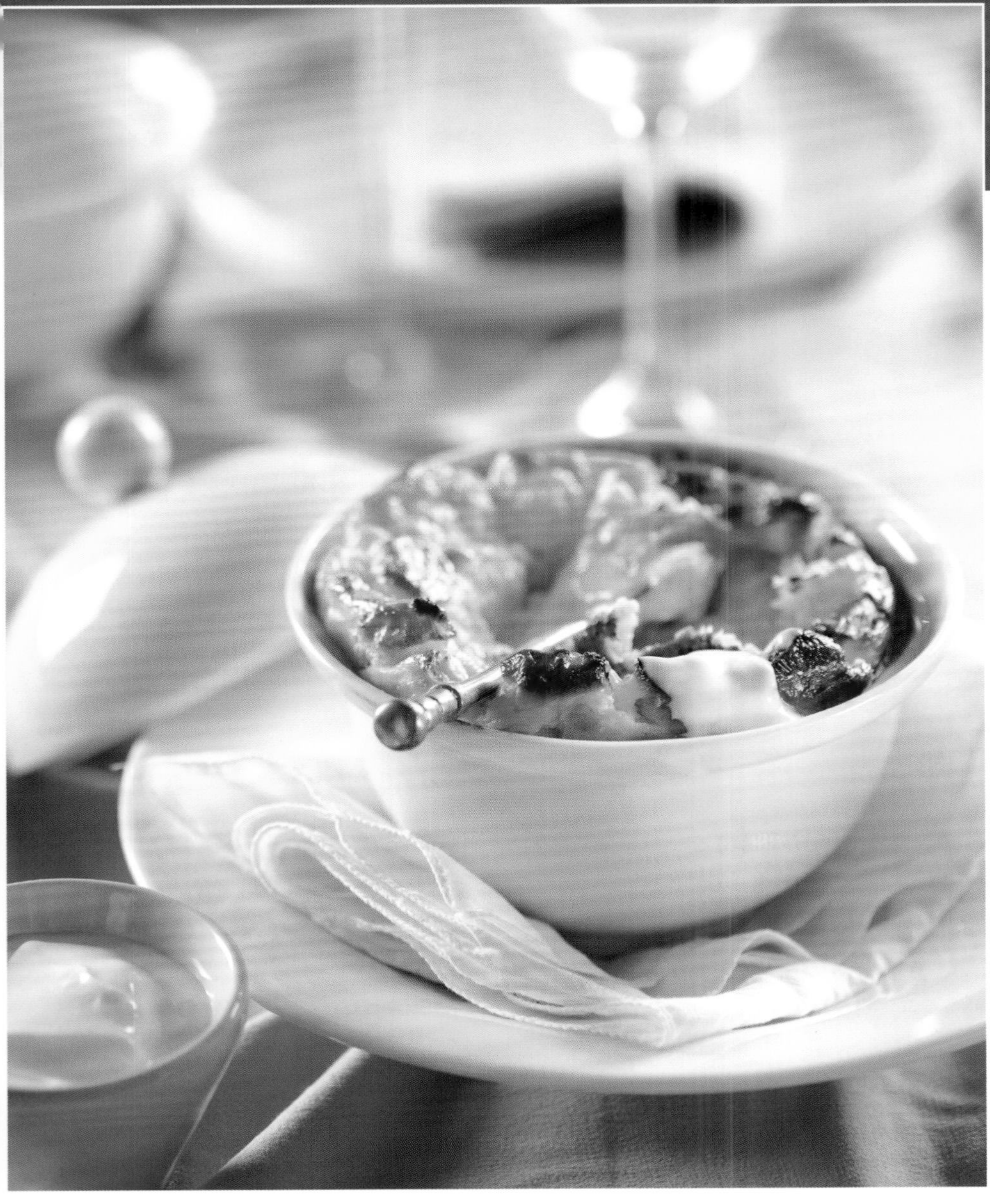

WHEN Victoria first told me about this quiche, I thought it sounded like something I'd really like. I was familiar with broccoli quiches and spinach quiches, but had never before seen one made from yellow squash. She laughed because, to her, this dish was hardly new. It's a traditional staple in Syrian-Jewish homes, where it's called kusa jiben, and has been one of her favorites her entire life. Now, we love it too. It's delicious both hot and at room temperature. –L.

Matzaroni and Cheese [GEBROKTS]

WHAT kids don't prefer mac 'n cheese over anything else? This is a easy dinner that will get all the troops running to the table when the hot, cheesy, and bubbling dish emerges from the oven. —V.

YIELD

6 to 8 servings

INSPIRED BY COOKKOSHER MEMBER
nashjille

INGREDIENTS

5	matzahs, broken into small pieces
5	eggs
1 (16-oz)	container sour cream
1 (16-oz)	container cottage cheese
3 Tbsp	butter, melted
1 tsp	salt
2 cups	shredded mozzarella or muenster cheese, divided

INSTRUCTIONS

1. Preheat oven to 350°F. In an 8 x 8-inch baking dish, arrange ⅓ of the broken matzah pieces.

2. In a medium bowl, beat eggs. Add sour cream, cottage cheese, butter, salt, and 1 cup shredded cheese. Pour ⅓ of the cheese mixture over the matzah. Repeat with two additional layers of matzah and cheese. Top with remaining 1 cup shredded cheese. Bake for 40 minutes. The cheese on top should be brown and bubbling.

Pineapple Pie

IN my brother and sister-in-law's home, this pie is a favorite all year round. Some say it tastes like a lighter and airier version of cheesecake. It's delicious served either hot or cold and it also works as a side dish or dessert. —L.

YIELD

8 servings

INSPIRED BY COOKKOSHER MEMBER
Dev

INGREDIENTS

½ cup	potato starch
½ cup	sugar
1 tsp	vanilla sugar
½ cup	oil
4	eggs
1 tsp	baking powder
1¾ cups	chopped fresh ripe pineapple or 1 (16-oz can) pineapple chunks, drained

INSTRUCTIONS

1. Preheat oven to 350°F.

2. In the bowl of a blender or food processor, combine potato starch, sugars, oil, eggs, baking powder, and pineapple. Texture should be runny. Pour into 2 pie plates or 1 (9-inch) round baking pan. Bake for 30-45 minutes, until pie is firm and golden on the edges.

TOP IT & MIX IT!

Use the components of our desserts to create your own ice cream treats. Use our vanilla ice cream base (page 106), store-bought, or your favorite homemade ice cream.

1 Make a fudge nut sundae by swirling in our Chocolate-Hazelnut Cream (from the Espresso Macarons, page 114).

2 Love cookie crunch? We show you how to make it on page 110. Keep extra on hand to top your ice cream or mix it with our chocolate ice cream mousse (page 114).

3 Break up Matzah Toffee Bars (page 120) into small bits to use as a candy bar-inspired mix-in or topping.

4 Mix the cookie crust from page 112 with some finely chopped chocolate. Bake and crush to small bits. Swirl it into ice cream along with the hot chocolate sauce (page 113).

5 Love tart and sweet? Swirl our lemon curd (page 104) into vanilla ice cream.

Dessert

Frozen Lemon Wafer Cake

INGREDIENTS

12	egg whites
1½ cups	sugar
2 Tbsp	potato starch
3 cups	ground almonds
	LEMON CURD CREAM
2	whole eggs
8	egg yolks
1 cup	sugar
¾ cup	fresh lemon juice
2 Tbsp	margarine or frozen oil

INSTRUCTIONS

1. Preheat oven to 350°F. Line 2 jellyroll pans with parchment paper.
2. In the bowl of an electric mixer, beat egg whites until foamy. Slowly add in sugar, beating until stiff peaks form. Add potato starch and ground nuts. Divide batter between pans and use a spatula to spread evenly. Bake until golden, 20-25 minutes.
3. Prepare the lemon curd cream: Combine eggs, yolks, sugar, and lemon juice in a double boiler. Cook, stirring occasionally, until mixture thickens, about 10-12 minutes. Mixture may curdle slightly. Blend mixture using an immersion blender (if using a standard blender, blend and return mixture to the pot). Whisk in margarine.
4. Using a spatula, spread half the cream over one cake. Carefully place second cake over the cream. Spread the remaining cream over the second cake. Freeze until firm. Slice into squares or bars and serve frozen.

   Optional: Garnish with whipped cream

YIELD

40 bars

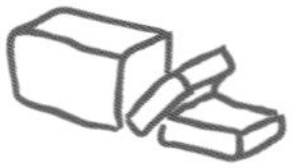

When you freeze most oils, they gain the consistency of shortening. If you're avoiding trans-fat, it's a good stand-in for margarine here.

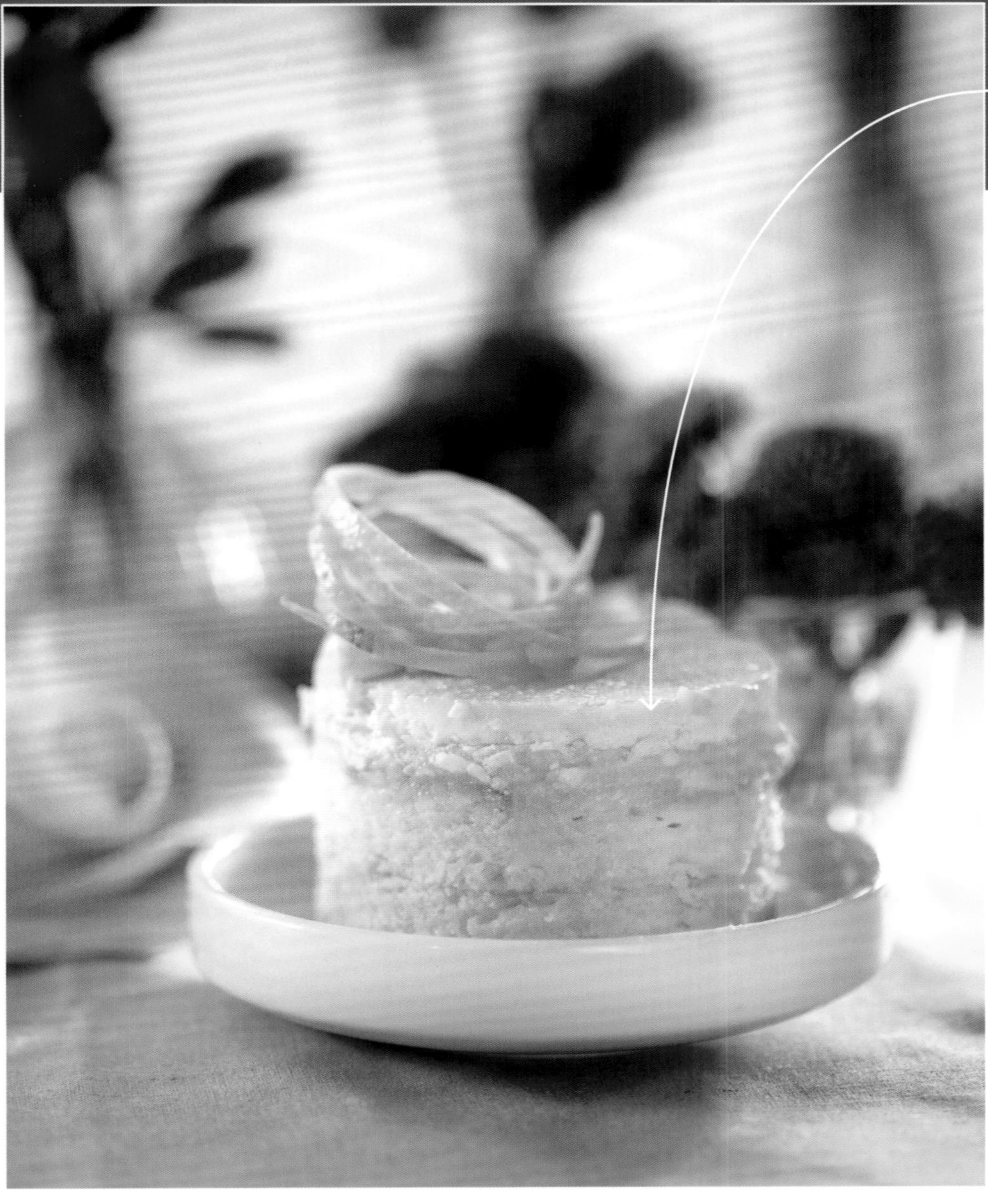

You can make more layers simply by cutting each layer in half and stacking them with cream between each to form a 4-layer cake.

EVERY year before Passover, the first cake I make is a chocolate wafer cake, which consists of two large sheet cakes with cream between them. It's been my most popular dessert over the years. I keep it in the freezer, and I slice off bars as needed. This year it was time to change things up. Light, refreshing, and lemony: this is the perfect dessert to finish off heavy holiday meals. –L.

Hot Apple Pie *with* Cinnamon-Streusel Ice Cream

INGREDIENTS

5	Granny Smith apples
½ cup	potato starch
5	eggs
½ cup	oil
1 cup	sugar
1 tsp	vanilla sugar
¾ tsp	cinnamon
	CRUST/TOPPING
1¾ cup	chopped walnuts
⅓-½ cup	sugar
	STREUSEL FOR ICE CREAM
¼ cup	potato starch
¼ cup	sugar
⅛ tsp	cinnamon
1 tsp	vanilla extract
1½ Tbsp	oil
	ICE CREAM BASE
6	egg yolks
2 cups	non-dairy whipped topping, divided
1 cup	sugar
1 tsp	vanilla extract
¼ tsp	cinnamon

INSTRUCTIONS

1. Preheat oven to 350°F.
2. Peel and core apples. Slice into rings.
3. In a large mixing bowl, combine potato starch, eggs, oil, sugars, and cinnamon. Add apples to bowl and coat well.
4. Prepare the crust/topping: Combine walnuts and sugar. Place half of the walnut/sugar mixture into the bottom of an 8-inch round baking dish to form a crust.
5. Layer battered apples neatly over crust. Pour remaining apple batter over apples. Let mixture settle into apples. Sprinkle with remaining walnut/sugar mixture. Bake, uncovered, for 1 hour or until golden brown. If top browns too quickly, cover with foil. Serve warm.
6. Prepare the streusel for the ice cream: In a small bowl, combine potato starch, sugar, cinnamon, vanilla, and oil to form crumbs. Spread in a baking pan and bake 20 minutes. Set aside.
7. Prepare ice cream base: In a heatproof bowl set over a pan of simmering water, combine yolks and ¼ cup whipped topping. Whisk often for 8 minutes (this will cook the yolks without scrambling them). Add ½ cup sugar and whisk until dissolved. Place bowl in refrigerator to cool.

YIELD

8 servings

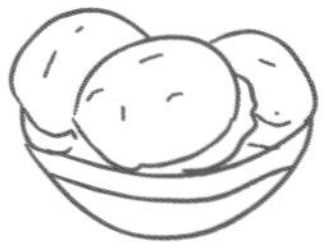

You can also replace the ice cream base with store-bought vanilla ice cream. Simply soften and stir in the streusel.

THE ingredients are nothing unusual, yet this yields a highly addictive pie — dare we say one of the best Passover pies.

My aunt's housekeeper knows the family recipes better than my aunt does. To keep herself indispensable, the housekeeper doesn't share any of the recipes. And when she does, there's always a missing ingredient. When I called her for this recipe, what she told me didn't seem right. After a couple of phone calls and some memory digging, I assembled it the way it was supposed to be. Share it. That's sweet revenge.

–L.

8. In the bowl of an electric mixer on high speed, whip remaining 1¾ cups non-dairy whipped topping until stiff. Add remaining ½ cup sugar, vanilla, and cinnamon. Add yolk mixture and mix to combine. Stir in streusel crumbs. Freeze overnight. Serve on hot apple pie.

Pecan Pie *with* Cookie Crust

INGREDIENTS

COOKIE CRUST

1	egg, separated
¼ cup	sugar, divided
⅔ cup	ground almonds

PIE FILLING

2	eggs
½ cup	margarine or butter, melted
1 cup	brown sugar
¼ cup	sugar
1 Tbsp	potato starch (heaping)
1 tsp	vanilla extract
1 cup	chopped pecans

INSTRUCTIONS

1. Prepare the cookie crust: Preheat oven to 350°F. Line the bottom of a 9-inch round baking pan with parchment paper (cut a circle from a sheet).
2. In the bowl of an electric mixer on high speed, beat egg white. When foamy, slowly add 2 tablespoons sugar and beat until soft peaks form. In a small bowl, combine yolk and remaining 2 tablespoons sugar. Add to beaten white. Fold in almonds. Pour into baking pan and spread evenly, using a spatula. Bake for 15 minutes. Raise oven heat to 400°F.
3. Prepare the filling: In the bowl of an electric mixer, beat eggs until foamy. Stir in melted margarine, sugars, potato starch, vanilla, and pecans. Pour over crust. Bake for 10 minutes. Reduce oven temperature to 350°F and bake until center of pie is set, about 25-35 minutes.

The cookie crust can be made into cookies too. Add chocolate chips to the batter, drop spoonfuls on a baking sheet, and bake for 15 minutes.

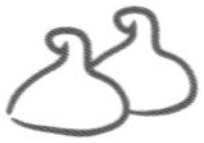

YIELD

8 servings

INSPIRED BY COOKKOSHER MEMBER

oreo20

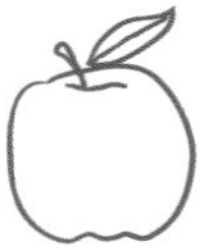

TIDBIT:

Just as one is not allowed to eat matzah on the day of the first Seder, there is a custom not to eat any of the charoset ingredients or marror vegetables then as well.

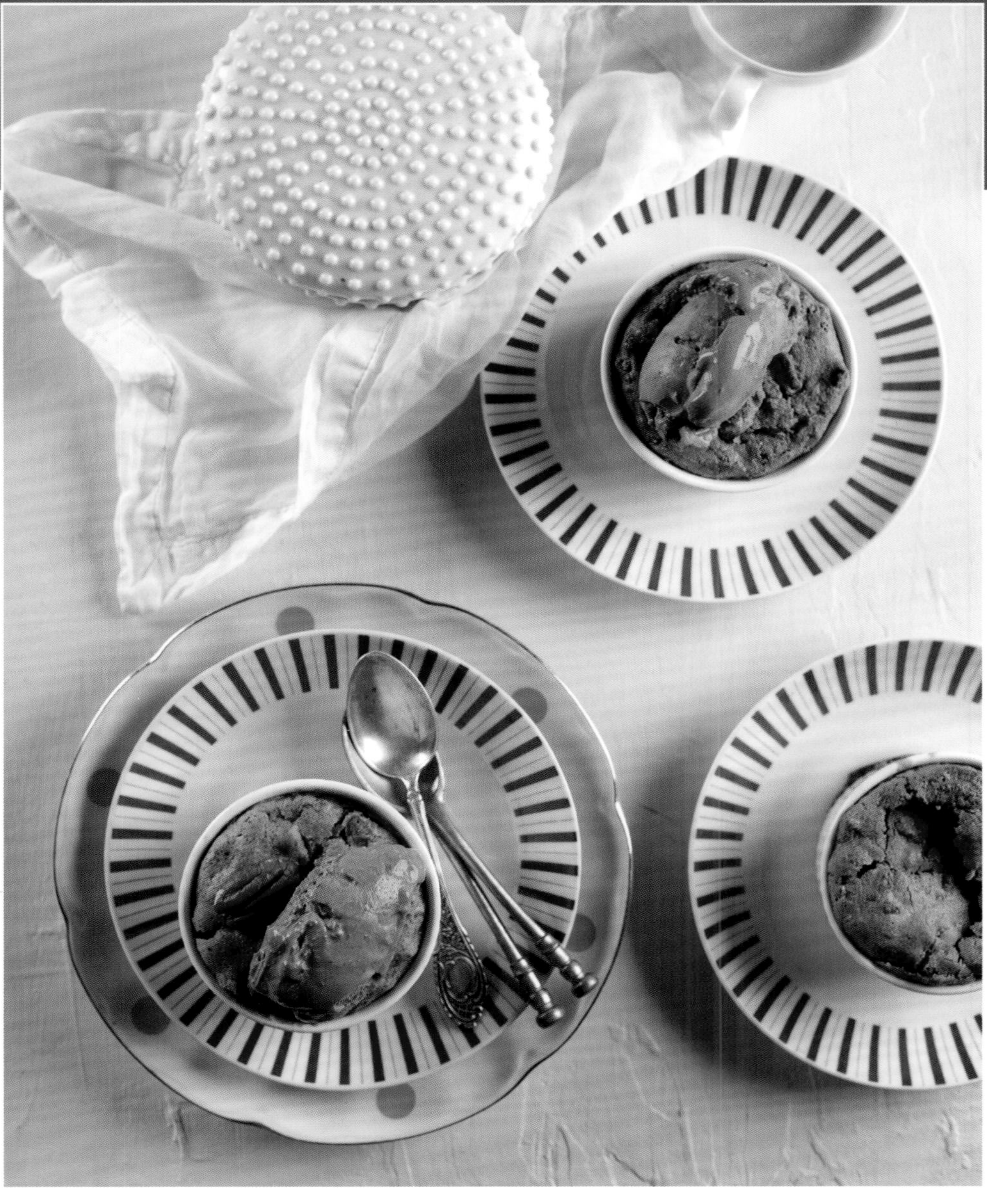

ON Passover, we have lots of chocolate desserts and meringue cookies. But have you ever had a pecan pie? I planned to make this to serve to my mother's guests on Friday night when we were doing the final round of recipe testing for this book.

When I told my mother I'd be bringing her desserts for Shabbat, she responded, "Real dessert or Passover desserts?"

"Don't worry," I told her.

She thought my brothers would complain about being guinea pigs. Come Friday night, they were too busy savoring this pie to care. –V.

Strawberry Fudge Cake

INGREDIENTS

CHOCOLATE CAKE

7	eggs, separated
1 cup	sugar, divided
7 oz	good-quality chocolate
½ cup	oil
1 tsp	vanilla extract
1 tsp	red wine

STRAWBERRY SORBET

1 (16-oz)	bag frozen strawberries, completely thawed
3	egg whites
¾ cup	sugar
¼ cup	water

You can also use mangos, pineapple, kiwis, or blueberries. You'll need 2 cups fruit puree. See replacement index, page 126.

INSTRUCTIONS

1. Preheat oven to 350°F. Line the bottom of a 10-inch springform pan with parchment paper and grease the sides. In the bowl of an electric mixer, beat egg whites. Slowly add in ¼ cup sugar and beat until soft peaks form.
2. Meanwhile, melt chocolate with oil in a double boiler. In a medium bowl, beat egg yolks with remaining ¾ cup sugar. Add melted chocolate mixture, vanilla, and wine and whisk to combine. Fold in egg whites. Separate ¾ cup batter and set aside. Pour remaining batter into prepared pan. Bake for 25-30 minutes.
3. Prepare the cookie crunch topping: Pour reserved ¾ cup batter into a greased baking pan. Bake 10 minutes. Using a fork, mix batter with a fork. Repeat twice, baking 10 minutes and then mixing with a fork, for a total baking time of 30 minutes. Let cool. (You can crumble to fine crumbs using your fingers or pulsing in the food processor.) Set aside.
4. Prepare the strawberry sorbet: In the bowl of food processor or blender, blend strawberries until completely liquefied. Set aside.

YIELD

12 servings

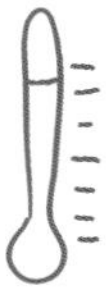

Don't have a candy thermometer? To tell whether your sugar has reached "soft ball stage," use a clean spoon to drop a teaspoon of boiling sugar into a cup of cold water. If you can pick the sugar out of the water and squish it with your fingers, it's ready.

We made our own kosher-for-Passover cookie crunch. Check out how we did it in step 3.

ONE of the classic, all-around favorite desserts on Passover is a flourless chocolate cake. There's no potato starch or nuts, and it's fudgy and intense, as it should be. We made it even better by balancing it with a creamy, light sorbet. I love this sorbet because there's nothing artificial. You can create different flavors of fresh fruit sorbets using this technique.

And while the cake and the sorbet are both awesome on their own, together they satisfy the craving for something rich and something refreshing in one bite.   –V.

5. In the bowl of an electric mixer, whip egg whites until soft peaks form. Meanwhile, combine sugar and water in a small saucepan and bring to a boil. Boil for 3-4 minutes, until mixture reaches between 235°F and 245°F on a candy thermometer.

6. With the mixer running at high speed, drip the boiling sugar into the whipped egg whites in a very slow trickle. Beat for 7 minutes (the mixture should be cool by then). Fold in strawberry purée until completely combined. Pour over cake. Freeze 30 minutes. Top with cookie crunch. Freeze overnight and serve.

Chocolate Crackel Sandwiches

INGREDIENTS

4 cups	confectioners' sugar
1 tsp	vanilla sugar (optional)
2/3 cup	cocoa (scant)
•	pinch salt
4	egg whites
3 cups	walnuts halves, toasted

CHOCOLATE ICE CREAM MOUSSE

15 oz	bittersweet chocolate
9	eggs, separated
2¼ cups	sugar, divided
¾ cup	oil
1 Tbsp	lemon juice

INSTRUCTIONS

1. Preheat oven to 325°F. Line 3 baking sheets with parchment paper.
2. In the bowl of a stand mixer (or using a hand mixer), combine confectioners' sugar, vanilla sugar, and cocoa. Add the salt and egg whites. Beat well. Add the walnuts and mix until incorporated. Do not let the batter sit.
3. Immediately spoon full tablespoons of batter onto each baking sheet. There should be 6 cookies per sheet for a total of 18 large cookies (the cookies spread). Bake for 12-15 minutes.
4. Prepare chocolate ice cream mousse: Line a 9 x 13-inch baking pan with parchment paper or plastic wrap. Melt the chocolate in a double boiler over low heat. In the bowl of a food processor or blender, combine egg yolks, 1 cup sugar, oil, and melted chocolate. Process until well combined.
5. In the bowl of an electric mixer, beat the egg whites until stiff, gradually adding in remaining 1¼ cups sugar. Add lemon juice. Lower speed and add chocolate mixture.

YIELD

9 sandwiches

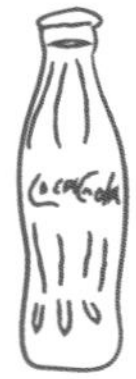

TIDBIT:

Coca-Cola makes a special batch of soda for Passover using real sugar instead of high fructose corn syrup, which is kitniot. A yellow cap identifies the special bottles.

THESE crackels are a simply delicious cookie that work well either on their own or paired with ice cream. There's just one major rule. Once you mix the batter, drop it onto the cookie sheet immediately. If it sits in the bowl, the batter becomes thick and chunky and result in cookies that aren't as appealing. I haven't yet figured out a way to reverse that — so work quickly! —L.

6. Pour ice cream into prepared pan. Freeze until firm.

7. Assemble the ice cream sandwiches: Pair the cookies that are the most evenly-sized. Using a deep cookie cutter the size of the cookie, cut the ice cream. The ice cream should stick to the sides of the cutter; when you lift the cutter, the ice cream should come out with it. Push it out onto a cookie. Sandwich it with the matching cookie. Freeze.

HOT CHOCOLATE SAUCE

1 cup	sugar
2 tsp	vanilla sugar
½ cup	cocoa, sifted
•	pinch salt
½ cup	water
2 Tbsp	oil

1. In a medium saucepan over high heat, combine the sugars, cocoa, salt, water, and oil. Bring to a boil. Lower heat and simmer, stirring occasionally, until sauce thickens to desired consistency

Espresso Macarons *with* Chocolate-Hazelnut Cream

INGREDIENTS

1 cup	ground almonds (100 grams)
1¼ cups	confectioners' sugar (175 grams)
2 tsp	instant coffee or espresso powder
3	egg whites
2 Tbsp	sugar

CHOCOLATE HAZELNUT CREAM

½ cup	hazelnuts, toasted
1 tsp	confectioners' sugar
2 oz	chocolate

Use only large egg whites.

INSTRUCTIONS

1. Line 2 baking sheets with parchment paper. Fit a piping bag with a medium round tip.

2. In a large bowl, thoroughly whisk together almonds, confectioners' sugar, and coffee. There should be no lumps.

3. In the bowl of an electric mixer, beat egg whites. When egg whites begin to foam, slowly add sugar. Beat until stiff peaks form.

4. Using a spatula, add half the egg whites to the dry ingredients. Fold in, just slightly. Add remaining egg whites and continue to fold gently until dry ingredients are completely incorporated. The batter should have some stiffness and not spread to fill the bottom of the bowl.

5. Fill the piping bag with half the batter at a time (I like to place the piping bag into a wide-mouthed jar and fold the top of the bag over the edges. This makes it easier to fill.) Pipe circles onto prepared baking sheets. Leave a bit of room, as macarons will spread slightly. Tap each tray on the counter 3 times. This releases the air bubbles. Let sit at room temperature for at least 1 hour. The surface of the macaron should be hard and smooth before baking.

YIELD
30 macaron sandwiches

You can also make plain almond macarons or one of our favorites: lemon macarons. Replace the coffee with lemon zest and fill with our lemon curd cream (page 104).

This heavenly chocolate-hazelnut cream makes great truffles. Pour into molds and freeze, or cut frozen cream into shapes.

IF you're ever going to try macarons, Passover is the time. After all, it's a cookie we savor all year long, and on Passover we can enjoy them in all their glory, without any substitutions. And these live up to all the hype.

Since you're probably also going to be making meringues at some point over Passover, it's worthwhile to purchase piping bags and tips. A set of disposable bags costs about $5 and metal tips cost only $1 to $1.50 each. Get a medium round tip for macarons and a jumbo star tip for meringues. They'll be a worthwhile addition to your Passover toolkit.   –V.

6. Preheat oven to 280°F. Bake 17 minutes. Let cool completely before removing from baking sheet. Macarons can be frozen at this point. Store in a single layer, separated by parchment or wax paper.

7. Prepare the cream: In the bowl of a food processor, process hazelnuts until they reach the consistency of a spread. Add confectioners' sugar and pulse again. Melt chocolate and add to food processor. Process again until smooth.

8. Spread cream onto macaron shells. Refrigerate overnight to let the shells soften. Serve at room temperature.

Chocolate-Nut Biscotti

INGREDIENTS

1/3 cup	oil
2/3 cup	sugar
2	eggs
1/3 cup	cocoa, sifted
1/2 cup	potato starch
1 1/4 cups	ground almonds
2 tsp	baking powder (optional)
1/2 cup	chocolate chips (or chopped baking chocolate)
1/4 cup	slivered almonds, toasted

GARNISH

6 oz	good-quality bittersweet chocolate
•	caramelized nuts, for sprinkling

INSTRUCTIONS

1. Preheat oven to 350°F. Line a baking sheet with parchment paper.
2. In the bowl of an electric mixer, cream oil and sugar. Add eggs and mix well. Gradually add cocoa.
3. In a small bowl, combine potato starch, ground almonds, and baking powder. Add to the mixer, alternating with chocolate chips. Add almonds. Do not overmix.
4. Place in the refrigerator for 1/2 hour.
5. With wet hands, form 2 loaves of batter on the baking sheet. Smooth with a few drops of water. Bake for 20 minutes. Let cool slightly.
6. Using a serrated knife, cut biscotti into slices about 1-inch thick. Return to baking sheet on a cut side. Bake for an additional 5 minutes.
7. To decorate, melt baking chocolate over a double boiler. Using a spatula, smear chocolate over the biscotti. Sprinkle on caramelized nuts. Biscotti freeze well.

YIELD

20 biscotti

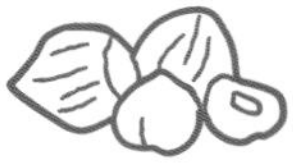

You'll need lots of nuts on Passover. For best results, toast any whole or chopped (not ground) nuts before using.

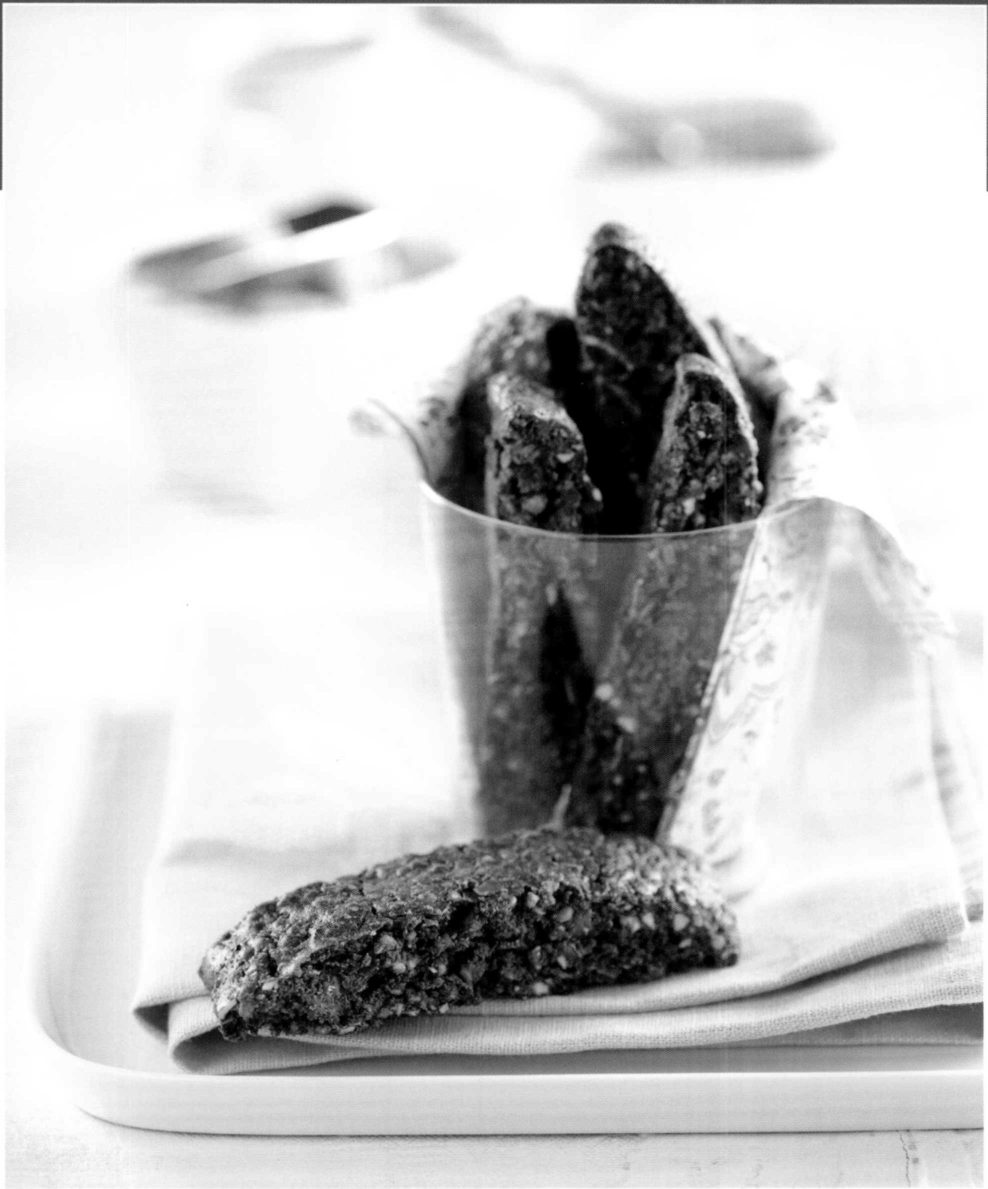

AFTER I made these, I left them in a cookie jar on the counter. Three days later, when I gave my neighbor one to taste, she asked, "It's she'hakol, right?" Oops. All along, my family had been saying the blessing of mezonos before eating these biscotti. I had forgotten to tell them these were Passover biscotti! –L.

Double Decker Bars

INGREDIENTS

CRUST

1 cup	ground nuts
1 cup	potato starch
2/3 cup	oil
1/2 cup	sugar

TOPPING

1 cup	sugar
2	eggs
2 Tbsp	lemon juice
1/2 tsp	baking powder
1/4 tsp	salt
1/4 cup	confectioners' sugar, for dusting

INSTRUCTIONS

1. Preheat oven to 375°F. Grease an 8 x 8-inch baking pan or line with parchment paper.
2. Prepare the crust: In a small bowl, combine nuts, potato starch, oil, and sugar. Press evenly into prepared pan. Bake for 15 minutes.
3. Meanwhile, prepare the topping: In a small bowl, combine sugar, eggs, lemon juice, baking powder, and salt. Mix until frothy. Pour over baked crust. Bake 18-22 minutes, or until lightly browned. Let cool. Dust with confectioners' sugar.

YIELD

16 bars

INSPIRED BY COOKKOSHER MEMBER

Sjs0219

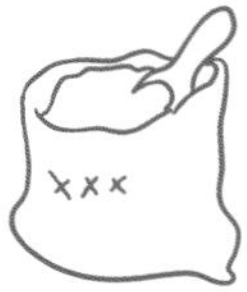

xxx

TIDBIT:

A select few have a custom not to use potato starch on Passover because it resembles flour.

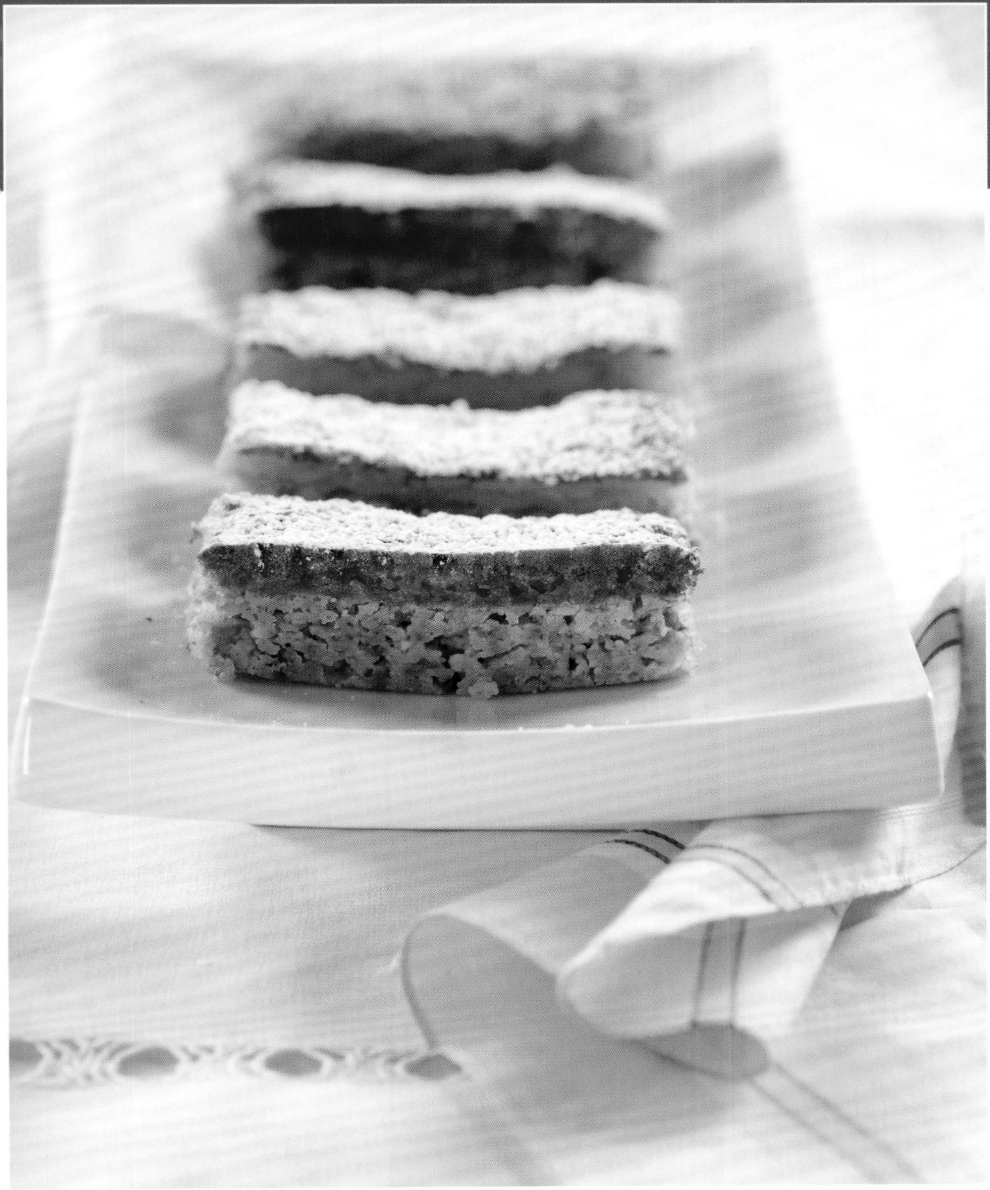

In some houses, people fight over the crispy edges. In other houses, they fight over the soft, gooey centers. These bars keep everyone happy with a little crunch and a little creaminess in every bite. –V.

Matzah Toffee Bar Crunch [GEBROKTS]

INGREDIENTS

6	sheets matzah (or enough to cover baking sheet)
1 cup	(2 sticks) margarine
1½ cups	brown sugar
1 tsp	vanilla extract
1¼ cups	chocolate chips

OPTIONAL GARNISHES

- sea salt
- slivered almonds, toasted

INSTRUCTIONS

1. Preheat oven to 375°F. Line a baking sheet with foil. Cover with matzah.

2. In a small saucepan over medium heat, bring margarine and brown sugar to a boil, stirring constantly as margarine melts. Add vanilla and boil 2-4 minutes. Pour over matzah. Bake for 15 minutes.

3. Immediately sprinkle with chocolate chips. Wait 5 minutes as chocolate melts. Using a spatula, spread chocolate in an even layer. Sprinkle with optional garnish. Chill in freezer to set. Break into pieces. Store in an airtight container.

YIELD

18 servings

INSPIRED BY COOKKOSHER MEMBER
trachtmj

TIDBIT:
There are more editions of the Passover Haggadah than of any other Jewish book.

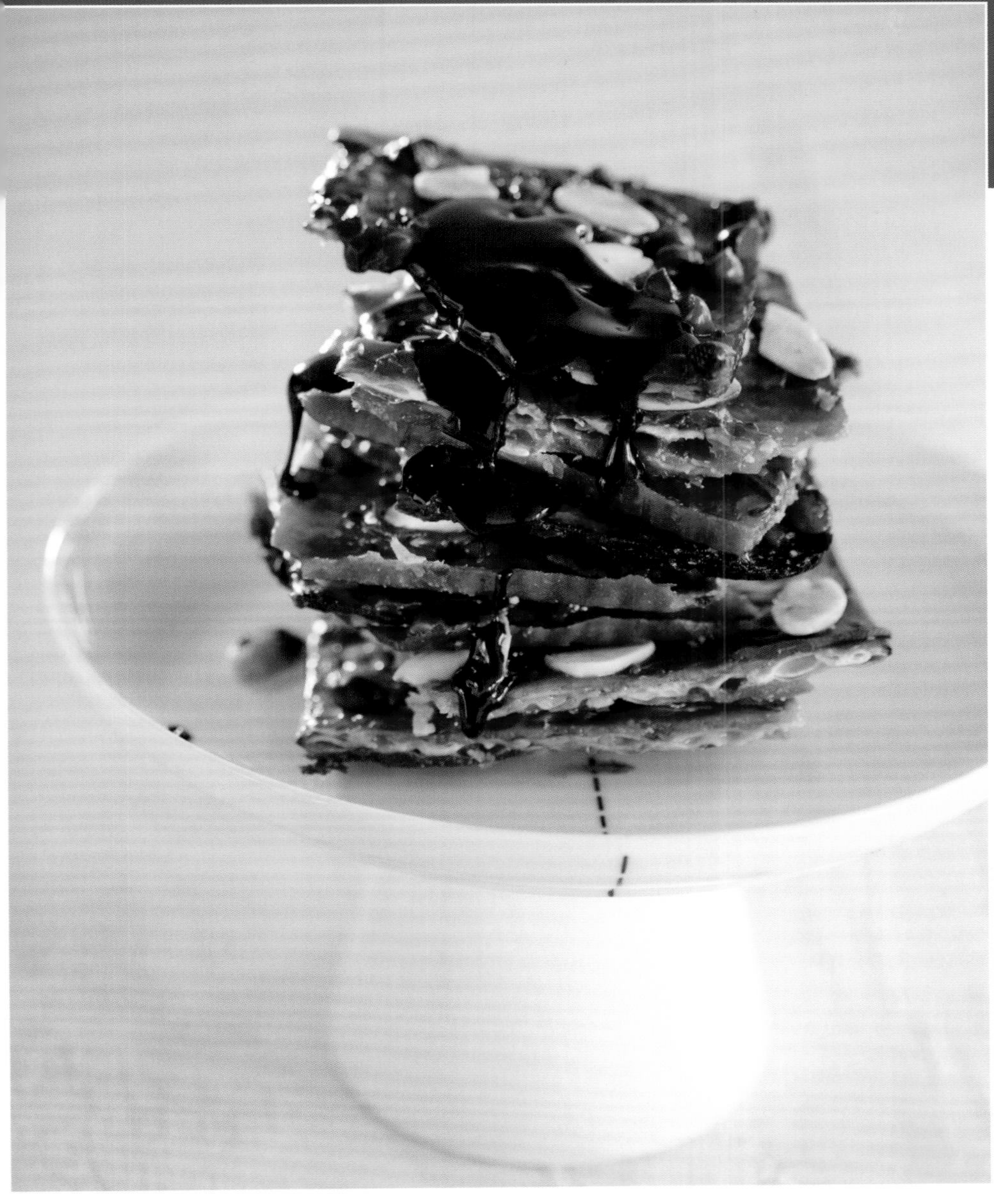

AFTER I made a batch of this classic Passover treat, we all tasted, and I put the rest in the freezer. Later that day, I sneaked some from the bag. Then I took the rest and stuffed it into my son's backpack so they'd be removed from the premises the next morning. I just couldn't trust myself not to finish the whole batch myself. I knew they weren't safe.

I'm sure, though, when Passover comes, you'll have lots of guests around to help you polish these off and sing your praises. –V.

Truffled Grapes

INGREDIENTS

50	red seedless grapes
7 oz	good-quality bitter-sweet chocolate
2 Tbsp	cocoa powder or confectioners' sugar

FRUIT ALTERNATIVES

1	mango, peeled and cut into cubes
½	pineapple, peeled, sliced, and cut into triangular wedges

INSTRUCTIONS

1. Clean and dry grapes. Melt chocolate in a double boiler. Let cool slightly. Place a grape into a spoon or on a skewer. Spoon chocolate over grape, letting the excess drip back into the pan. Repeat with remaining grapes. Place on a parchment- or wax paper-lined baking sheet.

2. Refrigerate 30 minutes and roll in cocoa or confectioners' sugar. Return to refrigerator until serving and eat chilled.

YIELD
50 truffles

INSPIRED BY COOKKOSHER MEMBER
fredericks

TIDBIT:
Many matzah bakers use oil left over from the Chanukah menorah to heat their ovens. Others use their old lulavim as fuel.

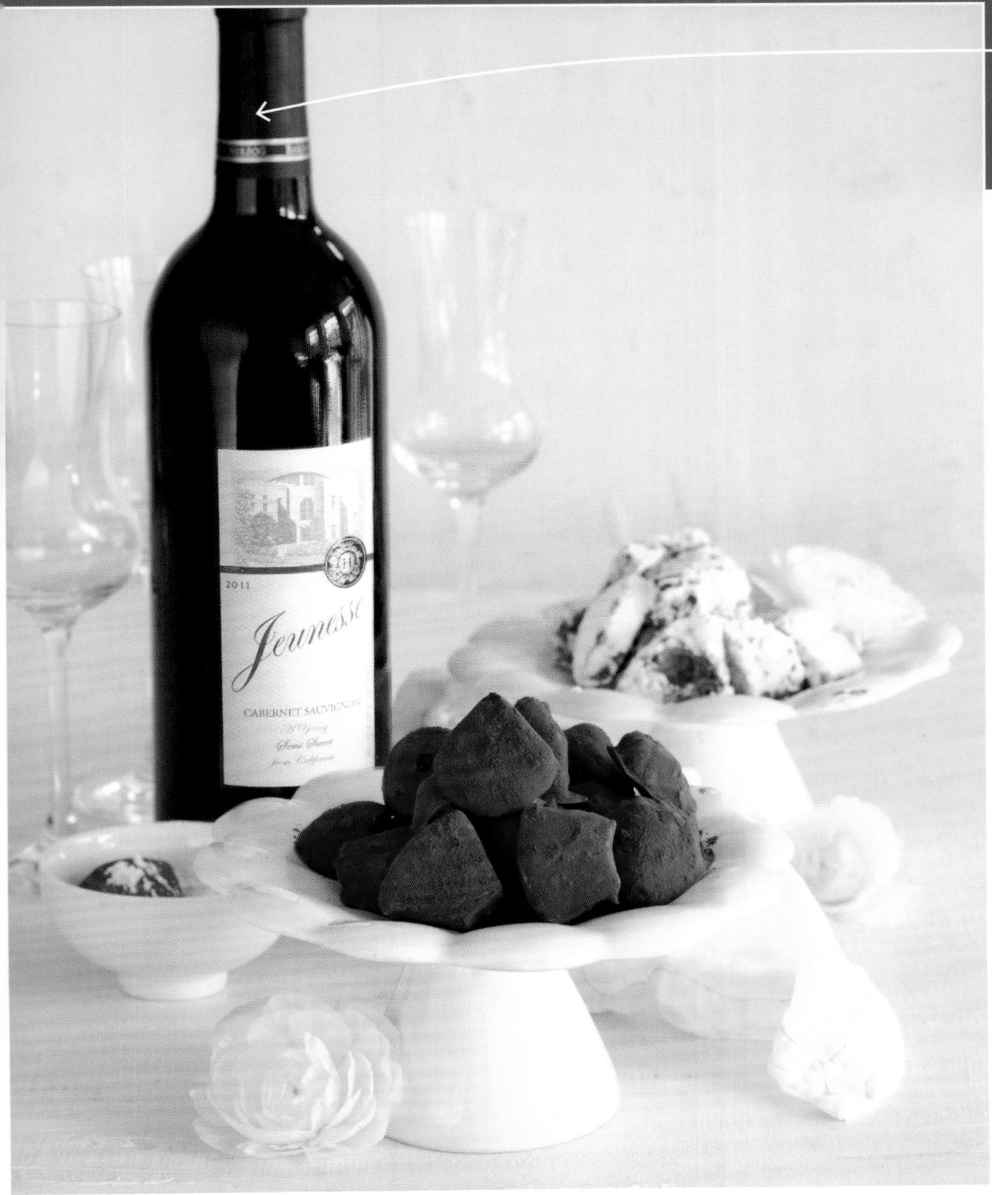
2011
Jeunesse
CABERNET SAUVIGNON

Wine Pairing:
Jeunesse Cabernet Sauvignon

THERE was only one way to eliminate the temptation of these refreshing little truffles. And that was to finish them all. Serve them in a bowl as a lighter alternative to chocolate covered nuts, or stick them on skewers. The grapes make the cutest truffles, but I also love the pineapple and mango versions (pictured). Unlike the grapes, though, the other fruits don't have to be coated completely. —L.

Passover Drinks

Citrus-Ade

I'M thirsty all Passover long because I can't satisfy my Snapple addiction. To quench my thirst, I end up combining seltzer with a bit of orange juice and sweetener. Here are more options to keep us thirsty folks happy. They're also lower in sugar than straight-up juice. —V.

YIELD *1 half-gallon*
INSPIRED BY COOKKOSHER MEMBER *mamaleh*

INGREDIENTS

1 cup	water
½ cup	sugar
½ cup	lemon juice
1 cup	orange juice
1 cup	grapefruit juice
1 quart	seltzer

INSTRUCTIONS

- In a small saucepan, combine water and sugar and bring to a boil. Let boil until sugar dissolves. Pour into a half-gallon pitcher. Add juices and seltzer. Serve chilled.

Apple Iced Tea

YIELD *1 half-gallon*
INSPIRED BY COOKKOSHER MEMBER *aidelK*

INGREDIENTS

4 cups	boiling water
4	fruit-flavored tea bags
4 cups	apple juice
•	sugar or artificial sweetener to taste

INSTRUCTIONS

- In a large measuring cup, steep tea bags in water for 10 minutes. Pour into half-gallon pitcher. Add apple juice and sweeten to taste.

Vanilla Banana Shake

I'LL take this shake over dinner any night. I'll take it over ice cream. My husband and kids beg me to make it. I don't mind because it's light, even though it tastes so indulgent. *–V.*

YIELD *2 servings*

INGREDIENTS

- *1 cup* ice
- *1 cup* whole milk
- *1* banana
- *2 Tbsp* sugar-free or regular vanilla pudding powder

INSTRUCTIONS

- In the jar of a blender, blend all ingredients. Shake will keep for 1 hour at room temperature, but do not refrigerate.

Replacement Index

This page is a guide for those who want to avoid using processed ingredients or who follow the stricter Passover customs of using only produce that can be peeled.

Note: *Garlic can be omitted from all recipes. Taste and adjust seasoning as necessary.*

Syrian Charoset *Page 9*
To avoid *gebrokts*, omit matzah meal.

Crispy Crackers with Mock Techineh *Page 18*
Omit parsley in techineh.

Chips and Dip *Page 24*
Peel peppers and omit basil in roasted pepper dip.

Antipasti Rolls *Page 26*
Omit basil.

Roasted Tomato and Eggplant Soup *Page 32*
Omit dried basil and adjust seasoning to taste.

Citrus Beet Salad *Page 36*
Omit imitation mustard and dill. Replace honey with sugar and adjust seasoning to taste.

Russian Coleslaw *Page 40*
Replace vinegar with lemon juice. Omit dill.

Turnip and Beet Pickles *Page 42*
Omit jalapeño pepper. Replace vinegar with lemon juice.

Grilled Vegetable Salad *Page 44*
Omit mushrooms in salad. In dressing, replace brown sugar with granulated sugar. Omit imitation mustard.

Apple Jam Chicken Drumettes *Page 48*
Replace apple juice with orange juice. Use Homemade Orange Jam (on recipe page).

Seder Night Chicken *Page 50*
Replace honey with sugar. Add 1 tablespoon liquid.

Schnitzel Nuggets *Page 52*
Omit baking powder in batter. Use Homemade Duck Sauce, page 60, as a dipping sauce.

Eggplant-Wrapped Chicken *Page 54*
Omit garlic powder and garlic cloves and adjust seasoning to taste.

Veal in White Wine Sauce *Page 56*
Omit mushrooms and parsley.

French Roast *Page 58*
Omit or peel the tomato.

Barbecue Rib Steak *Page 66*
Replace honey with 2 tablespoons sugar and 4 additional tablespoons olive oil.

Honey-Pecan Salmon *Page 72*
Replace honey with sugar.

Potato-Chip Zucchini Sticks *Page 76*
Replace store-bought potato chips with homemade potato chips (see Chips and Dip, page 24).

Vegetable Lo Mein *Page 88*
Omit honey, soy sauce, and garlic. Replace with 2 to 3 tablespoons Homemade Duck Sauce, page 60.

Sweet Potato and Beet Terrine *Page 90*
Omit portobello mushrooms. Replace balsamic vinegar with red wine, for 1 cup total red wine.

Hot Apple Pie with Cinnamon-Streusel Ice Cream *Page 106*
Replace ice cream base with your vanilla ice cream recipe.

Strawberry Fudge Cake *Page 110*
Replace frozen strawberries with ripe mangos, pineapple, kiwis, or papaya. You will need 2 cups puréed fruit.

Double-Decker Bars *Page 118*
Omit baking powder.

Vanilla Banana Shake *Page 124*
Replace pudding powder with vanilla sugar. Adjust sweetness to taste.